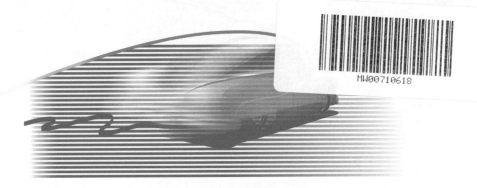

Special Edition
Using
Adobe
Illustrator 10

Peter Bauer

201 W. 103rd Street
Indianapolis, Indiana 46290

SPECIAL EDITION USING ADOBE ILLUSTRATOR 10

Trademarks

Warning and Disclaimer

Executive Editor
Jeff Schultz

Acquisitions Editor
Lloyd Black

Development Editors
Damon Jordan
Laura Norman

Managing Editor
Thomas F. Hayes

Project Editor
Karen S. Shields

Production Editor
Benjamin Berg

Indexer
Mandie Frank

Proofreader
Andrea Dugan

Technical Editor
Andrew Shalat

Team Coordinator
Sharry Lee Gregory

Interior Designer
Anne Jones

Cover Designer
Ruth Lewis
Dan Armstrong

Page Layout
Stacey Richwine-DeRome

Contents at a Glance

I Overview of Adobe Illustrator 10

1 What's New in Illustrator 10 13
2 The Illustrator Interface and Setup 23
3 Working with Files in Illustrator 41

II Basic Creation in Illustrator

4 Creating and Editing Paths 59
5 Shape, Drawing, and Graph Tools 83
6 Utilizing the Four Types of Brushes 119
7 Type and Text in Illustrator 137

III Manipulating Objects in Illustrator

8 Transforming and Distorting Objects 173
9 Working with Blends 211
10 Illustrator's Layers, Sublayers, and Groups 231
11 Output Options 255

IV Enhancing Illustrator Objects

12 Understanding and Applying Color 275
13 Applying and Defining Patterns 299
14 Using the Appearance and Style Palettes 323
15 The Gradient and Gradient Mesh Tools 337

V Getting the Most Out of Illustrator

16 Customizing Illustrator 357
17 Using Masks to Show and Hide 373

VI Between Vector and Raster

18 Raster Images and Rasterized Objects 389
19 Exploiting Illustrator's Transparency 405
20 Using Filters and Effects 429

VII Illustrator and the Web

21 Designing Web Sites and Web Pages 469
22 Saving Images for the Web 497
23 Flash and SVG Support 533

VIII Pre-Press and Four-Color Process Printing

24 Commercial Printing and Trapping Issues 569
25 Linking and Embedding Images and Fonts 603

IX Illustrator Efficiency and Interoperability

26 Automation Through Actions 625
27 Dynamic Data-Driven Graphics 645
28 Integrating Illustrator 10 and Photoshop 655

Appendixes

A Installing Illustrator 675
B Illustrator Assistance and Resources 687
C Illustrator to Go 697

Index 705

CONTENTS

Introduction 1

I Overview of Adobe Illustrator 10

1 What's New in Illustrator 10   13

Illustrator for the Web   **14**
   CSS, Object-Based Slicing, and SVG
   Effects   **14**
   Symbols and Selective
   Antialiasing   **14**

Envelope Distort, Warps, and
Liquifying   **15**
   Envelope Distort   **15**

Illustrator's Other New Tools   **17**
   The Magic Wand   **17**
   The Line and Arc Tools   **17**
   The Rectangular and Polar Grid
   Tools   **18**
   The Flare Tool   **18**
   The Slice and Slice Select Tools   **18**

Compound Shapes   **19**

Mac OS X and Windows XP   **20**

Dynamic Data-Driven Graphics   **20**

Integration with the Adobe Family of
Products   **21**

**2 The Illustrator Interface and
Setup   23**

A Quick Tour of the Illustrator
Workplace   **24**
   The Basic Interface   **24**
   Interacting with the Interface   **25**
   The Status Bar   **26**
   The Artboard   **26**
   Rulers, Guides, and Grid   **27**

Zooming   **27**

View Options   **28**
   View Modes   **28**
   The View Menu   **29**

Illustrator Terminology and Labels   **31**
   Interface Terminology   **31**
   The Creative Elements   **33**
   Techniques and Procedures   **35**
   Typography and Text Terms   **36**
   Color and Color Management   **38**

3 Working with Files in Illustrator   41

Determining File Format
Requirements   **42**
   Raster Versus Vector   **42**
   Web, Print, and Other File
   Destinations   **43**
   Compression Issues   **43**
   Platform Considerations   **43**

Illustrator's Commands to Save and
Export Files   **44**
   Save   **44**
   Save As   **45**
   Export   **48**
   Save for Web   **52**

Linking and Embedding   **53**
   Linking and Embedding Images   **53**
   Embedding Fonts   **54**

Troubleshooting   **55**

II Basic Creation in Illustrator

4 Creating and Editing Paths   59

Paths and Vector Art   **60**
   Basic Path Creation   **60**
   Types of Paths   **61**

How Anchor Points Shape Paths   62
Locating, Selecting, and Moving
Anchor Points   63
The Types of Anchor Points   64
The Anatomy of an Anchor Point   65

The Pen Tools   67
Creating Paths with the Pen
Tool   68
The Other Pen Tools   69

Editing Paths   70
Using the Direct Selection Tool with
Points and Segments   70
Manipulating Direction Lines with
the Direct Selection Tool   72

More Path Creation Tools   74
The Paintbrush Tool   74
The Pencil Tool   75

Additional Path-Related Tools   77
The Smooth Tool   78
The Erase Tool   78
The Scissors Tool   79
The Knife Tool   79

Non-Object Paths in Illustrator   80

Illustrator's Auto Trace Tool   80

Troubleshooting   81

**5 Shape, Drawing, and Graph
Tools   83**

Illustrator's Object Creation Tools   84

The Basic Object Creation Tools   85
The Rectangle Tool   85
The Rounded Rectangle Tool   86
The Ellipse Tool   87
The Polygon Tool   87
The Star Tool   88
The Line Segment Tool   89
The Arc Tool   89
The Spiral Tool   91

The Complex Object Creation Tools   92
The Flare Tool   92
The Rectangular Grid Tool   94
The Polar Grid Tool   95

Selection Tools and Commands   97
The Selection Tool   98
The Direct Selection Tool   99
The Group Selection Tool   99
The Magic Wand Tool   99
The Direct Select Lasso Tool   101
The Lasso Tool   102

Illustrator's Select Menu   102
Select, All   102
Select, Deselect   103
Select, Reselect   103
Select, Inverse   103
Select, Next Object Above   103
Select, Next Object Below   103
Select, Same   104
Select, Object   104
Select, Save Selection   105
Edit Selection   106
The Saved Selections   106

Compound Shapes and the Pathfinder
Palette   106
Compound Shapes   106
Expanding a Compound Shape   107
The Pathfinder Buttons   108
The Pathfinder Palette Menu   109

Graphs in Illustrator   110
The Types of Graphs and Graph
Tools   110
Adding a Graph to the Artboard   112
Adding Graph Data   113
Changing Graph Type and Graph
Data   113
Customizing Graphs   115

Troubleshooting   116

6 Utilizing the Four Types of Brushes 119

Working with Brushes 120
   The Four Categories 120
   The Brushes Palette 121
   Brushes and Strokes 122
   Editing and Transforming Brushed Paths 123
   Brush-Stroked Type 125

Creating and Modifying Brushes 127
   Creating or Modifying a Calligraphic Brush 129
   Creating or Modifying a Scatter Brush 130
   Creating or Modifying an Art Brush 131
   Creating or Modifying a Pattern Brush 133
   Loading Illustrator's Other Brushes 135

Troubleshooting 135

7 Type and Text in Illustrator 137

The Type Tools 138
   Type Tool and Vertical Type Tool 139
   Area Type Tool and Vertical Area Type Tool 140
   Path Type Tool and Vertical Path Type Tool 141
   Preferences and General Considerations 143

The Palettes 146
   The Character Palette 146
   The Paragraph Palette 147
   The Multiple Master Design Palette 148
   The Tab Ruler Palette 149

The Type Menu 149

Text Containers, Outlines, and Attributes 154
   Linking Text Containers 154
   Wrapping Text Around Objects 156
   Filling and Stroking Text Containers 158
   Converting Text to Outlines 158
   Copying Type Attributes 159

Fonts and Font Embedding 160
   Fonts and Font Families 161
   Multiple Master Fonts 161
   CID and OpenType Fonts 162
   Font Embedding 162

Typographic Terminology 163

.Troubleshooting 169

III Manipulating Objects in Illustrator

8 Transforming and Distorting Objects 173

Transformations and Distortions in Illustrator 174
   Transform, Envelope Distort, and Liquify 174

The Basics of Transforming 175
   Transforming with the Selection Tool and the Bounding Box 176
   The Point of Origin 176
   Transforming Objects, Patterns, and Both 178
   Scaling Strokes and Effects 179

The Transformations 180
   Free Transform 180
   Move 181
   Rotate 182
   Reflect 184
   Reshape 184
   Scale 185
   Shear 187

Twist **189**
The Transform Palette Menu **191**
The Transform Again Command **191**
The Transform Each Command **192**
The Reset Bounding Box
Command **194**

Envelope Distortions **194**
The Basics of Warping **195**
How Warps Work **197**
Editing a Mesh Object **198**
The Make with Mesh Command **200**
Reopening the Envelope Distort
Dialog Box **200**
Using the Make with Top Object
Command **201**
Envelope Options **202**
Releasing and Expanding Envelope
Distortions **203**
The Edit Contents Command **204**

Illustrator's Liquify Tools **206**
Working with the Liquify Tools **206**
The Liquify Tool Options **208**

Troubleshooting **210**

9 Working with Blends 211

Creating Blends **212**
The Blend Menu **215**
Using the Blend Tool **215**
The Blend, Make Command **216**

Examining the Blend Options **216**
Smooth Color **216**
Specified Steps **219**
Specified Distance **222**
Orientation **224**

Adjusting Blend Paths **226**
Editing Spines **226**
Replacing Spines **228**
Reversing **228**

Expanding a Blend **229**

Troubleshooting **229**

**10 Illustrator's Layers, Sublayers, and
Groups 231**

The Layers Palette **232**

Illustrator's Layers **232**

Working with Layers **237**
Creating New Layers and
Sublayers **238**
Moving Elements in the Layers
Palette **239**
Using Sublayers and Groups **240**

Templates **245**

Targeting Layers, Groups, and
Objects **246**

Release to Layers **249**

Special Utilization of Layers **252**

Troubleshooting **253**

11 Output Options 255

Differences Between Page and
Screen **256**
Color **256**
Resolution **259**
File Formats **262**

The PDF Option **262**

Other Output Options **265**
Presentation Programs **265**
Film Recorders **269**

Troubleshooting **270**

IV Enhancing Illustrator Objects

**12 Understanding and Applying
Color 275**

The Two Types of Color **276**
Additive Color **276**
Subtractive Color **277**

RGB Versus CMYK Versus Spot
Colors   278
  Defining RGB Colors   281
  Defining CMYK Colors   281
  Spot Colors   282

The Other Color Modes: HSB and
Grayscale   282

Reduced Palettes   284

Determining the Color Mode   284

Using the Color Palette   286

Applying Color   290

Using the Swatches Palette   291
  Global Colors   294
  Using the Swatch Library   294

Troubleshooting   297

**13 Applying and Defining
Patterns   299**

General Rules Governing Patterns   300

Fill Patterns   303

Brush Patterns   306
  Creating a Brush Pattern   307
  Designing Brush Patterns for Pattern
  Brushes   310
  Creating Brush Pattern Side
  Tiles   311
  Creating Brush Pattern Corner
  Tiles   313
  Creating Brush Pattern Start and End
  Tiles   320

Troubleshooting   321

**14 Using the Appearance and Styles
Palettes   323**

Appearances and Styles   324

The Appearance Palette   325

The Appearance Palette Menu   329

Applying Appearances to Groups and
Layers   331

The Styles Palette   333

Style Libraries   334

Troubleshooting   335

**15 The Gradient and Gradient Mesh
Tools   337**

Working with Gradients   338
  The Anatomy of a Gradient   339
  Using the Gradient Sliders   340
  Saving and Applying Gradients   341

Gradient Meshes   343
  Creating Gradient Mesh Objects   344
  Creating Gradient Mesh Objects from
  Raster Images   346
  Editing Gradient Meshes   348
  Printing Gradients and Gradient
  Meshes   350

Troubleshooting   352

V Getting the Most Out of Illustrator

16 Customizing Illustrator   357

Keyboard Shortcuts: Speed for Illustrator
Power Users   358

Setting Illustrator's Preferences   360
  General   360
  Type & Auto Tracing   362
  Units & Undo   363
  Guides & Grid   364
  Smart Guides & Slices   365
  Hyphenation   366
  Plug-ins & Scratch Disk   366
  Files & Clipboard   367
  Workgroup   368
  Online Settings   369

Creating Illustrator Startup Files   370

Troubleshooting   372

17 Using Masks to Show and Hide   373

Clipping Masks   374
  Creating Clipping Masks   374
  Editing a Clipping Mask   376
  Type as Clipping Masks   377

Opacity Masks   378
  Creating Opacity Masks   379
  Editing Opacity Masks   380
  Type as Opacity Masks   383

Troubleshooting   384

VI Between Vector and Raster

18 Raster Images and Rasterized Objects   389

The Difference Between Vector and Raster   390
  What Is Vector Art?   390
  What Is Raster Art?   394
  Comparing Vector and Raster   397

Rasterizing Objects in Illustrator   399
  The Rasterize and Raster Effects Settings Dialog Boxes   399
  Resolution and Antialiasing   401

Troubleshooting   403

19 Exploiting Illustrator's Transparency   405

Working with Transparency in Illustrator   406
  The Transparency Theory   406
  The Transparency Palette   409
  Transparency Preferences and Other Settings   411
  Opacity Masks   413

The Blending Modes   414
  Normal   416
  Multiply   416
  Screen   417
  Overlay   417
  Soft Light   418
  Hard Light   418
  Color Dodge   418
  Color Burn   419
  Darken   419
  Lighten   420
  Difference   420
  Exclusion   420
  Hue   421
  Saturation   421
  Color   422
  Luminosity   423
  Restricting the Effects of Blending Modes   423

Outputting Transparency   424
  Preparing Transparent Objects for Print   425
  Transparency and the Web   426

Troubleshooting   427

20 Using Filters and Effects   429

About Filters and Effects   430
  What They Do and How They Do It   430
  Filters Versus Effects   431
  Why Use Filters?   432

Illustrator's Filter and Effect Menus   433

The Top of the Menus   434
  Apply Last Filter/Apply Last Effect   434
  Last Filter/Last Effect   434
  Document Raster Effects Settings (Effect Only)   434

The Middle of the Menus—Vector   **435**
  Colors (Filter Only)   **435**
  Convert to Shape (Effects Only)   **436**
  Create (Filters Only)   **437**
  Distort/Distort & Transform
  (Filters/Effects)   **438**
  Path (Effects Only)   **441**
  Pathfinder (Effects Only)   **442**
  Pen and Ink (Filters Only)   **443**
  Rasterize (Effect)   **444**
  Stylize (Filters and Effects)   **444**
  SVG Filters (Effects Only)   **446**
  Warp (Effects Only)   **446**

The Bottom of the Menu—Raster   **446**
  Artistic (Filters/Effects)   **447**
  Blur (Filters and Effects)   **454**
  Brush Strokes (Filters and
  Effects)   **455**
  Distort (Filters and Effects)   **459**
  Pixelate (Filters and Effects)   **461**
  Sharpen (Filter and Effect)   **462**
  Sketch (Filters and Effects)   **463**
  Stylize (Filter and Effect)   **464**
  Texture (Filters and Effects)   **464**
  Video (Filters and Effects)   **465**

Troubleshooting   **466**

VII Illustrator and the Web

**21 Designing Web Sites and Web
      Pages   469**

Web Design with Illustrator   **470**
  A Few Web Graphic Basic
  Concepts   **470**
  Laying Out the Site   **472**
  Organizing the Pages   **474**

Preparing for Web Graphic
Creation   **475**
  Units of Measure   **475**
  Setting up the Other
  Preferences   **476**

  Page Setup   **477**
  View Options   **478**

Color on the Web   **479**
  Color Spaces for the Web   **479**
  HTML and Hexadecimal
  Notation   **479**
  The Return of the Web-Safe
  Palette   **480**

File Format Considerations   **480**
  Rasterization   **481**
  File Size and the Web   **482**
  Animation on the Web   **482**

Cascading Style Sheets   **482**
  CSS in Illustrator   **483**

Symbols and Symbolism for the
Web   **485**
  How Symbols Work in Illustrator   **485**
  Working with the Symbolism
  Tools   **485**
  Symbolism Tool Options   **489**
  Replacing a Symbol in an Image   **492**
  Updating a Symbol and Breaking
  Links   **492**
  Creating a Custom Symbol   **493**
  Expanding Symbol Sets and
  Instances   **494**

Slicing   **494**
  The Two Types of Slices   **494**
  The Slice Tool   **494**
  Using a Selection for Slicing   **494**
  Using Guides for Selections   **495**
  Object-Based Slicing   **495**
  Linking to a Slice in Illustrator   **495**
  Creating Image Maps   **495**

Troubleshooting   **496**

22 Saving Images for the Web   497

Control Graphic Images   **498**

Color and the Web   **499**

File Size and the Web   **500**

Image Formats for the Web   **501**
GIF   **501**
JPEG   **503**
PNG   **505**
SVG   **505**
SWF (Flash)   **506**

Pixel Preview   **506**

Save for Web and Image
Optimizing   **509**

The Color Table   **516**

The Optimization Settings   **518**
GIF Optimization Choices   **518**
PNG-8 Optimization Settings   **520**
JPEG Optimization Settings   **520**
PNG-24 Optimization Settings   **521**
SWF and SVG Optimization
Settings   **521**

Types of Dithering   **521**

Optimizing Slices   **525**

The Save Optimized As Dialog Box   **527**
Saving Images, HTML, or Both   **527**
Output Options   **528**

Troubleshooting   **530**

23 **Flash and SVG Support**   **533**

Animation on the Web   **534**

What Is Flash?   **537**

What Is SVG?   **538**

Preparing Vector-Based Animation for
Flash   **539**
Determining the Correct Size and
Adjusting Timing   **544**

Exporting to SWF   **552**

Creating SVG Output   **554**
SVG Filters   **558**
Raster Images in SVG Files   **559**

Dynamic SVG   **560**
The SVG Interactivity Palette   **561**

Saving as SVG   **562**
SVG Options   **562**
Font Subsetting with SVG   **563**

Save for Web with SWF and SVG   **564**

Troubleshooting   **565**

VIII **Pre-Press and Four-Color Process
Printing**

24 **Commercial Printing and Trapping
Issues   569**

Terms and Concepts   **570**

The Basics of Printing   **575**
Proofs   **576**
Color Separations   **577**
Imagesetters   **578**
Printing Plates   **578**

Color Issues   **579**
CMYK Versus RGB Color   **580**
Process Versus Spot Colors   **580**
Preparing Spot Colors for Print   **581**
The Separations Setup Options   **583**
Registration Color   **584**
Viewing and Correcting Colors   **584**

Preparing Artwork for Print   **586**
Overprinting and the Attributes
Palette   **587**
Overprint Preview   **589**
Knockout   **589**
Trapping   **590**
Potential Path Problems   **591**
Crop, Trim, and Printer's Marks   **591**
Document Info   **593**
Resolution Options   **594**

Service Bureaus, Print Brokers, and
Printers **595**
Service Bureaus **595**
Print Brokers **595**
Printers **596**

Trapping **596**
Trapping Software and Plug-ins **596**
General Trapping Techniques **597**
Avoiding the Need to Trap **600**

Troubleshooting **601**

**25 Linking and Embedding Images and
Fonts 603**

Linking Raster Images **604**
The Basics of Image Linking **605**
Working with Linked Images **607**
The Links Palette **610**

Embedding Raster and Vector
Images **612**
Embedding Raster Images **612**
Embedding Vector Images **615**
Embedding Photoshop Files **616**

Embedding Text Files and Fonts **617**
Embedding Text Files **617**
Embedding Fonts **619**

Troubleshooting **620**

**IX Illustrator Efficiency and
Interoperability**

26 Automation Through Actions 625

Actions in Theory and Practice **626**
What Is an Action? **626**
The Actions Palette **628**
Using Actions **629**
The Batch Command **630**

Recording Custom Actions **632**
Recording a New Action **632**
Inserting Nonrecordable
Commands **634**
Paths in Actions **635**
The Select Object Command **636**
Stops **638**
Modal Controls **639**
Editing Actions **640**
Saving and Sharing Action Sets **641**

Troubleshooting **642**

27 Dynamic Data-Driven Graphics 645

Dynamic Data-Driven Graphics—
Overview **646**
How They Work **646**
Dynamic Data-Driven Graphics
Terminology **647**
The Design Process **648**

Templates, Variables, and Data
Sets **648**
Creating and Using Templates **648**
The Variables Palette **649**
Creating Variables **650**
Working With Data Sets **651**
XML IDs **652**
Variable Libraries **653**

Troubleshooting **654**

**28 Integrating Illustrator and
Photoshop 655**

Illustrator Versus Photoshop **656**
Illustrator's Vectors, Photoshop's
Rasters **656**
The Raster Advantage **658**
The Vector Edge **659**

Moving Artwork from Illustrator to
Photoshop **660**
   Saving as Illustrator, Opening in
   Photoshop **660**
   Exporting from Illustrator in
   Photoshop Format **661**
   Editable Text from Illustrator to
   Photoshop **664**
   Copy and Paste, Drag and Drop **664**
   Alternative File Formats **667**

Moving Artwork from Photoshop to
Illustrator **668**
   Opening Photoshop Files in
   Illustrator **668**
   Copy and Paste, Drag and Drop **669**
   Exporting Paths to Illustrator **669**
   Round-Tripping **670**

Troubleshooting **671**

X Appendixes

A Installing Illustrator 675

Illustrator's Easy Installation
Process **676**
   Preparing for Installation **676**
   Installing Illustrator the Easy Way:
   Macintosh **676**
   Installing Illustrator the Easy Way:
   Windows (Generally) **677**

The Custom Installation Procedure—
Basic Files **679**
   Adobe Illustrator 10 **680**
   Mac OS 9 to OS X Updater
   (Macintosh Only) **680**
   Illustrator Plug-ins **680**
   File Format Plug-ins **680**
   Photoshop Filters & Effects **681**

Macintosh Custom Installation—
Additional Files **681**
   Presets **681**
   Color Settings **682**

   Helpers **682**
   ICC Profiles **682**
   Install SVG **682**
   Kodak Photo CD Support **682**
   Online Help **682**
   Sample Files Folder **682**
   Utilities Folder **683**
   Adobe Online **683**
   CMP Folder **683**
   Settings **683**

Windows Custom Installation—
Additional Files **683**
   Brush Libraries **683**
   Fonts **683**
   CMap Files **683**
   ICC Profiles **683**
   Calibration **683**
   Online Help **684**
   Libraries **684**
   Sample Files **684**
   Utility Files **684**
   Adobe Online **684**
   Color Settings **684**
   Style Libraries **684**
   Keyboard Shortcuts **684**

What Can Be Skipped? **684**

What Can Be Deleted After
Installation? **685**

**B Illustrator Assistance and
Resources 687**

Basic Troubleshooting Diagnosis and
Repair **688**
   Illustrator Performance Issues **688**
   File-Specific Issues **690**
   Interoperability Issues **690**
   Procedural Concerns **690**

Where to Go for Help **691**
   Special Edition Using Adobe
   Illustrator 10 **691**
   The Illustrator User Guide **691**

Illustrator's Help PDF   **691**

Illustrator's Help Menu   **691**

Internet-Based Help Options   **692**

Adobe Online   **693**

The Adobe Support Web Site   **693**

Tips for Searching and Asking   **694**

Searching the Support
Knowledgebase   **694**

Using the User to User Forum   **695**

The Adobe Expert Center   **695**

C Illustrator to Go   697

Taking Illustrator with You   **698**

Legalities   **698**

Preparing a Portable   **698**

Preparing an Image for the Client's
Computer   **699**

Separations and Proofing   **700**

Separation Problem Solving   **701**

Types of Color Proofs   **701**

Color Page Proofs   **702**

Press Check Checklist   **703**

Web Animation Checklist   **703**

Index   705

ABOUT THE AUTHOR

Peter Bauer is the help desk director for the National Association of Photoshop Professionals, the largest graphics association of its kind. He is an Adobe Certified Expert in both Adobe Illustrator and Adobe Photoshop. A computer graphics consultant, he writes a weekly column for the graphics portal `PlanetPhotoshop.com` and is a contributing editor for *Photoshop User* and *Mac Design* magazines. He is also a member of the instructor "Dream Team" for Photoshop World.

He is the author of *Sams Teach Yourself Adobe Illustrator 10 in 24 Hours* (with Mordy Golding), *Special Edition Using Illustrator 9*, and a contributing author for *Photoshop 6 Web Magic,* and has served as technical editor on a number of Illustrator and Photoshop books. Pete also writes software documentation and does software testing for a variety of Illustrator- and Photoshop-related products.

Pete and his wife, Professor Mary Ellen O'Connell of the Ohio State University Moritz College of Law, live in the historic German Village area of Columbus, Ohio.

Dedication

Special Edition Using Adobe Illustrator 10 is dedicated to my wife, Professor Mary Ellen O'Connell of the Ohio State University Moritz College of Law. Her dedication to providing the best possible education for her students is matched only by her desire to help international law make the world a better place for us all.

Acknowledgments

First, I must acknowledge the entire team at Que who made this book happen. Especially I'd like to recognize Jeff Schultz and Laura Norman. I cannot possibly express my thanks for your understanding during those difficult weeks following the events of the Fall of 2001. Lloyd, Andrew, and Damon worked to make sure that this book is worth your time (and money). Ben Berg, take a bow! Ben did a tremendous job of catching those little "oops!" things before they reached print and caused confusion for you. And, Karen, always a pleasure working with you!

I also need to express my sincere gratitude to Mordy Golding, Illustrator product manager at Adobe, and the rest of the Illustrator team. Not only have they produced yet again a top-flight product, they were always available to answer those difficult "waddif" questions. ("What if, for example, you take *this* and do *this* and then create *this*...?" "Why would anyone want to do *that*?" "I dunno. But what if...?") In the same vein, I'd like to thank my many colleagues on the Forum who were always willing to share their experience and expertise.

Thanks also go to Michelle Lindsey and Bill Lindsay at Wacom for their generous contribution of an Intuos tablet for production; to Bill Evans at Apple for providing Mac OS X; to Josh Bond for allowing me to work with the Columbus Chiefs logo; and to Hugo and (the late) Stanley, our English bulldogs, for helping me avoid any problems that may have stemmed from working more than twenty minutes at a time.

TELL US WHAT YOU THINK!

As the reader of this book, *you* are our most important critic and commentator. We value your opinion and want to know what we're doing right, what we could do better, what areas you'd like to see us publish in, and any other words of wisdom you're willing to pass our way.

As an executive editor for Que, I welcome your comments. You can e-mail or write me directly to let me know what you did or didn't like about this book—as well as what we can do to make our books stronger.

Please note that I cannot help you with technical problems related to the topic of this book, and that due to the high volume of mail I receive, I might not be able to reply to every message.

When you write, please be sure to include this book's title and author as well as your name and phone or fax number. I will carefully review your comments and share them with the author and editors who worked on the book.

Email: ctfeedback@quepublishing.com

Mail: Candy Hall
          Executive Editor
          Que
          201 West 103rd Street
          Indianapolis, IN 46290 USA

INTRODUCTION

Special Edition Using Adobe Illustrator 10 is a book for intermediate-to-advanced users. However, novices with a working knowledge of Illustrator's commands and tools will be able to understand the descriptions and explanations. Everything is clearly and concisely presented, from the discussion of what's new in version 10 and the exploration of the interface to the discussions of dynamic data-driven graphics and Flash animation.

In keeping with the *Special Edition* tradition, this book is factual, practical, and no-nonsense. It is designed for the reader who has work to do, deadlines to meet, visions to capture, concepts to digitize, images to create, dreams to fulfill. It is designed for users of Adobe Illustrator.

WHO SHOULD READ THIS BOOK?

Special Edition Using Adobe Illustrator 10 has been written primarily for higher-level users and for those who are striving for that status. Most readers are already Illustrator users and already work with Illustrator 10. They can come to this book for answers. Every aspect of this multifaceted program has been addressed, both in theory and in practice.

Even after months or years of working with Adobe Illustrator, most users still find areas that are foreign to them. The aspects of the program that you use rarely (if ever) may actually be the techniques and tools that are best for your daily work. This book is the place to find out. And sometimes a question about

Illustrator that's outside your area of expertise arises, yet you need an answer. For example, prepress specialists usually have little or no experience with Illustrator's SVG, animation, and optimization capabilities. Similarly, Web designers are likely to be unfamiliar with CMYK, trapping, and overprinting. But those questions and situations do arise from time to time, and the answers and solutions can be as close as your bookshelf.

Readers who work with Illustrator on a daily basis can reach for this book to check a specific detail, learn how to apply a new technique, or simply to find new ways of doing things. If you work with Illustrator less frequently, you'll find this book even more valuable. You can discover what a specific feature does, how a particular command works, and what technique is best for a certain job.

If you are brand new to computer illustration and drawing, in all honesty, this should not be your first book. You will not find here those simple step-by-step lessons that are basic to initial familiarity with a new program. Start with *Sams Teach Yourself Adobe Illustrator 10 in 24 Hours*, which I wrote with Mordy Golding, product manager for Illustrator at Adobe. Then make this your *second* book. When you have a basic understanding of the program and how it works, you'll be prepared for this more advanced look at Illustrator 10.

WHY YOU SHOULD USE ADOBE ILLUSTRATOR 10

First, let's note that Illustrator 10 is fully Carbonized and is a Mac OS X native program. It can also function fully under Windows XP.

Several top-notch computer illustration and drawing programs are available, and Adobe Illustrator is among the leaders. Illustrator can certainly be considered a full-featured illustration program.

What Sets Illustrator Apart from Similar Programs?

For many people, the biggest advantage to using Illustrator is its outstanding integration with the rest of the Adobe family. In addition to sharing interface components, tools, and commands with such important programs as Photoshop, GoLive, and InDesign, Illustrator integrates seamlessly in various ways. One example is Illustrator's Save for Web feature, which can tailor HTML for GoLive. And that's a two-way street. Users of the latest version of GoLive will find that they can now place native Illustrator graphics directly in their pages. LiveMotion also accepts Illustrator's native file format. The SmartObjects technology extends to InDesign as well.

Illustrator's integration with Photoshop is legendary. Illustrator can preserve a Photoshop file's masks, blending modes, and transparency, and individual Photoshop layers can become individual Illustrator objects. Likewise, putting each Illustrator object on a separate layer enables you to create Photoshop files with "objects." In addition, Illustrator and Photoshop can share files with text, and maintain the editability of the type. Now, Illustrator can even maintain ImageReady's rollovers and animations as files pass through on their way to the Web.

This latest version of Illustrator has added numerous features, including a number of new tools, more advanced Web creation features, and support for dynamic data-driven graphics.

Using the Adobe tabbed floating palettes puts everything within reach when you need it. Long-time users of Photoshop especially will be comfortable working with Illustrator.

Unmatched Web Workflow

If you are producing graphics for the Web (or eventually will be), Illustrator's enhanced Web workflow can maximize efficiency. Pixels as a unit of measure are critical for Web production, as is the capability of seeing how your final product will look. Illustrator offers pixels both as a global measure and Pixel Preview. In addition, you'll find the Save for Web feature invaluable. Preview up to four different optimizations settings and compare them head-to-head in one window. Save images effortlessly in GIF, JPEG, or PNG format (see Figure 1).

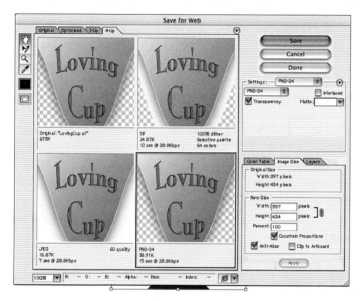

Figure 1
Save for Web enables you to compare various optimization settings in a single window.

Save for Web now offers SWF (Flash) and SVG as file formats. Improved support for SVG includes SVG Filters, which maintain the appearance of effects even when an SVG image is scaled, and a native Illustrator file format for SVG, which can be used as SmartObjects with both GoLive and LiveMotion, as well as templates in dynamic data-driven graphics.

Also new in Illustrator 10 are the Slice and Slice Select tools, along with object-based slicing. Object-based slices automatically update when a user-defined slice is moved on the artboard. No more deleting and re-creating slices!

Illustrator now supports cascading style sheets (CSS) through Save for Web. CSS offers the possibilities of overlapping objects, multi-purposed Web sites, and more complete control of fonts and page appearance.

Symbols, which can streamline the creative process and minimize file sizes, are now available. Illustrator also carries a full tool belt of things to use with symbols. The eight new Symbolism tools give you incomparable ways to manipulate those individual pieces of artwork. And Illustrator's symbols can be used when an SWF file is opened in Flash.

Illustrator also offers a Web-safe palette to supplement its RGB capabilities. You can even set the Color Picker to Only Web Colors. Save for Web allows you to select an exact color table for 8-bit images, including control over individual colors in the table.

Drop shadows, glows, and blending modes can all be employed before you optimize an image. Illustrator also offers live shape effects, allowing effortless re-editing of rounded rectangles and other button-like shapes. Converting type to an editable shape in this way makes button creation as easy as possible. The type remains fully editable, and the shape conforms instantly to changes in the text.

Don't forget Illustrator's support for exporting Flash and saving images as Scalable Vector Graphics (SVG), enabling you to produce top-of-the-line vector graphics for the Web. In addition, the new Release to Layers feature enables you to create multiple objects on a single layer for animation with a single click. Illustrator even enables you to produce cumulative content for layers, with each layer containing all the content of preceding layers, as well as an additional object. And that takes merely a simple Shift+click.

Prepress Power

Illustrator has improved color management, excellent tools for outputting the new transparency, and a host of other ways to make preparing four-color jobs easier. Trapping, overprinting, soft proofing, and knockout control help ensure that your images print just the way you want them to look.

The power of automation, although universally available in Illustrator through Actions, can be a very important part of the prepress workflow.

New Tools and Capabilities

From one-segment lines to lens flares, objects created with Illustrator 10's new tools range from the sublimely simple to the outrageously intricate. Rectangular and polar grids in a pair of clicks. Tools that manipulate paths far beyond the capabilities of basic transformations. A Magic Wand tool that selects based on a *range* of shared characteristics. Figure 2 introduces you to some of Illustrator's newest icons and palettes.

Figure 2
Some of Illustrator's new tools.

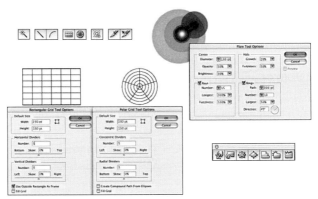

Of tremendous interest to most will be Illustrator's Envelope Distort capabilities. Taking a page from Photoshop's Text Warp, they work to pull and push objects in a variety of ways. Best of all, these distortions can be live through the Effects palette, fully editable using mesh objects, and completely customizable, using your own paths as the envelope distortion. Figure 3 has a sneak preview.

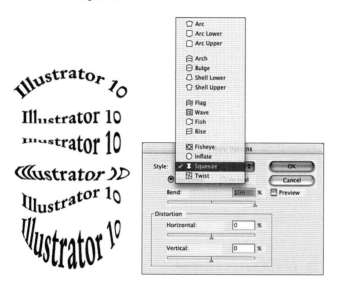

Figure 3
Envelope distortions can produce variations of 15 preset shapes.

Another new capability, although admittedly of less general attraction, is dynamic data-driven graphics. Dynamic data-driven graphics is an advanced technology that allows *templates* to hold one or more *variables* whose content is updated automatically from databases containing *data sets*. Imagine, if you will, a Web site for a hockey team. Instead of having a page for each of the players, there's a single page. And the player's name, number, statistics, and even picture are supplied by an easily updated database, on demand. Rather than re-creating a Web page every time the player's statistics change, the data is drawn from the team's database. Another marvel of XML!

WINDOWS AND MACINTOSH

No matter which platform you use, Illustrator offers the same powerful features. The interface is as close to identical as possible, with virtually the same tools, palettes, and commands. Many of the images in this book show Macintosh interface elements, such as palettes, menus, and windows. In those few specific instances in which a difference exists between Macintosh and Windows, the differences have been shown or noted. Keyboard shortcuts are shown for both platforms throughout.

The abbreviations used in this book are as follows:

- **Cmd [Ctrl]**—This identifies the Command key for Macintosh and Control key for Windows. The Command and Control keys are modifier keys; they do nothing on their own. They are always used in combination with another key or a mouse click. The key must remain pressed while you press the other key or click the mouse button.

- **Option [Alt]**—This identifies the Option key for Macintosh and Alt key for Windows. The Option and Alt keys are modifier keys, and they also must always be used in combination with another key or a mouse click. The key must remain pressed while you press the other key or click the mouse button.

- **Shift**—Like the keys described above, Shift is a modifier key and must remain pressed while you click or press another key.

- **Click**—A mouse button is clicked when it is pressed and released.

- **Double-click**—Very rapidly, press and release the mouse button twice. The two clicks must be very close together to be recognized by your computer as a double-click rather than two separate clicks. You can adjust the speed required to achieve a double-click on both Windows and Macintosh through the Mouse control panel.

- **Drag**—To drag with the mouse, press the left mouse button for Windows, the only button for Macintosh, and move the cursor onscreen by moving the mouse. To end a drag, release the mouse button.

- **Ctrl+click [Right-click]**—Macintosh users must press the Control key and click the mouse button; Windows users click the mouse's right button once.

HOW THIS BOOK IS ORGANIZED

Special Edition Using Adobe Illustrator 10 has nine parts, encompassing 28 chapters, and a tenth part, which consists of three appendixes. The nine parts are structured around central themes, with the chapters developing the part's concept. Readers new to Illustrator should explore the earlier parts before exploring the later chapters. Readers who have some familiarity with Illustrator 10 should also take a look at the first three parts. Although few high-level practitioners have the time to thoroughly explore a new version of a favorite program, often incredibly useful tools and techniques can be added to the reader's workflow.

The appendixes differ from the chapters; they are supplements. They cover such subjects as installing the program (along with what doesn't need to be installed and what can be deleted after installation), where to go for Illustrator assistance and resources, and checklists for folks on the go, for prepress, and for Web design.

Part I: Overview of Adobe Illustrator 10

The three chapters in this part provide a basis of reference for Illustrator 10. Chapter 1, "What's New in Illustrator 10," looks at what's new in the program, including envelope distortions, new tools, dynamic data-driven graphics, Web support, and productivity. Chapter 2, "The Illustrator Interface and Setup," focuses on the workplace and interface. This chapter is certainly valuable for readers both new to Illustrator and new to version 10. Chapter 3, "Working with Files in Illustrator," helps you understand both how file formats differ and which is appropriate for which project. Illustrator supports numerous file formats, each of which has its unique strengths, weaknesses, and applications. This version of Illustrator changes some file capabilities, too, such as new native support for the SVG file format.

Part II: Basic Creation in Illustrator

Four chapters look at the nuts and bolts of Illustrator's creative tools and techniques. Even readers with extensive experience with Illustrator will benefit from a look at Part II's chapters. Of particular note for advanced Illustrator users are Chapter 6, "Utilizing the Four Types of Brushes," and Chapter 7, "Type and Text in Illustrator." The many subtleties of these tools and techniques are examined in depth.

Part III: Manipulating Objects in Illustrator

Transformations, envelope distortions, and the new Liquify tools are explored. Illustrator's powerful blend capability gets a chapter all to itself. Chapter 10, "Illustrator's Layers, Sublayers, and Groups," takes an in-depth look at the power of Illustrator's Layers palette, which is important not just for work within Illustrator, but also for Photoshop compatibility and creation of animation. Part III also introduces the basic requirements for various types of output from Illustrator, including the difference between Web and print, and takes a look at such other output options as film recorders and presentation programs.

Part IV: Enhancing Illustrator Objects

Four chapters explore in depth many of Illustrator's more advanced concepts. This part starts with a thorough look at color in Illustrator, including the difference between RGB and CMYK, and a look at HSB and grayscale. Images critical to understanding the concepts are reproduced in full color in the book's color insert. Spot colors, global colors, and the Swatches palette are all discussed. Another chapter discusses patterns, including developing custom brush patterns. The Appearance and Styles palettes are the subject of Chapter 14, "Using the Appearance and Styles Palettes," which also looks at targeting groups and layers with appearance attributes using the Layers palette. Style libraries are introduced, and those included with Illustrator are examined. The topic of creating and applying gradients shares a chapter with a description of the Gradient Mesh tool. A tremendously powerful, but rather complex tool, its capabilities are explained and its use simplified.

Part V: Getting the Most Out of Illustrator

Although Illustrator utilizes Adobe's standardized interface, you can tailor it for your individual needs. Chapter 16, "Customizing Illustrator," looks at everything from the customizable keyboard shortcuts to creating startup files that save those initial steps required to prepare every new document. Masks, both clipping and opacity, get their own treatments in Chapter 17, "Using Masks to Show and Hide."

Part VI: Between Vector and Raster

Web graphic file formats, Photoshop interoperability, SVG—the need to understand raster artwork and images becomes more important than ever. This part of the book starts with an in-depth look at raster art and how it differs from Illustrator's native vector illustration capabilities. The concept of rasterizing vector artwork is discussed, along with a look at the options and possibilities. Chapter 19, "Exploiting Illustrator's Transparency," dives into Illustrator's powerful transparency capability, explaining how it works, why it works, and what has gone wrong when it doesn't work. Each of the 16 blending modes gets individual attention. The interactions among colors with each of the modes are shown in full color in the book's color insert. The filters and effects available in Illustrator are explained, as well as the differences between filters and effects.

Part VII: Illustrator and the Web

Designing Web sites and pages has never been easier in Illustrator. Chapter 21, "Designing Web Sites and Web Pages," presents the idea of color-coding a Web site for ease of design. The special requirements for Web graphics are explored, and the basic concepts of images on the Web are presented as well. Chapter 22, "Saving Images for the Web," concentrates on the details of saving images for the Web. Which file formats are appropriate in which situations, the difference between 8-bit and 24-bit color, and image compression are all covered thoroughly. The Save for Web feature is explained, along with the various optimization settings for GIF, JPEG, and PNG files. Chapter 23, "Flash and SVG Support," takes you to the cutting edge of Web graphics, presenting Illustrator's Flash and Scalable Vector Graphics (SVG) capabilities. Animation is the primary focus, but the additional potential is also discussed.

Part VIII: Prepress and Four-Color Process Printing

If you've never prepared a four-color job, you'll start with the basic concepts of printing. If you're a prepress professional, you, too, may learn a few things. Color, overprinting, knockouts, and trapping are presented, including a section on Illustrator's built-in trapping capabilities. The differences between linking and embedding images is critical to the success or failure of many projects. You'll read more than simply the differences; you'll get advice on which technique to use in which circumstances. A discussion of embedding fonts and the related legal issues also is presented.

Part IX: Illustrator Efficiency and Interoperability

Actions, how to use them, and how to create them are the subject of Chapter 26, "Automation Through Actions." Few, if any, readers would not benefit from developing and using custom Actions. You'll see a list of Illustrator's tools that cannot be recorded, as well as ways around most of those limitations. Readers who use Actions already likely know that paths can be inserted into a document using an Action. However, readers may be surprised when they see precisely what is recorded with the path, what is not, and what can make a path unrecordable. Likewise, Chapter 27 provides an introduction to dynamic data-driven graphics. This part also looks at interaction between Illustrator 10 and its sister program, Adobe Photoshop. You'll read about transferring artwork in either direction, the difference between transferring paths and moving art, and the parallel color management capabilities of the two programs.

Part X: Appendixes

The first appendix helps you with Illustrator 10 installation. Even if the program is installed already, take a look. You'll get an idea of how much unnecessary stuff is cluttering your hard drive, and guidance on what must stay and what can go. In Appendix B, you'll find resources galore. Where to go for help with Illustrator, how to help yourself, and some great additional resources—free resources—on the Web. Appendix C provides guidance on a variety of subjects, including how to take Illustrator on the road, how to help your clients view Illustrator documents, prepress checklists, and Web-related checklists.

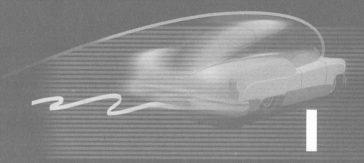

I

OVERVIEW OF ADOBE ILLUSTRATOR 10

IN THIS PART

1 What's New in Illustrator 10 **13**

2 The Illustrator Interface and Setup **23**

3 Working with Files in Illustrator **41**

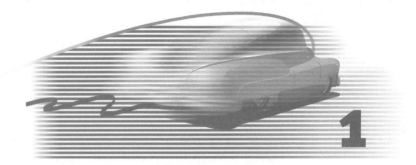

WHAT'S NEW IN ILLUSTRATOR 10

IN THIS CHAPTER

Illustrator for the Web   14

Envelope Distort, Warps, and Liquifying   15

Illustrator's Other New Tools   17

Compound Shapes   19

Mac OS X and Windows XP   20

Dynamic Data-Driven Graphics   20

Integration with the Adobe Family of Products   21

ILLUSTRATOR FOR THE WEB

Illustrator's new capabilities and improvements are nicely balanced between the creative and the productive. Web designers and creative professionals get several new capabilities and improved support for both SWF (Flash) and SVG (scalable vector graphics). Every Illustrator user, however, benefits from the new tools and even greater interoperability with other Adobe products. Adobe has also improved the way that Illustrator works with Photoshop and ImageReady, as well as GoLive, InDesign, LiveMotion, and AfterEffects.

The improvement that will be welcomed by all, regardless of how they use Illustrator, is performance. Illustrator 10 is substantially faster than the previous version. Illustrator 10 is also AltiVec capable, improving performance on Apple G4s and Apple's dual-processors machines.

A number of the new capabilities in Illustrator are designed for Web creation professionals. A number of the other improvements, while they have Web applications, are also very useful for other design projects.

CSS, Object-Based Slicing, and SVG Effects

Illustrator now supports cascading style sheets (CSS) through Save for Web. CSS offers the possibilities of overlapping objects, multi-purposed Web sites, and more complete control of fonts and page appearance.

Slicing can be object-based in Illustrator or you can use the Slice tool. Either way, precise and efficient slicing is as simple as designating an object as a slice or dragging the tool. And object-based slices update automatically as artwork is rearranged. Slices can be individually optimized using Save for Web, which also now offers SWF and SVG output.

SVG gets a major new capability with Illustrator 10: SVG Effects. Drop shadows, glows, and other effects are not applied until the SVG image appears in the browser window. That means that the effects are always applied after the SVG image is scaled, rather than having the raster effect scaled with the image. The result is a cleaner look to the effects, without the risk of pixelization.

Symbols and Selective Antialiasing

Symbols and the symbolism tools offer an incredibly easy way to create collections of identical objects—and then make them as different as you want them to be. And each of those objects, called *instances*, contained within a *symbol set*, is merely a representation. The artwork itself is actually added to the image only once, no matter how many instances appear on the artboard (see Figure 1.1). Illustrator's symbols can also be transferred to Flash.

Symbols are stored in the Symbols palette and can be loaded from document to document, just as styles, swatches, and brushes. Eight tools place the instances on the artboard and allow you to adjust the size, spacing, color, opacity, rotation, and even style of the individual instances.

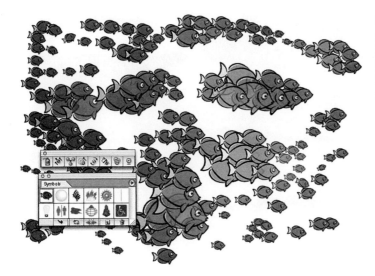

Figure 1.1
All of the fish in the sea, big and little, dark and light, are "symbol instances." The file actually stores the fish artwork only once, greatly reducing the file size.

Type objects can be antialiased separately from the rest of an image. This allows greater control over the appearance of the type in raster file formats, and is especially useful for small type destined for the Web. Illustrator 10 offers several ways to anti-alias text (and, of course, the option of no antialiasing), as shown in Figure 1.2.

Rasterized without anti-aliasing

Streamline anti-aliasing for type

Outline anti-aliasing for type

Standard anti-aliasing

Figure 1.2
The inset shows the type at 100% zoom, as it would be viewed on the Web.

ENVELOPE DISTORT, WARPS, AND LIQUIFYING

In addition to the distortion tools and effects, Illustrator 10 offers envelope distortions, warp effects, and a whole new set of tools for changing the shape of paths.

Envelope Distort

Extremely convenient, extremely flexible, and a whole lot of fun to use, Illustrator's new Envelope Distort commands can save hours of work with the Direct Selection tool (see Figure 1.3).

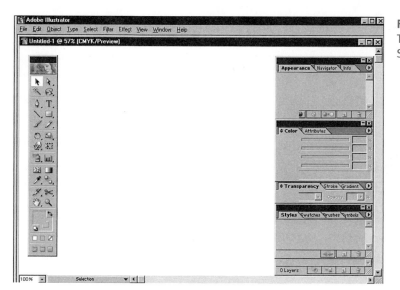

Figure 2.1
The Windows interface, using Standard Screen Mode.

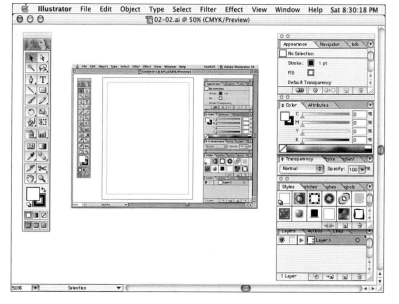

Figure 2.2
The Macintosh OS 9 interface (inset) and the Mac OS X interface, both using Standard Screen Mode.

Interacting with the Interface

You can select the tools from the Toolbox by using the cursor. Each tool works in a particular way within the illustration. Some are clicked, some are dragged, and some can be used in multiple ways.

You can bring palettes that are not visible to the front by clicking their tabs. Most palettes have a menu, which you access by clicking the small triangle in the upper-right corner of the palette. You can show or hide palettes by using the commands in the Window menu.

You access menu commands by clicking the menu heading at the top of the window and moving the cursor to the desired command. Some menu commands have submenus. When selected, some menu commands open dialog boxes, whereas others are executed immediately. In most cases, you can reverse the command by choosing Edit, Undo.

The Status Bar

Visible only in Standard Screen Mode, the status bar is located in the lower-left corner of the active window. (The screen modes are discussed in the section "View Modes.") To the left is the current zoom percentage. The small downward-pointing triangle represents a pop-up menu of preset zoom factors, from 3.13% to 6400%. Fit On Screen (comparable to the menu command View, Fit In Window) is also offered.

To the right of the zoom display is another status area. Using the pop-up menu, you can select the information to be displayed:

* **Current Tool**—This option is the default. The name of whichever tool is currently selected is displayed.

* **Date and Time**—This information is taken from the current system settings.

* **Free Memory**—Illustrator keeps you apprised of what percent of the assigned memory is still available and the amount of memory measured in megabytes.

* **Number of Undos**—Both the number of undos and the number of redos are displayed. Each undo represents an action that you can reverse in sequence by choosing Edit, Undo or its keyboard equivalent. Redos are available only when one or more undos have been used.

* **Document Color Profile**—This reading indicates the embedded color profile, if any.

The Artboard

The artboard represents the actual size of the illustration. In the document window, it is represented by a black rectangle. The size is specified in the New Document dialog box. You can alter it by choosing File, Document Setup (see Figure 2.3).

Figure 2.3
In addition to the standard sizes, you can enter custom artboard dimensions.

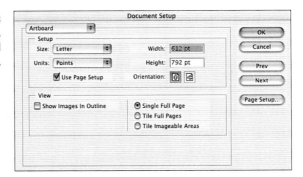

The artboard can be many times the size of the actual paper upon which the image will be printed. The printed pages are then *tiled*, or printed section by section. Page tiling is shown as a dotted line in the document window based on the paper size chosen in the Page Setup dialog box.

Rulers, Guides, and Grid

Proper placement of artwork is important to most illustrations created with Illustrator. Several interface elements are available to you to assist in the matter:

- **Rulers**—Shown and hidden with the View menu (or the appropriate keyboard shortcut), the rulers use the unit of measure selected in the preferences. By default, the rulers measure from the lower-left corner of the artboard, the *point of origin*. Although this point of origin is appropriate for most print applications, Web design and many other illustrations are better served by a point of origin in the upper-left corner. With the rulers showing, click and drag from their intersection in the upper-left corner of the document window and place the new point of origin as appropriate.

  The rulers and the point of origin affect many aspects of the Illustrator interface, including the Info palette, the Measure tool, and Document Setup, to name a few.

- **Guides**—You bring guides into a document by clicking and dragging from a ruler. Holding down Option [Alt] rotates a guide 90 degrees while dragging. You can place guides anywhere in a document. They are non-printing. When you use the command View, Snap to Point, objects you're dragging snap to a guide when within two screen pixels of it. Illustrator also offers Smart Guides. When activated, Smart Guides appear as needed in the window.

- **Grid**—Like guides, grids are non-printing lines used for alignment. The grid can be placed in front of or behind artwork on the artboard, and the unit of measure is determined by the general unit specified in the preferences. You can snap to the grid when moving objects by choosing View, Snap to Grid.

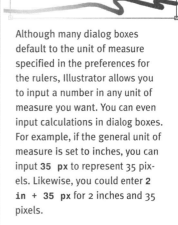

Although many dialog boxes default to the unit of measure specified in the preferences for the rulers, Illustrator allows you to input a number in any unit of measure you want. You can even input calculations in dialog boxes. For example, if the general unit of measure is set to inches, you can input **35 px** to represent 35 pixels. Likewise, you could enter **2 in** + **35 px** for 2 inches and 35 pixels.

In addition, Illustrator offers the Align palette and the Measure tool to help you properly place artwork.

ZOOMING

Zoom refers to the magnification of an image. To get a detailed look at a portion of an illustration, you can zoom in as closely as 6400%. To get a bird's-eye view, you can zoom out to 3.13%. Illustrator allows you to adjust the zoom factor in a variety of ways:

- The Zoom tool is available in the Toolbox. You can click to zoom in to the next standard magnification level, Option+click [Alt+click] to zoom out, or click and drag to zoom in on a specific portion of the artboard. When you're dragging the Zoom tool, Illustrator allows fractional zoom ratios.

- The View menu contains several zoom-related commands. In addition to Zoom In and Zoom Out, it offers Fit in Window and Actual Size. Fit in Window resizes the artboard to match the document's window onscreen. The command automatically makes the entire artboard visible. The Actual Size command changes the zoom factor to 100%, regardless of whether the artboard fits in the window.

- You can also control the zoom factor using the Navigator palette. The palette, which displays a rectangle indicating what part of an image is visible onscreen, offers three ways to alter the zoom. You can type over the percentage displayed in the lower left of the palette, you can click the Zoom Out and Zoom In icons, or you can drag the slider.

- When you're working in Standard Screen Mode, you can type a new zoom percentage in the lower-left corner of the window or select a zoom factor from the pop-up menu next to it.

VIEW OPTIONS

The basic display onscreen can be altered in several ways within Illustrator. The interface can be changed, the appearance of objects onscreen can be selected, palettes can be shown or hidden, and alignment aides can be used or not.

View Modes

You can make one of the most basic view selections by using the buttons at the bottom of the Toolbox. Illustrator offers Standard Screen Mode, Full Screen Mode with Menu Bar, and Full Screen Mode. By default, pressing F on the keyboard will rotate through the three view modes.

In the standard mode, Illustrator shows the document window and scrollbars, the window's title bar, the Illustrator status bar to the lower left, Illustrator's menu bar, and the appropriate operating system (OS) interface items. This last category can include the Windows Start menu and taskbar, or for Mac it includes the Apple menu and the optional display items (such as the time display) that appear in the menu bar. This is the default view mode.

The optional view modes eliminate much of the non-artboard information from the screen. Full Screen Mode with Menu Bar hides the scrollbars, the window's title bar, and the status bar. In Windows, the Start menu and taskbar are also hidden. Full Screen Mode hides everything except the work area.

No matter which of the three view modes you select, you retain control over whether palettes are visible or hidden. Zooming is also independent of the view mode.

The View Menu

The View menu contains numerous ways you can customize the appearance of the work area:

- **Outline/Preview**—Outline view shows only the path of each element on the artboard, without any appearance attributes. It redraws quickly and is efficient for laying out and organizing objects. Preview mode shows each object with all assigned attributes.

- **Overprint Preview**—This mode attempts to show the blending, transparency, and overprinting of overlapping colors. You use it to prepare images for four-color process printing.

- **Pixel Preview**—This option gives you the capability to preview artwork as it will appear on the World Wide Web. It simulates how the image will look when it is rasterized.

- **Proof Setup**—This setting determines the accuracy of the Proof Colors command.

  Custom allows you to select a specific output device's profile for soft proofing. Preserve Color Numbers shows how the image would print if the colors were not converted to the output device's color space. If this setting is not selected, the proof shows how the image will look if the colors are converted for the specified output device. You can also select rendering intent.

  Macintosh RGB assumes a standard Macintosh monitor gamut.

  Windows RGB assumes a standard Windows gamut.

  Monitor RGB uses the currently selected monitor calibration profile.

- **Proof Colors**—*Soft proofing* is the process of using a properly calibrated monitor to view how colors will print from a CMYK printer. (CMYK is described later in this chapter.) Rather than actually printing a sample (*hard proofing*), soft proofing allows the monitor to create a simulation. It is very important that the monitor be properly calibrated and that the appropriate CMYK profile be selected for soft proofing to be effective.

- **Zoom In**—This menu command or its keyboard equivalent increases the magnification of the image in the window to the next standard increment. Zoom can range from 6400% to 3.13%.

- **Zoom Out**—This menu command or its keyboard equivalent decreases the magnification of the image in the window to the next standard increment. Zoom can range from 6400% to 3.13%.

- **Fit In Window**—This command reduces the zoom of the image until the entire artboard is visible within the window. (This command is comparable to the status bar option Fit On Screen.)

- **Actual Size**—The zoom factor is set to 100%. This command is very important for previewing images or objects that will be viewed on the Web. With the exception of SVG graphics, all images you see on the Web are viewed at 100% zoom.

- **Hide/Show Edges**—The edges indicate an object's path. When a nonselection tool is active, the edges indicate what object or objects are selected.

- **Hide/Show Artboard**—The artboard, the area of the image that can contain printable artwork, is indicated by a solid black line when shown. The dimensions are established in the New Document dialog box and can be changed in Document Setup. This command determines whether the line will be visible in the document window.

- **Hide/Show Page Tiling**—The paper size and orientation, as selected in Page Setup, are shown with a pair of dotted lines on the artboard. The outer dotted line indicates the page size; the inner indicates the printable area. This command determines the visibility of those dotted lines.

- **Hide/Show Template**—All template layers present in the document can be shown and hidden using this command.

- **Show/Hide Rulers**—By default, the rulers are hidden in Illustrator. This command makes them visible along the top and left edges of the window.

- **Hide/Show Bounding Box**—Each object has a bounding box, which you can use to resize or scale the object. This command inactivates or activates the bounding boxes.

- **Show/Hide Transparency Grid**—A pattern of gray and white squares is visible in transparent areas of an illustration when this grid is visible.

- **Guides**—Guides, which you can use for references or to align objects within an illustration, can be dragged from the rulers onto the artboard. This command determines their visibility.

- **Smart Guides**—When you're working with an object on the artboard, you can use Smart Guides to help align to other objects, page corners, and guide intersections. The Smart Guides appear automatically, when activated, as an object approaches another object or an appropriate angle. Smart Guides indicate positions relative to the cursor. To snap to a designated point, select an object near the object's edge. Smart Guides are governed by settings established in the Smart Guides Preferences.

You cannot use Smart Guides when Snap to Grid is active.

- **Show/Hide Grid**—The grid is a pattern of horizontal and vertical lines, at intervals established in the preferences, that allow proper alignment and placement of objects on the artboard.

- **Snap to Grid**—When you activate Snap to Grid, the cursor automatically jumps to the nearest grid line or intersection when you're drawing, moving, scaling, or rotating an object. You can snap to the grid even when the grid is not visible.

- **Snap to Pixel**—When Pixel Preview is active, Snap to Grid changes its name. Snapping to the nearest pixel prevents unnecessary dithering and antialiasing when an image is rasterized.

- **Snap to Point**—When you're dragging an object, this option forces the cursor to snap to another object's anchor point or a guide when within 2 pixels.

- **New View**—With a particular set of options established in the window (zoom, position, rulers, and so on), this command creates and stores the view for later recall. Up to 25 views can be stored with a document. Saved views can be used to quickly show or hide rulers, guides, and grids all at once with a single command. In addition, separate areas of a large illustration can be saved as views to speed navigation.

- **Edit Views**—When views have been saved with the New View command, this command allows you to rename or delete them.

ILLUSTRATOR TERMINOLOGY AND LABELS

Most terms will be explained (or be obvious) within context throughout the book. Others, however, should be identified here to establish a firm foundation of understanding. The first set covers the basic Illustrator Interface.

Interface Terminology

- **Artboard**—The area upon which the illustration is created is the artboard. The artboard itself is, by default, outlined onscreen by a black rectangle. It should not be confused with page tiling (see later in this list).

- **Bounding box**—When an object is selected on the artboard, a rectangular outline appears. You can use the bounding box to move, rotate, or scale an object. When a transform tool is active, the bounding box can be used to further alter the object's path. To manipulate an object using the bounding box, use the mouse to drag within the object, or use the eight handles located around the bounding box to transform the selection. When multiple objects are selected, a single bounding box encompasses them all. You can hide or show this temporary outline by using the View menu.

- **Brush**—A selected brush determines the appearance of a path's stroke. Brushes are stored in the Brushes palette, and sets of brushes can be loaded and saved. The different kinds of brushes (calligraphic, scatter, art, and pattern) are discussed in Chapter 6, "Utilizing the Four Types of Brushes." You can apply a brush to a selected path or paths by clicking on it in the Brushes palette. The Paintbrush and Pencil tools can also use brushes.

- **Contextual menus**—You can access these options and commands by Ctrl+clicking [right-clicking]. They are called *contextual* because the choices available vary depending on what is clicked.

- **Dialog boxes**—Many commands open dialog boxes, which give you the option of adding or changing specific values before executing the command.

- **Guides**—These nonprinting vertical and horizontal lines can be used as alignment and spacing cues. You drag them from the rulers and lock/unlock and make them visible/invisible through the View menu.

- **Layers**—Artwork can be separated within a single document by using layers. Each layer is comparable to a sheet of clear acetate. Where no artwork appears, the underlying layers are visible. You use the Layers palette to organize and control layers. You can move objects from layer to layer and control their look by specifying an appearance for everything on a particular layer.

- **Menu commands**—You can interact with Illustrator and the artboard and objects on it by using the drop-down menus at the top of the screen. Some commands execute an action (Clear, Copy, Zoom In), whereas others open a dialog box (Save As, Check Spelling, Rasterize). Many menu commands have submenus, which open to the side of the drop-down list of commands.

- **Page tiling**—Shown onscreen by default as a dashed rectangle, page tiling represents the printable area of the page. It depends on the Page Setup options selected. It should not be confused with the artboard (see earlier in this list).

- **Palettes and tabs**—The so-called "floating palettes" appear by default along the right side of the screen. Many of the palette windows have multiple tabs, each representing a separate palette. Clicking a tab brings that palette to the front of the floating window. You can move palettes among the floating windows by dragging the tabs and can "dock" them at the bottom of another palette.

- **Pop-up menus**—Many palettes and dialog boxes have pop-up menus. To access a pop-up menu, click the option that is showing, and additional choices are made available.

- **Preferences**—Illustrator maintains a small file that records your particular choices for working with the program. This preferences file is updated every time you quit the program. You can select many of the choices by using the dialog boxes available when you choose Edit, Preferences. Others, however, are automatic, such as the location of palettes when you exit. This file, because of the nature of its contents and the fact that it is rewritten so often, can easily become corrupted. When Illustrator starts misbehaving, it is most often a preferences problem. If you quit Illustrator, delete the file, and restart the program, you often can set things right. You can find full instructions on replacing the preferences file in Chapter 16. Check the sidebar "Re-creating Illustrator's Preferences."

- **Ruler origin**—The rulers and the Info palette, among other aspects of Illustrator, measure distance from a set point. By default, Illustrator measures from the lower-left corner of a document. You can change the ruler origin to any point visible onscreen by dragging from the intersection of the rulers in the upper-left corner. (The rulers must be visible.) The ruler origin differs from the *point of origin* (although you will see the term used), which refers to transformation procedures (see "Techniques and Procedures," later in this chapter).

- **Tool**—The tools are the basic link between you and the creative process. Visible in the Toolbox (see the following description) along the left side of the screen, they each have certain properties and capabilities.

- **Toolbox**—This palette contains Illustrator's tools (see the preceding description). Many of the tools are hidden by default. When an icon in the Toolbox hides additional tools, a small triangle appears in the lower-right corner of the icon's box. To access the hidden tools, click and hold the visible icon. The hidden tool palettes can be "torn off" to become floating palettes of their own. Simply drag the palette away from the Toolbox.

- **Unit of measure**—Controlled by the Units & Undo preferences, this setting determines how the rulers, document setup and page setup, and several other interface elements express size. Typically, the term *unit of measure* refers to the setting in the General box of the Units & Undo panel in the Preferences dialog box. However, separate settings exist for both Stroke and Type.

- **Zoom**—Zoom can be controlled through a tool (the Zoom tool), a palette (the Navigator palette), menu commands (under the View menu), or the status bar (to the lower left of the screen in Standard View). It changes the appearance onscreen without affecting the actual artwork.

The Creative Elements

- **Actions**—A series of recorded commands is called an Action. These commands can be "played" on different images, executing the recorded commands in sequence. Illustrator ships with a variety of prerecorded Actions, and you can record and save your own. Actions are discussed in Chapter 26, "Automation Through Actions."

- **Anchor points**—A path (see later in this list) is defined by anchor points. Anchor points can be either corner points or smooth points. Smooth points link two curved segments of a path, whereas corner points link two straight segments or a straight and curved segment.

- **Appearance**—Properties that change or affect the look of an object without actually changing the object itself are called appearances. Effects, transparency, fills, and strokes are examples of appearances. Appearance attributes can be saved (see *style* later in this list).

- **Attributes**—Attributes should not be confused with appearance. The Attributes palette lists those items that actually fall into this category. In addition to overprinting information and output resolution, imagemap link information is displayed. The palette also offers the opportunity to reverse a path and to show or hide the center points of selected objects.

- **Bézier curves**—These editable vector paths are created with the Pen tool and other tools. (See *anchor points* earlier in this list, and *path*, *path segments*, and *vector objects* later in this list.)

- **Clipping mask**—A clipping mask uses the mask's shape to hide part of another object or objects. The object being masked appears to be cropped, but it is otherwise unaffected. (Contrast this with an *opacity mask*, described later in this list.) You create clipping masks by choosing Object, Clipping Mask, Make.

- **Direction points**—These points are used by smooth anchor points (see *anchor points* earlier in this section) to determine the shape of a curved segment of a path. You can manipulate them by using the Direct Selection tool.

- **Fill**—The area within a path, open or closed, is called its fill. The path can be filled with color, pattern, or gradient, or it can be left empty.

- **Gradient**—Gradients are smooth blendings of two or more colors. They, and gradient meshes, are discussed in detail in Chapter 15, "The Gradient and Gradient Mesh Tools." Gradients can be problematic for some printing operations. Illustrator can expand (see the next section) a gradient to create a series of individual objects that simulate the gradated blend between colors.

- **Mask**—See *clipping mask* (earlier in this list) and *opacity mask* (later in this list).

- **Object**—Any piece of artwork on the artboard can be considered an object. Such interface elements as guides and the grid do not count as objects.

- **Opacity mask**—An opacity mask, unlike a clipping mask (see earlier in this list), affects the appearance of the visible object being masked. Luminosity changes are used to show the mask's artwork on the masked object. Opacity masks are created using the Transparency palette.

- **Path**—A path is a vector object. It is defined and stored in a file mathematically. Paths can be stroked (colored) or left unstroked. They consist of path segments (see the following description), which are joined at anchor points (see earlier in this list). Paths can be closed (a continuous path with no apparent beginning or end) or open.

- **Path segments**—Each path consists of one or more segments, each defined by its two anchor points. A segment can be straight or curved, depending on those anchor points.

- **Pattern**—A pattern is a piece of artwork that can be used as a fill. It tiles, reproducing itself as many times as necessary, to fill the object to which the pattern is applied.

- **Pixel**—A pixel is a colored square. Images on monitors and in raster (see the following description) images consist of pixels. The pixels are arranged in rows and columns to create rectangular images. The term "pixel" derives from the longer term "picture element".

- **Raster image**—Raster images are created from individual colored squares called pixels (see preceding description). While Illustrator is primarily a vector art program, it has some powerful tools for working with raster images. Vector art can also be rasterized in Illustrator, changing it from path-based to pixel-based.

- **Stroke**—The color or pattern applied to a path is called its stroke. It can also be adjusted for width and the behavior of endpoints and corners.

- **Style**—One or more appearance attributes (see *appearance* earlier in this list) applied to an object or layer is called a Style. Styles can be saved in and applied from the Styles palette.

- **Swatch**—A swatch is a stored color, gradient, or pattern that can be applied through the Swatches palette. Sets of swatches can be saved and loaded, and exchanged between documents.

- **Vector objects**—Unlike raster objects and images (see earlier in this list), these objects are mathematically defined and can be edited and transformed. (See *paths* earlier in this list.)

Techniques and Procedures

- **Align**—Objects can be positioned precisely in relationship to themselves or to the artboard by means of the Align palette. The palette allows for both alignment and distribution.

- **Arrange**—See *stacking order* later in this list.

- **Effect**—An effect applies the appearance of a filter without changing the underlying object. An effect can be removed, unlike a filter (see later in this list).

- **Expand**—Illustrator allows you to create separate objects from a blend or a gradient (see the preceding section). The smooth transition between objects of different colors is maintained, but rather than a single object, a grouped series of objects is produced. Expanding a blend or gradient can simplify a file that won't print properly.

- **Filter**—A filter applies an artistic or other effect to an object. The object itself is changed, unlike using an effect (see earlier in this list).

- **Group/Ungroup**—When objects are grouped, they can be manipulated as a single entity. You can control grouping through the Object menu or from within the Layers palette.

- **Knockout**—This term refers to the behavior of overlapping objects. Within a group, knockout can visually block objects that are behind or below another. Transparency and masks can be used to define knockout behavior.

- **Lock/Unlock**—When an object is locked, it cannot be accidentally selected or altered on the artboard. You control locking through the Layers palette and with the menu commands Object, Lock and Object, Unlock All. Guides can also be locked or unlocked, but they are controlled through the View menu.

- **Point of Origin**—The point of origin determines the location from which an object will be transformed. By default, it is in the center of the object, but it can be dragged to any visible location within or outside the object. For the Rotate tool and command, this is the point around which the object will turn. It plays a similar role for other transform procedures. The point of origin should not be confused with ruler origin (see "Interface Terminology" earlier in this chapter), which determines the point from which Illustrator starts the rulers and measures. The term is also used for the point on the artboard from which the rulers measure (see *ruler origin*), the so-called zero-zero point. By default, that point is in the lower-left corner of the artboard.

- **Registration**—In addition to the process of becoming listed as an owner of the Illustrator software, the term *registration* also applies to a critical aspect of commercial printing. When printing presses are perfectly aligned, or in register, the colored inks will be perfectly placed. Misregistration, however, can result in minute shifting of the individual ink colors as they are printed. This topic is discussed in Chapter 24, "Commercial Printing and Trapping Issues." See also *trapping* later in this list.

- **Show/Hide**—Objects on the artboard, as well as interface options such as rulers, guides, and the grid, can be made visible or invisible. Interface options use commands in the View menu; objects are controlled through the Layers palette.

- **Snap To**—Available through the View menu, snapping precisely positions an object being created or transformed in relationship to the grid or to other objects or guides (Snap to Point). When you're dragging an object within two screen pixels of an anchor point or a guide, the object jumps to that position. When you use Pixel Preview, Snap to Pixel is available.

- **Stacking Order**—Objects have a three-dimensional relationship with each other. Each object is considered to be in front of (above) or behind (below) each of the other objects within an illustration. In addition to layers (see "Interface Terminology," earlier in this chapter), the objects on a single layer have positional relationships. An object in front of or above another hides the other where they overlap. (Whether the object is hidden, of course, depends on the higher object's transparency.)

- **Transform**—The Transform commands and tools affect the size, shape, or orientation of an object. They make changes to the object's path.

- **Transparency**—Transparency is the capability to see through an object to another behind it in the stacking order (see earlier in this list). It is measured in percent of opacity and controlled through the Transparency palette.

- **Trapping**—Trapping is discussed in Chapter 25. It refers to the slight overlap of colors that is designed to prevent unwanted bare areas during the printing process. Without trapping, minute discrepancies between the alignment of printing plates or press runs can result in registration (see earlier in this list) problems.

- **Undo**—Limited only by the memory available to Illustrator, Undo allows you to reverse steps taken in the creative process sequentially. Each step must be undone in order. Interface adjustments, such as repositioning palettes, cannot be undone. Undos are not saved with a document, existing only in memory. They are lost when a file is closed.

Typography and Text Terms

(Also see Chapter 7, "Type and Text in Illustrator.")

- **Alignment**—Alignment is the arrangement of ends of the lines of text in a paragraph. Because each line of text may have a different number of characters (or the characters may require a different amount of linear space on the line), text can be set to align to the right, the left, be center aligned, or have the spacing adjusted automatically to present even borders on both the right and left edges. Even a single word or character can be aligned to determine its location in relationship to the point where the cursor was clicked or to the object being used as a type container. When both the left and right margins of a paragraph are aligned, the text is said to be *justified* (see later in this list).

- **Area type**—Objects and open paths can be used as containers for text. When you're creating area type, the object's shape determines the layout of the text.

- **Baseline**—The baseline for text is an imaginary line drawn along the bottom of the majority of the letters and numbers. Several letters (specifically the lowercase *g, j, p, q,* and *y* in most fonts) drop below the baseline. Individual characters can be *superscript* (raised above the baseline) or *subscript* (dropped below the baseline).

- **Block type**—You can drag with the Type tool or use the Rectangle tool to define a box for text. You can use the box's bounding box (see "Interface Terminology" earlier in this chapter) to resize and reshape the object to accommodate the text.

- **CJK**—Chinese-Japanese-Korean fonts require substantially different handling than letter-based text. Illustrator has several special CJK text-handling capabilities.

- **Display font**—This term is used for those particular fonts that are designed for use at large sizes. They are specialty fonts, intended for use as headlines. Although they can be used at smaller sizes, they are often more difficult to read and visually unappealing when so employed.

- **Font**—A font, also known as a typeface or font family, is a set of characters designed to be used together. Typically, a font includes all the letters, numbers, and standard symbols in a particular alphabet. However, some fonts may include only a subset or consist entirely of symbols. Fonts are discussed in Chapter 7.

- **Leading**—Leading refers to the space between lines of type. It is pronounced *ledding* (as in the metal) rather than *leeding* (as in the verb *to lead*). The term dates from the times when type was set by hand, and thin strips of lead were placed horizontally between the lines of letters.

- **Justification**—Justification is the alignment of both the left and right margins in a paragraph (see *alignment* earlier in this list). Illustrator offers two types of justification. A paragraph can be justified using all full lines, leaving the last line aligned only to one margin, or the paragraph can be fully aligned, which results in justification of the last line, regardless of the number of words.

- **Kerning**—Kerning is the spacing between two adjacent characters. It should not be confused with tracking (see later in this list), which is the spacing of a series of characters. See also *ligature*.

- **Ligature**—Certain combinations of letters can be replaced with a single symbol. These combinations include ff, fi, ffi, fl, and ffl. In Illustrator, you control this use through the menu command Type, Smart Punctuation. Ligatures can improve the appearance, and legibility, of these letter combinations.

- **Multiple master**—Multiple master fonts are PostScript Type 1 fonts that can be adjusted for a variety of typeface characteristics. Depending on how the font will be used, you can customize it for optical size, weight, width, and style. Most multiple master fonts are supplied with a number of primary instances. Standard Type 1 and TrueType fonts, in comparison, have a single master.

- **Path type**—When text is applied to an open path so that it runs along the path (rather than flows inside a closed path), it can be considered path type (also called *type on a path*). You therefore can manipulate the appearance of the text by editing the path.

- **Point type**—Text that is entered directly into an illustration at a specific spot is considered point type. Such text is not linked to an object's shape or a container and can be manipulated by means of its own bounding box (see "Interface Terminology," earlier in this chapter). (See also *area type* and *path type*, both in this list.)

- **Tracking**—Tracking is the spacing among a series of characters. It should not be confused with kerning, which is the spacing between a particular pair of adjacent characters.

- **Type on a path**—(See *path type* earlier in this list.)

Color and Color Management

(See also Chapter 12, "Understanding and Applying Color.")

- **Banding**—Under some conditions, *gradients* (see "The Creative Elements," earlier in this chapter) and other gradual changes of color in an illustration may suffer from banding onscreen or in print. Banding occurs when similar colors are grouped together. For example, a gradient that runs from red to blue may be banded into a series of discrete colors. The visible bands of color no longer appear as a smooth transition from one color to another. Onscreen, this lack of transition is typically a function of having a monitor set to too few colors (8-bit color rather than thousands or millions of colors). Often you can minimize banding by expanding a gradient. (See *expand* under "Techniques and Procedures," earlier in this chapter.)

- **Bitmap**—This term has two distinct meanings. When referring to color, *bitmap* describes images that consist of only black and white pixels. This color mode is also called 1-bit color. The term bitmap can also be used to refer to raster art, as opposed to vector objects (see "The Creative Elements," earlier in this chapter, for both raster and vector objects).

- **CMYK (Cyan, Magenta, Yellow, Black)**—This color mode is used for commercial printing presses. The name refers to the four process color inks used to reproduce the spectrum. CMYK's gamut is substantially smaller than that of RGB. CMYK should be used only for images intended to be reproduced by four-color process printing; it is not for use with most inkjet printers. (See also *color mode, gamut, RGB,* and *separations* in this list.)

- **Color management**—Because different devices produce color differently, color management systems have been established. They are intended to standardize color from scanner to monitor, between monitors, from monitor to printer, and so on. The goal is to produce consistent color so that each image looks or prints exactly the same, regardless of computer or printer. Color management does not correct images that contain inaccurate color but rather helps portray the colors of the image exactly as recorded in the file.

- **Color mode/color model**—A document's color mode is determined by the color model. The color model is the specific way in which color is recorded and expressed within a document. Illustrator supports the CMYK and RGB color modes, and allows you to work in the CMYK, RGB, grayscale, HSB, and Web-safe RGB color models. CMYK is reserved for use with images that will be reproduced using four-color process printing, whereas RGB is intended for monitor, film, inkjet, and other output and display options. (See also *gamut* and *ICC profile* in this section.)

- **Color space**—See *gamut* in this list.

- **Gamut**—A color gamut or color space expresses the range of colors that can be produced by a particular color model (earlier in this list). For example, the CMYK gamut (earlier in this list) consists of all colors that can be reproduced by mixing the four colors of ink. The RGB gamut likewise consists of all colors that can be reproduced using red, green, and blue light. The RGB gamut (later in this list) is considerably larger than that of CMYK. RGB colors that cannot be reproduced with the four process inks are referred to as out of gamut (later in this list).

- **Grayscale**—The grayscale color model consists only of those colors that can be produced using various tints of black ink. Grayscale objects can exist in either RGB (later in this list) or CMYK (earlier in this list) Illustrator documents. Grayscale is normally expressed as 8-bit color, resulting in a total of 256 possible shades of gray.

- **ICC profile**—You can think of a profile as a translator, ensuring that the color information recorded in an image file is faithfully reproduced onscreen or in print. Each profile is designed to work with a specific device whose characteristics are understood. For example, if a particular monitor has a tendency to produce a slight reddish tint onscreen, a correctly recorded ICC profile compensates by slightly reducing the percentage of red sent to the monitor for display. ICC refers to the International Color Consortium, an organization entrusted with establishing color standards.

- **Jaggies**—This generally accepted term refers to the appearance of blocky edges on curved lines. A function of visible pixels, it produces a stair-step look to curves. Jaggies are discussed in Chapter 18, "Raster Images and Rasterized Objects."

- **Out of gamut**—RGB colors that cannot be reproduced using the four process inks (CMYK) are referred to as out of gamut. (See also *gamut* in this list.) Illustrator has several ways of warning you when a color is out of gamut. This is of importance only when an image will be sent to a four-color printing press. Artwork destined for the Web, for example, will be reproduced using RGB, so the CMYK gamut is of no concern.

- **Process color**—The four process colors are cyan, magenta, yellow, and black. They are referred to collectively as CMYK. CMYK colors are used only in commercial printing, which relies on the four colors of ink to reproduce the wide range of colors possible in images. (See also *CMYK*, *gamut*, *RGB*, and *spot color* in this list.)

- **RGB (Red, Green, Blue)**—This color mode is used for all images other than those destined for four-color process printing. The RGB gamut is larger than that of CMYK, meaning that it can reproduce a large range of colors. The three component colors, when added together at full strength, produce white. (See also *CMYK*, *color mode*, and *gamut* in this list.)

- **Separations**—Color separations are the representations of an image that show exactly where one of the four process (CMYK) colors or a spot color will be printed in an image. They are used to produce the actual printing plates in the traditional printing process (although some workflows are "direct-to-plate"). They are used only with CMYK images and are intended only for printing. (See also *CMYK* and *spot color* in this list.)

- **Spot color**—Specific ink colors added to a CMYK image are referred to as spot colors. These colors can be present only in a specific spot in an image or can be found throughout the image. The colors may require a particular ink from a specific manufacturer or might be reproducible using the standard four-color process (CMYK) inks. However, whether process or not, spot colors normally are printed separately, using a separate color separation. (See also *CMYK* and *separations* in this list.)

- **Web-safe**—This term refers to the 216 specific colors that can be viewed accurately on both Windows and Macintosh computers using only the systems' native color palettes. Both operating systems have system palettes that consist of 256 colors (8-bit); however, 40 of the colors differ. The Web-safe palette is of less importance than it was several years ago when more computers using the World Wide Web were restricted to 8-bit color.

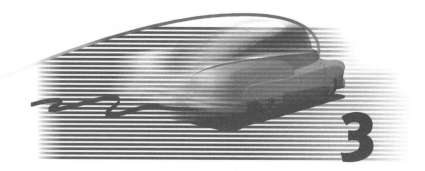

3

WORKING WITH FILES IN ILLUSTRATOR

IN THIS CHAPTER

Determining File Format Requirements   42

Illustrator's Commands to Save and Export Files   44

Linking and Embedding   53

Troubleshooting   55

DETERMINING FILE FORMAT REQUIREMENTS

A file's format determines how the file's information is stored. Different formats store information in different ways and, in some cases, store different information. How the file can be used, and for what, often depends on file format. Print and Web applications require different file formats. What works well for print is not even visible on the Web. Trying to use Web-formatted images to produce high-quality printed materials is an exercise in frustration. Knowing the destination of a file before you begin working can often help prevent serious errors later. Creating with the end product in mind is usually a good idea.

You also need to consider various other issues when working with files in Illustrator. You may need to consider whether to link or embed placed artwork. You may need to consider copyright issues when sending images with fonts to a printer. Even how and what you name a file may be problematic.

A file that's headed to the World Wide Web can be saved in one of several formats. Each format has its strengths and weaknesses. Images that are intended for four-color process printing can also be saved in several formats. There are, of course, several other possible destinations for your work. In this chapter, you'll look at appropriate file formats for those purposes, too.

More in-depth information on these specific issues is available in these chapters: Chapter 11, "Output Options"; Chapter 12, "Understanding and Applying Color"; Chapter 18, "Raster Images and Rasterized Objects"; Chapter 22, "Saving Images for the Web"; Chapter 23, "Flash and SVG Support"; and Chapter 24, "Commercial Printing and Trapping Issues."

Raster Versus Vector

File formats can be divided numerous ways and into numerous categories. One of the most important divisions is between *raster* and *vector*. Although these concepts are explained at length in Chapter 19, it's important to have the most basic of understandings for this discussion of file formats. In a nutshell, a raster file saves an image as a series of pixels, colored squares arranged in a series of rows. Vector data, on the other hand, consists of mathematical descriptions of shapes. When raster images are resized (enlarged or made smaller), the images can become blurry. Vector images, on the other hand, remain sharp and clear at any size.

More and more, the line between vector and raster is blurring. Illustrator is a vector art program, but it can and does work with raster data. Adobe Photoshop, on the other hand, is a raster image editor. The most recent version of Photoshop, however, does have vector text capabilities and simulates vector objects through the use of clipping paths. Despite these advances, however, the difference between the two types of data is important.

⇨ *If you're confused about the difference between raster and vector, see "Pixels and Paths" in the "Troubleshooting" section at the end of this chapter.*

Web, Print, and Other File Destinations

For the Web, the most common file formats are all raster: JPEG, GIF, and PNG. Some of the newer formats, such as Flash and SVG, are vector based. JPEG is designed for photographs and also does a very good job with other continuous tone images. GIF, on the other hand, is limited in the number of colors it can store and so is better suited to images with large areas of solid color, such as clip art, cartoons, and logos. (The differences are explored in depth in Chapter 22.)

In the print world, EPS and TIFF can both be raster formats, although the clipping paths embedded in the files are actually vector data. Chapter 24 provides more information.

Illustrator also supports several other file formats, which are used specifically with certain programs. Files can be prepared in the native formats of programs such as Photoshop and AutoCAD, and for specific platforms and systems, such as Amiga and Pixar. Most files, however, are saved in a limited number of formats. They will be discussed later in this chapter.

Compression Issues

Many file formats shrink the amount of space required on disk for the file through compression. Files can also be prepared for archiving using compressed file formats. The two categories of file compression are *lossy* and *lossless*. Lossy schemes discard data to reduce file size. Lossless compression schemes rarely achieve the tiny file sizes available to their lossy counterparts but retain all of an image's original data.

The content of a file also plays a role in file format and compression selection. Some images are better suited for one type of compression than others; some files are better suited for a specific file type that uses one type of compression.

JPEG uses a lossy compression system, discarding data to reduce file size. There are several levels of JPEG compression, and Illustrator allows you to balance file size against image quality. The smaller the file, the more data discarded. The more data discarded, the lower the quality of the image.

⇨ *Having trouble with JPEG? See "Lossy Compression" in the "Troubleshooting" section at the end of this chapter.*

GIF and PNG usually use lossless compression schemes. All the image's original information is retained. Illustrator offers a lossy GIF compression option within its Save for Web feature.

Platform Considerations

Filenames are still a consideration, despite the great strides that have been made over the past few years. The "eight-point-three" naming system is no longer required for Windows, but that doesn't mean that it's gone completely. (In computer jargon, "8.3" refers to a filename of up to eight characters followed by a period and a three-character file extension. This was and is the only acceptable way to name files in MS-DOS.)

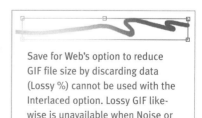

Save for Web's option to reduce GIF file size by discarding data (Lossy %) cannot be used with the Interlaced option. Lossy GIF likewise is unavailable when Noise or Pattern dither is selected.

The following are some considerations when you're naming files:

- Windows filenames can be up to 256 characters long, and they are not case sensitive (upper- and lowercase letters are seen as the same letter). Several characters cannot be used in filenames: forward and back slashes, colons, asterisks, question marks, quotation marks, left and right angle brackets, and vertical slashes. In order, these characters are as follows: / \ : * ? " < > |

- Macintosh filenames through OS 9 can be up to 31 characters long and are not case sensitive. The only forbidden character is the colon (:).

- Under Mac OS X, you can have file names as long as 255 characters, and the colon (:) is the only forbidden character.

- Unix filenames can be 256 characters long, cannot use the slash character (/), and are case sensitive.

- MS-DOS filenames can use only the 8.3 format and have the same character restrictions as Windows.

- ISO 9660 for CD-ROMs uses the 8.3 name format and allows only 26 letters, the numbers from zero to nine, and the underscore (_). These names are not case sensitive. (This standard is designed to allow a CD-ROM to be recognized by any computer.)

ILLUSTRATOR'S COMMANDS TO SAVE AND EXPORT FILES

When you start a new document, it is, by default, an Illustrator document. However, the file isn't actually recorded to disk until you use the Save, Save As, Export, or Save for Web command. When the file is written to disk, you must select a file format. The format (as noted previously) determines many important aspects of how the file will be recorded. File compatibility, compression scheme, and file size are just some of the factors that you must consider.

> **Caution**
>
> When you're preparing files for the Web, including the three-character filename extension is important. Although the platform and operating system (OS) may support filenames without extensions, Web browsers require them. Because of the peculiarities of the Web, my best advice to you is to be as conservative as possible. Unless you have direct knowledge of (and control over) the server upon which your files will be stored, use the lowest common denominator for filenames:
>
> - Use the 8.3 naming convention and never forget to add the filename extension.
>
> - Stick with the 26 letters, the 10 numerals, and the underscore (_).
>
> - Use only lowercase letters.

Save

The Save command maintains the file's existing format and simply updates the file's information. If a new file has not previously been saved, the Save As dialog box opens.

Save As

The Save As dialog box offers five file formats from which to choose:

- **Adobe Illustrator Document (.ai)**—This is the native file format for Adobe Illustrator. It supports all the features of the program. However, earlier versions also use the .ai file extension and do not support all the features of Illustrator 10.

  Illustrator offers you several options when saving a file in its native format. You can see them in the dialog box shown in Figure 3.1.

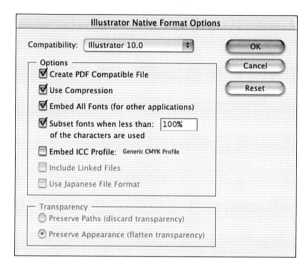

Using the Compatibility option, you can make the file emulate earlier versions of Illustrator. You should use this when the file will be opened in an earlier version of the program. You can also embed the fonts used in the document and subset them to reduce file size. (See "Embedding Fonts" later in this chapter.) Any specific ICC profiles in use when the file was created can be included, as well as any files that were placed but not embedded. (See "Linking and Embedding Images" later in this chapter.) If a version of Illustrator earlier than 9 was selected for Compatibility, you have the option of choosing how to handle transparency. If you choose to preserve the paths, the file will be fully editable in the earlier version of the program. If you opt to preserve the appearance, sections of the illustration that employ transparency will be flattened (rasterized and divided). Figure 3.2 shows the result.

Figure 3.2
The two objects on the left were flattened when the file was saved. To the right, the parts have been scattered to show them individually.

- **Adobe PDF (.pdf)**—The native format of Adobe Acrobat, PDF files are now very common. Acrobat Reader can be found on most modern computers and is freely available for others. Documents saved in PDF format can be viewed on almost any computer.

  PDF files support both vector and raster (bitmap) information. Although PDF pages are PostScript at heart, they can also contain annotations and notes, and can be searched and hold hyperlinks.

  You'll see two panels in the Adobe PDF Format Options dialog box after you've named and chosen a location for your file. On the General panel (shown in Figure 3.3), you can select general Acrobat options. On the Compression panel (shown in Figure 3.4), you can specify compression settings. In either panel, you can use the Options Set menu to select the prede-fined sets of options for Default (print) or Screen Optimized (Web).

- **Illustrator EPS (.eps)**—PostScript is a page descrip-tion language developed by Adobe. Encapsulated PostScript (EPS), like PDF, supports both vector and raster information. EPS is often used to put a graphic element into a page layout program. Typically, the EPS file is an image on a page, but it can be a com-plete page as well.

  EPS files can contain previews that are visible in a page layout program. When no preview is present, a placeholder (a box with two crossing diagonal lines) is shown on the page. Macintosh previews are avail-able in PICT (Macintosh) or TIFF format, and either can be 1-bit (black and white) or 8-bit (color). Windows EPS files can have previews in TIFF or Windows Metafile (.wmf) format.

  In addition to choosing the file format, you can opt to have transparency for Tiff previews in the EPS Format Options dialog box (see Figure 3.5).

If you exchange files with anyone using an earlier version of Adobe Illustrator, suggest that your col-league download the free Version Checker from Adobe. With this plug-in installed, users of earlier versions of Illustrator get a warning when opening a document created in Illustrator 9 or later. (Version 9 is a key cutoff point because that's when transparency was introduced.) The plug-in can be downloaded from the following sites:

Mac   `http://www.adobe.com/support/downloads/827a.htm`

Windows   `http://www.adobe.com/support/downloads/8276.htm`

Before saving complex illustrations as PDF files, you can take an extra step to help preserve the appear-ance of your image and ensure problem-free printing. Working on a copy of your original, open the Layers palette. From the palette menu (the little triangle in the upper-right corner of the palette), select Flatten Artwork. You can then save the file in PDF format with its original appearance intact.

Because TIFF previews are com-patible with both Windows and Macintosh, choose this option when saving as an EPS file. And, although the 8-bit color preview will increase the file size slightly, choose it rather than the 1-bit black-and-white version.

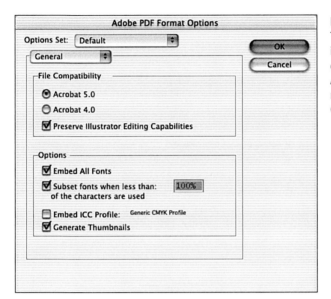

Figure 3.3
The General options for PDF files include compatibility and embedding. Thumbnails are used within Acrobat and Acrobat Reader, but not as previews in Illustrator's Open dialog box.

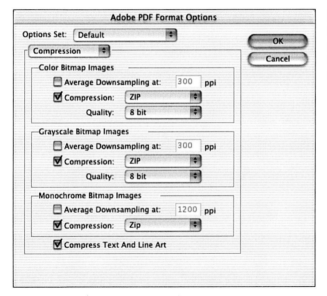

Figure 3.4
Note that in addition to allowing separate settings for different types of artwork, you have a separate check box for text and line art.

- **SVG (.svg)**—Scalable Vector Graphics are used on the World Wide Web. When saving in this format, you have the option of including part of a font or the entire font. Any placed images can be embedded or linked. You can retain the capability of editing the image in Illustrator if necessary. When you click the Advanced button, you'll see additional options (shown in Figure 3.6). The cascading style sheets (CSS) and encoding options will be discussed in Chapter 23, "Flash and SVG Support."

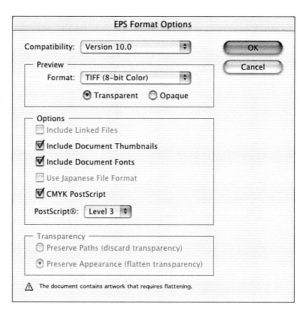

Figure 3.5
Among the other options on this dialog box is a choice of PostScript Level 2 or Level 3. PostScript Level 1 is supported only when you're saving as Illustrator 8 or earlier.

Figure 3.6
The SVG Options dialog box contains an Advanced button that opens the additional dialog box.

- **SVG Compressed (.svgz)**—The options for this file format are identical to those for the standard SVG format. The compressed version of the format is not supported by all SVG plug-ins.

Export

In addition to the three primary file formats and SVG available in the Save As dialog box, Illustrator offers a variety of export formats. Those formats that are unlikely to ever be needed can be deleted from the Photoshop Formats folder, found within Illustrator's Plug-ins folder.

A number of Illustrator's export formats require rasterization before you save the file. The Rasterize dialog box is shown in Figure 3.7.

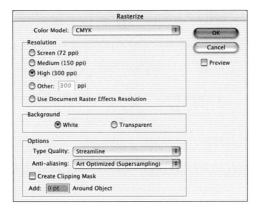

Figure 3.7
RGB, grayscale, and bitmap color modes are supported, as well as choices of resolution and antialiasing.

- **AutoCAD Drawing (.dwg)** — AutoCAD is a premier architectural and engineering design tool. DWG is the program's standard vector file format. DWG (and its sister format DXF) swaps white fills and strokes for black. The export dialog box is shown in Figure 3.8.

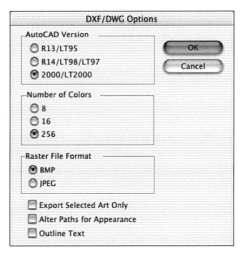

Figure 3.8
AutoCAD version, bit depth, and raster format for fills and textures are among the choices for the DWG format.

- **AutoCAD Interchange File (.dxf)** — This file format is used to exchange information between AutoCAD and programs that do not support the DWG format. From Illustrator, it can also be used to exchange information with those programs. When you're working directly with AutoCAD, however, DWG is usually a better choice. DXF is a tagged format. The dialog box is identical to that of DWG (shown in Figure 3.8).
- **Bitmap (.bmp)**— BMP requires that the image be rasterized before you save. The Rasterize dialog box is identical to the one shown in Figure 3.7. In addition, however, the BMP format offers compatibility with Windows or IBM's OS/2 format, a choice of color depth, and (in some cases) compression (see Figure 3.9) .

Figure 3.9
The Run Length Encoding (RLE) compression option is not always available.

- **Computer Graphics Metafile (.cgm)**—This format is designed for use with complex engineering and architectural diagrams. It is not suitable for illustrations that incorporate large amounts of text. It is a vector format. The export function has no user-definable options.

- **Enhanced Metafile (.emf)**—An advanced version of Microsoft's Windows Metafile (.wmf) format, EMF is available only for 32-bit Windows. The export function has no user-defined options.

- **JPEG (.jpg)**—One of the two main file formats on the Web, JPEG is a 24-bit file format best suited for photographs and other continuous-tone images. In addition to Export, JPEG is available through Illustrator's Save for Web feature. More information is available in Chapter 22, "Saving Images for the Web."

🖙 *Problems creating JPEG files for the Web? If they're valid JPEG files, but your browser won't show them, see "RGB for the Web" in the "Troubleshooting" section at the end of this chapter.*

- **Macintosh PICT (.pct)**—PICT is most effective when you're working with areas of solid color, rather than *continuous tone* images. (Continuous tone is the term used for the subtle transitions from color to color that can be found in photographs.) This Macintosh format has some (but limited) support in Windows programs.

- **Macromedia Flash (.swf)**—Although not the native Flash format, SWF fulfills the need for a vector-based, interactive file format. SWF is actually the Shockwave file format. (Flash's FLA is a proprietary format controlled by Macromedia.) This is a Web format, but viewers must use a browser equipped with the Flash plug-in. For more information, see Chapter 23, "Flash and SVG Support." Figure 3.10 shows the dialog box for Flash (SWF) Format Options.

- **Paintbrush (.pcx)**—Like TIFF, BMP, and a number of other formats, PCX requires rasterization before you save an image. (The Rasterize dialog box is shown in Figure 3.7.) PCX was developed for the PC Paintbrush program. Illustrator fully supports only version 5 of the format.

- **Photoshop (.psd)**—Photoshop native format files can now be created from Illustrator. Layered Illustrator documents can be exported to Photoshop with layers intact. Figure 3.11 shows the Photoshop Options dialog box.

Figure 3.10
The specific options in the SWF Format Options dialog box are discussed in Chapter 23.

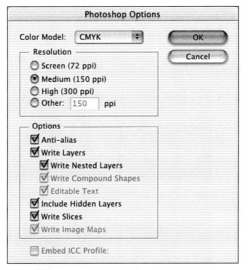

Figure 3.11
The available color models are RGB, CMYK, and grayscale.

For additional information, see Chapter 18, "Raster Images and Rasterized Objects," and Chapter 28, "Integrating Illustrator 10 and Photoshop."

- **Pixar (.pxr)**—Pixar is the file format used by PIXAR workstations for 3D and animation work. Saving in the Pixar format automatically rasterizes the image (refer to Figure 3.7 for the dialog box).

- **Targa (.tga)**—Targa files are designed for use with systems incorporating the Truevision video board. Numerous MS-DOS color applications can use the format. Artwork is automatically rasterized (refer to Figure 3.7) when saved as Targa.

- **Text (.txt)**—This "plain text" format is a most basic text format. It is a suitable choice when you need to move text to a word processor without fancy formatting. Such options as baseline shift and character scaling will be ignored.

- **Tagged Image File Format (.tif)**—TIFF (as the file format is known) is among the most common raster image formats. In addition to image-editing programs, many scanners produce TIFF files. This format is among the most common for placing rasterized images into page layout programs. In addition to the settings shown in the Rasterize dialog box (refer to Figure 3.7), the TIFF Options include LZW Compression settings and profile embedding.

- **Windows Metafile (.wmf)**—The basic file format of clip art from Microsoft Office for Windows (among other programs), WMF is a vector format.

Save for Web

The Save for Web command opens what is perhaps Illustrator's most impressive dialog box. Save for Web, which might be considered an independent program within Illustrator, will be fully explored in Chapter 22, "Saving Images for the Web." It even creates a separate and independent preferences file. Its entire function is to properly optimize graphic files for the Web in GIF, JPG, and PNG formats. As you can see in Figure 3.12, it offers up to four variations of optimization for comparison.

Figure 3.12
The Save for Web dialog box, despite its appearance, is actually quite user friendly.

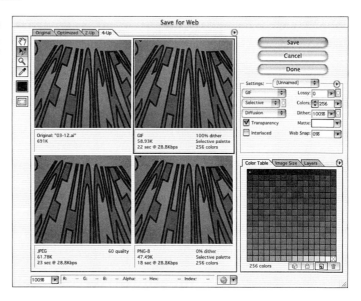

Save for Web allows you to balance the file's size against its appearance, even to the point of specifying exactly how many colors will be included (8-bit color only). Because it works only with GIF, JPG, and PNG, the files are rasterized when you save. Save for Web also allows you to specify a target file size and let the program make the decisions about how to optimize.

LINKING AND EMBEDDING

The process of linking and embedding objects is discussed fully in Chapter 25, "Linking and Embedding Images and Fonts." When you add artwork to an image from an outside file by using the Place command, it can be linked or embedded. Embedding places a copy of the artwork within the Illustrator file. Linking places only enough information to allow Illustrator to find the original artwork for display within the image. Linking placed images rather than embedding them keeps the Illustrator document's file size down and allows the placed artwork to be updated or changed as necessary in its own program.

Fonts can also be embedded in an image, ensuring that they will be available for later use with that file. To reduce file size, you can *subset* fonts. Subsetting a font allows you to include only the characters used.

Linking and Embedding Images

One of the two ways that you can place artwork in an Illustrator document from another file is *linking*. A linked image remains separate. This is somewhat similar to a hyperlink for the Web; only a pointer is placed in your illustration, and the external image is loaded when your file is opened. Illustrator notifies you if any changes have been made to the original. Keep in mind, though, that your image must always be able to find the external artwork. If you were, for example, to send out your image on disk without including a copy of the linked file, the linked artwork would not be available to anyone opening your image from the disk. A warning dialog box would appear. The Save As command (and Save the first time it is used) allows you the option of including linked files.

Embedding is the other way to include artwork from another file in an Illustrator document. When you embed an image, a copy of the artwork is incorporated into your Illustrator document. You are not notified of any changes to the original, and the only way to update is to replace the embedded image. The advantage is that the placed artwork becomes part of your image, and it doesn't have a link that can be accidentally broken. The Illustrator document's size increases by the size of the placed artwork.

Illustrator can place files of any format that it can open, with the exception of the Illustrator (.ai) format. Some formats, however, must be embedded rather than linked:

- CGM
- DOC
- DXF/DWG
- Freehand
- RTF
- SVG
- WMF

The Links palette, shown in Figure 3.13, is for use with linked and embedded images. Using the palette is an excellent way to maintain control of and to track images from other documents.

Figure 3.13
The Links palette allows you to view according to the status of a file.

Icons to the right of each image indicate the status. No icon, such as shown in Figure 3.13 next to <Image_002.tif>, indicates a linked file with no problems. A red octagon with a white question mark, like that next to <Image_004.tif>, indicates that the linked image's original is missing. The icon to the right of <Image_003.tif> indicates that it is embedded rather than linked. The symbol to the right of <Image_001.tif> indicates that it has been modified since it was placed into the Illustrator document and requires update.

Embedding Fonts

Illustrator allows you to include the fonts used when saving files in the Illustrator format. Embedding fonts ensures that they will be available when the image is opened on different machines or in different programs. When a font is not embedded and it is not installed on the computer opening the file, another font is substituted. However, that font may not have the same spacing, appearance, or size as the font originally used and, therefore, the appearance of your image can be altered, sometimes drastically.

You also have the option to subset a font, which results in only the characters used being embedded in the file. Subsetting helps keep file size small but restricts editing possibilities since not all characters will be available. In addition, font embedding is available only when the file is saved as an Illustrator document. Saving a file to be compatible with an earlier version of the program eliminates this option.

One other aspect of font embedding deserves attention. Most fonts are copyrighted. You may or may not have acquired the right to embed the font when you acquired the font itself. If you are sending a project to a print shop or service bureau, and it does not own copies of the fonts, you must have permission from the fonts' creators to embed them. Adobe allows embedding of all its fonts (as long as you have acquired the fonts properly). Other foundries may not. For information on how to determine the ownership of a font, check the Adobe Web site at www.adobe.com/type/embedding.html.

TROUBLESHOOTING

Pixels and Paths

I just don't get it. Shouldn't pictures be pictures? Why make a big deal out of this vector-raster stuff?

The two types of file formats are not generally compatible. Each has its strengths and weaknesses. Objects and lines created in Illustrator are typically made up of paths that may or may not be filled with color. These paths themselves may be colored or may be blank. The computer file that stores the image needs to know the relationship of each path to the others in the image and the colors used for each stroke and fill. When the file is opened and the image is viewed, the computer can make it any size required, as long as the relationships among the paths and their fills and strokes are maintained. The capability to resize images without degrading their quality is one of the things that can make vector formats preferable to raster formats in many cases.

Raster images, such as photographs taken with digital cameras or scanned into a computer, don't have paths and objects. You may see shapes and lines in the picture, but they weren't recorded as such in the image's file. Raster files record only a series of little squares (pixels), each a specific color. Neighboring pixels may be of the same color, different colors, or shades of the same color so close that you cannot see the difference. The picture is re-created by displaying those thousands or millions of little colored squares. Raster images are typically better than vector for displaying subtle shifts in colors and hues, such as those found in photographs.

Lossy Compression

I want to get my files really small for the Web, but it takes a long time. I save an image at one compression level and open it up to look at it. Then I have to go back and try a different compression level to get what I want. Isn't there a way to preview an image being saved as a JPEG?

Use the menu command File, Save for Web. This feature allows you to compare up to four versions of the same image, all at the same time. You pick the versions that best meet your needs for quality and file size, and click OK.

RGB for the Web

I created JPEG files of a lot of the images my company used in its latest brochure so that I could post them on the Web, but they don't show up. I exported them as JPEGs, so what's the problem?

For a brochure, eh? I'll bet those images were CMYK. Although that color mode is perfectly acceptable for JPEG, it's not acceptable on the Web. Your images need to be converted to RGB before they can be seen by a Web browser. Throw away the CMYK JPEGs and go back to the originals. Use Save for Web rather than Export, and the color mode will automatically be converted for you.

What's that? Why does JPEG accept CMYK if you can't see it on the Web? Well, JPEG does more than just Web graphics. It's also one of the major file formats used to compress images for storage or archiving. And many of those images are CMYK.

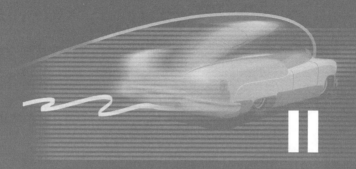

BASIC CREATION IN ILLUSTRATOR

IN THIS PART

4 Creating and Editing Paths **59**

5 Shape, Drawing, and Graph Tools **83**

6 Utilizing the Four Types of Brushes **119**

7 Type and Text in Illustrator **137**

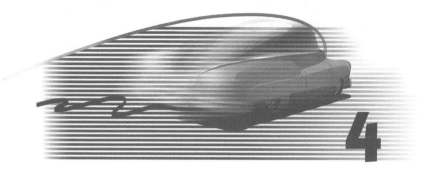

CREATING AND EDITING PATHS

IN THIS CHAPTER

Paths and Vector Art **60**

How Anchor Points Shape Paths **62**

The Pen Tools **67**

Editing Paths **70**

More Path Creation Tools **74**

Additional Path-Related Tools **77**

Non-Object Paths in Illustrator **80**

Illustrator's Auto Trace Tool **80**

Troubleshooting **81**

PATHS AND VECTOR ART

Illustrator is a vector art program. While it allows you to do some rather advanced work with raster images and rasterized artwork, it is at heart a vector art program. (The difference between vector and raster is addressed later in the sidebar called "Vector and Raster," as well as in Chapter 18, "Raster Images and Rasterized Artwork.")

Vector art is based on the concept of paths. Each item is a path, and the path is stroked and/or filled to produce artwork. Without the path, there's nothing to stroke or fill, so the artwork cannot appear on the page. Likewise, without a stroke or fill, the path may be there, but it is invisible. (Invisible paths are used in Illustrator. They are discussed later in this chapter.) The path defines the basic shape of an object, while the stroke and fill (and other characteristics) determine the appearance of the object.

Vector and Raster

The concepts *vector* and *raster* are very important in a discussion of computer graphics. To clarify, vector artwork is path-based. It consists of paths that determine the shape of objects and the colors that are applied to the path (stroke) and within the path (fill). Raster artwork consists of a series of small colored squares, called pixels. Raster artwork can be an object in an Illustrator document, but the raster art itself does not have objects within it. It may appear as a circle or a square, but the raster art is actually just those small colored pixels.

The differences between the two categories of computer graphics are discussed more fully in Chapter 18, "Raster Images and Rasterized Objects."

Basic Path Creation

Every time that you add a line or a shape to the artboard, you're creating a path. Rectangles, ellipses, stars, grids, graphs, and flares are just some of the examples of path-based objects that you can add to the artboard with a click and drag. The path is identifiable when an object is selected on the artboard (or in the Layers palette), as shown in Figure 4.1. The left and center objects are selected, and their paths are visible, but the object on the right is not selected and its path is not visible.

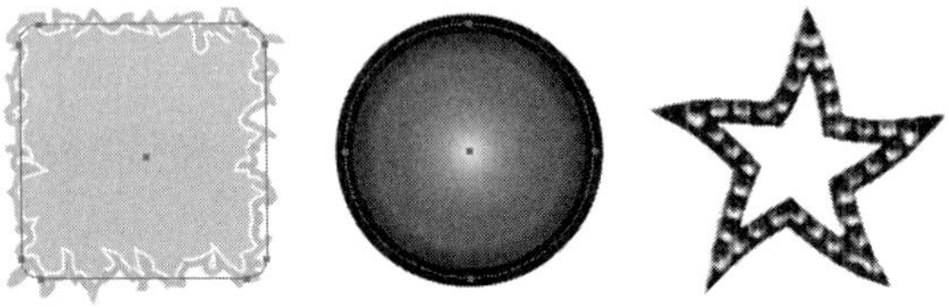

Figure 4.1
The color of the path depends upon the layer options, which are assigned through the Layers palette.

The menu command View, Hide Edges makes the path invisible, even when an object is selected.

Dragging or clicking one of the basic creation tools (Rectangle tool, Ellipse tool, Line tool, and so on) adds a path to the artboard. The path automatically assumes the current stroke and fill characteristics, as well as any characteristics assigned to the layer. (Chapter 10, "Illustrator's Layers, Sublayers, and Groups," discusses targeting appearances to a layer.)

There are many ways to add paths to the artboard in addition to the basic creation tools. The Pen, Pencil, and Paintbrush tools enable you to create paths in any shape. The Graph, Grid, and Flare tools create multiple paths at the same time. The Transform commands enable you to copy an existing path. Paste is another command that can add one or more paths. Figure 4.2 shows a variety of paths.

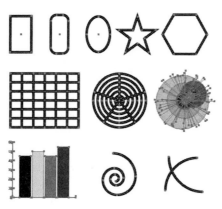

Figure 4.2
From simple objects and lines to grids and graphs, paths are the building blocks of artwork in Illustrator.

Types of Paths

Paths can be categorized in two ways. They can be either open or closed. A path consists of two or more *anchor points*, which bound a straight or curved *path segment*. Each segment must have an anchor point at either end. Paths can be open (with two distinct endpoints) or closed (with no endpoints). Consider the difference between a piece of string and a rubber band. The string, even if you tie the ends in a knot, has a pair of identifiable ends. The rubber band does not (unless broken). Figure 4.3 shows the examples of open paths.

Notice that the round path in the upper-right corner has two endpoints, even though the path crosses itself. Regardless of the enclosed area within the path, the endpoints make this an open path.

Closed paths, such as those shown in Figure 4.4, have no identifiable endpoints. Each and every anchor point has a path segment on either side of it. There are no end points.

Open paths can consist of a single path segment and so can have as few as two anchor points. Closed paths can also have only two anchor points (see Figure 4.5) .

Figure 4.3
All these paths have two identifiable end points, so all are open paths.

Figure 4.4
None of these paths have end points.

Figure 4.5
Each of these paths has exactly two anchor points.

HOW ANCHOR POINTS SHAPE PATHS

To understand how paths are shaped, it's important to understand how anchor points work. The path's segments are what we stroke and fill and otherwise use in Illustrator to produce art. However, it's the path's anchor points that actually determine the shape of those segments.

The location of an anchor point on the artboard is relatively insignificant in shaping a path. Rather, it is the relationships among anchor points that are important. The distance and direction among the anchor points determines the shape of an object. In addition, anchor points determine whether a path segment will be straight or curved.

The paths used in vector art are referred to as Bézier curves, named after the French engineer who pioneered their application, Pierre Etienne Bézier. (See the Sidebar "Why 'Bézier' Curves?" in Chapter 18 for more information on *Monsieur* Bézier.)

Locating, Selecting, and Moving Anchor Points

Each path segment is bordered by exactly two anchor points. The distance and angle between the anchor points is a major factor in determining the shape of the path. With straight path segments, this relationship between the anchor points is *the* determining factor.

⇨ *Think you've got an anchor point with more than two paths coming from it? See "That's No Path!" in the "Troubleshooting" section at the end of this chapter.*

When a path is selected, anchor points are shown as small squares along the path and at the ends of open paths. The path segments are indicated by a thin line. Both the path and the anchor points are shown in the color assigned to the layer upon which the path is located (see Figure 4.6).

Figure 4.6
Anchor points are visible, as are the path segments, when a path is selected on the artboard.

Normally, when an object is selected on the artboard, all of the object's anchor points are selected. However, when the Direct Selection tool or the Direct Selection Lasso tool is used, individual anchor points can be selected for manipulation. When selected, an anchor point is shown as a filled square on the artboard (see Figure 4.7). Unselected anchor points are shown as hollow squares.

Figure 4.7
The selected anchor points are filled squares, unselected anchor points are hollow squares.

When all anchor points are selected and you move an object on the artboard, the object moves as a unit but the appearance itself doesn't change. When some, but not all, anchor points are selected, you change the appearance of the object. In Figure 4.8, you can see that only the anchor points that were selected in Figure 4.7 are being dragged.

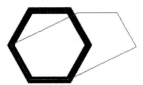

Figure 4.8
The three selected anchor points are being dragged; the other three remain stationary.

If all six anchor points had been selected, the entire polygon would have moved as a unit. Instead, its shape is changed (see Figure 4.9) .

Figure 4.9
The shape that results from the drag shown in Figure 4.8.

One or more selected anchor points can also be deleted to change the appearance of a selected object. The tool that you use makes a difference. In Figure 4.10, two copies of the object on the left had a single point deleted. In the middle, the point was selected with the Direct Selection tool and the Delete (Backspace) key was used. On the right, the Delete Anchor Point tool was used. (The Delete Anchor Point tool is discussed in the section "The Other Pen Tools," later in this chapter.)

Figure 4.10
The original object is on the left.

The first technique changed the closed path to an open path. The second simply altered the shape of the path.

The Types of Anchor Points

In addition to the locational relationship between anchor points, a path segment's shape is determined by the type of anchor points. There are two basic types of anchor points, *smooth* and *corner*.

In Figure 4.11, the middle anchor points of all six open paths are selected (they are within the dashed rectangles). On the left, all four points are corner points. On the right, both selected points are smooth points.

Figure 4.11
The middle of each path on the left has a corner anchor point. The two paths on the right have smooth anchor points in the middle.

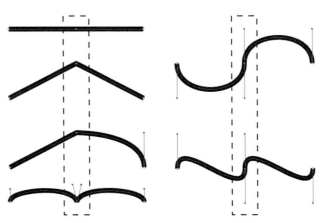

(In Figure 4.11 you can also see the *direction lines* and *control points* for a number of the anchor points. These lines, which control the shape of curved path segments, will be discussed in the next section.)

A smooth point has a curved path flowing continuously through it. The curve includes the curved path segments on either side of the smooth point. In contrast, a path abruptly changes direction at a corner point. The path segments on either side can both be straight segments, both be curved segments, or can be one of each. As you can see in the lowest example on the left in Figure 4.11, when two curved path segments meet at a point but do not flow smoothly through that point, the point is a corner point.

You may also hear the term *combination point* used. It typically refers to an anchor point where a curved path segment meets a straight path segment. While these anchor points are technically corner points, the unofficial term is certainly valuable for clarification.

As a rule, the key to differentiating between a corner point and a smooth point is the shape of the bordering path segments. If the path changes direction at the anchor point, the point is a corner point. If the path flows continuously through the point, it is a smooth anchor point.

Confused about how to tell a smooth anchor point from a corner anchor point? See "What's in a Name?" in the "Troubleshooting" section at the end of this chapter.

Remember that a straight path segment will always have two corner anchor points. A curved path segment may have two smooth points, one smooth and one corner point, or two corner points bordering it. (If a path segment appears to be perfectly straight but is bordered by one or two smooth anchor points, it is technically a curved path segment.)

The Pen tool creates corner points when you click with it. Smooth points are created by dragging. (Using the Pen tool is discussed in the section "Creating Paths with the Pen Tool," later in this chapter.)

The Anatomy of an Anchor Point

An anchor point's direction lines determine the shape of bordering curved path segments. Both corner and smooth anchor points can have direction lines. (Remember, though, that an anchor point with no direction lines must be a corner point.) The length and angle of the direction lines determine the shape of a curved path segment. Figure 4.12 shows several examples of how curved path segments can differ, even when their anchor points are exactly the same distance and direction apart.

At the end of each direction line is a *control point*. The control points can be dragged to change the length and angle of a direction line. In Figure 4.13, the path segment's anchor points are shown by a hollow square (left) to indicate an unselected anchor point and a filled square (right) to indicate a selected anchor point. The control points, visible at the ends of the direction lines, are solid diamond shapes.

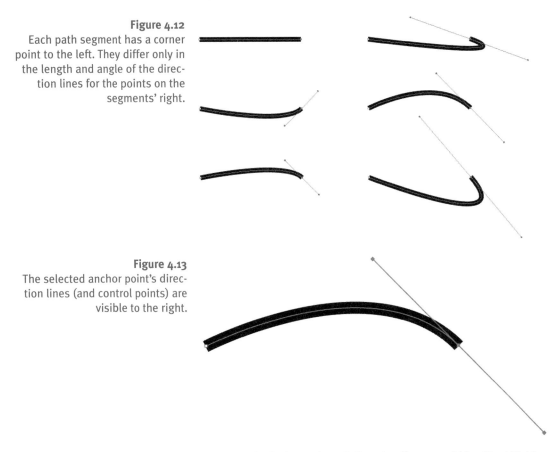

Figure 4.12
Each path segment has a corner point to the left. They differ only in the length and angle of the direction lines for the points on the segments' right.

Figure 4.13
The selected anchor point's direction lines (and control points) are visible to the right.

Even if the selected path was unstroked, the path and direction lines would be identifiable, thanks to the difference in appearance of the anchor points and the control points (see Figure 4.14).

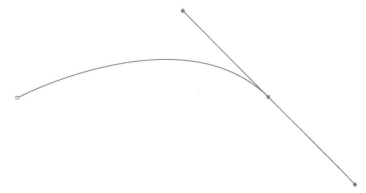

Figure 4.14
A path segment is bordered by squares, hollow or filled. A direction line has an anchor point (square) at one end and a control point (diamond) at the other.

A corner anchor point can have a single direction line. If the point is bordered by a straight path segment on one side and a curved path segment on the other, there can be but a single direction line, which will be used to control the curved segment (see Figure 4.17).

Figure 4.17
The path segment to the left is straight, that to the right is curved. The middle anchor point has only one direction line.

➡ *If you've never seen an anchor point with only one direction line (other than end points), see "Direction Line Demo" in the "Troubleshooting" section at the end of this chapter.*

THE PEN TOOLS

While all of the vector creation tools in Illustrator produce paths and anchor points as they add objects to the artboard, one tool gives you extremely precise control over the creation process. The Pen tool enables you to place each anchor point individually as you work, deciding between corner and smooth points on-the-fly. There are three additional pen tools to assist in the process.

Creating Paths with the Pen Tool

There are a few simple concepts behind the Pen tool:

- To place a corner anchor point with the Pen tool, simply click.

- To create a smooth point, click and drag. The direction and distance dragged sets the anchor point's direction line and determines the appearance of the curved path segment.

- To close a path, click (or click and drag) on the first end point. Clicking elsewhere with the Pen tool then starts a new path.

- To end an open path, either switch tools or Command-click (Control-click) away from the open path.

- To add to an existing open path, select the path on the artboard, click once with the Pen tool on an end point, and then continue creating anchor points.

The process of creating a path with the Pen tool can be as simple as clicking in two different locations on the artboard. A straight path segment will be created between the points. More complex paths can be created by clicking and dragging. The key to creation with the Pen tool is understanding how dragging affects curved path segments. In Figure 4.18, four paths were created by clicking and dragging with the Pen tool. In each case, the Pen was clicked and dragged straight up to form the left anchor point.

Figure 4.18
The dashed lines show the direction and distance of drag for each anchor point. Note that the points on the left of all of the path segments have the same direction line.

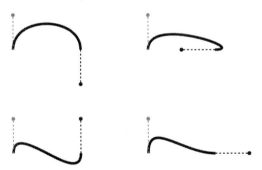

The only difference among the four path segments is the direction in which the Pen tool was dragged when creating the second anchor point. (The distance is identical in each case.)

Multiple-segment paths show the difference between dragging in opposite directions at each end of a path segment and dragging in the same direction (see Figure 4.19).

In Figure 4.19, the actual direction lines for the anchor points between path segments look identical. In Figure 4.20, you can see that, despite the radical difference in the shape of the curves, the direction lines are vertical.

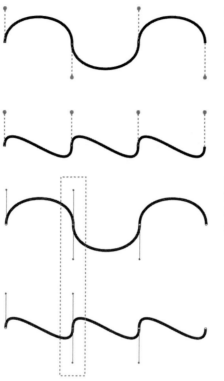

Figure 4.19
The dashed lines show the direction and distance of drag for each anchor point.

Figure 4.20
While the direction lines look the same, they were created by dragging in opposite directions.

In Figure 4.20, note that although only the two anchor points within the dashed box are selected (their squares are filled), one direction line for each of the neighboring points is visible. Even though those neighboring points aren't selected, the direction line for the path segment bordering the select anchor point is available. This enables you to use the Direct Selection tool to modify the path segments from either end.

Figure 4.20 shows a pair of excellent examples of smooth anchor points. Observe that the two direction lines for either anchor point are 180° from each other. The direction lines for a smooth point will always be 180° apart.

The Other Pen Tools

In addition to the Pen tool, Illustrator offers the Add Anchor Point tool, the Delete Anchor Point Tool, and the Convert Anchor Point tool. With an existing path selected on the artboard, the Add Anchor Point tool enables you to add both corner (click) and smooth (drag) anchor points to the path. Similarly, the Delete Anchor Point tool removes existing anchor points from a selected path when you click on them. The Convert Anchor Point can change a smooth anchor point to a corner point (click on it) or convert a corner point to a smooth point (click on the point and drag).

The Toolbox fly-out palette that holds these extra tools is shown in Figure 4.21, along with the preference that determines whether or not you'll ever need them.

Figure 4.21

The three additional pen tools are found in the Toolbox below the Pen tool. The General Preferences are accessed through the Illustrator menu in Mac OS X, or through the Edit menu in Mac OS 9 and Windows.

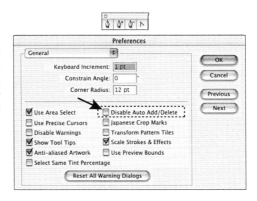

Wondering about that preference setting? See "Shutting Down the Auto" in the "Troubleshooting" section at the end of this chapter.

When you leave the preference Disable Auto Add/Delete unselected, you need never choose these additional pen tools from the Toolbox. Instead, Illustrator will automatically select the correct tool based on the cursor's location on a selected path. If the cursor is over a path segment, Illustrator assumes that you want to add a new anchor point. When the cursor is positioned over an existing anchor point, Illustrator assumes that you want the Delete Anchor Point tool. The cursor will change to indicate which tool is active. A small + or – will appear to the lower right of the Pen tool icon to indicate adding or subtracting an anchor point.

The Option (Alt) key converts the Pen tool to the Convert Anchor point tool.

EDITING PATHS

There are numerous ways to change paths in Illustrator. You can add and subtract anchor points. You can reposition one or more anchor points. You can apply various filters and use various tools to change a path. You can even manipulate a curve by changing the direction lines of one or more anchor points.

Using the Direct Selection Tool with Points and Segments

When you click on an object or drag across it with Illustrator's Selection tool, you select the object as a whole. The object's entire path will move as a unit. Using the Direct Selection tool enables you to select and move individual anchor points, one or several at a time. You can also select and move path segments with the Direct Selection tool.

To select a point, simply click on it. The path does not need to be selected first. To help you identify when the cursor is directly over an anchor point, a small hollow square will appear to the cursor's lower right. When the tool is positioned over a path segment, the square will be filled.

You can Shift-click with the Direct Selection tool to add additional anchor points and/or path segments to the selection. Both anchor points and path segments can be part of a single selection. You can also drag with the Direct Selection tool. Any anchor points within the drag will be selected.

With the appropriate point(s) and/or segments selected, you can drag to reposition. The elements of the selection will maintain their relationships to each other, but will be shifted in relationship to the other anchor points of the path. In Figure 4.22, the original object is on the left. In each of the other objects, several anchor points were selected with the Direct Selection tool and dragged upward. You can see by the filled squares which points were selected. You can also see how those selected points maintained their relationship as they were dragged.

Figure 4.22
Only the selected anchor points moved.

Selecting and dragging a curved path segment with the Direct Selection tool can help re-shape an object without moving anchor points (see Figure 4.23).

Figure 4.23
Click on a path segment with the Direct Selection tool and drag to reposition the segment.

Sometimes dragging a path segment can lead to undesirable changes in neighboring paths (see Figure 4.24) .

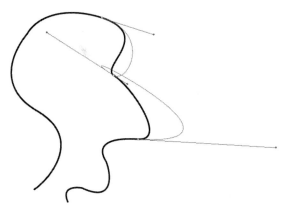

Figure 4.24
Dragging the same path in a slightly different direction causes it to double-back on a neighboring path.

Manipulating Direction Lines with the Direct Selection Tool

When you select a path segment with the Direct Selection tool, the direction lines that control the segment are active. When you click on a single anchor point with the tool, both direction lines for each of the neighboring path segments are activated (see Figure 4.25).

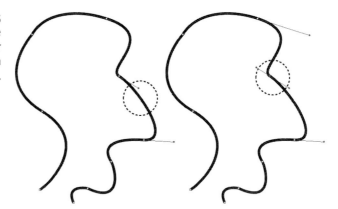

Figure 4.25
The dashed circles indicate the path segment (left) and anchor point (right) that were clicked with the Direct Selection tool.

Note in Figure 4.25 that two direction lines are active for the object to the left, while four direction lines are active on the right. When you select a path segment, Illustrator assumes that you will be editing that particular segment. When you select an anchor point, Illustrator is prepared for you to edit the path segments on either side.

You can use the Direct Selection tool to drag the control point of any active direction line. You cannot Shift-click to select multiple control points.

When you drag either control point of a smooth anchor point, the opposite direction line will also move. That preserves the flow of the curve through the anchor point. While the angle of the opposite direction line changes, the distance does not. The curves on both sides of a smooth anchor point are changed when you drag either direction line's control point.

In Figure 4.26, you can see how dragging one control point moves both direction lines of the smooth anchor point (and alters both adjoining path segments).

Figure 4.26
The anchor point's second direction line changes angle to remain 180° from the direction line being dragged. The second direction line's length remains unchanged.

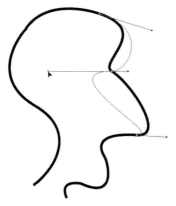

To edit only one adjoining path segment, the smooth anchor point must be converted to a corner anchor point. Clicking with the Convert Anchor Point tool would convert the anchor point to a corner point, but would delete both direction lines. This would, of course, alter both of the path segments.

To alter one direction line while leaving the other untouched, hold down the Option (Alt) key and then drag the control point with the Direct Selection tool. The path will no longer flow smoothly through the point, so it can no longer be considered a smooth anchor point. Instead, it becomes a corner anchor point with two direction lines. In Figure 4.27, the original path is on the left, with direction lines visible for the selected anchor point. In the middle, a direction line has been dragged, and the point's second direction line also moved. This alters the curved path segment above the anchor point. On the right, the control point has been Option-dragged (Alt-dragged). The curve below the anchor point has been altered without affecting the curved path segment above the anchor point.

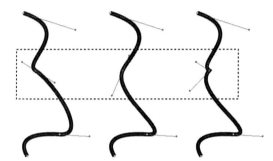

Figure 4.27
Option-dragging (Alt-dragging) enables you to edit one path segment without disturbing the adjacent curve.

Effects, Filters, and Paths

Illustrator offers some very sophisticated capabilities for manipulating the appearance of objects. Among them are filters and effects. (They are discussed in Chapter 20, "Using Filters and Effects.") Filters that are used with vector artwork change the path of an object. Effects, on the other hand, change the appearance without actually changing the path. Take a look at the three objects in Figure 4.28. On the left is the original object. In the middle, the Pucker & Bloat *filter* has been applied. Notice how the path conforms to the shape of the object. On the right, the Pucker & Bloat *effect* has been applied. Notice that the appearance is identical to the middle object, but the path remains identical to the first object. Filters change an object; effects change only the appearance of an object. This enables you to revert to the original appearance if necessary.

Figure 4.28
All three objects were identical until the filter and effect were applied.

MORE PATH CREATION TOOLS

Many of Illustrator's tools create paths while they create objects. A couple tools, however, are designed with path creation, rather than object creation, in mind.

The Paintbrush Tool

The Paintbrush tool (default keyboard shortcut B) creates freeform paths. The paths can be filled, stroked, and edited like any other path. While any path can be stroked with a brush, the Paintbrush tool and its cousin the Pencil tool (discussed in the next section) are well-equipped to work with the Brushes palette and its content. (Working with brushes is discussed in Chapter 6, "Utilizing the Four Types of Brushes.")

- Double-clicking the Paintbrush tool in the Toolbox opens the Paintbrush Tool Preferences dialog box. Here, you set the tool's options (see Figure 4.29).

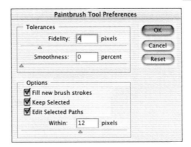

Figure 4.29
The Paintbrush tool is one of several that you can double-click to open a dialog box. It is, however, one of the few that has its own preferences.

Keep in mind that the Direct Select Lasso tool enables you to select individual anchor points, but does not enable you to manipulate them. For that, you'll need the Direct Selection Tool, not the Direct Selection Lasso tool. However, the Direct Selection tool can only select anchor points by clicking (and Shift-clicking) on them or by dragging a rectangular marquee. The Direct Selection Lasso tool, in contrast, can draw a selection marquee of any shape to select anchor points. You can weave in and out among anchor points, selecting with far more discrimination.

- Fidelity and Smoothness relate to the sensitivity of the tool to the movement of a mouse or stylus on a graphics tablet. In Figure 4.30, the same template was traced four times, using different Paintbrush options. They are, in order, low Fidelity/low Smoothness; low Fidelity/high Smoothness; high Fidelity/low Smoothness; and high Fidelity/high Smoothness. The third example is closest to the actual path as drawn.

Figure 4.30
Notice the difference in the number of anchor points produced by the Paintbrush at the different settings.

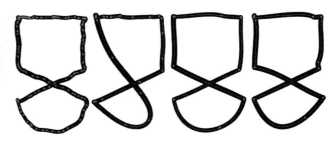

- Fidelity, which can range from 0.5 pixels to 20 pixels, determines how far from a path the stroke can drift to produce a smooth curve. Low Fidelity produces more points on a path.

- Smoothness, measured in percent, determines how tightly the stroke can handle corner anchor points. High Smoothness produces rounded paths.

- Fill New Brush Strokes, when unchecked, leaves the path unfilled. This option allows, among other things, Pattern Brushes to be stroke-only.

- Keep Selected leaves the just-drawn path active and selected after completion. The path is ready for editing or application of brush or style.

- Edit Selected Paths, which can range from 2 to 20 pixels, determines how far the cursor must be from a selected path to start a new path. The cursor changes appearance to indicate that the active path will be edited rather than a new path being started. (The small *x* to the lower right of the cursor, the New Path indicator, disappears when the cursor is within the specified distance of an active path.) When two or more paths must be drawn consecutively in a limited area, a small number for this option is preferable.

- Holding down Option [Alt] while drawing with the Paintbrush tool results in a closed path. No matter where you release the mouse button, the path is closed with a straight segment to the starting point if Option [Alt] is pressed.

- You also can use the Paintbrush tool to edit existing paths. Cmd+click [Ctrl+click] to select a path, release Cmd [Ctrl], and position the Paintbrush tool near the path to begin editing. The cursor must be within the distance specified in the tool's preferences under Edit Selected Paths.

The Pencil Tool

The Pencil tool (default keyboard shortcut N) is similar to the Paintbrush tool in a number of respects: They both draw open or closed paths, they both use the currently selected brush, and they can both edit paths. You can see one difference in the Pencil Tool Preferences (see Figure 4.31). Note that this tool lacks the Fill New Brush Strokes option of the Paintbrush tool.

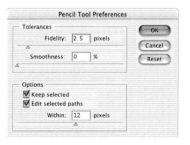

Figure 4.31
Like the Paintbrush, the Pencil tool has its own preferences.

- Fidelity can be set from 0.5 pixels to 20 pixels. It determines how far from a path the stroke can vary to produce a smooth curve.

- Smoothness, from 0 to 100%, allows the stroke to follow the path precisely or rounds off any corners. Refer to Figure 4.30 for examples of various Fidelity and Smoothness settings with the Paintbrush tool. The Pencil tool behaves similarly.

- Keep Selected leaves a new path active and selected for editing.

- Edit Selected Paths determines how close the tool must be to a selected path in order to edit that path. The lowest setting, 2 pixels, is appropriate when you're drawing several consecutive paths in a limited area. It allows the tool to begin a new path rather than edit the most recently created path. Higher settings, which can go up to 20 pixels, make it easier to begin the editing process when you want.

- While you're drawing with the Pencil tool, pressing Option [Alt] automatically forces it to produce a closed path. When the key is down and the mouse button is released, a final path segment is drawn from that point directly to the path's starting point.

- With the Pencil tool selected, but no path being drawn, pressing Option [Alt] changes the active tool to the Smooth tool (see the description in the following section of this chapter). As long as the modifier key is pressed, the Smooth tool is active.

- You can use the Pencil tool, like the Paintbrush tool, to edit existing paths. Cmd+click [Ctrl+click] a path to select it; then position the tool near the path and begin redrawing. The distance at which the tool will edit a path is set in the preferences (see the description of Edit Selected Paths earlier in the list). The cursor changes when it is within the predetermined range of a selected path; the small x to the lower right disappears.

Editing Paths with the Pencil and Paintbrush Tools

When you're first using the Paintbrush or Pencil tool to edit a path, their behavior may seem unpredictable. These tools, however, follow certain rules. Keep these points in mind:

- The cursor must be within a specified number of pixels of a selected path to begin editing. You select that distance in the Pencil Tool or Paintbrush Tool Preferences. Double-click the tool's icon in the Toolbox to open the dialog box.

- To alter the shape of one or more segments of an open path without changing the end points, start and end the new section with slight overlaps of the existing path. Make sure that the starting overlap moves away from the nearest end point and that the ending overlap finishes in the direction of the second end point. See Figure 4.32 for the difference between ending toward and away from the starting point.

- When you're editing a closed path, the cursor must start and end on (or near) the existing path to keep it closed (see Figure 4.33).

- You can transform closed paths into open paths by starting with the Pencil or Paintbrush tool on the existing path but ending away from the path. An end point is added to the first path at the position where the edit started. Figure 4.34 shows this graphically.

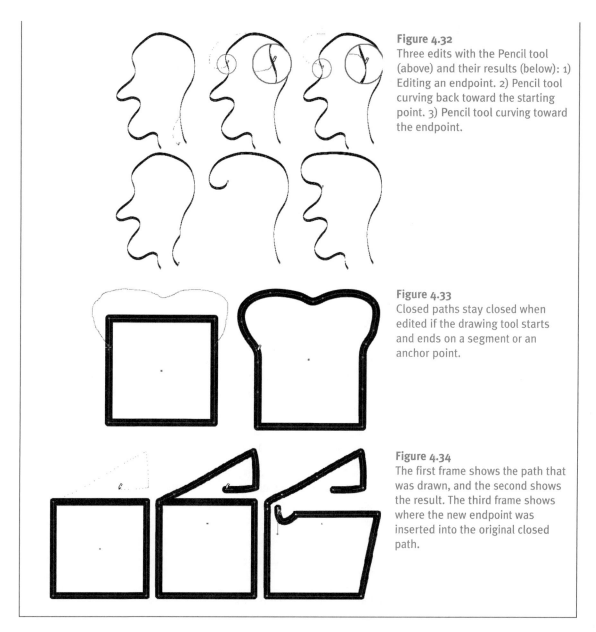

Figure 4.32
Three edits with the Pencil tool (above) and their results (below): 1) Editing an endpoint. 2) Pencil tool curving back toward the starting point. 3) Pencil tool curving toward the endpoint.

Figure 4.33
Closed paths stay closed when edited if the drawing tool starts and ends on a segment or an anchor point.

Figure 4.34
The first frame shows the path that was drawn, and the second shows the result. The third frame shows where the new endpoint was inserted into the original closed path.

ADDITIONAL PATH-RELATED TOOLS

Quite a few of Illustrator's other tools can be considered path manipulation capabilities. The transform and liquify tools, for example, change the appearance of objects by altering the objects' paths. (These tools are examined in Chapter 8, "Transforming and Distorting Objects.") Several other tools are designed to work directly with paths, rather than with objects.

The Smooth Tool

You can find the Smooth tool beneath the Pencil tool. It reduces sharp curves and angles in paths. Often you can simplify a complex path by using this tool. Additional application of the Smooth tool results in additional smoothing, as shown in Figure 4.35.

Figure 4.35
Multiple repetitions with the Smooth tool continue to reduce the sharpness of paths. From left, the original square, and after 2, 3, 4, 5, and 15 applications of the Smooth tool.

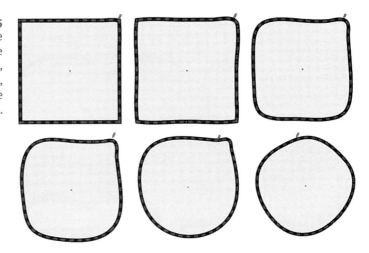

- You set preferences for the Smooth tool by double-clicking the tool in the Toolbox. This tool has only two options: Fidelity and Smoothness. As with the Paintbrush and Pencil tools, the sensitivity of the tools toward the mouse or stylus is determined by these two settings.

- Fidelity relates to how closely the path will follow the smoothed movement of the input device. Low values produce more angular corners and typically more complex paths with a greater number of points.

- The Smoothness setting controls what percentage of smoothing is applied to the path as drawn by the input device. Lower values produce paths that are closer to the actual movement of the mouse or stylus. Higher values compensate for minor irregularities of the input device.

- You also can activate the Smooth tool by pressing Option [Alt] with the Pencil tool selected.

- Use the Smooth tool along a path. Multiple repetitions continue to reduce sharpness in the path. The Smooth tool also works on corner points.

The Erase Tool

The Erase tool, located with the Smooth tool below the Pencil tool, removes portions of paths. When you use it on a closed path, the path becomes open and endpoints are created. Figure 4.36 shows one use of the Erase tool.

Figure 4.36
Dragging the Erase tool along a path, not across the path, eliminates one or more anchor points or segments. In this case, shortening the tail of the *e* with the Erase tool is easier than adjusting the path.

The Scissors Tool

The Scissors tool , which has no user-defined settings, divides both open and closed paths. The path need not be selected to apply this tool. Figure 4.37 shows the Scissors tool in action.

Figure 4.37
You can use the Scissors tool to clip off the end of a path. In this case, the upper path can be trimmed on the right to end the pattern with a large star.

The Knife Tool

The Knife tool is designed for use with closed paths. (It's found below the Scissors tools in the Toolbox.) Dragging the tool across one or more closed paths dived the objects into sections. In Figure 4.38, you'll see the original objects on the left. In the center are the divided objects, with a dashed line showing the path of the Knife tool. On the right, the pieces have been moved apart.

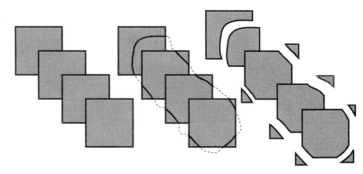

Figure 4.38
The Knife tool divides closed paths.

NON-OBJECT PATHS IN ILLUSTRATOR

While the most common paths in Illustrator are, without question, objects, there are a variety of other uses for paths in your documents. Here are some examples:

- Clipping masks are created from paths. They selectively expose parts of an image, hiding the rest without deleting. The path defines what part of the image will be visible (inside the clipping mask) and what will be hidden (outside the mask). (Clipping masks are discussed in Chapter 17, "Using Masks to Show and Hide.")

- Crop marks and trim marks, which indicate where a printed page should be cut, are formed from rectangular paths.

- Type on a path uses a path to create the baseline for type.

ILLUSTRATOR'S AUTO TRACE TOOL

Although no substitute for a dedicated tracing program such as Adobe's Streamline, the Auto Trace tool can do an adequate job of creating vector outlines of bitmap (raster) images. The tool has only two options, Auto Trace Tolerance and Gap, which you set in Illustrator's preferences. The Tolerance setting establishes how close the tool must be to an edge in the image being traced, and the Gap setting tells the tool which breaks in an edge to ignore. Figure 4.39 shows the Auto Trace tool's preferences, as well as a likely candidate for a successful trace.

- The Auto Trace tool works on the basis of color differences. An object that has several areas of different color should be traced manually or in segments.

Because the Auto Trace tool finds edges based on color differences, you can do several things (in Illustrator or in an image-editing program, such as Adobe Photoshop) to improve the tool's performance. As always, it's best to work on a copy of the image.

- You can blur images with texture near the edges.

- You can maximize the contrast and slightly decrease the brightness. You can produce a similar effect by using Photoshop's Levels adjustment and moving the middle slider to the far right.

- You can convert the image to Grayscale mode.

- You can use Photoshop's Threshold adjustment to reduce the image to black and white pixels.

- The crosshairs should be placed within the object to be traced, no more than six pixels from the edge.

- To trace the entire object, click once.

- To trace part of an object, drag the cursor, staying within two pixels of the edge.

- To connect Auto Trace paths, drag the second path from an anchor point of the first.

- You can edit Auto Trace paths like any other paths.

Figure 4.39
The Auto Trace tool performs best on uniformly colored objects against a contrasting background.

TROUBLESHOOTING

That's No Path!

I have an object on my artboard that seems to have three or four paths coming from each anchor point. How can that be?

The object is either a gradient mesh or an envelope mesh object. What look like extra paths coming from the anchor points are actually mesh lines. (And the points that seem to have four "paths" coming from them are mesh points, not anchor points.)

What's in a Name?

The difference between smooth anchor points and corner anchor points has me quite confused. How do I tell them apart?

If the anchor point has no direction lines, it's a corner point. If it has direction lines and they are exactly opposite each other (at 180°), it's *probably* a smooth point. If you click on the control point at the end of a direction line and drag and the other direction line moves, too, then it's *definitely* a smooth point.

But remember that these are just labels. You usually don't need to know whether an anchor point is a corner point or a smooth point, unless you're going to change a direction line. Click on the control point and drag. If it's a smooth point but you needed to change only one path segment, just hit Undo. Now you can hold down the Option (Alt) button and drag the control point without altering the adjoining path segment.

Direction Line Demo

Try as I might, I can't seem to create or find an anchor point with just one direction line. Did they get left off the ark with the unicorns?

They exist—really, truly. Typically you'll come across them in paths that have been edited. Here's one way to create these elusive creatures in your very own laboratory.

Select the Pen tool. Click on the artboard. Click in another spot to create a straight path segment. Click and drag to create a curved path segment. Command-click (Control-click) away from the path to deselect. Get the Direct Selection tool from the Toolbox. Click on that middle anchor point. No direction lines, right? Now click on the curved path segment and drag it in any direction. Watch a single direction line grow from that middle anchor point!

Shutting Down the Auto

Why would I want to disable the Auto Add/Delete Anchor Point function of the Pen tool?

If you ever find yourself creating multiple paths in tight quarters, or even starting just one new path within a few screen pixels of an existing path, you'll understand the option. When the Pen tool's cursor is within a few pixels of an existing path, the Auto capability switches tools—even if you're actually trying to start a new path rather than add a new anchor point to an existing path. With Auto Add/Delete disabled, you can even start a new path directly on top of an existing path.

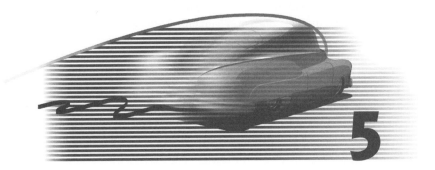

SHAPE, DRAWING, AND GRAPH TOOLS

IN THIS CHAPTER

Illustrator's Object Creation Tools　**84**

The Basic Object Creation Tools　**85**

The Complex Object Creation Tools　**92**

Selection Tools and Commands　**97**

Illustrator's Select Menu　**102**

Compound Shapes and the Pathfinder Palette　**106**

Graphs in Illustrator　**110**

Troubleshooting　**116**

If Illustrator offered only the Pen and Gradient tools and the Color palette, we would still be able to create the majority of the artwork we produce today. It would take a lot longer and would perhaps not be quite as precise. Thankfully, Illustrator offers a tremendous number of tools, palettes, and commands that make the creation process easier. Many of the capabilities we take for granted are simply shortcuts. The Rectangle tool, for example, does nothing more than create four-sided paths. These are quite easy to produce with the Pen tool, yet we think of the Rectangle tool as a basic component of Illustrator.

Efficiency means taking advantage of the capabilities Illustrator offers. That includes using the Rectangle tool to drag an object rather than trying to precisely place four corners with the Pen tool. *Maximizing* efficiency also includes knowing and taking advantage of the full potential of Illustrator's basic tools.

ILLUSTRATOR'S OBJECT CREATION TOOLS

Illustrator's Toolbox holds a variety of tools designed to simplify basic (and somewhat more advanced) object creation "click-and-drag." Generally speaking, these tools place an object on the artboard, using the current stroke and fill and other appearance characteristics, when you click, drag, and release. They also have dialog boxes that allow you to control the creation process numerically. Illustrator's Object Creation tools are shown in Figure 5.1.

Figure 5.1
These tools can be used to create Illustrator's basic objects (and some more advanced objects, too).

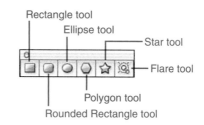

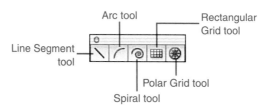

The object creation tools can be classified into a pair of categories, basic and complex. A basic object creation tool produces an object consisting of a single path, open or closed, in one of a variety of shapes. A complex object creation tool produces an object that consists of multiple paths.

New in Illustrator 10 are the Flare, Line Segment, Arc, Rectangular Grid, and Polar Grid tools.

THE BASIC OBJECT CREATION TOOLS

These eight tools include some of the most frequently used Illustrator capabilities. They include the Rectangle, Rounded Rectangle, Ellipse, Polygon, Star, Line Segment, Arc, and Spiral tools.

They produce objects consisting of a single path, which assumes the current appearance characteristics for stroke, fill, and effects. Each tool is designed to produce a single shape of object, but the dimensions of the object can be varied.

After selecting the appropriate tool in the Toolbox, you can drag to create an object or click the tool on the artboard and enter dimensions numerically in the tool's dialog box. For some of the tools, double-clicking the tool's icon in the Toolbox opens the dialog box so that numeric values can be pre-set. The dialog box otherwise assumes the dimensions of the object most recently created with that tool.

The following behaviors apply to all the basic creation tools, except as noted:

- Create objects by dragging.

- Clicking once brings up a dialog box, allowing you to enter numeric values for an object at the point clicked. The values you see in the boxes are those of the last object drawn. For the Rectangle, Rounded Rectangle, and Ellipse tools, the object will be created to the lower right of the point clicked. For the Polygon, Star, and Spiral tools, the point clicked will be at the center of the object. The Line Segment and Arc tools' dialog boxes allow you to specify in which direction the path will be created.

When created, objects will assume the current appearance characteristics for stroke, fill, and effects, as well as any appearance characteristics assigned to the layer upon which they are created. More information is available in Chapter 10, "Illustrator's Layers, Sublayers, and Groups," and in Chapter 14, "Using the Appearance and Style Palettes."

- Double-clicking the tool's icon in the Toolbox opens the dialog box for the Line Segment and Arc tools.

- Pressing the spacebar while drawing allows you to reposition the object while continuing to draw.

- Holding down Shift while dragging constrains the proportions of the object for the Rectangle, Rounded Rectangle, and Ellipse tools. (When proportions are constrained, the tools will produce squares and circles.)

- Holding down Option [Alt] allows you to draw from the center with several of the tools. You can use this technique in conjunction with the Shift key. This applies to the Rectangle, Rounded Rectangle, Ellipse, Line Segment, and Arc tools. The other three basic tools always create from the center.

The Rectangle Tool

The Rectangle tool (default keyboard shortcut M) is used to create rectangles and squares (which are simply rectangles with equal height and width dimensions). Select the tool and click once to access the variables. Figure 5.2 shows a series of rectangles and the dialog box for the last one created.

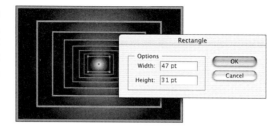

Figure 5.2
The Rectangle dialog box, by default, shows the exact dimension of the last such object created.

The Rounded Rectangle Tool

The Rounded Rectangle tool functions almost identically to its counterpart, the Rectangle tool, except for the corners of the shapes produced. The corners of the Rounded Rectangle tool can be controlled through its dialog box. Select the tool and click once to access the variables. Figure 5.3 shows the difference between the Rectangle and Rounded Rectangle tools.

Figure 5.3
The Corner Radius option is not found in the Rectangle dialog box.

The arc of the corners is adjustable from 0.001 points to 8192 points. Notice that the rectangle (left) has four anchor points. The rounded rectangle object has eight anchor points. The rectangle's anchor points are all corner points, while the rounded rectangle has smooth anchor points. (The difference between corner and smooth anchor points is discussed in Chapter 4, "Creating and Editing Paths.")

When you click the Rounded Rectangle tool on the artboard, the numeric values shown will be those of either the last rounded rectangle or the object last created with the Rectangle tool, which ever is most recent.

If an image is destined for the Web, create it using exact pixel dimensions. If you simply drag a rectangle or rounded rectangle that looks about the right size, it may end up with one or more sides that look "fuzzy" on the Web when the rectangle is resized to pixel dimensions. Instead, drag that "looks right" rectangle and delete it. Click with the Rectangle tool in the upper-left corner and see what the dialog box says. Round the dimensions to the nearest pixel and click OK.

The Ellipse Tool

The Ellipse tool (default keyboard shortcut L) is also sometimes referred to as the Oval or Circle tool. It creates elliptical objects, which have four smooth anchor points, as you can see in Figure 5.4.

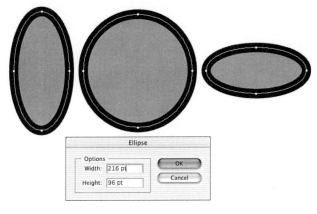

Figure 5.4
From the values in the dialog box, it is apparent that the object on the right was the most recently created.

The Polygon Tool

The Polygon tool creates multi-sided closed paths. The sides, which are path segments, are symmetrical in every variation. The minimum number of sides is 3 (triangle); the maximum is 1,000 sides. At the highest setting, an almost perfect circle is created. Figure 5.5 shows some polygons.

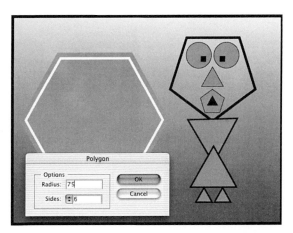

Figure 5.5
The Polygon tool produces closed paths. The circle for the eye on the left has 1,000 segments. The eye on the right has 50. There is no visible difference.

- Create a polygon by dragging. The object is drawn from the center, similar to holding down Option [Alt] while dragging the Ellipse or Rectangle tools.

- Clicking once with the tool brings up the dialog box, allowing you to enter numeric values for an object at the point clicked. The numbers in the boxes when the dialog box is opened are the dimensions of the most-recently created shape. The Radius is the distance from the center of the object to each anchor point.

- Pressing the spacebar while drawing allows you to reposition the object while continuing to draw.

- Holding down Shift orients the object to the top of the page. For polygons, a flat segment always appears at the bottom when you press Shift. With an odd number of segments, a point appears at the top; with an even number of segments, a flat side appears at the top. When you do not press Shift, you can rotate the object while drawing by moving the cursor in an arc.

- The up- and down-arrow keys allow changes to the number of sides of a polygon. Hold down the mouse button while drawing and press the up arrow to increase the number of sides or the down arrow to decrease the number.

The Star Tool

The Star tool always creates perfectly symmetrical objects. The number of sides can range from 3 to 1,000. Each star is measured according to two criteria: the distance from the center to the inner points and the distance from the center to the outer points. Figure 5.6 shows some variations among five-pointed stars.

Figure 5.6
Changing the ratio between the inner and outer points affects the general appearance of an object.

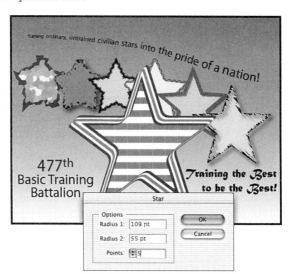

- Create a star by dragging. The object is drawn from the center.

- Clicking once with the tool brings up a dialog box, allowing you to enter numeric values for an object at the point clicked. The numbers in the boxes when the dialog box is opened are the dimensions of the most-recently created star. By default, the first Radius number is the distance from the center of the object to inner points. Radius 2 is the distance from the center to the outer points. However, as you can see in the dialog box in Figure 5.6, the numbers can be reversed. This, in effect, simply flips vertically a star with an odd number of points and has no effect on a star with an even number of points.

- Pressing the spacebar while drawing allows you to reposition the object while continuing to draw.

- When used with the Star tool, the Shift key orients the object toward the top of the page. A point is always straight up, regardless of whether the star has an odd or even number of points.

- Using the up- and down-arrow keys, you can make changes to the number of points on a star. Hold down the mouse button while drawing and press the up arrow to increase the number of points or the down arrow to decrease the number.

- Option and Cmd [Alt and Ctrl] alter the relationship between the inner and outer points of a star. Cmd [Ctrl] holds the inner points in position while you continue to draw, expanding or contracting the outer points. Option [Alt] holds the segments adjoining the topmost point parallel and at a 90° angle. (This is easiest to see when the Shift key is pressed, orienting the star toward the top of the page. The segments to either side of the top point are level.) This cannot apply to stars with four or fewer points.

The Line Segment Tool

New to Illustrator 10, this tool does one thing and does it very well. The Line Segment tool creates straight path segments, one at a time. It creates a single segment, with corner anchor points for endpoints. Click the tool where the line should start, click again where the segment should end. The path remains selected, yet the tool is ready to create another segment immediately. Previously, creating a single straight path segment required clicking with the Pen tool at the beginning and end points, and then Command-clicking (Control-clicking) away from the path to deselect and prepare to create the next line segment.

The Line Segment Tool's dialog box, shown in Figure 5.7, allows you to specify the length and angle of the segment, as well as offering the option to include a fill. (The fill normally would be unseen, but might be necessary when multiple segments are to be joined using a pathfinder command.)

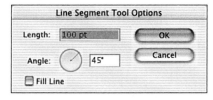

Figure 5.7
The path will extend the distance and direction chosen from the point on the artboard where the tool was clicked.

The Arc Tool

Also new with Illustrator 10 is the Arc tool. Like the Line Segment tool, this tool can create a single path segment, bordered by a pair of anchor points. Unlike the Line Segment tool, these anchor points have direction lines (although they are corner points, not smooth points). The direction lines allow the anchor points to produce a curved path segment. The Arc tool can also be used to create closed path with two straight sides and one curved side. The tool's behavior is governed by its dialog box (see Figure 5.8), which can be opened by double-clicking the tool's icon in the Toolbox or by clicking the Arc tool on the artboard.

Notice in the Arc Segment Tool Options dialog box the four-point grid to the left of the OK button. That grid allows you to specify the point of origin for the arc. For example, when the upper-left box is selected, the arc will be created to the lower right of the spot clicked on the artboard. When the upper-right square is selected, the arc will be created to the lower left.

The other settings in the dialog box determine the width and length of the arc (Length X-Axis and Length Y-Axis), whether the tool will create a single curved line or a three-sided object (Open/Closed), the orientation of the object (Base Along: Y Axis/X Axis), and the shape of the curve (Concave/Convex). There's also a check box that you can use to fill the path.

Figure 5.8
The Arc tool can create more than simple curved lines.

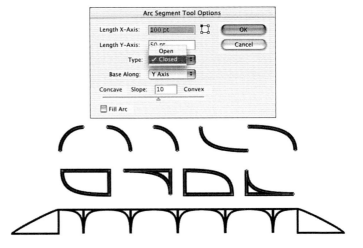

To see the differences among the settings, refer to Figure 5.8. The objects shown were created with the following settings in the Arc Tool Options dialog box:

- Top row, left: 50, 50, open, Base: X-axis, Convex: 50

- Top row, second: 50, 50, open, Base: Y-axis, Convex: 50

- Top row, third: 50, 50, open, Base: X-axis, Concave: -50

- Top row, fourth: 100, 50, open, Base: X-axis, Convex: 67

- Top row, right: 100, 50, open, Base: X-axis, Concave: -67

- Middle row, left: 100, 50, closed, Base: X-axis, Convex: 75

- Middle row, second: 100, 50, open, Base: X-axis, Concave: -75

- Middle row, third: 100, 50, open, Base: Y-axis, Convex: 75

- Middle row, right: 100, 50, open, Base: Y-axis, Concave: -75

- Bottom row: A series of arcs used to create a bridge.

The Spiral Tool

The Spiral tool creates open paths that are, as the name indicates, spirals. You draw the objects by dragging the tool in the document. (See the sidebar "Controlling a Spiral" for additional information on creating spirals.)

- The Spiral tool draws from the center. Position the cursor where you want the center of the new object.

- Dragging in an arc rotates the spiral.

- Pressing Shift constrains rotation to 45° angles.

- The up- and down-arrow keys add and subtract segments from the spiral.

- Although spirals are open paths, many Styles can be successfully applied (see Figure 5.9) .

Figure 5.9
Some Styles are more suitable for spirals than others, often tied to the stroke (or lack thereof) in the Style.

Controlling a Spiral

Like the Line Segment and Arc tools, with which it nests, the Spiral creates open paths. Its open paths can, indeed, be filled and stroked, much like closed paths. The differences in operation, however, are numerous between this tool and its more common cousins.

The Spiral tool, like the Polygon and Star tools, draws objects created with segments. These segments differ from those of a star or polygon in a couple of ways. First, they are curved. Polygons and stars are always created with straight sides. Second, the anchor points connecting the curved segments are, as you could imagine, smooth points rather than corner points. Once drawn, the anchors' direction lines can be modified with the Direct Selection tool. (The corner points of the stars and polygons must be converted with the Convert Anchor Point tool before they can have direction lines.)

An additional difference between the segments of a spiral and those created in other objects is that the spiral's segments are each one-quarter of a revolution around the object's center (called a *wind*). Because the spiral's segments move away from the center, the segments are not quarters of a circle.

You determine the direction of the spiral in a dialog box. To access the dialog box (shown in Figure 5.10), select the Spiral tool and click once in the document. In addition to controlling the direction of the spiral, you can enter numeric values for a precise object. Note that Decay rates (which can range from 50% to 150%) below 100% allow you to drag the spiral from the outside point. Decay rates above 100% result in drawing from the inner end of the path, and are a bit tougher to control. A spiral that decays at 100% is an open path shaped like a circle. If the spiral has more than four segments, they overlap.

Figure 5.10
In the Spiral tool dialog box, you can select a clockwise or counterclockwise rotation.

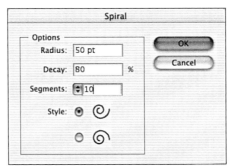

When you're dragging the Spiral tool to create an object, rotating the cursor in an arc rotates the spiral. Holding down Shift constrains the rotation to 45° angles. Pressing the up- or down-arrow key increases or decreases the number of winds, one segment at a time. Hold down Cmd [Ctrl] while dragging to increase or decrease the decay. When you start dragging a spiral and then press Cmd [Ctrl], moving the cursor toward the center of the spiral increases the decay percentage. This opens the center of the spiral and brings the winds closer together until the decay rate reaches 100%. Moving away from the center decreases the decay, tightening the center of the spiral and increasing the space between winds.

⇨ *Creating objects, but their appearance isn't coming out right? See "Check the Layers Palette" in the Troubleshooting section at the end of this chapter.*

THE COMPLEX OBJECT CREATION TOOLS

In addition to the tools that create objects consisting of a single path, Illustrator offers several more-complex creation tools. The objects created by these tools are actually multiple paths, working together to form a single object. All three of these tools are new with Illustrator 10.

The Flare Tool

Since the dawn of photography, artists have worked tirelessly to remove unwanted lens flares from their pictures. Now Adobe Illustrator offers us an easy way to *add* lens flare to an image with two clicks.

A flare consists of the bright center, some halos and rings, and some rays. In Figure 5.11, a flare is shown on the left. On the right, a copy of the flare is selected so that the complexity of its paths is visible. Below, the flare has been separated into component parts. (The Group Select tool can be used to take a flare object apart, and the command Object, Expand will separate it into components.)

Figure 5.11
The flare's halo and rays are very subtle accents to the highlights and the rings.

In Figure 5.12, the Flare dialog box is shown. Illustrator's default values are visible. The Flare Tool Options can be opened by double-clicking the tool's icon the Toolbox or by clicking the Flare tool on the artboard.

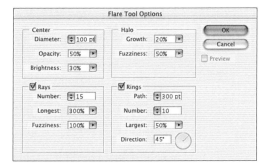

Figure 5.12
The center and halo are required parts of the flare. Rings and rays are optional.

You can bypass the dialog box and create flares directly with the Flare tool. Click on the artboard where you want the center to be, then drag to establish the center and rays. Click and drag a second time to create the rings. The process is shown in Figure 5.13.

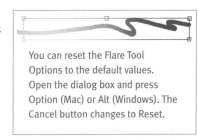

You can reset the Flare Tool Options to the default values. Open the dialog box and press Option (Mac) or Alt (Windows). The Cancel button changes to Reset.

Figure 5.13
In the upper-left, the first click and drag produces the center and rays. To the upper right, a second click and drag creates the rings. The finished flare is shown below.

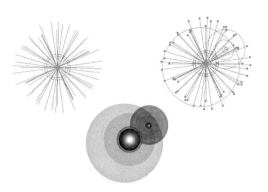

There are several modifier keys that can be used while creating with the Flare tool.

- Shift constrains the rays to the angles designated in the preferences (by default, 45° angles).

- The Up and Down Arrow keys add and subtract rings while you drag.

- In the first part of the flare creation process, holding down the Command (Mac) or Control (Windows) key while dragging will maintain the current size of the flare's center and allow you to continue dragging to change the size of the rays.

Want to edit an existing flare? Select it on the artboard. Select the Flare tool from the Toolbox. Press Return (Enter). The Flare Tool Options dialog box will open, allowing you to make changes. Check the Preview box to watch your changes in action.

- Holding down the Command (Mac) or Control (Windows) key while dragging during the second part lets you adjust the halo size.

- Pressing the tilde (~) key while dragging the rings creates new random patterns of rings.

Flare objects can be transformed and otherwise manipulated. Keep in mind, too, that flares are complex objects. Adding too many rays or rings in the dialog box can create objects that are difficult to output.

The Rectangular Grid Tool

The Rectangular Grid tool creates a grid of vertical and horizontal dividers. You can drag to create a grid or click with the tool to open its dialog box (see Figure 5.14).

The top section of the dialog box allows you to specify the outer dimensions of the grid. To the right, next to the OK button, is a grid that determines where the grid will be drawn in relationship to the point clicked on the artboard.

The dialog box also allows you to specify the number of horizontal and vertical dividers, as well as any skew. Skewing the dividers moves them proportionally closer together. Figure 5.15 shows some examples of skewed dividers.

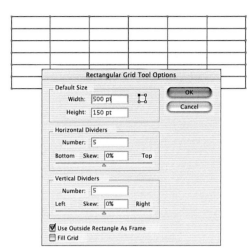

Figure 5.14
The dialog box can be opened by clicking with the tool on the artboard, or by double-clicking the tool's icon in the Toolbox.

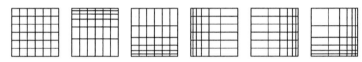

Figure 5.15
The examples are unskewed; horizontally skewed to the bottom and to the top 50%; vertically skewed to the left and right 30%; and skewed both vertically and horizontally 50%.

The check boxes at the bottom of the dialog box allow you to replace the outer dividers with a rectangle and to use the currently selected fill color. (By default, grids are unfilled.)

When dragging to create a rectangular grid, a number of modifier keys are available:

- Shift constrains the grid to a square.

- Option (Mac) and Alt (Windows) create the grid from the center. (Shift can be used in conjunction with Option and Alt.)

- Holding down the Spacebar allows you to reposition the grid as you drag.

- The Up and Down Arrow keys increase or decrease the number of horizontal dividers.

- The Left and Right Arrow keys decrease and increase the number of vertical dividers.

- F and V decrease and increase the horizontal skew in increments of 10%.

- X and C decrease and increase the vertical skew in increments of 10%.

- The Tilde key (~) creates multiple grids as you drag.

The Polar Grid Tool

The Polar Grid tool creates round grids either by dragging or numerically in the dialog box (see Figure 5.16).

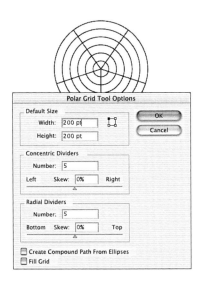

Figure 5.16
The dialog box can be opened by clicking with the tool on the art-board, or by double-clicking the tool's icon in the Toolbox.

Like the Rectangular Grid tool, the Polar Grid tool creates patterns of lines, which divide an object into sections. Rather than rectangles, the Polar Grid toolcreates concentric rings with radial dividers.

Skewing to the left and right moves the radial dividers. Skewing toward the bottom and top can perhaps be thought of as moving the concentric dividers inward and outward. Examples of skewing are shown in Figure 5.17.

Figure 5.17
Shown are (top) skewed right 50%, skewed left -50%; and (bottom) skewed top 50%, skewed bottom -50%, and skewed right and top 125%.

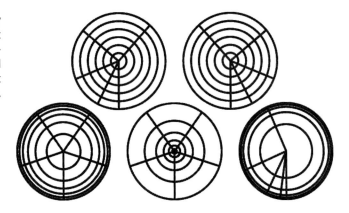

When dragging to create a polar grid, a number of modifier keys are available:

* Shift constrains the grid to a square.

* Option (Mac) and Alt (Windows) create the grid from the center. (Shift can be used in conjunction with Option and Alt.)

- Holding down the Spacebar allows you to reposition the grid as you drag.

- The Up and Down Arrow keys increase or decrease the number of concentric dividers.

- The Left and Right Arrow keys decrease and increase the number of radial dividers.

- F and V decrease and increase the skew of the radial dividers in increments of 10%.

- X and C decrease and increase the skew of the concentric dividers in increments of 10%.

- The Tilde key (~) creates multiple grids as you drag.

In addition to creating objects using the tools described in this chapter, Illustrator allows you to create objects and paths of any shape using the drawing tools. The Pen tool creates paths by placing each anchor point individually. The Paintbrush and Pencil tools create freeform paths as you drag, with Illustrator deciding where to put the individual anchor points.

Easy Targets

The Polar Grid tool can be used to create fast and easy target objects (see Figure 5.18). Check the box to create a compound object, check the box to fill the object, and set the radial dividers to zero.

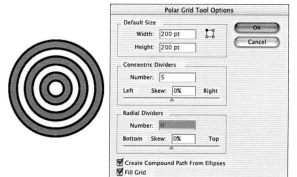

Figure 5.18
With no radial dividers, the Polar Grid tool creates concentric circles.

SELECTION TOOLS AND COMMANDS

After objects are created on the artboard, the work is rarely finished. Perhaps appearance characteristics must be applied, or one or more objects need to be rearranged on the artboard. For whatever reason, changes must be made.

The appearance of unselected objects can be altered if changes are targeted to its layer. Targeting layers is discussed in Chapter 10, "Illustrator's Layers, Sublayers, and Groups."

Before you can alter an object on the artboard, you have to identify it to Illustrator. This is the process of selection. When an object is selected on the artboard (or through the Layers palette), changes can be made to it. Unselected objects cannot be changed directly.

Illustrator has several tools and commands to help you select objects and paths.

The Selection Tool

The Selection tool (default keyboard shortcut V) selects an entire object. Select an object by clicking it or, if unfilled, its edge. Shift-clicking allows selection of multiple objects. The Selection tool can also be dragged on the artboard. All paths and objects that fall completely or partially within the dragged rectangle will be selected. (Objects partially within the selection marquee will be completely selected.)

By default, a selected object is surrounded by a rectangular bounding box. You can use the bounding box to manipulate the object(s). When the bounding box is visible, you use the Selection tool to change the shape or location of the object. By clicking within the object and dragging, you can move the object. By clicking one of the bounding box's eight handles, you can change the shape of the object. Notice how the cursor changes from the Selection tool to a two-headed arrow when positioned over a handle. The variations in the cursor's appearance are shown in Figure 5.19.

Figure 5.19
The Selection tool: Prepared to click an object to make a selection; prepared to move the object; ready to resize; ready to rotate; Shift+clicking to select multiple objects; and dragging to select multiple objects.

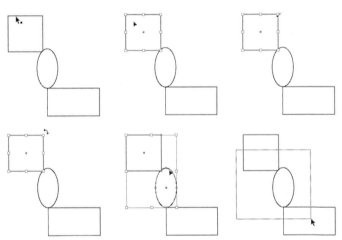

- You can access the Selection tool at virtually any time by pressing and holding Cmd [Ctrl].

- Click the fill or stroke of an object to select it for movement.

- You can select multiple objects in an image by Shift+clicking with the Selection tool. Dragging with the Selection tool across objects also selects them.

- When multiple objects are selected, Shift+clicking deselects an object.

- Click one of the bounding box's anchor points to edit the general shape of the object. The cursor changes to a two-headed arrow when over an anchor point.

- Holding the Shift key while dragging one of a bounding box's corner points constrains the object's proportions. The object's height-to-width ratio is maintained. If the object starts as a square or circle, it retains that quality; it does not become a rectangle or an oval.

- Option-dragging (Alt-dragging) one or more selected objects with the Selection tool will duplicate them on the artboard.

The Direct Selection Tool

The Direct Selection tool (default keyboard shortcut A) selects a portion of an object. Specifically, you use it to manipulate an anchor point or a segment of a path between anchor points.

- Click directly on an anchor point or path segment. An anchor point appears filled when selected, hollow when not.

- You can select multiple anchor points or segments by Shift+clicking or dragging.

- When multiple anchor points and/or segments are selected, Shift+clicking deselects each in turn.

- When a segment is selected, the bounding anchor points do not move when the segment is shifted.

- You can select segments and anchor points together by Shift+clicking.

The Group Selection Tool

The Group Selection tool selects one (or several) items from a group. When a number of objects are "grouped" (linked together as a single object, while retaining their individual attributes), the Selection tool selects them all. The Group Selection tool, on the other hand, can select an individual item from the group without your having to use the command Ungroup. (The Direct Selection tool operates on members of a group as it does with individual items.) With the Group Selection tool, the first click selects an object. An additional click selects the object's group. If that group is part of a larger group, a third click will select it, and so on.

- Using Option [Alt] with the Group Selection tool allows you to duplicate (copy) an individual segment.

- To copy more than one segment, Option+click [Alt+click] the first segment and, without releasing Option [Alt], Shift+click the remaining segments. Moving the cursor and releasing the mouse button complete the copy process.

The Magic Wand Tool

New in Illustrator 10, the Magic Wand tool (default keyboard shortcut Y) allows you to select objects on the artboard based on shared characteristics. Rather than a specific characteristic, such as the command Select, Same (discussed later in this chapter), you can use this tool to select based on a *range* of characteristics. Rather than an options dialog box, the Magic Wand has a palette, which is shown in Figure 5.20.

Figure 5.20
The Magic Wand tool's palette can be opened through the Windows menu or by double-clicking the tool's icon in the Toolbox.

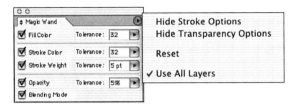

The Magic Wand palette can be expanded or contracted by double-clicking the palette's tab. You can choose to show just the Fill Color option, the Fill Color, Stroke Color, and Stroke Weight options, or the entire palette. Remember that a selection criterion will be applied, even if that part of the palette is hidden. Also keep in mind

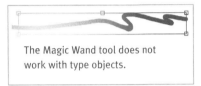

The Magic Wand tool does not work with type objects.

that the selection criteria are cumulative. If you check the boxes for Fill Color and Stroke Color, objects will be selected only if they fall within the tolerances for *both* fill *and* stroke color.

Notice in the palette that the Magic Wand has Tolerance sliders for fill, stroke, and opacity characteristics. When you click on an object with the Magic Wand, Illustrator will select all objects whose characteristics fall within the specified (and selected) tolerances. For example, check Stroke Weight in the palette and set the tolerance to 5 points, and then click on an object with a stroke of 7 points. Illustrator will select all objects with a stroke weight between 2 and 12 points (see Figure 5.21).

Figure 5.21
The stroke weight of the path segments ranges from 1 point to 15 points. The X marks the 7-point stroke, which was clicked with the Magic Wand, using the tolerance shown.

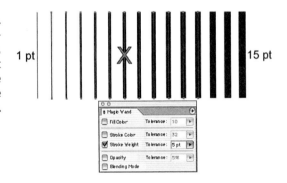

The opacity tolerance is also straightforward. It selects any object that falls within the specified tolerance. The Magic Wand is designed to select all objects with a specified blending mode. However, in the initial release of Illustrator 10, this functionality of the Magic Wand seems to be incompletely implemented.

⇨ *Can't get the Magic Wand to behave? See "Choosing What to Select" in the Troubleshooting section at the end of this chapter.*

The tolerance sliders for the fill and stroke colors require a bit more explanation. When working with an RGB document, the Fill Color and Stroke Color tolerance sliders range from 1 to 100. In RGB mode, the sliders range from 1 to 255.

In Figure 5.22, an RGB document, three objects are shown. Their fill colors are as noted. With the Magic Wand set to a Fill Color Tolerance of 18, click on the top object (fill: 255/0/0). The second object (fill: 253/16/16) was selected, but the bottom object (fill: 252/16/16) was not.

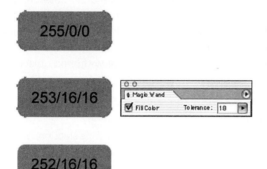

Figure 5.22
The Magic Wand was set to Fill Color Tolerance 18 and then clicked on the top object.

Slight variations in color tolerance can produce widely varying results with the Magic Wand tool's selections. The difference between fills 253/16/16 and 252/16/16 was enough to exclude the bottom object from a selection made with tolerance 18. However, still clicking on the top object, the bottom object is not included in the selection until the tolerance is raised to 34.

When clicking on the middle object with the Tolerance set to 16 (but not 15), the bottom object (but not the top) is selected. When the tolerance is raised to 18 (but not 17) and the Magic Wand is clicking on the middle object, all three objects are selected.

Like other selection tools, Shift-clicking with the Magic Wand will add to a selection. You can click on an object, change the selection options in the Magic Wand palette, and Shift-click on the same or a different object.

You can also remove objects from a current selection with the Magic Wand. Set the range of options for the object(s) that you want to remove from the current select and Option-click (Alt-click) on one of the objects.

The Direct Select Lasso Tool

Like the Direct Selection tool, the Direct Select Lasso selects individual anchor points. Drag the tool on the artboard to make a selection. All anchor points within the loop dragged will be selected. While the Direct Selection tool can be dragged to select anchor points as well, it always selects within a rectangular marquee. This tool, in contrast, can be dragged in any shape. You need not close the path of your drag, Illustrator will assume a straight line between the point first clicked and the point where the mouse button was released.

Dragging with the Shift key depressed allows you to add to an existing selection. Holding down Option (Alt) and dragging deselects.

The Direct Select Lasso tool cannot manipulate selected anchor points; it is used only for selection.

The Lasso Tool

Like the Selection tool, the Lasso tool can be dragged on the artboard to select objects. Unlike the Selection tool, the Lasso tool doesn't create a rectangular selection marquee. Rather, you can drag in any irregular pattern, just like the Direct Select Lasso tool. You need not drag a closed path. When you release the mouse button, Illustrator will assume a direct line from that point to the point where the mouse was clicked. An object whose path falls into the Lasso's loop will be selected. (If the Lasso is dragged entirely within an object, that object will not be selected because the tool did not cross the object's path.)

Holding down the Shift key while dragging adds to a selection. To subtract from an existing selection, hold down the Option (Alt) key while dragging.

Like the Direct Select Lasso tool, this tool is used only for selection. You cannot manipulate objects with the tool.

ILLUSTRATOR'S SELECT MENU

In previous versions of Illustrator, a number of handy selection-related commands appeared under the Edit menu. Those commands have been joined by another handful, and have been promoted to their own menu (see Figure 5.23).

Figure 5.23
The selection-related commands are consolidated under a separate menu in Illustrator 10.

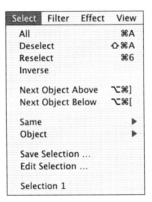

Select, All

As in previous versions of Illustrator, and many other programs, this command makes a selection of all available paths and objects on the artboard. Locked objects and groups, and objects on locked or hidden layers will not be selected.

The default keyboard shortcut is Cmd+A (Ctrl+A).

Select, Deselect

As the name implies, this commands deselects everything.

The default keyboard shortcut is Shift+Cmd+A (Shift+Ctrl+A).

Select, Reselect

The Reselect command works in conjunction with the Inverse and Select, Same commands. (It is not normally used when an object has been deselected with a selection tool.) Rather than reselecting a specific object or objects, the command applies the last used selection criteria again. Think of it as "select again," rather than "reselect."

For example, if a selection has been made of all objects with a specific fill color, using one object as an example, a different fill color can be used as a selection criterion again by simply clicking on a different object and using the Reselect command.

The default keyboard shortcut is Cmd+6 (Ctrl+6).

Select, Inverse

The Inverse command reverses the selection on the artboard. Objects that are selected become deselected, objects that were not selected become selected. Only objects that are not locked or hidden are considered.

When many but not all objects on the artboard need to be selected, consider whether or not it would be easier to select the ones you *don't* need and then use Select, Inverse.

Select, Next Object Above

Objects are considered by their position in the Layers palette and the stacking order for this command. When a single object or path is selected on the artboard, using Next Object Above switches the selection to the objects directly above in the stacking order. When multiple objects are selected, the topmost object is considered, and the object above it is selected.

Next Object Above, whose default keyboard shortcut is Option+Cmd+] (Alt+Ctrl+]), ignores layers and sublayers, but doesn't ignore groups. If the next "object" above is a group, the entire group is selected.

Select, Next Object Below

Like its counterpart, this command considers objects by their position in the Layers palette and the stacking order. When a single object or path is selected on the artboard, using Next Object Below switches the selection to the objects directly below in the stacking order. When multiple objects are selected, the lowest object is considered, and the object below it is selected.

Next Object Below, whose default keyboard shortcut is Option+Cmd+[(Alt+Ctrl+[), ignores layers and sublayers, but doesn't ignore groups. If the next "object" below is a group, the entire group is selected.

Select, Same

This series of commands is housed in a submenu (see Figure 5.24). Illustrator uses one or more already-selected objects as a guide and finds and selects all other objects on the artboard that match, using the selection criterion chosen from the menu.

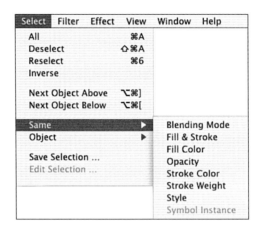

Figure 5.24
The submenu command Symbol Instance is only available when a symbol is selected on the artboard.

If multiple objects are selected on the artboard, they must match for Illustrator to use a characteristic as a selection criterion. For example, if you have several items selected on the artboard and want to use the command Select, Same, Stroke Weight, the already-selected items must have the same stroke weight.

Select, Object

This series of commands, shown in the submenu in Figure 5.25, has two groups. At the top of the submenu are All on Same Layer and Direction Handles. In the lower part of the submenu are commands to select certain types of objects throughout the document.

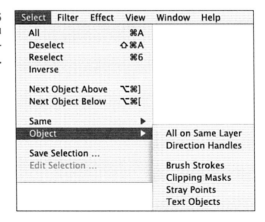

Figure 5.25
The two sections of the submenu hold different categories of commands.

The Select, Object commands are

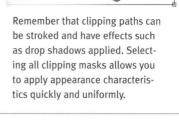

- The command All on Same Layer makes a selection of all unhidden, unlocked objects on the layer of the current selection. If multiple objects from different layers are selected when the command is chosen, all objects on all the represented layers will be selected.

Remember that clipping paths can be stroked and have effects such as drop shadows applied. Selecting all clipping masks allows you to apply appearance characteristics quickly and uniformly.

- Select, Object, Direction Handles shows the direction lines and control points for all anchor points of objects and paths selected on the artboard. (Remember that not all corner anchor points have direction lines, such as those in the corners of rectangles.) While the direction lines are all selected, you can manipulate only one control point at a time.

- Choosing Select, Object, Brush Strokes selects all objects and paths on the artboard that have a brush stroke (from the Brushes palette) applied. Some of Illustrator's Styles include brush strokes, and objects to which those styles have been applied will be selected.

- Selecting clipping masks selects only the paths being used as clipping masks, not the objects that are being masked.

- Stray points are anchor points that are not part of a path segment. They can be produced by accidental clicks of the Pen tool or be left over from various path editing procedures. It's good practice to select and delete all stray points as part of the work flow.

- The last command in the Select, Object submenu allows you to select all text objects in a document. Type on a path, area type, and point type will all be selected.

Select, Save Selection

Selections can be saved with a document. The saved selection will be listed at the bottom of the Select menu. (In Figure 5.23, "Selection 1" is a saved selection.) Once a selection has been saved, Illustrator will track the objects. The parts of a saved selection can be moved and edited, and even placed on a different layer or renamed in the Layers palette. When the selection is loaded, Illustrator will be able to find the objects.

To save a selection, first select the objects on the artboard or in the Layers palette. Next, simply choose the menu command Select, Object, Save Selection. You'll have an opportunity to name the selection (see Figure 5.26).

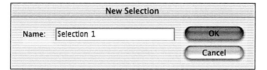

Figure 5.26
Illustrator offers numerically sequential names for saved selection. Descriptive names may be of more value with documents that will be re-opened at a later date.

Edit Selection

The Edit Selection command allows you to change the contents of a saved selection and delete saved selections using a dialog box (see Figure 5.27).

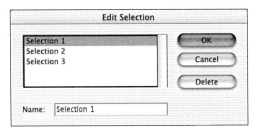

Figure 5.27
All selections saved with the document will be listed in the dialog box.

To edit a saved selection, first load the selection by choosing it from the bottom of the Select menu. Add or subtract objects from the selection. Next, choose the Edit Selection command and click on the appropriate selection name. Clicking OK overwrites the saved selection.

The Saved Selections

At the bottom of the Select menu will appear the names of all saved selections. To load a selection, select its name from the list.

COMPOUND SHAPES AND THE PATHFINDER PALETTE

Illustrator 10 changes the way paths are combined. Rather than simply creating compound paths from two or more objects, you can now create compound *shapes*. The difference is similar to that between filters and effects. Compound paths take two or more objects and combine them into a single object. However, to change the relationship among the parts, the compound shape must be released, the change made, then compound path restored. Compound shapes, on the other hand, are "live." You can use the Direct Selection or Group Selection tool to make changes to one of the components of the combined object without having to release or expand.

Compound shapes take the place of a couple of Illustrator's earlier pathfinder capabilities, but others remain.

Compound Shapes

Compound shapes are created through the Pathfinder palette (see Figure 5.28). Two or more overlapping objects must be selected on the artboard to create a compound shape. They should not be grouped.

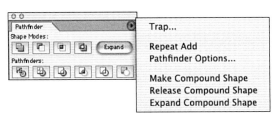

Figure 5.28
The buttons in the top row are used to create compound shapes.

Compound shapes combine objects in a variety of ways. In Figure 5.29, the original pair of objects is pictured in the upper left. All the compound shape examples have been created from copies of those objects.

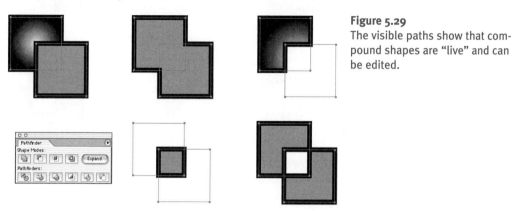

Figure 5.29
The visible paths show that compound shapes are "live" and can be edited.

The first compound shape button adds the selected objects (top row, middle). This replaces the former Unite pathfinder command. The resulting object takes on the fill and stroke of the topmost object.

The second button subtracts the topmost object from the lower object. The remaining object retains its original fill and stroke. Notice, however, that the center of the gradient is shifted to the center of the compound shape, rather than remaining at the center of the original object (top row, right).

Intersecting two objects (bottom row, left) retains only the overlapping area of the selected objects. The topmost object's fill and stroke are retained.

Excluding the overlapping area produces the opposite object (bottom row, right). Again, however, the topmost object's fill and stroke are retained.

⇨ *Can't create a compound shape from two selected objects? Check "Compounding Problems" in the Troubleshooting section at the end of this chapter.*

Expanding a Compound Shape

Clicking the Expand button in the Pathfinder palette with a compound shape selected on the artboard eliminates any hidden parts of the object. As you can see in Figure 5.30, the paths of the compound shapes are reduced to the visible areas.

Notice the resulting object in the lower-right corner. In this case, a pair of objects has been created by expanding. In Figure 5.31, one of the grouped objects has been selected to identify the paths.

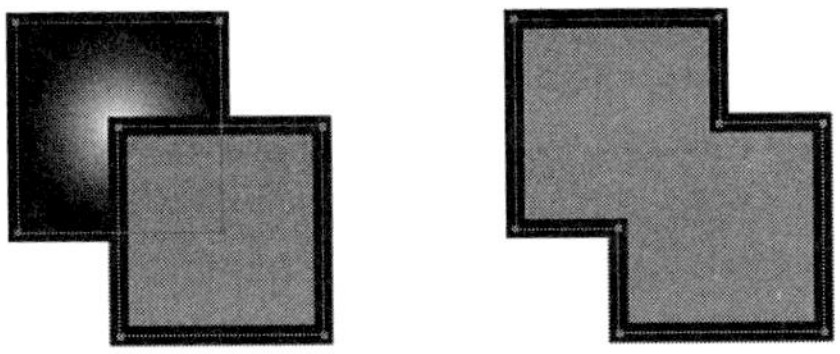

Figure 5.30
The compound shapes from
Figure 5.29 have been expanded.

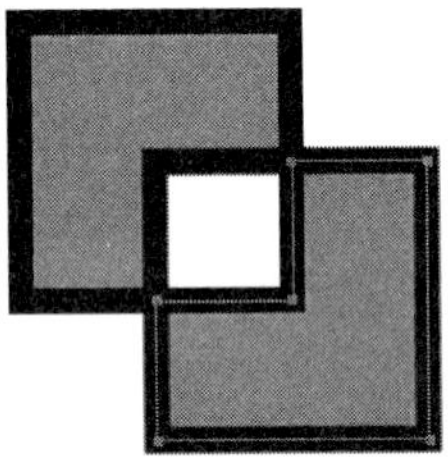

Figure 5.31
Expanding such a compound
object results in multiple objects,
which are grouped.

The Pathfinder Buttons

The lower half of the Pathfinder palette contains buttons that work with multiple shapes in a different way. The pathfinder capabilities are not live. Once they are applied, they can be removed with the Undo command (until the document is closed), but cannot be reversed, expanded, or released otherwise.

A number of general rules cover the use of the Pathfinder palette:

- Select objects before you access the Pathfinder palette.

- Resulting multiple objects are grouped.

- Gradient mesh objects cannot be altered from the Pathfinder palette.

- Many of the Pathfinder commands create *faces*, which are areas of color undivided by a path. The fill of a simple object is a face.

- Applying Pathfinder commands to complex objects, including blends, can be very memory-intensive.

You can choose from six basic operations in the lower part of the Pathfinder palette:

- **Divide**—Creates objects from overlapping areas, with each face becoming a separate object.

- **Trim**—Deletes hidden parts of objects, removing strokes and leaving objects of the same color as individual objects.

- **Merge**—Deletes hidden parts of objects, removing strokes, and merges objects of the same color as individual objects.

- **Crop**—Uses the front most object as the "cookie cutter," deleting anything outside it, and creates individual objects of the faces remaining. Strokes are changed to None.

- **Outline**—Creates unfilled open paths from the objects' path segments. Every place that one path crosses another, the paths are both divided.

- **Minus Back**—The opposite of Minus Front. The front most object is retained, after deletion of any part overlapping any selected object behind it.

The Pathfinder Palette Menu

The Pathfinder palette's menu allows you to make, release, and expand compound shapes, as well as repeat the last pathfinder operation. (Note that Make Compound Shape assumes the Unite operation.) The other two commands deserve a closer look.

The Trap command opens the dialog box shown in Figure 5.32. Trapping is a technique used to compensate for possible mis-registration during commercial printing operations. (Trapping is discussed in Chapter 24, "Commercial Printing and Trapping Issues.")

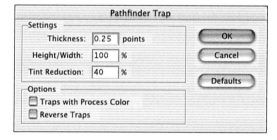

Figure 5.32
This dialog box offers the same trapping options (in a streamlined package) as those offered by the command Effect, Pathfinder, Trap.

The Pathfinder Options command opens the dialog box shown in Figure 5.33. You can select the accuracy with which Illustrator executes the pathfinder operations, as well as pair of other options. Redundant points are those anchor points that duplicate each others' effects on a path after a pathfinder operation. Removing them is usually a good idea. It's also a good idea to remove unpainted artwork after using the Divide and Outline capabilities. Redundant anchor points and unpainted artwork unnecessarily complicate documents and can lead to output problems.

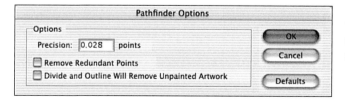

Figure 5.33
The Pathfinder options allow you to adjust accuracy and to clean up after pathfinder operations.

GRAPHS IN ILLUSTRATOR

While it doesn't compare to a dedicated graphing tool, Illustrator does offer some rather impressive graphing capabilities. In addition to placing a graph in a document, Illustrator allows you to import data from a variety of sources and update a graph at any time. Nine styles of graphs are offered, any of which can be added to a document in just a few quick clicks.

Illustrator also offers the full range of pathfinder operations as effects. The pathfinder effects are explained in Chapter 20, "Using Filters and Effects."

The Types of Graphs and Graph Tools

The first step in adding a graph to a document is deciding what type of graph to add. Illustrator offers you nine different types of graphs (see Figure 5.34).

By default, Illustrator installs several examples of graphs and graph designs on your hard drive. Look in the Sample Files folder.

Figure 5.34
The graph tools are shown on a Toolbox flyout palette.

The graph types, which correspond to the graph tools, are

- **Column Graph**—The most common type of graph, vertical bars are used to show the comparison between two or more sets of data (see Figure 5.35, top).

- **Stacked Column Graph**—Stacked columns use vertical bars stacked atop each other to produce the column. Each of the stacked pieces represents a subset of the column's value (see Figure 5.35, middle).

- **Bar Graph**—Bar graphs, counterparts to column graphs, use horizontal bars to show value. Like column graphs, each bar represents a single value (see Figure 5.35, bottom).

- **Stacked Bar Graph**—Similar to stacked column graphs, these graphs show partial values as subsections of the horizontal bar (see Figure 5.36, top).

- **Line Graph**—The line graph compares values over time. Typically, the horizontal axis represents time and the vertical placement of points represents value. Such graphs are often used for such data as stock prices (see Figure 5.36, middle).

- **Area Graph**—Area graphs have much in common with stacked column graphs, except they also make it easier to track horizontal comparisons and establish comparative subsections more easily (see Figure 5.36, bottom).

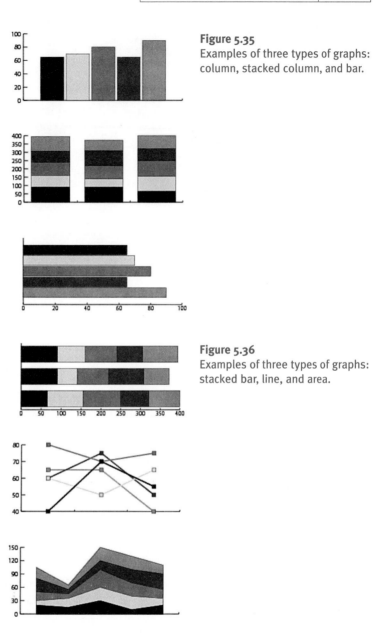

Figure 5.35
Examples of three types of graphs: column, stacked column, and bar.

Figure 5.36
Examples of three types of graphs: stacked bar, line, and area.

- **Scatter Graph**—Points are plotted against both the x-axis and the y-axis. These graphs are often used to spot trends or show a relationship between the x-axis and the y-axis variables (see Figure 5.37, top).

Figure 5.37
Examples of three types of graphs:
scatter, pie, and radar.

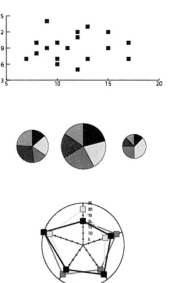

- **Pie Graph**—These graphs show subsections of a value as slices of the pie. Each pie represents a value. When the individual values of multiple pies are different, the diameter of the pies will vary. However, if all the pies total, for example, 100, the pies will be the same size (see Figure 5.37, middle).

- **Radar Graph**—Radar graphs plot comparative values around a circle. The x values are points around the circle, while the y values are the spokes (see Figure 5.37, bottom) .

Adding a Graph to the Artboard

Once you've decided what type of graph to add, select the corresponding icon from the tear-off palette of the Toolbox and either click once on the artboard or drag to determine the graph's size. Clicking opens the dialog box shown in Figure 5.38, which allows you to specify the dimensions of the graph.

Figure 5.38
Clicking a graph tool on the artboard allows you to specify
dimensions.

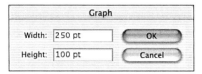

Adding Graph Data

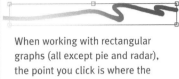

Once the dimensions are established, either through the dialog box or by dragging, a data window will appear (see Figure 5.39). You can enter data manually or import it from any tab-delineated text file.

The buttons to the right of the data entry field are, from the left, Import Data, Transpose Row/Column, Switch X/Y, Cell Style (which determines number of decimals and column width), Revert, and Apply. Transposing Row/Column and Switch X/Y are available for the appropriate graph types, and serve the same basic purpose: if the data across should be the data downward in the table, and vice versa, one click prevents having to re-enter all the data.

When working with rectangular graphs (all except pie and radar), the point you click is where the graph itself begins. The values for the vertical axis may fall to the left of that point. However, the overall width specified in the Graph dialog box includes those labels (if any).

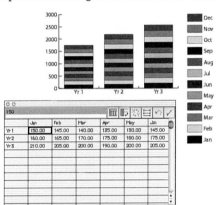

Figure 5.39
The data shown is for the graph pictured.

After you've entered the appropriate data, you must either click the Apply button or use the Enter key on the keyboard (the numeric keypad for Macintosh) to use the data in the graph.

Changing Graph Type and Graph Data

With a graph selected on the artboard, you can use the menu command Object, Graph, Type to open the Graph Type dialog box. You can change the type of graph and specify a variety of settings. Column, stacked column, bar, and stacked bar graphs use the same graph options (see Figure 5.40). The only differences are that for the two types of bar charts, the lower part of the dialog box asks for Bar Width rather than Column Width, and the Value Axis pop-up menu offers Top, Bottom, and Both, rather than Left, Right, and Both.

The line, scatter, and radar graphs use variations of the dialog box shown in Figure 5.41. Scatter graphs, however, do not have the option of Edge-to-Edge Lines.

Figure 5.40
The column and bar type graphs have similar options.

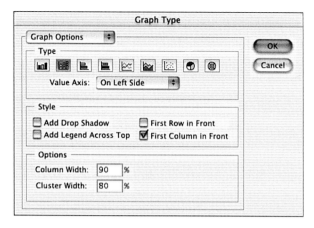

Figure 5.41
Graph options are similar for line, scatter, and radar graphs.

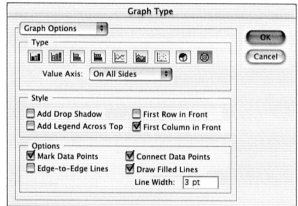

Pie graphs offer the graph options shown in Figure 5.42.

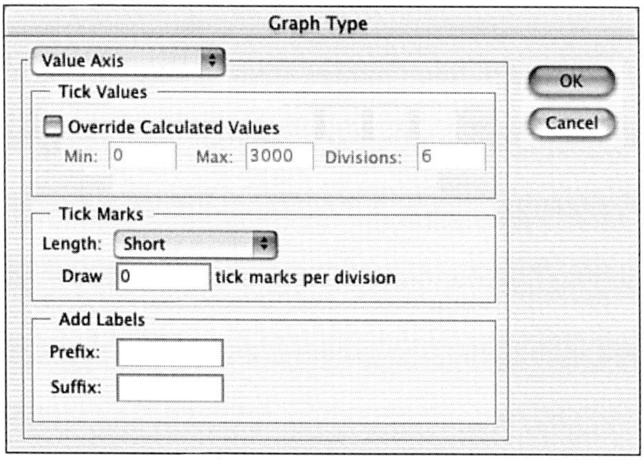

Figure 5.42
The pie graph options are shown here.

Area graphs have no options, offering only the possibility of changing the Style options (as shown in the previous figures).

All the graph types except the pie graphs offer customization of the value axis and the category axis. The options are shown in the dialog box in Figure 5.43.

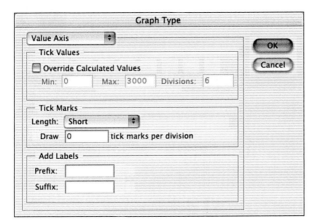

Figure 5.43
These settings determine much about how the graph will appear.

Radar graphs have only a value axis. With the exception of the scatter graph, all other graph types can customize the category axis only in terms of the tick marks. Scatter graphs offer the same options for both the value axis and the category axis.

Illustrator also allows you to update a graph's data using the menu command Object, Graph, Data. The current data will appear in the data window. Remember to either click the Apply button or use the Enter key to update the graph.

Customizing Graphs

One of the easiest ways to customize a graph in Illustrator is to add color. By default, all graphs are created in grayscale. Do not ungroup a graph to make changes to its appearance; the connection to the graph's data will be broken. The Group selection tool can select elements to add strokes and color, pattern, or gradient fills. Click once to select part of a "stacked" column or bar chart, click a second time to select all like items in the graph, and click a third time to include the identifying item in the legend (if any).

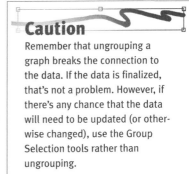

Caution

Remember that ungrouping a graph breaks the connection to the data. If the data is finalized, that's not a problem. However, if there's any chance that the data will need to be updated (or otherwise changed), use the Group Selection tools rather than ungrouping.

Graphs in Illustrator can be jazzed up with custom symbols to replace the standard bars and columns. Create the artwork, surround it with a rectangle to delineate the boundary (use a stroke and fill of None to make the rectangle invisible), and then use go to the menu command Object, Graph, Design (see Figure 5.44).

Clicking the New Design button adds the artwork to the list (as shown). You can also paste existing artwork onto the artboard to edit it and delete unneeded designs. (The Select Unused button can make it simple to delete any designs that are not in use in the current document.)

Figure 5.44
The Graph Design dialog box will list all available designs.

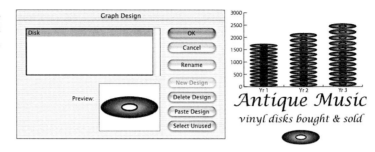

To apply custom artwork to a specific graph, select the graph on the artboard and use the menu command Object, Graph, Column or Object, Graph, Marker (depending upon whether you want to customize the columns or bars or the value markers). You'll be able to choose from any existing designs, and you'll have the option of how to apply the design (see Figure 5.45).

Figure 5.45
You can scale, repeat artwork to show value, or you can have the artwork slide (distort) to show value.

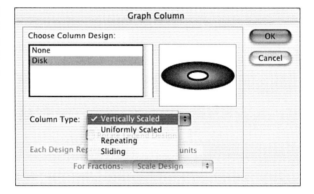

If you choose to have the artwork repeat, you must enter a value. Each occurrence of the artwork will represent that value.

TROUBLESHOOTING

Check the Layers Palette

Simple rectangles and ellipses are showing up on the artboard with all sorts of unexpected looks. What's going on?

Open Illustrator's Layers palette and take a look. If the layer upon which you're creating the objects has a small filled circle to the right of its name, appearance characteristics have been targeted on the layer. You can click the New Layer button to create an untargeted layer and create on it. (Targeting appearances to layers is discussed in Chapter 10.)

Choosing What to Select

I can't seem to get the Magic Wand to select properly. It either gets too many objects or not enough. I've tried fiddling with the settings, but that doesn't seem to help.

Remember that there are three parts to the Magic Wand palette. Click the palette's tab a couple of times until you've got the palette fully opened up. Take a look at the check boxes. In particular, uncheck Blending Mode (unless that's what you're trying to select). Any characteristic checked will be part of the selection criteria, whether visible or hidden by a partially collapsed palette.

Compounding Problems

Why can't I create a compound shape from the selected objects?

Make sure that the objects are not grouped. Grouped objects cannot be used in compound shapes.

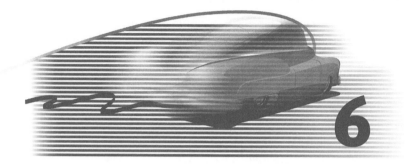

UTILIZING THE FOUR TYPES OF BRUSHES

IN THIS CHAPTER

Working with Brushes   120

Creating and Modifying Brushes   127

Troubleshooting   135

WORKING WITH BRUSHES

Illustrator not only gives you tools with which to draw paths, but it also gives you ways to add art to those paths while you draw them. By selecting a particular brush, you can decorate your path as it is created. Illustrator offers four types of brushes, each with its own capabilities. Brushes are stored in the Brushes palette. They can be applied to existing paths to change the stroke, or used to create new paths with various tools. Figure 6.1 shows the Brushes palette and several examples of each type of brush.

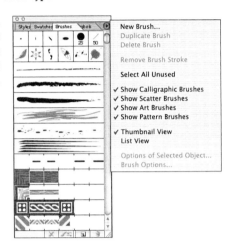

Figure 6.1
The Brushes palette menu allows you to streamline the palette's contents by showing only brushes of a certain type or types.

Illustrator's brushes are categorized as calligraphic, scatter, art, and pattern brushes. Several of each are installed by default with the program. In addition to the default brushes, extra sets are available on the hard drive and the program CD, and you can create your own.

To add brush artwork to an illustration, you either draw the art with a tool that uses brushes or apply a brush to an existing path. After a brush is applied to a path, the path can still be edited.

The Four Categories

Illustrator's brushes are grouped into four categories, each with its own unique applications. Descriptions of each of the four categories follow, and examples are shown in Figure 6.2:

- **Calligraphic brushes**—These brushes are designed to replicate calligraphy. The angled points of such pens produce lines that vary in width with the stroke as they curve.

- **Scatter brushes**—These brushes place copies of a piece of artwork along the path. How the individual objects are scattered is determined when the brush is designed.

- **Art brushes**—These brushes stretch a single piece of artwork along the path.

- **Pattern brushes**—These brushes tile a repeating pattern along the path.

Figure 6.2
From the top, examples of calligraphic, scatter, art, and pattern brushes.

The Brushes Palette

The Brushes palette, shown earlier in Figure 6.1, stores all four types of brushes. A number of general rules govern brushes:

- You can design and store custom brushes in the Brushes palette.

- When you select View By Name from the Brushes palette's menu, a small icon appears to the right of each brush to tell you what kind of brush it is.

- You can load brush libraries from other documents by choosing Window, Brush Libraries, Other Library.

- After you use a brush from another library, it is added automatically to your document's Brushes palette.

- With additional brush libraries open, you can drag brushes onto your document's Brushes palette to make them readily available.

- Double-clicking a brush in the palette opens the Brush Options dialog box. Making changes can affect all paths in the artwork that use the brush, just those selected, or none. The palette menu also contains the Brush Options command.

- To change a brush without changing pre-existing artwork, drag the brush to the New Brush button at the bottom of the palette or use the Duplicate Brush command from the palette menu.

- To change some but not all artwork using a specific brush, select the desired artwork and choose Options of Selected Object. You can also access this command through its button at the bottom of the Brushes palette.

- Illustrator installs nine additional brush libraries on your hard drive, ranging from animals to borders. You can find numerous others on the Illustrator CD.

Brushes and Strokes

The artwork you create with brushes is applied to paths. Both open and closed paths have strokes and can use brushes. You can apply a brush to an existing path in a variety of ways:

- Select the path (or paths) on the artboard with the Selection, Direct Selection, or Group Selection tool and then click the desired brush in the Brushes palette.

- Select the path (or paths) in the Layers palette by clicking the targeting icon and then click the desired brush in the Brushes palette.

- Drag the brush from the Brushes palette onto the path.

You can also select a brush for use with a tool. The Pen, Paintbrush, and Pencil tools all can be used with brushes. Any of the object tools also apply a selected brush. (See "Brush-Stroked Type" later in this chapter for information about applying brushes to text.) Figure 6.3 shows three different brushes used with the same tools.

Figure 6.3
Each brush was applied to identical paths created with (from the top) the Rectangle, Star, Pen, and Paintbrush tools.

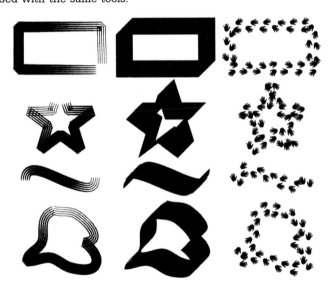

The appearance of the brush is affected by the stroke weight selected in the Stroke palette. The brush is scaled to match the weight. Figure 6.4 shows some examples of identical paths at different stroke weights.

Changing the stroke color in the Color palette affects some strokes but not others. Many pattern brushes, for example, are designed with specific color schemes. Some of the scatter brushes are also locked into particular colors. Generally speaking, though, the calligraphic brushes can be changed with the Color palette, whereas art, pattern, and scatter brushes cannot be changed unless designed with particular colors. (Locking in a brush's

A particular combination of brush and stroke weight can easily be saved for repeated use. Simply make it a style and store it in the Styles palette.

colors is a function of the Colorization option. See the sidebar "A Note About Colorization" later in this chapter.)

Figure 6.4
The left column shows stroke weight of 1; the right column is weight 2.

Editing and Transforming Brushed Paths

When a brush is applied to a path, the path can still be edited. Anchor points can be moved, segments can be reshaped, transformations can be applied. Especially with scatter brushes, identifying the anchor points can be challenging unless the path as a whole is selected. Figure 6.5 shows an example.

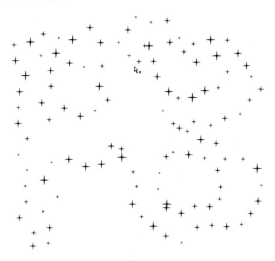

Figure 6.5
This image is an example of the challenge of finding anchor points when a scatter brush is applied. Dragging with a selection tool can help.

You can change a path both by editing its anchor points and by altering its bounding box. In Figure 6.6, a path has been changed using both techniques.

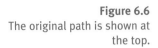

Figure 6.6
The original path is shown at the top.

In Figure 6.6, the middle copy of the arrow was edited by dragging up on the top of the bounding box. Notice how the tail and point are relatively unchanged, whereas the body of the arrow has been warped. The direction lines for the center anchor point were correspondingly extended vertically.

The bottom copy was changed by extending and angling the direction lines of the center anchor point. A different look has been created, curving the arrow throughout its length.

The point where Illustrator starts a brush, particularly the art brushes, may not produce the flow along a closed path that you want. You can alter the brush's appearance by changing the starting point of the path. Use the Scissors tool to cut the path and create a new starting point. Figure 6.7 shows an example.

Figure 6.7
The first star shows the default flow. The center and right stars were divided at the anchor point between the lower points.

The center star in Figure 6.7 was cut with the Scissors tool, and the two resulting anchor points were left, creating an open path. For the star on the right, however, those two points were selected and the command Object, Path, Join was used. In addition to reclosing the path, choosing this command re-established the original break in the artwork.

The Transform palette and transform commands can also play a large part in editing brushed paths. The dialog box for the Scale command contains a check box labeled Scale Strokes & Effects. The comparable option for the Transform palette appears in the palette's menu, as shown in Figure 6.8.

Figure 6.8
When checked, Scale Strokes & Effects preserves the relationship between the objects and the brushed stroke.

The original object is shown to the left in Figure 6.8. To the right, the upper object was scaled without scaling the stroke. The lower object was scaled with the option selected.

Effects added to a path are also added to the brush's artwork. For example, in Figure 6.9, a drop shadow has been applied to a scatter brush. Note that each element produces its own shadow. Also, note by comparing the upper and lower halves the difference between a fill of None and a white fill. The stroked path is still considered part of the object, and the object as a whole will cast its shadow. The stroke cannot cast its shadow on the fill, even when the stroke is above the fill in the Appearance palette.

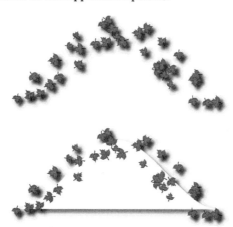

Figure 6.9
Each piece of a scatter brush pattern casts its own shadow, but an object's stroke cannot cast a shadow on the object's fill.

Brush-Stroked Type

Most appropriate for display fonts at very large sizes, Illustrator's default brushes can be applied to text. No stroke is required. Samples of each of the four types of brushes are shown applied to text in Figure 6.10.

Figure 6.10
The text is Adobe Myriad Roman
at 150 points.

Stroke

Stroke

Stroke

Stroke

After you apply these brushes to text, you cannot change the size and color of the brush artwork. You can, however, change the color of the text. To get, for example, blue scatter brush art on black text, follow these steps:

1. Select the Type tool.

2. Set the fill color to the desired shade of blue.

3. Place the text. The text should be the selected shade of blue.

4. Switch to the Move tool by clicking it in the Toolbox. The text should be within a bounding box.

5. Apply the scatter brush from the Brushes palette. Both the text and scatter brush artwork should be blue.

6. With the text still selected on the artboard, change the fill color to black. The text should change color, but not the scatter brush artwork.

Changing the stroke color in the Color palette or the Toolbox after the brush has been applied does not change the scatter brush artwork. It instead places a stroke around the text. You can also resize this stroke by using the Stroke palette.

⇨ *If the artwork applied with the brush seems too large, see "Type Size and Brushes" in the "Troubleshooting" section at the end of this chapter.*

Although Illustrator's default brushes are too large for most type sizes, that doesn't mean you can't use them. You just need to chop them down to size by following these steps:

1. In the Brushes palette, click the brush you intend to apply.

2. In the Brushes palette menu, select Duplicate Brush.

3. Double-click the copy of the brush to open its Brush Options dialog box.

4. To the right, under the Cancel button, you'll see the Size area. Change the percentage in the Scale box to fit your needs.

5. Click OK and apply the new brush to your text.

CREATING AND MODIFYING BRUSHES

You can create your own brushes in Illustrator, and you can alter the brushes supplied with the program to fit your needs. Because brushes are stored with a particular file, you can freely alter the default brushes without fear of causing problems for other documents. And, of course, you can reload those default brushes when needed.

However, because brushes are stored with a specific document, the brushes you create or modify are not automatically available for use with other images. Using a simple technique, though, you can make all your hard work available to other documents. See the sidebar "Creating Custom Brush Libraries."

Creating Custom Brush Libraries

Creating new brushes or editing existing brushes takes time and effort. But those brushes are saved only in the file in which you created them. Rather than creating brushes over and over for various files, you can create your own brush library, which you can load just like any other. Just follow these steps:

1. Create or modify the brushes that you want in your custom set.

2. Delete any other brushes from the Brushes palette.

3. Save a copy of the file with the name Custom Brushes or something else recognizable.

4. Put the file into the Brush Libraries folder, which you can find inside the Adobe Illustrator folder.

5. Restart Illustrator.

6. You can now load this set of custom brushes in any other document by choosing Window, Brush Libraries. Your file shows up right there in the list.

If you would like your custom brushes to be automatically available to every new and existing Illustrator document you open, see Chapter 16, "Customizing Illustrator." There, you can learn how to make customized startup files. As you follow those instructions, include your custom brushes in the Brushes palette and they will always be available.

The processes of creating and modifying brushes have much in common. In both cases (with the exception of calligraphic brushes), you start with one or more pieces of artwork and define some options. The difference between modifying a brush and creating an original brush is the source of the artwork. When you're modifying an existing brush, the artwork is ready for you rather than individually developed.

The easiest way to modify an existing brush is to double-click it in the Brushes palette to open the brush's options palette. You can also click a brush once to select it in the Brushes palette and choose the palette menu command Brush Options. You also can modify the artwork used for scatter, art, and pattern brushes. Simply drag the artwork to the artboard, make the changes, and drag it back to the Brushes palette. Illustrator prompts you to pick a type of brush and assign options. This type of change does not affect the original brush. Each of the four types of brushes has its own set of options. They will be discussed individually.

If the brush that you've modified has been applied in the document, you are asked how you want to handle existing strokes. The dialog box is shown in Figure 6.11.

Figure 6.11
You can apply your changes to previously created artwork, leave the older art as it is, or cancel the changes.

Illustrator also allows you to change a brush stroke that has been applied to one or more paths without changing other objects or the brush itself. Select one or more objects that have the same brush stroke and, from the Brushes palette menu, choose the command Options of Selected Object. You can then make modifications that will be applied only to those selected objects.

➪ *If your new brushes—or any brush artwork, for that matter—don't seem to print, see "Expanding Brush Artwork for Print" in the "Troubleshooting" section at the end of this chapter.*

A Note About Colorization

The scatter, art, and pattern brushes all contain artwork. The colors used to re-create that artwork with the brush depend on the settings selected in the brush's options. In the Colorization section of the Options dialog boxes, you'll find a button labeled Tips. It opens the window shown in Figure 6.12.

Figure 6.12
The Colorization Tips are not particularly useful, especially in grayscale.

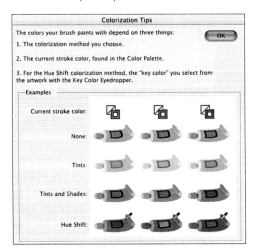

More complete explanations of the options may be helpful:

* **None**—With None selected, the artwork retains the colors with which it was created. Modification of the path's stroke color does not affect the brush stroke.

* **Tints**—The stroke color is applied to the artwork along the path. The various colors in the original artwork are replaced with tints of the stroke color. Black in the original artwork becomes the stroke color. White stays white. Illustrator uses the saturation and brightness values of the tints to maintain the relationships among the various components of the artwork. If a stroke color is a spot color, Illustrator automatically generates the appropriate tints (but they are not automatically added to the Swatches palette).

- **Tints and Shades**—As it does with Tints, Illustrator re-creates the artwork in tints of the stroke color, but black and white are maintained. When you're using a spot color as the stroke color, keep in mind that black is added, which prevents the artwork from separating to a single spot color plate.

- **Hue Shift**—The Eyedropper in the brush's Options dialog box designates the key color in the original artwork. The key color usually should be the most important color rather than the most prominent color. The designated color becomes the stroke color, and other colors become tints of the stroke color. Hue Shift maintains any black, white, and gray in the original.

Figure 6.13 shows one scatter brush colorized in each of the three ways. Even when the image is in grayscale, very large differences are apparent.

Figure 6.13
From the top, the samples are None, Tint, Tint and Shade, and Hue Shift.

In color, the image shows that the last example, Hue Shift, maintained the gray of the pushpin's pin. In the other two samples, the pin is colored with a tint of the stroke color.

In the Hue Shift sample, the center of the pushpin's shaft was designated the key color. This area was selected because it represents what could be considered the actual color of the pushpin, without highlight or shadow. Selecting a darker area would substantially lighten the resulting artwork, whereas selecting a lighter area would produce shadows that are too dark.

Creating or Modifying a Calligraphic Brush

The calligraphic brushes simulate the angled points of their nondigital counterparts. To create a new calligraphic brush or modify an existing calligraphic brush, do the following:

- Click the New Brush button at the bottom of the Brushes palette or use the palette's New Brush command. Select New Calligraphic Brush from the New Brush dialog box. The Calligraphic Brush Options dialog box then opens, as shown in Figure 6.14.

- Double-click an existing calligraphic brush in the Brushes palette to open the Calligraphic Brush Options dialog box, as shown in Figure 6.14.

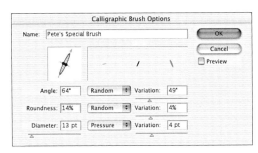

Figure 6.14
Changing the name prevents overwriting an existing brush.

The Angle and Roundness values can be fixed at a set value, random within a range of values, or set to respond to the pressure of a stylus on a graphics tablet (if one is installed and available). The Angle, when set to Random, can range from 0 to 180 degrees. Roundness as a random value can range from 0 to the amount specified in the Roundness field. Diameter is similarly limited, ranging from 0 to the number of points in the Diameter box.

You can also make changes by using the cursor to drag points in the sample above the Angle box. Dragging the arrowhead changes the angle (called the *eclipse angle of rotation*), and dragging either of the two side spots can change the roundness of the brush. You can set the diameter either by using the slider or by entering a value in the Diameter box.

Creating or Modifying a Scatter Brush

A scatter brush consists of a piece of artwork and the instructions for distributing that art along a path. To create a new scatter brush or to modify an existing scatter brush, do the following:

- Create or select a piece of artwork on the artboard. Click the New Brush button at the bottom of the Brushes palette or use the palette's New Brush command. Select New Scatter Brush from the New Brush dialog box. The Scatter Brush Options dialog box then opens, as shown in Figure 6.15. The Scatter Brush option is not available in the New Brush dialog box if no artwork is selected.

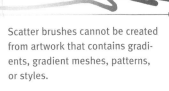

Scatter brushes cannot be created from artwork that contains gradients, gradient meshes, patterns, or styles.

- Double-click an existing scatter brush in the Brushes palette to open the Scatter Brush Options dialog box, as shown in Figure 6.15.

⇨ *If you would like to use a particular style but it knocks out your brush, see "Styles and Brushes" in the "Troubleshooting" section at the end of this chapter.*

You can choose from six options for scatter brushes. You can set Size, Spacing, Scatter, and Rotation to a fixed or random value within specified limits. If a graphics tablet is available, you can also set Size, Spacing, Scatter, and Rotation to vary according to the stylus pressure. Each setting is measured as a percentage of the size of the original artwork. You can rotate the artwork in relation to the page or the path. The other two scatter brush options are Colorization

Method and Key Color. All four of the Colorization methods are available. (Refer to the sidebar "A Note About Colorization.")

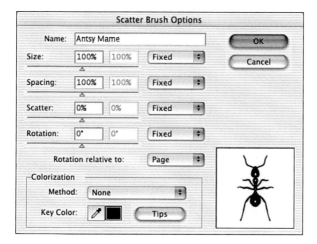

Figure 6.15
You can check Preview to see how the changes will look on artwork that was selected on the artboard.

When fixed settings are used for the first four options, each slider has a single adjustment triangle below. When an option is set to random, a pair of triangles is available. Use them to set the minimum and maximum values for each setting.

The scatter brush's artwork can also be dragged to the artboard and modified. After you change the artwork, drag it back to the Brushes palette. You then are prompted to select the type of brush, and the appropriate Brush Options dialog box will open. The original scatter brush is not changed.

Creating or Modifying an Art Brush

Like a scatter brush, an art brush consists of a single piece of artwork that is replicated along a path. To create a new art brush or modify an existing art brush, do the following:

- Create or select a piece of artwork on the artboard. Click the New Brush button at the bottom of the Brushes palette or use the palette's New Brush command. Select New Art Brush from the New Brush dialog box. The Art Brush Options dialog box then opens, as shown in Figure 6.16. The Art Brush option is not available in the New Brush dialog box if no artwork is selected.

- Double-click an existing art brush in the Brushes palette to open the Art Brush Options dialog box, as shown in Figure 6.16.

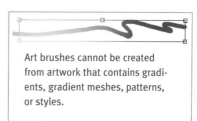

Art brushes cannot be created from artwork that contains gradients, gradient meshes, patterns, or styles.

The four Direction buttons indicate how the art will be drawn along the path. The arrow indicates the end of the path. Also important to the appearance of the art are the size and proportions selected. The length of the artwork is determined by the length of the path. The width is designated in the Options dialog box. The percentage is relative to the original artwork. Checking Proportional results in a width based not on the original art, but rather on the percentage specified for width. Flipping the artwork along a path is similar to using the Reflect tool or command.

Some samples of how the various options affect the appearance of the artwork are shown in Figure 6.17.

Figure 6.16
The 3D Arrow brush is not part of Illustrator's default collection.

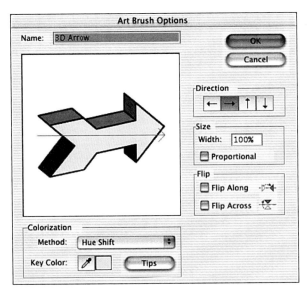

Figure 6.17
You can substantially change the appearance of a preset brush.

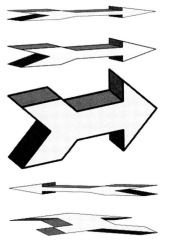

The first arrow uses a width of 50%. The second arrow in the figure is identical to the first except that the width has been changed from 50% to 100%. The middle arrow is set for 100% width, and the Proportional box is checked. The fourth arrow is again at 50% width, but the Flip Along box is checked, changing the alignment of the arrow on the path. The arrow at the bottom of the stack is also at 50% width, but a different Direction button has been selected. Rather than the right-pointing button, the upward-pointing button has been clicked.

The Colorization options were discussed earlier in this chapter in the sidebar "A Note About Colorization."

Like a scatter brush, an art brush can be dragged from the palette onto the artboard so that you can edit the image. Afterward, drag the image back to the Brushes palette, select the type and some options, and a new brush is created, leaving the original untouched.

An easy way to create a set of brushes is to make copies of an art brush and use the Options dialog box to flip the artwork. Create the original with neither box checked. Make a copy with Flip Along checked, another with Flip Across checked, and a third with both boxes checked. This way, you'll have a brush pointed in whichever direction you require.

Creating or Modifying a Pattern Brush

Using individual tiles, a pattern brush creates a pattern along an open or closed path. When you're modifying a pattern brush, you may see a single tile or as many as five tiles in the Pattern Brush Options dialog box. A side tile, one that places the pattern along segments of a path, is required. Optional are tiles for the beginning and end of open paths, and tiles used for corner anchor points that point inward and outward. To create a new pattern brush or modify an existing pattern brush, do the following:

- Click the New Brush button at the bottom of the Brushes palette or use the palette's New Brush command. Select New Pattern Brush from the New Brush dialog box. The Pattern Brush Options dialog box then opens, as shown in Figure 6.18.

- Double-click an existing pattern brush in the Brushes palette to open the Pattern Brush Options dialog box, as shown in Figure 6.18.

⇨ *The specifics of creating tiles for pattern brushes are discussed in Chapter 13, "Applying and Defining Patterns."*

Creating or modifying the tiles of a pattern brush is a simple matter of designating the appropriate pattern for the type of tile.

- Near the top of the dialog box, below the pattern's name, are the samples for each of the five types of tiles. The first, Side Tile, is required. The others are Outer Corner Tile, Inner Corner Tile, Start Tile, and End Tile.

- Below the five tile samples is a list of patterns available to create the individual tiles. Shown are the default patterns. (Chapter 13 discusses the specifics of creating tiles for use with patterns.)

- Click one of the five types of tiles and then click the pattern to use.

The Size options, Scale and Spacing, are set for the entire pattern brush, not for individual types of tiles. They are relative to the original artwork's size.

Figure 6.18
The Classical pattern is installed
by default into the Brushes palette
in Illustrator 10.

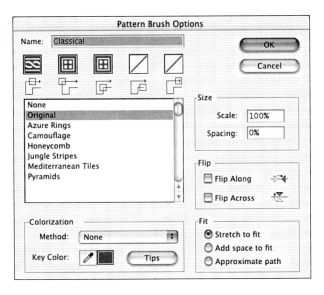

Flipping a pattern along or across the path is comparable to using the Reflect tool or command. The pattern is reversed across the designated axis. You can select Flip Along, Flip Across, both, or neither.

The Colorization options were discussed earlier in this chapter in the sidebar "A Note About Colorization."

Choosing the appropriate Fit setting can drastically affect the appearance of the pattern when it is used with a path that includes corner anchor points (see Figure 6.19).

Figure 6.19
The Pattern Brush Options dialog
box offers three Fit settings.

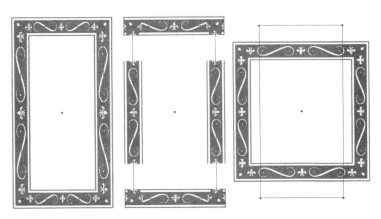

The first rectangle uses Stretch to Fit, the middle rectangle is set to Add Space to Fit, and the object to the right is set to Approximate Path. Note that the pattern is not centered on the bounding box of the last object (the three objects are of identical size and are aligned through their centers).

Loading Illustrator's Other Brushes

Before you spend too much time creating a new brush, check to see whether something similar is already available to you. Installed on your hard drive are a large selection of extra brushes, which do not, by default, load with the program. Choose Window, Brush Libraries to open them into your document (see Figure 6.20). They appear in a separate floating palette.

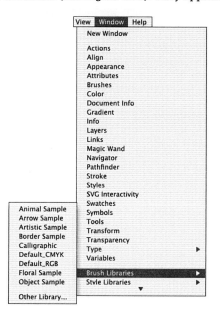

Figure 6.20
The Window menu allows you to load preset collections of brushes and custom brushes (by means of the Other Library command).

TROUBLESHOOTING

Type Size and Brushes

The art brush seems to overwhelm my font, but I can't find a way to resize it.

You can't resize the brush work, but you can resize the text. Set your type at a point size that's between one-half and three-quarters the desired size. Apply the art brush. Resize the type to the size you need in the illustration. The brush work should stay the same size.

Expanding Brush Artwork for Print

I created these really killer brushes, but my printer seems to lock up every time I try to use them. What can I do?

The artwork added to your image by the brushes is likely very complex. Try expanding it to simplify the printing. Select the object to which the brush is applied, and choose Object, Expand Appearance.

Styles and Brushes

I want to add a style to my artwork, but every time I do, it erases my brush.

Apply the style first; then add the brush. Many styles have a specific stroke assigned to them. That stroke overrides any stroke previously applied (including brushes). After the style is in place, however, you can override the style's stroke with a brush.

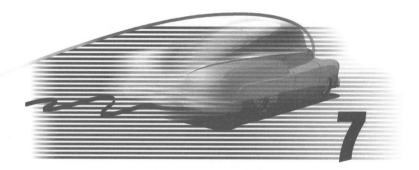

TYPE AND TEXT IN ILLUSTRATOR

IN THIS CHAPTER

The Type Tools 138

The Palettes 146

The Type Menu 149

Text Containers, Outlines, and Attributes 154

Fonts and Font Embedding 160

Typographic Terminology 163

Troubleshooting 169

THE TYPE TOOLS

Text is often a critical part of an illustration. Illustrator not only allows you to place and control text in an image, it also gives you advanced typographic capabilities. You can produce individual pages of text with the sort of refinement and precision associated with high-end page layout programs. (A short lexicon of typographic terminology appears at the end of this chapter.)

In addition, letters and words can be used as artwork. Not only can you strategically place characters, but you also can transform them into paths and use them as outlines.

Illustrator allows you to work with type in various ways. The primary means are the tab ruler, 6 type tools, 3 palettes, and 15 separate commands. The conglomeration is shown in Figure 7.1.

Figure 7.1
You can tear off the Type tools floating palette from the Toolbox and show or hide the three palettes and the tab ruler by using commands from the Window menu's Type submenu.

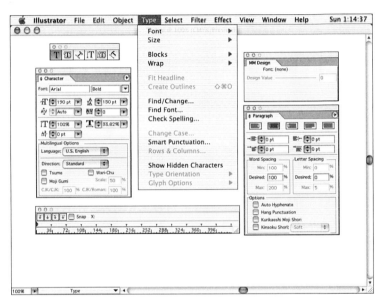

In addition to the tools, palettes, and commands shown in Figure 7.1, Illustrator enables you to interact with text, using everything from the Rectangle tool (to make text containers) and transform tools (to alter them) to the Eyedropper and Paint Bucket (to copy attributes).

The Type tool (default keyboard shortcut T) has six variations. You can choose from horizontal and vertical versions of three different functions. In Figure 7.1, the tools are shown in the floating palette in the upper-left. They are, in order, the Type tool, Area Type tool, Path Type tool, and their vertical counterparts.

In addition to inserting new text, you can use the Type tools to select text that is already present in the document. Click and drag with a Type tool to select all or part of a section of text. After you select the text, you can edit the type or change its attributes.

Type Tool and Vertical Type Tool

The Type tools place horizontal and vertical type at any point in a document. Select the tool in the Toolbox and click once anywhere on the artboard to begin entering type. If the point where you need to place text is already occupied by an object, lock or hide that object in the Layers palette to prevent it from being converted to a type container.

After you click with the Type tool, you can begin typing your text. While you're in this mode, Illustrator functions as a basic word processor. The single-key keyboard shortcuts (V for the Move tool, M for the Rectangle tool, Tab to show/hide palettes, Return or Enter to accept changes) are not available when you're entering text. Pressing those letters, most naturally, adds them to the text being entered. After you finish entering text, click another tool in the Toolbox or Cmd+click [Ctrl+click] away from the text to retain the Type tool.

You also can use these tools to create text boxes. Click and drag with either Type tool to create a rectangular area in which you can enter text. The text wraps from line to line to stay within the rectangle. Such text boxes are invisible and nonprinting unless you choose to fill or stroke them with color.

If the text you enter doesn't fit in the rectangle, you have several options. In addition to choosing a new font size, shortening the text, or adjusting spacing and leading, you can resize the rectangle or have the text continue in another box. A small indicator appears in the lower-right corner of the rectangle to indicate text overflow. When the small box with the plus sign appears, your text no longer fits in the rectangle. To resize the box, use the Selection tool and drag one of the bounding box handles. If the Type tool is active, you can simply hold down the Command [Control] key to activate the Selection tool. Illustrator gives you a live update of how the text will appear by indicating the baselines of the lines of text. As you drag the bounding box, the baselines shift and reposition themselves to show you how the text will flow in the resized box. Figure 7.2 shows how the lines appear as the box is dragged.

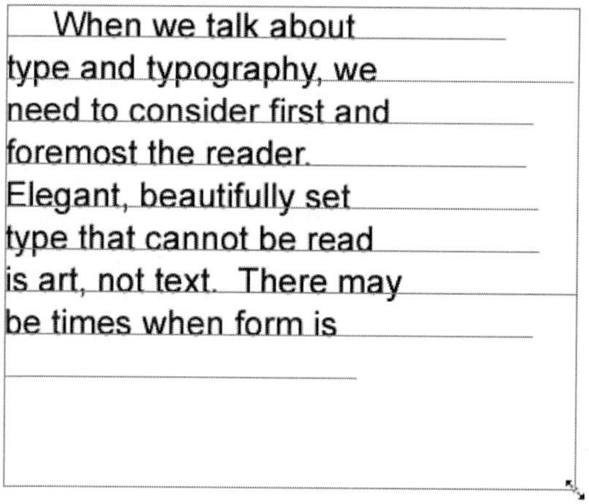

When we talk about
type and typography, we
need to consider first and
foremost the reader.
Elegant, beautifully set
type that cannot be read
is art, not text. There may
be times when form is

Figure 7.2
The disappearance of the text overflow indicator in the lower right means that the text will fit in the new rectangle.

⇨ *Do you absolutely have to make the text fit into a container of a specific size? Can't stand the thought of reducing your font size any further? See "Copyfitting" in the "Troubleshooting" section at the end of this chapter.*

Resizing a Text Rectangle

Be sure that you do not have anything else selected when resizing a text rectangle. If more than one object on the artboard is active, Illustrator treats the text within the rectangle as an object, scaling it along with the box. Figure 7.3 shows an example.

Figure 7.3
When you have both the text rectangle and object rectangle selected, Illustrator resizes the type.

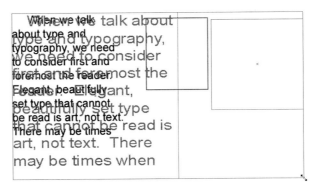

The text within the box is resized along with the rectangle. The overflow text is still not visible, and the text that was visible is distorted in size and shape.

When the Type or Vertical Type tool is positioned over an object or a path, it automatically changes to the Area Type or Path Type tool (or their vertical counterparts).

Area Type Tool and Vertical Area Type Tool

Using the Area Type tool, you can enter text into any shape, including open paths. Figure 7.4 shows some examples.

Figure 7.4
Whether you create a path with an object tool or Pen tool and whether it's open or closed, Illustrator can fill it with text.

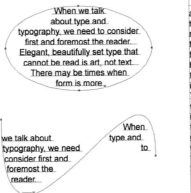

Notice that two of the three text containers in the figure show the text overflow symbol. Also, note that the oval's text is center aligned, whereas the open path and rectangle are left aligned. Alignment is controlled through the Paragraph palette.

When you select an open path, Illustrator fills an area with text just as it does with the fill color, drawing an invisible straight line between the two endpoints. Area type is also required to wrap text around an object. This will be discussed later in this chapter, in the section "Wrapping Text Around Objects."

By default, any object or path that is filled with text loses its fill and stroke. Any changes made to the fill and stroke swatches with the object and text selected are applied to the text. To add color to the fill or stroke of the text container, select it with the Direct Selection tool and use the Color or Swatches palette to add color. Figure 7.5 shows an example of coloring a text container.

Figure 7.5
Using the Direct Selection tool, you can select the text container independently of the text.

Path Type Tool and Vertical Path Type Tool

Just as a text container receives a stroke and fill of None, so too does a path along which type has been placed. Using the Type, Vertical Type, Path Type, or Vertical Type Path tool, you can click a path to have the text flow along it. In Figure 7.6, the text paths are invisible but loosely parallel stroked paths.

Figure 7.6
The text paths help convey the message.

The text can be repositioned along a path. Using the Selection or Direct Selection tool, click the text. Click directly on the I-beam and drag the text to a new position, as shown in Figure 7.7.

Figure 7.7
The text maintains its flow and attributes when repositioned.

You can also flip text by dragging the I-beam across the path. This technique also works with closed paths. Figure 7.8 shows an example.

Figure 7.8
The cursor shows the position of the I-beam, which regulates the start position of the text.

The initial direction of text flow is determined by the path's direction of creation. The order in which the path's anchor points were placed determines in which direction the text will flow. Figure 7.9 shows this flow graphically.

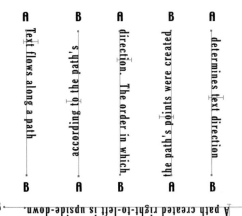

Figure 7.9
Each path was created from A to B. That is, the Pen tool was clicked near the letter A and then near the letter B to draw each path.

Preferences and General Considerations

Perhaps the most important Illustrator preference for type is not found with the others. When you open Preferences, Units & Undo, you'll find the setting that determines the unit of measure for type. It is shown in Figure 7.10.

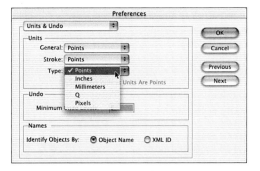

Figure 7.10
This dialog box contains several choices for measuring type.

Points are the standard unit of measure for type in the United States. There are 72 points in an inch. Illustrator also offers several alternatives. Inches and millimeters are self-explanatory. One Q is equal to one-quarter of a millimeter. Pixels are the same as points when you're working with a standard of 72 pixels per inch (ppi). The unit of measure selected here is used not only for font size, but also for all other type-related preferences and palettes. You can change the unit of measure for type by choosing File, Document Setup.

The remainder of Illustrator's type-related preferences have their own dialog box. You can access the Type & Auto Tracing panel of the Preferences, as shown in Figure 7.11, by choosing Preferences, Type & Auto Tracing.

Figure 7.11

The Auto Trace Options have nothing to do with type or text and merely share the Preferences dialog box.

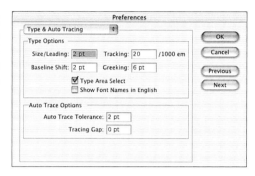

The type preferences are global, affecting all documents with editable type opened or created in Illustrator. You can change them at any time, but you cannot save them with individual documents. Three of the preferences listed here involve keyboard shortcuts:

Both the Macintosh and Windows versions of Illustrator use the 72ppi standard. You can verify this unit of measure by opening Preferences, Units & Undo and setting the General unit of measure to inches. Choose File, New and look at the default dimensions; then click Cancel. Now change the General unit of measure to pixels and check the default dimension of a new document. That 8.5- by 11-inch document is now listed as 612 pixels by 792 pixels. Dividing 612 pixels by 8.5 inches and dividing 792 pixels by 11 inches gives you 72ppi.

- **Size/Leading**—These preference values determine the increment when you use the keyboard to adjust type size or leading. *Leading* is the amount of space between lines of type, measured from baseline to baseline. The unit of measure is determined by that set for type size in the Units & Undo panel of the Preferences dialog box. The keyboard shortcuts to increase and decrease a font's size are Cmd+Shift+>> [Ctrl+Shift+>]> and Cmd+Shift+< [Ctrl+Shift+<]. To increase or decrease leading, you use Option [Alt] and the up or down arrows.

- **Tracking**—This preference value determines the keyboard increment for both tracking and kerning. The unit of measure is determined by that set for type size in the Units & Undo panel of the Preferences dialog box. The default value is 20/1000 of an em space. An *em space* is a distance equivalent to that needed for an em dash in the particular font being used. An em dash (—) is larger than a hyphen (-) and historically the width of the uppercase letter *M* in a typeface. You can change tracking and kerning from the keyboard by using Option [Alt] and the left and right arrows. If two letters are selected, kerning is changed. If more than two characters are selected, tracking is adjusted.

- **Baseline Shift**—This preference value determines the keyboard increment for baseline shift. The unit of measure is determined by that set for type size in the Units & Undo panel of the Preferences dialog box. Option+Shift [Alt+Shift] and the up and down arrows adjust the baseline of selected text.

- **Greeking**—Text is *greeked*, displayed as a linear placeholder, when it is too small to be displayed on the monitor. The value entered in the preferences is for use at 100% zoom. If you change the zoom factor to 50%, text at twice the specified size also gets greeked. Figure 7.12 gives a comparable demonstration.

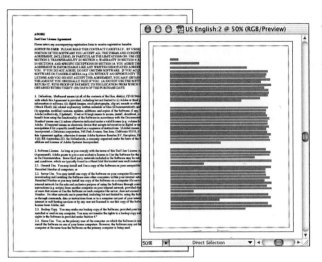

Figure 7.12
The inset window is zoomed out to 50%, and the body text must be greeked because it is too small to be displayed properly.

- **Type Area Select**—With this option checked, you can click with a selection tool anywhere on text to select it. When this option is unchecked, you must click the type's baseline to select it.

- **Show Font Names in English**—When you're working with double-byte fonts, specifically CJK (Chinese-Japanese-Korean), this option determines which language will be used to show the name of the font in the menu and palette listings.

Some general rules cover the Type tools:

- Click anywhere in a document with the Type or Vertical Type tool to start placing text.

- Click any shape with the Area Type or Vertical Area Type tool to place text in that shape.

- Use the Path Type or Vertical Path Type tool to place text along any open or closed path.

- Double-clicking with any text tool within text selects an entire word. Triple-clicking selects an entire paragraph.

- When a block or line of text is not selected, Shift+clicking with any Type tool at any point within text automatically highlights text from that point to the beginning of the text.

- Shift+clicking when the text is already active makes a selection from the point Shift+clicked to the previous blinking insertion point.

- When a text tool is active and the cursor is within text, hold down Shift and use the right or left arrow to add to or subtract from (or make) a selection one letter at a time. Add Cmd [Ctrl] to add or subtract entire words, one at a time.

- With the cursor inside a block of text, hold down Shift and use the up and down arrows to add an entire line to or subtract it from a selection. Cmd+Shift [Ctrl+Shift] and the up and down arrows alter the selection a paragraph at a time.

- When you're editing type, you can use any of the Type tools to highlight (select) text.

- Using the Selection tool to alter the bounding box of text set with the Type tools (vertical or horizontal) changes the size and shape of the text.

- Using the Selection tool to alter the bounding box of text set with the Area Type tools (vertical or horizontal) changes the shape of the object, and may change the amount of visible text within the object, but the type retains its size, shape, and other characteristics.

- Using the Selection tool to alter the bounding box of text set with the Path Type tools (vertical or horizontal) changes the path and the size and shape of the type, and may change the distribution of type along the path.

THE PALETTES

Four of Illustrator's palettes are devoted to text. Like other palettes in Illustrator, they are shown and hidden using the Window menu. However, you'll find them in the Type submenu.

The Character Palette

The default keyboard shortcut to show and hide the Character palette, shown in Figure 7.13, is Cmd+T [Ctrl+T]. It is normally grouped with the Paragraph palette.

Figure 7.13
By default, only the top two sections of the palette are shown. You show or hide the Options and Multilingual Options by using the commands in the palette menu or by clicking the two-headed arrow on the palette's tab.

The first of the palette's four sections determines the font. The pop-up menu uses submenus for font styles, such as bold, condensed, italic, and regular. The keyboard shortcut Cmd+Z [Ctrl+Z] works to undo font changes.

The second section determines font size, leading, kerning, and tracking. These concepts will be explained more fully later in this chapter in the section on typographic terminology. Briefly, *leading* (pronounced as in the metal *lead*, rather than the verb *to lead*) is the space between rows of type. *Kerning* is the space between two letters, and *tracking* is uniform space between letters in a word or several words.

The palette's third section, which you show by choosing the palette menu command Show Options, controls the appearance of individual characters. Using the designated font size, you can increase or decrease the height and width of one or more selected characters. *Baseline shift*, the placement of a character above or below the others as a superscript or subscript character, is also controlled here.

The bottom portion of the palette, displayed and hidden with the pop-out menu commands Show/Hide Multilingual, is designed for use with oriental character sets. Its primary use is to integrate Roman or other Western characters into CJK (Chinese-Japanese-Korean) text blocks.

The Paragraph Palette

You open the Paragraph palette through the Type submenu of the Window menu, or with the default keyboard shortcut Cmd+M [Ctrl+M]. Figure 7.14 shows this palette with its options visible, as well as the Hyphenation Options dialog box.

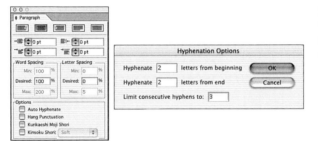

Figure 7.14
You access the Hyphenation Options dialog box through a command in the palette menu.

You can use the Paragraph palette to change the options for a selected paragraph or paragraphs or, if no text is selected, establish options for all later text:

- The five boxes across the top of the palette control paragraph alignment. Following left, center, and right alignment buttons are options to justify all full lines and to justify all lines, even if they are not full.

- Below the alignment buttons are two entry fields that control the left and right indent of a paragraph. The unit of measure is that specified for type size in the Units & Undo panel of the Preferences dialog box. Next are, on the left, indentation for the first line of a paragraph and, on the right, space before a paragraph. You can specify space to precede a paragraph only when you're using area type. The left indent and first line indent can also be controlled using the tab ruler.

- Word and letter spacing apply to entire paragraphs. To control a pair of letters, use kerning. To control three or more letters, multiple words, or even several lines, use tracking.

- When text is not justified, only the Desired option (your preferred spacing) is available within the Word Spacing and Letter Spacing sections. With justified type, you can set the minimum and maximum amounts of space to be added between words. At 100%, no additional space is added between words. Letter spacing works in a similar manner, allowing you to determine how much additional space will be added between each letter. At 0%, no additional space is added.

- Auto Hyphenate allows Illustrator to automatically hyphenate long words at the ends of lines. You access the options, shown in the Hyphenation Options dialog box in Figure 7.14, through the Paragraph palette menu.

- Hanging Punctuation, when selected, allows punctuation marks at the ends of lines to extend past the margin. This presents margins that are more sharply defined visually. Question marks and exclamation marks, because they are full-sized characters, are excluded. When a punctuation mark is followed by an end quotation mark, both are left outside the margin. While hanging punctuation primarily works with justified and right-aligned text, it can also affect the left margin. (See Figure 7.22 for an example. In the top example, the quote mark in the second-last line overhangs the left margin.)

- Kurikaeshi Moji Shori regulates how repeated characters are handled in Japanese text. If identical characters are separated by a line break, this option (when selected) retains both. When this option is not selected, Illustrator replaces the second character with a repeat character symbol.

- Kinsoku Shori allows for "smart" line breaks. It recognizes characters in CJK text that must not end or start lines, as well as characters that must remain together. In addition, the rules can be adhered to strictly (when you select the Hard option) or can be more loosely followed (when you select Soft) by using only a subset of the characters.

The Multiple Master Design Palette

The MM Design palette, shown in Figure 7.15, allows for adjustments to multiple master typefaces. To use the palette, select text that has been set in a multiple master font. If you're not using a multiple master font, the palette shows the name of the font and a grayed-out notation—(not MM). When you are using a multiple master font, two sliders allow for adjustment of the text's appearance. Multiple master fonts will be discussed later in this chapter.

Figure 7.15
The identical typeface and font size are used, but the weight and optical size have been adjusted for the lower samples.

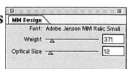

CHANGING WITH THE TIMES
CHANGING WITH THE TIMES
CHANGING WITH THE TIMES
CHANGING WITH THE TIMES
CHANGING WITH THE TIMES

The Tab Ruler Palette

The Tab Ruler palette controls the placement of tab stops in the document. You can also adjust a paragraph's left indent and first line indent here. Default tab stops are placed every one-half inch in an Illustrator document. (The tab ruler uses the unit of measure established in the preferences or specified in the Document Setup dialog box.) When you click the type of tab you want and then in the desired spot on the ruler, you can place a new stop for selected text. A paragraph of text can have up to 15 tab stops.

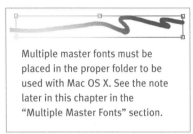

Multiple master fonts must be placed in the proper folder to be used with Mac OS X. See the note later in this chapter in the "Multiple Master Fonts" section.

The tab ruler offers four types of tab stops: left, center, right, and decimal. The decimal tab stop aligns numbers according to their decimal points (or according to where their decimal points would be). Placing any tab stop on the ruler erases all default stops to the left of it on the tab ruler. You can delete tab stops by dragging them off the ruler. You also can relocate them by dragging. Shift+dragging repositions all tab stops.

The tab ruler works with both horizontal and vertical text. It automatically aligns itself according to the type of text selected. In addition, Windows users can click the Alignment box to have the ruler line up with the selected text.

➪ *Can't get the tabs where you want them? See "Taming the Tab Ruler" in the "Troubleshooting" section at the end of this chapter.*

THE TYPE MENU

Many of the commands in the Type menu, shown in Figure 7.16, are available only when a selection has been made. Others can be used to establish settings that will be applied to text placed subsequently.

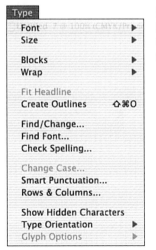

Figure 7.16
Some commands are available only when appropriate text is selected.

The commands include the following:

- **Font**—A list of all available fonts appears to the right when you drag the cursor to this command. Pick a font by dragging onto the list and releasing the mouse button while over the specific font's name. If text is selected in the document, it is changed to that font, with all other attributes and options unchanged. If none is selected, the font is used for text placed from that point on. Because of the way Adobe's type engine functions, third-party programs or plug-ins that show font names in their specific fonts won't work with Illustrator.

- **Size**—Like Font, this choice can be applied to existing type or specified for type placed in the document subsequently. In addition to the standard font sizes, this list contains the Other option, which opens the Character palette.

- **Blocks**—This command has two possible subcommands: Link and Unlink. The subcommands are grayed out if no appropriate type containers are selected. Linking type containers allows text to automatically flow from one container to the next. Linking text containers will be discussed later in this chapter.

- **Wrap**—Area text can be wrapped around paths or objects. This command offers Make and Release subcommands when appropriate selections are made. Wrapping text will be discussed later in this chapter.

- **Fit Headline**—This command is designed to work with multiple master fonts but can be used with others. It is designed to adjust type to fit into its container's width. When you're working with non–multiple master fonts, tracking is changed to spread or tighten the spacing of the letters. When you use a multiple master font, Illustrator also adjusts the optical weight to preserve the appearance of the type. In Figure 7.17, at the top are the before and after images using a multiple master font. In the middle is the error message received when Illustrator cannot squeeze a non–multiple master font into the required space.

Figure 7.17
The error message means that the non–multiple master font cannot be tightened enough to fit the allotted space.

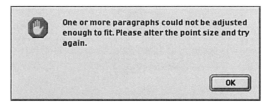

EXTRA! EXTRA! READ ALL ABOUT IT!

EXTRA! EXTRA! READ ALL ABOUT

> One or more paragraphs could not be adjusted enough to fit. Please alter the point size and try again.
>
> OK

EXTRA! EXTRA! READ ALL ABOUT

EXTRA! EXTRA! READ ALL ABOUT

- **Create Outlines**—This command changes type into compound paths. It is similar to the effect Outline Object. Text can no longer be edited after being converted. Create Outlines will also be discussed later in this chapter.

- **Find/Change**—Illustrator allows you to perform search and replace operations in your text as you do in a word processor. The dialog box is shown in Figure 7.18.

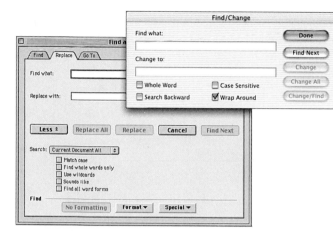

Figure 7.18
Although Illustrator's Find/Change feature is not as sophisticated as those found in dedicated word processors, such as Microsoft Word (shown behind), it is a useful tool.

- **Find Font**—A powerful tool, Find Font allows you to find and replace all instances of any font in your document. You can also print lists of included fonts, which can be of great assistance when you're troubleshooting a problem file. Illustrator compiles a list of all fonts used in the document, and you can choose to replace them from a list of fonts already in the document or fonts installed on your system. (Figure 7.19 shows the System option.) To help manage the list of replacement fonts, you can check or uncheck categories of fonts below the window. Type 1, TrueType, Multiple Master, CID (Character Identification), and OTF (OpenType font) can be considered technical classifications of fonts. (Note that if you want multiple master fonts to appear in the list, you must check the boxes for both Multiple Master and Type 1.) CID fonts allow extended character sets (including CJK fonts), as do OpenType fonts. When unchecked, the Standard check box excludes the following fonts from the list: Chicago, Geneva, Helvetica, Hobo, Monaco, New York, Courier, Souvenir, Symbol, and Times.

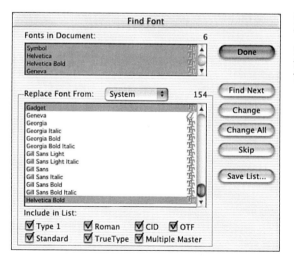

Figure 7.19
The Find Font dialog box also displays the type of font. Visible are the symbols for Type 1 and TrueType fonts.

- **Check Spelling**—Like Find/Change, Check Spelling is an adequate tool for most uses. As you can see in Figure 7.20, you can edit the list of words added to the dictionary.

Figure 7.20
Clicking the Edit List button opens the Learned Words dialog box.

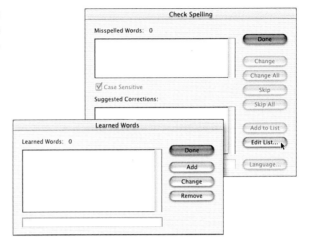

The custom word list is stored as AI User Dictionary inside Illustrator's Plug-in folder, which is inside the Text Filters folder.

Illustrator supports a wide range of languages. You can find spelling and hyphenation resources in the Text Filters folder. (If you don't work in multiple languages, you can delete the ones you don't need.)

- **Change Case**—With 1-byte Roman fonts (not CJK fonts), you can change selected text to and from all capital letters, all small, or titling (first letter of each word capitalized).

- **Smart Punctuation**—Using a find-and-replace technique, Smart Punctuation searches either the selected text or the entire document and replaces certain characters and symbols with their publishing equivalents. To change selected text, you must highlight it with one of the text tools. The list of possible changes is shown in the dialog box in Figure 7.21.

Ligatures are the lowercase letter combinations *ff*, *fi*, *fl*, *ffi*, and *ffl*. They are replaced with a single publishing symbol. Ligatures are available only when an appropriate Adobe Expert font is installed. Smart Quotes replace the straight quotation marks with the "curly" marks used in publishing. Smart Spaces changes a double space after a period to a single space. En, Em Dashes replaces a double hyphen with an en dash

You can open the AI User Dictionary in a word processor for editing. If you already have a custom dictionary for a word processor or other program, you can open it as a text file and copy and paste into the AI User Dictionary.

If you need multiple dictionaries for different projects, you can create them and name the files AI User Dictionary1, AI User Dictionary2, AI User Dictionary3, and so on. Simply remove the final digit from the filename when you need that particular dictionary and replace it when you're done. You don't need to quit Illustrator to make the change, but you should make sure that Check Spelling is not running.

and a triple hyphen with an em dash. Ellipses replaces three periods with the correct symbol. Expert Fractions (like Ligatures, available only when an appropriate Adobe Expert font is available) uses a single character for the most common fractions. Smart Punctuation also generates a report, telling you how many characters were changed. Such a report is shown in Figure 7.22.

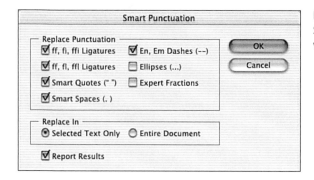

Figure 7.21
Smart Punctuation is available whether or not text is selected.

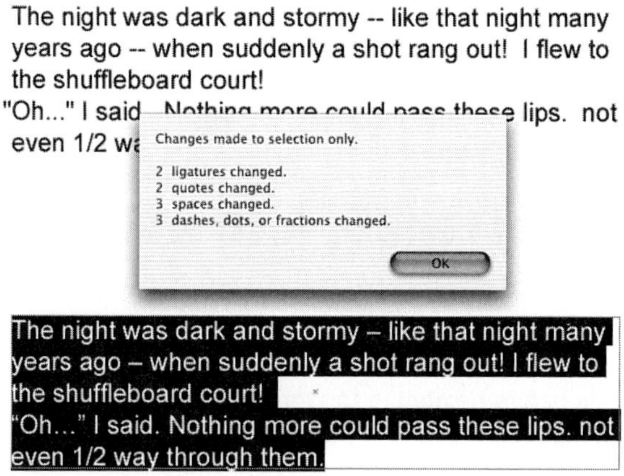

Figure 7.22
As you can tell by comparing the two passages, this Adobe Expert font does not contain the single-character fractions.

- **Rows & Columns**—Select any size or shape container filled with text, and Rows & Columns produces precisely defined text rectangles. Figure 7.23 shows an example.

  Rows & Columns can be used with empty rectangles as well to create grids or other sets of identical boxes.

- **Show Hidden Characters**—The hidden characters are nonprinting symbols. Among the hidden characters are those for spaces, tabs, and returns. They can be made visible for editing or troubleshooting. In Figure 7.24, the symbols for line breaks (returns), tabs, and spaces are visible.

- **Type Orientation**—Selected type can be switched from horizontal to vertical and vice versa with this command.

- **Glyph Options** (Mac only)—Some Japanese fonts include alternatives for some characters. With the appropriate Type 1 CID font, you can replace a standard character with a historical or alternative character from the Expert, Traditional, or JIS78 set.

Figure 7.23
What was one large text container has now become three linked columns.

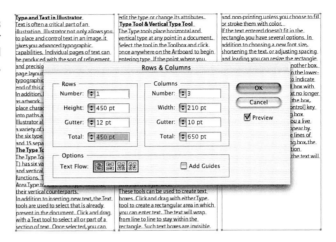

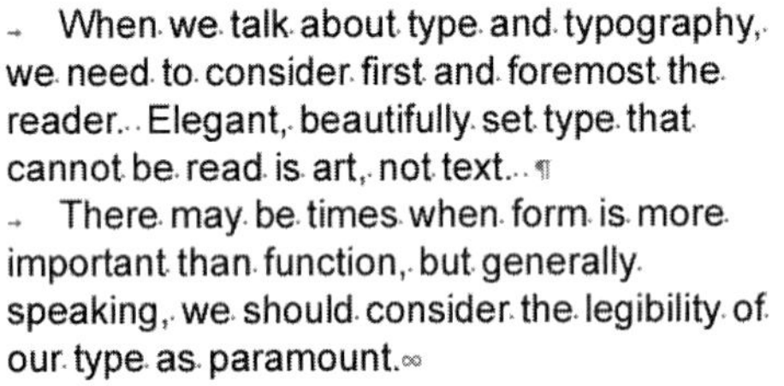

Figure 7.24
The now-visible characters can be selected and deleted just as you would delete an empty space, a return, or a tab when hidden.

→ When we talk about type and typography, we need to consider first and foremost the reader. Elegant, beautifully set type that cannot be read is art, not text. ¶

→ There may be times when form is more important than function, but generally speaking, we should consider the legibility of our type as paramount. ∞

TEXT CONTAINERS, OUTLINES, AND ATTRIBUTES

Any shape can contain text in Illustrator, including open paths. In addition, Illustrator can wrap text outside objects. One very important aspect of text containers is linking, being able to have text automatically flow from one container to the next. You should be familiar with two of the Type menu's commands before beginning to work with text containers. The Blocks command (discussed earlier in this chapter following Figure 7.16) and Rows & Columns command (explained before Figure 7.23) are very important to this subject.

Linking Text Containers

When two or more text containers (also called *text boxes*) are linked, their content works as a single piece of text. If words are added somewhere in the first container, the text near the bottom that no longer fits moves to the top of the next container automatically. Figure 7.25 shows how container linking works.

To link containers, select them on the artboard and choose Type, Blocks, Link. The containers are linked according to their place in the stacking order, not necessarily from left to right in the illustration. The alphabet was entered into a group of linked containers in Figure 7.26. From the flow of the letters, you can tell in what order the objects were drawn.

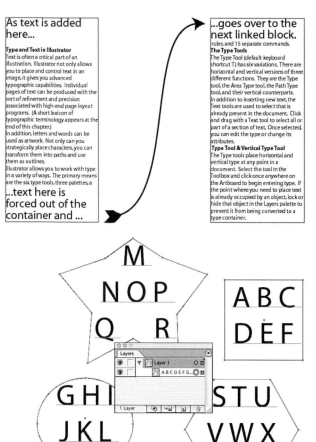

As text is added here...

Type and Text in Illustrator

Text is often a critical part of an illustration. Illustrator not only allows you to place and control text in an image, it gives you advanced typographic capabilities. Individual pages of text can be produced with the sort of refinement and precision associated with high-end page layout programs. (A short lexicon of typographic terminology appears at the end of this chapter.)

In addition, letters and words can be used as artwork. Not only can you strategically place characters, you can transform them into paths and use them as outlines.

Illustrator allows you to work with type in a variety of ways. The primary means are the six type tools, three palettes, a

...text here is forced out of the container and ...

...goes over to the next linked block.

ruler, and 15 separate commands.

The Type Tools

The Type Tool (default keyboard shortcut T) has six variations. There are horizontal and vertical versions of three different functions. They are the Type tool, the Area Type tool, the Path Type tool, and their vertical counterparts. In addition to inserting new text, the Text tools are used to select that is already present in the document. Click and drag with a Text tool to select all or part of a section of text. Once selected, you can edit the type or change its attributes.

Type Tool & Vertical Type Tool

The Type tools place horizontal and vertical type at any point in a document. Select the tool in the Toolbox and click once anywhere on the Artboard to begin entering type. If the point where you need to place text is already occupied by an object, lock or hide that object in the Layers palette to prevent it from being converted to a type container.

Figure 7.25
Linking the two rectangles allows text to flow from one to the other.

Figure 7.26
The stacking order of the objects, apparent from the alphabet, is square, circle, star, hexagon.

As you can see from the Layers palette in the figure, Illustrator creates a single object from the containers and their text. It is not a group of objects, but a single path. Therefore, to control the flow of text, arrange your containers in the Layers palette before linking.

Stacking Order

The stacking order is, by default, the order in which objects are created in Illustrator. The eldest object is at the bottom of the stacking order; the most recent, at the top. You can change the stacking order by using the Object, Arrange menu commands. Moving an object to the back makes it the lowest in the stacking order and the first in the text flow.

Likewise, you can rearrange the order of objects in the Layers palette. Objects closer to the bottom of the palette are farther down in the stacking order, farther back in terms of the Arrange commands.

Make sure the objects are in the order you want in the Layers palette before you link them as text containers.

If several objects are linked and you click with a text tool on any one of them, the cursor positions itself in the eldest of the objects.

You can bring text from word processing programs into Illustrator by cutting and pasting, placing, or opening the text file. If no text box or container is defined when you bring text into an Illustrator document, each paragraph is placed as point text, stretching as far as necessary off the artboard.

➥ *If you're having trouble getting text into Illustrator, see "Importing Text" in the "Troubleshooting" section at the end of this chapter.*

Wrapping Text Around Objects

Just as text can be placed inside objects, Illustrator can wrap text around objects and paths. You need to keep in mind a few important concepts:

- You must place a path around placed bitmap images. The text can wrap around identifiable paths only.

- The objects or paths around which the type will be wrapped must be in front of the type.

- Text flows directly against the path. Adding a path some distance beyond an object to create a margin is often worthwhile.

- An unstroked, unfilled path can create an invisible boundary around which you can wrap type. This boundary can be smaller than the object, as long as the object itself is not also selected for wrapping. Figure 7.27 shows an example.

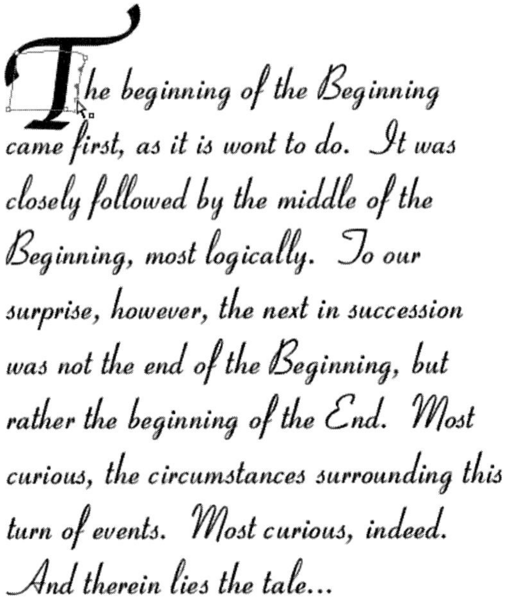

Figure 7.27
The unstroked, unfilled path is actually smaller than the capital *T*, allowing the text to wrap a bit more closely.

The beginning of the Beginning came first, as it is wont to do. It was closely followed by the middle of the Beginning, most logically. To our surprise, however, the next in succession was not the end of the Beginning, but rather the beginning of the End. Most curious, the circumstances surrounding this turn of events. Most curious, indeed. And therein lies the tale...

Note that the capital *T* in Figure 7.27 is technically neither a *drop cap* (top-aligned with the following text) nor a *raised cap* (bottom-aligned with the following text).

- After you wrap paths, you can select and edit them, and the wrap will reconfigure and adapt to the object's new path. This capability can be especially useful with unstroked, unfilled paths, such as described earlier in this list.

Figure 7.28 shows an example of text being wrapped around multiple objects. Notice that each placed bitmap image is surrounded by a path. Also, note that the text is very tightly aligned to those paths.

Figure 7.28

If the paths had been at the edge of the bitmap images, the text would have flowed to the very edge of the pictures.

Multiple text containers can wrap around one or more paths or objects. In Figure 7.29, two containers wrap around one path.

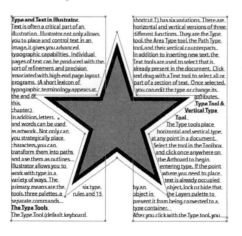

Figure 7.29

Like the previous figure, an additional path has been drawn around the object to prevent the text from wrapping too closely.

Filling and Stroking Text Containers

By default, when a path or an object becomes a text container, it automatically receives a stroke and fill of None. However, it often makes sense to have a text container with either a stroke or a fill or both. Illustrator allows you to colorize your text containers, but you must select them independently of the text. Using the Direct Selection tool, click the invisible path that constrains the text. You can then apply a fill and/or stroke as appropriate. Figure 7.30 shows an example.

Converting Text to Outlines

In addition to being used for text, type can be used as decorations or objects in an illustration. When type is used in these capacities, the characters may be converted to compound paths. As such, they can no longer be edited as text but can be edited as paths. Figure 7.31 shows the difference between a type character and an outline created from that character.

To easily create a margin around an object, follow these steps:

1. Select the object.

2. Copy the object using Cmd+C [Ctrl+C].

3. Paste the copy directly in front of the original object using the command Paste in Front. The keyboard shortcut is Cmd+F [Ctrl+F].

4. Choose Effect, Path, Offset Path. Enter an amount equal to the desired margin. Then click OK.

5. Change the stroke and fill of the enlarged copy to None, and wrap the text around it rather than the original.

Figure 7.30
The normally invisible text container was selected using the Direct Selection too, and a style was applied.

Figure 7.31
On the left is a letter; on the right is a compound path that can be edited with the Direct Selection tool.

More useful with type at very large sizes, the command Type, Create Outlines produces compound paths for each letter. Text—whether point, path, or area—must be converted together. You cannot convert, for example, a single word in the middle of a sentence.

Simplifying Type Outlines

When you're converting text to outlines, Illustrator is very precise. This precision can result in very complex paths. These paths are often too complicated to print properly. Illustrator usually returns a warning when you attempt to use extremely complex paths as masks, too.

The command Object, Path, Simplify can be of great help. You'll find that, in many cases, you can leave Curve Precision set to 100% and still have a dramatic reduction in the path complexity. Figure 7.32 shows an example of text converted to outlines and simplified to 90%. The resulting paths, not visually different from the originals, had a reduction in anchor points of more than 80%.

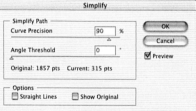

Figure 7.32
The more angular serif fonts benefit most from simplification, but all type outlines can benefit as well.

Copying Type Attributes

Typography can be considered the art of typesetting and printing. Although you can get beautiful results using the type defaults, taking advantage of Illustrator's advanced typographic capabilities can improve virtually any text. One of Illustrator's great time-savers is the capability to copy attributes from one set of characters to another.

The Eyedropper tool, in conjunction with the Paint Bucket tool, allows you to copy type attributes among text in an Illustrator file. The Eyedropper samples the attributes from the source text, and the Paint Bucket applies them to the target text.

You can copy attributes in two ways using the Eyedropper:

1. Use a type or selection tool to designate the text that is to receive the attributes, the *target* text.

2. Use the Eyedropper to click the *source* text, the text whose attributes you want to be copied to the target text.

Alternatively, you can use the Paint Bucket with the Eyedropper as follows:

1. Use the Eyedropper to copy attributes from the source text by clicking it.

2. Switch to the Paint Bucket tool and click the target text, or drag with the Paint Bucket to apply the attributes to only part of the target text.

When either the Eyedropper or Paint Bucket is selected in the Toolbox, you can switch to its partner tool by pressing and holding down Option [Alt].

To control which attributes are transferred from source to target, double-click either the Eyedropper or Paint Bucket tool to open the dialog box shown in Figure 7.33.

Figure 7.33
Checking or unchecking a box determines which attributes are copied.

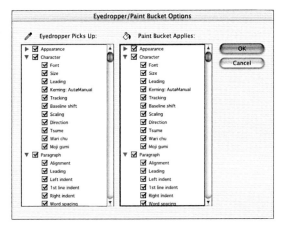

The following text attributes can be copied:

• **Appearance**—Transparency; Focal Fill color, Transparency, and Overprint; Focal Stroke color, Transparency, Overprint, Weight, Cap, Join, Miter limit, Dash pattern

• **Character**—Font, Size, Leading, Kerning (auto/manual), Tracking, Baseline shift, Scaling, Direction, Tsume, Wari-Chu, Moji Gumi

• **Paragraph**—Alignment, Leading, Left indent, First line indent, Right indent, Word spacing, Letter spacing, Auto-hyphenation, Kurikaeshi Moji Shori, Kinsoku Shori

Note that Leading appears twice, once under Character and again under Paragraph. The first refers to the leading (line spacing) set in the Character palette. The second refers to the amount of space added before a paragraph in the Paragraph palette. (Remember that the latter is available only for area type.)

FONTS AND FONT EMBEDDING

Many types of fonts are available today, in various qualities. Illustrator, like most high-end computer programs, works best with high-quality fonts. Although you can get good results with inexpensive and free fonts, they are often problematic. TrueType and Type 1 fonts are the most common high-quality fonts available today, with more and more multiple master and OpenType fonts reaching the marketplace.

Fonts (also called typefaces) that are classified as TrueType, Type 1, multiple master, and OpenType typically perform flawlessly with Illustrator. (Any font, however, is subject to corruption over time and may need to be reinstalled.) Bitmap fonts can be used, but not all of Illustrator's capabilities will be available. In addition, such fonts may not print properly.

Fonts and Font Families

Technically, a certain typeface at a certain size in a certain style constitutes a *font*. More generally, we tend to use the term to refer to an entire family of fonts. For example, Times 12 pt is different from Times 24 pt and Times (Italic) or Times (Bold). Each was designed to serve a separate purpose. Colloquially, we refer to all the Times typefaces as a single font. Technically, Times is a font family, with numerous individual fonts.

When does terminology make a difference? Primarily today, the subject comes up in marketing. Such-and-such a laser printer may have 52 fonts installed, and a competitor might claim more than 250 fonts. One font package could include more than 1,000 fonts, and another might have 85 font families. As long as you are aware of the difference in terminology, you can make informed decisions.

Multiple Master Fonts

Multiple master fonts allow customization of such design attributes as the weight, width, style, and optical size. The MM Design palette, shown in Figure 7.34, gives you access to weight and optical size. Using the Character palette, also shown Figure 7.34, to change the height and width of a font can result in distortion of the letter shapes and proportions. The optical weight is the visual appearance of a character at a particular font size.

Figure 7.34
The four lines of type are all Adobe Jensen MM Expert at 72 pt.

The top line in Figure 7.34 has a weight of 470 and an optical size of 72. The second line has a reduced weight of 340, but it retains the optical size. The third line of type has an increased weight of 600 and the same optical size of 72. The bottom line retains the original's weight of 470 but has an optical size of 36 points.

Using Illustrator's MM Design palette, you can customize a Multiple Master font one or more ways. Some multiple master fonts allow you to make other adjustments in Adobe Type Manager. (ATM is installed with Illustrator by default.) In addition, multiple master fonts adjusted in Illustrator are available only to that document. To make a customized font available to all documents, make the changes in ATM.

CID and OpenType Fonts

The CID and OpenType font families support extended characters rather than being limited to 256 letters, numbers, and symbols. The larger number of characters available makes these types of fonts highly appropriate for CJK character sets. CID fonts are an extension of the Type 1 architecture, so they perform well with Illustrator. CID (Character Identification) fonts use ID numbers to index and access characters. This system is more efficient than the name-based access system used by Type 1 fonts.

To use multiple master fonts with Illustrator 10 in Mac OS X (version 10.1 or later), the fonts must be installed in Illustrator's own Fonts folder. In OS X's Finder, open the Applications folder. Inside the Illustrator folder, Control-click (or right-click with a multi-button mouse) on the Adobe Illustrator 10 icon. From the contextual menu, select Show Package Contents. You'll find a folder named Required. Within the Required folder is the Fonts folder. Unless multiple master fonts are placed into that folder, they will not be available in Illustrator under Mac OS X. Remember, too, that you must be using version 10.1 or later to use MM fonts.

OpenType fonts are cross-platform, working on both Macintosh and Windows computers. In addition, each OpenType font requires a single file to include the entire font family. Multiple glyphs for each character are incorporated into many OpenType fonts. (*Glyphs* are the individual representations of a character, such as the lowercase and small caps versions of the same letter.)

Font Embedding

Illustrator allows you to include fonts used in a document when saving files in the Illustrator, PDF, and EPS formats. If a font is not embedded and it is not installed on another computer used to open the file, another font will be substituted. However, the substitute font may not have the same spacing, appearance, or size as the font you designated. That can lead to substantial changes in the appearance of the document. Additionally, missing fonts can generate PostScript errors, preventing the document from outputting properly at a service bureau or print shop.

Remember that fonts are copyrighted. You may or may not have received the right to embed the font when you purchased or otherwise acquired the font itself. If you are sending a project off to a print shop or service bureau and they do not own copies of those specific fonts, you must have permission from the font's copyright holder to embed it. (Adobe fonts typically include embedding rights.)

Font subsetting is designed to reduce the size of your file by including only that part of the font necessary to reproduce your image. Subsetting is available for Illustrator and PDF formats, but not EPS.

TYPOGRAPHIC TERMINOLOGY

An understanding of some basic typographic terminology can be helpful. Figure 7.35 defines several of the terms visually:

- **Alignment**—Also called (incorrectly) *justification*, this term refers to the positioning of lines of text within a paragraph. Text can be flush left, centered, flush right, or justified (flush left and right). Illustrator allows you to choose two types of justification: All Full Lines and All Lines. The difference is the last line of a paragraph. Under the first option, the last line (if it doesn't extend from margin to margin) is aligned left. With the second option, the word spacing is extended to stretch the line from margin to margin. Text that is flush left, centered, or flush right is sometimes referred to as *unjustified*. (See also *margin* and *indent*.)

Figure 7.35
The key terms are further defined in this section.

- **Ascender**—The part of a lowercase letter that extends above the x-height of the font is called an ascender (refer to Figure 7.35). In most fonts, the following letters have ascenders: *b*, *d*, *f*, *h*, *k*, and *l*. (See also *descender* and *x-height*.)

- **Baseline**—The baseline is the imaginary line along which the bottoms of most letters rest (refer to Figure 7.35). Typically, the baseline runs along the bottom of the ends of letter strokes rather than along the curves of rounded letters. In the font used in Figure 7.35, the baseline is established by the letters *x*, *r*, and *l*, whereas the rounded bottoms of the letters *p*, *e*, and *t* extend slightly below the baseline.

- **Body**—Also called *body text*, this is the majority of the text in most documents. The body text in an office memo or letter, as well as many publications, is typically 10-or 12-point type.

- **Bold**—Text that is visually heavier than the regular text of the same font family is bold. It is thickened, as if drawn with heavier strokes. Emphasis within body text is usually italicized rather than bolded; however, bold is often appropriate for headlines and as a visual reference to items in a list. Bold is a weight rather than a style. (See also *style* and *weight*.)

- **Cap height**—The height of most capital letters in a font, measured from the baseline, is the cap height (refer to Figure 7.35). It may or may not be the same height as the font's ascenders. (See also *ascender*.)

- **Character**—An individual letter, number, or symbol is a character. That particular character can be represented by numerous glyphs in a font family. For example, the lowercase letter *a* is a character, but it can be represented by regular, italic, bold, and small-cap glyphs. Note that the lowercase *a* and uppercase *A* are considered different characters. (See also *glyphs*.)

- **CID**—A type of font, CID (Character ID) allows for a vastly larger number of characters in a single font. CID, which is an Adobe technology, uses a different system of identification for each glyph. (See also *glyphs*.)

- **CJK (Chinese-Japanese-Korean)**—Rather than letters, CJK fonts consist of characters that represent words or ideas. CJK fonts require a very large number of characters, so they usually are double-byte fonts. CJK fonts have special rules and options within Illustrator. A computer's operating system must have the capability to use CJK fonts before they can be employed in Illustrator. (See also *double-byte fonts*.)

- **Condensed**—A version of a font in which each glyph is narrower than the regular version is called condensed. This is a style. (See also *extended* and *style*.)

- **Copyfitting**—The process of making a certain quantity of text fit into a specific area is called copyfitting. It is usually accomplished by adjusting the size and spacing of type, not by editing the text.

- **Descender**—The part of a lowercase letter that extends below the baseline is called a descender (refer to Figure 7.35). In most fonts, the following characters have descenders: *g, j, q,* and *y*. (See also *ascender* and *baseline*.)

- **Dingbats/wingdings**—See *symbol*.

- **Double-byte fonts**—These fonts, including most CJK fonts, use two bytes of information to record the character identification. Using two bytes allows for a far greater number of characters in a single font. (Single-byte fonts are limited to 256 glyphs.) (See also *CJK, glyphs,* and *single-byte fonts*.)

- **Drop cap**—An initial letter of a paragraph set in a larger size and top-aligned with the first line is called a drop cap. *Cap* is a shortened version of *capital*, referring to an uppercase letter. (See also *raised cap*.)

- **Ellipsis**—Three periods in a row, this symbol indicates that one or more words are missing, usually from a quotation. Rather than type three periods, you can insert the individual symbol in many fonts. Option+semicolon [Alt+semicolon] is the usual keystroke. Ellipses (the plural) are often smaller than three periods.

- **Em space/em dash**—A standard unit of measure within a font, *em* refers to the font's point size. The name comes from the width of an uppercase *M*. An em dash is a dash one em in width. (See also *en space/en dash*.)

- **En space/en dash**—A standard unit of measure within a font, an *en* is one-half the font's point size. The name comes from the width of an uppercase *N*. An en dash is a dash one en in width. (See also *em space/en dash*.)

- **Extended**—A version of a font in which each glyph is wider than the regular is called extended. This is a style. (See also *condensed* and *style*.)

- **Fixed pitch**—A font whose characters each require the same amount of space on a line is said to be fixed pitch. The terms *fixed width* and *monospaced* are also used. (See also *proportional*.)

- **Font/face/font family**—These terms are often used interchangeably, but technically they are not all the same. *Font* and *face* can be used to refer to a specific typeface in a specific weight and style. A group of related fonts is called a *font family*. For example, Times Roman 12 pt, Times Roman 18 pt, and Times Bold 12 pt are all fonts within the Times font family. (See also *style*, *typeface*, and *weight*.)

- **Font size**—See *point/point size* and Figure 7.35.

- **Glyphs**—A glyph is a particular character of a font. Although the lowercase *a* can be called a *character*, each separate rendition of the letter is a glyph. For example, the regular lowercase *a*, its italic and bold counterparts, and the small caps version are all separate glyphs of a single character. (See also *character* and *font/face/font family*.)

- **Greeking**—When type is too small to be properly displayed onscreen, it is replaced with a gray bar that represents the line at its approximate length. The size at which type is greeked is set in Illustrator's preferences (Preferences, Type & Auto Tracing). Greeking does not affect printed output.

- **Hanging indent**—When the first line of a block of type is left-aligned and the remaining lines are indented, the paragraph can be said to have a hanging indent.

- **Hanging punctuation**—Punctuation that extends past the margin of a block of text is called hanging punctuation. Typically, this refers to the right margin of text, although hyphens and dashes can extend past the left margin. The full-sized punctuation marks, such as the exclamation mark and question mark, are not included. The purpose of hanging punctuation is to give the margin of text a cleaner look.

- **Head/headline**—Type that is set apart from (usually above) the body text and is designed to introduce the subject of the body is headline text. It is usually larger or otherwise emphasized. The term can also refer to fonts and font families designed to be used for headlines.

- **Hinting**—Hints are the instructions included with a font to make it display and output properly at different sizes and resolutions.

- **Indent**—A block or line of text that is moved away from the edge of the text alignment is said to be indented. The first line of a paragraph, moved inward from the left alignment, is indented. An entire paragraph moved in from the left alignment shared by other paragraphs is indented. Paragraphs can be indented left, right, or both.

- **Italic**—A slanted version of a font is called italic. It is used for emphasis in both headline and body text.

- **Justification**—See *alignment*.

- **Kerning**—The spacing between a pair of adjacent letters is kerning. The goal of kerning is to produce uniform visual spacing between letters. Kerning is of particular importance for headline type. (See also *letter spacing*.)

- **Leading**—The space between lines of type is referred to as leading. (The term is pronounced like the metal, not like the verb *to lead*.) In the days when type was set by hand, thin strips of soft metal were added between lines to separate them.

- **Letterform**—The actual shape of an individual character or glyph is sometimes referred to as its letterform. Illustrator allows you to alter the paths that create the letterform. The type, however, becomes compound paths, can no longer be edited as type, and can no longer be hinted when scaled.

- **Letter spacing**—Although kerning applies to and is applied to a pair of letters, letter spacing (also called *tracking*) works with an entire block of text. It alters the average space between letters in the copyfitting process or to improve appearance. (See also *copyfitting*, *kerning*, and *word spacing*.)

- **Ligature**—Two lowercase letters combined into a single glyph are referred to as a ligature. Ligatures are designed to improve the look of the letter combinations. The letter combinations are *fi*, *fl*, *ff*, *ffi*, and *ffl*. The first two are often built into fonts and can be accessed with the keystrokes Shift+Option+5 [Shift+Alt+5] and Shift+Option+6 [Shift+Alt+6], respectively. The remaining ligatures are available in specialized fonts, usually those with the word *expert* or *pro* in their names.

- **Margin**—The empty spaces around the left, right, top, and bottom edges of one or more blocks of text are the margins. The term is often used to refer to the invisible line that runs along the alignment of one or more blocks of text, but should properly be used for the empty space beyond the line. Because most printers cannot print all the way to the edge of the paper, margins are necessary. In addition, properly balanced margins increase visual appeal and make text easier to read.

- **Monospace**—See *fixed pitch*.

- **Multiple master**—This type of font allows for customizable optical size, weight, and other adjustments. Such fonts typically have *MM* in their names. Depending upon the individual multiple master font, Illustrator's MM Design palette enables you to customize a number of appearance factors. Other characteristics, however, may need to be adjusted in Adobe Type Manager (ATM). (See also *optical size* and *weight*.)

- **Old-style figures**—The old-style figures are lowercase numbers. They are best used with lowercase type and in body text. Many old-style figures have ascenders and descenders. Old-style figures are usually not mixed with uppercase numbers. A font that includes old-style figures usually indicates this fact in its name. (See also *ascender* and *descender*.)

- **OpenType**—A recent type technology developed by Adobe and Microsoft, OpenType fonts are multiplatform and have extended character sets. Illustrator 10 has some support for OpenType fonts but cannot fully take advantage of the hinting capabilities. OpenType fonts can carry an entire font family in a single file, making font management much easier. Smart Punctuation for OpenType fonts in Illustrator 10 is limited to the Macintosh. (See also *hinting*.)

- **Optical size**—Fonts are designed to be used at a particular point size. The shapes of the individual glyphs are balanced for viewing at that size. This is the font's optical size. When a 12-point font is scaled to 72 points, its optical size may be skewed. Multiple master fonts allow adjustment of a font's optical size. (See also *multiple master*.)

- **Pica**—A pica is equal to 12 points. In PostScript printing, it is exactly one-sixth of an inch. (See also *point/point size*.)

- **Point/point size**—A point is 1/72 of an inch. Theoretically, each font is measured from the lowest **descender** to the highest **ascender** to determine its point size. There can be wide variances. Points are the most common unit of measure for type in the United States. In Europe, fonts are measured in millimeters using the cap height (refer to Figure 7.35). (See also *ascender*, *cap height*, and *descender*.)

- **Proportional**—Most fonts are proportional; each character is allocated a certain required amount of space on a line. The spacing is assigned to increase legibility and visual appeal of the type. (See also *fixed pitch*.)

- **Raised cap**—An initial capital (uppercase) letter of a paragraph that is substantially larger than the body text and aligned with the baseline of the following text is a raised cap. (See also *drop cap*.)

- **Regular**—This term refers to the visual weight of a font. Typical body text is usually regular, and the related fonts in the font family may include bold, light, and semi-bold. A font's weight differs from its style. (See also *bold*, *style*, and *weight*.)

- **Roman**—One of a font family's styles, Roman is the upright font usually used for body text. It is contrasted with condensed, extended, and italic. (See also *condensed*, *extended*, *italic*, and *style*.)

- **Rule**—Lines used to separate items on a page are called rules. They are sometimes used between paragraphs or around graphic elements. The current trend is to limit the use of rules.

- **Scaling**—To increase or decrease the size of a font is to scale the font. Using another font of the same font family, one designed for use at the size required, is usually better than transforming a font.

- **Serif/sans serif**—Serifs are the small flourishes at the end of the stroke of a letter, number, or symbol (refer to Figure 7.35). Serif fonts have such decorative strokes, whereas sans serif fonts do not. In most sans serif fonts, the stroke of a letter also has a uniform thickness. Serifs make text easier to read on the printed page, especially at small sizes. Sans serif fonts, on the other hand, are usually preferred when a document will be seen on a computer monitor (including text on the World Wide Web).

- **Single-byte fonts**—These fonts, which include most TrueType and Type 1 fonts, use eight bits (one byte) of information to record character identifications. That limits each font to a maximum of 256 glyphs. (See also *double-byte fonts* and *glyphs*.)

- **Small caps**—One of a font family's styles, small caps use smaller versions of the upper-case letters to substitute for the lowercase letters. This style is typically used for emphasis within body text and for headlines. It is contrasted with condensed, extended, and italic. (See also *condensed*, *extended*, *italic*, and *style*.)

- **Smart quotes**—Many fonts place straight quotes when you press the single or double quotation mark key. Such quotation marks are identical at the beginning and end of any quotation. Smart quotes, on the other hand, are the so-called curly quotes, which point inward toward the quote, at the beginning and end of the quoted material.

- **Spacing**—See *letter spacing* and *word spacing*.

- **Style**—Condensed, extended, italic, Roman, small caps, and underline are examples of styles. The term refers to the appearance of a character or font. Illustrator uses fonts within a font family for styles instead of adding faux styles as do many word processors. A font's style differs from its weight. (See also *font/face/font family* and *weight*.)

- **Superscript/subscript**—One or more characters raised above the neighboring text's base-line are said to be superscript. Subscript characters are dropped below the baseline. (See also *baseline*.)

- **Symbol**—Some fonts consist of special symbols rather than letters and numbers. Such fonts often have names that include the words *symbol*, *dingbat*, or *wingding*.

- **Tracking**—See *letter spacing*.

- **Typeface**—A specific group of letters, numbers, and symbols all designed to be used together at a specific size with a particular weight and style is a typeface. The term *type-face* is often used interchangeably with *font*. (See also *font/face/font family*, *style*, and *weight*.)

- **Underline**—Text with a line underneath was often used for emphasis with typewriters. Most typewriters had no alternative typefaces, such as italic or bold, available. Underlining is rarely used for emphasis now, with italic being the preferred style. One place where underlined text is common is the World Wide Web. On the Web, however, it should be restricted to indicating a hyperlink.

- **Unjustified**—See *alignment*.

- **Weight**—Bold, light, regular, and semibold are type weights. The term refers to the visual darkness of a font. Illustrator uses fonts within a font family for weight instead of adding a faux weight as do many word processors. (See also *font/face/font family* and *style*.)

- **White space**—See *margin*.

- **Width**—Variations in a font family's styles may include condensed and extended. They are changes in a font's width. (See also *condensed*, *extended*, and *style*.)

- **Word spacing**—Adjusting the space between words in a block of text can be done to improve legibility or for the purposes of copyfitting. Such adjustments usually change the average spacing throughout an entire block of text. (See also *copyfitting* and *letter spacing.*)

- **WYSIWYG**—This acronym, which is pronounced *WI-see-wig,* stands for *What You See Is What You Get.* It most commonly refers to having printed output match that which was designed on the computer screen. It can also refer to font management utilities that show the contents of the Font menu in the actual typefaces. Illustrator does not support such font utilities.

- **x-Height**—The distance from the bottom of a font's lowercase *x* to the letter's top is referred to as the font's x-height (refer to Figure 7.35). For many fonts, this is the height of all lowercase letters without ascenders or descenders. However, some fonts have variations in height among lowercase letters. The x-height can vary tremendously among fonts of the same point size. (See also *ascender* and *descender.*)

TROUBLESHOOTING

Copyfitting

I can't make the font any smaller because it won't be legible, but I need to squeeze another line or two into my text container. What can I do?

You've got several possibilities, all of which fit under the title *copyfitting.* First, reduce your leading in the Character palette. That will bring the lines of type closer together vertically. Remember that you can use fractions, too, so that the adjustment is the very smallest necessary. Next on the list (if your text is justified rather than aligned) would be word spacing from the Paragraph palette. (If the palette is not visible, expand it by clicking the two-headed arrow in the palette's tab a couple of times.) Word spacing, which works only with area type, allows you to change the amount of space between words in the selected text. After that, you've still got letter spacing (also in the Paragraph palette), which reduces the gap between each of the letters in the selected text. Think of it as mass-kerning. Using these three advanced techniques should bring those last two lines of your text into the allotted area.

Taming the Tab Ruler

The tab ruler is something new for me, but I can't seem to get it to work. No matter what I do, I can't get different parts of my text to have different tab stops.

Tabs established for a block of text apply to the entire block, even if only part of the text is selected. If you need different tab stops for different parts of the text, break the block into two separate text boxes.

In addition, did you know that you can change the indent and first line indent of selected text in the tab ruler? To the left, above the ruler and below the icon for the Left Tab Stop, are two small triangles. Drag the top one to change the first line indent; drag the lower one to change the paragraph indent.

Importing Text

When I bring text into Illustrator from my word processor, I have two problems: First, the text forms one long line, and it takes a lot of time to put back in all the returns to make a column. Second, even after I import the text, it doesn't look the same. It's close but not quite right.

First, identify a container for the text before putting it in your document. Either drag with the appropriate Type tool or click an object with a Type tool to make it a text container. The text may overfill the container, but you can resize it to fit. This way, you also avoid having a lot of hard returns at the ends of lines, which prevents text from reflowing when edited.

Second, it sounds as though the word processor has a font available to it that isn't available to Illustrator. If the text document was created on a different machine, find out what font was used, and either purchase a copy of that font or find one you own that's similar.

MANIPULATING OBJECTS IN ILLUSTRATOR

III

IN THIS PART

8   Transforming and Distorting Objects   **173**

9   Working with Blends   **211**

10   Illustrator's Layers, Sublayers, and Groups   **231**

11   Output Options   **255**

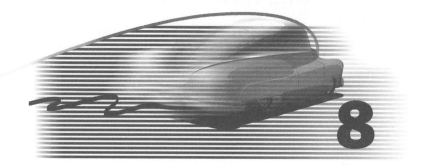

TRANSFORMING AND
DISTORTING OBJECTS

IN THIS CHAPTER

Transformations and Distortions in Illustrator   174

The Basics of Transforming   175

The Transformations   180

Envelope Distortions   194

Illustrator's Liquify Tools   206

Troubleshooting   210

TRANSFORMATIONS AND DISTORTIONS IN ILLUSTRATOR

Illustrator offers a variety of ways to alter the shape of an object or a path. Some are designed for convenience, some for precision, and some are targeted toward creativity. Illustrator 10 adds a couple of major new capabilities to this part of the creation process. The introduction of envelope distortions and the liquify tools open new doors on productivity and artistry.

When a transformation or distortion is applied to a path, open or closed, the anchor points and/or the direction lines for the anchor points are moved. Changing the path will alter not only the appearance of the stroke and fill, but also any effects applied to the selection.

Transforming vs. Effects

Illustrator also offers many of the capabilities discussed in this chapter as effects. Using the commands under the Effect, Distort & Transform or Effect, Warp menus does *not* alter the path of an object. As live effects, only the appearance is changed. The difference between transforming a path and applying an effect is shown in Figure 8.1.

Figure 8.1
The original object is on the left. In the center, the object has been transformed using a transform tool. On the right, an effect has been applied. Compare the three paths.

The first and third figures have a star-shaped path. The middle figure, transformed with the Twist tool, has a path that conforms to its appearance. For more information on the Effect commands, see Chapter 20, "Using Filters and Effects."

Generally speaking, a transformation is applied to paths, objects, or groups selected on the artboard. You can also use most of the transformation commands and tools with selected anchor points to change part of an object or path.

Transform, Envelope Distort, and Liquify

Three basic categories of path manipulation are discussed in this chapter. Each of the groups works in a different way to create different results. Each of the three categories has a number of different capabilities.

The transformation commands, tool, and palette offer predictable and regular control over the changes to a path (or a portion of a path). They work with the existing anchor points, moving them or changing the length and angle of the direction lines. In some instances, additional anchor points may be added to a path or object. Corner anchor points may have direction lines added, and smooth points might be converted to corner points.

The Envelope Distort commands create mesh objects that are used to alter the shape and appearance of paths or objects. A mesh object, which will be explained in depth later in the chapter, uses a series of path-like mesh lines to re-shape the fill of an object.

Illustrator's new liquify tools alter the shape of a path by adding, subtracting, and moving anchor points. The tools provide a variety of capabilities.

THE BASICS OF TRANSFORMING

There's nothing in the category of transformations that cannot also be done with the Selection and Direct Selection tools. However, using Illustrator's transformation commands and tools and the Transform palette allow you to quickly and precisely change the shape of paths and objects. Transformations can be performed on objects, open paths, selected anchor points of objects and paths, and on groups. The transformation tools and menu commands and the Transform palette are shown in Figure 8.2.

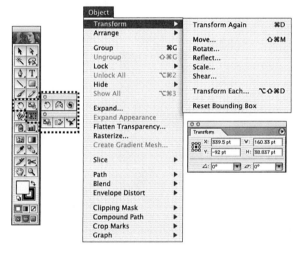

Figure 8.2
The transform tools are indicated by the dashed line. The Transform submenu is visible. Use the Window menu to make the Transform palette visible.

Illustrator's Toolbox has two hidden palettes that hold transformation tools. The Rotate, Reflect, and Twist tools share one flyout palette, while the Scale, Shear, and Reshape tools share the other. The Free Transform tool (default keyboard shortcut E) sits alone in the Toolbox. (It is the selected tool in Figure 8.2.)

Note that the Rotate, Reflect, Scale, and Shear tools are duplicated by menu commands. The menu also has commands for reapplying the most recent transformation (Transform Again), relocating a selection on the artboard (Move), applying a transformation individually to members of a group or selection (Transform Each), and a command to reset a selections bounding box.

The Transform palette, which can be used to move, scale, rotate, and shear a selection, can accept negative numbers and can accept values with precision to one one-thousandth of a point (three decimal places).

Illustrator offers 15 preset warps (which are also available under the Effect menu), user-defined mesh distortions, and distortions using user-created paths. The submenu Object, Envelope Distort contains the seven commands shown in Figure 8.31.

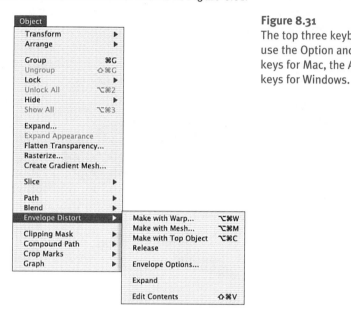

Figure 8.31
The top three keyboard shortcuts use the Option and Command keys for Mac, the Alt and Control keys for Windows.

The Basics of Warping

The easiest envelope distortions to make are those that use the ready-made shapes applied with the menu command Object, Envelope Distort, Create with Warp. Illustrator offers a variety of customizable preset distortions (see Figure 8.32).

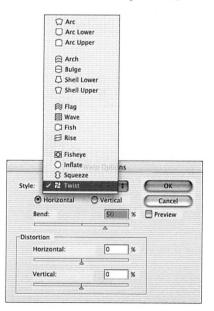

Figure 8.32
Illustrator's 15 preset warps are shown in miniature in the pop-up menu.

Warps can be applied to objects, paths, text, meshes, blends, and placed raster images. They cannot be used with graphs. To apply a warp, make a selection on the artboard and choose the menu command Object, Envelope Distort, Make with Warp to open the dialog box. In the dialog box, choose the desired preset from the pop-up menu, click horizontal or vertical, and adjust the sliders to achieve the desired shape.

While the preset warps do a good job of replicating the shape shown in the pop-up menu, the power of warping comes from the sliders in the dialog box. As you can see in Figure 8.33, adjusting the distortion sliders can add a 3D look to an object.

Figure 8.33
The warp samples are all created with the Arc preset.

In the upper-left corner, the default values are used: Horizontal, Bend 50%, Horizontal Distortion 0%, Vertical Distortion 0%. To the right, the only change was switching from Horizontal to Vertical. In the lower-left example, the setting included distortion: Horizontal, Bend 67%, Horizontal Distortion 50%, Vertical Distortion 50%.

Extreme Warping

Extreme warping can make objects appear to be twisted so much that the "back" of the object is visible. In Figure 8.34, for example, the type of the top object appears reversed when the object is warped.

Figure 8.34
The "back" of the text is visible when warped.

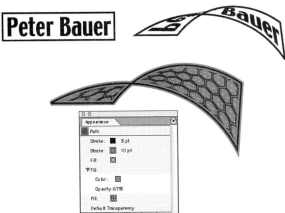

However, keep in mind that Illustrator is not actually manipulating objects in 3D. If it were, then the lower object would show a different fill appearance on the two sides. In the Appearance palette below, you can see that there are several layered fills in the object. If the "back" of the object were actually visible, the fills would be stacked in reverse order. Likewise, if a pair of objects are stacked and grouped and then warped, the lower object will not be visible as the "back."

Warps can be applied to a selection that includes multiple objects. Whether grouped or not, the warp will be applied to the selected objects as a single entity. In Figure 8.35, the difference between applying the same warp to three individual objects (left) is compared to applying a single warp to three selected objects (right) .

Figure 8.35
On the left, each object was warped individually. On the right, the three objects were selected together and the warp applied once.

How Warps Work

Notice in Figure 8.35 that the warp paths are visible. The warped object becomes a *mesh object*, whose shape is determined by mesh points and mesh lines. A closer examination, in Figure 8.36, shows the anatomy of a mesh object.

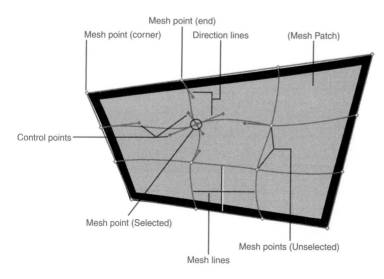

Figure 8.36
The selection is warped using mesh lines and mesh points. Direction lines with control points determine the shape of the mesh lines.

The parts of a mesh object are

- **Mesh Point**—Mesh points are comparable to a path's anchor points. They are found at every intersection of mesh lines and only at the intersection of mesh lines.

- **Mesh Line**—Like path segments, each segment of a mesh line is bordered by two points. Their ends are determined by the mesh point locations, and the shape of the segment is determined by the points' direction lines.

- **Direction Line**—Just as path anchor points can have direction lines to determine path segment geometry, so too do mesh points. The shape of a mesh line segment is determined by the length and angle of the mesh point's direction line. (A complete explanation of direction lines and how they work is found in Chapter 4, "Creating and Editing Paths.")

- **Control Point**—Each direction line has a control point at the end. Dragging the control point determines the length and angle of the direction line.

- **Mesh Patch**—An area surrounded by mesh lines can be called a mesh patch. Mesh patches can be dragged to reshape a mesh object.

When a mesh line ends at a mesh point, the point may be called an end point. Mesh points that join only two mesh line segments are corner points. Mesh points always have one direction line for each line segment that touches the point. There can be as few as two or as many as four direction lines. Corner points will have two, end points will have three, and other mesh points will have four direction lines.

When a mesh point is selected on the artboard, the diamond is filled. Unselected mesh points show hollow diamonds.

When a mesh point is selected on the artboard, its direction lines will be visible. In addition, the direction lines for the mesh points at the far end of each adjoining path segment will be visible. (This is depicted in Figure 8.36.)

Editing a Mesh Object

Mesh objects are manipulated like gradient mesh objects and, in many respects, paths. (Gradient meshes are discussed in Chapter 15, "The Gradient and Gradient Mesh Tools.") Changing the shape and fill appearance of a mesh object is similar to manipulating paths in Illustrator. The Direct Selection tool can be used to modify the mesh points. As you can see in Figure 8.37, mesh points can have as many as four direction lines. Mesh points will be found at the intersection of mesh lines, including corners. Each mesh point will have one direction line for each mesh line segment.

The following guidelines cover manipulating mesh points and mesh lines:

- Each mesh point has at least two direction lines, one for each mesh line segment that meets at the mesh point.

- The shape of the mesh object is governed by the location of the mesh points and the length and angle of the point's direction lines. (This is analogous to the way that anchor points determine the shape of paths.)

- Mesh points can be moved by selecting them and dragging with the Direct Selection tool.

- A direction line is manipulated by dragging the control point at its end. The Direct Selection tool is used to drag control points.

Figure 8.37
The selected mesh point is at the intersection of two mesh lines. It has four direction lines, one for each line segment.

- Shift-clicking with the Direct Selection tool allows you to select and move multiple mesh points.

- Only one control point can be manipulated at a time.

- The Direct Select Lasso tool can be used to select (but not move) mesh points. It cannot be used with control points.

- Holding down the Option (Alt) key and clicking on a mesh point with the Direct Selection tool will select all mesh points and dragging will make a copy of the mesh object.

- Mesh lines can be deleted by selecting a mesh end point and deleting the point. (Corner mesh points cannot be deleted.)

- Deleting a mesh point at the intersection of two mesh lines deletes both lines.

- The Direct Selection tool can be used to select and drag a mesh patch, an area surrounded by mesh lines. The surrounding mesh lines will be adjusted, but the mesh points' direction lines will remain unchanged in length and angle.

- When a mesh point has a mesh line running smoothly through it, changing the angle of direction line with the Direct Selection tool will have an equal and opposite affect on the opposite direction line. (The length of the direction line on the other side of the mesh point will not be affected.) This behavior is comparable to that of a smooth anchor point on a path.

- The Convert Anchor Point tool can be used to move a control point without altering the opposite direction line.

The Make with Mesh Command

The Object, Envelope Distort menu also offers a couple of ways to create custom envelope mesh objects. The Make with Mesh command opens the dialog box shown in Figure 8.38.

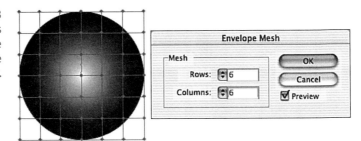

Figure 8.38
This simple dialog box offers tremendous control over the development of an envelope mesh object.

Illustrator will turn the selected object or objects into an envelope mesh object with the specified number of rows and columns. The mesh lines will be organized in an evenly-spaced grid.

Creating mesh grids allows you to customize the shape of the envelope from scratch.

Rather than counting the mesh lines, the Make with Mesh dialog box asks you for the number of rows and columns of *mesh patches*. The actual number of horizontal and vertical mesh lines will be one higher than the number or rows and columns.

Reopening the Envelope Distort Dialog Box

After a warp distortion has been applied, it can be altered. With an envelope mesh object selected on the artboard, the Object, Envelope Distort menu changes to that seen in Figure 8.39.

Figure 8.39
Envelope mesh objects can be altered through the original dialog boxes.

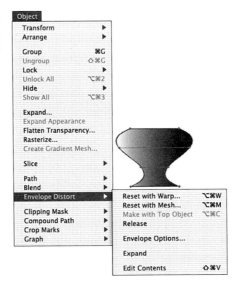

Selecting Reset with Warp reopens the Warp Options dialog box, allowing you to change the slider settings or even select a different preset. Using the menu command Reset with Mesh opens the dialog box shown in Figure 8.40.

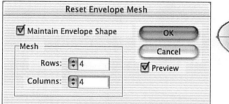

Figure 8.40
You can add or subtract rows and columns.

If the Maintain Envelope Shape box is unchecked, Illustrator will convert the envelope mesh object into a rectangle the size of the original object.

Using the Make with Top Object Command

Illustrator allows you to use an object as the basis for an envelope mesh object. Only a single path or mesh object can be used, which excludes compound paths and compound shapes. The command Object, Envelope Distort, Make with Top Object executes without a dialog box. Whatever path is top-most of those selected will be used to create the shape of the mesh object, distorting any selected object(s) below to create the fill. Figure 8.41 shows a pair of examples.

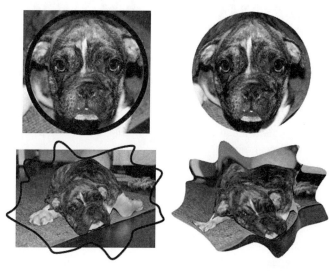

Figure 8.41
The original raster images and the paths used are on the left, the resulting mesh objects are on the right.

Any path, open or closed, stroked and filled or invisible, can be used at the top object. Illustrator will assume a direct line between end points of an open path.

In Figure 8.42, a path has been drawn that maintains the integrity of the upper two-thirds of the photograph, while distorting only the lower one-third.

Figure 8.42
The path is shown as a heavy
black outline.

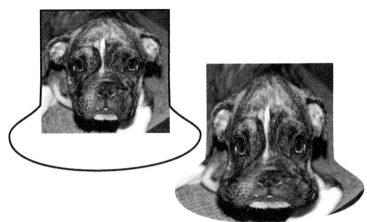

Where the top path follows the edges of the photo, the distortion is minimal. Where the path flares away from the photo, the distortion is much more pronounced.

Make with Top Object can also be very effective with type (see Figure 8.43).

Figure 8.43
The top object is the gray path on
the left. The mesh path is visible
on the right. Type is no longer
editable when part of an
envelope mesh.

When a gradient mesh object is used to create an envelope mesh, only the object's path is used. The gradient mesh lines within are ignored and colors can no longer be assigned to the mesh points or mesh patches. Similarly, when another object is used to create an envelope mesh from a gradient mesh, the gradient mesh is no longer editable. The gradient mesh object is rasterized to create the envelope mesh object.

Envelope Options

Illustrator gives you several options that can be preset for envelope distortions. The menu command Object, Envelope Distort, Envelope Options opens the dialog box shown in Figure 8.44.

The top section of the box, which applies only to rasterized artwork, allows you to use antialiasing to smooth the appearance of curves and to choose between a clipping path and a mask (alpha channel) to preserve the appearance of the artwork.

The Fidelity slider controls how closely the distortion will match the path. The slider ranges from zero to 100, with 50 as the default. Increased fidelity results in more points being added to the resulting object. In addition to requiring more time to produce the envelope distortions, higher fidelity can produce extremely complex paths.

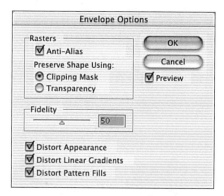

Figure 8.44
This dialog box determines what characteristics of an object will be distorted and how precisely.

Illustrator also uses the Envelope Options dialog box to determine whether a pattern fill of linear gradient fill will be distorted with an object. You can also elect to scale strokes and effects, much as they can be scaled when working with transformations.

The difference between distorting an object and distorting an object and its pattern fill is shown in Figure 8.45.

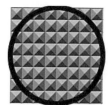  

Figure 8.45
The original pair of objects is on the left. In the center, the object alone was distorted. On the right, the object and pattern were distorted.

Releasing and Expanding Envelope Distortions

The menu commands Object, Envelope Distort, Release and Object, Envelope Distort, Expand are discussed together to avoid confusion. In execution they have similarities; in result they do not.

To either release or expand an envelope distortion, the envelope mesh object must be selected on the artboard and the command invoked. Multiple envelope mesh objects can be released or expanded at the same time.

The Release command removes the distortion, returning the object to its original state, and produces an object in the shape of the mesh. It is no longer a mesh object, but rather consists of an unstroked path filled with gray. It is always created on top of the original object(s). If no longer needed, the mesh shape can be selected and deleted.

The Expand command applies the envelope distortion permanently. The mesh is removed and the object retains the distorted shape.

Figure 8.46 shows the envelope mesh objects from the previous figure released (top) and expanded (bottom).

Figure 8.46
The two envelope mesh objects
from Figure 8.45 have been both
released (top) and expanded
(bottom).

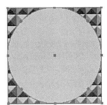
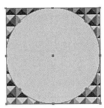

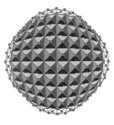

Note that there is no difference between the two released envelope distortions. Both now consist of the original object and a gray circle.

The expanded objects, however, differ substantially. On the left, only the object was distorted, so expanding the envelope mesh resulted in a simple change of shape from the original square to the circle. On the right, however, both the object and its pattern fill were distorted and expanded. The result is a very complex collection of vector objects. Each section of the pattern has been expanded to a separate object. (There are actually 275 separate vector objects, surrounded by a clipping path.)

The Edit Contents Command

The appearance of an object can be changed even after it is converted to an envelope mesh object. The menu command Object, Envelope Distort, Edit Contents gives you access to the underlying object through the Appearance palette. (After choosing this command, it will change in the menu to Edit Envelope.)

If this command isn't in effect, double-clicking the Contents line in the Appearance palette expands to show the mesh object (see Figure 8.47). No stroke or fill or other appearance characteristic can be applied directly to the mesh.

If you need to replicate a custom distortion again and again, you need to create it only once and you can apply it as often as you'd like. Make the envelope mesh object and manipulate it until it looks just right. Next, use the menu command Object, Envelope Distort, Release. A plain gray object will be created, representing the envelope mesh shape. Select just that shape and click the New Symbol button in the Symbols palette. The shape will be added to the palette as a symbol.

When you next need to create an envelope distortion with the shape, you can select it in the Symbols palette and either click once with the Symbol Sprayer or drag the shape to the artboard. Position it atop the object(s) to be distorted, and use the menu command Object, Envelope Distort, Make from Top Object.

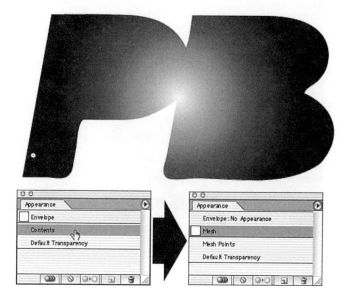

Figure 8.47
With an envelope mesh object selected on the artboard, double-clicking Contents in the Appearance palette (left) opens the palette content to show Mesh (right). Of course, only one Appearance palette will be visible.

After using the menu command Edit Contents, double-clicking Contents in the Appearance palette gives you access to the underlying object. You can add or change fills and strokes and opacity characteristics. The envelope mesh remains applied and the distorted shape remains unchanged. If necessary, Illustrator will re-center the mesh on the original object. Figure 8.48 shows one example of what can be done after an envelope distortion is applied.

Figure 8.48
Once the content is available for editing, additional stroke, fill, and opacity characteristics can be added through the Appearance palette, all without removing the distortion.

The Envelope Distort Menu

The Envelope Distort menu command alternates between Edit Contents and Edit Envelope, depending upon which you have chosen most recently. Illustrator does allow you to add strokes and fills directly to an envelope object itself. As you can see in Figure 8.49, adding a simple one-point stroke to an envelope mesh object can have very interesting results.

Figure 8.49
The mesh includes the original object's pattern fill, so the stroke is applied to it as well as the outer path.

ILLUSTRATOR'S LIQUIFY TOOLS

Illustrator 10 contains a group of tools that enable you to push and pull, swirl and scallop, expand and contract, and generally distort vector shapes (see Figure 8.50).

Figure 8.50
The flyout tool palette is found under the Warp tool in the Toolbox. The original object is shown at the top. Each tool was applied in turn.

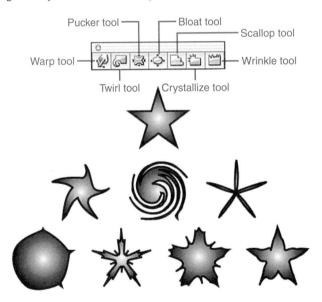

Working with the Liquify Tools

The liquify tools use round brushes to define the area of application. Selected paths within the diameter of the brush are modified by moving and/or adding anchor points.

- The Warp tool pushes and pulls on an object's anchor points as you drag. New anchor points are created as necessary to modify the shape.

- The Twirl tool modifies path segments by adding and moving anchor points and changing direction lines. Not to be confused with the Twist tool (one of the transform tools), it does not create smoothly-uniform changes to an entire object. Rather, it manipulates those path segments and anchor points within the brush's diameter. To use it, select the target object on the artboard and either click and hold to create uniform twirls or click and drag for non-uniform distortions. In Figure 8.51, a single line has been distorted three times with the Twirl tool.

  Note the number of anchor points added by the twirl tool. The original path was a single line segment with two anchor points.

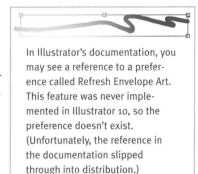

In Illustrator's documentation, you may see a reference to a preference called Refresh Envelope Art. This feature was never implemented in Illustrator 10, so the preference doesn't exist. (Unfortunately, the reference in the documentation slipped through into distribution.)

- The Pucker tool collapses the sides of an object inward. It can also be used to drag a path segment. Select an object on the artboard and click and hold to pucker it. In Figure 8.52, three pairs of squares are shown, one of each pair has been puckered. The dashed circles represent the brush size for the Pucker tool.

The Liquify tools have preferences (including brush size) that can be specified by double-clicking the tool's icon in Illustrator's Toolbox.

Figure 8.51
To the left, the twirl tool was applied with a click-hold-release. In the center, the tool was dragged in a small circle. To the right, the tool was dragged upward.

Figure 8.52
Whether or not an object's anchor points are within the brush diameter makes a large difference in the pucker distortion applied.

To the left, you can see that the anchor points and parts of the object's path that were outside the brush remain unaffected. In the center, the square was just slightly larger than the brush diameter. On the right, you can see the result when the entire object is within the brush diameter.

Figure 8.52 also shows the result of applying the Pucker tool to a straight path segment. The speed with which the tool is dragged affects its result. The Pucker tool was dragged upward three times from the path. From the left, the tool was dragged very slowly, slowly, and quickly.

- The Bloat tool is the counterpart of the Pucker tool. It expands the sides of an object. Apply the Bloat tool by clicking or dragging over a selected object. When the entire selected object fits inside the brush diameter, a single click can result in a near-circular object. Smaller brushes are usually more effective. When applied to a path segment rather than anchor points, drag in the direction opposite to that in which you want to bloat. Think of it as dragging away to create curves.

- The Scallop tool creates curves along the path of a selected object. Dragging the tool produces curves going in the direction of drag.

- The Crystallize tool creates pointed segments rather than curves. Drag away from the direction in which the points should go.

- The Wrinkle tool creates a series of angles along a path, like the Crystallize tool, but its angles are restricted by the Liquify options.

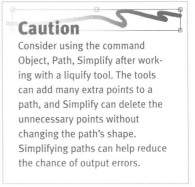

Caution

Consider using the command Object, Path, Simplify after working with a liquify tool. The tools can add many extra points to a path, and Simplify can delete the unnecessary points without changing the path's shape. Simplifying paths can help reduce the chance of output errors.

The Liquify Tool Options

Each of the liquify tools has its own options dialog box, which can be opened by double-clicking the tool's icon in Illustrator's Toolbox. The Warp Tool Options dialog box is shown in Figure 8.53.

Figure 8.53
This dialog box is typical of most of the liquify tool options.

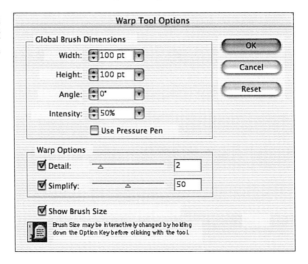

All of the liquify tools use the same Global Brush Dimensions options. In fact, all of the tools use the same brush. Changing the Warp tool's brush also changes the brush for each of the other liquify tools.

Modifying the width and height non-uniformly creates a non-round brush. Adding an angle other than zero produces a calligraphy-like brush.

Intensity determines how fast or slowly the tool works while the mouse button is held down. The Pressure Pen option is for use with drawing tablets, such as the Wacom Intuos line.

The lower part of the options dialog box varies from tool to tool. The Warp, Pucker, and Bloat tools use the options shown in Figure 8.53 as the Warp Options.

The Twirl tool adds an option for Twirl Rate.

The Scallop, Crystallize, and Wrinkle tools use a different set of options. The Wrinkle Tool Options dialog box is pictured in Figure 8.54. The Scallop and Crystallize tools do not have the Horizontal and Vertical sliders, but otherwise offer the same options.

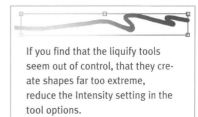

If you find that the liquify tools seem out of control, that they create shapes far too extreme, reduce the Intensity setting in the tool options.

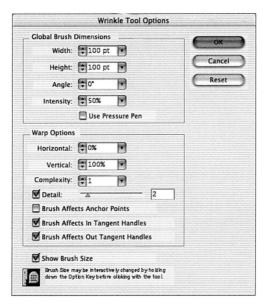

Figure 8.54
The Wrinkle, Scallop, and Crystallize tools have basically the same options.

You can modify anchor points and/or either of the tangent handle types, or you can choose just one of the three. You'll typically see little variation between the tangent handle options. However, checking and unchecking the Brush Affects Anchor Points box will typically produce a large difference in tool behavior.

Always check the Wrinkle tool options before working with the tool. Specifically, look to see if you'll be producing changes horizontally, vertically, or both. When horizontal is set to zero, you'll be adding anchor points to vertical lines without changing the path appearance in any noticeable way.

On the flip side, restricting distortion to either vertical or horizontal allows you to produce uniform perspective, motion, and gravity effects.

TROUBLESHOOTING

Showing and Hiding

Why is the bounding box sometimes visible and sometimes not?

First, remember that Illustrator uses the bounding box with only the Selection tool and the Free Transform tool. When any other tool is active, the bounding box is not. Second, it's possible to inadvertently hide the bounding box with the Show/Hide Bounding Box command's default keyboard shortcut. Shift-Command-B (Shift-Control-B) is very close to the keyboard shortcut for Paste in Back, Command-B (Control-B). You can check to see if the bounding box is hidden by pressing the Command (Control) key to temporarily switch to the Selection tool. Assuming that something is selected on the artboard, the bounding box will be visible while the key is depressed.

Checking Options

I get some pretty strange results when I use the Transform tools. Any suggestions?

When a Transform tool is acting strangely, double-click its icon in the Toolbox and look at the check boxes in the Options dialog box. You may (or may not) be scaling patterns, strokes, and effects as well as the object.

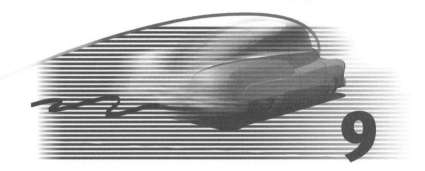

WORKING WITH BLENDS

IN THIS CHAPTER

Creating Blends **212**

Examining the Blend Options **216**

Adjusting Blend Paths **226**

Expanding a Blend **229**

Troubleshooting **229**

CREATING BLENDS

A *blend* is a series of objects created to show a linear progression between two objects. Each step (or intermediary object) created by Illustrator in a blend is unique, with characteristics of each of the objects being blended. As the blend progresses from one of the original objects toward the other, the balance of characteristics shifts.

Blends are created along straight paths (called *spines*), but the paths can be edited as any other. The shapes from which the blend was created can be edited, and the blend is automatically updated.

You can create blends by using the Blend tool or choosing Object, Blend, Make. You can create them among an unlimited number of objects, but Illustrator blends only adjacent objects. See Figure 9.1 for an example.

Figure 9.1
The blend among the three objects is actually a pair of blends. The first is a blend between the square and star; the second, between the star and circle.

In Figure 9.1, notice that the path along which the blend was created is visible, as are the paths of the three objects used in the creation. Making an adjustment to one of the objects produces the result shown in Figure 9.2. The intermediary objects, created by Illustrator for the blend, cannot themselves be edited unless the blend is expanded. (See "Expanding a Blend" later in this chapter.)

Blends can be created between multiple filled or unfilled objects, multiple open paths, or among a combination of open and closed paths. As you can see in Figure 9.3, Illustrator can also blend grouped objects and unfilled/unstroked objects.

Depending on the current options, Illustrator produces a specified number of intermediary objects, produces objects at a specified distance from each other, or creates a smooth blend of colors.

Figure 9.2
Using the Direct Selection tool to move an anchor point results in changes to all the intermediary objects in the blend.

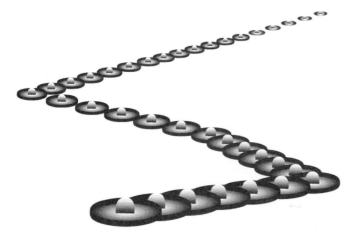

Figure 9.3
The object appears to fade in because the first object in the upper-right corner has a stroke and fill of None.

The following rules govern the creation of blends:

- The objects must be vector (not rasterized) and cannot be gradient mesh objects.

- The paths can be open or closed.

- You can blend between gradients.

- You can blend between open and closed paths.

- You can create a blend from numerous objects.

- After you create a blend, the parts of the blend are joined into a single object. You can access individual parts of the blend after choosing Object, Blend, Expand.

- You can transform or edit the unexpanded blend like any other single object.

- You can edit the path along which the blend is created like any other open or closed path.

- Intermediary objects are always distributed evenly along the blend spine.

- You can select and manipulate individual points on the blend's original objects with the Group Select tool.

- When you're blending among more than two objects, the order of blend follows the stacking order in the Layers palette.

- You can blend among grouped objects, but when you're blending between members of a group and another object, each group member blends independently.

- Objects with multiple attributes, such as strokes, fills, and effects, can be blended. Illustrator attempts to determine the averages of the attributes to create the intermediary objects.

- When you're blending objects filled with patterns, the pattern of the topmost object overrides the others.

- When you're blending objects with differing opacities, the blend adopts the transparency of the topmost object.

- When you're blending paths with different miter limits, caps, or joins, the intermediary objects assume the appearance of the object uppermost in the stacking order.

- When you're blending objects on different layers, Illustrator moves the entire blend to the layer of the topmost object.

Complex blends, especially when you're blending different colors, can substantially slow screen redraw times in Preview Mode. Outline Mode shows only the paths of the original objects and the path along which they were blended. If you create your blend on a separate layer, you can show that individual layer in Outline Mode by Cmd+clicking [Ctrl+clicking] the layer's eye icon in the Layers palette. You can leave the rest of the image in Preview Mode, with just the blend's layer in Outline Mode.

Several issues related to printing involve blends. Illustrator uses process colors to blend between two spot colors or between a spot color and process color. When you're blending between two tints of the same spot color, the intermediary shapes are also tints of the spot color. To control whether transparent objects in a blend knock out those below, select the blend and expand the Transparency palette to show its options.

- You can edit the blend itself after creating it by using selection and transformation tools.
- Illustrator attempts to blend multiple effects, fills, and strokes.

The Blend Menu

The following commands are available in the Blend menu:

- **Make**—Creates the blend according to the options specified.

- **Release**—Deletes all intermediary objects in a selected blend.

- **Blend Options**—Opens the Blend Options dialog box. There, you can specify the number of intermediary objects (Specify Steps) to be created or how far apart to place the new objects (Specify Distance). You also can allow Illustrator to choose the number of steps and their distance by opting to blend for Smooth Color. You can also choose the orientation of the intermediary objects, whether they will be aligned with the page or the path.

- **Expand**—Comparable to the Object option of the menu command Object, Expand.

- **Replace Spine**—Allows you to substitute a new path for the straight path along which the blend was created.

- **Reverse Spine**—Somewhat comparable to using the Reflect tool and reflecting perpendicular to the spine's path. Reversing the spine may give more precise results than Reflect with complicated paths.

- **Reverse Front to Back**—Reverses the stacking order of the original and intermediary objects. If the pattern or transparency of the original topmost object was imposed on the blend, it is not changed.

Using the Blend Tool

The Blend tool allows you to click objects sequentially to determine the order of blend. In addition, you can click specific anchor points of the objects to force Illustrator to create the blend with the designated points aligning. The intermediary objects are rotated. The difference between the two techniques is shown in Figure 9.4.

Figure 9.4
In the lower example, the Blend tool was clicked on the uppermost anchor point of the five-point star and then on the point indicated on the second star.

Designating anchor points with the Blend tool will create a blend that rotates to align the points. This technique can be accomplished only with the Blend tool; the menu command cannot assign anchor points:

- To simply blend two or more objects, click them sequentially with the Blend tool.
- To rotate a blend between two objects, click corresponding anchor points. For example, if a point at the top of one object and a point at the bottom of the second object are clicked, the intermediary objects appear to rotate 180°. When the cursor is directly over an anchor point, it changes appearance, darkening and adding a plus sign.

The Blend, Make Command

The actual process of making a blend can be as simple as selecting two objects on the artboard and choosing Object, Blend, Make. Illustrator uses the currently specified blend options (see the next section).

Unlike the Blend tool, which allows you to specify the order of blend, the Make command uses the stacking order found in the Layers palette. To change the order, rearrange the objects, groups, or layers in the Layers palette.

➪ *If an illustration isn't printing properly, see "Printing Blends" in the "Troubleshooting" section at the end of this chapter.*

EXAMINING THE BLEND OPTIONS

In the Blend Options dialog box (see Figure 9.5), you can specify that the blend be created with smooth color, a certain number of steps (intermediary objects), or with a specified distance between objects. In addition, you can choose to maintain the orientation of the objects on a curved path or create each object perpendicular to the path.

Figure 9.5
For the Specified Distance option, you can input a specific number and unit of measure. Smooth Color has no numeric option.

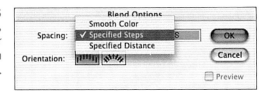

Smooth Color

Illustrator determines how many intermediary objects are required to produce a smooth color blend between two objects. If the colors are identical, or if the objects have gradient or pattern fills, Illustrator calculates the number of new objects based on the distance between bounding boxes (see Figure 9.6).

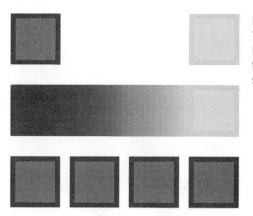

Figure 9.6
The top pair of boxes were blended using Smooth Color to produce the blend in the second row.

In Figure 9.6, two squares of differing stroke and fill (shown at the top of the image) were blended. Illustrator created 254 intermediary objects to bridge the gap between the colors. The third and fourth pairs of squares show how Illustrator blends two identically colored squares when Smooth Color is selected. The third pair has two intermediary objects because that is how many would fit between the originals without overlapping bounding boxes. A blend of the bottom pair produced only a single intermediary object for the same reason. When Objects with identical colors are blended with the Smooth Color option, Illustrator produces only as many intermediary objects as will fit between the originals without overlapping.

Figure 9.7 illustrates how the number of intermediary objects created depends on the color difference between the two originals. All the squares have the same color stroke. All the squares on the left have the same fill, an RGB value of 255/0/0. The squares with which they have been blended, on the right, have varying fills. The RGB values are, from the top down, 250/0/0, 240/0/0, 225/0/0, and 200/0/0.

Figure 9.7
To bridge the gap between a red value of 255 and, from the top, red values of 250, 240, 225, and 200, Illustrator created, respectively, 5, 15, 30, and 57 new objects.

You can use Smooth Color to create shaped gradients. Figure 9.8 shows a star-shaped example. To create this gradient look, the large star was created with a fill, but no stroke. It was duplicated using Copy and Paste in Front. The duplicate was scaled to 25% of its original size using the command Object, Transform, Scale. Its fill was changed to white, and the command Object, Blend, Make was used, with the Blend Options set to Smooth Color.

Figure 9.8
The small white star (on top) is blended into the larger star to create the gradient look.

You also can use Smooth Color to create shaded objects with unusual shapes. Figure 9.9 shows a blend between two open paths.

Figure 9.9
Using vector paths and Smooth Color blends can produce precisely proportioned objects.

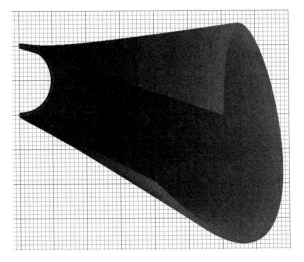

Smooth Color Blends

Smooth Color blends are excellent for customizing certain types of graphs. Figure 9.10 provides some suggestions.

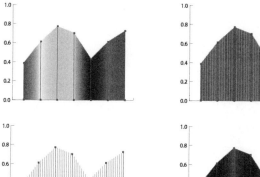

Figure 9.10
As is evident from the selections, the four graphs use the same seven open paths as values.

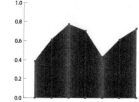

The rainbow pattern in the upper left is created by using different color values for each of the seven paths that are blended. In the upper right, grayscale values of 100% and 75% are alternated. To the lower left, the grayscale values are 100% for each path. In the lower right, the alternating grayscale values are 50% and 100%.

You can make blends from graphs created with the Graph tools after ungrouping. Remember, however, that ungrouping a graph prevents further changes to graph data, styles, or designs (see Chapter 5, "Shape, Drawing, and Graph Tools").

Specified Steps

When you select Specified Steps, you are instructing Illustrator on how many intermediary objects to create. The program automatically calculates the proper proportion of each original object's appearance for the intermediary objects. The objects are evenly spaced between the original objects.

The Specified Steps setting is especially appropriate for creation of Web-based animation. Whether you're working with animated GIF or Flash format illustrations, you can simplify frame-based animation by using Specified Steps blends. After you expand and ungroup the blended objects, choosing Illustrator's Release to Layers command puts each object on a separate layer, ready to become an individual frame of the animation. (Animation will be discussed in detail in Chapter 23, "Flash and SVG Support.")

In Figure 9.11, a grouped object has been duplicated using the command Object, Blend, Make. The option Specified Steps produced 13 intermediary objects, to bring the total to 15. Using the typical animation frame rate of 15 frames per second, the Little Blue Car will take one second to cross the screen.

Figure 9.11
The first and last cars (which are identical) were blended using Specified Steps to produce the 15 objects necessary for a one-second animation.

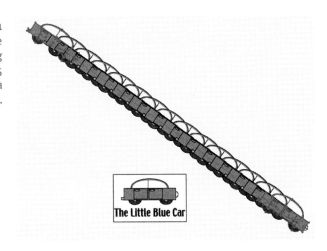

In addition to creating simple frames, you can create more complex animation by blending groups of several different objects. In Figure 9.12, three objects have been grouped at the beginning of the sequence and copied to the end. Illustrator's Blend command produced the intermediary steps in the sequence.

Figure 9.12
Separating each object into its own frame results in an animation that shows the figure walking across the page. Enlarged versions of the three original objects are shown below.

Specifying the number of intermediary objects can serve a variety of purposes in addition to creating animation. For example, when you're creating a custom graph, rather than using one of the Graph tools, you can apply tick marks uniformly to the x and y axes. Figure 9.13 shows one technique.

Figure 9.13
Adding the 13 intermediary paths gives a total of 15 tick marks for the graph.

Intermediary objects can also be used to fill in a graph, as shown in Figure 9.14. In this case, the curve will be more apparent with additional columns. By using Specified Steps, you can add two columns between each of the existing objects. The result is shown in Figure 9.15.

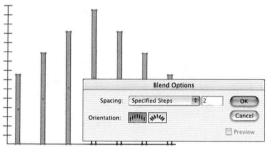

Figure 9.14
Because the data for this graph is assumed to be uniform, you can add the additional columns by blending.

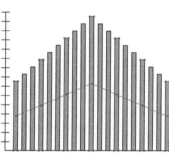

Figure 9.15
The completed graph consists of the path creating the axes, the blend of the tick marks, and the blend of the columns.

You can add virtually anything that you need to uniformly add to an illustration by choosing Object, Blend, Make using Specified Steps. Figure 9.16 shows some varied ideas.

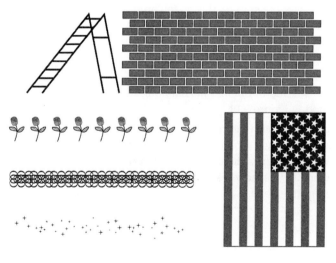

Figure 9.16
All these samples employ one or more blends using Specified Steps.

Blending Multiple Objects

When you're blending multiple objects, keep in mind that blends depend on the stacking order of objects. Even when all objects are on the same layer, the order in which they were drawn determines the order in which they will be blended. Figure 9.17 shows 20 numbered tiles, drawn sequentially, and how they blend.

Figure 9.17
Note that the spacing of the intermediary objects varies, depending on the distance between the two objects being blended. The number of intermediary objects, however, is the same for each segment of the blend.

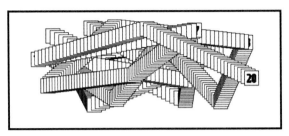

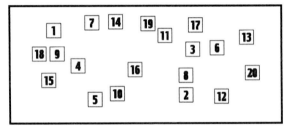

Specified Distance

The third choice for spacing in the Blend Options dialog box is Specified Distance. Especially useful for blends that include multiple objects, this option attempts to place intermediary objects at a set distance from the original objects and from each other. However, if the distance isn't a multiple of the specified distance, Illustrator will shift the intermediary objects to maintain uniform distance between all of the objects.

When you're using Specified Distance, the relative positions of the original objects being blended are irrelevant to the spacing of the intermediary objects. Specified Distance and Specified Steps are contrasted in Figure 9.18.

In Figure 9.18, the upper blend has each intermediary object evenly spaced. The lower blend has an equal number of objects in each segment of the blend, but because the distance between blended objects differs, so does the spacing. As you can see in Figure 9.19, with Specified Distance, all intermediary objects are equally spaced, regardless of the spacing of the two original objects bordering the blend.

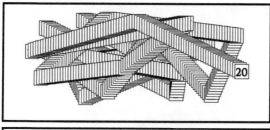

Figure 9.18
Compare the upper blend, created with Specified Distance, to the lower blend, shown in Figure 9.17, created with Specified Steps.

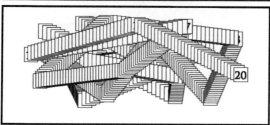

Figure 9.19
The 10 original objects are at the corners, with intermediary objects between.

⇨ *If you can't seem to get that last intermediary object in exactly the right spot using Specified Distance, see "Correcting Blend Spacing" in the "Troubleshooting" section at the end of this chapter.*

The spacing of the intermediary objects created with the Specified Distance option is based on paths. Observe in Figure 9.20 how the stroke of a path can change the perception of spacing.

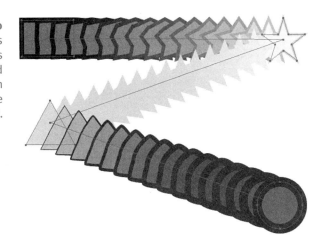

Figure 9.20
Because the stroke of the circle is heavy, the intermediary objects toward the end of the blend appear to be closer together than those near the triangle. They are all equidistant.

An increase in stroke, especially combined with a change in transparency, can alter the perception of distance created with a blend. Figure 9.21 shows two different examples.

Figure 9.21
The increased stroke on the left adds a perception of distance. On the right, an enlarged stroke is combined with a change in transparency for a different look.

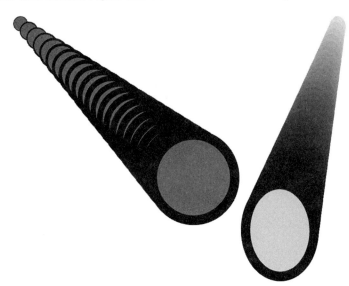

Orientation

The Orientation options in the Blend Options dialog box are Align to Page and Align to Path. The former maintains the vertical orientation of each intermediary object created; the latter rotates each object so that it is perpendicular to the path. Although this pertains to all paths, it is significant only with nonlinear paths. (Editing the straight path of a blend as created by Illustrator is discussed in "Adjusting Blend Paths.") The difference between the two choices is shown in Figure 9.22.

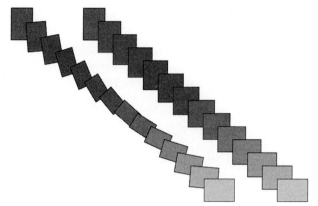

Figure 9.22
On the left, the intermediary objects maintain orientation to the page. On the right, they rotate and remain perpendicular to the angled path.

At first glance, the caption for Figure 9.22 may seem to be reversed. Note, however, that the two original objects (at either end of the blends) are perpendicular to each other. Because of the 90° rotation between the original objects, the intermediary objects in the blend on the right are the ones that are rotated.

The orientation of the blend can also make a subtle but important difference when you're blending with scatter brushes. Figure 9.23 shows a basic set of paths (upper left) and a pair of blends created after the path has the Grape Leaves brush applied (which you can find in the Default_RGB and Default_CMYK brush libraries). To the right, the blend was created with the orientation set to Align to Page. The lower example shows the same blend, but with orientation set to Align to Path.

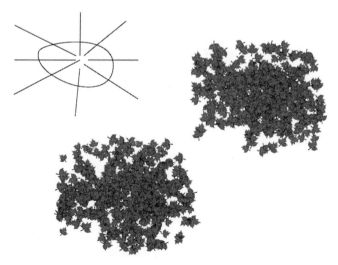

Figure 9.23
Both of the blends were created with the option of five steps for spacing.

ADJUSTING BLEND PATHS

After you create a blend, you can change the path (spine) along which the intermediary objects were drawn. Illustrator always creates the blend along a straight path. You can edit that spine with the same tools you use to edit any other path. You can also replace it with another existing path.

Editing Spines

As with any path, the two basic types of editing involve moving anchor points and changing the curve of segments. When you move an anchor point, the appearance of the blend changes. How it changes depends, to a large degree, on the options with which the blend was created. As you can see in Figure 9.24, you can predict the results of editing spines based on the type of blend.

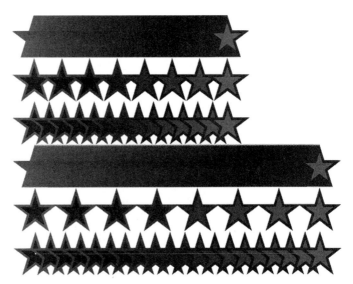

Figure 9.24
The first and fourth blends are Smooth Color; the second and fifth are Specified Steps; the third and last are Specified Distance.

Each of the top three blends was duplicated, and the spine was edited. In each case, the Direct Selection tool was used to drag the end of the path to the right. The results included the following:

- Smooth Color had already added the proper number of intermediary objects to ensure a proper transition between the objects. When the blend was extended, the intermediary objects were simply spread out slightly.

- Specified Steps had produced a blend with the exact number of intermediary objects requested. Extending the spine maintained that required number of objects and adjusted their spacing.

- Specified Distance continued to approximate the requested distance between intermediary objects, adding additional objects at the necessary interval.

Because a blend is created along a straight path, the spine's anchor points are always corner points. When you use the Convert Anchor Point tool to change a corner point into a smooth point, a straight spine can be curved. Note, however, that even with Specified Distance selected, curving a spine does not produce additional intermediary objects. Figure 9.25 gives an example.

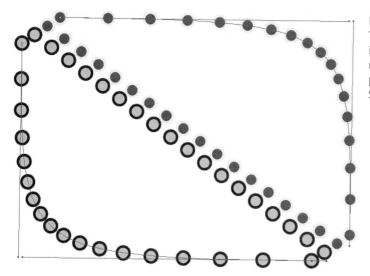

Figure 9.25
The four paths were originally identical except for color. The upper pair are Specified Steps paths, whereas the lower are Specified Distance.

When the duplicate paths were curved (as shown by the anchor points' direction lines), the number of intermediary objects remained the same, even for the Specified Distance blend.

As mentioned previously, the Orientation blend option is very important to the appearance of a curved spine. Figure 9.26 shows the difference between Align to Page (top) and Align to Path (bottom) .

Figure 9.26
Other than the orientation option, the two blends are identical.

Replacing Spines

In addition to editing spines, you can replace them with any other path, open or closed. In Figure 9.27, the top blend and open path just below have been combined to create the third object at the bottom of the page.

Figure 9.27
The original blend was created with the option Orient to Path, resulting in the confusion of arrows after the spine is replaced.

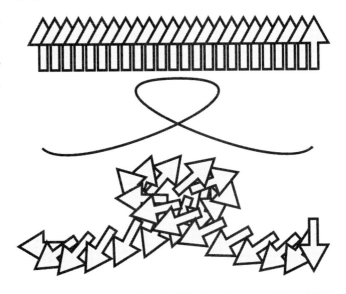

To place a blend along a different path, simply select the blend and new path and then choose Object, Blend, Replace Spine.

Sometimes Illustrator doesn't cooperate when you're trying to wrap a blend around an object. See "Different Spines" in the "Troubleshooting" section at the end of this chapter.

Reversing

Illustrator also gives you two additional commands for editing blends. As you can see in Figure 9.28, Reverse Spine and Reverse Front to Back are different.

Figure 9.28
The top blend is the original; the middle has the spine reversed; the bottom has the stacking order of the objects reversed by the command Reverse Front to Back.

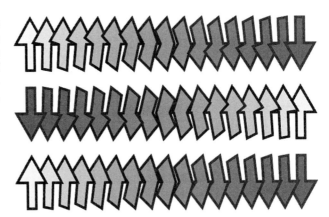

EXPANDING A BLEND

Expanding a blend creates editable objects from each of the intermediary objects. There are two major reasons for expanding a blend. First, expanding complex objects is often a cure for printing problems. Second, the objects created with an expanded blend can be used independently. Figure 9.29 shows an example of the latter.

Figure 9.29
Using Specified Steps and a value of three, a door one-quarter open is produced. The other four doors can be discarded.

For a particular series of illustrations, an image of a partly opened door was required. The closed and open doors were available, so rather than drawing a new door, a blend was created and expanded. After expansion and ungrouping, the partially open door (the second object) could be moved to the new illustration. The first, third, and fourth doors could then be deleted or saved for future use.

Of course, after a blend is expanded, the individual objects can also be ungrouped and edited as any other path or group. Figure 9.30 shows a smooth color blend that was used to create color samples.

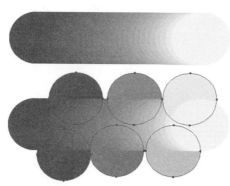

Figure 9.30
Using Smooth Color created the blend at the top. A copy of the blend was expanded and ungrouped, allowing the individual disks to be extracted as color samples.

TROUBLESHOOTING

Printing Blends

Ever since I added a blend, my artwork seems to be crashing my printer. What can I do?

Expanding blends often cures printer trouble. Blends are highly complex objects, which can put a lot of strain on printers. Expanding the blend creates a series of individual objects, much easier for the printer to digest.

Correcting Blend Spacing

I've got my distance almost exactly right, but the final blend object is too far away from my last original object. I don't want to move the original object, but it is a noticeable difference in spacing.

You can do one of several things, including expanding the blend and moving the intermediary objects. But here's an easier way. You're just a little bit off, so count the number of objects created by Specified Distance blending and then Undo the blend. Now switch the Blend Option to Specified Steps and input that number. When you remake the blend, that difference in spacing will be spread out among the intermediary objects, resulting in an unnoticeable variation.

Different Spines

No matter what I do, my blend goes only three-quarters of the way around my object when I choose Object, Blend, Replace Spine.

The easiest workaround is to create an open path on top of your object. Use the Pen tool to re-create the object, leaving a tiny gap or tiny overlap where the first and last points meet. Give the path a stroke and fill of None and replace the spine of your blend.

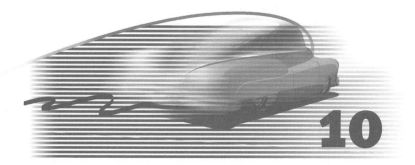

ILLUSTRATOR'S LAYERS, SUBLAYERS, AND GROUPS

IN THIS CHAPTER

The Layers Palette   **232**

Illustrator's Layers   **232**

Working with Layers   **237**

Templates   **245**

Targeting Layers, Groups, and Objects   **246**

Release to Layers   **249**

Special Utilization of Layers   **252**

Troubleshooting   **253**

Just as objects and paths are arranged back-to-front according to the order in which they are drawn, they can be organized using *layers*. Rather than back and front, the terms *top* and *bottom*, *above* and *below*, and *up* and *down* are used with layers.

Each layer, in and of itself, is transparent. The typical analogy is to a sheet of clear plastic, acetate, or glass. If you put artwork on an upper layer, it obscures the artwork below. You can make the lower artwork visible by moving it to a place not obscured by the upper layer's artwork. You can also make it visible by moving that layer above the other.

THE LAYERS PALETTE

Illustrator offers layers and sublayers, as well as the capability to rearrange specific groups of objects and paths within the Layers palette. You can also *target* layers and groups. Using this capability, you can assign appearance attributes to an entire layer, and any object moved to or created on the layer will assume the attributes. Layers can also work with Illustrator's effects and transparency. Rather than merely a handy way to keep track of your artwork, layers are now a very powerful, creative tool.

The features of the Layers palette, include the following:

- Thumbnails (icon-sized views of the contents of layers and groups, and pictures of individual paths)

- Sublayers and the capability to nest layers

- The capability to target a layer, group, or object for styles, effects, or transparency (discussed separately in this chapter)

- Groups and paths (objects) within the palette

- The capability to move objects and groups among layers directly in the palette

- Increased flexibility in palette display

- Several powerful commands available from the palette menu, including Locate Object, Collect in New Layer, Release to Layers, and Reverse Order

> ➪ *The Collect in New Layer command is a great time-saver in Illustrator 10. If it's grayed out when you're trying to use it in conjunction with the Layers palette, see "Collect in New Layer Unavailable" in the "Troubleshooting" section at the end of this chapter.*

ILLUSTRATOR'S LAYERS

A thorough understanding of Illustrator's capabilities, including the sublayers, forms the basis upon which you can build your mastery of layers. Even with all the powerful new capabilities, the most important aspects of layers remain your ability to create without destroying artwork below and to organize and rearrange the elements of your artwork. Figure 10.1 shows how layers interact in the most basic fashion. At the top, the three layers are separated so that the content is visible. To the lower-left, they overlap. To the lower-right, they are aligned.

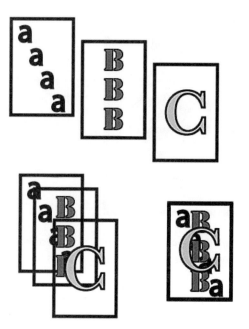

Figure 10.1
Although each of the three layers is independent and has its own artwork, when viewed together, artwork on an upper layer blocks the artwork below.

Also note in Figure 10.1 that lower artwork shows through when nothing is above. Keep in mind that Illustrator's transparency capabilities make this explanation a bit simplistic. For more details on transparency, see Chapter 19, "Exploiting Illustrator's Transparency."

You can rearrange layers by dragging and dropping them in the Layers palette. You can achieve similar effects by using the menu commands Object, Arrange, Bring to Front or Bring Forward, Send Backward, and Send to Back to move individual objects or paths. Figure 10.2 shows how the Layers palette looks for the three layers of objects in Figure 10.1.

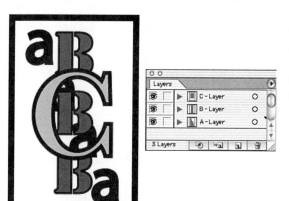

Figure 10.2
The three layers, named for their content in this case, appear in the Layers palette in the same order as their contents appear in the document.

When a layer is moved, the artwork on it is also moved. Figure 10.3 shows the difference in both the artwork and the Layers palette when C-Layer is dragged to the bottom of the palette.

Figure 10.3
Dragging the C layer to the bottom of the palette is the equivalent of using the command Send to Back. If you had dragged the layer to the spot between B-Layer and A-Layer, the equivalent command would have been Send Backward.

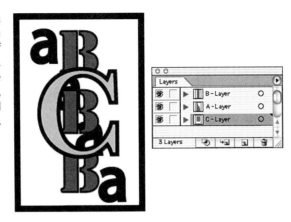

If you're having trouble with the appearance of an object or objects changing when moved from layer to layer, see "Moving a Group or Object Changes Appearance" in the "Troubleshooting" section at the end of this chapter.

Notice the triangles to the left of the layer names. They indicate that the layer contains one or more elements. Clicking the Create New Layer button at the bottom of the palette adds Layer 4, a blank layer numbered sequentially (see Figure 10.4) .

Figure 10.4
Notice that Layer 4 is highlighted. A newly created layer is automatically made the active layer.

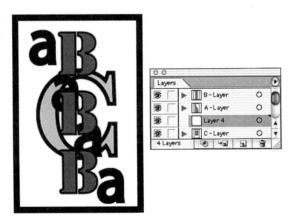

In Figure 10.4, the new layer is placed immediately above the layer of the document that was last active—in this case, C-Layer. A new layer appears immediately above any active layer when the Create New Layer button is clicked. Also note that no triangle appears next to the name, indicating that Layer 4 has no content.

You can drag Layer 4 upward to the layer named A-Layer. When you do, it becomes a sublayer of A-Layer. (Sublayers are discussed in detail later in this chapter.) To make a layer a sublayer of another, or to *nest* a layer, drag it to the name of the second layer and release the mouse button.

Understanding how (and when) to expand a layer or sublayer to view its contents can help simplify the process of learning how to use the new layer capabilities. Figure 10.5 shows the Layers palette with the full range of possibilities.

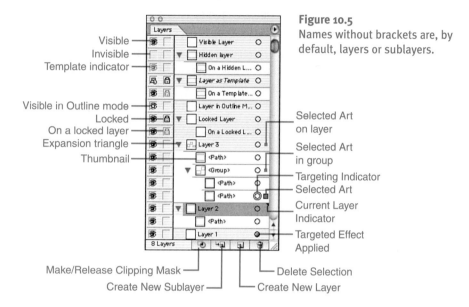

Visible
Invisible
Template indicator
Visible in Outline mode
Locked
On a locked layer
Expansion triangle
Thumbnail

Selected Art on layer
Selected Art in group
Targeting Indicator
Selected Art
Current Layer Indicator
Targeted Effect Applied

Make/Release Clipping Mask
Create New Sublayer
Delete Selection
Create New Layer

Figure 10.5
Names without brackets are, by default, layers or sublayers.

By default, layer names are capitalized, and the names of groups and paths are enclosed in angle brackets. Double-click a layer, sublayer, group, or path to open the Layer Options dialog box and rename it.

Figure 10.5 indicates the names of the various parts of the Layers palette. They are described here:

- Show/Hide is the visibility column. An eyeball in this column indicates that the layer, group, or object is visible. When the column is empty, that layer, group, or object is hidden. A hollow eyeball indicates that the layer, group, or object is visible in Outline mode. An icon constructed of a triangle, a circle, and a square indicates that the layer is a template.

- Lock/Unlock determines whether a layer can be changed, edited, altered, added to or subtracted from, deleted, or given a sublayer. A locked layer, indicated by a Lock icon in the second column, can be duplicated. When the icon is grayed out, the parent layer or group is locked. Groups and objects can also be locked independently in the layers palette.

Be aware that locked objects (paths) and groups can still be deleted if the layer upon which they are located is deleted in the Layers palette.

- Expand/Collapse allows you to view the sublayers, groups, and paths (objects) that are part of a particular layer. You can also expand or collapse sublayers and groups to see their contents.

- Thumbnails give you a visual reference for the content of a layer, sublayer, group, or path. Their visibility and size are controlled through the Layers palette menu.

- An active layer, sublayer, group, or path is highlighted. If you don't want any layer highlighted, you can click in the blank space at the bottom of the Layers palette, below the lowest layer, group, or path. Illustrator, however, still recognizes the active layer through the small black triangle at the far right of the layer's row, the Current Layer indicator. When you click this indicator, all art at that particular level is selected. You should not confuse it with the Selected Art indicator (described next).

- The Selected Art indicator tells you which particular element of your artwork is selected. You can also use it to move artwork by dragging the icon to a different layer. Especially useful when layers or groups are collapsed are the mini-indicators that show on which layer or in which group the selected art can be found.

- A targeted layer, sublayer, group, or object can have one or more appearance attributes assigned to it. Anything created on or added to such a targeted layer has that attribute applied. Any object moved to another layer does not take the particular characteristic with it. The various possible icons are described later in this chapter in the section "Targeting Layers, Groups, and Objects."

- The four buttons across the bottom of the palette perform their functions according to their names. The special capabilities of the Create New Sublayer and Create New Layer buttons are described later in this chapter in the section "Creating New Layers and Sublayers."

The Selected Art indicator can be a great help in locating or moving a specific element in a complicated document. When a large square, in the layer's designated color, appears to the right of the layer's name, the entire layer is selected. When a smaller square appears, a group or object on that layer or sublayer is selected. With all layers collapsed or only top layers showing, you still get an indication of where the particular element is located. You can even move the selected artwork without expanding the layer. Simply drag the icon to another unlocked layer or group.

The name of a non-printing layer will be italicized. The layer options can be used to make a layer non-printing, and templates are automatically non-printing.

A look at the Layers Palette Options dialog box (see Figure 10.6) shows several choices for how the contents of the Layers palette will be presented. The Show Layers Only check box hides all information other than layers and sublayers. The groups and paths themselves are not affected; they simply are no longer visible in the palette.

The Row Size adjusts the height of each row in the palette to the thumbnail size. If you set it to Small, no thumbnail appears (rows are minimized to the height of the font). At Medium, the default size, the thumbnail is 20 pixels square. Large thumbnails are 32 pixels square. Custom thumbnails can range in size from 12 to 100 pixels. Text size is not affected by Row Size, and visibility, lock, and target icons appear one pixel smaller in Small Row Size than in the other possibilities.

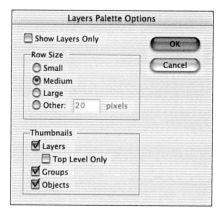

Figure 10.6
In the Layers Palette Options dialog box, you can control how the palette is viewed, as well as how much of it viewed.

The Thumbnails area of the Layers Palette Options dialog box controls which thumbnails are visible. These check boxes hide only the thumbnail at the left of the row; the rows themselves remain visible. Checking Top Level Only hides the thumbnails of all sublevels nested in other layers.

The procedure for expanding and collapsing the various layers, sublayers, and groups in a complicated document can be streamlined with a modifier key. Option+clicking [Alt+clicking] the expand/collapse triangle next to a layer's name expands or collapses all sublayers and groups, as well as the layer itself.

Every element in the Layers palette—layers, sublayers, groups, and paths—has its own options. Double-clicking the item's name opens its options dialog box. The name and color of a layer or sublayer can be changed; it also can be made a template (discussed later in this chapter), be hidden, be shown in Preview or Outline mode, be locked, made nonprinting, and dimmed to a specified percentage. Groups and objects (paths) can be renamed, hidden, or made nonprinting through their options. (Nonprinting layers, sublayers, groups, and objects are indicated by italicized names in the Layers palette.)

Redrawing the object thumbnails and group thumbnails in the Layers palette can significantly slow down your work. Using the triangle to the left of the layer name to hide nested sublayers, groups, and paths can speed things up. Another way to minimize the amount of time required to show the palette is to name the various layers, groups, and paths so that the thumbnails are unnecessary. Double-click the name of a layer in the Layers palette to bring up the Layer Options dialog box, rename it according to content, and use the Layers Palette Options dialog box to hide thumbnails.

WORKING WITH LAYERS

In early versions of Illustrator, the Layers palette was a convenience for organizing artwork. Now, you can not only arrange your artwork on layers, but you also can use the Layers palette to rearrange those elements. No longer do you need to select an object or a path on the artboard to move it from one layer to another. The procedure is as simple as dragging and dropping right in the Layers palette.

Creating New Layers and Sublayers

When you click the Create New Layer button at the bottom of the Layers palette, a new layer is created directly above your currently active layer. This new layer is always at the same hierarchical level as your current work. In other words, if you are working on a sublayer that is a sublevel of a sublayer, the Create New Layer button gives you a new sub-sublayer. See the sidebar "Exploring New Layers and Sublayers" for clarification.

Exploring New Layers and Sublayers

Figure 10.7 shows an example of the Layers palette with several nested layers and sublayers. The image that this Layers palette represents would have a minimum of 13 items. You can't see exactly how many layers there are because Sublayers 2-a and 2-b are collapsed in the palette. You can tell, however, that each of the two has at least one sublayer, group, or path because of the presence of the expansion triangle to the left of the sublayers' names.

Figure 10.7
For simplicity, the layers have been renumbered in reverse order. If they were named as created, the higher numbers (later layers) would be above the earlier layers in both the palette and the image.

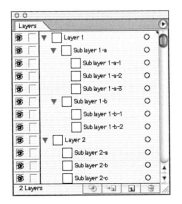

The location and hierarchical level of the active layer determine the location and level of a new layer or sublayer. If, for example, the active layer is Sublayer 1b2 when the Create New Layer button is clicked, the new layer would be placed between Sublayer 1b1 and Sublayer 1b2. It would be at the same hierarchical level as the two, so its thumbnail would be even with theirs (justified left, so to speak). If the active layer is Sublayer 1b when a new layer is created, it would appear between Sublayer 1a2 and Sublayer 1b, with its thumbnail at the same level as Sublayer 1b.

Clicking the Create New Sublayer button creates a new layer subordinate to the active layer. Using the hierarchy shown in Figure 10.7, clicking the Create New Sublayer button with Sublayer 1b2 active would create a new layer between Sublayer 1b2 and Sublayer 1b3. The new sublayer would be indented to the right of Sublayer 1b2, and Sublayer 1b2 would then have a triangle to the left of its thumbnail. If the naming convention being used here were followed, the new sublayer would be named Sublayer 1b2a.

New Layer Options

The modifier keys are partially active with both the Create New Layer and Create New Sublayer buttons. (Only the Mac shortcuts are listed for brevity and clarity, with the Windows equivalents following.)

Create New Layer (menu command/button alone) = Creates a new layer directly above the active layer, at the same hierarchical level.

Cmd + Create New Layer = Creates a new layer at the top of the Layers palette (the highest hierarchical level).

Option + Create New Layer = Creates a new layer directly above and at the same level as the active layer (as normal) and opens the Layer Options dialog box.

Create New Sublayer (menu command/button alone) = Creates a new sublayer directly below and subordinate to the active layer.

Option + Create New Sublayer = Creates a new sublayer as normal, but also opens the Layer Options dialog box.

The Shift key has no effect. The Command key has no effect with the Create New Sublayer button.

Cmd (Mac) = Ctrl (Windows)

Option (Mac) = Alt (Windows)

New layers can also be created with the Layers palette menu (the triangle at the upper-right corner of the palette). Both the Create New Layer and Create New Sublayer menu commands automatically open the Layer Options dialog box. The default keyboard shortcut for New Layer is Cmd+L[Ctrl+L] . The Option and Alt keys are not available with the keyboard shortcut. In the Keyboard Shortcuts dialog box (Edit, Keyboard Shortcuts), you can find the New Layer command under Menu Commands in the Other Palette category. There is no default keyboard shortcut for New Sublayer, nor is it available for customization.

Moving Elements in the Layers Palette

The Selected Art indicator in the Layers palette (see Figure 10.5) tells you what layer, sublayer, group, or object is currently selected on the artboard. You can move that element to another layer by dragging its name to the new layer and releasing the mouse button. To make this process even easier for you, the Layers palette shows a smaller version of the Selected Art indicator throughout the element's location hierarchy. For example, Figure 10.8 revisits the A-B-C image as last modified.

In Figure 10.8's Layers palette, note that the individual letter is marked by the Selected Art indicator (a box filled with the layer's designated color). Smaller boxes indicate the letter's group (<Group>) and its layer (A-Layer). If the group were on a sublayer or part of another group, those intermediate levels would also be designated with a smaller box.

The little boxes that indicate the location hierarchy of the selected artwork are more than just indicators. Even with the Layers palette collapsed to Top Layers Only, you can rearrange your artwork. Simply drag the little box to a different layer and release. You don't need to open all the layers, sublayers, and groups to find the particular element you want to move. Figure 10.9 represents the same situation as Figure 10.8, but the Layers palette is collapsed. Here, you can move the selected letter to Layer 4 by dragging the Selected Art indicator's small box to the lower layer and releasing the mouse button.

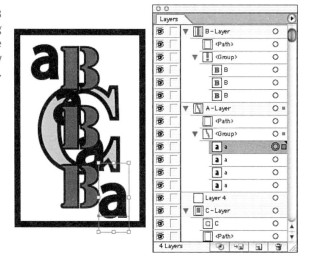

Figure 10.8
As you can see from the bounding box in the artwork itself, the lower-right letter "a" is currently selected.

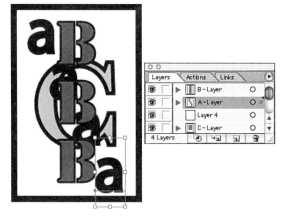

Figure 10.9
This figure represents exactly the same situation as the previous figure. The same letter is selected on the same layer.

Note that although you can move the selected artwork to Layer 4 by dragging the Selected Art icon, you would not be able to move it to a locked layer.

Using Sublayers and Groups

The relationship between layers and their sublayers is similar to that between groups and the objects or paths in the group.

A sublayer is, in fact, a layer in and of itself. It works like a layer, has a name like a layer, has content like a layer, has a designated color like a layer, and can be rearranged like a layer. However, it is called a sublayer when it is subordinate to a layer. (Sublayers can be moved to the top level and become layers.) The advantage is in having what amounts to groups of layers. Rather than Shift+click to select multiple layers, you can just click to select the topmost layer and all its sublayers. An appearance attribute (including style, effects, and transparency) can be applied to the layer and all its sublayers through targeting (explained later in this chapter). Only the top layer (or the highest sublayer you want) need be targeted; subordinate sublayers, groups, and objects are automatically selected. Of course, a sublayer can be targeted individually, too. A layer and all its subordinate components can be locked, deleted, or made invisible or a template simply by making the desired change to the top layer (or the highest subordinate layer you want) .

Clicking the name of a layer automatically selects all objects and groups on that layer. The modifier keys work to add to or subtract from a selection according to the Windows paradigm:

- **Individual selection**—Cmd+click [Ctrl+click] to add (or subtract) a layer's contents or a specific group or object to the selection.
- **Contiguous selection**—Shift+clicking adds all the items between that or those originally selected and the item that was Shift+clicked.

You can also hold down the Cmd and Option keys [Ctrl and Alt keys] and drag through the Layers palette to make selections.

You also can select an individual object, even when it's part of a group, by clicking the far right of its row (name) in the Layers palette. The Selected Art indicator appears in the row, and the object's bounding box becomes visible in the document, but the row in the Layers palette is not highlighted. An additional indicator, targeting, will be discussed later in this chapter. When an individual object is selected in the Layers palette, it can be manipulated individually, including movement and appearance, without altering any other part of the group. This capability is comparable to clicking the object itself in the document with the Direct Selection tool (white arrow icon) rather than the Selection tool (black arrow icon).

➪ *If your Layers palette doesn' t show all the thumbnails you would like to see, check "Layers Palette Viewing Options" in the "Troubleshooting" section at the end of this chapter.*

As noted previously, you can move an object from one layer (or sublayer) to another by dragging within the Layers palette. Groups can also be managed through the Layers palette using this drag-and-drop capability. Rather than select a group on the artboard, ungroup it, deselect one item, and regroup the remainder, you can move an object (path) out of a group or add it to a group by dragging within the palette. An object added to a group automatically is moved to the same layer as the group, and it assumes all attributes and styles applicable to that layer, while losing any that were applied to the former layer.

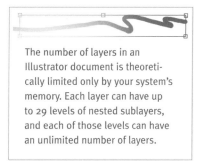

The number of layers in an Illustrator document is theoretically limited only by your system's memory. Each layer can have up to 29 levels of nested sublayers, and each of those levels can have an unlimited number of layers.

Styles and attributes applied specifically to the individual object or path transfer with the object to the new group's layer without affecting other objects in the group.

The power of the Layers palette truly comes into play with very complicated documents. Illustrator gives substantial flexibility with the Show/Hide option. Rather than simply toggle the visibility/invisibility of a layer, you can change a layer to Outline View mode by Cmd+clicking [Ctrl+clicking] the eye icon in the Layers palette. This capability applies only to layers and sublayers; groups and objects cannot be viewed differently than the other content of their layers. Additionally, you can make a layer into a template through its Layer Options dialog box. Templates are discussed in detail later in this chapter.

One other aspect of working with the Layers palette deserves attention. The palette menu, which you access by clicking the triangle in the upper-right corner of the palette, contains numerous commands. Many of these commands need little explanation.

New Layer and New Sublayer were discussed previously; Duplicate Layer and Delete Layer are just as you would expect. Layer Options also were discussed earlier in this chapter. Make/Release Clipping Mask functions the same as the commands Object, Clipping Mask, Make and Object, Clipping Mask, Release. The remainder of the palette menu commands deserve specific attention, although some may be familiar from earlier versions of Illustrator:

- **Locate Object**—Useful for those incredibly complicated illustrations that are possible with so powerful a program, this command finds an object in the Layers palette. Click an object or group, select Locate Object from the palette menu, and the Layers palette automatically scrolls to or opens to the object's row in the palette. See Figure 10.10 and Figure 10.11 for before and after images of searching the Layers palette for a specific object.

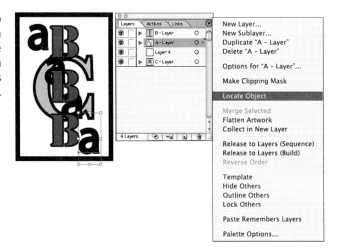

Figure 10.10
On the artboard, the letter "a" in the lower-right is selected. The menu command Locate Object can then be chosen from the Layers palette menu.

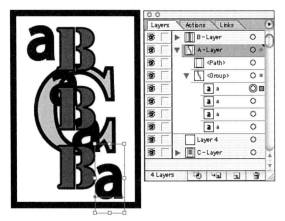

Figure 10.11
After Locate Object is chosen, the Layers palette automatically opens the layers and sublayers necessary to show the object's row in the palette.

The Selected Art indicator is visible as a large box on the object's row and smaller boxes on the group, sublayer, and layer under which it falls. Also, note that the Layer Targeting indicator shows two hollow circles, indicating that the object is selected (the outer circle) and that no attribute has yet been targeted on that object (the hollow inner circle).

- **Merge Selected**—Select layers, choose the command, and the layers are merged. To select layers that are adjacent in the Layers palette, Shift+click the highest and the lowest in the palette. To select layers that are not contiguous in the palette, Cmd+click [Ctrl+click] each of them. Keep in mind that you can merge locked and hidden layers without changing their status. Artwork is merged onto the highest visible, unlocked layer. The content of each layer or sublayer is collected as a group. The stacking order of all objects as they appeared on the artboard is retained on the remaining layer.

- **Flatten Artwork**—This command works much like Merge Selected, but affects all layers and sublayers. There is one major difference, however. Rather than automatically creating a group from a hidden layer, Flatten Artwork deletes the layer and its contents. You are given a warning that artwork appears on the hidden layer or layers, and you are asked whether you would like to save the artwork or delete it. The artwork is flattened to the active layer. Effects are carried from layers and sublayers into the groups that are created. Effects for the top-level layer are discarded rather than applied to all other art. Illustrator attempts to preserve exactly the look of your art at the time you chose Flatten Artwork. Choosing this command is usually a final step, taken after all creative work is finished, and is used with a copy of the original file.

- **Collect in New Layer**—You can gather together the contents of various layers, sublayers, groups, or objects and place them on a new layer by using this command. You are, however, limited as to what you can select for collection. Only those items that have their next-higher level in common can be Shift+clicked to select. Because of the selection capabilities of the Layers palette, you can select, for example, only objects on the same sublayer or layer. You can select only those sublayers that are part of the same higher layer and are themselves at the same hierarchical level. All objects in a group are at the same level. All groups on a single sublayer are at the same level. A group on that sublayer and an object in a different group on that sublayer are not at the same level. A group on that sublayer and a group on a different sublayer are not on the same level. (See Figure 10.12 for a visual guide to the relationships among layers, sublayers, groups, and paths.) You can select objects and groups on any level of the Layers palette by using the Selection tool or the Direct Selection tool on the artboard and then placing them onto a new layer by using this command.

The largest box, Layer-1, contains all the other elements. Both Sublayer-1a and Sublayer-1b have elements, but no element can belong to both sublayers. Within the individual sublayers are paths (objects) and groups. Paths can be at the same level as groups. Not depicted here are sublayers within sublayers and groups within groups. Both are available to you in Illustrator 9.

Figure 10.12

The relationships among items in the illustration are comparable to those shown in the Layers palette.

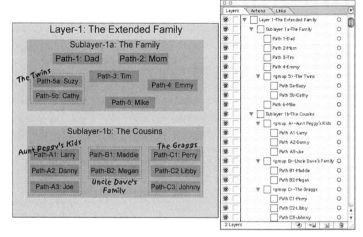

- **Release to Layers (Sequence)** and **Release to Layers (Build)**—These commands will be discussed independently later in this chapter.

- **Reverse Order**—Like the Collect in New Layer command, Reverse Order works only with items that can be selected together: Layers, sublayers, groups, and objects that are all part of the same group, sublayer, or layer and must be immediately subordinate to that "parent" level.

- **Template**—This command will be discussed independently later in this chapter.

- **Hide Others/Show All Layers**—With one or more layers selected, the Hide Others commands makes all other layers and sublayers and their contents invisible. In the Layers palette, invisible artwork, both groups and objects (paths), are indicated by grayed eye icons in the visibility column. For layers and sublayers that are hidden, nothing appears in that column. Any new layers or sublayers created while this command is active are visible. The Show All Layers command restores visibility.

- **Outline Others/Preview All Layers**—These commands work like Hide Others/Show All Others, except that instead of becoming invisible, the nonselected layers, sublayers, groups, and objects are viewed in Outline or Preview mode. The fact that these other elements retain their visibility means that they can be selected, moved, deleted, edited, and so on. Hidden elements cannot be selected.

- **Lock Others/Unlock All Layers**—Designed primarily to prevent unintended alteration of artwork, this is another command that is available only when you have selected one or more layers or sublayers. This command can be very effective when used in combination with Outline Others, allowing you to unclutter the artboard and speed screen redraw.

- **Paste Remembers Layers**—When this command is active, a check mark appears next to it in the Layers palette menu. When it is active, you can choose Edit, Paste or one of its related commands, Paste in Front and Paste in Back, to place an object from the Clipboard onto its original layer (assuming you copied it from a layer in the existing document). If that layer has been renamed or deleted, a new layer is created. When this command is unchecked (inactive), the Paste commands add from the Clipboard to the active layer. If more than one layer is active, the lowest layer receives the artwork.

- **Palette Options**—This command was discussed earlier in this chapter.

Paste Commands

You can find the Paste commands, used in conjunction with the Paste Remembers Layers command, under the Edit menu. Here's how they work with Paste Remembers Layers active:

- **Paste**—The command places the contents of the Clipboard onto the layer from which it came. If multiple objects are on the Clipboard and they came from different layers, they are returned to the layers from which they came. Objects are pasted in the center of the layer.

- **Paste in Front**—Objects are pasted to their original layers, in front, but rather than being pasted into the center of the layer, they are pasted in their original positions. If an object or path is selected, the Clipboard's contents are pasted in front of it.

- **Paste in Back**—Objects are pasted to their original layers, in back, but rather than being pasted into the center of the layer, they are pasted in their original positions. If an object or path is selected, the Clipboard's contents are pasted in back of it.

If no layer has the same name as the layer from which the objects came, a new layer is created and given the original layer's name, and the Clipboard is pasted there. The original layer need not exist, merely a layer with the same name.

Here's how these commands work with Paste Remembers Layers inactive:

- **Paste**—This command places the contents of the Clipboard into the center of the active layer. If more than one layer is selected, the lower layer receives the objects. The artwork is pasted to the front of that layer.

- **Paste in Front**—Pasting into the artwork's original positions on the active layer, it becomes the frontmost artwork. If a group is selected, it becomes part of the group.

- **Paste in Back**—Pasting into the artwork's original positions on the active layer, it becomes the rearmost artwork. If a group is selected, it becomes part of the group.

Remember, too, that Paste Remembers Layers works when pasting (or dragging and dropping) between Illustrator documents.

TEMPLATES

Double-clicking the name of a layer or sublayer opens the Layer Options dialog box. A check in the Template box makes several decisions for you. Templates are automatically made nonprinting and locked. They are dimmed to a default of 50% opacity, but that level can be adjusted on a individual basis, layer by layer. Three changes take place in the Layers palette:

- The eye icon is replaced by the template icon, a triangle-circle-square.

- The Locked icon appears in the second column.

- The name of the layer or sublayer appears in italics to indicate that it is a nonprinting layer.

You'll also notice that all subordinate sublayers, groups, and objects have a dimmed Locked icon in the second column of the Layers palette. The icon is dimmed to indicate that the locked status has been applied to a higher level in the hierarchy and must be removed at that level.

Templates

Templates are designed to allow you to trace over an item or to use it for reference. By default, checking Template in a layer or sublayer options dialog box automatically switches the view mode to Preview. If you would rather have an object or group in that template in Outline view, select the layer to be made a template and give it a sublayer. Move the elements that are to be in Outline view to the sublayer. Cmd+click [Ctrl+click] the eye icon to change the view mode of the sublayer to Outline. Now change the original layer to a template, and the elements on the sublayer remain in Outline view. Figure 10.13 shows an example.

Figure 10.13
Although the circles and stars must be in Preview mode because the top layer is a template, the Squares sublayer remains in Outline mode. This change in view mode must be made prior to the top layer becoming a template because all subordinate elements of templates are locked.

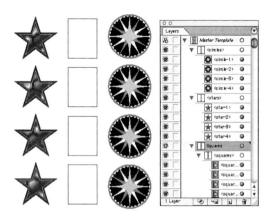

TARGETING LAYERS, GROUPS, AND OBJECTS

Targeting is the designation of a layer, sublayer, group, or object for application of an appearance attribute, including style, effect, and transparency. A targeted layer and all its subordinate elements take on the specific appearance when applied. From that point forward, any element added to that particular layer, sublayer, or group will also assume the attribute. If an object, group, or sublayer is moved from a layer to which an attribute has been targeted, the attribute is left behind, and the element moves to its new layer or sublayer as originally created. Any change to appearance that is applied directly to an individual element remains intact when the element is relocated.

⇨ *If you're having trouble with the appearance of an object or objects changing when moved from layer to layer, see "Moving a Group or Object Changes Appearance" in the "Troubleshooting" section at the end of this chapter.*

In the Layers palette, to the right of the row's name, a single hollow circle indicates that the layer, object, or group is not targeted. A double concentric circle icon indicates that it is targeted, but no attribute has been applied. A single filled circle means that an attribute has been applied to the layer, sublayer, group, or object, but that the layer, group, or object is not currently targeted. A filled circle in a hollow circle tells you that the level is targeted and has had an attribute applied. When this symbol is next to an object, it indicates that the object is more complex than a simple fill and stroke. Figure 10.14 uses the layer names to describe the status of its targeting.

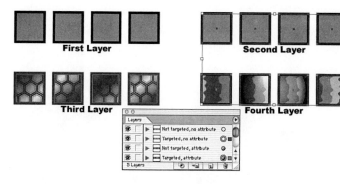

Figure 10.14
The objects on the layers targeted in the Layers palette are selected and their bounding boxes visible on the artboard.

The first layer in the Layers palette has no appearance attribute applied, nor is one targeted. The squares have only a simple fill and stroke. The second layer has been targeted, but no attribute has yet been applied. The third layer has an attribute applied, but it is not currently targeted. The last layer in the Layers palette has an attribute applied and is targeted.

If, at this point, a style or other attribute is selected from its palette, it will be applied to both the second and fourth layers (both are targeted), but not the first or third. You can think of the outer circle of the Layer Targeting icon as a visual bounding box. Just as a selected object on the artboard has its bounding box visible, so too do targeted layers have a "bounding circle" around the Layer Targeting icon.

Expressed in simplified form, the rules governing targeting are reasonably easy to understand. They are as follows:

When a layer is targeted and an appearance attribute (style, effect, or transparency) is applied

- Every item (sublayer, group, and object) already on the layer is modified according to the new attribute.

- Every item added to the layer receives the new attribute.

- Any item moved from the layer loses the attribute.

When an item is moved to a layer, sublayer, or group that has been targeted for an appearance attribute

- The element adopts the attribute of the layer.

- The element retains any attribute applied to it individually *and* attempts to apply the attribute of the layer, even if a conflict occurs. (For example, an object that has individually been given the style Starburst, when moved to a layer that has been given the style Caution Tape, attempts to display both styles. See Figure 10.15.)

When an item is moved from a layer, sublayer, or group to which an appearance attribute has been applied

- The item loses the attributes of the layer, sublayer, or group.

- The item retains any attribute applied individually to it, as well as its original stroke and fill.

- The item adopts any attribute applied to the new layer, sublayer, or group.

Figure 10.15
Two circles on each layer, one black and white, one with the Starburst style applied. To the left, the objects on one layer have no additional applied characteristics. On the right, the layer has the style Caution Tape applied.

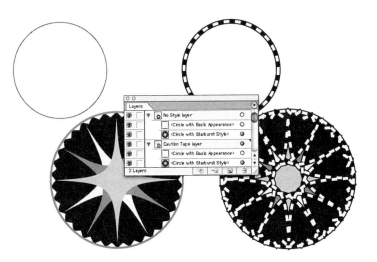

Appearance attributes can be dragged from element to element. Option+dragging [Alt+dragging] copies rather than transfers the attributes. Dragging from the Layer Targeting icon of a layer or sublayer to another layer or sublayer transfers some, but not all, attributes to existing elements on that layer. New objects created on the layer have all the attributes. When you're transferring or copying from layer to layer, attributes such as effect, transparency, and drop shadows are applied to existing objects. Stroke and fill do not override the element's existing attributes, unless they have been applied through targeting.

↪ *One potential problem with dragging attributes from layer to layer is discussed in "Disappearing Objects During Attribute Transfer" in the "Troubleshooting" section at the end of this chapter.*

Copying or transferring by dragging the Layer Targeting icon from a layer or sublayer to a group likewise does not apply all attributes to the elements of the group. The original fill and stroke are not replaced, unless applied through targeting.

Copying or transferring from a layer or sublayer to an individual object (path) overrides all previous attributes.

Dragging the Layer Targeting icon from a group or from an object to a layer, sublayer, another group, or another object works the same way.

The following can be applied to layers sublayers, groups, and objects (paths) using targeting:

- Fill color
- Stroke color
- Stroke weight
- Calligraphic, Scatter, Art, and Pattern brushes
- Style
- Transparency

- Gradient

- Fill pattern (swatch)

- Printing attributes (Attributes palette)

- Object menu commands

- Effects

- Filters

When you apply effects and filters through the Layers palette, Illustrator follows the same rules and guidelines as when you apply them directly. As an example, most filters are available only for RGB images. (For more information, see Chapter 20, "Using Filters and Effects.")

In the preceding list, you can see that Object menu commands are available to targeted layers. Because targeting, in effect, selects the groups and objects on a layer, the Transform commands, as well as such commands as Rasterize, Clipping Mask, and Compound Path, are available. Note that these commands work differently from attributes. They are available only when objects appear on a layer. They affect only those objects already on the layer, not any objects later added to the layer. They do not affect locked objects (paths) .

RELEASE TO LAYERS

The Release to Layers commands are located in the Layers palette menu, which you access through the triangle in the upper-right corner of the palette. Release to Layers (Sequence) places each object of a selected group or layer onto its own sublayer. Release to Layers (Build) puts the first object on one layer, the first and second on the next layer, the first, second, and third on the third layer, and so on. These commands are invaluable in the creation of Web-based animation. See Chapter 23, "Flash and SVG Support," for specific information about Web animation.

The objects on a layer or sublayer or in a group are each placed on a new layer according to their stacking order. The objects behind the others are placed on a layer lower than the others. When you're preparing illustrations for separation to layers, it is a good idea to rearrange the elements in the Layers palette before using the Release to Layers command. The success or failure of an animation depends, in part, on the layers (frames) being displayed in the correct order.

Figure 10.16 shows a simple series of objects on a single layer in a document. Note the order in which the objects appear in the Layers palette. This is the order in which the individual sublayers will be created. The layer that contains the objects or groups (or the group that contains the objects) must be active, or the Release to Layers commands will not correctly produce a series of layers. The actual sublayers created from this image with Release to Layers (Sequence) are visible in Figure 10.17.

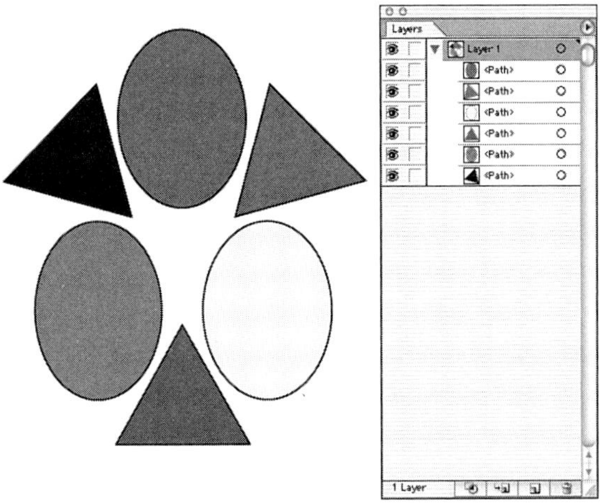

Figure 10.16
In this example, it is important to click Layer 1 to make it active prior to choosing Release to Layers.

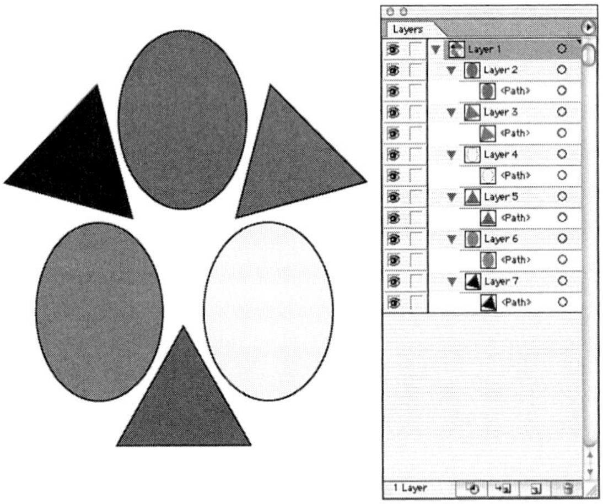

Figure 10.17
The newly created sublayers appear in the order in which their objects appeared. Note that each layer contains only a single object. Layer 1, of course, contains all the sublayers.

When you're working with animation, you often need to create what is referred to as a "typewriter" effect. In such an animation, objects appear cumulatively. That is, in the first frame (or layer, in this case), Object #1 appears. In the second frame, Object #1 remains and Object #2 appears. In the third frame, Objects #1 and #2 remain, and Object #3 appears. And so the string continues throughout the animation. Just as new letters appear after the old on a typewritten sheet, so do the objects appear onscreen in a parade of images. The manual technique involves laboriously copying a layer, adding an object, copying that layer, adding an object, copying that layer, adding yet another object, and so on, until the final layer has all the objects required for the typewriter effect. Illustrator 10's Release to Layers (Build) command offers one-click access to such frame creation.

In Figure 10.17 you saw how each element of the original figure was released to its own layer. Figure 10.18 shows the resulting Layers palette when the Release to Layers (Build) command is used.

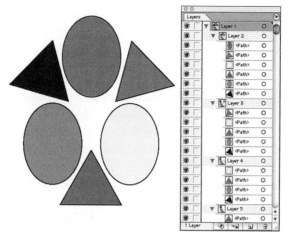

Figure 10.18
Notice how, from the bottom up, each layer incorporates the content of the previous layer.

Reverse Order

In Figure 10.18, note that Illustrator has numbered the layers in the reverse order. Normally, the first-created layer is at the bottom and has the lowest number. In this case, Illustrator has apparently created layers from the top down. If your animation program produces a backward graphic from this sequence (objects leaving the picture rather than entering), you have an easy solution. Click the bottom sublayer that contains a frame (or image) for your animation. Hold down the Shift key and click the top sublayer of your future animation (not the top layer in the Layers palette, just the top sublayer of the animation). Now choose Reverse Order from the Layers palette menu. The sublayers are then swapped from top to bottom, leaving you with your desired frame order. Figure 10.19 shows the result.

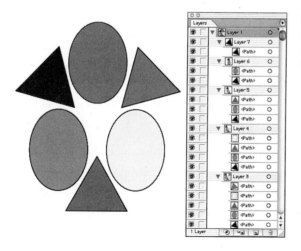

Figure 10.19
Although the order of the sublayers is reversed, their names and contents remain unchanged.

SPECIAL UTILIZATION OF LAYERS

The use of layers can make many tasks in Illustrator much simpler. You can accomplish some tasks, however, *only* by using layers. Animation is discussed earlier in this chapter and in Chapter 22, "Saving Images for the Web," and Chapter 23, "Flash and SVG Support." Using the standard Web file formats, you can create animation only through layers.

The Layers palette can be a major tool in the actual design of Web pages and sites. Using the layers for individual pages and sublayers for the components of those pages, you can design an entire Web site in a single Illustrator document. See Chapter 21, "Designing Web Sites and Web Pages," for specifics.

Effects can be applied much more easily when targeted to a layer rather than applied individually to a series of objects. Not only is this approach easier, it is often more accurate. Getting the same effect setting used 20 minutes earlier on some forgotten object is much more difficult than simply Option+dragging [Alt+dragging] an effect within the Layers palette. Filters can also be applied using targeting in the Layers palette. However, unlike effects, they permanently change all objects targeted or on the targeted layer, and are applied to only those objects that exist at that time.

One example of using effects with layers is simulating depth of field. By applying increasing amounts of blur to deeper and deeper layers, you can achieve an illusion of distance in your illustration. The foremost layer, the subject of the illustration, should be in sharp focus, as in a photograph. Objects immediately behind the subject can be slightly out of focus. Objects in the near distance should be a bit more out of focus, and objects in the far distance can be blurry (see Figure 20).

Figure 10.20
The blur effect is cumulative.

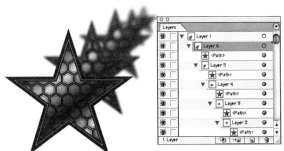

In Figure 10.20, each path has the same style applied, and each of the sublayers has a 2-pixel Gaussian Blur targeted. Because the sublayers are sublayers of each other, the effect is cumulative. The lowest sublayer effectively has four 2-pixel blurs applied.

TROUBLESHOOTING

Disappearing Objects During Attribute Transfer

I transferred the attributes of one layer to another, and everything on my first layer disappeared. Is something broken?

The fill and stroke of the objects was transferred to the second layer. The objects are still there, but they're invisible because they now have a fill and stroke of None. To maintain attributes on the first layer and apply them to the second, hold down Option [Alt] when dragging the filled circle of the Layer Targeting icon from one layer to another.

Collect in New Layer Unavailable

I have a number of objects that I want to put together on a separate layer, but I can't Shift+click to select them all in the Layers palette. How do I use the Collect in New Layer command?

The Collect in New Layer command, located in the Layers palette menu, is available only when you have selected elements at the same level hierarchy (when selecting in the Layers palette). You can use this command with objects of any level that are selected on the artboard. Shift+click the objects themselves, rather than their names in the Layers palette. When you're working in the palette, each object or group needs to be part of the same group, sublayer, or layer—whichever is the next level up in the Layers palette.

Moving a Group or Object Changes Appearance

I dragged a group and a few objects from one layer to another, and they look completely different. Why did they change appearance?

Either the layer that they came from or the layer they went to, or both, were targeted for attributes. Look in the Layers palette. To the right of each layer's name is a circle. If the circle is filled, the layer has one or more attributes applied to it. Those attributes, because they are at the layer level rather than applied to an individual object, affect every object added to the layer. Likewise, when an object is moved from the layer, it loses the layer's attributes.

Layers Palette Viewing Options

I can't see thumbnails for any of my objects, groups of objects, or sublayers in the Layers palette. How do I get to view them?

The Layers palette menu, which you access by clicking the triangle in the upper-right corner of the palette, has the Palette Options command. Open the Layers Palette Options dialog box with this command and look in the lower part of the dialog box. Put check marks in the boxes next to Layers, Groups, and Objects, and make sure that no check mark appears next to Top Level Only. After you click OK, you'll see the thumbnails for all the elements of your illustration.

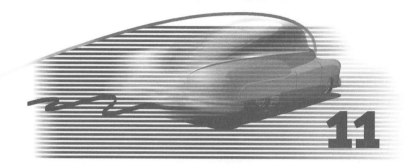

OUTPUT OPTIONS

IN THIS CHAPTER

Differences Between Page and Screen   256

The PDF Option   262

Other Output Options   265

Troubleshooting   270

DIFFERENCES BETWEEN PAGE AND SCREEN

The differences between the printed page and monitor screen are many. However, do not overlook the differences that exist within those two categories. There is often a huge difference between preparing artwork for newsprint and for a glossy magazine (see Chapter 24, "Commercial Printing and Trapping Issues"). And not all RGB work is destined for the World Wide Web. Nonetheless, the major categorical differences must be examined before any specialized discussion.

In a discussion of "print" output, it is important to differentiate between commercial four-color presses and other types of output. Inkjet, grayscale laser, dot-matrix, thermal, and dye-sublimation printers are not generally CMYK devices. (However, CMYK inkjet printers are available, and color laser printers are typically CMYK devices.)

In general, this discussion will consider the term *print* to encompass only CMYK output, and primarily four-color process printing. The subject of printing will be discussed in depth in Chapter 24.

Inkjet Input: CMYK or RGB

The vast majority of inkjet printers, especially those for home and small office use, have four ink colors. If you look under the lid, you're likely to see either four separate cartridges—one each for cyan, magenta, yellow, and black—or two cartridges—one for black and one for the CMY inks. (Some photorealistic printers add two colors: light cyan and light magenta.)

Despite the CMYK inks, almost all inkjet printers need RGB image data. The software (print drivers) for the printers convert the color information to CMYK. If you send CMYK data to the printer, the colors get converted twice and may come out muddy.

One exception to this rule is high-end inkjet printers used for *proofing* (printing test copies of images destined for four-color process printing). These printers, used in printing and prepress operations, replicate how files will come off the printing press. They require CMYK input.

Color

The largest difference between print and Web output is color. Commercial printing presses reproduce color using four process color inks. This is the *CMYK color model*. The Web, on the other hand, requires color made of three different components. This is the *RGB color model*. (Grayscale and black-and-white images can be used both in print and on the Web.) Color, which will be discussed in depth in Chapter 12, "Understanding and Applying Color," can be considered to be of two types. *Additive* colors combine to create white; *subtractive* colors create white by their absence. The difference is in how light reaches the eye. Additive colors are seen as they come from the colored light source; subtractive colors are white light reflected to the eye from a colored surface.

For a discussion of color and computers, you can classify the additive colors as those you see on a computer monitor or projected onto a screen for display. (A good projection screen adds no color to the image, allowing you to see the additive colors as they are projected, rather than as subtractive colors.) All the colors on a monitor are produced using red, green, and blue (RGB). The mixture of these three component colors produces the range of color required to reproduce most images.

Subtractive colors, on the other hand, are those used to reproduce an image on paper. They are the colors of the actual inks used by the printing press. Theoretically, the entire range of colors can be reproduced using mixtures of three colored inks: cyan, magenta, and yellow (CMY). In reality, however, the inks are limited in both the range of color that they can reproduce and their capability to combine to create black. To solve the second problem, a fourth color is added to the presses, black (K). (The letter *B* is used for blue in RGB, so black is represented by the letter K, which you can also think of as standing for "key color.")

The two color modes have different *gamuts*. Each gamut, or color range, includes all the colors that can be reproduced using the particular color model. Illustrator allows you to work in either RGB or CMYK color. A single document can contain objects and images of that color model, grayscale, and bitmap (black and white). You cannot mix RGB and CMYK elements in a single Illustrator document. Objects and images are automatically converted to match the document's color mode.

⇨ *Think you're seeing a CMYK object in an Illustrator document? See "One Color Mode per Illustration" in the "Troubleshooting" section at the end of this chapter.*

The relationship among the six colors (RGB and CMY) is interesting to note and useful to understand:

- The colors alternate on a color wheel: red, yellow, green, cyan, blue, magenta, and back to red.

- Mixing two additive colors gives you one of the subtractive colors; mixing two subtractive colors gives you an additive color (see Figure 11.1).

Red + Green = Yellow
Green + Blue = Cyan
Blue + Red = Magenta

Cyan + Magenta = Blue
Magenta + Yellow = Red
Yellow + Cyan = Green

Figure 11.1
The additive colors are red, green, and blue; the subtractive colors are cyan, magenta, and yellow.

- When working with color, you can often add one color by subtracting the two other component colors.

- While working in RGB color mode, you can increase a subtractive color (CMY) by adding both of the two additive colors that create the subtractive color.

- You can easily access Illustrator's Color Picker and Color palette to see the relationship among the six colors (see Figure 11.2).

Figure 11.2
When in Hue mode (the default), the Color Picker's color slider (the vertical bar in the center) shows the range of colors available. The Color palette's color ramp (the horizontal bar at the bottom) does likewise.

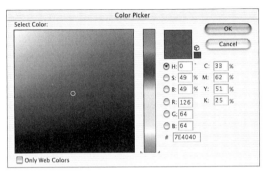

To ensure precise reproduction of specific colors and to add additional range to the printed page, CMYK inks can be supplemented with *spot colors*. Spot colors are inks that are specially formulated and manufactured to produce consistent color. Specific sets of inks are used for specific types of paper and printing procedures; inks in neon and metallic colors and clear varnishes are available as well. Their application during the printing process is controlled through their use in the image-creation process. Illustrator allows you to specify spot colors through the use of the Swatches palette and swatches libraries. When a custom color is added to an illustration from a supplemental swatch library, it is added to the document's Swatches palette. The Color palette also shows a selected spot color, as you can see in Figure 11.3, and allows you to create a *tint* of that color. (A tint is a lighter shade of a specific color. The color value remains the same, but the lightness or brightness value is altered.)

Figure 11.3
Pantone colors are the most commonly used spot colors in North America.

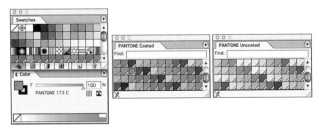

Monitors and other devices that produce light require RGB images. A computer screen can, of course, show a CMYK image. Because the RGB gamut is larger, virtually all CMYK colors can be reproduced onscreen. However, keep in mind that, even when you are working in CMYK color mode, the monitor is projecting RGB colors. The software simulates the conversion from monitor to paper for some colors.

➪ *Having difficulty with the difference between seeing RGB and CMYK on the monitor? Check "Seeing Colors" in the "Troubleshooting" section at the end of this chapter.*

In addition to computer monitors, RGB color is used for video and film, output to film recorders (which produce photographic slides and negatives), interactive kiosks and display terminals, CDs and DVDs, and other devices that rely on additive color.

Resolution

Another major difference between print and display applications is image *resolution*. Resolution is the relationship between the image's size digitally and its size on paper. When an image contains *raster* images, resolution determines how large or small an image will print and how fine or coarse its detail will be. To simplify, raster images are stored and displayed as a series of tiny squares called *pixels*. They are printed as a series of dots. Each pixel produces a tiny colored area on the page. The higher the resolution of an image, the smaller the colored areas and the finer the detail. However, to fill an equivalent space on a printed page, a high-resolution image must have more pixels with which the printer can produce colored spots. (For a more complete discussion, see Chapter 18, "Raster Images and Rasterized Objects.")

Figure 11.4 shows a single raster image, which measures 600 pixels by 250 pixels, and how it would appear on a printed page at three different print resolutions.

The image, in all three cases, has exactly 150,000 pixels (600×250). In the top example, the pixels are packed onto the page at a rate of 300 dots (pixels) per inch. The resulting image on the printed page is 2 inches by 0.83 inches. The middle example has the same number of pixels printed at 150dpi. That image prints on the page at 4 inches by 1.67 inches. The bottom example has that exact same number of pixels spread over a much larger area, at a rate of 72dpi. It prints with the dimensions 8.33 inches by 3.47 inches.

Resolution is measured for the printed page in *dots per inch (dpi)*. When you're working with digital imaging devices, such as scanners and digital cameras, resolution is measured in *pixels per inch (ppi)*. The terms are often used interchangeably, but the correct usage is *dpi* for the printed page and *ppi* for digital images. After all, the image on the page is reproduced with dots of ink, whereas that on the monitor or stored in a computer file consists of pixels. Computer monitors, on the other hand, have no resolution. Because monitors vary in the number of pixels displayed, the term *inch* in *ppi* is meaningless. For example, a monitor set to 800 × 600 pixels shows an image at a certain size. When the same monitor is set to 1024 × 768 pixels, that image is substantially smaller. (For a full discussion, see the sidebar "The Resolution-less Web" in Chapter 22, "Saving Images for the Web.")

Figure 11.4
The same image was placed on the artboard with three different resolutions. Illustrator uses the resolution with which the image was saved.

 300 dpi

 150 dpi

 72 dpi

If you need the image to fill this larger space on the page but require a resolution of 300dpi, the image must be *resampled*. (Resampling is the process of increasing or decreasing the number of pixels in an image to achieve a specific size and resolution.) In this example, the image would have to go from 600 pixels by 250 pixels to a size of 2,500 pixels by 1,042 pixels. The total number of pixels would increase from 150,000 to 2,605,000, and result in a file more than 17 times as large. Illustrator does not resample the image if you scale it. Rather, it adjusts the resolution, keeping the same number of pixels.

▷ *Confused about resampling? See "Changing the Number of Pixels" in the "Troubleshooting" section at the end of this chapter.*

Resampling

Although resampling is best done in an image-editing program, such as Photoshop, you can use Illustrator for the job as follows:

1. Open the image to be resampled in Illustrator.

2. Select it on the artboard.

3. Choose Object, Rasterize.

4. Select the desired resolution. In addition to the preset values of 72ppi, 150ppi, and 300ppi, you can enter any value in the Custom field.

5. Select other desired options, such as background, antialiasing, masking, and padding (added space around the image).

6. Click OK.

7. Choose Export to save the file in an appropriate file format, such as TIFF.

The quality of the resampling cannot compare to Photoshop but may be adequate. Figure 11.5 shows a comparison of Illustrator and Photoshop resampling results. The image on the left was resampled in Photoshop from 72dpi to 300dpi. The image on the right was resampled in Illustrator, using the technique described here, also to 300dpi.

Figure 11.5
Each of the visible "pixels" in the Illustrator image (right) is actually a box of four identically colored pixels.

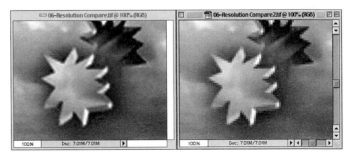

In addition to size, as noted previously, resolution affects the fineness or coarseness of an image's detail. In Figure 11.6, the three images have been masked to show only one area of detail, and the zoom factor has been increased to 400%. Note the graininess *(pixelization)* of the largest image. The "stars" in the distance show the relative size of the pixels in each image.

Figure 11.6
The smallest white spots in the background are 1 pixel each, showing the relative size of each image's pixels.

Scanners and many digital cameras can acquire images at varying resolutions. They use pixels per inch as the unit of measure. As seems logical, the greater the number of pixels captured, the better the resolution at a given size and the larger an image can be printed with adequate resolution.

When you're working with images for the Web or other monitor-based output, it's best to think in terms of raw pixels rather than pixels-per-unit-of-measure. Computer screens display varying numbers of pixels, with resolutions of 640×480, 800×600, 1024×768, and larger. Images, which have a certain number of pixels, occupy a different amount of screen space, depending on the monitor's resolution. And, because most modern monitors can be set for different resolutions, the number of pixels per inch on a given monitor can change.

The image in Figure 11.7 is 800×600 pixels (saved at 72ppi, although that is irrelevant). It is shown as it would be displayed on the same monitor at the three different monitor resolutions mentioned in the preceding paragraph.

Figure 11.7
The same image, at the same resolution, requires the same number of pixels to be displayed but uses different amounts of screen space.

File Formats

When considering a file's final destination, you must also consider the file format. Print and the Web require and use different file formats, although there is some overlap. In most cases, however, you should keep the original file as an Illustrator file and save a copy in the required format. You then can go back and edit the original, if necessary, and make a new copy.

Illustrator files that are destined for print are often placed into a page layout program, such as InDesign or PageMaker from Adobe or QuarkXPress. You can use the page layout program to integrate an illustration with text. The most common file formats for use with page layout programs that you can produce from Illustrator include EPS (Encapsulated PostScript), DCS (Desktop Color Separations), and TIFF (Tagged Image File Format). Various other file formats are available for use with page layout programs, including the Illustrator native file format (.ai), GIF (Graphics Interchange Format), JPEG (Joint Photographic Experts Group), PICT (Macintosh Picture format), and BMP (Bitmap). (The individual file formats were discussed in Chapter 3, "Working with Files in Illustrator.")

Web pages require specific file formats. Those available include GIF, JPEG, PNG (Portable Network Graphics), and the Flash and SVG (Scalable Vector Graphics) formats (see Chapter 22, "Saving Images for the Web," and Chapter 23, "Flash and SVG Support"). An image saved in any other file format on a Web page will almost certainly not be viewable by a visitor's Web browser.

Presentation programs, such as Microsoft PowerPoint, can use EPS and WMF files, in addition to several others. Many CAD programs can use several different file formats, including AutoCAD's DWG and DXF formats and (in some cases) Illustrator format.

Preparing illustrations or animations for incorporation into film or video requires that the appropriate file format be used. Adobe Premiere, for example, can import native Illustrator files, as well as Photoshop, PICT, PCX, TIFF, BMP, JPEG, GIF, and Targa. On the other hand, Illustrator can export an illustration for Strata VideoShop in JPEG, PICT, and Photoshop formats. Some digital film recorders (discussed later in this chapter) can produce film-ready images from various file formats.

THE PDF OPTION

Adobe's Portable Document Format (PDF) is used with the free Acrobat Reader and has a growing presence in the print industry and many other aspects of electronic document creation and management. The Illustrator-native file format (.ai) is PDF-based. PDF is a cross-platform format, which can be viewed on all major computer platforms (see Figure 11.8).

Acrobat documents are displayed exactly the same, regardless of platform. Graphics, fonts, formatting, and color are maintained. PDF files can be viewed onscreen or printed, and can also be viewed with a Web browser (with a plug-in). Other advantages of the PDF format include navigation and links, security, and sound and video annotations.

At the heart of the PDF format is a PostScript page. Like EPS and Illustrator's native format, PDF supports both vector and raster image data. Unlike an EPS file, a PDF file can be (and usually is) a multipage document. In Illustrator, you can open, edit, and save existing PDF documents one page at a time. Because Illustrator is a PDF-based format, you can save images as PDF and later reopen them in Illustrator for editing.

Figure 11.8
Adobe Acrobat Reader is freely downloadable for the computer platforms shown.

Acrobat's PDF files are also becoming more and more common in press workflows. It is not uncommon for PDF to replace page layout formats for submission to service bureaus and printing departments. In addition, you can prepare images for use on the Web. (See the sidebar "Saving as PDF" for information about the file format's options.) PDF files can also be linked or embedded within Illustrator files.

Saving as PDF

With PDF growing in importance as a document distribution format, understanding how to properly save such a file is important. PDF is an option in Illustrator's Save As dialog box. The PDF dialog boxes are shown in Figure 11.9.

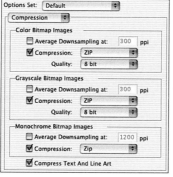

Figure 11.9
A pair of dialog boxes show the range of PDF options.

You have a number of options from which to choose, spread across two dialog box panels, General and Compression.

Your first choice in the PDF options is among predefined sets of options:

- **Default**—The Default set (for press) uses the settings shown on the left in Figure 11.9. The default compression settings are 8-bit Zip for color and grayscale bitmap images, and Zip for monochrome, with Compress Text and Line Art selected. Resolution values are left empty, using the resolution of the image's raster components (if any).

- **Screen Optimized**—The Screen Optimized (for Web) settings retain Acrobat 4 compatibility, but uncheck Preserve Illustrator Editing Capabilities. Fonts are embedded and subsetted, but the ICC profile is not. Thumbnails are not generated. For compression, Screen Optimized downsamples color and grayscale images at 72dpi, with Automatic selected for Compression mode and Medium for Quality. Monochrome images are downsampled at 300dpi and compressed using CCITT Group 4. Line art and text are compressed.

- **Custom**—This set allows you to pick your own settings.

The options, and your choices, for the two panels of the dialog box are as follows:

- **File Compatibility (General)**—Selecting Acrobat 5.0 preserves transparent artwork; Acrobat 4.0 does not.

- **Options (General)**—Font embedding and subsetting are the same as for Illustrator files. If a font is not embedded and not available on a computer that opens the file, another font is substituted. Subsetting fonts helps reduce file size by including only required characters. You can also embed the color mode used to create the document and embed thumbnails. Acrobat's thumbnails are used in the Reader's navigation system.

- **Color Bitmap Images (Compression) Average Downsampling At**—This option allows you to specify the resolution of the document's color images. The compression options are Automatic, JPEG, and Zip. You can select either downsampling or compression or both.

  Automatic offers five levels of quality, ranging from Minimum to Maximum. The lower the quality, the smaller the file. Automatic allows Illustrator's PDF engine to evaluate the image and choose between JPEG and Zip.

  JPEG offers the same five levels of quality as Automatic. Remember that JPEG is a lossy compression scheme and that image data is discarded during compression. Because it is lossy, JPEG usually achieves much smaller file sizes than Zip.

  Zip should be used only with images that contain large areas of solid color or distinct repeating patterns. Zip's 4-bit option should be selected only with images that contain a maximum of 16 colors. The 8-bit option allows up to 256 colors. Zip should not be used with photographic pictures or other continuous tone images. Nor should 4-bit compression be used with 8-bit images.

- **Grayscale Bitmap Images (Compression)**—The options for grayscale images are identical to those for color.

- **Monochrome Bitmap Images (Compression)**—Monochrome (black-and-white) images are 1-bit images. Every pixel is either black or white, no shades of gray, no colors. In addition to specifying a downsampling rate, you can choose a compression scheme. Zip is very good for 1-bit images that have large blocks of black or white or repeating patterns. The other choices include CCITT-3, CCITT-4, and Run Length Encoding (RLE). CCITT-4 is fine for general monochrome images, whereas version 3 was designed for faxes. RLE, like Zip, is best for images with large areas of solid color. It is a lossless compression scheme.

- **Compress Text and Line Art (Compression)**—If text and line art (black and white) are present in an image and this option is selected, Zip compression is applied.

OTHER OUTPUT OPTIONS

Although the vast majority of Illustrator's RGB documents end up on the World Wide Web, not all go down that cable. Presentations, 35mm slides and large-format film, information kiosks, and CD-ROMs and DVDs are just some of the other destinations.

The following are among the specific concerns when you are preparing illustrations for these various options:

- **File format**—Just as when you are preparing a document for inclusion into a page layout program or a Web page, most of these output alternatives involve additional software. You must be familiar with the destination software's file format requirements to properly prepare an image.

- **Resolution or image size**—Different output options have differing image size and resolution requirements. Some options accept vector files, but most require that the illustration be saved in a raster image format. The pixel dimensions or print resolution may be critical to proper image appearance.

- **Color depth**—When outputting to film, you can usually be assured that the image's entire RGB gamut will be used. Other options, however, may have restrictions on image bit depth.

- **File-naming conventions**—Especially important when you're working with CD/DVD output, ensuring that your images have appropriate filenames and extensions can prevent an unviewable image. (CDs using the ISO 9660 standard require that files be named using the old DOS "eight-point-three" convention. The name can be up to eight letters or numbers, followed by a period and a three-character file type extension.)

- **Frame rate and image size (animation)**—When you're preparing animation, remember to use an appropriate frame rate and image size. Too large an image or too many frames per second can result in choppy playback. Too few frames per second can produce an animation that stutters or looks jumpy. (Fifteen frames per second is usually a good compromise between speed and file size.)

Presentation Programs

Perhaps the most important presentation program today is Microsoft PowerPoint. It accepts Illustrator documents saved or exported in the following file formats: BMP, EMF, EPS, GIF,

JPEG, Photoshop, PICT, PNG, Targa, TIFF, and WMF. (You can find descriptions of the individual file formats in Chapter 3.) Other popular presentation programs may be limited to BMP, EPS, GIF, JPEG, and TIFF.

When you're inserting a file into a PowerPoint or other presentation as a picture, the various file formats have strengths and weaknesses. Many of the file formats require rasterization. You can accomplish this by choosing Object, Rasterize. Using this command gives you control of clipping paths and transparency. You can also specify resolution.

Although Illustrator now supports transparency, that capability doesn't completely translate to PowerPoint. Drop shadows, for example, can be problematic. Clipping paths (available in EPS, TIFF, and GIF files) draw a sharp edge around an image. With a drop shadow, the path is drawn at the outermost edge of the shadow and includes the background color beneath, by default, the white of the Illustrator artboard.

Figure 11.10 shows a logo with a drop shadow and, behind, a typical example of what happens when a drop shadow is taken into PowerPoint.

Figure 11.10
The logo was inserted into PowerPoint as an EPS file.

When you're working with shadows or other effects, the safest course is to work with a background identical to that of the presentation. You can use the Eyedropper tool to sample a PowerPoint background color (or a color from anywhere on the screen). Just follow these steps:

1. In its host application, open an image that contains the color you need to duplicate. In the case of the example, shown in Figure 11.11, a document is open in PowerPoint.

2. Open a document in Illustrator. It should be the document into which you want to insert the color.

3. Position the windows of the two images as shown in Figure 11.11, with both visible, and the Illustrator window on top and active.

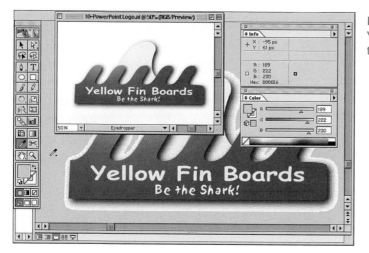

Figure 11.11
You must be able to see the color
that you want to sample onscreen.

4. Select Illustrator's Eyedropper tool from the Toolbox.

5. Click anywhere in the Illustrator document and drag the Eyedropper into the other image. You must start in Illustrator.

6. As you drag the Eyedropper through the non-Illustrator document, the swatch in the Toolbox, Color palette, and Info palette are all updated live. Watch the display to ensure that you get the desired color. Remember that Illustrator's Eyedropper uses a point sample (a single pixel). Antialiasing or other small variations in color can result in fluctuating readings.

7. Release the mouse button when the appropriate color is visible in the Color palette or swatch.

You can now use that color as you would any other in Illustrator, and it is a good idea to click the New Swatch button in the bottom of the Swatches palette. Creating a swatch allows you to maintain the color throughout the creative process. For the illustration in these examples, an unstroked rectangle was drawn, filled with the sampled color, and moved behind the logo.

Figure 11.12 shows how the background match allows you to use a drop shadow or other effect on an image destined for another program. The inset image is the Illustrator file with the background color. Behind is the PowerPoint file, with the inserted image's bounding box handles visible.

Figure 11.12
This image was saved as a Targa file for insertion into PowerPoint, but any one of a number of formats would have produced the same result.

Color Management

Not all programs use sophisticated color management. You may see variations in color, sometimes substantial. In Figure 11.13, you can see the extreme difference in how identical HSB values might be handled. (The difference in color is obvious even in a grayscale image.) The backgrounds of the Illustrator and PowerPoint documents are far from matching.

Figure 11.13
Differences in color variation can often be attributed to monitor calibration and color settings.

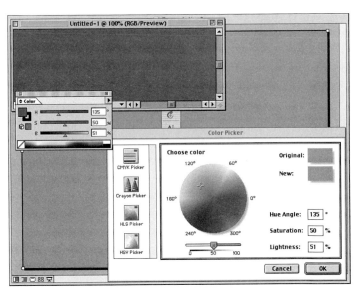

Although clipping paths are not suitable for illustrations that include shadows and some other effects, they are perfectly acceptable with hard-edged transparency.

Another concern when you're preparing images for inclusion in a presentation program is gradients. Depending on the file format selected, gradients may or may not dither. TIFF, Targa, and JPEG maintain gradients (as do most file formats that use 24-bit color modes) .

Film Recorders

Film recorders, sometimes referred to as slide printers, are printers. However, instead of using paper, they print to photographic film. The most common recorders typically print to 35mm slide film. Other, especially high-end professional, models can print to negative as well as transparency film and can handle large-format film. Recorders designed for 35mm slide film often produce foggy images when photographic negative film is used. Images are often printed to slides for presentation purposes, and printed to negative or positive for printing and archiving.

Illustrations and other images to be output to film need to be measured a bit differently. Most film recorders measure resolution as a series of vertical lines across the film. The standard resolutions are 4,000, 8,000, and 16,000 lines. Note that these are not "lines per inch," but total lines. Each line represents a dot. The higher the number, the more information sent to the film.

The sharpness of the output can vary widely among film recorders of the same resolution. One recorder may use 4,000 lines on a CRT (cathode ray tube) measuring 4 inches wide. Another may place 4,000 lines on a 6-inch CRT. The actual size of the dots (measured in millimeters) can also vary from recorder to recorder. As the image is projected onto the CRT, each dot "blooms" or spreads. The more overlap, the softer the image. Typically (but not always), larger CRTs have less overlap. However, a smaller dot on a 4-inch CRT may produce a sharper image than a larger dot on a 6-inch CRT.

Another feature of film recorders is 33-bit or 36-bit color. This feature allows for a wider range of colors, often more than the source program can produce. Images being recorded to film almost always are RGB. The exceptions usually are CMYK images that are being archived or must be duplicated from film.

Some programs can print directly to a film recorder, as they would to an imagesetter, laser printer, or inkjet printer. The film recorder is selected just as you would select a printer. This is typically a function of the film recorder's software or print driver. In other cases, the image must be prepared to be opened in or imported into a program that serves as the interface with the recorder. Among the most common file formats required are TIFF, EPS, BMP, PICT, and JPEG. PostScript is often an option on film recorders.

The documentation of many film recorders suggests appropriate sizes for images to be output in terms of file size. For example, the documentation may recommend that a 24-bit image be 5MB to fill a 35mm slide. If the image will occupy only part of a slide (in a presentation, for example), the file size can be reduced proportionally.

However, when you're preparing an image for a film recorder, it's better to know the actual *addressable* dimensions, in pixels. This is the number of pixels needed for an exact fit onto the film. A number of popular slide printers use the dimensions 4,096 pixels by 2,732 pixels for 35mm film.

When you're working with film recorders to produce images that fill a frame, the aspect ratio is important. The ratio for 35mm film is 3:2. Film called 4×5 actually has an aspect ratio of 54:42, and 6×7 film is 11:9. (By convention, the larger number comes first when you're discussing aspect ratios. The names of the film sizes list height before width.)

If an image is not proportioned properly, you can either resize it or add a border. When you're working with presentation slides, a border is often preferable to a blinding white reflection from the projection screen.

Some digital film recorders are designed to use 35mm or 16mm movie film. These cameras require aspect ratios appropriate for the film being used.

TROUBLESHOOTING

One Color Mode per Illustration

I dragged an object from a CMYK document to an RGB document. The Color palette shows CMYK values. Is it still CMYK?

No, it's an RGB object. Illustrator allows only one color mode per document. To check, open the Info palette and click the object. You'll see its true color mode and color values. When you transfer an object from a document of one color mode to a document of the other color mode, it is automatically converted.

Although moving an object from a CMYK document to an RGB document doesn't usually change its appearance, moving from RGB to CMYK can result in drastic—and unexpected—changes. And keep in mind that going from RGB to CMYK and then back to an RGB document does not restore the original RGB color values.

Seeing Colors

Okay, what's this about the difference in gamut between RGB and CMYK? Colors are colors, aren't they?

Actually, colors *are* colors. It's a question of which ones are available. Because of the way that light creates colors (RGB), it can reproduce more different colors than can the standard four printing inks (CMYK). Virtually all the CMYK colors can be reproduced on your screen using RGB, so you can think of CMYK as a subset of RGB. If you change a document's color mode from RGB to CMYK, your computer translates any RGB colors to the nearest CMYK equivalents.

Changing the Number of Pixels

Why should I resample an image? Why can't I just grab the corner and drag to make it larger or smaller?

Certainly, you can scale instead of resampling, but the quality of the raster object will suffer. Raster images are made up of pixels, and each image has a certain number of pixels. Think of them as the tiles in a mosaic. If the mosaic measures 3 feet by 2 feet, using tiles exactly 1-inch square, it is 36 tiles by 24 tiles. Standing a few feet away from the mosaic, you can see each of the individual tiles. Figure 11.14 shows a representation in the upper-left corner.

If you want the mosaic to show the same picture, but at a size of 6 feet by 4 feet, you need new tiles. If you want to use 1-inch tiles, like that of the original, you need a lot more of them. Instead of 864, you need 3,456 tiles. In Figure 11.14, this image is shown in the upper-right corner.

If, on the other hand, you want the mosaic to remain 3 feet by 2 feet, but you don't want the individual tiles to be as prominent, you need smaller tiles. If you use tiles that are one-quarter inch square, you need 13,824 to do the same three by two area. In Figure 13.14, this image is in the lower-right corner.

Dragging to scale a raster image is equivalent to changing the mosaic from 3 feet by 2 feet to 6 feet by 4 feet, while retaining the same number of tiles. Suddenly, those tiles are a massive 2 inches square. With tiles that large, the mosaic's picture might get lost. Can't see the forest for the trees.... In Figure 11.14, this image appears in the lower-left corner.

3' x 2' (1" tiles)

6' x 4' (1" tiles)

Figure 11.14
The four "mosaics" and their "tiles" are to scale.

6' x 4' (2" tiles)

3' x 2' (1/4" tiles)

As you can see by comparing the upper-right and lower-left images, resampling is better than simply scaling. And, as you can see by comparing the original "mosaic" in the upper-left with the image in the lower-right, using smaller tiles produces a cleaner look. For digital images, this is equivalent to printing at a higher resolution (using more pixels in the same space).

IV

ENHANCING ILLUSTRATOR OBJECTS

IN THIS PART

12 Understanding and Applying Color **275**

13 Applying and Defining Patterns **299**

14 Using the Appearance and Styles Palettes **323**

15 The Gradient and Gradient Mesh Tools **337**

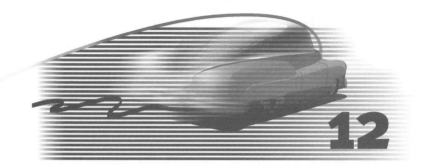

UNDERSTANDING AND APPLYING COLOR

IN THIS CHAPTER

The Two Types of Color   276

RGB Versus CMYK Versus Spot Colors   278

The Other Color Modes: HSB and Grayscale   282

Reduced Palettes   284

Determining the Color Mode   284

Using the Color Palette   286

Applying Color   290

Using the Swatches Palette   291

Troubleshooting   297

THE TWO TYPES OF COLOR

Without color, there is no illustration, merely invisible paths. A path is an abstract concept, conveying no information to the viewer, until the application of a fill and/or a stroke. It's color that produces the image, attracts the attention, AND conveys the message. Virtually everything done in Illustrator is about putting color in the correct places to create an image.

It's important, therefore, that you know a few things about color so that you can use it properly to communicate effectively with your audience. Color selection and combination are best left to the design school. Here, the discussion looks at the technical end of color use.

The two types of color are *additive* and *subtractive*. These two categories parallel another pair of categories you'll read about shortly—RGB and CMYK. The difference between the two is how white is created. They are also differentiated by how the color reaches the eye—directly or by reflection. Pure white light shining through a red filter can give a beautiful and brilliant color. That same white light reflecting off a wall painted red can also give a lovely and vibrant color. But how the eye perceives the two colors can be radically different, as is how the "red" is created.

Additive Color

Additive color gets its name because white is created by adding together the colors of the spectrum. White is the inclusion of all colors. A typical example of additive color is a stage with three spotlights, one each of red, green, and blue, as shown in Figure 12.1. Where the three lights overlap, you see white. Where two of the three overlap, you see cyan, magenta, or yellow. The combination, in varying proportions, of red, green, and blue can produce all the colors of the spectrum—up to a point. The absence of all three of the colors is black.

Figure 12.1
Conceptual view of RGB interaction. This cartoon assumes a uniform brightness for each of the lights, as well as uniformity across each light's splash.

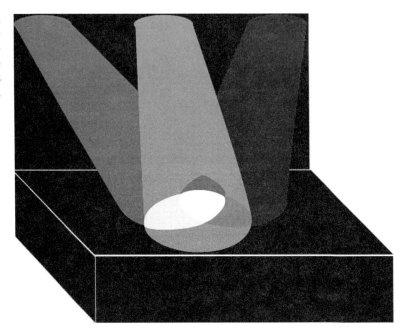

You see additive color when you look at a source of light, such as a bulb behind a colored lamp shade, a television, or a computer monitor. When this light reflects off a surface, like a lamp shining through its shade onto a wall, you see a combination of the additive colors of the lamp and its shade and the subtractive colors of the wall's surface. Consider this to be subtractive color.

Additive color is used in Illustrator when producing artwork that will be displayed on a monitor (such as Web graphics) or by means of another light source (projection, video, film, and so on) .

Subtractive Color

Subtractive color is thusly called because the lack of color produces white. White is the absence of color. The color that you see is reflected rather than directly generated like the spotlights mentioned in the preceding section. Think of the wall painted red. When white light hits the wall, all the colors of the spectrum are absorbed except red. That red is reflected back from the wall to the eye. Hence, you see the color red. Theoretically, the majority of the visible spectrum can be reproduced by using combinations of cyan, magenta, and yellow ink or paint. By careful proportioning of the inks, you can control exactly what shade is reflected back to the viewer's eye. When all the colors are absorbed and none reflected, the eye perceives black. Figure 12.2 shows the relationship among the various key colors discussed.

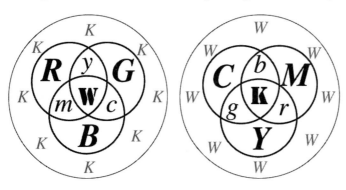

Figure 12.2
You can see how the RGB colors can be blended to create cyan, magenta, and yellow, and how the three together form white (W) and their absence results in black (K). Although the CMY values can produce shades of red, green, and blue, their absence results in white (W), and when combined fully, they theoretically produce black (K).

Even those who spend their days in front of computer monitors and television screens see far more subtractive color than additive during the course of a day. The plastic case of the monitor, the paper of the text being transcribed, the desk and keyboard, the remote control and couch—all are seen by virtue of reflected light. Consider, if you will, the movie theater with your favorite film playing. The bucket of popcorn in your lap and the face of your date are viewed by reflected light, subtractive light. The image on the screen, due to the highly reflective nature of the screen itself, is additive; you're actually seeing a near-mirror image of the light from the projector.

Subtractive color is used in Illustrator when preparing images that will be printed.

Before you embark on a project that will end up in four-color process inks, talk with your printer. Don't, for example, use a set of spot colors that requires your printer to import inks from Japan. Pantone colors are usually safe to use in North America.

Also, note that opening many Swatch Libraries can slow down Illustrator. Having large, wide-open Swatches palettes and lots of visible swatches can also slow down screen redraw and scrolling among the swatches.

Additional Swatch Libraries are available on the Web and from other sources. Hexachrome, for example, is Pantone's name for its own six-color printing process, which includes, in addition to CMYK inks, an orange and a green ink. This should not be confused with the photo-realistic inkjet printers that use six inks. In addition to CMYK, they include a light cyan and a light magenta. That six-color printing is usually abbreviated CcMmYK.

As mentioned previously, you can create your own Swatch Libraries and share them among Illustrator documents by choosing Window, Swatch Libraries, Other Library. You can also make your custom swatches available automatically in every new document by creating a new startup file. See Chapter 16 for instructions.

The Find field works somewhat differently with the Swatch Libraries listed earlier. If you ignore the name of the set, typing the first numeric takes you to the first instance of the number, not necessarily the first color whose number starts with that digit. For example, using the Pantone Process library, typing **2** takes you to Pantone 1-2 CVS. Quickly typing **20,** however, activates Pantone 20-1 CVS. Using the Find field with the Trumatch library requires that you type the hyphen in the middle of the name to get a specific color. For example, typing **5-b3** takes you directly to swatch Trumatch 5-b3. Typing **5b3** without the hyphen activates Trumatch 1-a.

TROUBLESHOOTING

Legacy Documents with Both RGB and CMYK Objects

I opened one of my old Illustrator files and got a warning that the document contained objects of both CMYK and RGB color. The warning box wanted me to change them, but I was afraid of messing up my artwork, so I clicked Cancel. What should I do?

The Convert Color Mode dialog box is, indeed, formidable. Illustrator now allows only one color mode per document. Here are the guidelines for choosing between RGB and CMYK: If the document is intended for a four-color process printing job, click CMYK and let Illustrator convert your RGB colors. Any colors that were outside the CMYK gamut (and would therefore not be reproduced accurately by the four-color process inks) are converted to the nearest CMYK color. If you don't plan to use the document in a four-color job, select RGB. Because virtually all CMYK colors fall within the RGB gamut, no conversion is necessary.

Multiple Color Modes

I'm preparing several illustrations that I would like to use both in print and on the Web. Considering the differences between RGB and CMYK, is this possible?

Some images, including logos and other small art, are multipurpose. When you're preparing an image for both RGB (Web or monitor) and print (CMYK), consider the following:

- If the colors must match exactly for every employment of the image, ensure that your RGB version doesn't contain any out-of-gamut colors. One way to do so is to work in CMYK and then convert a copy to RGB when finished.

- If a piece of art is headed for both print and the Web, and the colors must match, consider working in the Web Safe RGB palette. Those 216 colors don't give you any out-of-gamut warnings.

- If color matching is not critical, take advantage of RGB's larger gamut by doing your work in that mode. At the end of the creation process, reduce a copy for your Web needs and convert a copy to CMYK for print. Maintain the original in the full RGB spectrum for later use.

Changing Nonglobal Colors

I defined a color and added it as a swatch to my Swatches palette. I created a bunch of objects using that color as a fill. When I changed the color of my swatch, the objects didn't change. How come?

When you added the color to the Swatches palette, you didn't check the Global box. If you had, you would have seen a little white triangle in the lower-right corner of the swatch. Global colors can be updated throughout the document; nonglobal colors cannot be as easily updated.

Okay, so I should have made it a global color, but I didn't. Do I now have to Shift+click all those little objects to make the change?

No, you don't. Simply click any one of those little objects and choose Edit, Select, Same Fill Color or Edit, Select, Same Stroke Color. You can then make the change to all objects using that color.

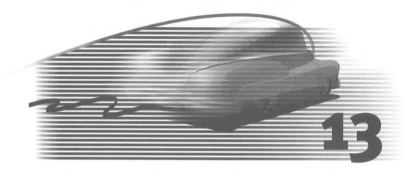

APPLYING AND DEFINING PATTERNS

IN THIS CHAPTER

General Rules Governing Patterns **300**

Fill Patterns **303**

Brush Patterns **306**

Troubleshooting **321**

GENERAL RULES GOVERNING PATTERNS

Patterns, like colors, can be customized, saved, and applied to individual objects. The two basic types of patterns are fill patterns and brush patterns. Brush patterns are intended to be applied to paths, including the stroke of an object. They are used exclusively with pattern brushes. Fill patterns, on the other hand, are designed for use as an object's fill. Fill patterns are stored in the Swatches palette; you can load them by choosing Window, Swatch Libraries. (The Swatches palette and Swatch Libraries are discussed in Chapter 12, "Understanding and Applying Color.") Brush patterns are stored in the Brushes palette; you can load them by choosing Window, Brush Libraries. (Brushes and the Brushes palette are discussed in Chapter 6, "Utilizing the Four Types of Brushes.")

Loosely, a *pattern* is a piece of artwork that repeats throughout the object into which it is placed (or along a path). This repeating is called *tiling*, much as a kitchen floor or a bathroom wall is made of individual tiles that repeat a pattern. A pattern is artwork that is available for fills or paths and is stored in the Swatches palette.

A pattern can contain objects and text, paths and compound paths, and fills or no fill. Several tools and techniques *cannot* be used to create patterns:

- Other patterns
- Gradients and gradient meshes
- Blends
- Brush strokes
- Bitmap images
- Placed files
- Graphs
- Masks

To see how you can use varying levels of transparency in a pattern, look at Figures 13.1 and 13.2, in which a simple target pattern was developed. The progressive circles are all set for 25% opacity in the Transparency palette, and the cross is set at 100% opacity. These figures show how the different opacities interact with each other and the background.

In Illustrator 10, you can use transparency with objects, paths, and text that are destined to become parts of a pattern. The transparency affects not only the interaction among the parts of the pattern, but also the pattern itself. Chapter 19, "Exploiting Illustrator's Transparency," describes how such interactions are controlled.

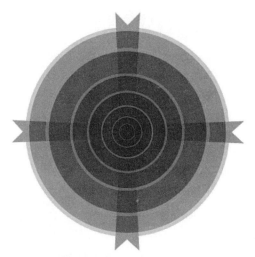

Figure 13.1
As the number of semi-transparent circles increases, the visibility of the background cross decreases, particularly within the inner pair of circles.

Figure 13.2
This close-up view shows how the cumulative opacity of the pattern in the foreground eventually obscures the background cross.

To see some of the differences in behavior between fill patterns and pattern brushes, see Figures 13.3 and 13.4.

Figure 13.3
Illustrator installs these six standard fill patterns in the Swatches palette.

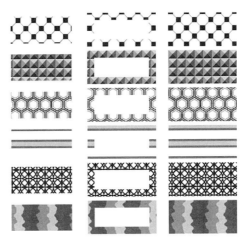

Figure 13.4
The top three objects have fill patterns applied to their strokes; the lower three have brush patterns.

In Figure 13.3, the rectangles in the left column have the pattern fill and no stroke; the center column shows no fill and a stroke of 15 points; the right column has both pattern fill and a stroke of 15 points. Note how the patterns flow seamlessly outward from the fill into the stroke.

In Figure 13.4, observe the difference between fill patterns and brush patterns when they're applied to a stroke. A brush pattern (bottom row) normally rotates around the object, whereas a fill pattern (top row) remains oriented to the vertical and horizontal axes.

Fill patterns tile (replicate to cover an area or stroke) from the ruler's point of origin. By default, the zero-zero point of the ruler is in the lower left of the document. When the rulers are visible, you can change this point by dragging from the intersection of the rulers in the upper left of the screen to the new point of origin. From the point of origin, patterns tile from left to right, from bottom to top. You can shift a pattern within an object or along a stroke (not a path) by holding down the tilde key (~) and dragging.

The tilde key can also be used in conjunction with the Rotate, Scale, and Reflect tools to change a fill pattern without altering the object itself. As with any use of these keys, the object must first be selected before it can be altered with the specific tool. You also can use these tools to transform fill patterns applied to strokes, but you cannot use them with brush patterns. Also, be aware of the Transform Pattern Only command from the Transform palette pop-up menu. When using this option, the pattern is altered without affecting the object itself.

FILL PATTERNS

Fill patterns can be complex or simple, plain or ornate. All, however, have several things in common. As discussed earlier, a number of tools and techniques cannot be used to create patterns. In addition, all fill patterns tile from the ruler origin. All fill patterns are stored in the Swatches palette and are kept with a particular document. More complex patterns should be smaller for efficiency. Simple patterns can be larger. Most fill pattern swatches should be between 1/2- and 1-inch square.

The process of creating a fill pattern is rather simple. You draw the artwork, place a *bounding box* behind the artwork to designate what will be included in the pattern, and save the pattern to the Swatches palette by choosing Edit, Define Pattern. Creating a good fill pattern, however, requires some planning.

The bounding box controls the size of an individual tile of the pattern. A bounding box substantially larger than the artwork it surrounds produces lots of whitespace between elements in an object filled with the pattern. Although it isn't required, a bounding box is useful for regulating how each tile aligns.

Bounding boxes are great for planning and for regulating space around your artwork within the pattern. They are not, however, always necessary. If, for example, you want a simple star as your fill pattern, draw the star, select it, and choose Edit, Define Pattern. That's all there is to it. Your star will repeat in nice, orderly rows throughout any object you choose.

You can think of fill patterns as falling into two distinct categories: repeating patterns and seamless patterns. A *repeating pattern* has individual elements that are obvious in the object that is filled. *Seamless patterns*, on the other hand, have hidden edges. They are meant to appear as one continuous pattern within the object rather than as a series of tiles. Examples of the two types are shown in Figure 13.5.

The basic technique for creating a seamless pattern is to have elements that cross the boundary of the tile into the neighboring tile. Although this isn't possible because only a single tile is used, you can create such an illusion. When an element starts on the left side of the tile, appears to go off the edge, and then reappears on the right side, the eye cannot tell where one tile ends and the next begins. Two approaches are shown in Figure 13.6.

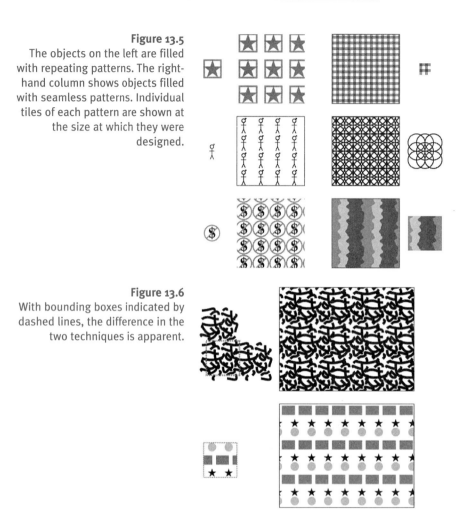

Figure 13.5
The objects on the left are filled with repeating patterns. The right-hand column shows objects filled with seamless patterns. Individual tiles of each pattern are shown at the size at which they were designed.

Figure 13.6
With bounding boxes indicated by dashed lines, the difference in the two techniques is apparent.

In the upper example in Figure 13.6, duplicates of the pattern were dragged above and to the right to add the ends of the lines that extended past the bounding box. Those parts of the lines that extend beyond the dashed lines to the left and the bottom are reproduced in the right and top of the box by the copies. The bounding box, in the process of producing the pattern, chops off any part of the pattern sticking out of it. The lower example is much more straightforward. Elements of the pattern are "halved" in the creation process, with one half on each side of the pattern.

To create a fill pattern, follow these basic steps:

1. Draw a square of the required dimensions (but typically no larger than 1 inch × 1 inch). It will become your bounding box and must be the furthest back of any object in the pattern.

2. Within the bounds of the square, draw and color your art. Remember which techniques cannot be used in a pattern. (See "General Rules Governing Patterns" at the beginning of this chapter.)

3. Group your art (but not the bounding box).

4. Select the bounding box; then give it a fill of None and a stroke of None.

5. With the bounding box still selected, Shift+click your grouped artwork to select it as well.

6. Choose Edit, Define Pattern to open the New Swatch dialog box.

7. Give your pattern a name and click OK.

If you want to create a seamless pattern as shown in the upper half of Figure 13.6, the technique is a bit different:

1. Establish your future bounding box and begin drawing your art as described in the preceding steps. Artwork can extend past all four sides of the bounding box for this procedure.

2. When the art is ready, select it all and the bounding box.

3. Ensure that Snap to Point is selected under the View menu.

4. Press Shift+Option [Shift+Alt] and drag the selection toward the bottom of the bounding box. When the edges of the boxes are aligned and snap together, release the mouse button.

5. Release the modifier keys, click again on the still-selected artwork, repress Shift+Option [Shift+Alt], and drag at a 45° angle until the copied artwork aligns with the right side of the original bounding box.

6. Release the modifier keys, click again on the still-selected artwork, repress Shift+Option [Shift+Alt], and drag at a 45° angle until the copied artwork aligns with the top of the original bounding box.

7. Release the modifier keys, click again on the still-selected artwork, repress Shift+Option [Shift+Alt], and drag at a 45° angle until the copied artwork aligns with the left side of the original bounding box.

8. Delete the four surrounding boxes, leaving only the original bounding box.

9. Select all the artwork (but not the bounding box) and group it.

10. Select the original bounding box. (It should be the only one left.) Give it a fill of None and a stroke of None.

11. Shift+click the grouped artwork. Everything, including the bounding box, should now be selected.

12. Choose Edit, Define Pattern to open the New Swatch dialog box.

13. Give your pattern a name and click OK.

You can edit a pattern after adding it to the Swatches palette. To do so, simply drag the swatch to the artboard, ungroup if necessary, do the editing, and Option+drag [Alt+drag] the modified swatch back on top of the original in the Swatches palette. All objects in the document that had been filled with the original pattern are updated to the new pattern. And, of course, anything new to which the pattern is applied uses the edited version.

☞ *If you're having trouble getting your new patterns to appear properly in the Swatches palette, see "Trouble Defining Patterns" in the "Troubleshooting" section at the end of this chapter.*

Often you can solve printing problems with documents that contain complex patterns by using the Expand command. The Object, Expand command can turn an object filled with a pattern into an object filled with objects.

☞ *Images with complex (or many) patterns can drown a printer in data. If your image isn't printing, check "Expanding Patterns for Print" in the "Troubleshooting" section at the end of this chapter.*

BRUSH PATTERNS

A brush pattern is actually a series of patterns combined into one brush. Unlike a fill pattern, a brush pattern must be able to rotate itself around corners and adapt to curves. To create such a pattern, you must actually create the individual parts that serve as the outer and inner corners. See Figure 13.7 for the difference between these two types of corners. If the brush pattern is to be used with open paths, start and end tiles must also be created.

Notice how, in making all the corners except one, the brush pattern has pointed the fleurs-de-lis outward, away from the corner. They are outer corners. The one exception (in the center of Figure 13.7) is the inner corner, in which the fleurs-de-lis are pointed toward each other. When you're designing a nonsymmetrical pattern brush, you must construct both outer and inner corners.

Caution

Patterns, especially very complex patterns, can cause trouble for printers. Rather than waiting for a printer error, consider the complexity when you're designing your custom patterns. Remove any unnecessary artwork (including details that will be obscured by other artwork placed on top). Objects of the same color should be grouped so that they are adjacent in the stacking order. Arranging similarly colored items in the stacking order can affect layers, so planning is required.

If you want to edit the pieces of an object whose fill has been expanded, you can do so. You'll often see masked objects and paths that extend well beyond the limits of the original object. Select the pattern and start with a couple of Ungroup commands (until the command is grayed out in the Edit menu). Next, zoom in very closely on a corner of the visible fill. Using the Direct Selection tool, and watching its cursor change to indicate that you're over a point, click to select the invisible bounding box. Press Delete twice. The once-masked objects and paths are now available for you to edit or copy as you will.

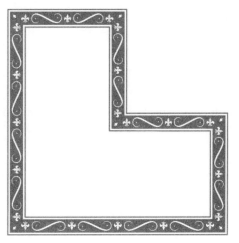

Figure 13.7
This pattern contains five outer corners and one inner corner.

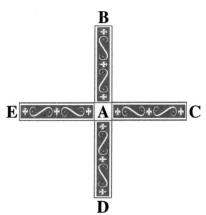

Figure 13.8
When you're using the Pen tool from a central point, Illustrator orients a pattern with the assumption that you are working clockwise.

In Figure 13.8, from point A to point B, the pattern points to the left. From A to C, it points upward. From A to D, the top of the pattern points to the right. From A to E, it's toward the bottom. This rule applies to any tool utilizing a pattern brush.

When you're drawing with the Pen tool or the Pencil, Illustrator assumes, for the purposes of applying a pattern, that you are working clockwise. See Figure 13.8 for a visual explanation.

Creating a Brush Pattern

You can create a new brush in two ways. In the first, you simply use the built-in Illustrator artwork found through the Brushes palette, as described in Chapter 6. Using the Brushes palette's pop-up menu, select New Brush. In the dialog box, choose New Pattern Brush. Illustrator gives you a large selection of parts with which to work.

You also can use the Brushes palette pop-up menu in the creation of original pattern brushes. All parts of the new brush pattern must be saved as patterns in the Swatches palette before you can access them from the New Pattern Brush dialog box. The process of creating a brush pattern is not as complicated as it seems. (The specifics of creating side, corner, and end tiles will follow.)

1. Create the side tile of your new brush and choose Edit, Define Pattern to add it to your Swatches palette.

2. Create the corner pattern or patterns (you need both outer and inner corner patterns if you're creating a nonsymmetrical pattern) and use the Define Pattern command.

3. Create end patterns and add them, too, to the Swatches palette.

4. After you've created all your required parts, click the Brushes palette tab to make it visible.

5. From the palette's pop-up menu, select New Brush.

6. Choose New Pattern Brush. Your new swatches should appear in the list of available art in the Pattern Brush Options dialog box.

7. At the top of the dialog box are five squares, each with a depiction of its purpose (see Figure 13.9). From left to right, they are Side Tile (straight segment), Outer Corner Tile, Inner Corner Tile, Start Tile, and End Tile. Click the leftmost one and then select your side tile pattern from the list below.

Figure 13.9
The Brush Pattern Options dialog box shows all available patterns from the Swatches palette.

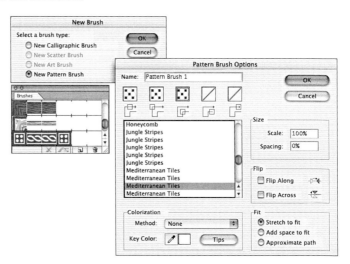

8. Do the same for all other required parts. If you accidentally choose the wrong artwork, simply reclick the correct swatch's name. If you add a swatch where you would rather have no swatch (an end tile, for example), you can choose None from the top of the list.

9. Select the appropriate size ratio. Choosing 100% tiles the brush pattern at the original creation size. The value must be between 1% and 10000%, although very large values are usually impractical. Consider a pattern designed and created at 1/4 inch × 1/4 inch. A size value of 10000% would produce tiles 25 inches × 25 inches.

10. Choose one, both, or neither Flip option. Flip Along reverses each tile, whereas Flip Across changes all tiles by swapping the top and bottom.

11. Choose the appropriate Fit setting (see Figure 13.10).

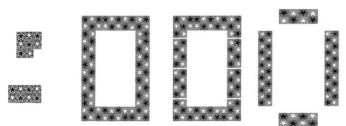

Figure 13.10
The Brush Pattern Options dialog box offers three Fit settings.

To the left in Figure 13.10 are an outer corner and a side tile from this particular pattern brush. The first rectangle uses Stretch to Fit, the middle rectangle is set to Add Space to Fit, and the object to the right is set to Approximate Path. Note that the pattern is not centered on the bounding box of the last object (the three objects are of identical size and are aligned through their centers). Also, be aware of the lack of corner tiles and the fact that only a single tile is used vertically, which distorts the pattern. Some other types of pattern brushes, however, behave excellently with this setting.

12. Choose your method of colorization. None keeps the pattern's colors as they were when created. Tints uses the currently active stroke color. The darkest parts of the brush pattern will be that color, whites will remain white, and everything in between will become a tint of the stroke color. Tints and Shades keeps black and white, and creates shades (and tints) of the stroke color for the rest of the pattern. This option is designed to be used with brushes created from grayscale art. (See the warning following these steps.) Hue Shift is designed for use with color patterns. It takes the dominant color (key color) and transforms it into the currently active stroke color. Other colors in the pattern are transformed accordingly. Black, white, and gray retain their respective values. You can designate a new key color by using the Eyedropper and clicking a color in one of the tiles at the top of the dialog box. Note that you should select your desired stroke color prior to opening the New Brush dialog box.

13. If you haven't yet, assign a name to your new pattern brush.

14. Click OK. The pattern is automatically applied to any currently selected object. It is added to the bottom of the Brushes palette as a new pattern brush.

15. (Optional) You can now delete your artwork from the Swatches palette unless you have further use for it.

Caution

The Tints and Shades colorization option adds black to the pattern brush's color palette. When you're working with a spot color for your pattern brush, be aware that this option could prevent the artwork from separating completely to a single plate. The addition of black could result in part of the pattern brush's stroke appearing on a spot color plate and the rest on the black plate.

Designing Brush Patterns for Pattern Brushes

Several key concepts deserve attention during the planning of a brush pattern:

- As side tiles are placed along the path, the top always faces "outward" from the center of an object.

- No artwork can protrude beyond the bounding box without being chopped off in the pattern.

- Like fill patterns, brush patterns should be kept as simple as possible to avoid long redraws and potential printing problems.

- The more complex a pattern, the smaller the individual tiles should be. Although more tiles are required to complete the path, the file itself will be less likely to present printing problems.

- A side tile should usually be from one to two inches long and half that high.

- Corner tiles must be square; each end of the pattern meets up with the same size tile. The pattern must be centered along the two sides where it will meet the side tiles (assuming that the side tiles are also centered).

- There are both continuous patterns and repeating patterns for both fill and brush. A continuous pattern would be one without a discernible repetition of elements. A repeating pattern, while perhaps having neither beginning nor end, does have individual elements that can be seen to reoccur. See Figure 13.11 for a visual comparison.

- If the pattern is symmetrical from top to bottom, the same tile can be used for outer and inner corners.

Figure 13.11
The examples on the left are continuous patterns; they have no obviously repeating elements. The double-line border, for example, has just one of each of the two lines. The examples on the right have repeating patterns.

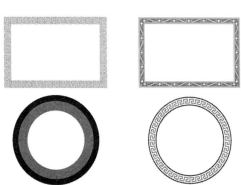

⇨ *If the brush pattern you've designed just doesn't seem to be proportional to your artwork, see "Resizing Brush Patterns" in the "Troubleshooting" section at the end of this chapter.*

Creating Brush Pattern Side Tiles

Among the handiest features of Illustrator for use during the brush pattern creation process are grids and guides. Using the commands View, Show Grid and View, Guides, Show Guides should be part of setting up the workplace for this type of operation.

As noted previously, the best dimensions for a side tile are between 1/2 and 1 inch tall and 1 to 2 inches wide. Simpler patterns are more efficient at larger sizes because fewer copies are required to cover a path.

If your brush pattern is to be a repeating pattern, you must decide whether you want the end of each tile to be in the middle or at the edge of an object. You can see the difference in Figure 13.12.

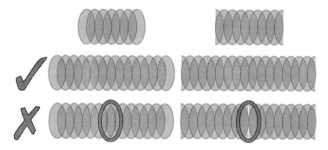

Figure 13.12
The patterns are shown at 200% zoom.

In Figure 13.12, the top row shows single tiles that end at the edge and in the middle of an object. The second row shows how two of the tiles should match. The third row shows what is to be avoided. Notice the misalignment of the center ovals on the left, which leads to a slight doubling of the stroke for the objects in the middle (where the pattern tiles join). On the right, the pattern is just a bit too short, resulting in a gap between tiles. A gap in the middle of an object is far more distracting than it would be between objects.

To create "seamless" patterns, many designers split each tile in the middle of an object rather than at its edge. When the object matches with the other half of the object in the abutting tile, an illusion of flow is maintained. The eye is prevented from seeing any place that the pattern could be split vertically. In the top example in Figure 13.13, the black and white blocks align, allowing the eye to see a potential seam between tiles. In the bottom example, a "seamless" pattern, no such break is visible between tiles. This illusion is maintained because the top block and bottom block do not align. The original patterns for the two lines are shown below with their bounding boxes visible.

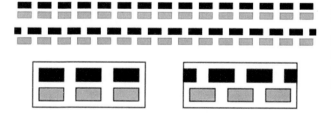

Figure 13.13
The two lines of blocks are actually the same length, although the upper line looks shorter because of the whitespace at the end of the tiles.

In addition to the decorative borders with which you are familiar, brush patterns can serve in more mundane (yet important) ways. Maps, for example, can contain patterned lines that represent such things as warm and cold fronts (weather maps), unit sector borders and minefields (military maps), and, of course, the borders that appear on political maps. Figure 13.14 shows some examples of various possible delineation and border patterns, along with examples of their side tiles.

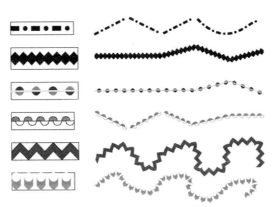

Figure 13.14
Using pattern brushes is the easiest way to make and store such delineation markers.

The first example in Figure 13.14 is a very basic combination of rectangles and circles. The second through fourth examples were created with two filled paths (the third pattern also has a third path for the yellow line). The bottom pattern is created with basic shapes. Note that items of similar color are grouped individually to ensure that they are on the same stacking order to simplify the pattern. Observe how the lack of corner tiles in the first, fourth, and fifth examples results in irregular spacing when the path changes direction sharply. (Creation of corner tiles is discussed in the next section.) Also note how irregular spacing is not a problem with the bottom example, which consists of discrete objects rather than a continuous segment.

Maps can also contain features such as roads, railroads, rivers, and other items that may be a bit more complex. See Figure 13.15 for some samples.

Figure 13.15
Brush patterns differ in complexity, resulting in a variety of potential concerns.

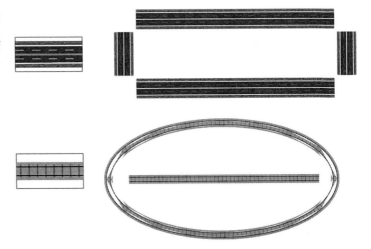

These two examples are a bit more complex and require some additional effort to design. So that the complexity of the top pattern was minimized, layered lines of varying sizes were used, rather than duplicating the edge lines and center lines. Although both of these samples appear fine in the horizontal and vertical, the lack of corner tiles ruins the effect for rectangles and ovals.

Creating Brush Pattern Corner Tiles

As you saw previously in this chapter, corner tiles are an important part of most (but not all) brush patterns that are applied to curves and shapes. Corners come in two types: outer and inner. (Refer to Figure 13.7 for a visual depiction of the difference.) The construction of a corner tile can be a very simple or an arduous task, depending in part on the complexity of the pattern. Using a simple pattern, you can examine many of the techniques of corner construction.

Remember that a corner tile's bounding box must be square to properly match both the vertical and horizontal side tiles. The center of the corner pattern will be centered on the adjoining sides.

In Figure 13.16, you can see how Illustrator handles curves differently from actual corners. The star pattern was added as a corner tile to the pattern brush. When the Pen tool is used with this pattern, corner tiles are placed only where corner anchor points exist. When smooth anchor points are created, the pattern continues without a corner tile.

Figure 13.16
Chapter 4, "Creating and Editing Paths," described the difference between a corner anchor point and smooth anchor point. These two examples show yet another reason why the difference is important.

If you want to explore the differences among square, curved, and angled corners, a continuous pattern is suitable. The pattern in Figure 13.17 is constructed of two stacked lines. The bottom line is 21 points wide, and the top is 7 points. The corner tiles are shown below, with bounding boxes simulated by dashed lines. The square and curved corner tiles are also two stacked lines with the same stroke specifications as the side tile. The angled corner, however, requires (at a minimum) that a path be drawn from corner to corner for each of the two lines, as shown in Figure 13.18.

Figure 13.17
These three objects use the same side tiles, but the corner tiles differ as shown.

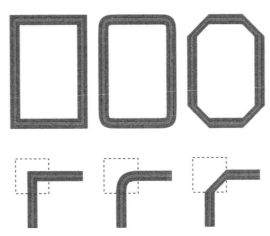

Each of the two lines of the square corner tile's path was constructed with the Pen tool and consists of a simple three-point open path with corner anchor points. The curved corner tile is a two-point open path with smooth anchor points on each end. The angled corner tile was constructed by making paths that outline the two lines (see Figure 13.18).

Figure 13.18
This image represents the paths required to produce the angled corner tile in Figure 13.17.

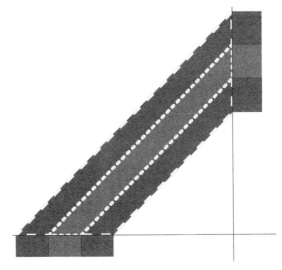

The dashed lines indicate the two paths that were drawn with the Pen tool to create the two lines. Both of the paths are set to a stroke of None and the appropriate fill color. With a stroke of None, the corners of the paths can easily match those of the horizontal and vertical side tiles. With a positive value for the stroke, the line caps force the edges beyond the desired point of junction.

Note that the angled corner tile in Figures 13.17 and 13.18 has thinner lines than the side tiles. To compensate for the angle, the outer edges of each line must be offset slightly. Figure 13.19 shows the difference.

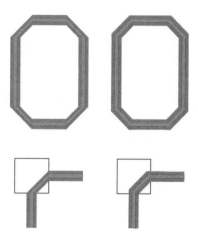

Figure 13.19
Notice the difference when angled corners are offset to maintain line width (right).

The corner tile on the left was drawn corner-to-corner (or point-to-point). Notice how much thinner the lines are across the angle than they are in the vertical and horizontal. To maintain the integrity of the pattern's lines (or other elements in various patterns), the outer edges of the lines must be extended slightly beyond the point where the inner edge angles away. Look at the corner tile on the right as three distinct lines, from the inner (right) side to the outer (left). The right edge of the right (innermost) line begins to angle from the bottom toward the top directly at the edge of the bounding box. The outer edge of the rightmost line proceeds vertically for a short distance before angling off. The edges of the other two lines follow similar patterns.

As you saw in Figure 13.19, drawing a path on an angle that maintains the width of the vertical and horizontal strokes is a bit more complicated than simply going corner-to-corner. The outer corners of the elements must be offset slightly, but how much is the question.

Here's an efficient technique to ensure that your angled corners maintain the integrity of your pattern. You should work within the document that you're using to create the elements of your brush pattern. Having the grid visible can make alignment much easier. The following example is based on the pattern shown on the right in Figure 13.19, but you can easily adapt it for other patterns.

1. Copy the pattern of your side tile by Option+dragging [Alt+dragging] to a free corner of the document. (This is the tile in the upper-right of Figure 13.20.)

2. With the side tile pattern still selected, choose Object, Transform, Rotate, or press R on the keyboard to select the Rotate tool. Then Option+click [Alt+click] the segment. Enter **90** degrees (or **-90** degrees, as appropriate) and click Copy in the dialog box. (This is the tile in the lower-center of Figure 13.20.)

3. Holding down the Shift key to constrain proportions to a square, use the Rectangle tool to draw a box to serve later as the bounding box of the corner tile. In this case, the box measures 1 inch by 1 inch.

4. Using the grid as a guide, position the two segments perpendicularly to each other at the centers of the bottom and right sides of the bounding box. (In Figure 13.20, they are the horizontal and vertical segments.)

5. Again using the Rotate tool, Option+click [Alt+click] the horizontal side segment. Enter 45 degrees (or -45 degrees) and again click Copy. This produces the segment that you will use as a template for your offset. (This is the angled segment shown in the center of Figure 13.20.)

6. With the angled copy still selected, press Cmd+X [Ctrl+X] to place the segment onto Illustrator's Clipboard.

7. In the Layers palette, click the New Layer button. (Layers are discussed in depth in Chapter 10, "Illustrator's Layers, Sublayers, and Groups.") If no other layers have yet been created in the document, this new layer is named Layer 2. Double-click the name in the Layers palette and rename the layer Angle Template or something similar.

8. Still in the Layers palette, drag the newly named layer below the layer upon which the pattern segments lie and release.

9. Ensuring that your new layer is active (highlighted in the Layers palette), press Cmd+F [Ctrl+F] to place the segment from Illustrator's Clipboard onto the front of your layer, in its original position. (This is a good time to save your document.)

10. Using the Selection tool (V), drag the angled segment to the point where its inner edge (the lower-right side) touches the inner corners of both the vertical and horizontal side tiles (see Figure 13.20).

Figure 13.20
It's not important whether the angled segment is centered. It should, however, overlap both the vertical and horizontal side tiles.

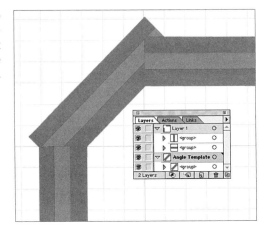

11. Returning to the Layers palette, create a third layer, name it as you will, and move it above the layer containing the original segments. This will be the layer upon which you actually create the corner tile.

12. Using the Pen tool, click the point where the inner corner of the vertical segment meets the inner corner of the angled segment (see Figure 13.21).

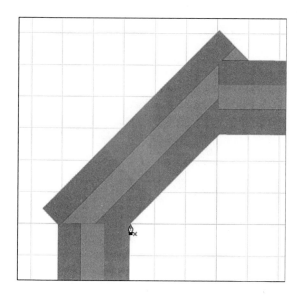

Figure 13.21
The starting point should be one that is easily identifiable, such as the inner junction of the template for the angled segment with the vertical or horizontal side tiles.

13. Click, in order, the point where the inner corners of the angled segment and the horizontal segment meet; the point in the horizontal segment where the lower and middle lines meet; and moving directly to the left (remaining horizontal) from that point, the start of the middle line in the angled segment. See Figure 13.22 for a view of how the path should look at this point.

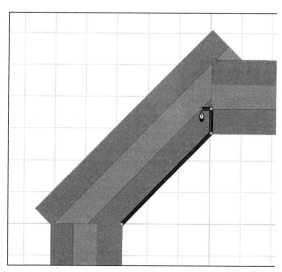

Figure 13.22
For the proper effect, it's important that the lower edge of the middle stripe be continued horizontally to the angled segment.

14. The next point on the path should be along the angled segment's middle line to the point where it is directly above the middle line of the vertical side tile. Figure 13.23 identifies the location.

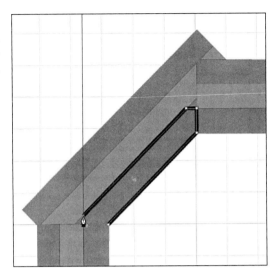

Figure 13.23
You can position a guide, as shown here, to help identify the exact position for a path point.

15. The last two points on the path should be directly below the previous point, at the end of the vertical side tile, and the point that closes the path. Ensure that the stroke of the path is then set to None. The completed path is shown in a contrasting color in Figure 13.24.

Figure 13.24
When the actual corner tile is created, this line will be the same color as the corresponding line of the side tiles.

16. Repeating the process for the other two lines of the angle segment should yield a result similar to that in Figure 13.25.

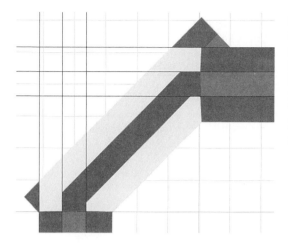

Figure 13.25
While the contrasting colors here are for illustration and are used on the angled segment that will become the corner tile, it is advisable to change the colors of the "template" segment on the lowest layer for improved contrast and ease of path creation.

17. Group the three paths, ensuring that their fill colors are correct and they are unstroked.

18. Delete all other artwork, with the exception of the bounding box. (That includes the "template" copy that was angled at 45% and the two original side tiles.)

19. Remember that the bounding box must have a fill and stroke of None and select it as well as the grouped paths.

20. Choose Edit, Define Pattern to create the swatch for your angled corner tile.

21. If your pattern is not symmetrical, you will also need an inner corner. Reflect the two side tiles and the "template" to reverse their patterns and repeat.

You can modify this technique to help maintain the proportions of virtually any pattern element in an angled corner tile. The keys to success are using layers to place your template below the layer upon which you are working and zooming to a view appropriate to the precision required. In cases of very fine detail, using transparency can be very helpful. Remember, though, to restore your artwork to the proper opacity upon completion.

A curved corner tile, in addition to being easier to create than an angled corner, is appropriate for many uses. Paths like the one shown in Figure 13.26 can use the same tile for both outer and inner curves.

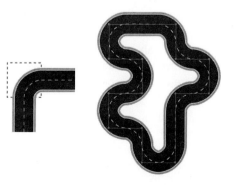

Figure 13.26
A simple curve can often be used for both inner and outer corner tiles.

The curved corner tile in Figure 13.26 was made by simply copying the side tile and curving it using a combination of the Direct Selection tool and the Convert Anchor Point tool. The Test Track path to the right is shown with the path itself selected.

Corner Bounding Boxes

Although the bounding box of a corner tile must be square, there is no requirement that it be the same size as the side tile's bounding box. Figure 13.27 shows how a corner tile can be of a substantially different size than the side tiles.

Figure 13.27
The corner tiles and their bounding boxes appear to the upper-left and lower-right.

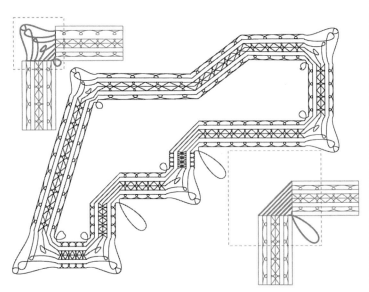

Notice how the bounding box of the outer corner tile (upper left) extends past the side tiles. The inner corner tile (lower right) is a much more dramatic example. The large amount of empty space in the inner corner's bounding box is required to ensure that the center of the bounding box aligns with the centers of both the horizontal and vertical side tiles.

Creating Brush Pattern Start and End Tiles

End tiles are required only when a brush pattern will be used with an open path, and not all patterns require end tiles for open paths. Unlike corner tiles, the bounding boxes of end tiles do not have to be square because they abut on only one side. Some patterns require closure at the start and end, such as those patterns that utilize a fine line or border near the top and bottom, and some patterns that are designed specifically for open paths. Figure 13.28 shows a couple of examples.

Because of the line at the top and bottom, the upper example requires end tiles when used with open paths. In this case, the start tile was simply reflected vertically to create the end tile. The lower example requires start and end tiles for obvious reasons. It does not require a corner tile because the side tile consists of a simple line.

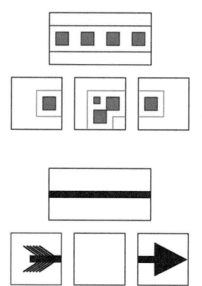

Figure 13.28
Both patterns show their side tile above and the start, corner, and end tiles below.

TROUBLESHOOTING

Trouble Defining Patterns

When I define a new pattern, sometimes all I get is a blank white box. Other times I get a border around my pattern that I don't want. What am I forgetting?

To ensure that your artwork actually becomes part of the pattern, make sure that the objects are selected (and grouping them is a good idea) before choosing Edit, Define Pattern. To avoid an unintended box around your pattern, check that your bounding box has a stroke (and fill) of None.

Expanding Patterns for Print

I send my image to the printer (or image setter), things start off fine, spooling is proceeding, and then everything locks up. What's the cure?

If the image contains complex patterns, blends, or gradients, select them and choose Object, Expand to create objects and paths from the more complex data. Printing should go much more smoothly.

Resizing Brush Patterns

I spent hours and hours designing the perfect pattern brush, but it looks terrible because it's too big to fit around my objects. Have I wasted all that time?

No, you haven't. In the Brushes palette, double-click your design. When the Pattern Brush Options dialog box opens, reduce the percentage in the box labeled Scale.

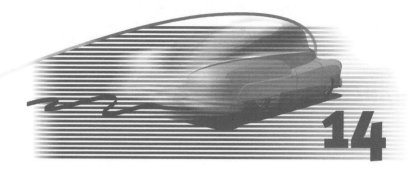

USING THE APPEARANCE AND STYLES PALETTES

IN THIS CHAPTER

Appearances and Styles   324

The Appearance Palette   326

The Appearance Palette Menu   329

Applying Appearances to Groups and Layers   331

The Styles Palette   333

Style Libraries   334

Troubleshooting   335

Appearances and styles are among the most powerful tools in Illustrator. They allow you to change the look of objects without actually changing the objects themselves. You can later edit the original object and have all the appearances update themselves automatically. Whether you need to change the size, shape, color, or effects applied to an object, the other characteristics will conform to the new look. They can be applied to objects, groups, or layers.

APPEARANCES AND STYLES

Appearance characteristics are applied to objects and groups and can be assigned to layers. Fill color, gradient, and pattern; stroke color, weight, and brush; effects; and transparency are all appearance characteristics. A selected object's characteristics are shown in the Appearance palette (see Figure 14.1).

Figure 14.1
This is a single object, a rectangle, with multiple appearance characteristics.

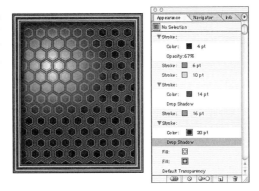

Appearance characteristics are sometimes referred to as appearance *attributes*. However, because that term is also used in Illustrator to refer to the Attributes palette (which contains printing and imagemap information), the term *characteristic* will be used throughout this discussion.

Styles are the various appearance characteristics, collected, named, and saved in the Styles palette. You can apply a style by selecting an object and clicking the style in the palette. Developing consistency and ease of application are the two main reasons to use styles. Style libraries can be loaded when needed, and custom libraries can be saved and opened in other documents.

In Figure 14.2, you can see that the little window has the same characteristics as the larger window. Instead of being applied individually, these characteristics are from a custom style named Grated Moon.

If you've created elaborate appearances or styles and now your document won't print, see "Expanding Appearances" in the "Troubleshooting" section at the end of this chapter.

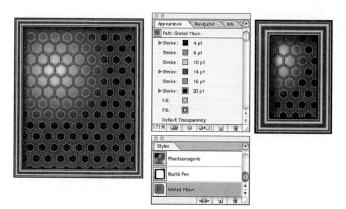

Figure 14.2
Notice that the name of the style is visible to the right of Path in the Appearance palette.

THE APPEARANCE PALETTE

The Appearance palette shows a list of every characteristic of the selected object or group. Before you even create an object, the Appearance palette is recording the characteristics: The current fill, stroke, and transparency settings are automatically tracked in the palette (see Figure 14.3).

Figure 14.3
The Appearance palette allows you to track various settings even when the individual palettes are not visible. For example, a glance at the Appearance palette can tell you the current settings in the Color, Stroke, and Transparency palettes.

The Appearance palette also allows you to view a layer's characteristics. In addition to fill, stroke, and transparency, any effects are shown (see Figure 14.4). (Effects and filters are discussed in Chapter 20, "Using Filters and Effects." See also the sidebar "Effects Versus Filters.")

 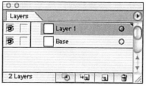

Figure 14.4
Any object created on or moved to this layer assumes the layer's characteristics, which are shown in the Appearance palette.

Effects Versus Filters

Illustrator supports a wide range of effects and filters. Discussed in Chapter 20, they can change the appearance of an object or group in many ways. Of key importance to a discussion of appearances and styles is the primary difference between effects and filters.

When something is applied as an effect rather than as a filter, you can edit or remove changes by using the Appearance palette. The effects of a filter, on the other hand, cannot be altered or removed except with the Undo command.

A filter, when applied, changes an object. If you apply the command Filter, Distort, Punk & Bloat to a rectangle, the object's path, which is virtually impossible to determine from this image, is permanently changed (see Figure 14.5).

Figure 14.5
When you're distorting with a filter, you can return the path's anchor points and control lines to their original positions only by using the Undo command.

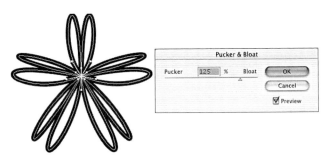

In comparison, when you're applying the same distortion as an effect, the path's anchor points and control lines are not changed; merely the appearance is altered. In Figure 14.6, notice that the effect's preview does not show new anchor points, as does the filter's preview. The original object's shape, now visible as a star, is unchanged by the effect.

Figure 14.6
The preview shows the appearance change rather than an actual change in the object itself.

In Figure 14.7, the characteristic Punk & Bloat was double-clicked in the Appearance palette to reopen the effect's dialog box. The setting can now be changed, and the object's appearance will be automatically updated. To remove an effect from an object, drag it to the trash can or use the palette menu command Remove Item.

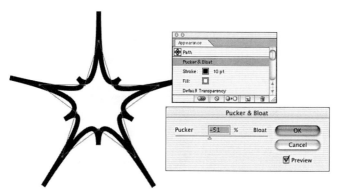

Figure 14.7
Any changes are automatically reflected in the object.

Filters applied to an object or a group cannot be reversed, as can effects. They, therefore, are not visible in the Appearance palette. You may, however, see one or more of the filter's options listed. They include settings that override the layer's setting, such as transparency. Figure 14.8 shows an application of a drop shadow as a filter. The drop shadow actually becomes rasterized pixels with an assigned opacity, which can be changed through the Appearance palette.

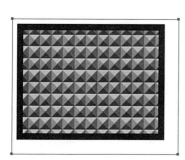

Figure 14.8
The drop shadow's opacity and blending mode differ from that of the layer, so they are listed. Even though a filter was applied, double-clicking allows you to change the settings.

When several appearance characteristics have been applied to a single object, they often interact. For example, the weight of a stroke may determine the impact of artistic effects. Changing one characteristic allows you to alter the entire appearance. In Figure 14.9, the weight of the stroke has been changed from 1 point (left) to 4 points (right), strengthening the impact of the effects.

The order of the effects in the palette can also make a difference in the appearance of an object. The lower an effect is in the Appearance palette, the later it was applied. Effects are applied to all existing artwork, so a later effect is applied on top of an earlier effect. In Figure 14.10, on the right, the Ocean Ripple effect has been dragged above the Colored Pencil and Neon Glow effects.

You can drag an object's appearance from the Appearance palette to another object. Grab the icon to the left of the word `Object` and drag it to an object on the artboard. The source object should be selected; the destination object should not be selected.

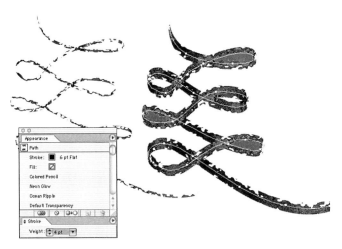

Figure 14.9
Colored Pencil and Neon Glow are Artistic effects, whereas Ocean Ripple is located under the Effects menu's Distort submenu.

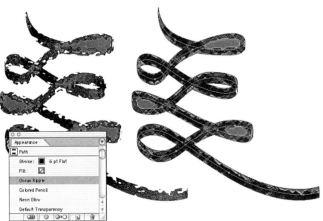

Figure 14.10
Altering the order in which effects are applied can dramatically change an object's appearance.

Effects can also be applied to just a fill or a stroke, without affecting the other. In Figure 14.11, a fill has been added to the artwork. For the image on the left, the Appearance palette would show, in order, Stroke, Fill, Colored Pencil, Neon Glow, Ocean Ripple, and Default Transparency. Notice that for the image on the right, the Neon Glow effect has been moved in the Appearance palette and now is applied only to the stroke.

Moving the Ocean Ripple effect in the Appearance palette so that it is applied only to the fill further changes the appearance of the object. Figure 14.12 shows both the result and the change to the Appearance palette.

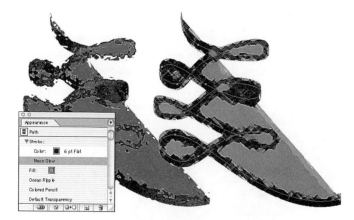

Figure 14.11
Effects can be subsetted in the palette, which applies them only to the stroke or the fill.

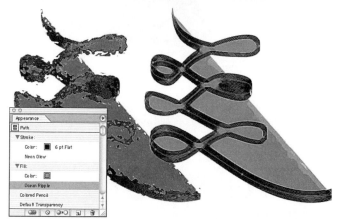

Figure 14.12
Both the stroke and the fill can have effects applied individually.

THE APPEARANCE PALETTE MENU

You can access the Appearance palette menu (shown in Figure 14.13) through the small triangle in the upper-right corner of the palette.

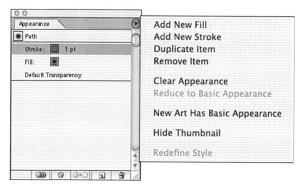

Figure 14.13
Not all the commands are available at all times. Some might be grayed out because they cannot be applied to the current selection.

The commands Add New Fill and Add New Stroke actually adds another fill or stroke on top of the one or more strokes already in place for an object. In Figure 14.14, several strokes have been layered to the road. Although you could create the same appearance by creating several objects and aligning them next to each other, there is no reason why you cannot do it by layering strokes in a single object.

Figure 14.14
Layering strokes and fills can create complex appearances for a single object.

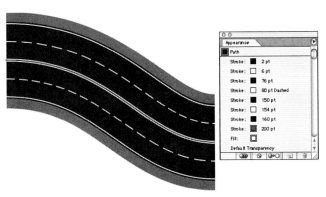

Text Effects with the Appearance Palette

Using the Appearance palette, you can create superior text effects. You can add additional strokes and fills to type objects, as shown in Figure 14.15.

Figure 14.15
The type object remains editable.

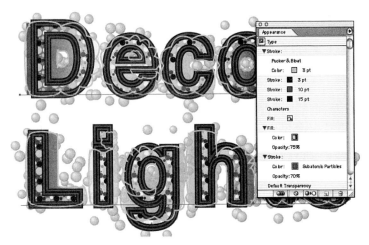

Remember that you can also add brushes to an appearance or style. However, keep in mind that you cannot apply multiple strokes and fills to the text within type objects. The appearance characteristics can be applied to the container, but the text inside the container will accept only one stroke and one fill. When you're creating complex text, it's usually best to choose Object, Expand Appearance before you print.

➡ *There is a difference between multiple appearance charac-teristics and a style. See "Appearances Versus Styles" in the "Troubleshooting" section at the end of this chapter.*

The Appearance palette com-mands Duplicate Item and Remove Item and their button counterparts use the term *item* to refer to a specific appearance characteristic, such as a stroke, fill, or effect. The object on the artboard is not duplicated or removed, simply the one charac-teristic.

To duplicate or delete an object or group, use the Layers palette.

You can duplicate individual appearance characteristics by using the Duplicate Item command from the Appearance palette menu or by dragging to the Duplicate button at the bottom of the palette. You can also remove an appearance characteristic by using a menu command or the appropriate button at the bottom of the palette.

The commands Clear Appearance and Reduce to Basic Appearance are similar and can have the same effect. However, if an object or group is on a layer to which appearance characteristics have been applied, the two commands perform different jobs. Clear Appearance reduces an object to a fill and stroke of None, and it will show only characteristics targeted to the layer that the object is on. Reduce to Basic Appearance removes targeted effects and appearance characteristics and the object retains its originally assigned fill and stroke.When selected, the Appearance palette's command New Art Has Basic Appearance has a check mark next to it in the menu. When this option is checked, any new objects will have the fill and stroke active in the Toolbox (plus any characteristics applied to the layer). When this option is unchecked, new objects will assume the characteristics of that object most recently created or edited.

The command Layer/Group Overrides Color makes the group or layer characteristics superior to those of the object. When an object is moved onto a layer or into a group that has assigned characteristics, it will assume those characteristics (until removed from the group or layer). When this option is not selected (no check mark appears next to its name in the menu), the object will retain its own stroke, fill, transparency, and effects when moved to a new layer or group.

The Appearance palette also allows you to show or hide thumbnails and replace a style in the Styles palette. When a selected object has an assigned style and a modification has been made, the menu offers you the option of updating the style in the Styles palette. Doing so updates all objects with the assigned style to the new appearance. (Styles will be discussed later in this chapter.)

APPLYING APPEARANCES TO GROUPS AND LAYERS

Just as appearance characteristics can be applied to objects, they also can be applied to groups and layers. By default, any object added to that group or layer is automatically updated to show the appearance characteristics assigned. Conversely, any object removed from a group or layer that has assigned characteristics loses them. As discussed earlier, this is controlled in part by the Appearance palette's menu command Layer/Group Overrides Color. Figure 14.16 shows some of the possibilities when this option is active.

Figure 14.16
The objects and Layers palette on
the right reflect several changes.

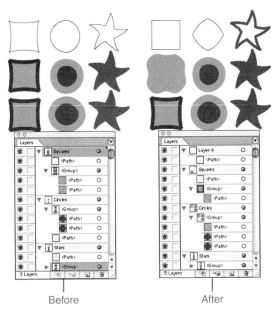

Before   After

The original objects (on the left in Figure 14.16) have been arranged with several conventions to clarify this demonstration:

- The top three objects have the default black stroke and white fill.

- All like shapes are on the same layer.

- Fills were assigned to individual objects.

- Strokes (both color and weight) were assigned to the groups.

- Effects were assigned to layers.

For the set of images on the right, several changes were made in the Layers palette, changing the appearance of the objects:

- A new layer (Layer 4), with no assigned attributes, was created.

- The top square was moved to the new layer. Its appearance remains unchanged.

- One square was moved from its group to the group on the Circles layer in the Layers palette. That square left behind the stroke of its original group, as well as the effect of the Squares layer. It assumes the stroke of the group on the Circles layer, as well as that layer's effect.

- The empty circle was moved in the Layers palette to the Squares layer, but not into the group on that layer. It therefore adopts the effect from the layer, but no stroke.

- The empty star remained on the Stars layer but was moved into the group. It adopts the stroke of the group.

⇨ *Confused by how appearances work with groups and layers? See "Stationary Characteristics" in the "Troubleshooting" section at the end of this chapter.*

THE STYLES PALETTE

Styles are collections of appearance characteristics (attributes) that are named and saved and can be applied together to an object or a group, or assigned to a layer. Styles can be saved in the Styles palette, and collections of styles (called *libraries*) can be loaded into a document.

Because styles are based on appearance characteristics, they can be edited and reversed later, even after the file has been closed and reopened. Styles themselves can be deleted, duplicated, and edited and reapplied.

To create a style, you need not have an object selected on the artboard. In fact, you can develop a style before you even create an object. Stroke color, weight, and brush; fill color, pattern, and gradient; and effects can all be selected without an object in the document. After you make these choices, you can click the New Style button at the bottom of the Styles palette or select the New Style command from the palette's menu. Likewise, clicking the button or selecting the command creates a new style from a selected object's appearance characteristics.

Several guidelines affect styles:

* Styles can include strokes, fills, effects, patterns, gradients, blending modes, and transformations.

* Styles are nondestructive. The original object is not changed; merely its appearance is changed. When a style is removed, an object reverts to the basic appearance (black stroke, white fill, 100% opacity).

* To apply a style to a selected object, group, or layer, you simply click it in the Styles palette. You can also apply a style by dragging it from the palette onto an object.

* You can apply a style to layers, groups, objects, or type (although some restrictions apply with type).

* When you're applying a style to type, you must select the entire type object. Styles cannot be applied to individual words or characters within a text object.

* You cannot apply a style to fixed-outline (outline-protected) fonts or bitmap fonts.

* You can apply multiple fills (with transparency) and strokes to a style.

* You can change a style globally; that is, when you modify a style, all objects, groups, and layers to which it has been applied are automatically updated.

* When you apply a style to a layer, any object added to the layer adopts the style.

* Selecting an object and changing an attribute break the link between that object and the style. The attributes of the style remain (unless changed), but if the style is modified, that object is not updated.

- The Styles palette can display swatches of each style or list them by name with a large or small thumbnail.

- You can apply a style by selecting an object (or targeting a group or layer in the Layers palette) and clicking the style in the Styles palette. A style can be dragged from the palette onto an object, whether or not the object has been selected.

- To create a new style, assign the desired attributes to an object and drag the object to the Styles palette or the New Style button at the bottom of the palette.

- Double-clicking a style in the palette opens the Style Options dialog box, allowing you to rename it.

- Choosing New Style from the Styles palette menu allows you to name a style while you're creating it.

- Option+dragging [Alt+dragging] an object from the artboard on top of a style in the Styles palette globally replaces that style with the new.

- Using the Appearance palette command Replace (Style) also creates a global change.

- You can delete styles from the palette by selecting them and then clicking the Delete Style button at the bottom of the palette, or by dragging them to the button's trash icon.

- You can select multiple styles in the Styles palette by Cmd+clicking [Ctrl+clicking].

- You can select multiple styles and use the command Merge Styles from the palette menu to create a new style with all the other styles' attributes.

- You can duplicate a style by using the Duplicate Style command from the palette menu or by dragging the style to the New Style button at the bottom of the palette. The duplicate style, which you can use as a template for a new style, will have the original style's name, followed by a numeral.

- You can disassociate a style from all objects, groups, and layers by highlighting it in the palette and clicking the Break Link to Style button at the bottom of the palette. There will no longer be a connection with objects, groups, or layers that have the style applied. The palette menu contains the comparable command.

STYLE LIBRARIES

Illustrator installs, by default, several libraries of styles. One appears in the Styles palette; the others are available to load from the Adobe Illustrator folder on the hard drive. The default library for the document's color mode is automatically loaded when the file is opened (unless the document has been saved with changes made to the Styles palette).

The Styles palette menu offers the command Select All Unused. Selecting and then deleting styles that aren't used in a document slims the document a little, and it streamlines the Styles palette. This is especially useful when a document contains numerous custom styles.

The command Window, Style Libraries allows you to add additional sets of styles to the document. The libraries appear in a separate floating palette. Although the available libraries for CMYK and RGB documents are parallel, they are not identical. Figure 14.17 shows the basic complement of CMYK styles.

When a style from an additional library is used in the document, it is automatically copied to the document's Styles palette. It is then saved with the document. If the style is discontinued in the document, it is not automatically deleted from the palette.

When a style has been created and saved in another document, you can load it by choosing Window, Style Libraries, Other. You must then navigate to the document in the dialog box and select it. The styles available in that document (including default styles, if loaded into the document's Styles palette) are loaded. They, like other loaded libraries, appear in a separate floating palette. And, also like other libraries, when a style is used in a document, it is added to the document's Styles palette.

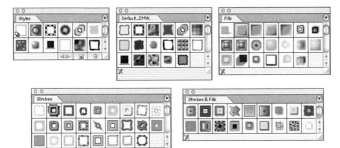

Figure 14.17
Other than the Styles palette itself (upper left), these palettes are opened using the menu command Window, Style Libraries.

TROUBLESHOOTING

Expanding Appearances

I've spent a lot of time getting my appearances just right, but now the illustration doesn't output. Have I wasted my time?

Appearances and styles can be expanded to simplify printing. Expanding (by choosing Object, Expand Appearance) creates a separate object from each stroke and fill of the object. The various components maintain the assigned effects and brushes. Figure 14.18 shows an example.

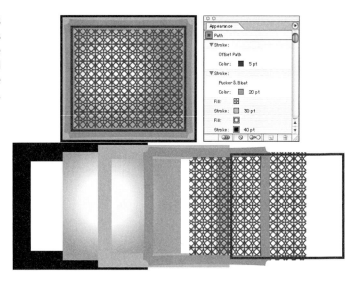

Figure 14.18
The object above, whose various characteristics are shown in the Appearance palette, is expanded and separated below to show the individual objects.

Appearances Versus Styles

I've assigned multiple strokes and fills to my object. Is that a style or not?

It's not a style until you give it a name and save it in the Styles palette. Until then, you've got an object, group, or layer with a bunch of appearance characteristics.

Stationary Characteristics

How do appearances and styles work with layers and groups? When does an object change and when doesn't it?

The layer or group can be assigned appearance characteristics. When an object is added to the layer or group, it puts on that appearance, just like slipping on the blazer from your new country club. If you are asked to leave the country club, you'll take off the jacket. So, too, will an object moved from a layer or group leave behind appearances assigned to the group or layer. However, you were wearing your own slacks and shirt when you put on that blazer and, so too, will the object retain any characteristics it had before being added to the group or layer.

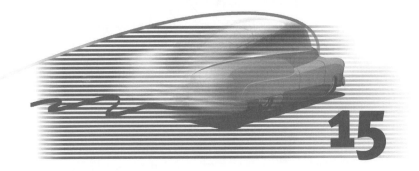

THE GRADIENT AND GRADIENT MESH TOOLS

IN THIS CHAPTER

Working with Gradients **338**

Gradient Meshes **343**

Troubleshooting **352**

WORKING WITH GRADIENTS

The Gradient and Gradient Mesh tools produce blends between colors. These subtle blends from one color to another help Illustrator produce the illusion of three dimensions and light. These tools enable you to produce top-notch illustrations. The simple addition of a gradient or two can change a piece of flat, two-dimensional artwork into an image with depth and perspective. Figure 15.1 shows the difference between a couple shapes filled with color and those same shapes filled with simple gradients.

Figure 15.1
The addition of gradients gives the illusion that the "pipe" is round and hollow.

Gradients are blends of two or more colors, either in a straight line or as concentric rings of color. Gradient meshes, on the other hand, allow you to blend numerous colors, and at whatever angle is necessary. In addition to being used to portray depth, gradients and meshes can be decorative. In Figure 15.2, a gradient mesh is used to portray a flame.

Figure 15.2
From the left, the basic star, the gradient mesh object, and a view of the mesh paths that create the design.

Gradients and meshes, however useful, can present some production problems. You might need to rasterize them before printing. The Document Settings dialog box contains fields for automatically selecting rasterization resolutions for gradients and gradient mesh objects. You can find them in the Printing & Export panel.

Gradients are designed and applied primarily through the Gradient palette, Color palette, Swatches palette, and Gradient tool. The Gradient palette determines which type of gradient you will be using and, in conjunction with the Color and Swatches palettes, allows you to customize the colors and blending. Also valuable in the development of a gradient are the Transparency and Appearance palettes and the Object and Effect menus.

After you design gradients, you can save them in the Swatches palette for future use. You can load them, like any swatches, into the current document from another by choosing Window, Swatch Libraries, Load Library.

The Anatomy of a Gradient

Whether linear or radial, a gradient can contain numerous colors, but only two colors can be blended at a time. A single color in the middle of a gradient blends with each color on either side, but each side blends independently. For example, in Figure 15.3, the gradient goes between left and right, through the color in the center. However, this is (for practical purposes) not one gradient, but two color blends. The color on the left blends with the color in the center. And then it stops. That color does not continue past the midpoint. The center color then blends with the color on the right. At no time does the color on the left pass through the center; at no time does the color on the right pass through the center.

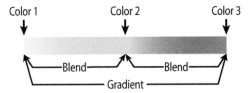

Figure 15.3
Each gradient is a series of colors, blended two at a time.

The point in a gradient that represents an unblended color is called a *stop*. From the stop, the color then begins to blend with the neighboring color. A gradient can have as many color stops as you would like, although there is a practical limit of about 25. More than that and the gradient bar in the Gradient palette gets too crowded to select individual stops. You can add (and delete) stops in the Gradient palette and control them by using the sliders (see Figure 15.4).

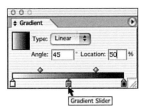

Figure 15.4
Each gradient slider represents a color stop.

A stop consists of a small square color swatch and the triangle above it. A darkened triangle, as shown for the middle stop in Figure 15.4, represents the active stop. The stop's location, given in percent, is shown in the palette. You can drag stops to reposition them. Option+dragging [Alt+dragging] a stop duplicates it.

The diamond above the gradient bar represents the 50% point between two colors. At this point, the two colors being blended are at equal strength. You can reposition it by dragging, which changes the distribution of the blend. As you drag it, the Location field is updated to show the position of the midpoint between the two color stops (in percent).

The Angle field represents the direction of the gradient when applied (see Figure 15.5). Rather than a particular gradient slider, this field affects the entire gradient. Dragging from left to right on the artboard creates an angle of 0, and the colors blend in that direction. Angle is available only for linear gradients.

Figure 15.5
The Angle field in the Gradient
palette determines the direction of
the blends.

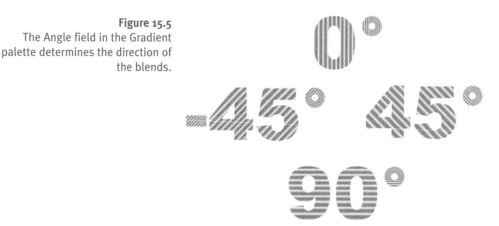

The Gradient palette shows you a thumbnail of your work. As you add, move, and change stops and midpoints, Illustrator updates the preview in the upper-left corner of the palette.

Using the Gradient Sliders

The area between two stops on a gradient slider is blended from one color to the other seamlessly. The default gradient has two color stops, one at each end. They are black and white, and their color mode is grayscale. When you're creating a custom gradient, it is often easier to use one from the Swatches palette as a starting point.

To edit an existing gradient or create a new one, choose Linear or Radial from the Gradient palette's Type pop-up menu. Choosing one of these options automatically makes the default or last-used gradient the fill and makes it available in the palette for editing. Most of the changes to a gradient are made through the sliders. Several rules govern changes to them:

- You can copy an existing color stop (with its assigned color value) by Option+dragging [Alt+dragging] it along the gradient bar. You can drag past an existing stop to place the new stop.

- You can click any place along the gradient bar to add a new color stop. It automatically assumes the color value directly above it.

- To change the color of a stop, click it and use the Color palette. If the Color palette isn't visible, double-click the slider.

- To delete a stop, drag it off the bar.

The gradient bar in the Gradient palette is rather small, which makes it difficult to see subtle changes in the gradient as you edit. When you're creating a new gradient, you can get a good look at your changes by creating a large rectangle on the artboard (perhaps on a new layer) and filling it with the gradient. As long as the rectangle is selected, the changes made in the Gradient palette are shown. If the gradient is to be applied to existing objects, select them before editing the gradient to see the changes as they're made.

- You can drag a swatch from the Swatches palette onto a stop to change its color.

- Option+clicking [Alt+clicking] a swatch in the Swatches palette assigns that color to a selected stop in the Gradient palette.

- You can drag a swatch from the Swatches palette directly onto the gradient bar to create a new stop of that color.

- You cannot have a color stop with a color value of None, nor can you use patterns or other gradients in a gradient.

- You can assign the locations of stops precisely by clicking a stop and typing the location (in percent) in the Location field.

If you plan to create a complex gradient, create swatches for the stops first. Using the Color palette, define each color and then add it to the Swatches palette by clicking the New Swatch button. After you have all the colors you need, creating the new gradient is simply a matter of dragging the swatches to the gradient bar in the Gradient palette.

By default, the blend is smooth and consistent, with the midpoint representing 50% of each color value. You can adjust the flow from one color to another by dragging the slider positioned above the gradient bars. You cannot drag the slider closer than 13% to either color stop. (Less than 13% gives a severe and distinct change in color, with little or no blending.)

⇨ *Do you have gradients that print okay but look lousy onscreen? Check "Monitor Settings" in the "Troubleshooting" section at the end of this chapter.*

Saving and Applying Gradients

After you create a gradient, you can save it in the Swatches palette for future use:

- Drag the gradient thumbnail from the Gradient palette to the Swatches palette.

- Drag the gradient swatch from the Fill swatch of the Toolbox or Color palette to the Swatches palette.

- Click the New Swatch button at the bottom of the Swatches palette.

- Use the command New Swatch from the Swatches palette menu (which you access by clicking the black triangle in the upper-right corner of the palette).

Gradients added to the Swatches palette in one document can be used in other documents. Choose Window, Swatch Libraries, Other Library and navigate to the file that contains the gradients. That file's gradients, along with all other swatches, are loaded into a separate floating palette. Swatches can be dragged from that palette into the Swatches palette, or they can be applied directly to an object. After a swatch (a gradient or any other swatch) is applied to an object from the new palette, it is added to the open document's Swatches palette.

After you create gradients, you can apply them to one or more objects in various ways:

- Select one or more objects on the artboard and click the gradient swatch at the bottom of the Toolbox, the gradient swatch in the Gradient palette, or the gradient swatch in the Swatches palette (if the gradient has been saved).

- Dragging the Gradient tool applies the current gradient to an object.

Linear Versus Radial

A linear gradient blends colors in straight lines, whether vertically, horizontally, or at an angle. Radial gradients use concentric circles. They are designed and constructed in the Gradient palette the same way. When you use the Gradient tool to create a linear gradient, the color on the left of the gradient bar (in the Gradient palette) is the start point and appears at the place clicked. With radial gradients, that point is the center of the gradient. That point does not have to be located in the center of the object. You can drag from any point, including outside the image, to create the effect you want. Figure 15.6 shows how both radial and linear gradients are dragged.

Figure 15.6
The Gradient tool was dragged along the dashed line. Note that in both cases, it was dragged from left to right.

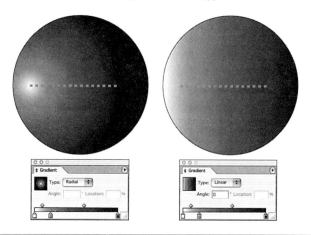

- If you select more than one object, the Gradient tool creates a gradient that encompasses the entire area of the selected objects. Parts of the gradients appear, as appropriate, in the selected objects. Figure 15.7 shows the difference. To the left, the gradient is applied to each object individually. To the right, the gradient works on the objects as a single entity.

Figure 15.7
The same gradient as it appears on individual objects and on a collection of objects.

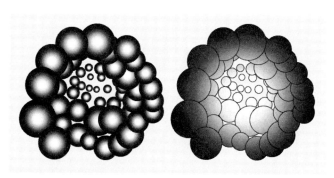

- You can reapply a gradient by redragging the Gradient tool.

- The direction in which you drag the tool determines the direction in which the gradient's colors are applied.

- The angle at which you drag the tool determines the angle of a linear gradient, and is shown in the Gradient palette.

- Shift+dragging constrains the Gradient tool to 45° angles.

- You can start dragging the Gradient tool from outside the object or from well inside the object. A gradient need not be applied from stroke-to-stroke. Areas before the start or after the end of the drag are the color of the last stop.

Combining Gradients

You can create complex patterns of gradients by layering fills within an object. In the Appearance palette, you can add additional fills to a selected object. (The Appearance palette menu command Add New Fill adds a fill to the palette.) Gradients are assigned to fills by selecting the fill in the Appearance palette and dragging the Gradient tool or clicking on the appropriate gradient in the Swatches palette.

If you use lessening opacity from bottom to top, a number of gradients can interact in a single object. Before you print, however, such an object is a likely candidate for high-resolution rasterization. Figure 15.8 shows several radial gradients applied to the same object. In the Appearance palette, note that the opacity of each layer is low, allowing those below to show through.

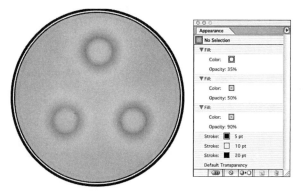

Figure 15.8
The higher the gradient is in the stacking order, the lower the opacity. The center points of the three radial gradients are identifiable as concentric circles.

GRADIENT MESHES

Gradient mesh objects can be created from vector objects or raster images embedded in an Illustrator document. A mesh is a single object with colors blending in various directions. The difference between objects with gradient fills and gradient mesh objects is shown in Figure 15.9.

A gradient mesh is created from an existing object or image and can then be edited. *Mesh points*, which control the placement of color, can be added, deleted, and moved, and the color can be changed, as can the spread of the color. The mesh points, which appear on *mesh lines*, appear as diamonds rather than squares on the lines. Regular anchor points (seen as squares) can also appear, but they lack the capability of affecting color.

Figure 15.9
To the left are simple gradients. In the center are gradient mesh objects created from those gradients. To the right, the meshes used to create the objects are visible.

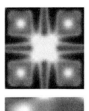
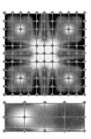

Creating Gradient Mesh Objects

With an object or embedded raster image selected, you can create a gradient mesh in three ways:

- Choose Object, Create Gradient Mesh.

- Click the object's stroke or fill with the Gradient Mesh tool.

- If the object is filled with a gradient, you can choose Object, Expand and then choose the Gradient Mesh option.

Caution

When an object is turned into a gradient mesh object, only the Undo command can convert it back to its original state. There is no way to convert a mesh object to a vector object. For that reason, it is usually a good idea to work with a copy of an object, with the original hidden away on an invisible layer.

When you use the Create Gradient Mesh command, you can specify the number of rows and columns and what type of mesh to start with in the resulting dialog box. The options are shown in Figure 15.10.

Figure 15.10
When applied to a vector object, the Create Gradient Mesh command produces either a solid color (Flat) or a two-color gradient (To Center, To Edge), no matter what the object's original fill. Colors in rasterized objects retain their general locations when a gradient mesh object is created with either of the latter Appearance options.

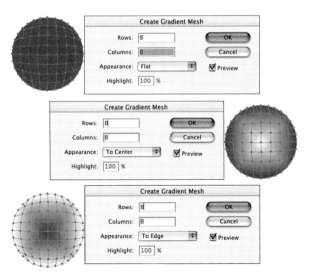

Although *Rows* and *Columns* are handy terms to work with, they actually refer to the spaces between the lines. A gradient mesh object is controlled with the points at the intersections of the lines.

When you select Flat for Appearance, the gradient mesh object has a solid color fill, the same color as the original object's fill. When you select To Edge or To Center, that color is blended in a gradient with a shade of itself determined by the Highlight percentage. A value of 100% produces white; lesser values give you a color closer to the original. When you're working with spot colors, tints are produced.

Using the Gradient Mesh tool to produce a mesh object is simply a matter of clicking the object's fill or path. When you click the fill, a pair of mesh lines with a single mesh anchor is produced. When you click a path (stroked or unstroked), a single mesh line, perpendicular to the path, is created. Figure 15.11 shows both a fill and a path that have been clicked.

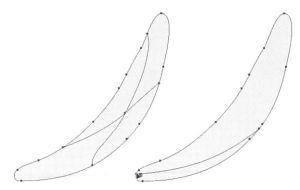

Figure 15.11
The Gradient Mesh tool was clicked in the center of the object on the left. The cursor indicates where the path was clicked on the object on the right.

After you use the Gradient Mesh tool to click an object, it is converted into a mesh object. You can use the Gradient Mesh tool only on vector objects; it is not available for raster images.

When you expand a gradient object using the command Object, Expand (see Figure 15.12), the option to create a gradient mesh object is available. Although the dialog box seems to indicate that both the fill and stroke can be used to create a mesh object, only the fill is actually available. (Remember that Illustrator does not allow gradient strokes.)

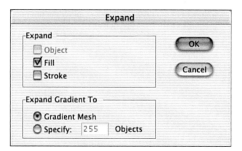

Figure 15.12
The Stroke option is designed for use with the Specify field, which you can use to create a specific number of objects from a gradient. It has no effect on the Gradient Mesh option.

When you use the Expand command to create a gradient mesh object, the object is given mesh lines that correspond to the color stops in the gradient. That pertains to both radial and linear gradients, as shown in Figure 15.13.

Figure 15.13
The mesh lines are visible, along with their mesh points. Note that the original rectangle shape serves as a clipping mask for the mesh object.

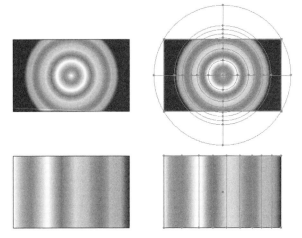

There are several guidelines and restrictions for the creation of gradient mesh objects in Illustrator:

- The Gradient Mesh tool creates the minimum number of mesh lines and points necessary when converting an object. Typically, that will be two lines with their end points and a fifth point where the lines intersect.

- If a specific point on an object requires a specific color (a highlight or button, for example), click that point with the Gradient Mesh tool when converting an object.

- You can use the Create Gradient Mesh command to specify a number of rows and columns, producing a given number of mesh points.

- You cannot create a gradient mesh object from a linked raster image, a compound path, or text.

- When an object becomes a gradient mesh object, it can no longer be considered a vector object, although the shape can still be manipulated.

Creating Gradient Mesh Objects from Raster Images

Linked and embedded raster images can be turned into gradient mesh objects. However, a linked image, after it is converted, becomes a mesh object and loses its link. In addition, gradient mesh objects from images can create very large files and may lead to print problems. One way to limit the size of the files is to compromise on the amount of detail and control. Figure 15.14 shows a comparison of two different settings for Create Gradient Mesh.

The number of mesh points makes a great difference in file size. The 50×50 mesh in Figure 15.14 produced an Adobe Illustrator file almost two and a half times bigger than the 25×25 mesh setting. However, notice the difference in detail between the two mesh settings. Obviously, images with more detail demand finer meshes.

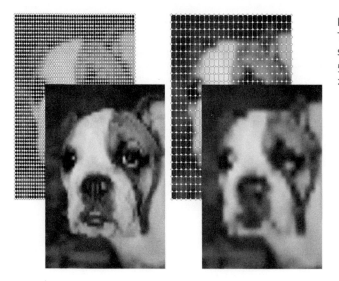

Figure 15.14
The meshes for the two objects are shown behind. On the left is a 50×50 mesh; on the right is a 25×25 mesh.

Creating Efficient Meshes

One way to reduce file size when you're creating a gradient mesh object from a raster image is to reduce the area being used. By copying the image and cropping away all but the area that needs to have colors adjusted through the mesh, you can keep the file small and reduce potential printing problems. In Figure 15.15, for example, the original image was copied and cropped down to just the portion that needed to be mesh. That smaller image was superimposed on the full image and then turned into a gradient mesh object. As you can see, the mesh involves only part of the image (which is actually on a separate layer). The file size was reduced to one-seventh, while maintaining the detail of a 50×50 mesh.

Figure 15.15
The image was copied and the copy was cropped to just the nose, the section where the gradient mesh was required. That nose was superimposed (on its own layer) and the colors adjusted.

You can minimize printing problems if you create and combine several smaller mesh objects rather than make one large object. The image in Figure 15.14, for example, can be quartered in an image-editing program, and separate mesh objects can be created from each.

⇨ *Having trouble outputting a gradient mesh object to an inkjet printer? See "Outputting Gradient Mesh Objects" in the "Troubleshooting" section at the end of this chapter.*

Simulating Meshes

Don't forget that you can simulate gradient meshes by using objects and the Blend command. If a gradient mesh is proving difficult to print, you might be able to easily simulate the mesh using blends. Figure 15.16 shows an example of blended objects that produce an effect similar to the gradient mesh shown in Figure 15.2.

Figure 15.16
The stacked objects are shown on the left; the blend, on the right.

Editing Gradient Meshes

After you create a gradient mesh object, whether from a vector object or raster image, you can edit it. To understand the process of editing a gradient mesh, you need to understand the components. Examining Figure 15.17, you'll see familiar-looking parts and some that look strange.

Figure 15.17
Mesh points have much in common with anchor points, but they have several important differences.

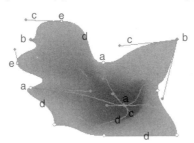

a. Mesh point
b. Corner Mesh point
c. Direction line
d. Mesh line
e. Path Anchor point

As you can see in Figure 15.17, gradient mesh objects, like other objects, are constructed of points and lines between those points:

* **Mesh point**—A mesh point, which is always shown as a diamond, can exist at the end of a mesh line or somewhere along the line. These points always exist at the intersection of two lines. (See also *corner mesh point*) Mesh points control the coloring of a mesh object. The color is applied to a point, and it spreads from there, based on the relationship to the point's direction lines and neighboring points. When a mesh point is located at the end of a mesh line, it has two direction lines. When it is found at a location where two mesh lines cross, it has four direction lines.

* **Corner mesh point**—Like any other mesh points, these points have direction lines and can be colored. They, too, exist at the intersection of two mesh lines. They are created when an object that contains corner anchor points is converted into a mesh object. An object's smooth anchor points are converted into regular mesh points when they coincide with mesh lines. Otherwise, they may be left as smooth anchor points (see Figure 15.18).

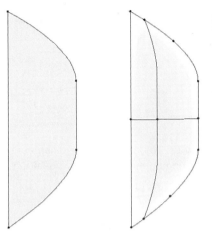

Figure 15.18
The object on the left was created with the Pen tool. The copy on the right was converted to a gradient mesh object using the command Object, Create Gradient Mesh.

As you can see, two mesh lines were created, and the object has nine mesh points. The two original smooth anchor points (on the right side of the objects) have been retained. The original corner anchor points have been converted to mesh points.

- **Direction line**—Just as control points and direction lines regulate the shape of paths, so do they regulate the shape of mesh lines. In addition, however, they also determine the interaction of colors (see Figure 15.19).

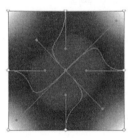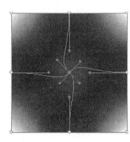

Figure 15.19
The difference between these two examples is only the length of the direction lines from the center mesh point. Note that, in addition to the color change, the direction lines control the shape of the mesh lines, just as with paths.

- **Mesh line**—You can add mesh lines by using the Create Gradient Mesh command or Gradient Mesh tool. Mesh lines extend across an object, whether horizontally or vertically. Every place where two mesh lines intersect, a mesh point is created. When you're converting an object, path segments may be subdivided by mesh points.

- **Path anchor point**—As you saw in Figure 15.18, regular anchor points can be retained when a mesh object is created. Path anchor points differ from mesh points in two respects. First, they cannot have an assigned color. Second, they appear at the ends of path segments rather than at intersections of paths. As usual, they are shown as squares on the artboard. (Mesh points are shown as diamonds.) You can add and delete these points by using the appropriate Pen tools.

- **Mesh patches** (not indicated in Figure 15.17)—The area bounded by mesh lines is referred to as a *mesh patch*. It always has four mesh points on its perimeter, even if there are not four places where mesh lines intersect. See Figure 15.20.

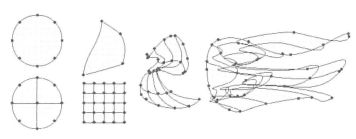

Figure 15.20
The top-left object has only one mesh patch and its four mesh points. It also has the original four smooth anchor points. Knowing that each patch has exactly four mesh points can help in deciphering the object on the right.

You can edit mesh objects by changing the color of mesh points, moving mesh points, adding mesh points (and the corresponding mesh lines), and deleting mesh points (and their lines):

- Before you can change the color of a mesh point, you must select it with the Direct Selection or Gradient Mesh tool.

- To add or change the color of a selected mesh point or points, you can use the Color palette, Swatches palette, or Paint Bucket. Gradients and patterns cannot be used.

- Clicking with the Direct Selection tool in a mesh patch selects the four surrounding mesh points.

- Clicking in a mesh patch with the Gradient Mesh tool adds a pair of mesh lines, perpendicular to each other, extending across the object.

- Clicking with the Gradient Mesh tool on a mesh line adds a single line, perpendicular to the existing line.

- If the mesh object is already colored, you can add a mesh point and corresponding mesh lines of the same color by Shift+clicking with the Gradient Mesh tool.

- Option+clicking [Alt+clicking] on a mesh point with the Gradient Mesh tool deletes the point.

- You can modify direction lines for an active mesh point by dragging the control points at the ends of the direction lines.

- To relocate a mesh point along the mesh line without disturbing the line itself, use the Gradient Mesh tool and hold down the Shift key.

- You can manipulate mesh points and mesh lines by using the Transform commands and tools.

⇨ *Having difficulty manipulating mesh points? See "Working with Mesh Points" in the "Troubleshooting" section at the end of this chapter.*

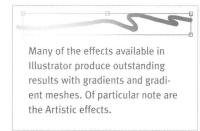

Many of the effects available in Illustrator produce outstanding results with gradients and gradient meshes. Of particular note are the Artistic effects.

Printing Gradients and Gradient Meshes

Printing gradients and especially gradient meshes can be a problem. The complexity of the objects can choke an imagesetter or result in banding. Chapter 24, "Commercial Printing and Trapping Issues," provides specific guidance on the physical length and composition of gradients. The following guidelines pertain primarily to preparing CMYK images for four-color process printing:

- Short, distinct blends print better than longer, more subtle blends.

- Lighter colors blend better than darker colors. Blending between a very dark color and white is worst.

- Use PostScript Level 3 devices when possible. When you must print a gradient mesh or gradient to a PostScript 2 device, be sure that you have appropriate settings in the Printing & Export panel of the Document Setup dialog box.

- Some lower resolution printers are not well-equipped to handle gradients. Try deselecting the Use Printer's Default Screen option.

- Ensure that the imagesetter's resolution and line screen frequency allow the full range of 256 levels of gray. Using too high a line screen actually reduces the number of grays available. As a general rule, the line screen frequency should be one-sixteenth the imagesetter or printer resolution.

When printing to low-resolution or inkjet printers, you may be able to solve problems by simply rasterizing the gradient or gradient mesh object.

You should also keep in mind several rules that Illustrator uses for separating and printing colors in gradients and mesh objects:

- If a process and a spot color are blended in a gradient, all colors are converted to process colors.

- When you're blending a spot color with a tint of itself, the gradient separates as a spot color.

- When you're creating a gradient between a spot color and white, make "white" a 0% tint of the spot color. This technique ensures that the gradient will separate to a single plate.

- When you're creating separate plates for spot colors, make sure that you have the correct options in the Separations Setup dialog box (which you access by choosing File, Separation Setup). See Figure 15.21 for an example of the dialog box.

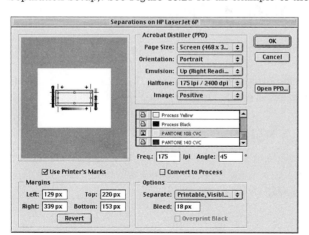

Figure 15.21
The printer icon next to a color's name in the list indicates that a separation will be printed. The four-part square indicates that a spot color will be converted to process colors.

TROUBLESHOOTING

Monitor Settings

My gradients look very dithered or banded onscreen, but when I send them to my inkjet printer, they come out fine. What's the solution?

Your monitor is probably set to too few colors. See Figure 15.22 for an example.

Figure 15.22
The same gradient as viewed on monitors set to (from top) 256 colors (8-bit), thousands of colors (16-bit), and millions of colors (24-bit).

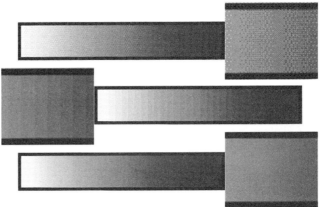

For Macintosh OS X, changes to monitor settings are made in the Displays panel of the System Preferences. For Macintosh OS 9, make the adjustment in the Monitors control panel. Access it through the Apple menu. For most Windows users, from the Start menu, go to Settings and open the Control Panel window. Display is the control panel; Settings is the tab. Look for Color Palette.

Outputting Gradient Mesh Objects

I'm having problems printing gradient meshes on my inkjet printer. What can I do?

Rasterize. The gradient mesh object is a combination of vector and raster information. Converting it to all-raster makes it easier for your printer to handle.

Working with Mesh Points

Trying to get that perfect look for a gradient mesh is driving me nuts! I can't seem to get the points to cooperate with each other.

First, keep in mind that having more points is not always better. Every time you add a mesh point, you're actually adding one or two mesh lines, with new mesh points every place they cross existing lines. Next, keep in mind that each mesh patch has four mesh points controlling it. When mesh lines curve and overlap, you may have trouble recognizing that fourth point. Click somewhere in the patch, and the four points will automatically be selected. One more tip: When a color fades as it moves away from a mesh point, but a second mesh point stands in the way, remember that you can use the HSB sliders in the Color palette to make the second point a tint of the fading color.

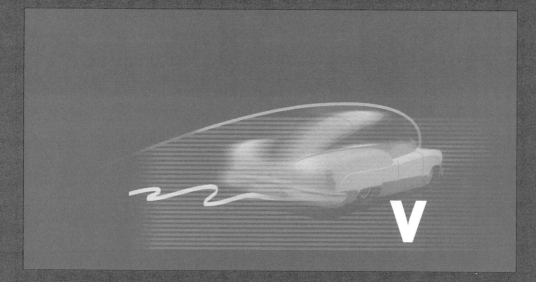

GETTING THE MOST OUT OF ILLUSTRATOR

IN THIS PART

16   Customizing Illustrator   **357**

17   Using Masks to Show and Hide   **373**

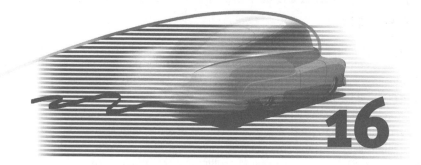

CUSTOMIZING ILLUSTRATOR

IN THIS CHAPTER

Customizing Illustrator's Keyboard Shortcuts   **358**

Setting Illustrator's Preferences   **360**

Creating Illustrator Startup Files   **370**

Troubleshooting   **372**

KEYBOARD SHORTCUTS: SPEED FOR ILLUSTRATOR POWER USERS

One of the keys to efficient production with Illustrator is customization. The Preferences file, default keyboard shortcuts, and palettes are set for the general user. And they work fine. But to improve efficiency, and perhaps to let Illustrator keep up with your creative flow, you can take a little bit of time to save a lot of time.

Spending a few minutes customizing Illustrator can save you a minute or two or three every time you start the program, every time you open a file, every time you start a new document. Those minutes add up quickly when you use Illustrator regularly. In addition, setting up the program correctly can help you avoid costly mistakes down the road.

With the introduction of graphical user interfaces (GUIs) almost two decades ago, we started to say good-bye to keyboards for anything other than text entry. Mouse clicks replaced text-based coding and commands. Since then, such issues as repetitive motion injuries, monitor size, and just plain speed have taken us away from the mouse. Sending a cursor from the lower-right corner of a 21-inch monitor to the upper-left corner just to save a document is far more time consuming and much more inconvenient than pressing Cmd+S [Ctrl+S] .

Illustrator has the capability to assign custom keyboard shortcuts to the majority of the menu commands and all the tools. Sets of shortcuts can be saved, which is extremely convenient for multiple-user environments. The utility of multiple sets of shortcuts for an individual is substantially less. (Memorizing one set of shortcuts is usually sufficient and slow.) Figure 16.1 shows the Keyboard Shortcuts dialog box. You can open it with the menu command Edit, Keyboard Shortcuts, or with its own keyboard shortcut, Cmd+Option+Shift+K [Ctrl+Alt+Shift+K].

Figure 16.1
The Set menu offers a choice between Illustrator Factory Defaults and Illustrator 6, as well as any custom sets that you've created with the Save command.

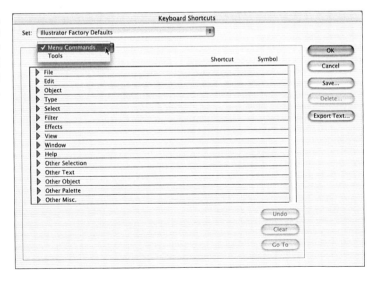

To assign a new keyboard shortcut, find the menu command or tool in the lists and click under the Shortcut column. When a box appears, you can press the key combination of your choice. In Figure 16.2, a new combination is being assigned for the Navigator Options palette menu command. Illustrator automatically assigns the menu symbol, although you can override this symbol with any single character. If you leave this action to Illustrator, the letter or number character is shown with the appropriate modifier keys. If you override it, no modifiers appear.

If you attempt to assign a keyboard shortcut that is already in use, Illustrator will warn you. When telling you which command or tool already uses that particular combination, Illustrator offers you the choice to Undo, to Clear, or to Go To, which takes you to the conflicting item and enables you to modify it. If you choose to ignore the warning, the menu item or tool that originally had the keyboard shortcut in question has none assigned. Note that Illustrator enables you to export your customized keyboard shortcuts as a text file that you can print for quick reference.

➡️ *If you can't seem to make your keyboard shortcuts stick, see "Saving Your Shortcuts" in the "Troubleshooting" section at the end of this chapter.*

Illustrator's top users have long written Actions to execute repetitive or often-used commands. Assigning keyboard shortcuts can simplify things even a bit more.

For example, the creation of a manuscript with illustrations requires that crop marks be prepared for every image. Rather than use the mouse to activate the menu command Object, Crop Marks, Make, you can create an Action that invokes this command and assign it to one of the 12 or 15 function keys. The number of function keys available is limited, but the wealth of modifier key combinations for shortcuts removes any realistic limitation. In addition, you can assign keyboard shortcuts that are easier to remember. To continue the earlier example, you might find it easier to remember using Cmd+Option+ C [Ctrl+Alt+C] to make crop marks than F5.

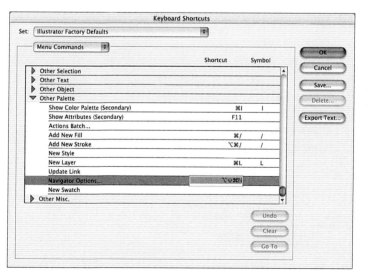

Figure 16.2
The modifier key symbols shown are those for Macintosh systems. The corresponding Windows keys assigned for Navigator Options would be, in order, Alt+Shift+ Ctrl+N.

ILLUSTRATOR'S ARTISTIC FILTERS

Smudge Stick

 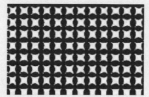 

ILLUSTRATOR'S ARTISTIC FILTERS

Sponge

ILLUSTRATOR'S ARTISTIC FILTERS

Underpainting

  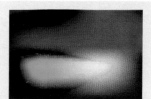

ILLUSTRATOR'S ARTISTIC FILTERS

Watercolor

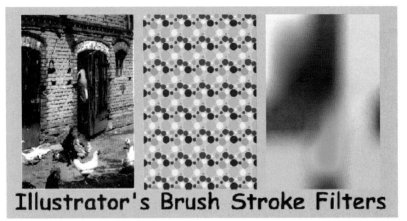

Originals

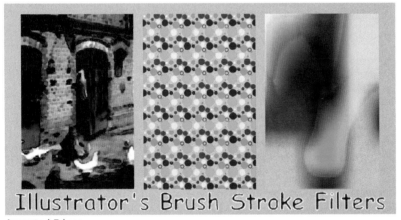

Accented Edges

Angled Strokes

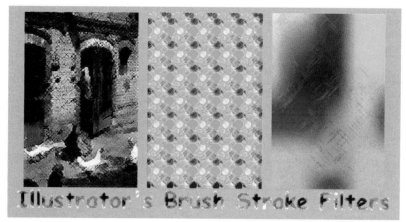

Crosshatch

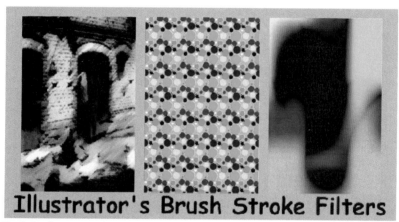

Dark Strokes

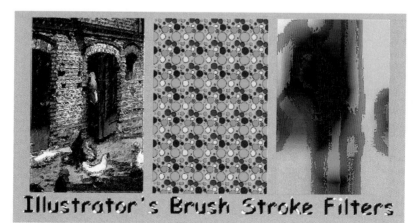

Ink Outlines

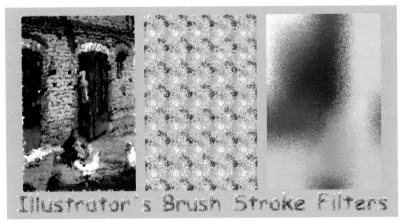

Spatter

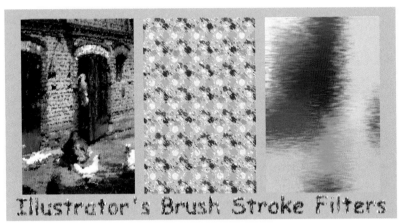

Sprayed Strokes

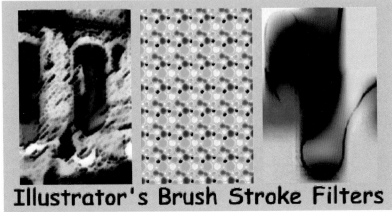

Sumi-e

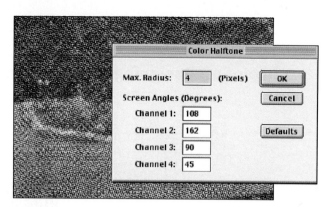

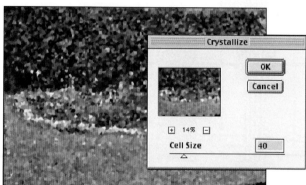

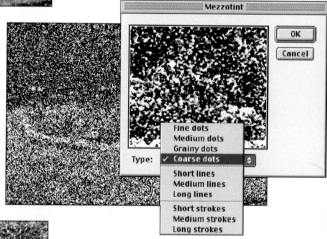

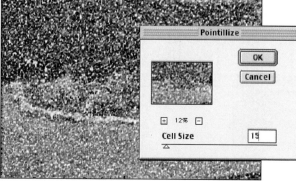

Chapter 21: Designing Web Sites and Web Pages

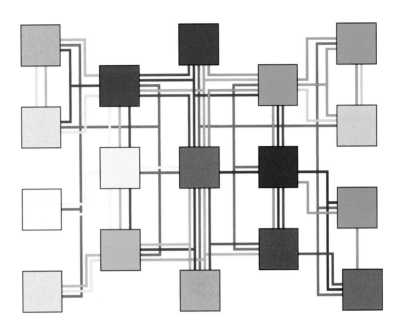

Figure 21.2

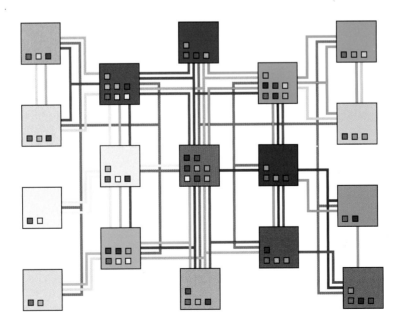

Figure 21.3

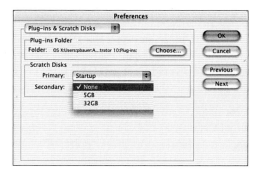

Figure 16.9
The two halves of this preferences dialog box are, again, unrelated.

- **Plug-ins Folder** enables you to select a folder of plug-ins. Note that Illustrator recognizes only one plug-ins folder at a time. Because plug-ins add to loading time, if you have many, you might want to split them into separate folders. If you do, make sure that you copy key plug-ins to each folder. Such things as tools and file formats might be needed with all sets. You also might want to delete unnecessary plug-ins from the default folder.

- **Primary** shows all available hard disks in a pop-up menu. Choose the fastest disk (assuming it has adequate available space) as the primary disk.

- **Secondary** shows None and the names of available hard disks.

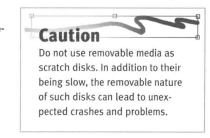

Caution
Do not use removable media as scratch disks. In addition to their being slow, the removable nature of such disks can lead to unexpected crashes and problems.

Files & Clipboard

The Files & Clipboard preferences, shown in Figure 16.10, involve saving files and exchanging information between programs.

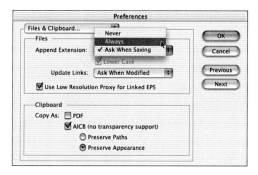

Figure 16.10
Appending the extension is a requirement when preparing files that will be used on Windows machines.

- **Append Extension** offers a choice of when to add the file format extension to a filename when saving. The choices are Never, Always, and Ask When Saving.

- **Lower Case** ensures maximum filename compatibility when checked.

- **Update Links** offers Automatically, Manually, and Ask When Modified. When a linked file has been modified, Illustrator can make sure that the most recent version is the one placed in your illustration automatically. It can assume that you are aware that a file has been modified and will update if desired, or it can keep track of each placed and linked file and let you make the decision at the time.

- **Copy As PDF** uses the Portable Document Format for Illustrator's Clipboard, in addition to the PICT data. The internal Clipboard can be used among Adobe products or can transfer data to another program. Some programs, such as Adobe InDesign, require the PDF version of the data.

- **Copy As AICB** adds a copy of the selection to the Clipboard as Adobe Illustrator Clipboard data. Similar to EPS, it simulates transparency. This is the preferred format for Adobe Photoshop.

- **Preserve Paths** maintains the integrity of the vector paths, allowing them to be edited.

- **Preserve Appearance** forgoes paths to maintain the look of an object.

Workgroup

When enabled, Illustrator's Workgroup functionality enables multiple users to work on the same project without losing track of changes (see Figure 16.11). Managed documents are stored on a server, "checked out" from the server, and updated from the server. Linked files can also be "managed" from the server.

Figure 16.11
Workgroup functionality allows several people to work on the same project without having to manually send updated files back and forth.

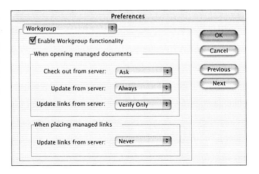

Re-creating Illustrator's Preferences

Every time you quit Illustrator, the program saves your latest settings and choices. These details, which make it more efficient to use Illustrator in your next session, are stored in the Preferences file. In addition to the eight screens of information identified here, Illustrator records the contents of palettes, color settings, and even your choice of keyboard shortcut settings.

This file is easily (and relatively often) corrupted. Such corruption manifests itself as strange or unusual behavior by the program. Suddenly, cursors don't appear with the correct shape. The program hangs or crashes. The screen doesn't redraw properly. The list is nearly endless.

Rather than reinstall Illustrator, you can replace the preferences. Here's the step-by-step checklist:

1. Quit Illustrator.

2. Delete the Preferences file. In Mac OS X, the Adobe Illustrator 10 Prefs file is stored individually for each user, in the user's Library: Preferences: Adobe Illustrator 10 folder. Mac OS 9 users will find the Adobe Illustrator 10 folder inside their System/Preferences folder. On the Windows side, the file can be found inside the Adobe Illustrator Settings folder. Find the Settings folder by opening the Program Files folder and looking inside the Adobe and Illustrator folders.

3. Restart Illustrator.

4. Reload any custom palettes required.

5. Re-establish your choice under the menu command Edit, Color Settings.

6. Reselect your choice of custom keyboard settings under Edit, Keyboard Shortcuts.

7. Review the settings in the nine preferences dialog boxes.

Online Settings

Although not technically part of Illustrator's preferences, the Online Settings are also located in the Preferences submenu. They are used with Adobe Online, which provides a variety of Internet-related services. You can update the program, get technical assistance, and even look for tips and case studies. Access Adobe Online from the Help menu or by clicking the icon at the top of the Tool palette.

These options control how often Adobe Online automatically checks for updates to Illustrator (and Adobe Online itself), and what it does when updates are found. A functioning Internet connection is required. If you set the pop-up menu to Never, you can use the Updates button to manually search for new software (see Figure 16.12).

Figure 16.12
Even when the Installer automatically launches, you'll still be able to control which, if any, updates are added to your local drives.

When you connect to Adobe Online for updates, you will see a list of available downloads (see Figure 16.13).

Figure 16.13
You can get updates for all
installed versions of Illustrator,
as well as Adobe Online, when
available.

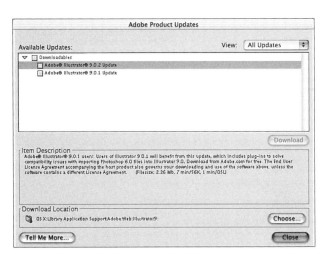

CREATING ILLUSTRATOR STARTUP FILES

Everything in a new Illustrator document, from the size of the artboard to the contents of the Swatches palette, is determined by the startup file. The default startup files are designed to fulfill most of the needs of most Illustrator users, but they rarely fulfill all the needs of any individual user. There is one for CMYK documents and a separate startup file for RGB documents.

Creating your own custom startup files is a relatively simple and painless process, as long as you understand that the file must have exactly the same name as the original to function. The sidebar "Changing Illustrator's Startup File" has step-by-step instructions.

Before you begin, decide what you want to change. The following are some things to consider:

- Page layout, including size and orientation.

- Document Setup, including Printing & Export and Transparency.

- The contents of the various palettes. Delete any unused swatches and brushes and the like, and load any libraries that are used regularly, including custom libraries.

- Initial zoom level. If you prefer to work at Actual Size rather than Fit In Window, make the change now.

- Show/Hide Artboard and Page Tiling.

- Window size and scroll.

- Any default artwork. If the same logo needs to appear in the same place in a series of images, make it part of the default setup.

Using Multiple Startup Files

Nothing says you can't have several startup files. If you have certain basic requirements for one set of jobs but different requirements for other repeat assignments, make separate startup files. If you'll be doing a series of illustrations for a one-time job, create a new startup file for its requirements, but save your regular startup file for later use. You must, however, be careful not to get them confused.

One suggestion is to create a folder called Startup Files. Inside that folder, create a series of folders, one for each situation. One might be called The Complete Idiot's Guide to Tree Painting to prep illustrations for a book job. Another could be Prepress-Murphy Printing, and a third might be Prepress-Uptown Print Shop. Make a folder for Default Startup, too. Each folder can contain one startup file (or one for each color mode).

When it's convenient to use a startup file with a certain bunch of settings, move the current startup file to its folder, and move the new one to the Plug-ins folder. (Make sure to move the old one out first.)

Changing Illustrator's Startup File

Every time you start Illustrator, certain things happen. The palettes are arranged a certain way. The default artboard size is set when you start a new document. Certain swatches are available in the Swatches palette. Particular graph styles are available. Windows open at a certain size and zoom.

All these factors are determined by the Illustrator startup files. Illustrator has two separate startup files, one for CMYK and one for RGB. You can modify Illustrator's default behavior by replacing these startup files. The following example is for the CMYK startup file. The same instructions apply to the RGB startup file, with the exception, of course, of the names.

1. In the Finder (Macintosh) or Windows Explorer (Windows), locate a file named Adobe Illustrator Startup_CMYK. Duplicate this file and rename the copy `AI Startup_CMYK_Old` or something else recognizable.

2. Double-click Adobe Illustrator Startup_CMYK to open the program and the file. The default swatches are then displayed in the document.

3. Delete any color swatches that you don't need, and add any that you do. Note that you must delete unwanted swatches from both the artboard and the Swatches palette. You can add swatches both from swatch libraries and from other documents (by choosing Window, Swatch Libraries, Other Library).

4. Create any patterns and gradients you'll need. Use the Graph sign dialog box to save any graph designs you want to have readily available.

5. Establish your preferred defaults for Page Setup and Document Setup, as well as your preferences for view, page origin, and ruler origin.

6. Save the document.

7. Quit Illustrator and restart, opening a new CMYK document to test your new settings.

TROUBLESHOOTING

Saving Your Shortcuts

I spend all kinds of time customizing my shortcuts, but later they never seem to work. Is something wrong?

No, nothing's wrong. There are three steps to using customized keyboard shortcuts. The first, and longest, step is making the assignments. The second step is saving them. Illustrator gives you this prompt when you leave the Keyboard Shortcuts dialog box. The third step, and where the trouble likely lies, is that the set of shortcuts needs to be active.

Press Cmd+Option+Shift+K (Ctrl+Alt+Shift+K), or choose Edit, Keyboard Shortcuts to open the dialog box. At the top of the dialog box is a pop-up menu labeled Set. Choose your custom collection there and click OK.

Setting the Point of Origin

I like to use pixels as my "general" unit of measure, but it doesn't do me any good when the rulers seem to start in strange places. What can I do to fix things?

Because your unit of choice is pixels, my guess would be that you work with the Web. Typically, a Web page begins measurement from the upper-left corner of the page. Print pages, on the other hand, default to the lower-left corner as the so-called "point of origin." Show the rulers by choosing View, Show Rulers or press Cmd+R (Ctrl+R). Go to the upper-left corner of the screen, where the vertical and horizontal rulers come together. Click and drag from that point to the upper-left corner of the document and release. The rulers are then reset to that spot as the point of origin.

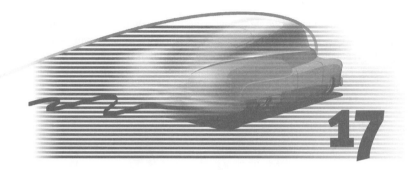

USING MASKS TO SHOW AND HIDE

IN THIS CHAPTER

Clipping Masks   374

Opacity Masks   378

Troubleshooting   384

CLIPPING MASKS

Masks in Illustrator come in two varieties: clipping and opacity. *Clipping masks* hide part of an object or image. *Opacity masks* use a pattern or gradient to selectively expose parts of an object or image. A practical difference is that opacity masks can be semitransparent, whereas clipping masks cannot. Figure 17.1 shows an image and how it can be affected by the two types of masks.

Figure 17.1
The selection in the center shows how the clipping mask hides part of the image. To the right is an opacity mask using a pattern.

A clipping mask is like an empty frame that hides part of an image. In this case, the frame is usually invisible, and it makes the hidden part of the image invisible, too. An opacity mask, on the other hand, has a fill and that fill reacts with the image underneath. Clipping masks can contain multiple paths and mask multiple objects or images. Clipping masks are grouped with the objects they mask, and the group is referred to as a *clipping set*.

Clipping masks, which can be any shape or size, are created with a menu command. They typically have no stroke or fill. They can be locked or unlocked so that you can reposition the artwork within the mask or the mask in relation to the artwork.

In some respects, clipping masks are similar to the compound shape mode Intersect (found on the Pathfinder palette). Like Intersect, the artwork is restricted to the area of overlap.

Creating Clipping Masks

A clipping mask, at its most basic, consists of a piece of artwork that is partially hidden and the path that defines the visible area. To create a mask, simply select the artwork to be masked and the path that will be doing the masking; then choose Object, Clipping Mask, Make. The following are some basic guidelines for creating clipping masks:

- Any vector object can be used as a clipping mask, regardless of its fill or stroke.

- The path or object to be used for the clipping mask must be on top of the artwork to be masked.

It's easier to comprehend the topic of masks when the terminology is clear.

- **Clipping Paths**—Define areas of visibility and invisibility. They are paths, and can be edited like those used to create objects.

- **Clipping Masks**—The clipping paths in action. A clipping mask is used to reveal and hide portions of an underlying object or objects. Normally, the clipping mask is not visible, consisting of a clipping path or paths with a stroke and fill of None. Multiple clipping paths can be used in one clipping mask.

- **Clipping Groups**—Compound paths used as clipping paths.

- **Clipping Sets**—Clipping masks grouped with objects that they mask.

- Both the fill and stroke of the upper path become None when the command is invoked (see Figure 17.2). The masking path's fill and stroke can be changed after it becomes a mask, however.

- Raster images and gradient mesh objects cannot be used as masks.

- If the object to be masked and the masking path are on separate layers, unselected objects on intervening layers are ignored. Figure 17.3 shows an example.

In the middle example, just the layers containing the ellipse and the rectangle were selected, and the command Object, Clipping Mask, Make was selected. You can see that the star (on the layer in between) was unaffected. Note also that the rectangle was moved to the layer of the clipping ellipse. The rectangle's original layer is now empty. In the lower example, the star's layer was included in the clipping set. It is shown for reference.

In the Layers palette, if the layers are expanded to show the individual paths, the names of the paths that make up the clipping masks are underlined. By default they are named <clipping path>, but they remain underlined even if the name is changed.

Caution

Clipping masks, especially those that use complex paths, can create printing problems.

When clipping masks are causing printing problems, the standard advice is to simplify the paths used to make the clipping masks or avoid using clipping masks completely. Before you do that, though, make a copy of the document and try rasterizing the masked objects and images. When rasterized, the vector path that may be causing the problem is eliminated.

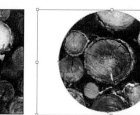

Figure 17.2
The gradient in the circle is lost when you choose Object, Clipping Mask, Make.

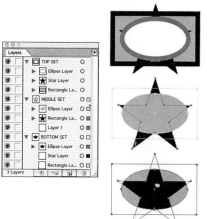

Figure 17.3
In the original, the star is on the layer between the ellipse and the rectangle. The ellipse masks the rectangle, ignoring the star.

- Text can be used for masking. (See "Type as Clipping Masks" later in this chapter.)

- Compound paths and compound shapes can be used as masks. Figure 17.4 shows a comparison of a simple path as a clipping mask, a compound path as a clipping mask, and a compound shape as a clipping mask. The top pair shows before and after images of a circle as a mask. The middle pair shows before and after with a compound path as a clipping mask. The lower pair shows the before and after using a compound shape as a clipping mask.

Figure 17.4

For the bottom pair, the compound shape was created using the Exclude Overlap button of the Pathfinder palette.

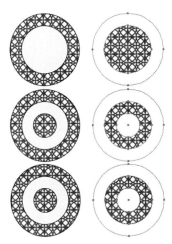

- Choosing Object, Clipping Mask, Release undoes a selected clipping mask but does not restore the original fill and stroke of the object used as a mask. The path that had been used as a mask will have a stroke and fill of None, unless you have specifically applied a stroke or fill.

⇨ *Having trouble creating a clipping mask? See "Clipping Creation Conflicts" in the "Troubleshooting" section at the end of this chapter.*

Editing a Clipping Mask

You can edit clipping masks in a variety of ways after you create them. The path being used as a clipping mask can be assigned a fill and stroke, and it remains a path, subject to manipulation.

Both fills and strokes can be assigned to a path being used as a clipping mask. The stroke is visible, but the fill remains hidden unless the object being masked has reduced opacity, is hidden, or does not occupy the entire area of the mask. If you select the clipping mask's path with the Direct Selection tool, you can assign a stroke and fill as you would to any other object.

Interestingly, reducing the opacity of the fill of a path being used as a clipping mask has no effect unless the mask is released. While acting as a clipping mask, the fill's opacity will not be changed. If the mask is released, the reduced opacity will be apparent. You can, however, control the opacity for both the object that is being masked and, by using the Appearance palette, its fill.

You can use the Direct Selection tool to manipulate individual anchor points on the clipping mask, just as you would any other path. You can also, when the mask is selected, change the path's appearance attributes. Figure 17.5 shows an example.

Figure 17.5
In this example, a stroke has been applied to a compound path being used in a clipping mask.

The Group Selection tool enables you to reposition a clipping mask. This includes repositioning a path that is part of a compound path being used as a mask (see Figure 17.6).

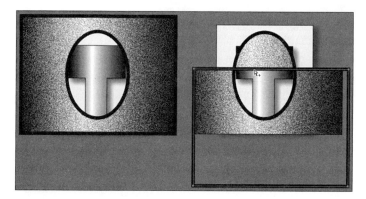

Figure 17.6
On the right, you can see the mask being dragged. The rectangle and ellipse are a compound path being used as a mask on the frontmost rectangle.

Illustrator enables you to cut an object from the artboard and then use the Paste in Front and Paste in Back commands to add it to a clipping mask. To determine where the new object will be added, use the Direct Selection tool to select a member of the clipping set. Keep in mind that Paste in Front and Paste in Back remember the object's location on the artboard. Position the object before cutting. Likewise, you can use the Direct Selection tool to select an object to be removed from a clipping set. Choosing Edit, Cut or pressing Delete [Backspace] removes a selected object from the artboard without disturbing the rest of the clipping set.

Type as Clipping Masks

You do not need to convert type to outlines to use it as a clipping mask. As you can see by the Type tool selection in Figure 17.7, the text remains fully editable.

Note that the type loses its drop shadow when it's made into a clipping mask. The shadow can be reapplied to the type while the type is being used as a mask, but the shadow isn't visible unless the mask is released.

Large amounts of type or area type can provoke a warning from Illustrator that previewing and printing might cause problems. See Figure 17.8 for such an example.

Figure 17.7
The word Mask is selected and can be overtyped to edit.

Figure 17.8
Text is created from complex compound paths, which can lead to problems.

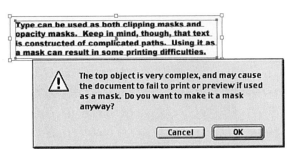

⇨ *Having trouble printing, but afraid to rasterize? See "Protecting Editable Type" in the "Troubleshooting" section at the end of this chapter.*

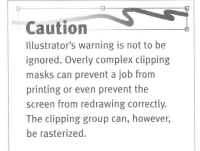

Caution

Illustrator's warning is not to be ignored. Overly complex clipping masks can prevent a job from printing or even prevent the screen from redrawing correctly. The clipping group can, however, be rasterized.

OPACITY MASKS

Opacity masks use the luminosity of the uppermost object to produce a transparent pattern on lower objects. When the masking object is filled with a solid color, the mask is uniform. If the luminosity is high (bright colors), the mask appears to have little or no effect. If the masking object is filled with a dark color, the artwork below appears more transparent. When the masking object is filled with a pattern or a gradient, the results can vary substantially. Figure 17.9 compares opacity masks created with various solid color, gradient, and pattern fills.

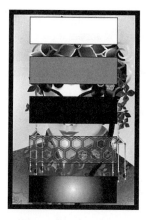 

Figure 17.9
On the left are the original objects. To the right, the background image has been divided into five pieces and different opacity masks have been applied to each. From the top: white, neutral gray, black, pattern, and gradient.

Creating Opacity Masks

Unlike clipping masks, opacity masks are created through the Transparency palette. Figure 17.10 shows the Make Opacity Mask command.

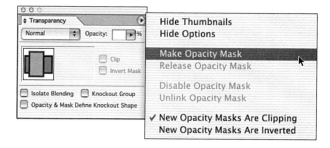

Figure 17.10
You must use the Transparency palette menu to create opacity masks.

When expanded, the Transparency palette shows the masked object and its opacity mask and enables you to manipulate them. The expanded palette is shown in Figure 17.11. The masked object is shown in the thumbnail to the left; the mask, in the right thumbnail. The icon between indicates that the masked object and mask are linked together. (Linking is explained later in this chapter in "Editing Opacity Masks.")

Figure 17.11
You can expand and contract the Transparency palette by clicking the double arrow in the palette's tab.

In the Transparency palette menu you also have the option of disabling an opacity mask without removing it. When the mask is disabled, it has a large red X across it (see Figure 17.12).

Figure 17.12
The opacity mask can be enabled again through the Transparency palette menu.

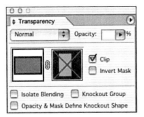

One of the simplest changes that you can make to an opacity mask in the Transparency palette is inversion. By checking the Invert Mask box, you reverse the effect of the opacity mask. Rather than dark areas of the mask having the greatest impact, the lighter areas produce greater transparency.

If you refer to Figure 17.10, you'll see the menu command New Opacity Masks Are Inverted. When you select this option, all new masks are reversed, with the lighter areas of the pattern or gradient providing greater transparency.

➯ *Confused by the concept of opacity masks? See "Clarifying Opacity" in the "Troubleshooting" section at the end of this chapter.*

Even when you have only one object selected, the command Make Opacity Mask is available. A blank mask is created, and the masked object shows no change. The mask, although created blank, can be edited.

Editing Opacity Masks

When an opacity mask is created, it is *linked* to the object being masked. When the object is moved, the opacity mask will move with it, maintaining its position. The opacity mask, when selected in the Transparency palette, can be repositioned without moving the masked object.

To unlink a mask, simply click the icon between the two thumbnails in the Transparency palette, as shown in Figure 17.13.

Figure 17.13
Clicking the icon unlinks the mask from the object. Clicking in the empty spot re-establishes the link. You cannot unlink a mask while it is active and being edited.

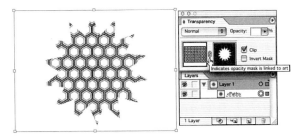

In Figure 17.13, a black border surrounds the thumbnail to the left. It indicates that the masked object, rather than the mask itself, is selected. When the object is selected on the artboard, it is shown as selected in the Transparency palette (and the Layers palette, as well). In Figure 17.14, the Transparency palette, Layers palette, and artboard all show that the object is selected. In the Layers palette, note that the opacity mask is indicated by the dashed underlining of the object name (<Path>, in this case).

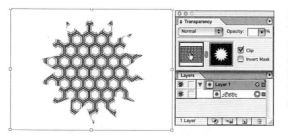

Figure 17.14
The bounding box, Selected Art indicator in the Layers palette, and dark border around the thumbnail in the Transparency palette all indicate that the rectangle is selected.

When the original object's path is selected, it can be manipulated as normal with, for example, the Direct Selection tool. You can alter the object's path without changing the opacity mask. Figure 17.15 shows an example.

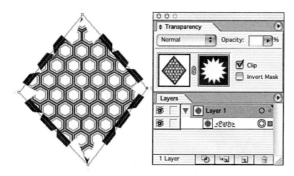

Figure 17.15
Notice that the changing shape of the object is reflected in the Transparency palette's thumbnail. And because of how the object falls behind the clipping path, you can now see parts of the heavy black stroke.

When you click the thumbnail image of the mask (to the right of the link icon), you can alter the mask's path. In Figure 17.16, the Direct Selection tool is being used to drag an anchor point of the mask.

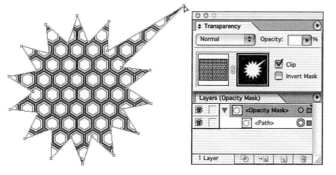

Figure 17.16
Note that when the opacity mask is selected in the Transparency palette, Illustrator changes the Layers palette to match.

When the mask itself is selected in the Transparency palette, the link between it and the object being masked is grayed out. The link is retained during the mask editing. To use the Selection tool to reposition the mask without moving the masked object, you must unlink before selecting the mask. When unlinked, the mask can be moved independently of the original object, as shown in Figure 17.17.

Figure 17.17
Observe how the thumbnails change to show the relationship between the two elements.

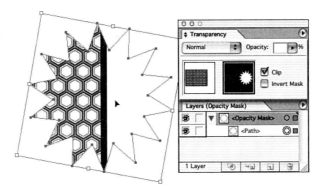

The transparency options of the mask can be altered when it is active. Changing the blending mode of the mask, for example, may change its effect on the underlying object. See the comparison in Figure 17.18.

Figure 17.18
The original objects are shown to the left. To the upper right, the opacity mask has a blending mode of Normal. In the lower right, the blending mode has been changed to Screen.

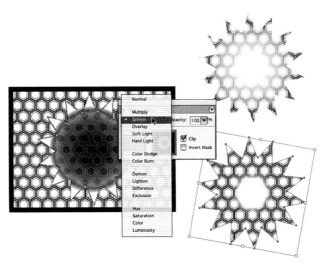

Effects and filters can also be applied to opacity masks when selected. In Figure 17.19, the command Filter, Distort, Twist was applied to the lower copy's mask.

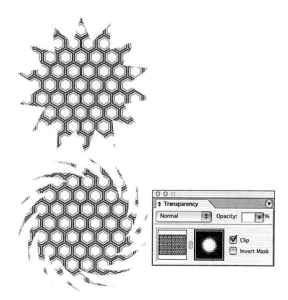

Figure 17.19
Virtually all effects and some filters, as well as Transform commands, are available when the mask is selected.

Type as Opacity Masks

You also can use type as opacity masks. Figure 17.20 shows a type opacity mask.

Figure 17.20
The Transparency palette shows the background object and opacity mask.

You can still edit type after you create the opacity mask. However, the mask itself must be active in the Transparency palette. Click the mask's thumbnail in the Transparency palette and use the Type tool to select the text for editing (see Figure 17.21).

Figure 17.21

With the mask active in the Transparency palette, you can edit the type.

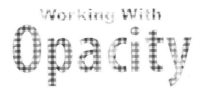

Figure 17.21

With the mask active in the Transparency palette, you can edit the type.

TROUBLESHOOTING

Clipping Creation Conflicts

I can't seem to create a clipping mask. What could I be doing wrong?

First, make sure that you have both (or all) objects selected. Second, make sure that the path to be used for clipping is on top. Third, remember that the clipping mask cannot be made from a raster or gradient mesh object.

Protecting Editable Type

I can't print, yet I can't rasterize my clipping set. I'll need to change the text later. Suggestions?

Elementary. Make a copy of the file, rasterize the clipping set in the copy so that it will print, and keep the original for future editing. Assuming you have the storage space, it's a good idea to save a copy of any image with its vector art before rasterizing any artwork.

Clarifying Opacity

I don't understand how opacity masks work. I see the examples and think they are something I want to use, but I just don't get the concept.

Opacity masks are based on the masking object's *luminosity*. Luminosity is the lightness value of a given color. Using the Hue-Saturation-Brightness (HSB) color model (also known as Hue-Saturation-Lightness), you can break down any given color into three values. Hue is the color, saturation is the purity or the amount of gray in the color, and brightness (lightness) is the relative darkness or brightness of the color. (Color theory is explained in depth in Chapter 12, "Understanding and Applying Color.")

Opacity masks look only at the lightness/brightness value of the color. By default, the darker the color's lightness/brightness, the more transparent the resulting image will be in that area. (You can, of course, reverse this by selecting the Invert Mask option in the Transparency palette.)

In other words, the actual color of the mask is ignored. The transparency applied to the object or image below is based strictly on the lightness or brightness of the mask.

VI

BETWEEN VECTOR AND RASTER

IN THIS PART

18   Raster Images and Rasterized Objects **389**

19   Exploiting Illustrator's Transparency **405**

20   Using Filters and Effects **429**

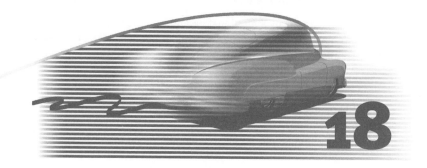

RASTER IMAGES AND RASTERIZED OBJECTS

IN THIS CHAPTER

The Difference Between Vector and Raster 390

Rasterizing Objects in Illustrator 399

Troubleshooting 403

THE DIFFERENCE BETWEEN VECTOR AND RASTER

The two basic classifications of digital images are *vector* and *raster*. Vector image files, such as those native to Illustrator, contain descriptions of geometric objects. Raster image files (also known as *bitmap* images) contain descriptions of colored pixels arranged in a grid or raster.

The two types of artwork have their strong points and their weaknesses. They are designed for different jobs, and they do their jobs well. Determining when to use which, when you have a choice, depends on a variety of factors. Sometimes file format requirements dictate whether your illustration can remain vector or be rasterized into a series of pixels. Sometimes you need to incorporate a raster image into an illustration, and such artwork needs to be properly prepared for best results.

Vector art generally produces sharper images than raster. Raster, however, can incorporate special effects and techniques that are impossible to reproduce in a vector art program, and can reproduce fine variations in color. Illustrator is, at heart, a vector illustration tool. Its sister program, Adobe Photoshop, is the premier raster program. With the releases of Illustrator 9 (with its transparency capability) and Photoshop 6 (which now employs vector type and simulates vector objects), the line is blurring between the programs. Each program, however, specializes in one type of artwork and has some capability with the other.

What Is Vector Art?

To understand the difference between raster and vector, you need to understand how vector art works. Vector art is recorded in a file as a series of mathematical relationships. If you were to translate the file data into English, it might read something like this:

    Start an oval shape near the upper-left corner and go to the middle of the page. It
    should be almost round, but taller than wide. Make the line that draws the circle
    about one-twentieth as wide as the page and color it black.

The result would look the same, regardless of page size (see Figure 18.1). Of course, the computer file would be far more precise, never recording data as "near" or "almost" or "about."

In addition, the mathematically defined vector objects enable you to control their characteristics when editing. When changing the size of a vector object, called *scaling*, you can choose to have its appearance attributes change proportionally or remain static. For example, when scaling a circle that consists of a single black line, you can choose to have the line remain the same size (stroke width) or have it change proportionally to retain the overall look of the circle. The difference is shown in Figure 18.2.

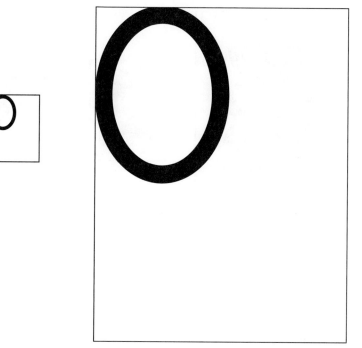

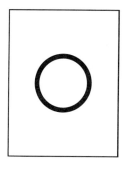

Figure 18.1
Regardless of page size, the relative terms produce an object that is relationally the same.

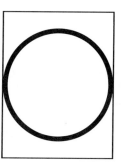

Figure 18.2
The original circle (left) is scaled without resizing the stroke (center) and with the stroke also scaled (right).

When you resize the stroke, the circle retains its appearance. The image on the right in Figure 18.2 is proportionally identical to the one on the left. It could be used, for example, as a "zoomed-in" look at the circle. The image in the center, on the other hand, could not be used in such a manner because the stroke size is smaller in relation to the diameter of the circle.

The capability to adjust the appearance of an image during scaling is just as important when you're reducing the size of an illustration. An example is shown in Figure 18.3.

Figure 18.3
The original is on the left, a copy scaled without resizing strokes is in the center, and a copy with strokes also scaled is on the right.

As you can see, leaving the strokes at their original weights in an illustration one-half the size (center) can seriously degrade the integrity of the image. Rescaling the strokes (right) along with the image size maintains the appearance. Often, however, it's better to leave the stroke unscaled when you change an image's size. In Figure 18.3, for example, the boxes that indicate page outlines for the second and third images are actually copies of the rectangle on the left. Leaving the stroke unscaled maintains the relationship between the two sizes of the rectangle.

One of the most important features of vector art is the way it prints. When you're using a page description language, such as PostScript, the lines are crisp and sharp, no matter how they are rescaled, rotated, or distorted. The entire image can be resized to meet page requirements with no noticeable loss of quality.

The reason that vector art prints and scales cleanly stems from how it is created. Vector art consists of objects, each made from a series of anchor points and the line segments between them. These points and segments, called *paths*, do not themselves have any size or color. Rather, they are stroked (color applied along the path) and filled (color applied within the path) to produce the artwork. In addition to colors, patterns and gradients can be used for strokes and paths. (Illustrator does not support gradient paths, although some other vector art programs do.)

When you're rescaling a vector object, then, the program must only re-create the shape of the object at the new size, remember what fill to use, and determine a stroke width and color. For example, a circle 2 inches in diameter is scaled to 200%. The fill is 30% gray; the stroke is 80% gray and 4 points wide. The new circle will be 4 inches in diameter, the fill color will be 30% gray, and the stroke will be 80% gray and 8 points wide.

The paths, made up of the anchor points and segments, are called *Bézier curves*. Each segment is defined by four points: the anchor points on either end, and direction points, which control the shape of the path between the endpoints. The anatomy of a Bézier curve is shown in Figure 18.5.

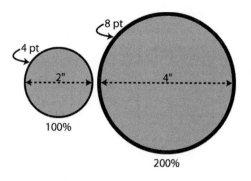

Figure 18.4
The calculations for rescaling a simple object are basic.

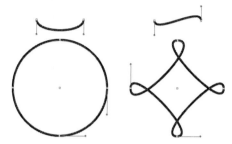

Figure 18.5
The anchor points appear as white spots on the paths, and the direction lines extend out from them. At the end of the direction lines are the direction points.

As you can see, the direction lines determine the shape of the path. In Illustrator, you typically adjust the direction lines by dragging the direction points with the Direct Selection tool. The term *vector art* comes from the direction lines, which are the mathematical *vectors* that define the path. A vector is a quantity that has both magnitude (in this case, the length of the direction line) and direction (its angle from the anchor point).

Paths can be *open*, with distinct endpoints, such as the upper paths in Figure 18.5, or *closed*, continuous paths with no visible start nor end. Whether open or closed, paths can be filled. The paths in Figure 18.5 were stroked (color was applied to the paths) but unfilled. In Figure 18.6, the same paths are both stroked and filled.

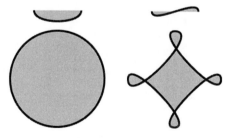

Figure 18.6
The path is mathematically defined, and the strokes and fills are recorded as colors, gradients, or patterns.

Note that the open paths are filled to an imaginary line that could be drawn between the endpoints. The closed paths are filled everywhere that the path encloses.

Why "Bézier" Curves?

Bézier curves are named for the man who defined them, Pierre Etienne Bézier (1910–1999). A long-time employee of the French automaker Renault, Bézier had degrees in mechanical and electrical engineering, and was awarded a doctor of science degree from the University of Paris in 1970.

Bézier began researching Computer-Aided Design/Computer-Aided Manufacturing (CAD/CAM) in 1960. In 1965, he began lobbying Renault in favor of a manufacturing process that would use mathematically defined curves to send car body designs to the factory. It wasn't until 1972 that his ideas were adopted.

Since that time, Bézier's work has indeed become widely accepted. The PostScript page description language, which is one of the keys to the desktop publishing revolution, relies on Bézier curves. In fact, the font in which this passage was typed and the font in which it is printed are created with outlines defined by Bézier curves.

What Is Raster Art?

The term *raster* refers to a grid. In the case of digital art, the grid consists of rows and columns of *pixels*. A pixel is the lowest common denominator in raster art. Each image is made of a series of squares, each of which can be exactly one color. These squares (pixels) cannot be subdivided. They are the smallest element in an image, and all images are made of them. Figure 18.7 shows a raster image and a close-up of the pixels used to display the image.

Figure 18.7
The close-up is of the third pane in the left column of the original.

One of the most important concepts to understand about raster art is that each pixel can be one color and one color only. As you can see in Figure 18.7, none of the small squares are multicolored; none blend from one shade to another. Some of the pixels are the same color or very close to those neighboring, but there can also be very definite color differences between adjacent pixels.

Because each pixel can contain only a single color, each has distinct corners and edges. In Figure 18.7, the left image is shown at 100% zoom. The individual pixels are not visible. In the inset (400% zoom), however, each pixel is visible. Figure 18.8 shows two versions of another image prepared to print at a size of 2 inches by 2 inches. On the left, the image is 300 dots per inch (dpi), appropriate for a glossy magazine. On the right is a version at 128dpi, a resolution you might use for newsprint.

Figure 18.8
These images occupy the same space on the page, but one uses smaller (and more) pixels for finer detail.

The difference in resolution for these two small images results in a large difference in quality. The high-resolution image contains far more pixels, each one much smaller than the low-resolution image's pixels. To be precise, the "hi-res" image contains 360,000 pixels. (That's 300 pixels per inch, times 2 inches wide, for a width of 600 pixels. The height is also 300 pixels times 2, therefore another 600 pixels. You calculate the total number of pixels by multiplying the number of pixels wide by the number of pixels high.) The "lo-res" image has 20,736 pixels (128 ppi × 2 inches = 256 pixels, 256 × 256 = 65,536).

Although the difference in resolution is a factor of a bit more than 2-1/3 (300 divided by 128 equals 2.34), the difference in the number of pixels is a factor of 5-1/2 (360,000 divided by 65,536 equals 5.49). The high-resolution image contains more than five times as many pixels in the same physical amount of space on the printed page; therefore, each printed dot is less than one-fifth as large and that much more difficult to see. And the harder it is to see the individual pixels, the finer the detail of the

The difference between the terms *dots per inch* and *pixels per inch* involves hardware. Use dots (dpi) when referring to physical output from a printer or an imagesetter, or when discussing the resolution of images that will be printed. Use pixels (ppi) when discussing digital data, such as images shown or stored on a computer, or captured by a digital camera or scanner. Other than that, there's no practical difference; both terms are used for that smallest building block of which raster images are constructed. Since most of the examples in this chapter are print-oriented, you'll often see "dpi."

image. Figure 18.9 shows close-ups of how these two different resolutions might be printed by a four-color press. Notice the relative dot size.

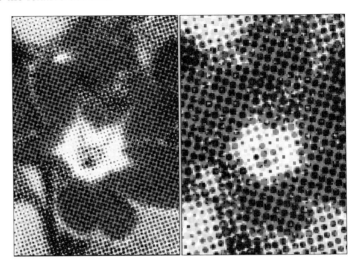

Figure 18.9
The image on the left represents printing at 150 lines per inch (lpi), whereas the image on the right might be produced by an 85lpi screen. Lines per inch is discussed in the sidebar "How Many Pixels Are Enough?"

Confused by the math? See "Calculating Resolution for Print" in the "Troubleshooting" section at the end of this chapter.

Because the difference in dot size can be so dramatic, why not save all images at the highest resolution the computer can support? Because there are limits to the capability of the printer. See the sidebar "How Many Pixels Are Enough?"

How Many Pixels Are Enough?

You've seen that more pixels means smaller pixels, and smaller pixels means finer detail. But where do you draw the line? When do you reach the maximum number of pixels that can effectively be printed? When is enough finally enough?

The number of pixels in a raster image for print—whether commercially printed using a four-color press and CMYK inks, or output on a home inkjet—depends on the printer's capabilities. You do not benefit from sending more pixels than the printer can handle and, in some cases, that can lead to printing problems.

In commercial printing, the press's *line screen frequency* determines detail and therefore the number of pixels the press can handle. A raster image should have a resolution of between 1.5 and 2 times the line screen frequency, which is measured in lines per inch (lpi).

The line screen frequency refers to the number of dots of ink that the press can physically place on the paper. The image covers the same area, with the difference being the size of the dots. Typically, newsprint and other absorbent papers are printed with lpi values between 85 and 100. Uncoated paper (not glossy) used for magazines may be printed at 110 to 133lpi, whereas glossy magazines are usually run at 133 or 150lpi. The highest-quality printed work, such as art books, may be between 200 and 250lpi.

For most inkjet printers, the maximum quality can be reached with image resolutions as low as 240ppi.

Comparing Vector and Raster

Despite the radical differences in the way that vector and raster art record data, they can coexist in a number of file formats. (Chapter 3, "Working with Files in Illustrator," discusses file formats.) Illustrator's native format, DCS, EPS, and PDF are examples of formats that can contain both types of artwork. Common raster file formats that cannot include vector data include BMP, GIF, JPEG, PICT, and PNG.

One of the advantages of raster artwork is the capability of displaying subtle variations in color. Although vector artwork in Illustrator can be filled with gradients or gradient meshes, only rasterized art can achieve the subtlety of pixel-by-pixel color variation. (Compare the relative smoothness of the tunnel walls in Figure 18.10 and Figure 18.11.) Photographs, for example, cannot be stored in vector format. Although the contents of a photo consist of actual objects in reality, once captured on film or digitally, the contents of the image no longer exist as separate objects. You could not, for example, open a picture of a city in a vector art program and click a building to drag it to a new location. In a raster art program, however, you could select the pixels that represent the building and move *them* to a new location in the image. On the other hand, selecting a circle or square in a vector art illustration and dragging it to a new spot on the artboard are far easier than selecting some of the pixels in a rasterized version of the image. In addition, in most raster image formats, moving pixels results in empty space or whitespace being left behind. (Most raster formats readable by Illustrator do not support layers.)

In Figure 18.10, a vector ring and its shadow have been grouped. They can easily be moved by dragging with the Selection tool.

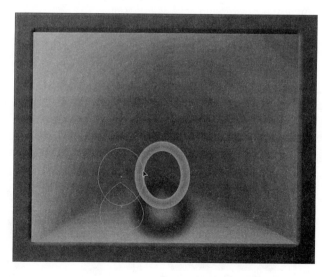

Figure 18.10
In vector art, the ring and its shadow remain objects that can be selected and moved, independent of the background or other objects.

In comparison, see Figure 18.11, which shows a rasterized version of the same image.

Figure 18.11
The ring and its shadow are no longer objects; rather, they are represented by individual pixels. The checkerboard pattern represents transparency.

Attempting to move the ring and its shadow causes several problems:

- Most obviously, the tunnel floor and walls are not behind the pixels that make up the ring and its shadow. Transparency (or white) is left behind when moving pixels.

- Selecting the correct pixels can be difficult and time-consuming.

- Selecting a drop shadow (or any of a number of other effects) cannot be done properly. Because a shadow or glow fades toward the edges, the background color shows through. Separating the shadow from the background color is impossible.

➡️ *Have a scan or other raster image that you need to turn into vector art? See "Vector-izing" in the "Troubleshooting" section at the end of this chapter.*

In Illustrator, many filters and effects are available for both raster and vector artwork. In a dedicated raster-imaging program such as Photoshop, however, you have far more control over the appearance of the image. Image adjustments for color correction, color selection and replacement, and manipulation (via commands such as Liquefy) are available. In addition, image-editing software has tools you can use to select and edit pixels.

One area where vector is almost always superior to raster is text. Type set at very small sizes and very large sizes almost always is sharper and clearer as vector (see Figure 18.12) .

Figure 18.12
The lower word was rasterized at 72ppi. While not horrible at full size, the inset shows a good comparison of vector and raster type.

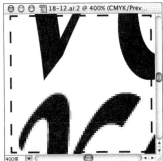

Font selection can make a difference when type will be rasterized. In Figure 18.13, you can see 20 different fonts and how they rasterize at a low resolution. The top row is vector type, and the second row has been rasterized at 72dpi with antialiasing selected. Both are shown at 100% zoom. In the inset, the text and rasterized letters are shown at 150% zoom.

Figure 18.13
For most fonts, antialiasing does a good job of disguising the pixel edges at 100% zoom.

Note that when this text is viewed at 150% zoom, the rasterization becomes quite apparent. This gives an indication, too, of how the low-resolution text may appear on a printed page.

As you can see, fonts with straight vertical and horizontal lines suffer least from the jaggies, whereas curly and angular fonts suffer most.

RASTERIZING OBJECTS IN ILLUSTRATOR

Illustrator gives you two ways to rasterize an object: through the Object menu or through the Effect menu. When you're rasterizing as an effect, the appearance is changed, but the object or text remains vector artwork. You can reverse the rasterization by selecting the object and deleting the effect from the Appearance palette. (Chapter 20, "Using Filters and Effects," discusses the nature of effects.)

Knowing when and why to rasterize and understanding the basic settings are key to preserving the appearance of artwork in Illustrator.

The Rasterize and Raster Effects Settings Dialog Boxes

When you are rasterizing a selection, the dialog box offers you the choice of Grayscale, Bitmap (black and white), or the color mode of the document. (You cannot rasterize an object as CMYK in an RGB document or vice versa. Illustrator does not allow objects of more than one color mode in the same document.) Figure 18.14 shows the Rasterize and Document Raster Effects Settings dialog boxes.

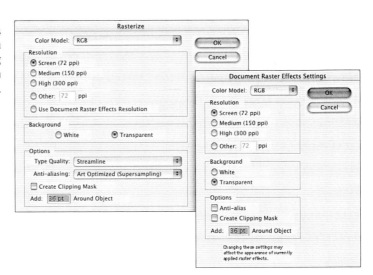

Figure 18.14
The Rasterize dialog box offers a bit of control over anti-aliasing that isn't required when Rasterizing effects.

The resolution of an object or text to be rasterized should depend on the final destination of the object. Images destined for the Web should be rasterized at low resolution to keep the pixel dimension comparable to those at which the element was designed. Images created for commercial printing should be of an appropriate resolution for the line screen frequency of the press. (See the sidebar "How Many Pixels Are Enough?" earlier in this chapter.)

The Type Quality choices are Streamline and Outline, while the Anti-Aliasing pop-up menu offers None, Art Optimized (Supersampling), and Type Optimized (Hinted). With large type, you may see a slight improvement with curvy fonts if you rasterize using the Streamline option with Type Optimized (Hinted) options.

You use the settings in the Document Raster Effects Settings dialog box to rasterize drop shadows, glows, and other live effects when artwork is exported or printed. Objects that are rasterized when exported or printed use the settings located in the Printing & Export panel of the Document Info dialog box.

You should select a transparent background if the rasterized object will be placed in front of or otherwise interact with another object. Figure 18.15 shows the difference between white and transparent backgrounds.

The Rasterize command also enables you to apply antialiasing (discussed later in this chapter) and add background pixels around the object. This extra space is sometimes referred to as *padding*. In Figure 18.15, note that the lower text is clipped on the left side, despite being left-aligned. The Rasterize command uses the baseline of a type object to determine left and right edges. The upper example includes all the letters *j* because padding of 36 pixels was selected in the dialog box.

Rasterized at the wrong settings? Can't use Undo? See "Rerasterizing" in the "Troubleshooting" section at the end of this chapter.

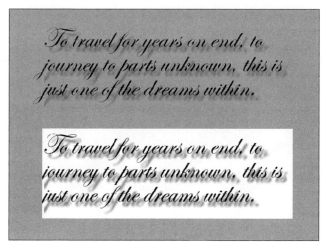

Figure 18.15
Rasterization produces a rectangular object. Both pieces of text are rasterized, but the upper example has a transparent background.

Resolution and Antialiasing

The resolution (dpi/ppi) at which artwork is rasterized can make a large difference in its appearance. In Figure 18.16, four identical paths were created, each with a one-point black stroke and no fill. Three of the lines were rasterized at different settings, using the command Object, Rasterize.

The bottom line remains vector art, with sharp edges that ignore the raster. The next were rasterized at 300dpi, 150dpi, and 72dpi, respectively. Note that the top line, rasterized at 72dpi, does not conform to the 300ppi grid in the background. That grid, created separately, is visible only to show the pixels.

In addition to the resolution, you must select or forego antialiasing. *Antialiasing* is a technique whereby the sharp, jagged edge of pixels is disguised. As you saw in Figure 18.16, rasterized curves are constructed of pixels, which have sharp corners. The antialiased lines soften those edges visually by adding in lightly colored pixels along the edges. Figure 18.17 shows the differences among lines rasterized at various resolutions, with and without antialiasing selected.

Caution

Using the command Object, Rasterize changes an object into pixels. You cannot alter this change later (except with the Undo command before you close the file). You can reverse the command Effect, Rasterize, Rasterize by selecting the object and deleting Rasterize from the Appearance palette. The difference between the two commands is the difference between changing an object into pixels and giving an object the appearance of being made of pixels. Effects can be reversed and edited.

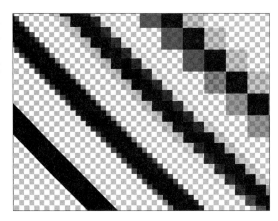

Figure 18.16
Zoomed to 4800%, the three top lines are rasterized at the three basic settings, all with antialiasing selected.

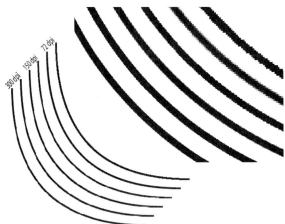

Figure 18.17
These identical lines were rasterized with and without antialiasing at 300, 150, and 72dpi. The close-up is at 500% zoom.

300 dpi   150 dpi   72 dpi

As you can see, the three antialiased lines, despite the difference in resolution, are very similar at 100% zoom. You can also see that antialiasing is far more important at lower resolutions than at high resolutions. At 100% zoom, antialiasing makes a substantial difference for the 72dpi lines. The stair-step pattern of pixel edges visible along the edges of the non-antialiased curves is a problem called *jaggies*. As you can see in the 100% zoom comparison, antialiasing is very effective in minimizing the appearance of jaggies.

You need to keep in mind a few points when considering rasterization for a vector object. Solid color objects that consist entirely of horizontal and vertical edges can be rasterized without antialiasing. Objects rasterized through the Object menu cannot be used in blends, but those rasterized using the Effect menu can be blended. A blend can be rasterized as an effect or using the Object menu.

Illustrator does an adequate job of rasterizing most artwork. However, when it comes to gradients and gradient meshes, you may experience *banding*. Banding occurs when similarly colored pixels are grouped together into a single color. The subtle variations within gradients can be lost, replaced by linear or ovoid stripes.

You can avoid this problem simply by saving the file as an Illustrator file and opening it in Photoshop. Photoshop rasterizes the artwork much more smoothly.

Preparing Raster Images for Use in Illustrator

When you're using an image-editing program to prepare raster artwork for inclusion in an Illustrator document, you need to keep three concepts in mind: dimensions, color mode, and file format.

Illustrator can accept raster artwork in any size and resolution and resize it to fit the allotted space. However, such resizing may degrade the quality of the image. It is preferable to prepare the artwork in the exact size and, if for print, resolution required. If the image must be resized, using a pixel-based program, such as Photoshop, to resample yields better results. Remember that images that will end up on the Web should be measured in pixels, not inches or centimeters.

Preparing an image may require a change in color mode. Remember that Illustrator no longer allows RGB and CMYK objects in the same document. Let your raster image editor do the color conversion; you'll have more control over the process.

Lastly, the file must be in a format that Illustrator can read. Although you can open and place the majority of the most common bitmap (raster) image formats, some proprietary files are not readable. Those programs can usually allow you to save or export in a usable format. Deneba Canvas's native file format, for example, cannot be imported into Illustrator, but Canvas allows you to save in several formats that can be read.

TROUBLESHOOTING

Calculating Resolution for Print

The numbers are mind-boggling. What do I need to know to get the right resolution for my print job?

You need to know the line screen frequency (in lines per inch, or lpi) that will be used to print the job. Call the printer that will handle the actual production. Multiply the number you get by 1.5 and you have your minimum safe image resolution. You can go as high as two times the lpi and often as low as 1.2 times the lpi. There's no reason to go above twice the screen frequency, however, because of the way the printer's dots are calculated. (See Chapter 24, "Commercial Printing and Trapping Issues," for details.)

Vector-izing

Changing an image from vector to raster is called rasterizing, but is there a way to go backward? I need to make editable paths from some line art I scanned.

Illustrator comes complete with the Auto Trace tool. It can follow the lines of the artwork and produce usable vectors. However, you'll get much better results with a dedicated program, such as Adobe's Streamline. Virtually any image can be converted to vector art for use in Illustrator, and line art is right at the top of the list.

Rerasterizing

I've made a mistake and need some help. I rasterized an object at the wrong resolution. What can I do?

The easiest thing, of course, is to use Undo. If that's not available because the file was closed and reopened, or because of intervening actions, you may still be okay. If you choose Effect, Rasterize, Rasterize, you can change the settings by selecting the object on the artboard or in the Layers palette and using the Attributes palette. Double-click the Rasterize entry, and the dialog box opens for you to make changes.

If you chose Object, Rasterize, the steps are a little different. If the object was rasterized with a white background, you're stuck with it. If you need to add a white background or change the resolution, simply rerasterize with the same command and different settings. Figure 18.18 shows an object that was rasterized at 72ppi and then again at 300ppi. The antialiasing tells the story.

Figure 18.18
The smaller pixels of the image on the right, which was rasterized at 300ppi, are visible in the antialiasing.

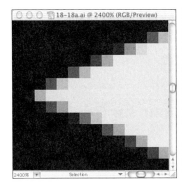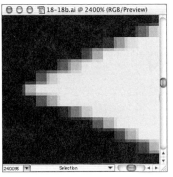

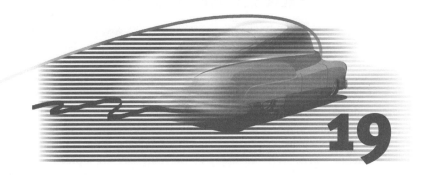

EXPLOITING ILLUSTRATOR'S TRANSPARENCY

IN THIS CHAPTER

Working with Transparency in Illustrator 406

The Blending Modes 414

Outputting Transparency 424

Troubleshooting 427

WORKING WITH TRANSPARENCY IN ILLUSTRATOR

Illustrator offers the capability to change the opacity of objects and images, much like Adobe Photoshop. In early versions of the program, an object could have a fill and stroke of None, making it invisible on the artboard, and the GIF file format supported invisible backgrounds. However, you could not make an object semi-transparent, easily apply a realistic shadow or glow that fades with distance, or change the way the colors of overlapping objects blend.

Transparency brings to Illustrator a tremendous creative boost, but also brings with it the potential for compatibility and printing problems. When it comes to actually outputting to paper, film, or plate, the concept of transparency disappears. Objects are printed as raster or vector, or a combination of both. Illustrator allows you to specify a preference for how transparency is handled in print output. In addition, there are restrictions on file formats for using transparency on the Web. However, during the creative process in Illustrator, you can work with transparency without regard for output issues, giving you near-complete control of opacity and color blending. In this respect, while you're producing artwork, Illustrator can be said to offer real transparency.

The *appearance* of transparency has always been available in Illustrator, but in the past, it has been difficult to achieve. For example, a drop shadow can be simulated with a gradient, as shown in Figure 19.1.

Figure 19.1
Placing a copy of an object that is filled with a black-to-white gradient behind the object can simulate the transparency of a drop shadow.

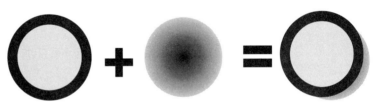

The gradient runs from black to white and in the shape of the object. In this case, with a simple circle, a radial gradient suffices. Drop shadows that can be directly applied rather than simulated with another object are just one example of transparency effects and filters in Illustrator. You can apply transparency to an object, its fill or stroke, or a group, or even assign it to a layer.

The Transparency Theory

Although *transparency* is the term we use, it's not exactly correct. Transparent objects, technically, are clear, such as window glass. In the case of Illustrator, that would make them invisible with a stroke and fill of None. *Translucent*, on the other hand, is also not quite appropriate for our purposes. It implies distortion of the light coming through, such as frosted glass.

In Illustrator, we can use the term *transparency* much as it is used in photography, where it refers to the amount of light passing through the film's emulsion. However, rather than measure an object's transparency, we work backward and describe its opacity. An object can be from 100% opaque (solid) to 0% opaque (invisible). In simpler terms, an object's opacity refers to whether or not (or how much) you can see an object behind it on the artboard. In Figure 19.2, a series of rectangles show the range of opacity against Illustrator's grid. The right-most rectangle, with an opacity of 0%, is selected.

Figure 19.2
If the rectangle on the far right was not selected, it would not be visible.

⇨ *Confused about the difference between transparency and opacity? See "Two Terms, One Concept" in the "Troubleshooting" section at the end of this chapter.*

Opacity is not the same as color value. Figure 19.3 compares transparency with grayscale fill values, each in increments of 10%. While the results may appear comparable on the artboard, an object's interaction with other objects may depend upon the difference between tinted fill and opacity changes.

100%   Opacity   0%

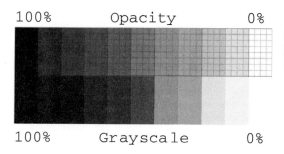

Figure 19.3
Note that the grid is not visible behind the color value swatches.

100%   Grayscale   0%

In addition, observe in Figure 19.4 that only in a couple of these cases do grayscale tint and opacity produce comparable appearances at comparable values.

At a couple of other places along the bars, opacity and grayscale values are very close. As you can see in Figure 19.5, a grayscale value of 70% is comparable to an opacity of 90%, and 50% gray is comparable to 70% opaque. These values, of course, are valid only against a white background and with these color settings.

The grayscale "matches" illustrated here are examples. Your choices in the Color Settings dialog box will determine how Illustrator displays color. In this example, the monitor profile is selected for RGB and the CMYK working space is ColorSync.

100%   Opacity   0%

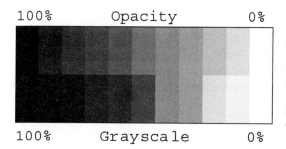

Figure 19.4
You can see that 100%, 40%, and 0% (invisible at the right end of the bars) produce comparable appearance for both grayscale and opacity using the current color settings.

100%   Grayscale   0%

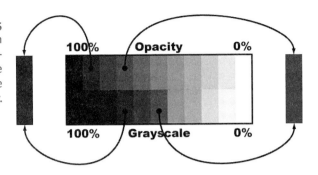

Figure 19.5
When compared next to each other, the swatches are very similar. To the left are 90% opaque and 70% gray; to the right are 70% opaque and 50% gray.

Opacity is much more difficult to simulate against a colored background. As you saw in Figure 19.1, creating a drop shadow for an object on a white background is relatively simple. Simulating such a shadow becomes a bit more difficult on a colored background. The gradient must then run from black to the background color. Figure 19.6 shows a comparison.

Figure 19.6
The "shadow" on the left is a black-to-white gradient and stands out from the background. The shadow on the right is from black to the background color and looks more natural.

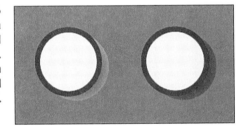

The technique becomes very complicated when the object sits on a multicolored background. If the shadow is to look as if it actually interacts with the background, it would have to be made up of numerous small segments, each of which would blend from black to that area's background color. This is no problem when transparency is available, as shown in Figure 19.7.

Figure 19.7
The "shadow" on the left is a gradient, whereas that on the right is an effect. (You can get this effect by choosing Effect, Stylize, Drop Shadow.)

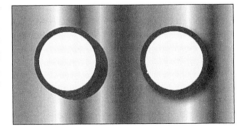

Opacity allows objects to interact in ways that are difficult (but not impossible) to reproduce. For example, in Figure 19.8, a single rectangle with an opacity of 50% overlaps several objects of different colors and different opacities. At the top, several objects are selected. Below, you can see how many objects it would take to re-create this look without opacity. Each individual object would be filled with a specific blend of the two colors to simulate the overlap.

Figure 19.8
One object using opacity to overlap four other objects requires 19 separate objects to re-create without opacity.

Bear in mind that the example shown in Figure 19.8 is actually very simplistic. All the objects have simple, one-color fills and they are unstroked. Adding strokes or complex fills greatly increases the difficulty of simulating transparency.

The division of overlapping objects into discrete components (as shown in Figure 19.8) is related to the way Illustrator prepares transparency for printing to both PostScript and non-PostScript printers. (This subject is discussed in more detail later in this chapter.)

Transparency works by calculating the effect of the two or more superimposed images upon each other. You can alter this interaction by changing an object's *blending mode*. Changing the blending mode, discussed in depth later in this chapter, alters the way two or more colors are calculated as they overlap.

The Transparency Palette

The primary way to control transparency in Illustrator is to use the Transparency palette. The palette allows you to specify percentage of opacity, blending mode, and several other variables. You can expand or reduce the palette, shown in Figure 19.9, by clicking its tab to cycle through the views. This figure shows it fully expanded, with the palette menu showing.

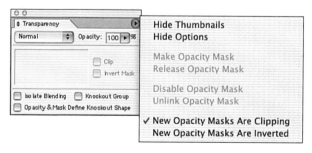

Figure 19.9
You access the palette menu through the small black triangle in the palette's upper-right corner.

You can change the transparency of an object selected on the artboard by either typing a new value (default: 100%) or using the Opacity field's slider. You change the blending mode (default: Normal) by choosing from the pop-up menu. The middle section of the palette controls opacity masks, which are discussed briefly later in this chapter and in depth in Chapter 17, "Using Masks to Show and Hide." The lower section is used primarily for printing preparation and is also discussed later in this chapter.

You also can use the Transparency palette in conjunction with the Layers and Appearance palettes. Using the Layers palette allows you to target a group or layer. Every object created in or pasted into that group or layer then assumes the designated level of transparency.

▷ *Unsure about how group and layer opacity affects objects with opacity values other than 100%? See "Multiple Transparencies" in the "Troubleshooting" section at the end of this chapter.*

Transparency and Groups

Transparency can affect groups differently from individual objects. When transparency is applied to individual objects in a group, their opacity is cumulative. When the change is applied to the group as a whole, the opacity affects how the group interacts with objects it overlies, but not how the members of the group affect each other.

Figure 19.10 shows three identical groups. The first group and the individual squares within it all have an opacity of 100%. In the middle, the three squares were selected individually, and their transparency was changed to 70%. Note how they interact with each other. The cumulative opacity in the center almost completely blocks the background. On the right, however, the group was targeted in the Layers palette. The changes affect the group as a whole. The relationship among the squares is consistent, and the group has a uniform level of difference with the background.

Figure 19.10
Targeting groups for opacity changes can protect the color relationships among the elements of the group.

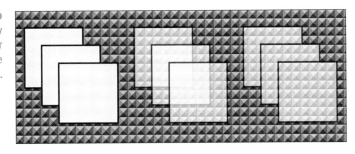

When used with the Appearance palette, multiple fills and/or strokes can be applied to an individual object. Without transparency, strokes of decreasing width can be layered. Transparency allows strokes of the same or narrower stroke to be layered, as well as fills. Figure 19.11 shows some of the potential.

Figure 19.11
This single object has five fills, all visible to some degree or another because of the varying opacity and blending modes. Additional fills are added to an object through the Appearance palette menu.

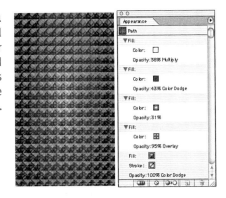

Transparency Preferences and Other Settings

Several settings affect transparency in Illustrator. In the Files & Clipboard preferences, for example, you can control how Illustrator handles transparency when copying. The Document Setup dialog box (shown in Figure 19.12) regulates, on a document-by-document basis, the printing and export of transparency, as well as some interface issues.

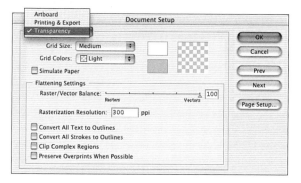

Figure 19.12
You access the Document Setup dialog box through the File menu.

The transparency grid, designed to aid visibility of objects with lowered opacity, is controlled with Document Setup, but shown and hidden through the View menu. The command is View, Show Transparency Grid, and the default keyboard shortcut is Cmd+Shift+D [Ctrl+Shift+D]. Figure 19.13 shows the grid with its default settings and how it works with opacity.

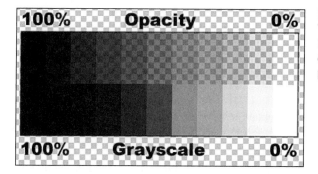

Figure 19.13
The transparency grid is hidden by objects with higher levels of opacity and visible behind transparent objects.

The transparency grid is not limited to the artboard; it extends across the entire work area. The size of the grid (determined in the Document Setup dialog box) is relative to the screen, not the artboard. In Figure 19.14, note that the zoom factor has been reduced to 50%, yet the grid remains the same size.

The Document Setup dialog box offers you a choice of three grid sizes, as well as three shades of gray and five preset colors. In addition, you can designate your own color for the grid by choosing the Custom option. You can also click either of the two color swatches to open the Color Picker and designate custom color combinations for

When you're working with grayscale objects of variable opacity, it's often better to designate a bright color for the grid. When you're working with illustrations that are primarily of a specific hue, using a contrasting color rather than gray for the transparency grid often makes it more effective.

the grid. The upper swatch controls the background (paper) color, and the lower swatch controls the grid squares themselves.

The Document Setup dialog box also offers the option Simulate Colored Paper. The color for the paper is controlled through the upper swatch in the Document Setup dialog box. Like the transparency grid, the color of the simulated color paper extends throughout the work area and is not limited to the artboard or the page tiling. Also like the transparency grid, it is nonprinting.

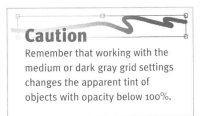

Caution

Remember that working with the medium or dark gray grid settings changes the apparent tint of objects with opacity below 100%.

Figure 19.14
The transparency grid is unaffected by changes in zoom or view.

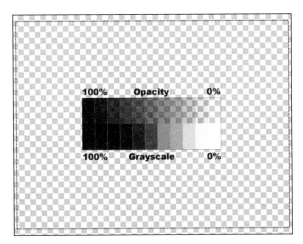

Figure 19.15 shows an example of using the Simulate Paper option. Even in grayscale, certain aspects of the option are apparent:

- The color "white" disappears. The comparison bars are the same used earlier in this chapter, with transparency changes on top and tint (grayscale) changes below. (Refer to the original in Figure 19.13.)

- The horizontal bar in the lowest group has a white fill. Although the fill doesn't show against the colored paper background, it is visible in the Layers palette and is listed in the Appearance palette. (The rectangle is the selected path at the bottom of the Layers path.)

- Notice that the grayscale samples in the middle group knock out the horizontal bar. (*Knockout* is a printing term. When an upper color knocks out a lower color, the lower color is not actually printed.)

➪ *Wondering what use you might have for simulated color paper? See "Picturing It on Paper" in the "Troubleshooting" section at the end of this chapter.*

The Document Setup dialog box's Quality/Speed option is explained in the section "Outputting Transparency" later in this chapter.

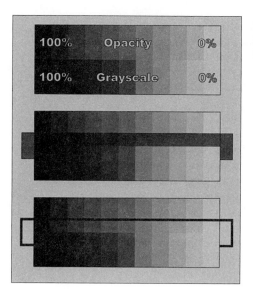

Figure 19.15
Simulated Colored Paper adds a background of the selected color.

Opacity Masks

Opacity masks, which are discussed in detail in Chapter 17, use the luminosity of the upper-most object to produce a transparent pattern on lower objects. When the masking object is filled with a solid color, the mask is uniform. If the luminosity is high (bright colors), the mask appears to have little or no effect. If the masking object is filled with a dark color, the artwork below is made more transparent. When the masking object is filled with a pattern or a gradient, the results can vary substantially. Opacity masks can be inverted so that the lighter values have a higher impact. Examples of opacity masks are shown in Figure 19.16.

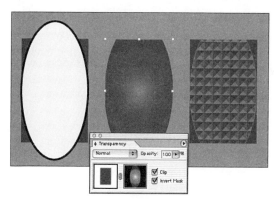

Figure 19.16
The original objects are shown to the left. In the center, a gradient creates an inverted opacity mask. On the right, a pattern fill is used and the mask is not inverted.

By changing an object's fill to a gradient or a pattern, you can use opacity masks to create transparency effects. You must keep in mind several guidelines when planning opacity masks:

- The uppermost object creates the mask for all selected objects below.

- If objects in different groups or on different layers are selected, they are moved to the layer of the lowest selected object.

- If one selected object is a member of a group on the lowest layer, all the selected objects are moved to that group.

- If a selected object is a member of a group that is on a layer other than that of the lowest selected object, it is removed from its group and moved to the lowest object's layer.

- If an effect, such as a drop shadow, is targeted on the layer of the lowest object, all objects affected by the opacity mask assume the effect.

- If one selected object is on a layer with specific attributes, it does not carry the layer's effects with it if moved to a lower layer.

- If the object you're using to create the opacity mask is on a layer with an effect such as a drop shadow, the effect is discarded. If, on the other hand, the effect is applied to the object itself, it becomes part of the opacity mask (see Figure 19.17).

Figure 19.17
On the left, the object used to create the mask was on a layer with a drop shadow. The shadow is not part of the mask. On the right, the drop shadow effect was applied to the object itself, so it is part of the opacity mask.

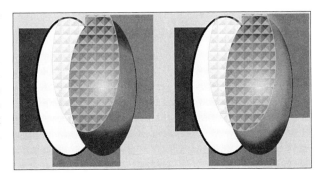

THE BLENDING MODES

Any time two colors overlap, one of two things can happen: The upper color can block the lower completely, or the two colors can interact. Blending modes determine how a color interacts with colors below it. As you can see in Figure 19.18, blending modes are controlled through the Transparency palette.

Figure 19.18
Several of the 16 blending modes have near-identical effects on any two colors but may have radically different effects on another pair of colors. Select an object on the artboard or in the Layers palette to change its blending mode.

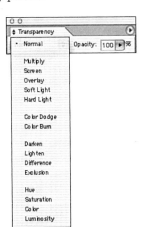

In a discussion of blending modes, Illustrator uses the terms *base color*, *blend color*, and *resulting color*. They are, respectively, the color in back or below, the color in front or above, and the color that results from their interaction.

A set of samples has been prepared to show the differences among the blending modes. (The samples are shown in Figures 20.19 through 20.34.) Because these samples will be used throughout this section to demonstrate how colors interact, it is worthwhile to explore them.

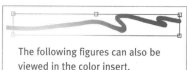

The following figures can also be viewed in the color insert.

- The samples appear on two distinct backgrounds. The larger area, to the left, is blue, with an RGB value of 0/0/255. The HSB value is Hue: 240, Saturation: 100, Brightness: 100. To the right, the background is yellow, with an RGB value of 255/255/0. The HSB value is 60/100/100. The blending mode of the two background rectangles will remain set to Normal throughout the examples.

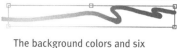

The background colors and six rainbow rectangles, discussed in the preceding two bullets, constitute the *base colors* for the blending mode demonstrations. The gradients and grids discussed in the following six bullets represent the "samples" themselves, the *blending colors*. Remember that in all the examples that follow, the base colors, which will retain a blending mode of Normal, are below the blending colors. Only the blending colors will have altered blending modes.

- Just above the background colors are six horizontal rectangles, filled with rainbow gradients. The rectangles stretch the width of the images. They are between the background colors and the sample swatches and gradients. They, like the background colors, have a blending mode of Normal. They will demonstrate how blending modes can affect a range of colors. The blending mode of the six thin rectangles will remain set to Normal throughout the examples.

- Across the top on both sides are RGB rainbow gradients. They will show how the range of colors interacts with the various blending modes. The blending mode of the gradients will change from example to example.

- The three grids are designed to show how blending modes affect changes in saturation and brightness. As the rows move upward, the saturation value decreases in increments of 25%. The columns, moving from left to right, decrease in brightness value, also in increments of 25%. Each upper-left square has a saturation of 25% and a brightness of 100%. The opposite square, in the lower right of each grid, has a saturation of 100% and a brightness of 25%. The upper right is 25/25 and the lower left is 100/100. Although the combination of saturation and brightness changes from square to square, each square in a grid has the same hue value. The blending mode of the squares that make up the three grids will change from example to example.

- The grid on the left uses yellow as a base color (RGB: 255/255/0, HSB: 60/100/100) in the lower-left square. From that value, the grid progresses uniformly to an HSB value of 60/25/25 in the upper right.

- The middle grid uses a base color of HSB: 150/100/100, a hue that is halfway between the yellow (H:60) and blue background (H:240). The RGB equivalent is 0/255/127. Like the other two grids, the higher rows have lower saturation values, while the columns decrease in brightness from left to right.

- The third grid, on the yellow background, uses a base color of HSB: 240/100/100, the same blue as the background on the left. This combination of blue on yellow reverses that of the left-hand grid.

- The larger grayscale gradient on the left has 11 color stops, evenly spaced between 100% gray and 0% gray. On the right, the smaller grayscale gradient is a simple black-to-white gradient, without the intermediary color stops. The blending mode of these gradients, too, will change from example to example.

Normal

Normal is the default, and the most common, blending mode. The top color supercedes the bottom color. Figure 19.19 shows the samples, all with a Normal blending mode.

Figure 19.19
This is what the samples look like without any interaction with the background colors.

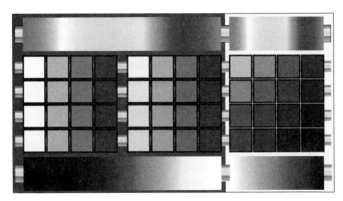

Multiply

The Multiply blending mode calculates the color values (RGB or CMYK) of both the top and bottom colors and multiplies them. Because it is a multiplication calculation, the resulting color is always darker than the original top color. Figure 19.20 shows the samples when their blending modes are Multiply.

In areas where the grids overlap only the background colors, notice the difference between the left and middle grids. The multiplication of the color values pushed more of the left grid's squares into black than in the middle grid. Because the two factors were the same (the color values being multiplied) where they overlap only their respective background colors, the right and left grids are identical except for the hue values.

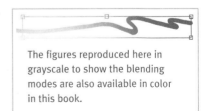

The figures reproduced here in grayscale to show the blending modes are also available in color in this book.

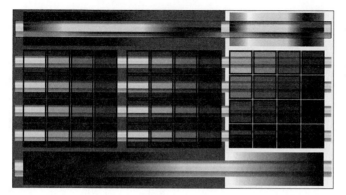

Figure 19.20
The Multiply blending mode always results in a darker color, except when the lower color is white (which results in no change).

Screen

Screen is, mathematically, the opposite of Multiply. The inverse of each color value is multiplied. The resulting color is always lighter. Figure 19.21 shows the result of changing the color mode of the samples to Screen.

Figure 19.21
If the upper color is black when you use Screen as the blending mode, no change is observed. White, however, always produces white when screening.

Although not apparent in the grayscale version of the figure, the screening of blue over red produces magenta, and green over blue produces cyan. Also nearly impossible to see in the grayscale is the effect of screening the yellow grid squares that have 100% brightness (the leftmost column). The gradient below has become shades of yellow, with saturation varying by row.

Overlay

Overlay serves as a cross between Multiply and Screen (see Figure 19.22). The lower color's values for brightness are retained (highlights and shadows). If the background color is dark, it is multiplied and becomes darker. If it is light, it is screened and becomes lighter. Often a hue shift also occurs.

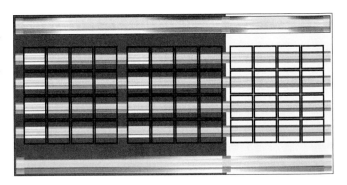

Figure 19.22
Overlay is a mix of Multiply and Screen, as you can see in the gradients.

Where they overlap only the background colors, both the grid squares and the gradients have disappeared. You can see this change in both the grayscale version of Figure 19.22 (pictured here) and in the color version (elsewhere in this book). This is a function of using the Overlay blending mode on top of areas of flat color.

Soft Light

Soft Light is a mixture of Color Dodge and Color Burn (explained later). If the top color is light, the bottom color is lightened; if dark, the lower color is darkened (see Figure 19.23). The effects of soft light are more subtle than many of the other blending modes. Some shifting of hues can be expected.

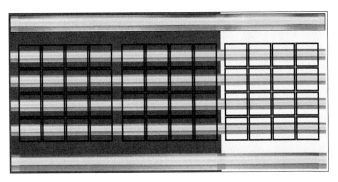

Figure 19.23
Using Soft Light with light colors is comparable to using Color Dodge; with dark colors, it is comparable to Color Burn.

Hard Light

Although pure black or white is ineffective with the Hard Light blending mode, shades of gray are very effective for adding highlights and shadows to an image (see Figure 19.24). Like some other blending modes, Hard Light acts like Multiply when colors are dark and like Screen with light colors.

Color Dodge

Dodging is a darkroom technique designed to lighten certain areas of a photograph. When you partially block the light before it reaches the paper, the image in that area is neither as dark nor as saturated. The Color Dodge blending mode is typically used with lighter blending colors. Blending with black produces no change (see Figure 19.25).

Figure 19.24
In this particular instance, you can see the best example of how the Hard Light blending mode works in the grayscale image. Look at the center one-third of the gradient example to the left at the bottom of the image. The highlights and shadows are emphasized.

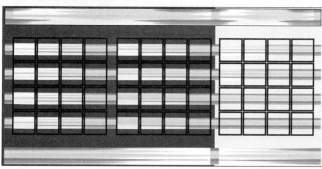

Figure 19.25
Looking at the lower gradient bars, you can see that the darker gray values produce little or no change, whereas the lighter grays create extreme change.

Color Burn

Color Burn is the complement to Color Dodge. As dodging is a darkroom technique to lighten parts of an image, so burning results in darkening of an image. Blending dark colors over a base color results in darkening. Blending with white produces no change in the lower color (see Figure 19.26).

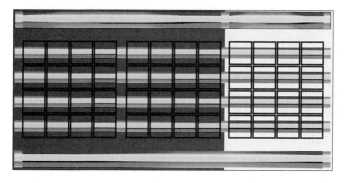

Figure 19.26
Here, you see that the lighter grays in the bottom gradient bars have very little effect. The darker grays produce dramatic changes in the underlying colors.

Darken

The Darken blending mode does a comparison of the upper and lower colors. If the underlying color is lighter than the blending color, it is darkened. If the lower color is already darker than the upper, it is unchanged (see Figure 19.27).

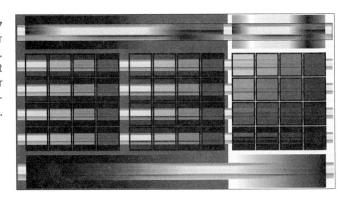

Figure 19.27
In the areas where the upper color is lighter, it appears to disappear. Note that this happens not just with the white areas of the lower gradients, but also with other colors, including the upper gradient.

Lighten

The Lighten blending mode is the complement to the Darken blending mode. It determines whether the upper or lower color is lighter and makes changes accordingly. If the lower color is lighter, it is left unchanged. If it is darker, the top color is blended (see Figure 19.28).

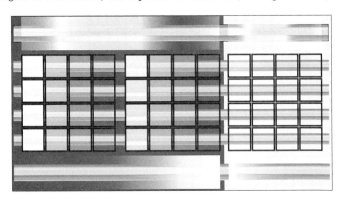

Figure 19.28
Notice in comparison with Figure 19.27 that the darker ends of the blending gradients have disappeared.

Difference

Difference can create among the most dramatic of blending changes. The brightness values of the upper and lower colors are compared, and then the color values of the lesser are subtracted from the greater. Because black has a brightness of zero, no change is made. When you're blending with white, expect colors to be inverted. In Figure 19.29, blending the yellow grid square in the lower left (HSB: 60/100/100) with the blue background (HSB: 240/100/100) results in white. Likewise, blending the comparable blue square with the yellow background results in white.

Exclusion

The results of blending with Exclusion are very similar to, but less dramatic than, those of the Difference blending mode. The best comparison can be made in the third column of each set of grid squares, the 50% brightness column. Comparing Figure 19.30 with Figure 19.29, you'll see much less definition and contrast with Exclusion. This is also apparent in the middle areas of the grayscale gradient bars at the bottom of the figures.

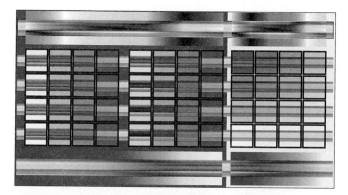

Figure 19.29
Even in grayscale, the results of the Difference blending mode are noticeable.

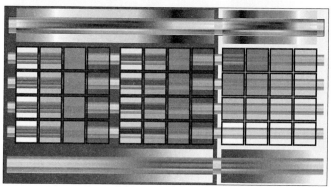

Figure 19.30
Exclusion has a tendency to flatten contrast when working with brightness values approaching 50% in the upper color.

Hue

The Hue blending mode uses the saturation and brightness of the lower color and the hue of the upper color. For that reason, in Figure 19.31, all the squares in each grid are identical. Because the brightness and saturation of the underlying background color and that of the gradients never vary from square to square, and within each grid each square has the same hue, the results are predictable and consistent. Additionally, note that you can see exactly where in the upper gradients the hue matches the background color. In each of the two gradients, you can see a small break in the pattern, a place where the gradient disappears. In the stepped grayscale gradient in the lower left, the points where the gradient are broken show where the background color and gradient values canceled each other out. Contrast this with the grayscale gradient in the lower right, where it overlaps only the background color. This gradient was made with tints of black, so the actual hue remained consistent throughout, and it becomes uniform in appearance when it adopts the uniform saturation and lightness from the background color.

Saturation

In contrast to the Hue blending mode, Saturation uses the hue and brightness from the lower color and the saturation of the upper color. When the upper color is a shade of gray, that neutral saturation overrides the hue. In Figure 19.32, the grayscale gradients at the bottom have superceded the hue values of both the underlying gradients and background colors.

Figure 19.31
When the lower color has consistent saturation and brightness, the results of the Hue blending mode are more predictable.

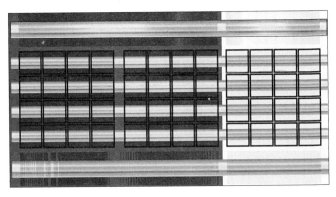

Figure 19.32
The upper (blending) color's saturation value is used with the hue and brightness of the lower (base) color.

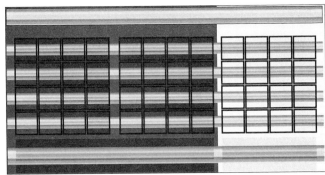

Color

The brightness of the lower color is retained in the Color blending mode, and the other two components (hue and saturation) are contributed by the upper color. In Figure 19.33, another example has been added to the samples. Because the primary use of the Color blending mode is to colorize or tint grayscale images, a grayscale bar has been overlaid with a rainbow gradient. Not apparent in the grayscale rendition of the figure, but visible in color, the hue of the upper (rainbow) gradient has been imposed upon the lower (grayscale) gradient.

Figure 19.33
The lowest sample is a grayscale gradient below and a rainbow gradient above.

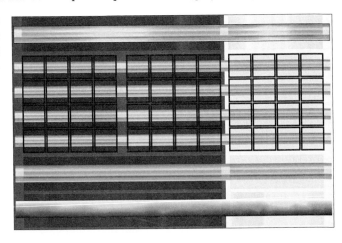

Luminosity

Using the brightness of the upper color and the hue and saturation of the lower color, Luminosity is the reverse of the Color blending mode. As you can see in Figure 19.34, a high brightness value can overwhelm colors with low saturation.

The last four blending modes—Hue, Saturation, Color, and Luminosity—take HSB values from either the lower or upper color to create the resulting color. The chart shown in Table 19.1 simplifies the equation for you.

Caution

The Hue, Saturation, Color, and Luminosity blending modes do not work with spot colors. Convert both upper and lower spot colors to process colors before applying these blending modes.

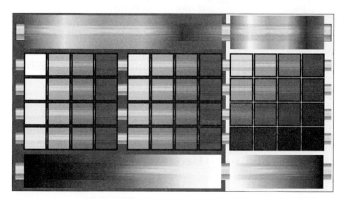

Figure 19.34
Luminosity retains the color values for the lower colors but applies the brightness of the upper color.

Table 19.1 Blending Modes

Blending Mode	H	S	B
Hue	Upper	Lower	Lower
Saturation	Lower	Upper	Lower
Color	Upper	Upper	Lower
Luminosity	Lower	Lower	Upper

The four blending modes take HSB components from the two colors being blended to create the resulting color. Illustrator refers to the upper color as the blending color and the lower color as the base color.

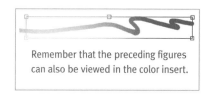

Remember that the preceding figures can also be viewed in the color insert.

Restricting the Effects of Blending Modes

Unless you specify otherwise, an object's blending mode affects its interaction with all colors below it. In the Transparency palette, you can choose the option Isolate Blending. When this option is checked, the interaction of colors created by a blending mode is constrained to a group. As you can see in Figure 19.35, you can have members of a group interact with all colors below (left) or restrict the blending to the group itself (right).

Figure 19.35
The stars on both the left and right have the blending mode Multiply. On the left, the stars are blended with each other and with the oval and rectangle below. On the right, with Isolate Blending checked, the stars blend only with each other.

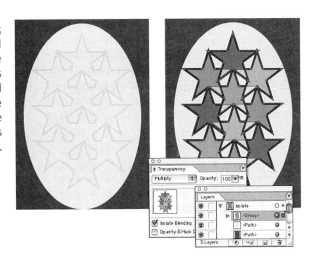

OUTPUTTING TRANSPARENCY

Transparency can be a problem for printing. When two objects with 100% opacity overlap, Illustrator need print only the top object because the lower object is totally obscured. When the upper object has opacity of less than 100%, or a blending mode other than Normal is applied, additional objects may have to be created from the area of overlap. Figure 19.36 shows an example.

Figure 19.36
The figures on the top left (Normal blending mode) would be printed as two objects, as shown in the bottom left. The figures on the top right (Multiply blending mode) would be printed as three objects, as shown on the bottom right.

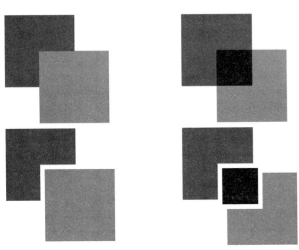

Although the example in Figure 19.36 seems simple enough, complex illustrations can lead to extremely complex printing problems. Merely adding strokes to the objects in Figure 19.36 complicates matters. Rather than three separate objects, the number balloons to nine, as you can see in Figure 19.37.

Adding additional objects and multiple layers of overlap, as well as gradients, can make matters extremely complicated. Figure 19.38 shows an image that requires a great deal of calculation before printing.

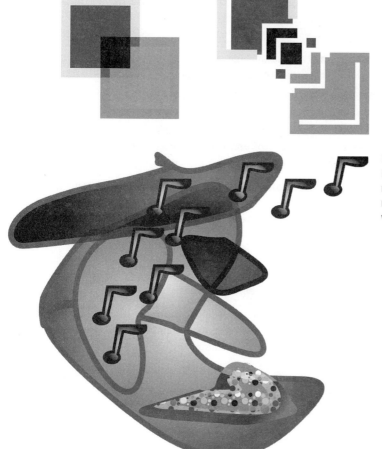

Figure 19.37
When a lowered opacity or blending mode is used, each area where two colors overlap becomes a separate color.

Figure 19.38
Every place where a blending mode changes or opacity is reduced results in additional work for printers.

Preparing Transparent Objects for Print

The primary tool for print preparation of illustrations containing transparency is the Document Setup dialog box. Figure 19.39 shows the options, including the Printing & Export slider.

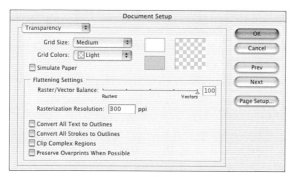

Figure 19.39
The dialog box's grid options were discussed earlier in this chapter, as was Simulate Paper.

Using the Transparency panel of the Document Setup dialog box, you can choose from five levels of compromise between quality and printing speed. Illustrator's descriptions of the five levels of Quality/Speed are as follows (from Lower/Faster to Higher/Slower):

● The entire illustration will be rasterized. Use this setting for printing or exporting very complex illustrations with many transparent objects. Ideal for fast output at low resolution; higher resolution will yield higher quality but increase processing time. Size of saved files or print spool files may be large.

● Maintains simpler vector objects, but rasterizes more complex areas involving transparency. Ideal for artwork with only a few transparent objects. Some printers may yield rough transitions between bordering vector and raster objects and make hairlines appear thicker. Appropriate for low-memory systems.

● Maintains most objects as vector data, but rasterizes very complex transparent regions. Generally the best setting for printing and exporting most illustrations. With some printers, improves transition issues between bordering vector and raster objects.

● Maintains most of the illustration as vectors, rasterizing only extremely complex areas. Produces high quality output that is generally resolution independent. Higher occurrences of transparent regions will increase processing time. With some printers, improves transition issues between bordering vector and raster objects.

● The entire illustration is printed or exported as vector data, to the greatest extent possible. This produces the highest quality resolution-independent output. Processing of complex illustrations may be very time and memory intensive.

Despite appearances, the Quality/Speed "slider" actually only has five settings available. Additional information about four-color process printing is available in Chapter 24, "Commercial Printing and Trapping Issues."

Transparency and the Web

Most graphic images on the World Wide Web are in JPEG or GIF file formats. Both of them are raster formats. As such, the issue of whether areas of color should be vector or raster disappears when you save images in either of these formats. The entire illustration or image becomes a single raster image. The file is automatically flattened and becomes a series of individually colored pixels. (See Chapter 18, "Raster Images and Rasterized Objects," for a full explanation of the difference between vector and raster.) PNG is another raster image format, and it is becoming more common on the Web.

Images in the Flash and SVG formats are also becoming more common. They, however, are vector formats. They are discussed in Chapter 23, "Flash and SVG Support."

The term *transparency* applies to Web graphics in another sense as well. GIF images can have irregular outlines with uncolored areas becoming transparent on the Web. JPEG, on the other hand, can have no such transparency. Every JPEG image must be rectangular. If an area of an illustration is not filled with color, it appears as white in a Web browser. Figure 19.40 shows examples.

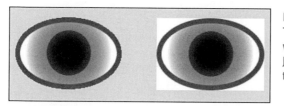

Figure 19.40
The image on the left is GIF, whereas the copy on the right is JPEG. JPEG does not support transparent backgrounds.

TROUBLESHOOTING

Two Terms, One Concept

What exactly is the difference between opacity and transparency?

Opacity is the way you measure transparency in Illustrator. An object through which you can see other objects below it on the artboard is said to be transparent. *How* transparent is a question of opacity. Using the Transparency palette's slider, you can assign an opacity of 0% to 100% to an object. In this respect, transparency and opacity are opposites; an object that has a 75% opacity setting is 25% transparent.

Don't forget, too, that there's more to transparency than just opacity. An object with an opacity of 100% can still be partially or fully transparent, depending on its blending mode and the interaction of its fill and stroke with colors below. In addition, an object with an opacity of 100% is still fully transparent if the fill and stroke are both None.

Multiple Transparencies

What happens if an object with, say, 75% opacity is moved to a layer that has, say, 50% opacity? Which takes precedence?

You could say that neither takes precedence. The effects are cumulative. Therefore, the object no longer is 75% opaque, nor is it 50% opaque. Its opacity is $50 \times .75 = 37.5\%$.

Picturing It on Paper

Why would I want to use the Simulate Paper setting?

Not all projects are printed on white paper. Remember that inks are not truly opaque and that the color of the paper shows through. When you're printing on bright white stock, coated or uncoated, this is not a particular problem. This option allows you to see what your illustration will look like as it goes to print on colored stock. It can also be very valuable when you're preparing jobs that will run on white paper of a lower brightness.

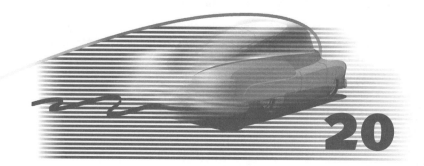

20

USING FILTERS AND EFFECTS

IN THIS CHAPTER

About Filters and Effects   430

Illustrator's Filter and Effect Menus   433

The Top of the Menus   434

The Middle of the Menus—Vector   435

The Bottom of the Menu—Raster   446

Troubleshooting   466

ABOUT FILTERS AND EFFECTS

Filters and effects, in most cases, are simply shortcuts. They do automatically, or with the drag of a slider and the click of a button, what could take hours to do manually. There are some filters and effects that would be almost impossible to replicate step by step in Illustrator. Illustrator installs, by default, nearly 140 filters and effects.

What They Do and How They Do It

Most of the filters and effects in Illustrator work in one of two ways. They either manipulate the appearance of an object by changing the way its path looks, or they alter the appearance by rasterizing and manipulating pixels. (Some do both, and so fall outside these general statements.) The difference can be categorized as similar to the difference between vector and raster artwork. One works with paths, one works with pixels. (And one set of effects is for use strictly with scalable vector graphics files.)

Some of Illustrator's "raster" filters and effects are not available for use with CMYK images. All can be used with both RGB and Grayscale images. Because these raster filters and effects work by manipulating the color information, the difference between RGB's three color channels and CMYK's four color channels presents a barrier.

An example of a path-manipulation effect/filter is seen in Figure 20.1.

Figure 20.1
The original object is on the left, the Pucker & Bloat filter/effect has been applied on the right.

In Figure 20.2, a pair of raster-based effects has been applied to the same object.

Figure 20.2
On the left, the effect Brush Strokes, Spatter has been applied. On the right, the effect is a Gaussian Blur.

➪ *Filter grayed out and unavailable? See "Circumventing the Unavailable Filter" in the "Troubleshooting" section at the end of this chapter.*

Most filters and effects parallel one another; the same appearance can be generated by a filter and its effect counterpart. There are some filters that are not duplicated by effects, and some effects that do not have comparable filters.

Filters Versus Effects

The primary difference between filters and effects is permanence. When applied as a filter, a change to an object's appearance can only be reversed with the Undo command. When altered with an effect, the object's appearance can be restored or changes to the effect can be made at any time. The effect does not actually alter the object, it just changes the appearance. Filters, on the other hand, do make changes to the object itself.

In Figure 20.3, the original object is seen on the left. In the center, the Pucker & Bloat filter has been applied. On the right, the Pucker & Bloat effect has been used. Observe the difference among the paths.

Figure 20.3
The objects are on separate layers so that the paths can be shown in contrasting colors.

The object in the middle has a different path from those to either side. The original object has the paths with which all three objects were created. The object that has an effect applied (on the right) retains that original path, although the appearance is changed. In the center, the filter has changed the path to match the appearance.

The same Pucker & Bloat effect was applied to three more identical objects to show how effects maintain the original object. In Figure 20.4, all three objects had the same effect applied. On the left, the effect is unaltered (for reference). In the center, the effect was removed using the Appearance palette. On the right, the Direct Selection tool was used to alter the object's path. Notice how the effect was updated to match the change in the object's path.

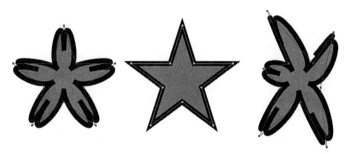

Figure 20.4
If the Pucker & Bloat filter had been used instead of the effect, you would have to manipulate the puckered path.

"Live" Effects

We often use the term "live" when referring to effects in Illustrator. This simply means that the effect can be removed or its settings altered at any time. Many of Illustrator's other capabilities can also be considered live. Strokes, fills, and even styles can be applied and removed at will. Compound paths and crop marks can be made and released. Type can be edited. (Consider, if you will, how much more difficult working with type would be if it were not live. To make a simple change of a word or kerning would require resetting an entire text block.)

On the other hand, many of the things we do in Illustrator are not live. If you use the Direct Selection tool to drag an object's anchor point, that point can be restored to its original position with the Undo command or by dragging it back. If you close and re-open the file, Undo is not available. Trying to put an anchor point back to exactly the same spot later could prove to be an exercise in frustration. Likewise, the Liquify tools are not live, nor is the simple process of deleting an object

One of the keys to working with the concept of live in Illustrator is the Appearance palette. When an effect (not a filter) has been applied to an object, you can re-open the effect dialog box and change the settings. Simply double-click the effect in the Appearance palette (see Figure 20.5). Likewise, you can use the Appearance palette to remove an effect from the object by dragging it to the trash icon at the bottom of the palette.

Figure 20.5
The Appearance palette allows
you to change or remove an effect.

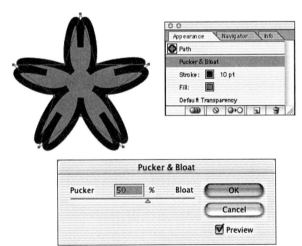

⇨ *Want to remove an effect but forgot how? See "Back to Normal" in the "Troubleshooting" section at the end of this chapter.*

Why Use Filters?

The advantages of using an editable effect rather than a permanent filter are obvious. It's usually a good idea to protect the original artwork as much as possible, just in case you need to make changes from an earlier state. However, there are several situations in which a filter is preferable to its effect counterpart.

- Images with filters applied rather than effects can be substantially smaller.

- Using a filter rather than an effect minimizes the chance that artwork will be inadvertently altered.

- If the file will be saved in an earlier version of Illustrator or exported as a raster image, the advantages of live effects will be lost.

- Additional editing of a path may require that a filter be applied to make permanent changes first. In some cases, the fact that an effect retains the original path can limit additional editing.

ILLUSTRATOR'S FILTER AND EFFECT MENUS

Filters and effects fall into two categories: those applied to vector (Illustrator) objects and those applied to rasterized artwork. At the top of each menu are a couple of commands that allow you to quickly re-apply a filter or effect. The Effect menu also has a command that governs rasterization. The remainder of the two menus are divided into two sections. Generally, the commands located in the middle section of the menus are for vector, whereas those in the lower parts are raster filters (see Figure 20.6). One exception is Pen and Ink, Photo Crosshatch, which works on a raster image to produce a series of vector objects. Such filters as Drop Shadow can be applied to both vector and rasterized artwork.

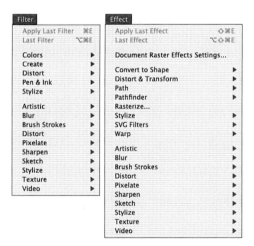

Figure 20.6
When a filter or effect has been used, the top two menu commands will be available and will indicate by name which filter or effect they will apply.

THE TOP OF THE MENUS

At the top of the Filter menu, you'll find a pair of commands that make re-applying the last filter quick and easy. The upper portion of the Effect menu has comparable commands, as well as one that controls how effects are rasterized.

In the descriptions that follow, there will be a notation about whether a particular capability is available as a filter, an effect, or both. In addition, if there is a difference in the behavior or interface between filter and effect versions, that will be noted.

Apply Last Filter/Apply Last Effect

When a filter has been applied, the first command in the Filter menu shows its name. Likewise, when an effect has been applied, it will show in the top command of the Effect menu. Using the Apply Last Filter/Apply Last Effect command reapplies the filter or effect, with whatever settings were last used, to the current selection.

Last Filter/Last Effect

When a filter or effect has been applied, its name is shown in this spot. Using the Last Filter/Last Effect command opens the filter's dialog box. The filter will not be applied until you have had a chance to make any changes and have clicked the OK button.

Document Raster Effects Settings (Effect Only)

These settings (shown in Figure 20.7) determine how Illustrator will work with objects when applying certain effects. With some commands, objects must take on a rasterized appearance. Such effects as glows and drop shadows are raster themselves. Screen resolution (72 ppi) is appropriate for Web graphics and other low-resolution work. Higher resolutions should be reserved for print.

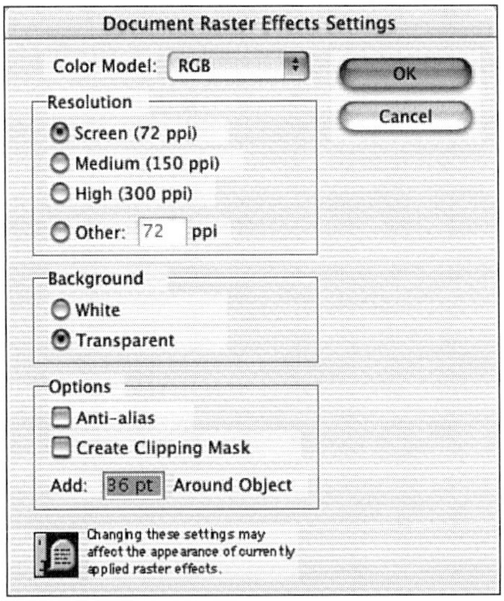

Figure 20.7
These settings affect existing effects as well as those applied later.

THE MIDDLE OF THE MENUS—VECTOR

The filters and effects listed in the middle of the menus are, as mentioned previously, designed for use primarily with vector objects.

Colors (Filter Only)

The following set of filters works with one or more selected objects. The object's stroke color or fill color or both can be adjusted, depending on the specific filter selected.

- **Adjust Colors (filter)**—This command's dialog box uses sliders to change the percentage of each component color in an object (see Figure 20.8). The object can be converted between the document's color mode and grayscale, but not between RGB and CMYK. (Illustrator supports objects of only one color mode per document.) The changes can be applied to the object's fill or stroke. Tints can also be adjusted. Adjust Colors can be used with both vector and raster objects.

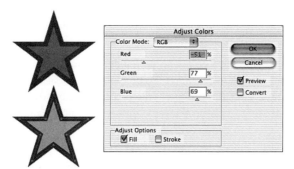

Figure 20.8
You have the option of adjusting the fill, the stroke, or both. In this sample, the lower object's fill is being modified.

- **Blend Front to Back (filter)**—Working with three or more objects, this filter creates intermediate colors in the objects between the front and rear objects. It works only on fills, ignoring all strokes and fills of None.

- **Blend Horizontally (filter)**—Like the other Blend filters, this one works with three or more objects, changing those in the middle to intermediate shades and tints. As the name implies, stacking order is ignored over placement from left to right.

- **Blend Vertically (filter)**—Like the other Blend filters, this one works with three or more objects, changing those in the middle to compromise shades and tints. As the name implies, stacking order is ignored over placement from top to bottom.

- **Convert to CMYK (filter)**—Available only for documents in CMYK mode, this command can bring grayscale objects into the CMYK gamut. However, the color value is still gray. Convert to CMYK can be used with both vector and raster objects.

- **Convert to Grayscale (filter)**—Any selected objects, regardless of the document's color mode, are converted to grayscale. After you execute this command, you can reverse it only by choosing Undo. Using a command to convert back to RGB or CMYK produces an image in the correct color mode but does not restore the former colors. Gradients and patterns cannot be converted to grayscale with this command. Convert to Grayscale can be used with both vector and raster objects.

- **Convert to RGB (filter)**—This command is grayed out when a CMYK document is active. In RGB documents, it can change the color space of a grayscale object to RGB, although it does not change the actual colors of the fill and stroke. Convert to RGB can be used with both vector and raster objects.

- **Invert Colors (filter)**—When you use this command, have the Color palette visible. You'll see the sliders for each value jump to positions opposite their original spots. Invert Colors can be applied to RGB, CMYK, or grayscale images. Each color changes to its opposite on the color wheel. Invert Colors can be used with both vector and raster objects.

- **Overprint Black (filter)**—Overprinting, which is discussed in Chapter 25, "Linking and Embedding Images and Fonts," determines how overlapping colors are printed. This command works with selected objects to determine how black ink will be applied. Note that the selected objects must create black through the K color value to be able to overprint it; any black created by mixing CMY or through transparency is not affected with this command.

- **Saturate (filter)**—The vibrancy of a color can be adjusted with this command. Most colors can be lightened by reducing the saturation. You cannot adjust patterns and gradients with this command, however. Although grayscale objects are already completely desaturated, Illustrator adjusts their brightness levels when you use this command on them.

Convert to Shape (Effects Only)

The three Convert to Shape commands change a selected path into the selected object. The source path can be open or closed. The commands share a single dialog box with a pop-up menu to select the choice of object (see Figure 20.9).

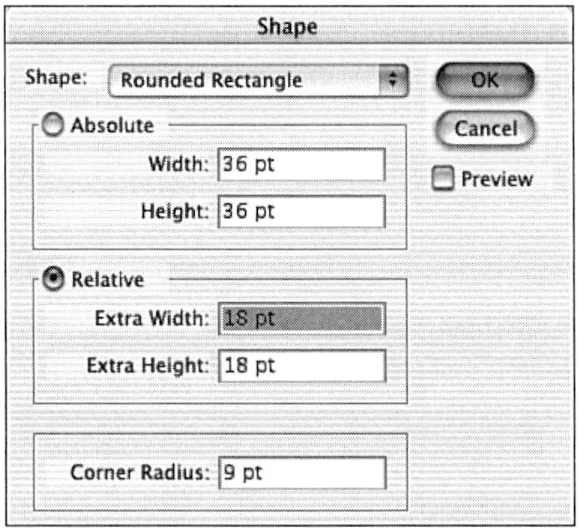

Figure 20.9
The Corner Radius option is available only for conversion to rounded rectangles, otherwise the dialog box is identical for all three options.

Shape

Shape: Rounded Rectangle

Absolute
Width: 36 pt
Height: 36 pt

Relative
Extra Width: 18 pt
Extra Height: 18 pt

Corner Radius: 9 pt

OK
Cancel
Preview

- **Rectangle (effect)**—A selected path (open or closed) is converted to a rectangle, maintaining the stroke and fill of the original object. An absolute height and width can be assigned, or the resulting object's dimensions can be expressed relative to the source path's size.

- **Rounded Rectangle (effect)**—A selected path (open or closed) is converted to a rounded rectangle, maintaining the stroke and fill of the original object. An absolute height and width can be assigned, or the resulting object's dimensions can be expressed relative to the source path's size. The radius of the corners can be determined in the dialog box.

- **Ellipse (effect)**—A selected path (open or closed) is converted to an oval or circle, maintaining the stroke and fill of the original object. An absolute height and width can be assigned, or the resulting object's dimensions can be expressed relative to the source path's size.

Create (Filters Only)

- **Object Mosaic (filter)**—Working with placed raster images or rasterized vector art, this filter creates blocks of color that approximate the colors in the raster image. The blocks are vector objects. The Object Mosaic dialog box (see Figure 20.10) allows you to control the resulting size of the object, the number of tiles and the spacing between them, and whether the original object is deleted. The button Use Ratio works with the Constrain Ratio option to adjust the Number of Tiles fields to proper proportions.

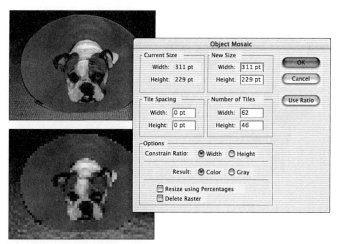

Figure 20.10
The upper figure is the original. The lower figure was created using the settings shown. It is a series of small vector rectangles, grouped together.

- **Trim Marks (filter)**—Similar to the Crop Marks command, this command identifies usable areas of an image. An artboard can have multiple sets of trim marks, identifying different areas that a prepress technician should trim. A single sheet with four three-by-five inch copies of an image could have each defined by trim marks.

Distort/Distort & Transform (Filters/Effects)

Under the Filter menu, these capabilities are listed under Distort. Under the Effect menu, you'll see Distort & Transform. The difference is that Transform is available only as an effect. The distortions are available as both filters and effects.

- **Free Distort (filter/effect)**—This command allows you to manipulate an object in two dimensions. The dialog box provides a preview and a Reset button for experimentation (see Figure 20.11).

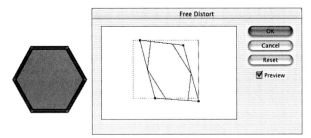

Figure 20.11
The Preview check box allows you to see an outline of the image in the dialog box rather than a live preview on the artboard. If the box is unchecked, only the bounding box is represented.

- **Pucker & Bloat (filter/effect)**—Puckering takes a vector object's existing anchor points and drags them outward, creating corner points and sharp extensions. Bloating, in contrast, drags existing anchor points inward, creating extensions from the original object that are smooth. In the dialog box (see Figure 20.12), you can set a slider that ranges from extreme puckering (–200%) to extreme bloating (+200%). A Preview check box allows you to track your work.

Figure 20.12
The original object is in the center. To the left, it is shown after a Punk distortion of –40%. To the right is a 40% Bloat.

- **Roughen (filter/effect)**—Points are added to a path according to a number of settings selected in the Roughen dialog box (shown in Figure 20.13). Size determines the amount of change (relative or absolute), Detail controls the number of anchor points added, and Points can be either smooth or corner points.

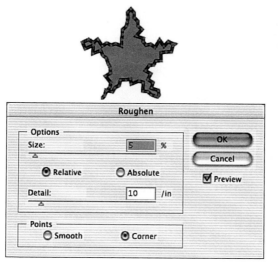

Figure 20.13
The original object was a star, with a total of 10 anchor points.

- **Scribble and Tweak (filter/effect)**—This dialog box allows you to distort existing anchor points in both the vertical and horizontal, either relative or absolute. The dialog box (see Figure 20.14) also allows you to apply the changes to anchor points or control points or both.

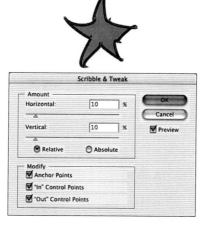

Figure 20.14
If Relative is selected, the amounts are measured in percentage; for Absolute, they are listed in the unit of measure specified in the preferences.

- **Transform (effect only)**—This command allows you to transform an object as an effect. The dialog box offers scaling, moving, reflecting, and rotating. In addition, you can make up to 360 copies of an object, each transformed by the amount and value you assign. The Transform Effect dialog box (see Figure 20.15) is identical to the Transform Each dialog box, opened by the menu command Object, Transform, Transform each. Consider Transform Each to be the filter version of this effect.

- **Twist (filter/effect)**—This command distorts an object according to the angle (degrees) input. Additional anchor points are added as needed. The Twist command offers no preview. Consider using the Twist tool instead.

- **Zig Zag (filter/effect)**—Points are added to each segment of a path according to Ridges per Segment. The distance each point varies from the original path is governed by Size, which can be measured relatively or absolutely. The added points can be smooth or corner anchor points. This filter can turn a circle into a star (corner) and a star into a puddle (smooth). See Figure 20.16 for an example.

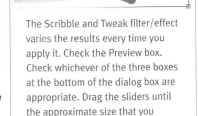

The Scribble and Tweak filter/effect varies the results every time you apply it. Check the Preview box. Check whichever of the three boxes at the bottom of the dialog box are appropriate. Drag the sliders until the approximate size that you desire is shown. Then check and uncheck the Preview box until you see a shape you like. The shape changes every time you click a box. The results are sometimes subtle, sometimes drastic. Keep clicking until you see the perfect shape.

Figure 20.15
Transforming as an effect allows you to retain the object's original path.

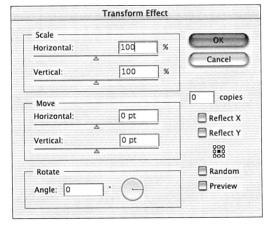

Figure 20.16
The effect of this filter is far more uniform than that of Roughen.

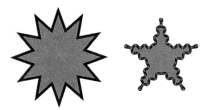

Path (Effects Only)

You can often use the Path effects to avoid or cure printing problems. Here they are presented only as effects, because they are not found under the Filter menu. However, you'll also find these commands under the Object, Path menu. Applying the command from that menu is equivalent to applying a filter.

- **Offset Path (effect)**—This command creates copies of paths, open or closed, filled or unfilled, and relocates the copy according to the distance specified in the Offset Path dialog box (shown in Figure 20.17). Negative numbers in the Offset field produce smaller copies, positive numbers produce enlarged copies. The original path remains unchanged.

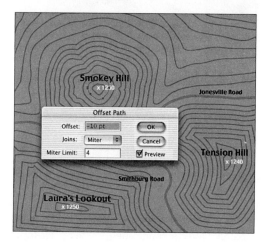

Figure 20.17
Illustrator 10 offers a Preview checkbox. The cursor indicates the smaller path copy that will be produced.

Because the copy is created to all sides of a path, copying an open path results in a closed-path copy. The copy retains the fill and stroke of the original, but not all filters or effects applied to the object are duplicated. When a filter or effect that alters the path (Punk & Bloat, Roughen) has been applied, the altered shape is copied. Stylize effects (Drop Shadow, Inner Glow) are not copied.

- **Outline Object (effect)**—This command generates a stroke with a value of None around an entire object.

Fixing "Clipped" Output

If text or an object with an effect or filter applied seems "clipped" on output, use Outline Object. When a drop shadow is clipped, for example, the fade isn't complete and may cut off abruptly at some point. Illustrator is not allowing enough of a cushion around the basic object to accommodate the shadow. Adding an invisible stroke with Outline Object forces Illustrator to recognize the true boundaries of the object with its effect.

This command is also a good safety net when stroked text is rasterized. Normally, Illustrator allows space for just the text—that is, the fill. When the text is stroked, the width of the stroke must be added to the space allocated for the text. Outline Object forces that to happen.

- **Outline Stroke (Effect)**—This command creates a filled object in the shape and location of any selected path. In addition to adding a great deal of flexibility in the modification of shapes, Outline Stroke can be useful when you're preparing trapping. (Trapping is discussed in Chapter 24, "Commercial Printing and Trapping Issues.") Figure 20.18 shows a compound path created when a heavy stroke is outlined.

Figure 20.18
The Gradient fill becomes a separate, unstroked object. The former stroke is also now an unstroked fill.

Pathfinder (Effects Only)

The Pathfinder effects work with multiple objects to create a single object. Unlike the Pathfinder palette, these commands apply effects, which can be reversed. Only the appearance is changed, not the objects' paths. Objects should be grouped prior to using these commands. Pathfinder commands can also be applied to layers and to type objects.

- **Add (effect)**—Simulates combining the selected objects, retaining the fill and stroke of the topmost object.

- **Intersect (effect)**—Retains the appearance of only areas of overlap in a stack of objects, again using the fill and stroke of the topmost object.

- **Exclude (effect)**—Hides areas of overlap where you have an even number of objects. Non-overlapping areas and areas where an odd number of objects overlap are retained, and assume the fill and stroke of the top object.

- **Subtract (effect)**—The upper paths are used as a "cookie cutter" to hide the lowest object. All parts of the bottom object that are below other objects in the group are hidden. The resulting object retains its original stroke and fill.

- **Minus Back (effect)**—The opposite of Subtract, the front-most object is retained, after hiding of any part overlapping any selected object behind it.

- **Divide (effect)**—Creates the appearance of multiple objects, with a new object created from area where multiple paths overlap. Because this is an effect, no objects are actually created.

- **Trim (effect)**—Hides underlying parts of objects, removing strokes.

- **Merge (effect)**—Hides parts of objects that were not visible, removing strokes and seeming to merge objects of the same color.

- **Crop (effect)**—Uses the front-most object as the "cookie cutter," hiding anything outside it, and creates the appearance of individual objects of the faces remaining. Strokes are changed to None.

- **Outline (effect)**—Creates unfilled open paths from the objects' path segments. Every place that one path crosses another, the paths are both divided.

- **Hard Mix (effect)**—Blends the color by using the higher percentage for each of the CMYK values.

- **Soft Mix (effect)**—Allows the underlying color to show through according to the percentage selected.

- **Trap (effect)**—Produces a slight overlap to compensate for mis-registration of a printing press. This command is discussed in Chapter 24.

Pen and Ink (Filters Only)

- **Hatch Effects (filter)**—Lines are used to fill a vector object. This filter has numerous presets (see Figure 20.19), and you can create, name, and save sets. The resulting image uses the original object as a clipping path for the hatching.

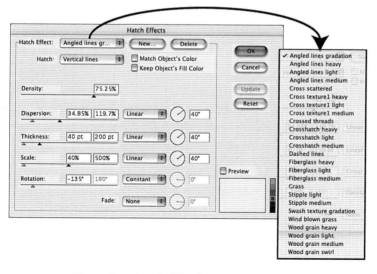

Figure 20.19
The options available vary with the different presets. The Preview shows only in the small preview area, not on the artboard.

- **Photo Crosshatch (filter)**—This filter creates a line-art sketch from a raster image. The dialog box (see Figure 20.20) gives you precise control over the placement of the lines. The number of different angles used is controlled by the Hatch Layers option, with a maximum of eight. If the resulting image is ungrouped, individual lines can be selected and edited.

Figure 20.20
The settings shown created the image on the right.

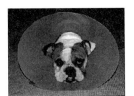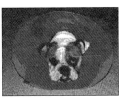

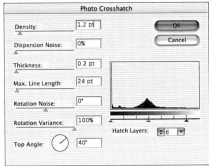

- **New Hatch (filter)**—This command defines hatches. You can paste the component of an existing hatch into the document for editing and then later resave it as a new hatch, or you can draw a new hatch mark from scratch.

- **Library Open (filter)**—You can load collections of hatch effects into the Hatch Effects filter. The previous library is replaced rather than supplemented. Illustrator has several libraries of hatches inside the Sample Files folder.

- **Library Save As (filter)**—You can save groups of hatch effects with this command for later use with the current or other documents. You load saved hatch libraries by using the Library Open command.

Rasterize (Effect)

Rasterization, the process of converting a vector object to pixels, is covered in Chapter 18, "Raster Images and Rasterized Objects." When used as an effect, Illustrator simulates a conversion to pixels. The original object is maintained, and the rasterization can be reversed later. In contrast, the menu command Object, Rasterize permanently changes the artwork, as if applying a filter. The settings in Effect, Document Raster Effects Settings can be used with this command, or you can specify other settings in the dialog box (see Figure 20.21).

Stylize (Filters and Effects)

- **Add Arrowheads (filter/effect)**—Illustrator has 27 different arrowheads that you can add to open paths. Using the dialog box, you can put them on the beginning, end, or both. The size of the arrowhead can be scaled relative to the stroke of the path from 1% to 1000%. Arrowheads assume the stroke and fill of the path, including None. After arrowheads have been applied, a path's stroke can be altered, which adjusts the size of the arrowhead's stroke without affecting its scale. There is no preview available for the Arrowhead filter, although that is an option for the Arrowhead effect.

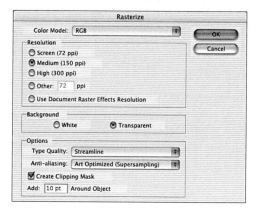

Figure 20.21
The settings in this dialog box are applied only to the current selection.

- **Drop Shadow (filter/effect)**—A drop shadow is created as a separate object. When you select Create Separate Shadow, the shadow is grouped with the original object. When you select Color, the original object is treated as opaque. When you select Darkness, the original is considered to be translucent. The difference is shown in Figure 20.22.

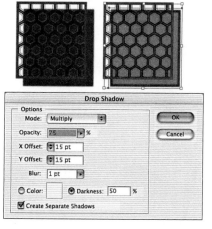

Figure 20.22
Note that the shadow and the object have separate edges, but because they're grouped, they share a bounding box.

- **Feather (effect)**—This command, which is available only as an effect, fades a selected image over a specified distance.

- **Inner Glow (effect)**—Available only as an effect, this command applies a feathered effect to the selected object. In the dialog box, you can specify color, opacity, blur, and blending mode. In addition, you can determine whether the glow will start at the center of the object and fade outward, or start at the edge of the object and fade inward.

- **Outer Glow (effect)**—An outer glow, similar to the inner glow, is available only as an effect. The feathered appearance extends outward from the stroke of a selected object. You can specify color, opacity, blur, and blending mode.

- **Round Corners (filter/effect)**—Any corner anchor point on a path, open or closed, can be smoothed with this filter. You can apply it only to corner points; it allows adjustments from 1/100 of a point to 4,000 points (from 1/1,000 of an inch to more than 55 inches). The unit of measure is that specified in the preferences.

SVG Filters (Effects Only)

These effects are actually JavaScripts that are applied to scalable vector graphics (SVG) files for use on the Web. SVG files, which are discussed in Chapter 23, "Flash and SVG Support," are vector artwork that can be rasterized when downloaded to a Web browser over the Internet. These effects are applied at the time of rasterization. That avoids scaling the effect to match the size of the vector artwork, and therefore avoids a degradation of the appearance.

Warp (Effects Only)

The results of the Warp effect commands are comparable to those created with the Object, Envelope Distort, Make With Warp dialog box. However, rather than producing an envelope mesh than can be edited, the effects change only the appearance of the selection. Figure 20.23 shows a comparison of the envelope mesh (top), the warp effect (middle), and how editing the path of an object affects the warp effect (bottom).

Figure 20.23
The settings shown were applied to three identical objects. The bottom object's path was changed with the Direct Selection tool, and the warp effect automatically conformed to the new shape.

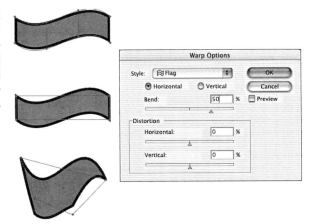

Both the envelope distort and effects versions of Warp offer employ the Warp Options dialog box. They offer the same 15 variations.

THE BOTTOM OF THE MENU—RASTER

Below the vector-related filters and effects is a blank line in the menus. Below the line, the lowest set of commands, are the filters and effects designed for use with raster artwork and rasterized objects.

Artistic (Filters/Effects)

The Artistic filters and effects apply fine art looks to the selected artwork. They are meant to simulate natural or traditional art media. When applied as effects, a vector selection is rasterized as an effect. The effect and filter versions can be applied to raster artwork that is opened or placed into an Illustrator document, or to rasterized objects. With filters the objects must be rasterized using Object, Rasterize rather than Effect, Rasterize.

The Artistic filters and effects are some of the most demanding on your computer, requiring large amounts of memory. The amount of time required to preview and apply Artistic filters and effects depends on the size and resolution (pixels per inch) of the image and the speed of the computer's processor.

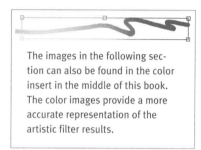

The images in the following section can also be found in the color insert in the middle of this book. The color images provide a more accurate representation of the artistic filter results.

The filters/effects were sampled using the images shown in Figure 20.24. On the left is an embedded EPS file with a resolution of 300ppi. The pattern in the center was rendered at 150ppi, as was the gradient mesh object to the right. The text below was rendered at 300ppi. The filters and effects are, for these purposes, equivalent

Figure 20.24
Each object will be subjected to all appropriate filters/effects, using settings that might be applicable to a commercial illustration.

- **Colored Pencil (filter/effect)**—This filter/effect simulates, as the name implies, the look of a colored sketch. It is not suitable for gradients, although it produces interesting effects on gradient mesh objects. Used subtly, it can greatly enhance many of Illustrator's patterns. See Figure 20.25 for examples.

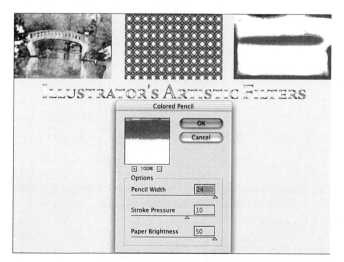

Figure 20.25
The first two objects had the filter/effect applied with settings of 3, 7, 50. The gradient mesh object requires a much higher Pencil Width setting, as shown in the dialog box's preview area.

- **Cutout (filter/effect)**—Using the edges defined by changes in color, this filter/effect simulates a collage effect. Figure 20.26 shows samples.

Figure 20.26
No. of Levels defines the color difference to determine edges, and Edge Simplicity and Edge Fidelity change the relationship of those edges to the shapes that will be created.

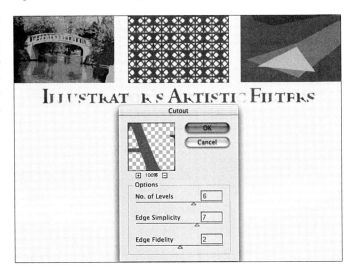

- **Dry Brush (filter/effect)**—For this next painterly filter/effect, the Brush Size and Brush Detail settings can produce gross effects, such as that shown for the letter *R* in the preview area of Figure 20.27, or (when moderated) have more subtle impact on an image. When Brush Size is minimized and Brush Detail is maximized, many computer-generated images can be softened just enough to look natural.

Figure 20.27
The attempt to find edges in the gradient mesh object has produced an interesting effect, and use of a small brush with medium detail has produced a painted look to the photograph.

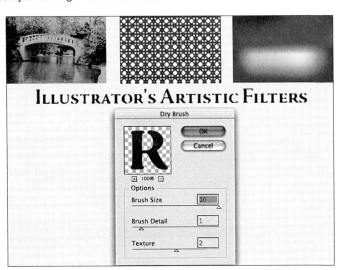

- **Film Grain (filter/effect)**—This filter/effect adds an even layer of noise to the midtones and shadows of an image. The noise, when applied minimally, can reproduce the grain of film and can be used with images from digital video. The dialog box, shown in

Figure 20.28, has three sliders. Grain controls the amount of noise, Highlight Area defines how much of the lighter areas of the image will have a smoother pattern of noise applied, and Intensity determines how much those highlight areas will be smoothed.

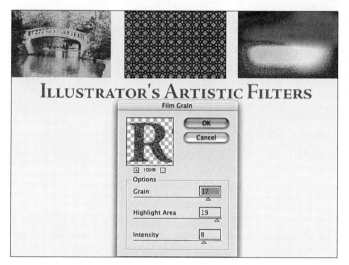

Figure 20.28
The gradient mesh object serves as a good example of how the Highlight Area and Intensity sliders reduce the amount of noise in lighter-colored parts of an image.

- **Fresco (filter/effect)**—Fresco uses short, round strokes to reproduce the image. As you can see in Figure 20.29, it has no effect on the pattern and a very substantial effect on the gradient mesh.

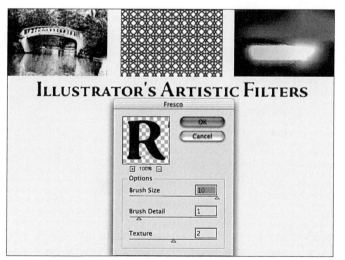

Figure 20.29
The Fresco filter/effect is intended to portray short, coarse strokes, as if the surface had been dabbed with a brush.

- **Neon Glow (filter/effect)**—Surrounding edges with a neon glow can do great things for flat or grayscale images. Depending on the settings, this filter/effect can also work to change a color image into a "colorized" image (see Figure 20.30).

Figure 20.30
The settings for the first image were high for both Size and Brightness, producing the colorized look. Notice that the text is changed using a negative number for Size, which brings the neon glow into the fill rather than surround it.

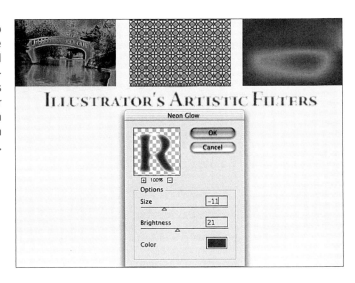

Figure 20.30
The settings for the first image were high for both Size and Brightness, producing the colorized look. Notice that the text is changed using a negative number for Size, which brings the neon glow into the fill rather than surround it.

- **Paint Daubs (filter/effect)**—This filter/effect simulates another painting technique. Brush sizes can range from 1 to 50, and several brush types are available in the dialog box (see Figure 20.31).

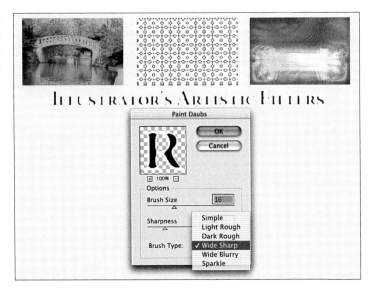

Figure 20.31
The Brush Type has greater effects on detailed images than on simple ones.

- **Palette Knife (filter/effect)**—This filter/effect is designed to create the appearance that the texture of the canvas is showing through a thin layer of paint. Figure 20.32 shows some examples of the effect.

- **Plastic Wrap (filter/effect)**—This filter/effect reproduces the effect of plastic wrap on wet paint. In the dialog box (see Figure 20.33), Highlight Strength, Detail, and Smoothness all refer to the surface of the imaginary plastic.

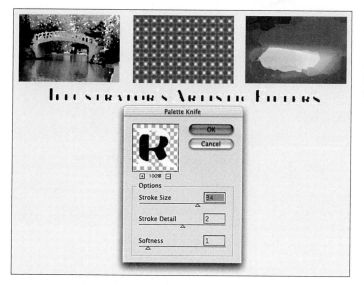

Figure 20.32
The Stroke Size has a significant impact on detailed images, such as the photograph, as well as gradated images, such as the gradient mesh.

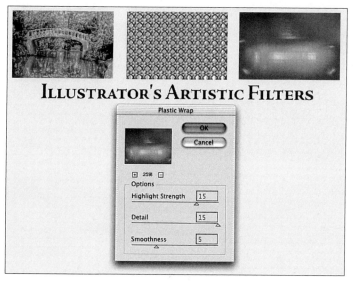

Figure 20.33
A lower Detail setting on the photographic image would produce a smoothing effect. It had virtually no effect at any setting on the text.

- **Poster Edges (filter/effect)**—Posterizing reduces the number of colors in the image. This filter/effect also isolates areas of color with black lines along the edges. Figure 20.34 shows the effect on various types of images and on text.

- **Rough Pastels (filter/effect)**—This filter/effect simulates chalk on rough surfaces. The textures available include canvas, burlap, brick, and sandstone, and custom textures can be loaded. Figure 20.35 shows how effectively this filter/effect can be applied to rasterized text. Note also how well the texture shows up in the darker areas of the gradient mesh.

Figure 20.34
Poster Edges had no effect on the pattern in the center nor on the text because they have no areas of solid color large enough to be filtered. Notice in the preview area the effect of a second application of the filter/effect on the gradient mesh object.

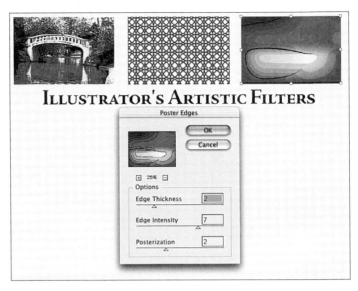

Figure 20.35
The Rough Pastels filter/effect shows more texture in shadow and darker areas, and the "chalk" appears thicker in highlights and lighter-colored areas.

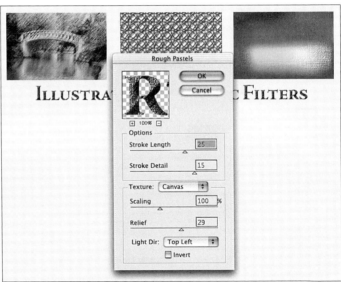

- **Smudge Stick (filter/effect)**—As if the darker areas had been smudged, this filter/effect uses diagonal strokes to smear those areas. Lighter areas of an image become brighter and lose contrast. Figure 20.36 shows some examples.

- **Sponge (filter/effect)**—The Sponge filter/effect produces areas of contrast with high texture. The effect can be subtle or extreme, depending on the source image and the settings. The dialog box is shown in Figure 20.37.

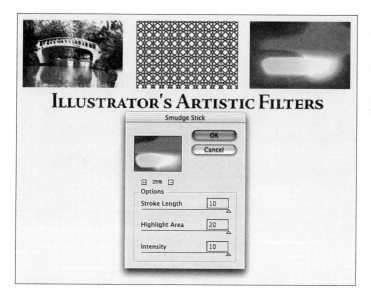

Figure 20.36
The gradient mesh object to the upper right was "smudged" with settings of Highlight Area 10 and Intensity 5. The preview area shows what would happen if these values were doubled.

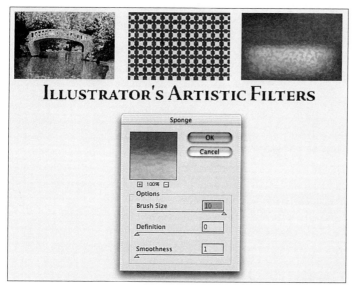

Figure 20.37
The preview area shows alternative settings for the gradient mesh object. The original was filtered with more moderate settings, which produced a more visible effect.

- **Underpainting (filter/effect)**—Another filter/effect that uses textures, Underpainting overlays the image on itself, with the bottom image appearing texturized. Figure 20.38 shows several possible applications of this filter.

- **Watercolor (filter/effect)**—As if painted with watercolors and a medium brush, images subject to this filter/effect lose detail and can experience high saturation at contrasting edges. See Figure 20.39.

Figure 20.38
Several preset textures are available, or a custom texture can be loaded.

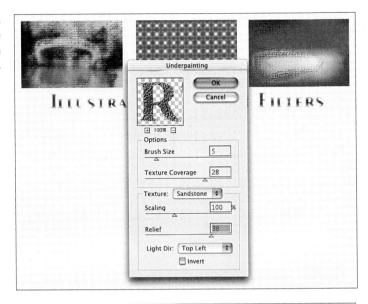

Figure 20.39
Because there is no contrast within the solid-color text, the filter/effect has no effect.

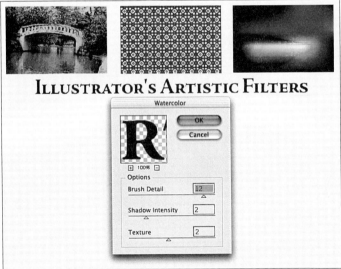

Blur (Filters and Effects)

Blur filters and effects unfocus a raster image or a rasterized object. They soften edges and edge contrast. Figure 20.40 shows a comparison of Gaussian and radial blurs.

- **Gaussian Blur (filter/effect)**—Among the most commonly applied raster filter/effect, the Gaussian blur is a workhorse. It is especially valuable for smoothing images and can be very effective in eliminating noise and pixelization in an image.

The images in the following section can also be found in the color insert in the middle of this book. The color images provide a more accurate representation of the artistic filter results.

Figure 20.40
The original is on the left, the center shows a Gaussian blur of 1 pixel radius, and the right shows a radial zoom blur of 41.

- **Radial Blur (filter/effect)**—As a special effect, the Radial Blur filter/effect has few equals. In either Zoom mode (refer to Figure 20.33) or Spin mode (see Figure 20.41), it is highly effective at what it does.

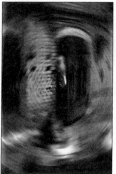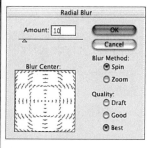

Figure 20.41
The filter and effect dialog boxes offer settings for Amount, Blur Method, and Quality, but do not offer a preview area.

Brush Strokes (Filters and Effects)

The various Brush Stroke filters and effects are explored using the images shown in Figure 20.42. The test images include a raster image, an Illustrator pattern (rasterized at 150ppi), a gradient mesh object (also rasterized at 150ppi), and a line of text (rasterized at 300ppi).

The images in the following section can also be found in the color insert in the middle of this book. The color images provide a more accurate representation of the artistic filter results.

- **Accented Edges**—Working with the edges of an image, this filter/effect can be set to accent the edges with white or black. Figure 20.43 shows examples.

- **Angled Strokes (filter/effect)**—With light areas stroked in one direction and dark areas stroked in a perpendicular direction, this filter/effect produces interesting effects on images with fine detail and on text (see Figure 20.44).

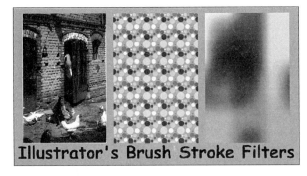

Figure 20.42
The Brush Stroke filters/effects will be applied to each image in a manner suitable for commercial application.

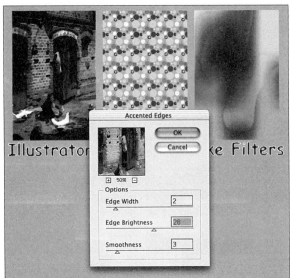

Figure 20.43
Changing the Edge Brightness value from below 25 to above 25 changes the edge accent from black to white.

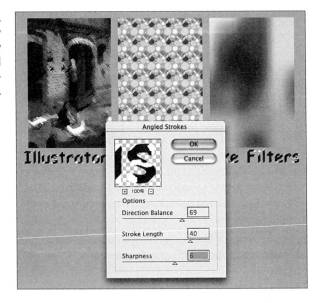

Figure 20.44
Because the text contains only dark areas, strokes appear in only one direction. This filter/effect had no effect on the rasterized gradient mesh object.

- **Crosshatch (filter/effect)**—This filter/effect roughens edges and applies pencil strokes but preserves more of the image's detail than the two previous filters/effects. Figure 20.45 shows how the filter/effect alters the text images. The Strength option determines the number of passes made by the filter/effect, from 1 to 3.

Figure 20.45
As you can see in the dialog box's preview area, a larger Stroke Length setting substantially changes the effect of the Crosshatch filter/effect on the gradient mesh object.

- **Dark Strokes (filter/effect)**—An image's shadow areas are painted by this filter/effect with short dark strokes, and highlight areas are treated with long white strokes. Figure 20.46 has examples.

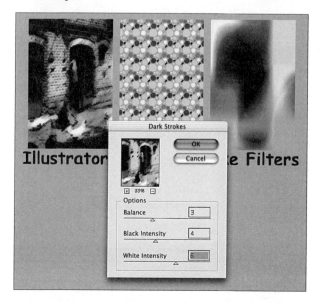

Figure 20.46
This filter/effect has no effect on the text because the lettering consists of only black.

- **Ink Outlines (filter/effect)**—This filter/effect overlays black lines, as if the image had been sketched in ink. It follows edges and allows for control of both light and dark areas (see Figure 20.47).

Figure 20.47
Note how the Ink Outlines filter/effect ignores the non-edge areas of the gradient mesh object.

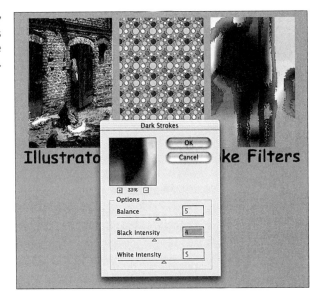

- **Spatter (filter/effect)**—The Spatter filter/effect is designed to replicate an airbrush. Figure 20.48 shows various applications.

Figure 20.48
This Brush Stroke filter/effect is highly effective on text.

- **Sprayed Strokes (filter/effect)**—Using the colors that appear most prominently in an image, this filter/effect repaints with angled strokes (see Figure 20.49).

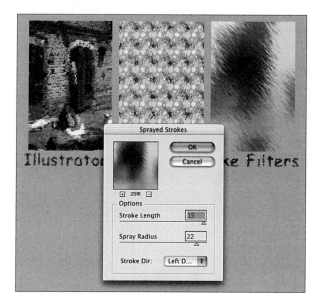

Figure 20.49
In the Sprayed Strokes dialog box, you can choose from four angles for the filter/effect. Notice the difference in the appearance of the gradient mesh object when the Stroke Length is changed from 7 (upper-right image) to 19 (preview area).

- **Sumi-e (filter/effect)**—Dark blacks and soft edges mark this command's attempt to replicate a Japanese painting technique that calls for a brush heavy with black ink applied to rice paper. See its results in Figure 20.50

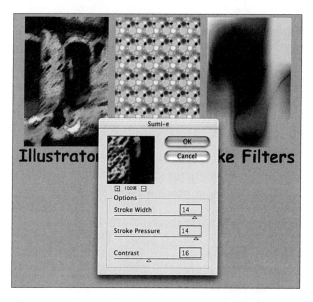

Figure 20.50
As you can see in the preview area, the effects of higher Stroke Width and Stroke Pressure settings on the photographic image are extreme. Meanwhile, none of the possible settings increased the effect on the text sample.

Distort (Filters and Effects)

These distort filters/effects should not be confused with those introduced earlier. While the first set of distort capabilities (including Pucker & Bloat, Roughen, Twist, and Zig Zag) work with vector objects, these filters/effects are for use with raster and rasterized objects.

- **Diffuse Glow (filter/effect)**—Transparent white noise is added to the rasterized selection to create a glow. The glow fades along the edges. Figure 20.51 shows a preview in the filter's dialog box.

Figure 20.51
The Glow Amount and Clear Amount sliders are used in tandem to control the glow.

- **Glass (filter/effect)**—This filter/effect distorts shapes, as though you're looking through different kinds of glass windows and blocks, while leaving colors virtually unchanged. See Figure 20.52.

Figure 20.52
The filter/effect allows you to choose types of glass and other distortion patterns, including custom textures.

- **Ocean Ripple (filter/effect)**—Attempting to show an object as if under water, this filter/effect applies a pattern of random curved distortions. You can control the size and intensity of the ripples, as you can see in Figure 20.53.

Figure 20.53
On the left, the Ripple Size and Ripple Magnitude applied were lower than those shown in the dialog box.

Pixelate (Filters and Effects)

Pixelization can be a bad thing or a good thing in images. The visible appearance of individual pixels in, for example, a digital photograph taken at a wedding is unwelcome. On the other hand, the introduction of pixelization, when controlled, can produce artistic effects. In general, these filters and effects group pixels of similar colors into groups, called *cells* that simulate a reduced resolution of the image.

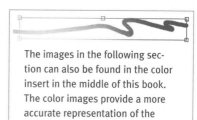

The images in the following section can also be found in the color insert in the middle of this book. The color images provide a more accurate representation of the artistic filter results.

- **Color Halftone (filter/effect)**—The filter/effect creates halftone-like circular cells by dividing the image into rectangular areas. The brighter an area, the larger the circle that's substituted for the pixels in that area. In the dialog box, shown in Figure 20.54, the dot size can range from 4 (as in the sample image) to 127.

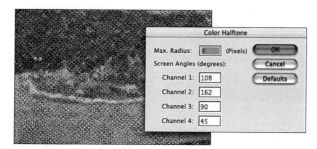

Figure 20.54
The halftone filter/effect simulates a close-up of a four-color print.

- **Crystallize (filter/effect)**—Pixels are grouped into polygons and assigned one of the group's colors. Figure 20.55 shows that the only option is Cell Size.

- **Mezzotint (filter/effect)**[md]A random pattern is created according to the option selected. For color images, each element of the pattern is a fully saturated color. Grayscale images are reduced to black and white. Figure 20.56 shows the filter's dialog box.

If the Color Halftone filter's 4-pixel radius (the minimum) seems too dramatic for your purposes, you can re-rasterize an object to a higher resolution, apply the filter, then re-rasterize back to the original resolution.

Figure 20.55
The preview area shows the cell size 40, and the image behind was created with cell size 10.

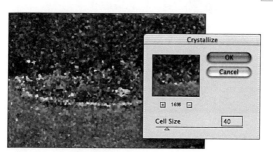

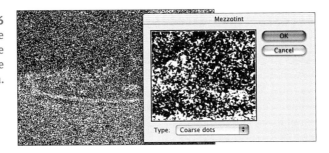

Figure 20.56
The image behind shows the Fine Dots setting, in contrast to the Coarse Dots shown in the preview area.

- **Pointillize (filter/effect)**—A series of large dots are placed to represent the image (see Figure 20.57). The smallest dot size available is 3.

Figure 20.57
The difference between a setting of 6 (background image) and 15 (preview area) is substantial. Note that the preview area is showing the entire image, not just part of the image. The maximum value of 300 creates fewer than a dozen cells for the entire image.

Sharpen (Filter and Effect)

Illustrator's default installation includes only one Sharpen filter, but it is certainly the most valuable of those found in Adobe Photoshop.

- **Unsharp Mask (filter/effect)**—This filter/effect simulates a sharper focus on an image by increasing the contrast along edges. Where the filter/effect finds a significant difference between colors, it emphasizes the breaks. Figure 20.58 shows how Unsharp Mask can improve the detail of an image. Unsharp Mask is always worth considering when a raster image has been resized.

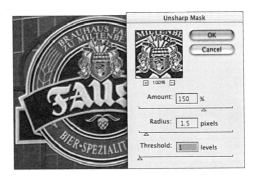

Figure 20.58
Compare the original image with the preview area to see the significant effect even a slight bit of sharpening can have on a detailed image.

Sketch (Filters and Effects)

The Sketch filters include some that produce a fine-arts effect and some that attempt to portray 3D. Most of these filters produce a grayscale image. Examples of each of the filters are shown (in alphabetical/menu order) in Figure 20.59.

The following image can also be found in the color insert in the middle of this book. The color image provides a more accurate representation of the artistic filter results.

Figure 20.59
The original image is shown in the upper left. Each of the Sketch filters has been applied with an appropriate setting to produce an image in this figure.

- **Bas Relief**—(Figure 20.59, top row, number 2.) The image looks as if it had been carved in stone. The dialog box allows you to control the amount of detail and smoothness, as well as the angle of lighting.

- **Chalk & Charcoal**—(Figure 20.59, top row, number 3.) This filter works with a gray background and uses dark strokes (charcoal) for darker and shadow areas and light strokes (chalk) for highlights.

- **Charcoal**—(Figure 20.59, top row, number 4.) The Charcoal filter is similar to the Chalk & Charcoal filter, but the background is paper rather than chalk. Prominent edges are drawn; midtones are stroked.

- **Chrome**—(Figure 20.59, top row, number 5.) The image is prepared as if polished chrome, with highlights as elevations and shadows as recesses.

- **Conté Crayon**—(Figure 20.59, middle row, number 1.) This filter offers several textures (including brick, shown in Figure 20.59). The image can be incorporated into the background or placed above it.

- **Graphic Pen**—(Figure 20.59, middle row, number 2.) This filter uses short diagonal lines to create a black-and-white version of the image.

- **Halftone Pattern**—(Figure 20.59, middle row, number 3.) You can reproduce a moiré pattern by using the Dots option with this filter. In addition, you can use circles and lines to re-create the image.

- **Note Paper**—(Figure 20.59, middle row, number 4.) The image is reproduced as if made from layers of paper. Dark areas of the image are cut out of the top layer of paper.

- **Photocopy**—(Figure 20.59, middle row, number 5.) As if the image had been put on a photocopier, midtones run to black or white, and areas of solid darkness are copied around the edges.

- **Plaster**—(Figure 20.59, bottom row, number 1.) Creating a 3D image, as if from plaster, this filter's lighting direction has several options.

- **Reticulation**—(Figure 20.59, bottom row, number 2.) This filter produces a grained effect, more pronounced in the highlights than in the shadows.

- **Stamp**—(Figure 20.59, bottom row, number 3.) High-contrast or bitmap (black-and-white) images are best for this filter.

- **Torn Edges**—(Figure 20.59, bottom row, number 4.) Another filter that is best with high-contrast images, the subject is reproduced as if made from ripped paper.

- **Water Paper**—(Figure 20.59, bottom row, number 5.) As if painted with watercolors on a highly absorbent paper, the colors run and bleed with this filter.

Stylize (Filter and Effect)

The single Stylize filter included with Illustrator is Glowing Edges. As you can see in Figure 20.60, the filter finds and emphasizes edges, allowing control over brightness, width, and smoothness.

Figure 20.60
The settings shown in this dialog box produced the image shown.

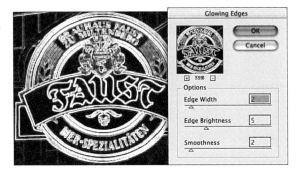

Texture (Filters and Effects)

The Texture filters/effects are designed not so much to add texture to an image as to portray the image as having been painted on a textured surface.

Examples of the filters/effects are shown in Figure 20.61.

- **Craquelure (filter/effect)**—(Figure 20.60, top row, number 1.) The image is painted on a surface resembling a plaster wall, complete with cracks. The cracks follow the edges within the image. The dialog box offers control of crack spacing, depth, and brightness.

The following image can also be found in the color insert in the middle of this book. The color image provides a more accurate representation of the artistic filter results.

Figure 20.61
The effects of the six filters are shown here.

- **Grain (filter/effect)**—(Figure 20.60, top row, number 2.) This filter/effect offers ten different varieties of grain to add to an image. In addition, intensity and contrast can be modified.

- **Mosaic Tiles (filter/effect)**—(Figure 20.60, top row, number 3.) The size of the tiles used to reconstruct the image can range from 2 to 100. The width and lightness of the grout between tiles can be optimized for each image.

- **Patchwork (filter/effect)**—(Figure 20.60, bottom row, number 1.) The image is divided into squares, and the dominant color of each is used for the entire segment. The "depth" of each tile is adjusted by the filter/effect to control highlights and shadows. The size of the squares and the relief are adjustable.

- **Stained Glass (filter/effect)**—(Figure 20.60, bottom row, number 2.) Individual cells are created, outlined in black, to reproduce the image. The size of the cells, the thickness of border between, and the back lighting intensity are all adjustable.

- **Texturizer (filter/effect)**—(Figure 20.60, bottom row, number 3.) This filter/effect offers a choice among brick, burlap, canvas, sandstone, and custom-made textures. The scaling, relief, and lighting direction are options.

Video (Filters and Effects)

The two Video filters/effects approach an image from opposite directions. The first is designed to clean up images taken from video, whereas the second prepares images for video.

- **De-Interlace (filter/effect)**—Video images are broadcast one-half at a time. Every other line of an image is sent separately. Between these lines of the image are lines of black. When a video image is captured digitally, those black lines are prominent. De-Interlace replaces the black lines either by interpolation (calculating what color each pixel should be based on neighboring pixels) or by duplication (copying the neighboring line of image). Odd or Even scan lines can be selected.

- **NTSC Colors (filter/effect)**—This filter/effect restricts an image to colors with appropriate saturation for broadcast. The filter/effect desaturates highly saturated colors, which can bleed across scan lines.

TROUBLESHOOTING

Circumventing the Unavailable Filter

Sometimes the filter I want to use is grayed out and unavailable. What can I do?

Try the Effect menu. If the selection isn't rasterized, the effect may work when the filter won't. In other cases, you may be trying to apply an RGB filter in a CMYK document.

Back to Normal

If I apply an effect and want to remove it later, what do I do?

Immediately after an effect if applied, Undo can be used. After that, select the object(s) on the artboard and open the Appearance palette. Find the effect in the Appearance palette and drag it to the trashcan icon at the bottom of the palette. Remember that filters cannot be removed—they are permanent.

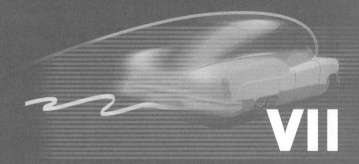

VII

ILLUSTRATOR AND THE WEB

IN THIS PART

21   Designing Web Sites and Web Pages **469**

22   Saving Images for the Web **497**

23   Flash and SVG Support **533**

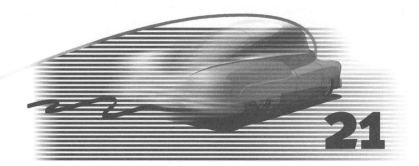

21

DESIGNING WEB SITES AND WEB PAGES

IN THIS CHAPTER

Web Design with Illustrator   **470**

Preparing for Web Graphic Creation   **475**

Color on the Web   **479**

File Format Considerations   **480**

Cascading Style Sheets   **482**

Symbols and Symbolism for the Web   **485**

Slicing   **494**

Troubleshooting   **496**

When people discuss Illustrator and the Web, conversation generally divides into two subjects: using Illustrator as a design tool and using Illustrator as a production tool. As a design tool, it excels in capturing the layout of each page and producing flow charts of the site links. As a production tool, it cannot be matched for creation of vector-based images.

With Illustrator's Layers palette and its sublayers, groups, and objects, you can design an entire site in one document. Transparency, Save for Web, Web-safe palette, Pixel Preview, file optimization control, the Release to Layers command, and expanded file format import/export make Illustrator a virtual one-stop shop for graphic production. Illustrator also has support for Flash (SWF) and Scalable Vector Graphics (SVG) output, keeping it on the leading edge of Web technology. (These file formats and Illustrator's support for them are discussed in Chapter 23, "Flash and SVG Support.")

WEB DESIGN WITH ILLUSTRATOR

Most professionally designed Web sites start life as pencil on paper or their digital counterparts. Good planning leads to good Web sites. A site's layout is drafted and individual pages are designed. Specific graphics, such as buttons and banners, are given preliminary shape and size before being created. Illustrator has long been a part of this process. The vector-based illustrations are perfect for laying out individual pages, as well as diagramming entire sites.

You can organize and plan a Web site in many ways. In the past, a separate folder may have been generated for each page of a Web site, with all the pages of a Web site stored in one master folder. Each folder for an individual page may have contained dozens of component pieces, including frame outlines, frames, buttons, button text, page text blocks, scrollbars, banners, and a multitude of other individual pieces. Organizing and tracking each of these components could be difficult. Many components reoccurred on multiple pages, meaning a change to, say, a button shape involved identifying, locating, and changing each button in perhaps dozens of folders.

These images of the future Web pages (you can think of them as "sketches") were opened and viewed individually. Using Illustrator's layers, however, every page of a Web site can be stored in one document, with each page independently available to view, edit, or print. You can exchange or copy elements of the pages during the design phase with drag-and-drop ease directly within the Layers palette.

Illustrator enables you to have and manipulate sublayers in the Layers palette. In addition, you can also see, rearrange, copy, delete, and even edit (to some degree) groups of objects and individual objects themselves. (See Chapter 10, "Illustrator's Layers, Sublayers, and Groups," for full information.)

A Few Web Graphic Basic Concepts

A few issues deserve attention prior to development of individual Web components:

- Each component of a Web page must be saved as a separate file for use in a Web design program, such as Adobe GoLive. Additional enhancements, such as GIF animation, button rollovers, and image slicing can be added in Adobe ImageReady (the Web production tool of Photoshop) or with Adobe LiveMotion.

- Images that are not square or rectangular require special preparation unless they are to appear on a plain white background. By default, raster images (including most Web graphics) are rectangular. With some file formats, transparency can be used to give the impression that an image is not rectangular.

- Special effects such as drop shadows must be handled with care. Despite Illustrator's transparency capabilities (see Chapter 19), variable or graduated transparency is not generally supported on the Web.

The actual process of producing the objects relies on the preceding principles: Create it at the actual pixel size, use appropriate colors, and save it in an appropriate file format.

Producing shadows and other semi-transparent effects for the Web using the standard GIF and JPEG formats is not possible. However, you can simulate soft effects such as shadows by matching the Web page's background. In Figure 21.1, the left figure is on a background the same color as the Web page into which it will be placed. The background is large enough to contain the foreground object's shadow. That object is duplicated to the right, without the background.

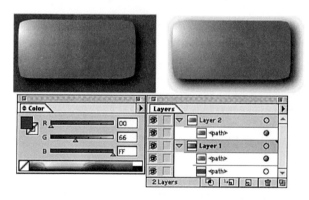

Figure 21.1
Each of these objects was rendered individually and saved separately as a GIF file, using Save for Web.

The separate files created were each placed into an Adobe GoLive Web page. The background of the GoLive page is the color to which the first image was matched. The results are shown in Figure 21.2.

You can also preview GIF and JPEG images in any browser installed on the computer. Start the browser and, rather than load a Web page, use the keyboard shortcut Cmd+O [Ctrl+O] or choose File, Open File (Internet Explorer) or File, Open, Page in Navigator or Communicator (Netscape) and navigate to the files. The images from Figure 21.1 are shown in Internet Explorer in Figure 21.3.

➪ See "Web Images Unavailable" in the "Troubleshooting" section at the end of this chapter if your graphics do not show up.

- If a symbol in the Symbols palette is redefined, all artwork using that symbol will be updated, unless the link is broken.

- To redefine a symbol, add a single instance to the artboard, make changes, and then use the Symbols palette menu command Redefine Symbol. (The symbol to be redefined must be selected in the Symbols palette, and the new symbol artwork must be selected on the artboard.)

- After adding a symbol instance to the artboard, you can rotate, scale, and shear; you can apply effects and styles; and you can make changes in the Appearance and Transparency palettes.

- You can also alter a symbol by using the menu command Object, Expand. You can ungroup and alter anything about the symbol's appearance.

- When multiple symbols occur in a symbol set, redefining a symbol affects only those instances that were originally that symbol.

- To break a link, select the symbol set on the artboard and click the Break Link to Symbol button (shown in Figure 21.32).

- Breaking a link severs the connection between a symbol set and the Symbols palette. If multiple symbols appear in a set, all links are broken.

Creating a Custom Symbol

Virtually any Illustrator artwork (except linked files) can be used as a symbol. Select the artwork on the artboard and use the Symbols palette menu command or New Symbol button (see Figure 21.33). The artwork is added to the Symbols palette, ready to go.

 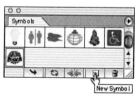

Figure 21.33
New symbols are added to the bottom of the Symbols palette.

As with other libraries in Illustrator, you can add the contents of an other document's Symbols palette to the current document. Use the menu command Window, Symbol Library, Other Library. Navigate to the document whose symbols you want to add and select it. A separate palette will open, with the source document's name in the tab.

Any artwork can be stored in the Symbols palette, even if you never use it with the symbolism tools. A company logo, for example, can be defined as a symbol and then added to any image, any time, with the Place Symbol Instance button at the bottom of the Symbols palette.

Expanding Symbol Sets and Instances

The Expand menu command object works with both symbol sets and symbol instances. The difference between the two uses is shown in Figure 21.34. The top fish is an expanded instance, while the others in the school were expanded as a set.

Figure 21.34
When a symbol set is expanded, the symbol instances become individual objects in a group. The instances can then be expanded to grouped paths.

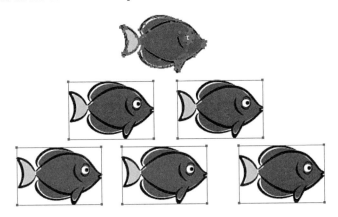

SLICING

Slicing an image for the Web identifies sections of a single file that can have some independent functions. For example, the slices of an image load into a Web browser's window individually. You can also assign specific optimizations settings for each slice of an image. Illustrator allow you to slice an image using a variety of techniques.

The Two Types of Slices

When you designate a slice, using any of the techniques described in this section, you've created a user-defined slice, or a user slice. Illustrator automatically divides the rest of the image into appropriate rectangles so that the entire image is represented by slices. Those slices are called automatic slices, or auto slices. All slices are rectangular. If an image is not rectangular, surround parts of the artboard are included so that each slice is rectangular, as will be the image overall.

The Slice Tool

Drag to identify an area of an image as a slice. Illustrator automatically creates the other slices necessary to fill the HTML table in which the image will be displayed.

Using a Selection for Slicing

Create a selection, including one or more objects on the artboard. Use the menu command Object, Slice, Create from Selection. A user-generated slice will be created, along with the required auto slices.

The user slice will be defined by the edge of the stroke (if any) or fill, not by an object's path. In addition, any effects (such as outer glows or drop shadows) will also be included.

Using Guides for Selections

Illustrator enables you to create extremely precise slices by using the guides. Place each guide where you want the image to be sliced, and then use the menu command Object, Slice, Create from Guides.

Object-Based Slicing

The command Object, Slice, Make creates a slice from the currently selected object. The slice is tied to the object; therefore if the object is moved on the artboard, slices are automatically redrawn to maintain the object-oriented slice.

In contrast, slices created with the command Create from Selection remain in place, even if that original selection is moved.

⮕ *Need to change the type of slice you're using from selection-based to object-based? See "Resetting Slices" in the "Troubleshooting" section at the end of this chapter.*

Linking to a Slice in Illustrator

Another of the great advantages to using slices in a Web image is hyperlinking. Each slice can be used as a link to another Web page. A Web address, known as a URL (uniform resource locator), is assigned in the Slice Options dialog box. Access the dialog box through the menu command Object, Slice, Slice Options.

Creating Image Maps

An image map is similar to a slice in that a URL can be assigned to it, turning it into a hyperlink. When the image map is clicked in a Web browser, the viewer will be taken to the designated Web page.

Unlike slices, image maps do not have to be rectangular. Any object can be used. To assign a URL, open the Attributes palette (see Figure 21.35), select either rectangular or Polygon from the pop-up menu, and enter the URL.

Figure 21.35
Assigning URLs to image maps is just one of the purposes of the Attributes palette.

TROUBLESHOOTING

Correcting Banding in Images

My images are starting to look like targets at a bow-and-arrow convention. The concentric circles in areas that should be gradients are driving me crazy. What's wrong?

You're experiencing banding. The reduction in the number of colors results in grouping of several colors into one. For example, in a 24-bit image, a certain area might transition from light red to medium red to dark red. With a reduction of colors, it all becomes medium red. If the original transition were actually "dark purple—medium purple—light purple—light red—medium red—dark red," the result could be medium purple and medium red side-by-side. The visible banding created by two dissimilar colors next to each other can be eased with dithering. Dithering uses dots and/or patterns of the two colors in differing densities to simulate shades between the colors. Save for Web offers options and controls for dithering.

Web Images Unavailable

I worked very hard to optimize my images, choosing quality over size, and now that I have them posted, I can't see them. Did I make them too big?

No, the problem isn't likely to be size. Patience allows even the largest Web images to download. Perhaps, however, your browser isn't the latest and your images are in a format it doesn't support. Did you, by chance, save the images in PNG or Optimized JPEG format?

Resetting Slices

I thought my image was finished, so I sliced it up. Now, however, I have to shift one piece of artwork a little bit. Since I didn't use object-based slices, everything will be messed up. How do I handle it?

You can use the Slice Select tool to adjust the boundaries of a slice. Click on the slice, and then use the handles in the corners of the box to resize, or simply drag to reposition. Illustrator updates the other auto slices automatically. (Be aware that it is possible to overlap user-defined slices. This can create problems for some Web browsers.)

The menu Object, Slice includes a handy command for situations that get out of hand. The Delete All command removes all slices and lets you start over.

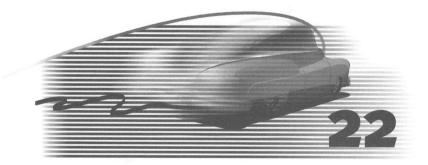

SAVING IMAGES FOR THE WEB

IN THIS CHAPTER

Control Graphic Images **498**

Color and the Web **499**

File Size and the Web **500**

Image Formats for the Web **501**

Pixel Preview **506**

Save for Web and Image Optimizing **509**

The Color Table **516**

The Optimization Settings **518**

Types of Dithering **521**

Optimizing Slices **525**

The Save Optimized As Dialog Box **527**

Troubleshooting **530**

When discussing Web graphics, you need to know basic information about the file formats available. In addition, you need to have an understanding of color and how it relates to both the file formats and the Web itself. The basic goal is, of course, to have the viewers of your Web pages and your site see exactly what you intend for them to see. The epitome of this goal would be to have each and every visitor see precisely what is portrayed on your monitor.

That goal is not within reach of today's technology. Different visitors use different sizes and resolutions of monitors, set to various numbers of colors (and actually different colors when you consider the difference between the Macintosh and Windows system palettes). And, until such time as every monitor is automatically self-calibrating and adjusts to ambient lighting changes, you cannot be assured that any given visitor to your site is seeing anything remotely close to the color scheme you spent hours devising.

CONTROL GRAPHIC IMAGES

So why worry about this problem at all? Why spend time picking color schemes and worrying about file optimization? Because you can have an impact on what the viewer sees. By following certain conventions, you can limit the amount of variance from your design. You can even control exactly what your viewer sees and make a page look identical to every browser, regardless of version, platform, or color setting. Unfortunately, doing so requires using only black and white, and rather than text, each page would have to be rendered as a graphic. See Figure 22.1 for an example. Using color and modern Web technologies, such as animation, requires compromises. Limiting file size and reducing color palettes often restrict creativity, but these techniques help ensure that your message or vision is communicated.

Figure 22.1
The appearance of a black-and-white GIF file is nearly universally consistent on the Web.

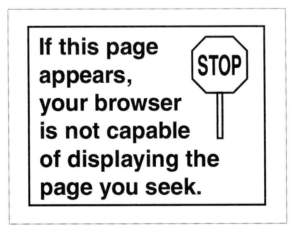

The image in Figure 22.1, saved in GIF format, is theoretically capable of appearing exactly the same with any browser capable of displaying graphics. (The original Web browsers were text-only.) The only colors used are black and white, which are common to all computer system palettes, and because the text is rendered as a graphic, you don't need to be concerned about installed fonts or the difference between Windows and Macintosh font display.

COLOR AND THE WEB

Among the concepts that you must consider when designing for the Web is color. As explained in Chapter 12, "Understanding and Applying Color," not all computers can display all colors. Older computers might be restricted to 8-bit color, limiting them to a palette of only 256 possible colors. This is particularly true of older laptop computers. But today, most Web surfers are equipped with video cards and displays that are capable of millions, if not billions, of colors. So, is the Web-safe palette really necessary?

Reducing an image to the 216 colors in the Web-safe palette accomplishes two things. In addition to making an image look better on older computers and with older browsers, it also reduces the file size, leading to faster download and less waiting. There are, most certainly, Web sites to which neither of these issues is applicable. For example, an intranet or internal network, in an organization whose computers are all powerful, modern machines equipped with high-speed access would not require such limitations. Or perhaps considerations in one direction override the other. For example, a site on the Web whose intended audience is all computer artists and illustrators might require accurate color at the expense of download speed. If the work being shown on the Web site would be significantly lessened in the eyes of the viewers by a reduced palette, then perhaps longer download times become more acceptable.

⇨ *When the number of colors is reduced, some images show stripes of solid color where smooth transitions should appear. If this is a problem for you, see "Minimizing Banding" in the "Troubleshooting" section at the end of this chapter.*

8-Bit and 24-Bit Color

The concepts of *8-bit color* and *24-bit color* are important in discussions of Web graphics. When you refer to an 8-bit image or a video card capable of only 8-bit color, the discussion is not at its root about color, but rather about how much information a computer records. Each individual "bit" can be zero or one, on or off, yes or no, up or down. There are, so to speak, no shades of gray.

Computers, in essence, are binary machines. Every single piece of information is recorded in a series of zeros and ones, which are grouped together by the computer to form a comprehensible (to the computer) piece of information. Each pixel displayed on the monitor has a color value recorded by the computer and transmitted to the monitor. The color value is recorded like other information, in a series of zeros and ones. That series, or number of possible zeros or ones, for 8-bit color consists of eight digits, each a zero or one. Because each of the digits can have only two possible values, the total number of combinations is 256 (2×2=4, ×2=8, ×2=16, ×2=32, ×2=64, ×2=128, ×2=256).

Using a series of 24 zeros or ones (for 24-bit color) gives a computer more than 16.7 million different combinations with which to record the color value of a single pixel. The term *millions of colors* refers to 24-bit color, whereas *thousands of colors* is 16-bit, and 32-bit color is referred to as *billions of colors*. Black and white, by the way, are recorded with a single bit, hence the term *bitmap* for black-and-white artwork.

Be aware, however, that the same term *bitmap* is also often used to refer to raster art. Raster art (as opposed to vector art such as that native to Illustrator) is created from a series of pixels rather than mathematical paths. (Chapter 18, "Raster Images and Rasterized Objects," discusses in depth the difference between raster and vector art.)

Furthermore, be aware of the difference between 8-bit color (256 total colors) and 8-bits per channel (24-bit color for RGB, 32-bit color for CMYK). Adobe Photoshop, Illustrator's raster art sibling, also uses the term *16-bit color* to refer to 16 bits per channel. This format actually produces 64-bit color for CMYK images and 48-bit color for RGB.

All Web graphics should be created and saved in the RGB or Web Safe RGB color mode. Although CMYK contains virtually no colors that cannot be reproduced in the RGB gamut, it has several disadvantages for the Web. First, and of critical importance, is the lack of CMYK support by most Web browsers. They are not capable of displaying a JPEG image that is in CMYK color mode. Second, CMYK produces larger files. Four color channels, rather than three, must be stored with every file. Third, color values have to be converted to be displayed on monitors. Finally, the PNG file format (for one) does not support CMYK colors.

The Web Safe RGB palette uses the subset of colors common to the system palettes of both Macintosh and Windows. If a Web site is targeted to, say, only Windows users, using the system palette rather than the Web-safe palette adds 40 colors without substantially changing file size or compatibility with the target audience.

The computer language used by Web browsers and servers to communicate is Hypertext Markup Language (HTML) and its derivatives. HTML records colors as hexadecimal (base 16) values. Many designers prefer that any color that will be described in HTML be a Web-safe color. This includes Web page backgrounds and text but does not include the colors of an image saved in a graphics file format (such as JPEG, GIF, and PNG). You can find a discussion of hexadecimal with a chart showing the conversion from RGB in the sidebar "Hexadecimal Colors" in Chapter 12.

FILE SIZE AND THE WEB

Visitors to a Web site access the information remotely. The data is sent to their computers and forwarded to their monitors by means of wires and cables (and in some cases, wirelessly). Very often, the information travels, in part, along telephone cables. Such transmission of data has some limitations, not the least of which is speed. Only so much information can pass along the cables and wires during a specified period of time. The typical unit of measure is one second. The data transfer rates are measured in kilobits per second (Kbps) or megabits per second (Mbps). Some internal networks can handle gigabits per second, and one day soon that might be the norm for home Internet links. In the meantime, a massive number of Web surfers are surfing with download times measured at 53Kbps or slower.

To efficiently serve visitors who don't have access to DSL, cable modem, or other high-speed connections—those who still depend upon dial-up Internet connections—you should keep file size to a minimum. The balance between size and speed can be hard to find. Keep in mind, however, that many Web surfers are not patient. They will not wait for a large image to download unless, perhaps, that particular image is the reason for their visit to your site. Art-related Web sites are one example of an exception. The connection speed is just one of many factors that affect how quickly a Web page downloads. A network server's traffic load, the route that the data must travel, and even how many people are surfing the Web at a particular time are just some of the others.

There are two types of file sizes for Web graphics. One is the actual pixel space occupied by the image on the computer screen, and the other is the file size as it is transmitted to the viewer's computer. A distinct relationship exists between the two, but you also can find ways to reduce the file size without changing the pixel size of an image.

The pixel dimensions of a graphic are typically determined by the Web page designer. Aesthetic and artistic considerations are often balanced with practicality. In some cases, a single image occupies an entire page. The image's dimensions in such a situation could depend on the expected monitor resolution of the typical visitor, with download times as an additional concern.

The file size and download time for individual images of a given size depend on file format and compression. Compression reduces a file's size by using various types of "shorthand" to record the file's content. For example, rather than record a series of three pixels as

```
"pixel 1-blue; pixel 2-blue; pixel 3-blue."
```

compression could shorten the series to

```
"pixels 1-3-blue."
```

(This example is, of course, a simplification.)

IMAGE FORMATS FOR THE WEB

Of the hundreds of file formats available for recording digital information, only a few are appropriate for graphics on the Web. The two most common are JPEG and GIF. Improved compatibility with the latest Web browsers from Microsoft and Netscape has allowed the PNG format to be more widely used, but it is still not universally supported. Other major formats require that a plug-in be available to the browser in order for a graphic to be properly displayed. Flash (SWF) (discussed in Chapter 23, "Flash and SVG Support") and PDF are two examples.

GIF

GIF (Graphical Interchange Format), also known as CompuServe GIF and in a variation as GIF89a, is an 8-bit color format designed for illustration-type graphics. This format excels at storing and reproducing images with large areas of solid color but, because it is 8-bit, is limited to 256 colors. GIF does not do a good job with continuous tone images, such as photographs, having to reduce them to the smaller number of colors. Areas in an image that should blend smoothly from one color to another become banded or dithered. *Banding* occurs when a large number of colors across an area must be reduced to a smaller number. The colors are then grouped into stripes of a color that is available in the reduced palette. *Dithering* is the technique of applying a pattern of two colors to represent a third, intermediate color. S~ Figure 22.2 and Figure 22.3 for examples of banding and dithering. Banding can be c~ to a large degree, with dithering. See "Types of Dithering" later in this chapter. ~ able in Illustrator through the command Save for Web and will be discussed f~ section of this chapter.

GIF employs a patented technology and is used under license from CompuServe. You personally need not pay CompuServe directly. However, part of the price you paid for software that uses the format was a licensing fee.

Figure 22.2
The vertical banding is quite noticeable, and a wide variety of dithering patterns can be seen. Notice how the two shades are blended using a variety of different sized dots and some patterns.

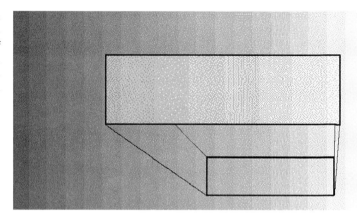

Figure 22.3
A circular gradient begins to look more like concentric circles with high degrees of banding. Seen from a distance, however, the dithering can be quite effective in disguising the lack of color range.

⇨ *If banding is appearing on your monitor but not in printed images, see "Onscreen Images Show Banding but Print Is Fine" in the "Troubleshooting" section at the end of this chapter.*

CompuServe, GIF, and LZW Compression

The aspect of GIF that is subject to licensing fees is actually the compression system, LZW (named after Lempel-Ziv-Welch, who were the developers). Patented in 1985 by Sperry (the forerunner of Unisys), it was designed to compress ASCII text files. Searching for repetitive 8-bit patterns in a file, such as the regular use of the ASCII codes for T, H, and E in sequence, it replaces the string with a shorter code. In early applications, primarily data transmission, a dictionary of the coded sequences had to be sent with or before the compressed text.

Some time after the introduction of GIF, Unisys decided to exercise its right to receive royalties for use of the patented algorithm. CompuServe paid a one-time fee that was reportedly under $150,000 and now charges a licensing fee for each copy of a program that uses the GIF file format. Interestingly, LZW is based on the Lempel-Ziv compression algorithm, which is in the public domain and therefore free.

JPEG

JPEG (Joint Photographic Experts Group) is designed to record *continuous tone* images. It cannot truly be called a file format but rather is a compression algorithm. The actual file format is properly known as JPEG File Interchange Format (JFIF). Images such as photographs are classified as continuous tone because one hue or color blends seamlessly into another. Nonphotographic images that contain gradients or blends should also be considered continuous tone. JPEG uses a *lossy* file compression scheme. Some data is actually discarded to reduce the size of the file. JPEG allows control over the amount of compression applied to an image. The compression setting is a compromise between image quality and file size. When an image is opened for viewing, it is decompressed. Sometimes in the compression process, some data that affects the image is discarded. The resulting randomly colored pixel or patch of color is often noticeable in the image and is called an *artifact*. At higher compression/lower quality settings, JPEG can produce noticeable 8×8 blocks of pixels. JPEG is a 24-bit color format.

JPEG can store both RGB and CMYK images but cannot store additional alpha channels, nor does it support transparency. You can access JPEG through both the Save for Web command (which will be discussed separately later in this chapter) and the Export command. When you're exporting, Illustrator presents you with a number of options, as you can see in Figure 22.4.

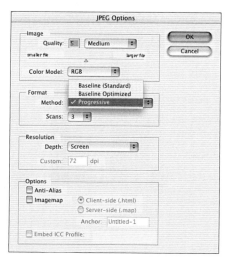

Figure 22.4
The JPEG Options dialog box offers control over both the file size and how it appears.

The options when you're exporting an image as a JPEG are as follows:

- **Image Quality**—This option controls the compression of the image and, therefore, the quality of the image. Remember that JPEG is a lossy file format. The slider actually has

11 predetermined stops and snaps to those positions. The pop-up menu offers Low (0–2), Medium (3–5), High (6–7), and Maximum (8–10).

- **Color Model**—The choices are RGB, CMYK, and Grayscale. CYMK is, of course, unacceptable for Web work.

- **Format Method**—You have three choices. Baseline (Standard) is compatible with virtually all Web browsers. Baseline Optimized is not supported by all browsers but maintains color quality better than Standard. Progressive is also not supported by all browsers and produces a slightly larger file size. It allows the image to be viewed as it downloads instead of just appearing after all image information is received by the browser. If you select Progressive, you can choose the number of Scans. The choices—3, 4, or 5—represent how many levels of appearance the image will have as it is downloading. Three is usually sufficient.

- **Resolution Depth**—The options are Screen (72 dpi), Medium (150 dpi), High (300 dpi), and Custom. For the Web, always use Screen. (See the sidebar "The Resolution-less Web" in this chapter.) This setting has a large effect on file size. See Figure 22.5 for a look at how much depth and quality affect file sizes.

- **Options**—Antialiasing uses a slight blending of colors to make edges look smoother. Imagemapping uses inline graphics with multiple "hotspots" to create hyperlinks. A client-side imagemap uses the viewer's browser to process the links, whereas a server-side imagemap is handled by the Web server. Embedding ICC profiles allows you to specify color information for a specific output device and is typically used with four-color process printing.

Figure 22.5
The size goes down as compression is increased, but so does image quality when you reopen the picture. Web work is a balancing act between small file sizes for quick downloading and better image quality. When you're preparing images for the Web, never use a resolution setting other than Screen.

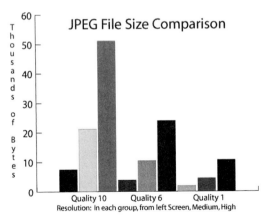

PNG

PNG (Portable Network Graphic) was, at least in part, inspired by the licensing fee for GIF. It is not supported by older browsers. (See the "Troubleshooting" section at the end of this chapter for specific information about Web browser support.) Illustrator uses PNG, like GIF, in conjunction with Save for Web (discussed later in this chapter). This file format supports indexed color, grayscale, and RGB images. In grayscale and RGB images, PNG supports a single alpha channel to define areas of transparency. It uses a *lossless* compression system, meaning no data is discarded during the compression process. When you reopen an image later, all the original information is present.

Illustrator supports two varieties of PNG: 8-bit and 24-bit. PNG-8 is comparable to GIF in application. It is designed for work with images that contain large areas of solid color and no gradients. It typically produces files up to 30% smaller than GIF from the same image. (A single, solid color block or similar image with one or few colors might be smaller in GIF.) PNG-24 is employed as a substitute for JPEG. Because it uses a lossless compression scheme, the file sizes are typically not as small as JPEG. However, the image quality remains the same as the original's, and transparency through an alpha channel is supported. And, unlike JPEG, PNG-24 retains the sharp detail of vector art, line art, and type.

Caution

Save your original file in its original format. Re-editing a JPEG file is usually a bad idea. After you compress a file with JPEG, you should try to avoid recompressing it. To compress more than once is to invite artifacts and distortion. Because JPEG is a lossy compression system, data is discarded. A second compression compromises the areas surrounding the discarded data. How do you avoid recompressing? If a file is a JPEG file, don't use the Export command or the Save for Web feature to produce another JPEG file from the image. If you must edit a JPEG and resave it as a JPEG (for Web use, for example), use maximum quality to minimize visible damage. However, it is certainly preferable to return to the original file, make the changes, and create a new JPEG file.

➡ *If PNG images do not display properly, check "Viewing PNG Files" in the "Troubleshooting" section at the end of this chapter.*

SVG

SVG (Scalable Vector Graphics) is less a file format and more a computer language. Exporting as SVG takes vector graphics and prepares them for use with Extensible Markup Language (XML) on the Web. *Scalable graphics* are artwork that can automatically be resized to appear correctly on monitors of any resolution or size, and are platform independent. These high-resolution vector graphics can include gradients, filters and effects, and animations. JavaScript interactivity is supported. SVG uses JPEG for rasterized portions of the image that do not contain transparency and PNG for those that include an alpha channel.

Illustrator 10 uses a version of SVG that's fully compatible with Illustrator. Rather than exporting, Illustrator now generates SVG files using the Save command and Save for Web. SVG is discussed in depth in Chapter 23.

SWF (Flash)

SWF (Shockwave Format) is commonly referred to as *Flash*. Like SVG, it will be discussed in the following chapter. Flash is the name of a program from Macromedia that produces scalable graphics. Viewers must have a Flash-enabled browser (via a Flash plug-in) to see the graphics. Illustrator produces SWF files with the Export command and Save for Web.

The Resolution-less Web

For years, graphic designers, illustrators, and Web designers have been told that the proper resolution for monitor-viewed images (including Web) is 72 pixels per inch (ppi) or dots per inch (dpi) — any higher resolution will result in files that are slow to download and too large for the Web. Many Web designers and graphic artists are now rejecting that theory in favor of a different one: There is no resolution on the Web. (The term *resolution* actually refers to printing an image. An image contains a certain number of pixels, and resolution tells the printer how tightly to pack those pixels.)

The argument against using the term *resolution* with the Web is founded in both technology and in common sense. What, exactly, is an inch on a monitor? A 17-inch screen set to display at 800×600 pixels shows a "life-size" image of a six-inch ruler at 72 ppi in just over half of its width (432 pixels is 54% of 800). Set that same monitor to 1,024×768 pixels, and that same image takes up just 42% of the width of the screen. Which is a correct inch? Well, the 800×600 pixel resolution for a 17-inch monitor comes close, depending on the actual viewable area of the screen. But remember that same 800×600 resolution on a 14-inch laptop screen gives a much smaller inch.

The current thinking is strictly in terms of pixels. An image is not "two inches by four inches at 72 dpi" for the Web; rather, the image is "144 pixels wide by 288 pixels high." Web pages are designed and viewed in pixels, not in inches. The term *resolution* will long be a part of Web design, however, and is present in Illustrator in, among other places, the Export JPEG dialog box. When you're forced to make a choice, Web work should be at 72 dpi. When you have the option, consider thinking strictly in pixel dimensions for the Web.

PIXEL PREVIEW

Despite starting life as vector art, when saved in any of the top three Web file formats (JPEG, GIF, or PNG), Illustrator documents have more in common with Photoshop files than with their own Illustrator-native siblings. All three file formats support only raster images. (Vector images contain shapes and text that are mathematically described, whereas raster images are merely collections of different colored pixels. See Chapter 18.) When you export to one of these file formats to prepare an image for the Web, the conversion changes the art to pixels. Layers are flattened, and text and objects are no longer editable.

Rasterization can cause severe degradation of image quality. Perfect curves and circles are created from little rectangles, leading to a problem called *jaggies*. Jaggies are the little steps that are created by the rectangular pixels attempting to represent curved segments. Figure 22.6 shows the problem.

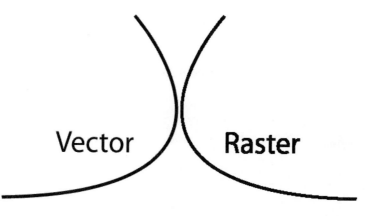

Figure 22.6
The difference is obvious. The appearance of the curve and text on the right were identical to those on the left until the command Effect, Rasterize was applied. All vector artwork is rasterized when saved to JPEG, GIF, or PNG formats. Antialiasing helps control the jaggies.

Although the effect can be severe, it can also be managed to some degree. *Antialiasing* uses pixels that are intermediates between two bordering colors to soften an edge. The sharp contrast between the corners of a black pixel and the corners of a white pixel are very noticeable. Adding a few gray pixels around the edges eases the transition. See Figure 22.7 and Figure 22.8 for examples of antialiasing.

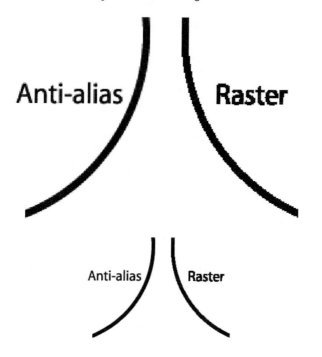

Figure 22.7
While better than those on the right, the curve and text on the left still leave much to be desired from a vector art point of view. The gray squares that are the antialiasing pixels are especially visible at the top of the curve in this 250% zoom.

Figure 22.8
This image shows the same two curves and their text when viewed at 100% magnification, as they would be on the Web. At the proper viewing percentage, the antialiasing is very effective. Notice how the text on the left has lost the softness and grayness that seemed apparent in Figure 22.7.

Illustrator helps you prepare for rasterization of your vector artwork and text with the menu command View, Pixel Preview. This command has no effect on your artwork itself, merely on how it is displayed. Figure 22.9 shows a section of a Web page prior to Pixel Preview, and Figure 22.10 shows how the same image looks with the Pixel Preview turned on.

Figure 22.9
Even at 300% magnification, the vector art and text look very sharp and clean. For reference, the text on the upper button (Ohio Inline Hockey) is Arial 12-point.

Figure 22.10
At 300% magnification, the antialiasing is evident. At 100% magnification, as this image will be seen on the Web, the button text is crisp and legible.

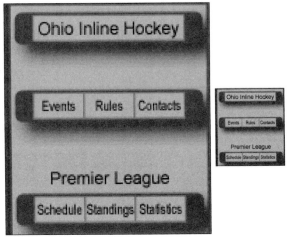

Although the Rasterize command works on elements that have been selected, Pixel Preview affects the entire document. You can use it as a preview or as a creation mode. When you're creating in Pixel Preview, objects automatically snap to a pixel-sized invisible grid. With Pixel Preview activated, the menu command View, Snap to Grid automatically becomes Snap to Pixel. The rulers and units of measure remain unchanged, but the snap increment, as pixels, no longer conforms to the ruler. Just like Snap to Grid, the command Snap to Pixel can be deactivated in the View menu.

SAVE FOR WEB AND IMAGE OPTIMIZING

At first glance, the Save for Web dialog box (see Figure 22.11) looks daunting. It almost seems to be a program in itself, with an entirely new interface to learn. It is not very imposing after the features are identified and explained. In fact, using this feature is far simpler than using the trial-and-error method often employed to optimize images for the Web.

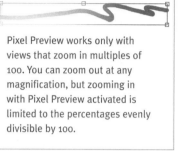

Pixel Preview works only with views that zoom in multiples of 100. You can zoom out at any magnification, but zooming in with Pixel Preview activated is limited to the percentages evenly divisible by 100.

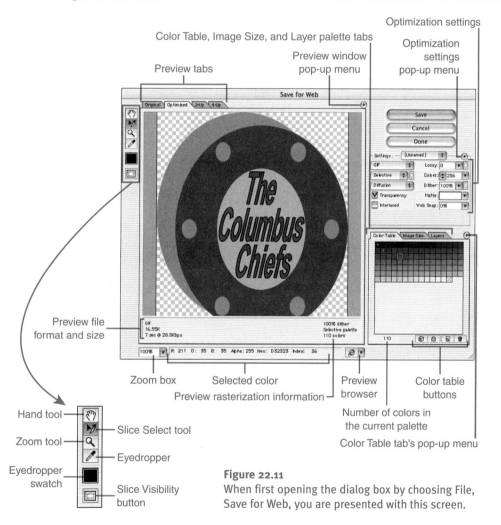

Figure 22.11
When first opening the dialog box by choosing File, Save for Web, you are presented with this screen.

Optimization is the process of selecting the balance between file size (download time) and image quality (compression and number of colors in the image). Illustrator's Save for Web feature offers you choices and helps you make your decisions.

Figure 22.11 identifies the elements of the default Save for Web view. Here is further explanation:

- The four tabs in the preview window present the panels as labeled. Examples of the other panels and how they differ from the Optimized panel are shown in Figure 22.14 through Figure 22.16.

- The four tools available to you in Save for Web are the Hand tool, the Slice Select tool, the Zoom tool, and the Eyedropper. The swatch below the Eyedropper shows what color was most recently clicked with that tool. The button below the swatch allows you to toggle the visibility of slices.

- The information at the lower left of the preview window tells you what you are looking at in the preview window. Here, you can find the file format, the size of the file, and how long it will take to download from your Web site onto your visitor's screen (more or less). The connection speed shown is the default 28.8Kbps, but you can select a faster or slower modem speed from the preview window pop-up menu. The values are taken from the optimization settings.

- The Zoom box has a pop-up menu of nine levels, from 12.5% to 1,600%, as well as Fit in Window. You can double-click in the box and type any value from 1 to 1,600.

- The line at the bottom of the preview window tells you the color value under the cursor, either in the preview window or in the color table. When the cursor is over transparency or outside the preview area, the R, G, B, Alpha, and Hex values are empty. With the cursor over a color or over transparency, if there is any, the *Index number* of the Save for Web window is shown. It refers to the specific swatch in the color palette that represents a particular color. The Alpha information refers to transparency. When a channel is used to store the information, it has 256 levels of transparency. The values in this item range from 0 to 255. Hex refers to the hexadecimal name of the Web-safe color. See the sidebar "Hexadecimal Colors" in Chapter 12 for more information about this color numbering system.

- The information at the lower right tells you what you are seeing in the preview window. Whereas the information to the left of the window describes the file format and size, this section describes the number of colors and how they are handled. You can adjust the values by manipulating the optimization settings.

Caution

Despite the size and complexity of the Save for Web feature, remember that it is a dialog box. As such, when it is open, you have certain restrictions that you don't have in an Illustrator document window. For example, you cannot click to access Help (although it is not grayed out); no Undo is available, even with the keyboard shortcut Cmd+Z [Ctrl+Z]; there is no obvious way to save your work in the middle—you are offered OK and Cancel; and you cannot collapse the window (Macintosh). Some tricks, however, are built in to Save for Web. You'll find them in the sidebar "Taming the Save for Web Dialog Box," later in this chapter.

- The Preview browser button allows you to preview your choices in an actual browser window. Your choices are the browsers installed on your computer. Illustrator starts the browser (if it is not already running) and opens a window with the image as it appears in the current window. (In 2-Up and 4-Up views, whichever preview is selected appears in the browser window.)

- The number in the lower left of the color table tells you how many colors actually are used in the image.

- The icons in the lower right of the color table are, from the left

  - Snap to Web Palette

  - Lock Color

  - Add Eyedropper Color

  - Delete Selected Color(s).

  Respectively, they change any swatch selected in the color table to a Web-safe color; prevent a color swatch from being deleted or changed in the color table or in the image; add to the color table a color that has been sampled with the Eyedropper tool (which is useful in the 2-Up and 4-Up windows when a variation has altered a color); and delete from both the color table and the image itself any swatches selected in the table.

- The color table holds a swatch for each color currently in use in the image. This table, of course, is available only for the indexed color modes (GIF and PNG-8). Showing all 16.7 million possible colors of a continuous tone image is not practical in table form. See the section "The Color Table" later in this chapter for more details.

- The Color Table tab's pop-up menu will also be discussed in the section "The Color Table" later in the chapter.

- The Optimization Settings are the core of the Save for Web feature. Changes are made here during the optimization process. See the section "The Optimization Settings" later in this chapter for more details.

- The Optimization Settings pop-up menu will be described later in detail in the section "The Optimization Settings."

- The Preview window pop-up menu offers the option of previewing how an image will look when dithered by a browser using 8-bit color. Browser dithering is not available for the original in 2-Up or 4-Up mode and can be turned on or off individually for each of the other three panes in 4-Up. You can also adjust the calculation of download time by selecting the target speed of the Internet connection. Save for Web calculates approximately how long it will take to download the image over a connection with speeds of 14.4Kbps, 28.8Kbps, or 56.6Kbps. Faster connections, such as

Save for Web is much like a stand-alone application in more respects than one. In addition to having a complex interface, it has its own preferences file. If you start having problems with Save for Web, delete this file. You'll find it in the same location as the Adobe Illustrator 10 preferences folder.

cable modem, DSL, and T1, are not considered because of the minimal amount of time required for most graphics to download with them.

Optimizing a vector art illustration can be as simple as choosing the GIF format. With its built-in compression, the GIF format can produce very small files from images such as that shown to the left in Figure 22.12. This image has large areas of solid color, with no areas where the color value changes gradually (such as a gradient). The Save for Web feature allows you to make simple decisions as well as fine-tune an image until you achieve the perfect balance between file size and image quality.

Figure 22.12
Before you explore the Save for Web options, take a look at the subject images. The image on the left is all vector art, with no gradients or rasterized objects. The logo on the right contains several gradients.

GIF, JPEG, and PNG all require a rasterized image—that is, an image turned into a series of pixels that can be displayed by a Web browser. This is best done in Illustrator by Save for Web. Figure 22.13 shows the results of choosing Effect, Rasterize.

Figure 22.13
For reference, copies of the two pucks in Figure 22.12 were rasterized using the menu command Effect, Rasterize.

When the two images in Figure 22.13 were rasterized, the resolution was set for Screen (72 dpi), with antialiasing checked. Note the degradation of the text and the slight banding in the gradated center of the image on the right.

In addition to the Optimize panel of the Save for Web feature (shown in Figure 22.11), Illustrator enables you to do head-to-head comparison of your image with possible optimization configurations. The three additional tabs of the window allow you to visually see the effects of the various potential file format, color, and compression changes. The first of the other panels of Save for Web is Original (see Figure 22.14), which allows you to refer to a large version of the artwork as created. The third tab, after Optimize, is 2-Up (see Figure 22.15), which gives you two panes in which to work. By default, the left pane is the original image, and the right pane is the place where you view your potential changes. However, you also can change the left pane as desired for comparison. Whichever pane is active (selected) at the time the OK button is clicked is the version saved. This is also true of the 4-Up version, which offers you three variations of optimization, as well as the original (see Figure 22.16).

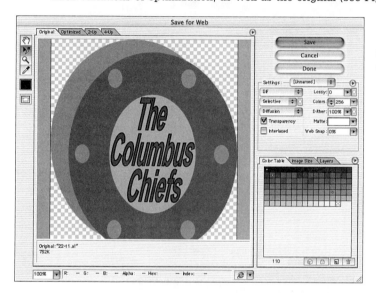

Figure 22.14
On the first tab in the Save for Web screen, you can easily view the original artwork with a single click.

In the lower-left corner of the Original tab in Figure 22.14, the zoom factor has been set to 100%. Note the other differences between this screen and that of the Optimized screen shown in Figure 22.11. In the lower-left corner, in addition to the zoom factor, the file size information lacks any reference to download speed, and rather than a file format, the filename is listed. The rasterization information to the lower right of the image is missing, as there is no rasterization. Also note that, although you can change the optimization settings, the changes will not be reflected in the original. Any changes, however, are carried over to the Optimized panel, the 2-Up panel, and the top-right pane of the 4-Up panel.

Figures 23.15 and 23.16 show the other two panels of the Save for Web dialog box. These two panels allow comparisons between an original and one or three possible optimization schemes, or between two or four possible optimization settings.

In the 2-Up screen in Figure 22.15, the default is to have the original image on the left and make changes to the image on the right. However, this isn't mandatory. You can click the original image once, use the Optimization

Always make your final selections in 100% zoom mode. Using zoom in conjunction with the Hand tool to check details of the artwork and zooming out to get an overall view are good working habits, but always base your decisions on the 100% view. Not only is it what your visitors will eventually see, it is a more accurate rendering of the rasterization.

Settings pop-up menu to make changes, and have two different optimized versions for comparison. At any time, you can switch back to the original image using the pop-up menu. Notice the several differences in the Save for Web feature between this image using 24-bit color and Figure 22.14, which showed the options for an 8-bit image. For example, no color table is available for 24-bit color, so the Image Size palette has been activated.

Figure 22.15
The 2-Up panel allows comparison between the original and the selected optimization settings. The zoom factor has been returned to 100%.

Figure 22.16
The 4-Up panel functions much like the 2-Up window, except that you can experiment with three panes, along with the original image. As you can do with the 2-Up panel, click in an individual pane to make it active.

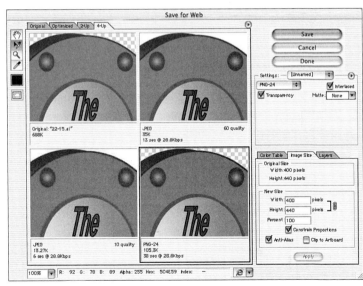

As you can see in Figure 22.15, Save for Web also works with continuous tone images, such as those with gradients. Rather than GIF and PNG-8, the formats of choice are JPEG and PNG-24. The options and controls vary because of the nature of the images. For example, the Color Table tab is inactive. Figure 22.17 and Figure 22.18 illustrate some of the differences between the PNG-24 and JPEG file formats as employed by Save for Web.

In Figure 22.17, the order of figures is (clockwise from top left) as follows: Interlaced PNG, non-Interlaced PNG, JPEG-Medium quality, JPEG-High quality. The JPEG-Medium file is less than one-fifth the size of the PNG-Interlaced file, yet the differences would not be apparent to a casual Web surfer.

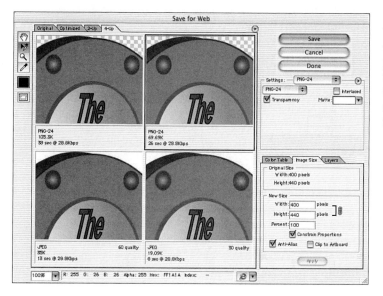

Figure 22.17
The Save for Web feature allows you to compare file formats, not just for quality, but for size and format options as well. Note that the Interlaced option for PNG had added about 50% to the image size.

The image in Figure 22.18 is reduced by PNG to 38% of its original size. In comparison, the hockey puck in Figure 22.17 was reduced to approximately 10% of its original size with the same PNG settings. The difference can be attributed to the fact that the previous image had a large area of transparency and more uniform colors. On the other hand, JPEG at 60% quality reduces either image to under 5% of its original size.

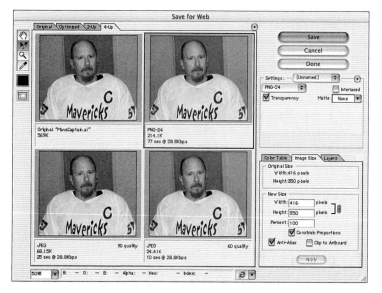

Figure 22.18
Because it doesn't have large areas of transparency, this image is less compressed by the PNG-24 format than that in the previous figure. (Figure 22.17 was originally 688KB.)

Taming the Save for Web Dialog Box

The warning near the beginning of this chapter said that the Save for Web feature has no Undo and no obvious way to save your work in the middle of an optimization. That is correct. However, a couple of features can take the place of those capabilities. Rather than an option to save your work in the middle of an optimization, after you've made perhaps a dozen changes and still have a dozen to go, Illustrator offers you Remember. When you press Option [Alt], the OK button changes to Remember. It records the settings as they are at the time. For example, say you have edited several colors to make them Web-safe and adjusted the dithering, but have not yet decided on GIF or PNG and are still considering lossiness. Then the phone rings, and an emergency project lands on your desk. Looking at the monitor, you decide that your options are to optimize your image half-finished or cancel and lose the work you've done. By employing the Remember capability, you can store the settings as they are for the next time you open the image in the Save for Web feature. The changes are saved with that file and have no effect on other images being optimized. You cannot, however, use Remember and then return to the default Save for Web settings.

Also, when you press Option [Alt], the Cancel button changes to Reset. With 2-Up and 4-Up panes, it works with the active pane only, allowing you to return that individual pane to its original values. Rather than the last operation, this removes all the settings since the last time the feature was started or the last time you used Remember. This capability can be a big help if you accidentally delete several key colors from the image while using the color table. Although it is not the same as Undo, it can salvage work that you would otherwise lose when you click Cancel.

You also can access Illustrator's Help files while working with Save for Web. Switch applications through your operating system and open your Web browser. (For Macintosh users, Cmd+Tab is the default keyboard shortcut to switch applications, and the application menu in the upper-right corner of the screen is available. Windows users can use the Start menu.) Use the keyboard shortcut Cmd+O [Ctrl+O] to open the Open dialog box. Navigate to the Adobe Illustrator folder, inside of which you can find the folder Help. Open that folder and press H on the keyboard to jump to files starting with that letter. Select Help.html, and Illustrator Help starts right up. You can bookmark this page or add it to Favorites for easy access.

THE COLOR TABLE

The Color Table tab is available when you're working with GIF or PNG-8 file formats only. These formats use indexed color mode, whereas JPEG and PNG-24 use the full RGB gamut. The table displays all the colors currently in use in the 8-bit image. With the 2-Up and 4-Up tabs, it displays the colors of the currently selected version. Figure 22.19 shows the color table.

The color table in Figure 22.19 shows four Web-safe colors (indicated by the white diamond in the middle of the swatch), three colors that have been edited (with a black diamond in the middle), and some swatches that have been locked (a symbol in the lower-right corner of the swatch). Edited colors are automatically locked. Note that the last swatch in the color table represents transparency. In the bottom row, five colors have been selected, as indicated by the boxes around them.

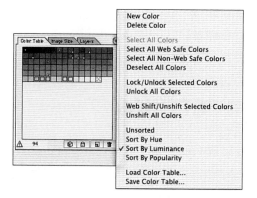

Figure 22.19
The color table is available only for GIF and PNG-8, the 8-bit file formats.

To select a color (for deletion or to use a menu command, for example), click its swatch. To select two or more contiguous colors in the table, click the first and Shift+click the last. You can select noncontiguous colors, those whose swatches are not consecutive in the color tables, by Cmd+clicking [Ctrl+clicking].

Colors can be deleted using the color table. Select a swatch and click the Delete Color button or choose the command from the table's pop-up menu. When a color is deleted from the table, it is also deleted from the image. In the image, the nearest remaining color is substituted. This is used to reduce not only the number of colors in the image, but also to reduce file size.

Editing colors by double-clicking a color table swatch opens the Color Picker. After you change colors, clicking the OK button does several things. The new color is added as a swatch to the color table, the color is updated throughout the particular pane (but not other panes in the case of 2-Up and 4-Up modes), and the new color is locked.

In the event that a color is missing from the color table, you can add it by using the Eyedropper. This feature can sample a color in the original or an optimization pane. The color is added to the swatch below the Eyedropper tool on the left. To add it to a color table, click the image for which you've selected the color to make it active, and click the New Color button at the bottom of the color table.

The color table's pop-up menu, accessible through the arrow to the right of the tabs, is shown in Figure 22.19. In addition to the commands represented by the buttons on the bottom of the tab, it allows you to select colors based on a couple of criteria and to rearrange the swatches.

The selection criteria of the color table's pop-up menu allow you to lock or shift the colors that fall into the two major categories—Web-safe and non–Web-safe—as well as work with all colors in the table. The Select commands are most often used with the Lock and the Shift commands. Unshift All Colors returns colors forced to Web-safe values, as well as returns edited colors to their original values. Locked swatches remain locked.

The Unsorted command puts the colors into their original order in the color table. Sort by Hue works within the HSB color mode. Neutrals are placed with the reds. Sort by Luminance relies on the B, or brightness, value of HSB. Sort by Popularity ranks the colors according to how many pixels contain each color. This command can be very useful for eliminating colors to reduce file size but can destroy antialiasing.

The final two commands in the color table's pop-up menu are Load Color Table and Save Color Table. Any collection of swatches from an optimization pane can be saved and accessed later on for a different image. Remember that only GIF and PNG-8 images can use color tables. This feature could be useful for producing uniformity in a series of images.

THE OPTIMIZATION SETTINGS

The choices for optimization vary according to the file format selected. The pop-up menu at the top of the Settings area allows you to choose a number of predetermined setting sets. They include PNG-8; PNG-24; JPEG with settings for Low, Medium, or High compression; GIF, with sets of 32, 64, or 128 colors, and each setting can be either dithered and undithered; and also a choice of GIF with the Web-safe palette. Any change you make to a set of settings changes the pop-up menu to [Unnamed]. Like color tables, sets of settings can be saved and later exchanged between files. The Save Settings command is located in the Settings pop-up menu. Any sets saved appear with the Settings sets in the pop-up menu just below the Cancel button.

Also found in the Settings pop-up menu are the commands Delete Settings, Optimize to File Size, and Repopulate Views. Delete Settings removes the predetermined set of values currently active in the pop-up menu. Optimize to File Size allows you to determine the file format and the target size, leaving Illustrator to make decisions regarding the color table and compression. Repopulate Views, in the 2-Up and 4-Up modes, creates new compression options based on those of the active pane.

GIF Optimization Choices

Figure 22.20 shows the Settings area that appears when any of the six sets of GIF settings are selected from the pop-up menu or when GIF is chosen as a file format.

Color palette pop-up menu
File format pop-up menu
Setting sets pop-up menu

Figure 22.20
The fields do not vary among the predetermined GIF setting sets, but the values in the fields change.

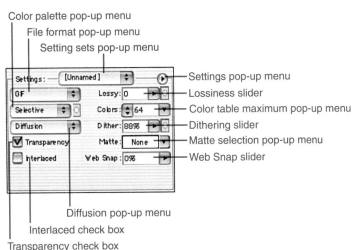

Settings pop-up menu
Lossiness slider
Color table maximum pop-up menu
Dithering slider
Matte selection pop-up menu
Web Snap slider

Diffusion pop-up menu
Interlaced check box
Transparency check box

The Settings pop-up menu is the same for all versions of the Settings area, giving a choice of the 12 predetermined sets described in Figure 22.20. The file format menu changes among the four possible formats, selecting by default the highest quality of each.

The Color palette pop-up menu allows a choice of Perceptual, Selective, Adaptive, Web, or Custom. Perceptual color palettes give priority to those colors that appear dominant to the human eye. Selective, the default, modifies the Perceptual palette to maintain priority for colors that appear in large areas of the image and for Web-safe colors. This option produces a palette closest to the image's original palette. Adaptive assigns the available number of colors in the color table to shades of the colors (hues) that are most common in an image. (For example, the image used in Figure 22.14 is almost exclusively reds and grays.) Choosing Web from the pop-up menu ensures that any color appearing in the color table is Web-safe. Custom is automatically selected if colors are deleted from the color table.

The Dithering pop-up menu allows you to choose among Diffusion, Pattern, Noise, or No Dither. These options are explained later in this chapter in the section "Types of Dithering."

The Transparency check box toggles the appearance of any areas of the image that do not contain color. By default, it is checked. When the box is unchecked, any pixels that had been transparent become white or the color selected under Matte (see the following description). The transparent swatch is also removed from the color table.

Interlacing is the gradual appearance of an image in the browser's window as it downloads. Although interlacing adds somewhat to file size, it is becoming increasingly rare for any but the smallest images to be noninterlaced.

The Lossiness slider allows you to override GIF's default lossless compression. The amount of lossiness, from 0 to 100, does not directly correlate with a reduction in file size. Linear artifacts (lines of color) can start appearing at settings as low as 10 for many images. These lines give some indication of how the compression algorithm functions.

The maximum number of colors in the color table must be between 2 and 256 for GIF images. Reducing the number does not necessarily reduce file size. When you use dithering, the extra compensation can actually increase file size slightly when you remove a color from the table.

The Dithering slider is used in conjunction with diffusion dithering and is explained later in this chapter in the section "Types of Dithering."

The Matte selection pop-up menu offers choices of how the image interacts with its background. It works in conjunction with the Transparency check box. When the box is checked, transparency is maintained and Matte works with pixels that are semi-transparent for antialiasing. When the box is unchecked, the entire range of transparency is used for matting. GIF supports transparency through the use of clipping paths. When the Web page upon which the image will be placed has a solid color background, you can use this feature to help blend the image into its page. Areas that appear as transparent in the optimization window can be filled with the page's background color. The pop-up menu offers Black, White, Eyedropper Color, None, and Other. Selecting Other opens the Color Picker. Partially transparent pixels that are used to soften edges through antialiasing, when not matted, can produce a halo effect around the image. Selecting None from the Matte pop-up menu results in hard-edge transparency for GIF images. These hard edges can produce jagged lines on curves. In hard-edge transparency, any pixel more than 50% transparent becomes fully transparent; any pixel less than 50% transparent becomes fully opaque in its original color.

Web Snap refers to colors. The higher the value selected, the more colors of the color table are automatically converted to Web-safe colors. By selecting individual colors in the color table and shifting them using the palette's button or pop-up menu command, you get much more control.

PNG-8 Optimization Settings

Figure 22.21 shows the Settings area when PNG-8 is selected from the Format pop-up menu or from the Settings pop-up menu. The options and choices are virtually the same as for GIF. Note that PNG-8 does not offer the Lossiness slider because the format does not support lossy compression. For an explanation of the various settings, refer to the preceding section, "GIF Optimization Choices."

Figure 22.21
Other than the removal of the Lossiness slider and the subsequent relocation of the Interlaced box, the PNG options are identical to GIF.

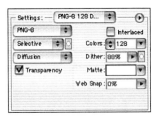

JPEG Optimization Settings

As a 24-bit format, JPEG has a different group of optimization settings. Because 24-bit images do not offer direct control over the color table, several settings seen for GIF and PNG-8 are missing. The Settings pop-up menu offers JPEG High, JPEG Low, and JPEG Medium. Figure 22.22 offers a view of the JPEG Settings area.

Figure 22.22
The pop-up menus for Settings, file format, and Matte are the only items that the JPEG Settings area has in common with GIF or PNG-8.

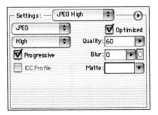

Beneath the file format pop-up menu (showing JPEG in Figure 22.22), you can see the pop-up menu for image quality. The choices are Low, Medium, High, and Maximum. This box automatically sets the value for the Quality slider to its right but does not override the slider. When the slider is moved to a value that is in a classification other than that shown in the pop-up menu, the menu automatically changes. The quality value is directly related to the number of colors saved with the file and, therefore, the file size.

The Progressive check box functions similarly to the Interlaced check box for GIF and PNG-8, allowing the image to appear gradually as it downloads.

The Optimized check box, when checked, produces a slightly different version of JPEG, known as Optimized JPEG or Enhanced JPEG. This version of the format results in slightly smaller file sizes but is not supported by all browsers.

Blur applies a Gaussian blur to the image, reducing artifacts but softening the overall appearance of the image. Named for the nineteenth-century German astronomer and mathematician Carl Friedrich Gauss, a Gaussian blur uses a mathematical formula to determine the relationship among adjoining pixels. Possible values range from 0 to 2.0 for this feature and represent the pixel radius of the blur. Save for Web actually calculates and redraws the screen for values as low as or lower than 0.000001 pixel, but this is a waste of time. No radius under approximately 0.1 pixel will have any effect on the image. Blurs can reduce file sizes by reducing the number of colors needed to display the image.

Because JPEG does not support transparency in any form, the Matte control takes on a larger role. A single circle in a JPEG image, unless modified, appears as a circle in a white square when placed into a Web page. When you're using JPEG, any pixel that does not have an assigned color value is, by default, white. To avoid a white rectangle or square around your image, use the Matte feature to match your image's background to that of the Web page. As noted previously, only solid colors can be matted.

PNG-24 Optimization Settings

The simplest of all settings, PNG-24 offers the Settings pop-up menu, the file format pop-up menu, and only three options: Transparency, Interlaced, and Matte. These three options are virtually identical to those described in the preceding sections, with one exception. Although both PNG-8 and PNG-24 support transparency, PNG-24 supports up to 256 levels of transparency. However, not all browsers support multilevel transparency. Figure 22.23 shows the PNG-24 Settings area.

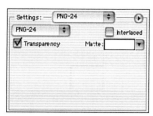

Figure 22.23
This set of options is both the simplest and most restrictive. As a 24-bit color mode, PNG-24 has no direct control over the color table. And unlike JPEG, PNG-24 offers no control over quality and cannot apply a Gaussian blur.

SWF and SVG Optimization Settings

Illustrator 10 allows you to use Save for Web to produce both Flash (SWF) and SVG images. The optimization setting options parallel the options when exporting to SWF or saving as SVG formats. They will be discussed in the following chapter.

TYPES OF DITHERING

Diffusion, pattern, and noise are the three types of dithering available in Save for Web. Dithering is used to perceptually ease the transition between two colors by arranging pixels to create the appearance of intermediate colors. Much the way that a photograph in a newspaper creates the illusion of numerous shades of gray using only black ink, so this dithering creates the perception of several colors or shades when only two colors of pixels are being used.

Diffusion dither, when used with either GIF or PNG-8, allows control of how much dithering is applied. The Dither slider in the Settings area ranges from 0% to 100%. Figure 22.24 and Figure 22.25 show the difference between 50% and 100% dither in close-up, respectively, and Figure 22.26 and Figure 22.27 show the effects as they would be viewed on the Web.

Figure 22.24
Diffusion dither at 50% is magnified to a zoom level of 250%.

Figure 22.25
Diffusion dither at 100% is magnified to a zoom level of 250%.

Increasing the amount of diffusion dithering greatly reduces the width of the individual bands, while increasing the areas of dither proportionally. This is far more noticeable in the center of the puck (toward the lower-right corner) than in the outer areas or the round stud.

Pattern dithering can be very effective. Rather than rely on interspersing dots of the two colors, it uses dots to create, as you could guess, patterns between the two bands of color. Figure 22.28 shows pattern dithering, and Figure 22.29 shows the effect at 100% zoom. When you use pattern dithering, Illustrator controls the amount of dithering, and the Dither slider is unavailable.

Figure 22.26
At 100% view, the banding is very recognizable, although the edges are not as hard as they would be without the 50% dithering.

Figure 22.27
At 100% view, the 100% dithering has virtually eliminated the banding. This image was reduced from 24-bit color to a total of 32 colors. You can see the 24-bit version, for comparison, in Figure 22.11.

Figure 22.28
Most noticeable as a series of "x" shapes in the center of the puck, the pattern is virtually undetectable in the round stud, although some red pixels appear there.

Figure 22.29
The pattern dithering is very effective in parts of the image, primarily in the outer face of the puck. It is less successful with the outer edge of the puck, which has taken on a tread-like appearance.

Noise dithering, like diffusion dithering, relies on interspersing dots of the two colors to reduce perceptual banding. However, it does not allow control over the amount of dithering. Figure 22.30 shows noise dithering in the test image, and Figure 22.31 shows the result at 100% zoom.

Figure 22.30
Noise uses dots much like diffusion dithering and in close-up looks almost identical to 100% diffusion dither.

Figure 22.31
At 100% zoom, as it would be viewed on the Web, this image is virtually indistinguishable from Figure 22.27, which showed 100% diffusion dithering at actual size.

The type of dithering selected plays a role in file size. Working with the identical image, whose original size was 691KB, and optimizing for GIF with a palette of 32 colors and 0% lossy, the following file sizes were produced:

- Diffusion dither at 50%: 20.6KB

- Diffusion dither at 100%: 26.75KB

- Pattern dither: 27.11KB

- Noise dither: 31.37KB

Although noise and diffusion dither at 100% produced almost identical images, diffusion resulted in a file some 17% smaller.

Keep in mind that you should make all dithering choices, like color and compression decisions, with the view at 100% zoom.

OPTIMIZING SLICES

It's not unusual to have an image that combines a variety of artwork. You might have, for example, an image that contains both a photograph and large areas of solid color, such as that shown in Figure 22.32.

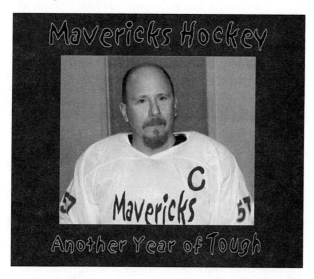

Figure 22.32
This image contains continuous tone areas (the photo) and large blocks of solid color.

Such images used to pose problems for optimization. The photo would be best as a 24-bit image, such as JPEG or PNG-24. However, the areas of solid color are better optimized as GIF or PNG-8. If you optimize the entire image as JPEG, you run the risk of artifacts and other compression damage in the background areas. If you optimize the image as GIF, you lose quality in the foreground area.

Illustrator 10's Save for Web feature includes the capability of optimizing different slices separately. (Slices are further discussed in Chapter 21, "Designing Web Sites and Web Pages.")

In Figure 22.33 you can see that the image was sliced to create a separate area for the photographic image.

Figure 22.33
The photo is a user-defined slice, while the rest of the image has been automatically sliced by Illustrator.

In Save for Web, select a slice and assign the appropriate optimization settings. In Figure 22.34, the photo has been selected with the Slice Select tool, and JPEG settings have been determined.

Figure 22.34
The optimization settings shown will be applied only to the single selected slice.

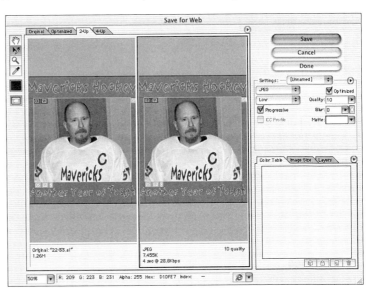

Again using the Slice Selection tool, you can Shift-click to select the remaining slices (or any combination thereof). Different settings can be assigned (see Figure 22.35).

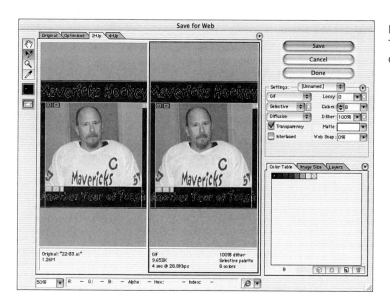

Figure 22.35
The four other slices will all be optimized as GIFs.

When Save for Web generates the optimized slices, one will be JPEG, the others will be GIF.

THE SAVE OPTIMIZED AS DIALOG BOX

Because Save for Web generates images for the World Wide Web, it offers you the opportunity to get a head start on creating a Web page. You can even generate the necessary HTML file to create a Web page itself from Save for Web.

Saving Images, HTML, or Both

After clicking the Save button in the Save for Web dialog box, you're presented with the Save Optimized As dialog box (see Figure 22.36).

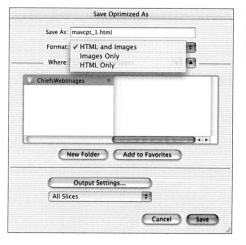

Figure 22.36
These options determine what files will be generated by Save for Web.

You have the option of saving just the image or images (when sliced), the HTML code, or both. When saving sliced images, typically both the HTML file and the images are required (see Figure 22.37). When optimizing a non-sliced image that will be placed into a Web page using a Web development tool such as GoLive, only the image is required.

Figure 22.37
In this instance, both an HTML file and a folder of images have been generated.

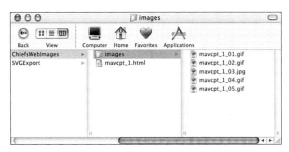

The HTML file contains all the Web-ready code necessary to recreate a sliced image in a Web browser. In Figure 22.38, you can see that a table is generated.

Figure 22.38
The HTML tags <TABLE> and </TABLE> indicate the beginning and end of the table.

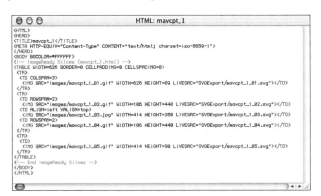

In contrast, if an HTML file is generated for an unsliced image, the code references only a single slice, the image itself, and so is hardly necessary unless the image is to stand alone as a Web page in and of itself.

Output Options

The Output Settings dialog box offers four panels of options. The pop-up menu directly below Settings changes the panel. In Figure 22.39, you can see the HTML options panel.

Unless you work with HTML, the only option that needs to be addressed is Include GoLive Code. If you are saving an image with an HTML file and will be adding the HTML to an Adobe GoLive page, check this box. If not, leave the box unchecked.

In Figure 22.40, the Background panel allows you to create an image to be used as the background of a Web page.

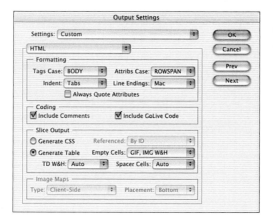

Figure 22.39
Those unfamiliar with HTML might find these options unintelligible.

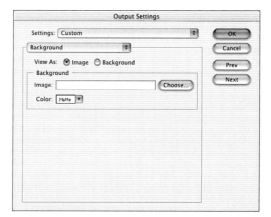

Figure 22.40
Unless actually generating a background to be added to a Web page, leave View As Image selected.

The Saving Files panel (see Figure 22.41) gives you some control over how Save for Web will name the files it generates.

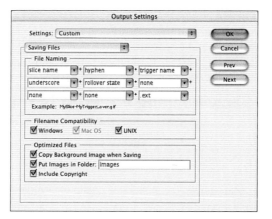

Figure 22.41
Each of the fields includes a pop-up list of options.

The fourth panel of Output Settings options controls slice naming (see Figure 22.42) .

Figure 22.42
This panel is important when saving sliced images.

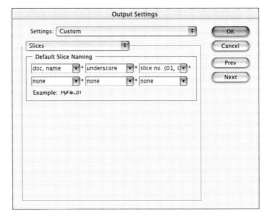

TROUBLESHOOTING

Minimizing Banding

How do I eliminate the bands of color that sometimes show up in a transitional color?

Banding occurs when a gradation from one color to another is forced into several distinct colors. The reduction in the number of colors results in grouping of several colors into one. For example, in a 24-bit image, a certain area might transition from light red to medium red to dark red. With a reduction of colors, it all becomes medium red. If the original transition was actually "dark purple–medium purple–light purple–light red–medium red–dark red," the result could be medium purple and medium red side-by-side.

There are two solutions: Use a file format that supports 24-bit color (JPEG, PNG-24) or dither an 8-bit image. Dithering uses dots and/or patterns of the two colors in differing densities to simulate shades between the colors. Save for Web offers options and controls for dithering.

Onscreen Images Show Banding but Print Is Fine

My printed images are fine. Everyone else says they look okay, but my monitor shows severe banding. Is the monitor broken?

No, probably not. Check the color depth. If the monitor is showing only 256 colors, gradated images without dithering appear banded. For Windows, use the Start menu's Settings to access the Control Panels. Double-click Display to open the Display Properties dialog box. Click the Settings tab and adjust the Color Palette to High Color or True Color. For Macintosh, use the Apple Menu's Control Panels to access Monitors. Click the Monitor button (not Color) and set the Color Depth to thousands or millions.

Viewing PNG Files

I only get an "image not available" icon when trying to view a PNG image in my browser. Any help?

Check first to see that your browser supports PNG. Here's the status:

- **Microsoft Internet Explorer for Windows**—Version 5 and higher support PNG with limited transparency. Version 4 can see in-line (using an HTML IMG tag) PNG files but does not open a referenced file. IE4 has no support for transparency.

- **Microsoft Internet Explorer for Macintosh**—IE5 and higher for Macintosh have full support for PNG, including alpha channel transparency, and support for gamma, sRGB, and ICC profiles.

- **Netscape Navigator/Communicator for Windows and Macintosh**—Versions 4.0 through 4.5 had limited PNG support, and numerous plug-ins are available as freeware to extend the capability. Version 4.7 has improved support, and Navigator 6 (and later) offers the same high-quality PNG support as Mozilla.

Next, check to see that PNG is properly associated with the browser application. (See your particular browser's Help for specific information.)

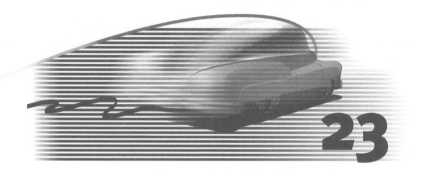

23

FLASH AND SVG SUPPORT

IN THIS CHAPTER

Animation on the Web 534

What Is Flash? 537

What Is SVG? 538

Preparing Vector-Based Animation for Flash 539

Exporting to SWF 552

Creating SVG Output 554

Dynamic SVG 560

Saving as SVG 562

Save for Web with SWF and SVG 564

Troubleshooting 565

ANIMATION ON THE WEB

The most common file formats for the Web (discussed in Chapter 22, "Saving Images for the Web") have their individual strengths and weaknesses, but they all have one common weakness. JPEG, GIF, and PNG are all raster formats. Raster art, defined later in this chapter and discussed in Chapter 18, "Raster Images and Rasterized Objects," changes appearance as it is altered in size. Flash and SVG formats, on the other hand, rely on vector art, which can be scaled to virtually any size without losing its shape, and can incorporate raster art. Both Flash and SVG are excellent formats for animation. Additionally, the vector formats (SVG, SWF) typically produce smaller file sizes than raster formats (JPEG, GIF, and PNG) for comparable images. Smaller files result in faster downloads and quicker display over Internet connections. However, both Flash and SVG require the newer Web browsers or plug-ins to view the images. SVG is not natively supported at all on Macintosh by Internet Explorer 4 or 5, but can have some functionality with the appropriate SVG plug-in.

Illustrator supports Flash format through the Export command and SVG through the Save As command, and both file formats can be created with Save for Web.

Both the SWF and SVG formats rely on Illustrator's layers to produce the frames of an animation. (Layers are discussed in depth in Chapter 10, "Illustrator's Layers, Sublayers, and Groups.") The differences between adjacent layers determine the differences between consecutive frames. SVG can also incorporate JavaScripts directly from Illustrator, and Flash files can be made interactive in the Flash program. Flash is a mature technology, whereas SVG as a standard was not yet finalized at the end of 2001. (The World Wide Web Consortium, known as the W3C, announced the public release of the draft standard SVG 1.1 in October 2001.) Illustrator uses the SWF (Shockwave) file format for Flash files.

Illustrator 10's version of SVG is fully compatible with all standard SVG viewers, but also retains complete Illustrator editability. Adobe's GoLive version 6 will also work with the new AISVG file format as a SmartObject, allowing it to be placed in a GoLive document as an Illustrator file.

Illustrator 10 is also capable of opening SVG files.

Neither SVG nor Flash is limited to animation. Both have far more capability. Animation, however, is one of the primary purposes of these formats for Illustrator users. Additional SVG potential will be discussed in the section "Creating SVG Output." However, Illustrator cannot fully take advantage of the Shockwave format (SWF), which requires Macromedia's Flash program itself.

Animation is becoming more and more common on the Web as the technology matures. Not only are the file formats becoming compact enough for speedy downloading, but the creation tools are also becoming more and more accessible. Illustrator is an excellent example. With its support for Flash and SVG, Illustrator puts animation creation in anyone's hands.

You may hear several terms in conjunction with animation:

* *Animation* itself can be described as a series of images that portray movement or, perhaps more accurately, a series of images that give the illusion of a single image with movement.

- *Raster* images are files in which the image is recorded as a series of colored pixels. The term *bitmap graphics* is often used as well. Each *pixel* (the rectangles that make up the image on the monitor) is a specific color, and the image appears because of the differences in the colors. Because pixels are always the same size relative to each other on a monitor, changing the size of a raster image requires either increasing (to enlarge an image) or decreasing (to shrink an image) the number of pixels used in the image. Adding or subtracting pixels requires *interpolation*, a process of estimating the color of a new pixel based on the colors of the surrounding pixels, or choosing which pixels to eliminate.

- *Vector* art is a series of geometric objects whose shapes and relative positions are described mathematically. Vector images can be scaled to any size without loss of quality because the file information is recorded according to how the parts of the image relate to each other. If one circle is half the size of a second circle, the actual size of either circle doesn't matter. The image appears based on the relationship between the two circles. Remember that when it is viewed onscreen, vector art is portrayed with pixels.

- *Frame* refers to a single image within an animation. A series of frames produces the illusion of motion.

- *Animated GIF* is a file in GIF format that simulates motion through the use of frames. Illustrator cannot directly produce an animated GIF, but it can save a file with layers in Photoshop format. Adobe ImageReady uses the individual layers of a Photoshop file to create the frames of an animation. GIF is a raster image file format.

- *Flash* is the name of both a program from Macromedia and the file format produced by and for it. Flash will be described in the section "Preparing Vector-Based Animation for Flash," later in this chapter. The filename extension for the Flash file format is .fla; it works in conjunction with the Shockwave format, which has the extension .swf.

- *SVG* is a vector format that can be used to create animation. It will be described later in this chapter.

- *Shockwave* is Macromedia's file format (with the extension .swf) that is used to produce Flash-compatible images. Shockwave Player is a plug-in required to view Director content.

- *Director* is Macromedia's multimedia authoring tool. Using art, text, sound, and interactivity, Director produces everything from games to interactive learning tools and professional-level presentations. Director produces Optimized Shockwave files.

- *LiveMotion* is a program from Adobe that is more or less comparable to Flash. It is used to create Web animations and graphics. It can produce both animated GIF and SWF files. LiveMotion can maintain layers when opening images from both Illustrator and Photoshop. Its output is fully compatible with Adobe GoLive.

- *XML (Extensible Markup Language)* is the computer language of the Web that enables SVG to produce interactivity and vector graphics.

- *Video* can refer to photographic-style images recorded in series by analog or digital means to produce a movie or film. When discussing animation, video may incorporate computer-generated images, but should consist primarily of recorded images. Video that is created by *analog* means (recorded to tape) is later *digitized* (translated to computer-readable information) to produce computer-readable images. Until video (or any other recorded matter) has been digitized, it cannot be viewed or transferred by computer.

- *Streaming video* refers to video delivered over an Internet connection that is viewed as it downloads. Alternatively, nonstreaming video must be downloaded to the viewer's hard drive as a complete file before it can be seen. (Streaming video is a delivery technology rather than an actual form of animation or file format.) The term *streaming video* can also encompass streaming animation, as long as the concept of viewing-while-downloading is maintained.

- *Full-motion video* can be considered a series of images of an action that were captured in progress. Consider watching television or a movie. See the description of *video* earlier in this list.

- *Frame-based animation*, on the other hand, is more akin to a cartoon. The frames, rather than being a series of photographic representations of an event, are a series of drawings, if you will. Rather than capture images on film, you create each image individually.

Illustrator, as a vector art program, can produce animations, but not video as defined here. It can, however, incorporate raster images along with vector art. Limitations on incorporating raster images (or rasterizing vector art) will be described in the corresponding sections later in this chapter. In general, complex gradients and blends are transformed into raster art when necessary to preserve appearance. This may result in some degradation of the overall image if it is scaled.

Animations can be grouped into two categories. *Cumulative animations* build from frame to frame, with objects from the first frame appearing in the second. They are also called *typewriter* animations because each character or object appears one-after-another, much like a typewriter puts letters on a page (or, perhaps, the way a keyboard enters letters on a monitor). *Noncumulative* animations do not build. When the second frame appears, the objects in the first frame disappear. A graphic representation of a cumulative animation is shown in Figure 23.1. A contrasting example, noncumulative, appears in Figure 23.2

Illustrator 10 has a pair of commands that transfer objects from a single layer to multiple layers. The difference between Release to Layers (Build) and Release to Layers (Sequence) is the same as the difference between cumulative and noncumulative builds. The first command (Build) puts one object on the first new layer and then adds another object for each additional layer. The second (Sequence) puts only one object on each new layer.

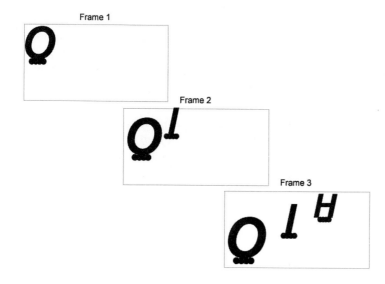

Figure 23.1
The simulated frames show the progression from one frame to the next in the animation. Observe how the first character is both moved and scaled in Frame 2 and how both the first and second characters are moved and scaled for Frame 3.

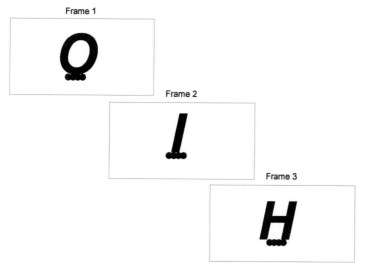

Figure 23.2
These three frames would show a flashing O-I-H on the screen, with each letter appearing individually and then making an exit as the next frame is loaded.

WHAT IS FLASH?

The term *Flash* properly refers to a program rather than a file format. The true Flash file format (using the filename extension .fla) differs from the Shockwave format (using the extension .swf) produced by Illustrator. Macromedia, the company that owns Flash, has chosen to retain the full file functionality as proprietary. Only part of the code has been released for public development and standardization.

Macromedia has, however, loosened its hold on the format and is allowing more and more external development and production. Part of that expansion is the inclusion of Illustrator and Adobe LiveMotion as Flash-capable programs. SWF is not certified by the International

Standards Organization (ISO), nor accepted by the World Wide Web Consortium (W3C) as a Web standard. Nonetheless, it is likely that well over 95% of the browsers in use at the beginning of the year 2002 were Flash-capable with or without a plug-in. The majority of the remaining minority were thought to be Flash-capable through a plug-in. In other words, using Flash on your Web site no longer restricts the site to the cutting-edge viewer. The vast majority of Web surfers can now view Flash animations without experiencing difficulty.

Flash itself incorporates far more than just animation. Using the parent program, you can incorporate animation, sound, interactivity, and form input into a Web site. Illustrator's support for Flash ends at animation. However, Illustrator can produce SWF files optimized for further creative work within the Flash program. (See "Exporting to SWF," later in this chapter.) Likewise, Illustrator can produce SWF files that are ready to be incorporated directly into your Web pages.

WHAT IS SVG?

SVG (Scalable Vector Graphics) is an open-standard language for describing two-dimensional vector and vector/raster images in XML, rather than a file format as such. In addition to animation, SVG promises support for gradients, embedded fonts, transparency, and filters and effects. Interactivity in SVG files can be developed through the use of JavaScript. An SVG file is actually a text file, and SVG animated and interactive files can theoretically be written in a text editor.

SVG continues to be developed under the auspices of the W3C, the body charged with promoting the evolution of and maintaining the universality of the Web. Using the XML (Extensible Markup Language) of the Web, it allows vector (and mixed vector/raster) graphics, improved text support, and interactivity. Illustrator produces SVG files with graphics and the XML required to display them on the Web. Web browsers normally must use a plug-in to display SVG graphics.

As an *open standard*, SVG does not belong to any one company. Any company or individual can implement SVG without payment of any licensing fees. Among the companies participating in the SVG Working Group are Adobe, Apple, Microsoft, Netscape, Macromedia, Corel, Quark, and Xerox. SVG, through the development efforts of the Working Group, evolved from earlier proposals that included Vector Markup Language (VML) and Page Graphics Markup Language (PGML).

Among the other advantages of SVG over GIF for animation are 24-bit color, zoom without pixelization, support for gradients and masking, and embedded ICC profiles. (The term *pixelization* refers to the problem encountered when a raster image is viewed at too high a magnification. Rather than a smooth image, individual pixels are visible, resulting in a blocky, unattractive image. The term *jaggies* is also used, primarily to refer to visible pixels creating blocky curves.) The International Color Consortium (ICC) is the body responsible for maintaining the standards that keep colors uniform. ICC profiles are specific values saved with a file to tell the receiving machine, whether monitor or printer, what colors were actually used in the creation of the image.

Web browsers must be SVG capable, or they require the SVG Viewer plug-in to display SVG graphics. The plug-in is free and available from a variety of sources, including Adobe's Web site. Web sites implementing SVG may have a link to the download area for the convenience of non–SVG-capable visitors. The plug-in is installed by default with Illustrator 10.

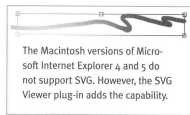

The Macintosh versions of Micro-soft Internet Explorer 4 and 5 do not support SVG. However, the SVG Viewer plug-in adds the capability.

In addition to its other benefits, SVG Web graphics sent to a printer print at full resolution rather than the 72dpi that is standard for JPEG, GIF, and PNG Web graphics.

PREPARING VECTOR-BASED ANIMATION FOR FLASH

Creating a Flash animation (or *movie*, as it is called in Flash) is as simple as creating a layered document. Each layer represents a frame of the movie. The lowest layer in the Layers palette represents the first frame. When you export to SWF, layers and sublayers are treated equally, each creating an individual frame.

A few limitations and restrictions are placed on what you can export to Flash:

* Flash supports only rounded caps and joins for stroked paths. Mitered and beveled joins and projecting and butt caps assigned in the Strokes palette are converted upon export.

* Simple opacity of an object is exported, but any transparency attributes of blending modes, knockout groups, isolated blending, and opacity masks are flattened. The original art is written to the SWF file along with the flattened art, which should retain the look of the transparency.

* Flash doesn't support gradient meshes. An object containing a gradient mesh is rasterized to retain its appearance.

* Any gradient with more than eight stops is rasterized and retains its appearance. This limit is imposed by Flash. Gradients with fewer than eight segments are exported as vector gradients.

* Patterns used as strokes are rasterized.

* Pattern-filled text is converted to shapes (paths) with a rasterized fill. The text can no longer be edited.

* Text used as a clipping mask also is converted to paths and can no longer be edited. The art behind the text mask appears as rasterized fill within the paths.

* Flash does not support leading, kerning, or tracking, so these text attributes are lost upon export. Flash converts the text into several text objects and positions them to retain their appearance.

* Flash does not support dashed lines. Illustrator simulates dashed lines upon export by creating a series of objects.

Virtually all the tools in Illustrator are available for creation of the individual layers that will become frames in the movie or animation. The preceding restrictions have little effect on the final appearance of the frames, with the exception of round caps and joins.

Illustrator offers a number of tools that can speed the process of creating animation. For instance, rather than draw a progression of 12 objects to represent a single object approaching from a distance, you can draw the first and last and use the Blend command to create the intermediate steps (see Figure 23.3 and Figure 23.4).

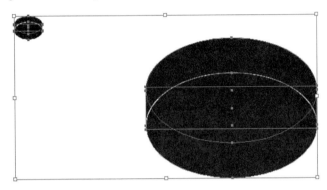

Figure 23.3
Two hockey pucks ready for blending.

The small, distant hockey puck in Figure 23.3 was drawn first and then copied and scaled to 600% to create the near puck. The two are selected and ready for the menu command Object, Blend, Make, with the Blend Options set to create 10 intermediate copies at Specified Steps. With the two originals, the puck will approach in 12 steps, and at the default 12 frames per second, the animation will last one second and then repeat. (Blending is discussed in Chapter 9, "Working with Blends.")

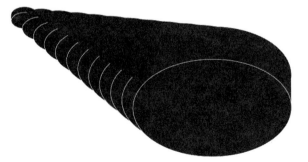

Figure 23.4
The Blend command has created an object that encompasses the 12 hockey pucks.

The objects are then expanded (by using the menu command Object, Blend, Expand), and the Release to Layers (Sequence) command is employed from the Layers palette pop-up menu (see Figure 23.5 and Figure 23.6).

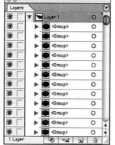

Figure 23.5
The Expand command has created a series of groups, one for each puck. The groups are placed on the same layer as the original object.

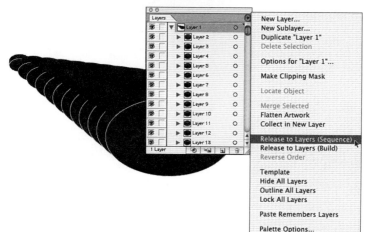

Figure 23.6
The 12 groups become 12 sub-layers of the original layer. So that the animation will be created correctly, the sublayers should be moved to the top level of the Layers palette and Layer 1 deleted, although the Export command creates frames from sublayers, too.

As noted in Figure 23.6, the sublayers of the animation should be moved to the top level and, in this case, the original Layer 1 (which will then be empty) should be deleted. If left as is, Layer 1 will also produce a frame, which will alter the timing of the animation and cause a flicker. Although the Layer 1 thumbnail shows all the pucks, the layer is actually empty except for the sublayers. See Figures 23.7 and 23.8 for a comparison of exporting with and without an empty Layer 1.

Remember the difference between Release to Layers (Sequence) and Release to Layers (Build). The first puts one object on each layer; the second puts one object on the first layer, and then adds one more to each layer, with the last layer having a copy of each object. This is the difference between noncumulative and cumulative builds in animations.

When the animation consists of one or more static objects (objects that appear in every frame) and one or more moving objects, the static elements must be on every layer of the document. Think in terms of frames. For an object to appear in a frame, it must be on the layer that will create the frame. In Figure 23.9, as you can see in the layers palette, the net appears only on the layer with the final puck the topmost layer. If this file were exported to SWF now, for almost a full second the puck would be approaching the viewer and then, suddenly, the net would appear.

Figure 23.7
On the left is an animation exported from the file shown in Figure 23.6. The 12 pucks are sublayers of Layer 1, which itself is empty. On the right, the animation was exported after the 12 sublayers were moved to the top level and Layer 1 deleted. They start their cycles together.

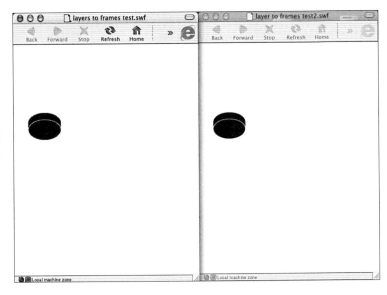

Figure 23.8
After a few cycles, the extra frame in the animation on the left has slowed it considerably. After the thirteenth cycle, the two animations will again be in sync.

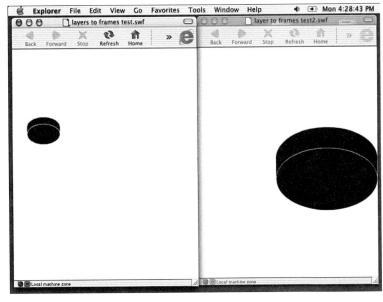

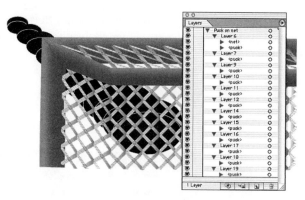

Figure 23.9
Of the 12 layers, only one contains the group <net>. Each of the other layers produces a frame that shows only the group <puck>.

In contrast, Figure 23.10 shows what the Layers palette looks like for a proper SWF file, with the puck changing size and location from frame to frame, but the net remaining stationary and visible in each frame.

The Flash authoring program itself can use symbols to represent objects or elements that repeat from frame to frame. Illustrator 10's symbols (discussed in Chapter 21, "Designing Web Sites and Web Pages") can be used in Flash.

If you want to organize your animation in segments within the Layers palette, you can use the final frame in a sequence as a layer, with all the sequence's preceding frames as sublayers. This technique ensures that no blank frames are inadvertently added to the movie.

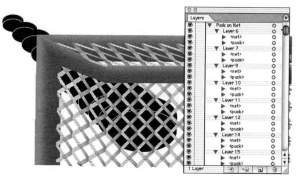

Figure 23.10
Here, the group <net> has been Option+dragged (Alt+dragged for Windows) to each of the other layers. An animation created from this file will have the net in each frame, apparently motionless while the puck approaches.

Outline Mode

When you're copying among layers in the Layers palette, especially when working with complex groups, remember the Outline view mode. You can also use the palette menu and Palette Options to change the view to Small Rows. You'll be amazed at how much faster—and more accurately—you can work when you're not waiting for screen and thumbnail redraws. If you need to stay in Preview view mode, use the Hand tool to scroll the window until none of your art is showing while you work in the Layers palette.

You can see how the animation appears in a browser window in Figure 23.11. Note how the gradients of the hockey net have been rasterized, with dithering used to reproduce the gradient. (Dithering and the rasterization process are discussed in Chapter 22.)

Figure 23.11
The animation, which was created on a page 620×318 pixels, is shown in a browser window on a monitor set to display 800×600 pixels. It has resized itself to fill the width of the window, while maintaining the appropriate height-to-width ratio.

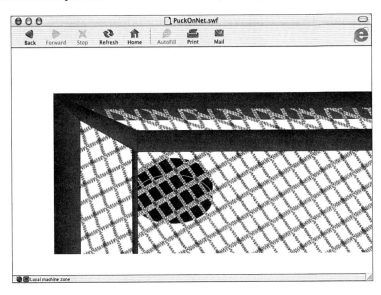

Determining the Correct Size and Adjusting Timing

Although SWF automatically resizes an animation to fit a browser window, it does not reproportion the image. Rather, to maintain the image's integrity, it maintains the same height-to-width ratio. Figure 23.12 shows two browser windows displaying the same SWF animation. Note that the larger window, behind, is filled from side-to-side and, as you can estimate from the smaller image, it also fills the window from top-to-bottom. The smaller window, on the other hand, is filled to the maximum height but cannot fill the width of the window without severe distortion.

Despite the obvious size difference, the browser's Flash plug-in maintains the rate of play as well as the proportions of the image. With raster images, smaller sizes mean smaller files, which appear (display) in a browser window more quickly. The loading time for these two windows was identical because it is actually the same file. The speed of screen redraw, however, can be a factor. It is based on the viewer's video card and VRAM.

The default background color for SWF files is white. If you must blend the animation with an existing Web background, you should add it in Illustrator. A solid color works best, especially Web-safe colors.

A textured or patterned Web page background can be duplicated in Illustrator, but scaling becomes a factor. Remember that the Flash animation (and therefore any background included) resizes to fit the browser's window and so increases the size of the pattern to fit a larger window. The HTML that tiles the page's background image, however, retains the size of the tile and simply increases the number of tiles for a larger window.

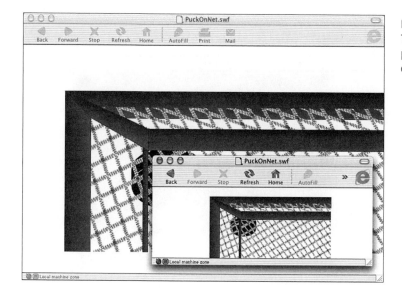

Figure 23.12
The two browser windows display the same Flash graphic at different sizes.

Determining the correct starting size and, perhaps more importantly with scalable graphic formats, the proportions of the frames is not as simple as choosing monitor resolution. Some of your Web site's visitors may have their screens set to 640×480 pixels. Others may be surfing at 800×600. Some 17-inch monitors may be set for 1024×768 or 1280×862 pixels, and 21-inch monitors can support much higher resolutions. All are common, although the very largest are not too frequent among the general Web-surfing public, and the smallest are fading away. Most modern 14-inch (laptop) and 15-inch monitors (iMac and other all-in-ones) are capable of 800×600 pixel resolution. However, if you want to include all potential viewers in your animation visitation, do not overlook the 640×480 monitors. With scalable vector graphics, this is not too much of a problem.

The larger consideration is Web browser configuration. Although a monitor may be set for 800×600 pixels, not all the screen "real estate" is on the market. You need to take the browser's title bar, frame, toolbar, and scrollbar into consideration. They can eat up a lot of the available monitor. Figure 23.13 shows an animation frame sized at 800×600 pixels on a monitor set for 800×600 resolution. Note the white area outside the image on either side. Because SWF maintains proportions, the width is compromised to compensate for the height. Internet Explorer's default interface requires substantial space at the top of the screen, like most browser configurations. The compensation for this lost height results in more than 20% of the horizontal space being wasted on plain white filler.

If you properly compensate for the browser's own use of space, you can size an animation to perfectly fit a given screen resolution. Using the same settings on the same monitor, the animation frame in Figure 23.14 fits perfectly in the default Internet Explorer 5 window.

Figure 23.13
When the height is shrunk to fit the available space, the animation frame's width is reduced proportionally. This results in wasted space on either side of the animation. For reference, the text in this and the related figures is Arial at 72 points.

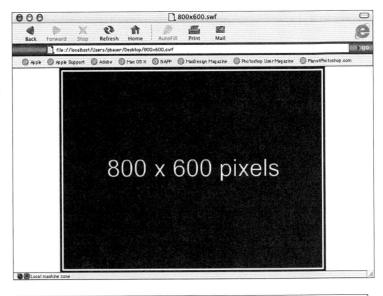

Figure 23.14
There will always be variations in window size. Factors such as which browser is being used, maximization, visible toolbars, and horizontal and vertical sizing can play a role in whether an image is a perfect fit for the monitor upon which it is viewed.

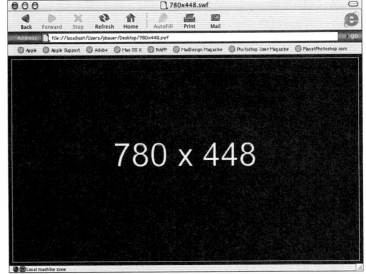

Animations that are properly proportioned look acceptable on virtually any monitor, regardless of screen resolution. Figure 23.15 shows an animation frame designed for a much larger monitor, whereas Figure 23.16 shows a frame designed for a smaller monitor. In both cases, some whitespace is showing in one dimension. In neither case is the whitespace as severe as in Figure 23.13.

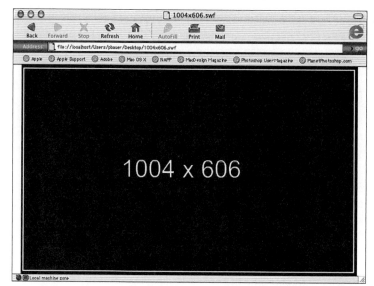

Figure 23.15
This frame is sized for a typical 17- or 21-inch monitor set to 1024×768 pixels. It was recorded on a monitor set for 800×600 resolution. It has room for a vertical scrollbar on the right and an equal amount of wasted space on the left.

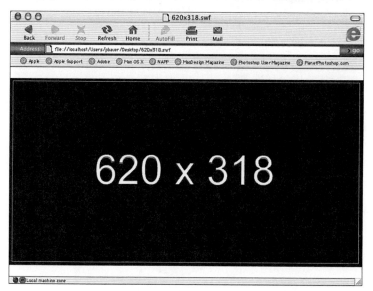

Figure 23.16
Designed for a smaller monitor, this frame is displayed on a screen set for 800×600 pixels. It has considerable wasted space at the top and bottom, but because of the location of the toolbars, such whitespace in the vertical dimension is less noticeable than in the horizontal.

It is important to remember that different browsers, or the same browser on different platforms, require different amounts of vertical space. In addition, an imperfectly sized animation frame may require a vertical scrollbar, which can further distort proportioning.

There is substantial variation in browser interface requirements. The difference between, for example, Internet Explorer 4 and Internet Explorer 5 is a few pixels vertically. The difference between Netscape Navigator 3 and Netscape Navigator 4 is 2 pixels. However, the difference between Explorer and Navigator is about 16 pixels for comparable versions. (Explorer allows the larger animation frame.) And the individual preferences of the viewer play a considerable role in browser configuration. Which toolbars and menu bars are visible, whether a window is maximized, the physical dimensions of the screen, and the screen resolution all play a part in determining what space is available for your images.

Generally speaking, you need to determine what size and resolution monitors your target audience is likely to be using. Subtract 20 pixels horizontally (or four pixels with no vertical scroll-bar) and subtract 175 pixels vertically. Although your animation is certainly not going to fit every screen exactly, these dimensions will provide a suitable height-to-width ratio for the majority of your viewers.

One of the great advantages to Scalable Vector Graphics for animation is the fact that they can automatically resize to fit the browser window. That can also be a production problem. Figure 23.17 shows the Ohio Inline Hockey opening animation at its intended size near the beginning of the animation (previewed in Internet Explorer). Figure 23.18 shows what happens when production specifications fall prey to creativity.

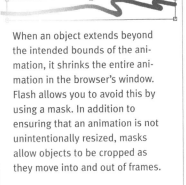

When an object extends beyond the intended bounds of the animation, it shrinks the entire animation in the browser's window. Flash allows you to avoid this by using a mask. In addition to ensuring that an animation is not unintentionally resized, masks allow objects to be cropped as they move into and out of frames.

Figure 23.17
This is the intended size of the animation when viewed in a browser window of a monitor set to 800×600 pixels.

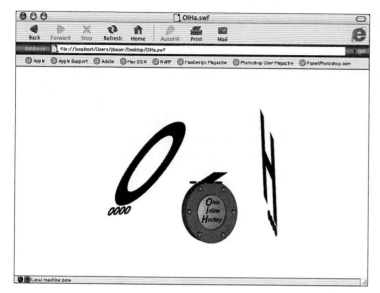

Figure 23.18
The animation in the browser window is considerably smaller than designed. You can easily determine the source of the problem and correct it through the Layers palette.

The problem in this case is that an element of a frame sticks beyond the target-size document layout. Although it makes the arrival of the *H* more dramatic, Flash's automatic resizing changes the entire scale of the animation to ensure that the one part isn't cut off. In this case, that reduces the overall size of the animation below what was intended. The solution is to find the offending frame and correct it.

In the Illustrator file (not the SWF file), the Layers palette makes this task simple. With all layers visible, the element that is causing the resizing is apparent. As you can see in Figure 23.19, clicking the object to select its group forces the Layers palette to scroll to that layer.

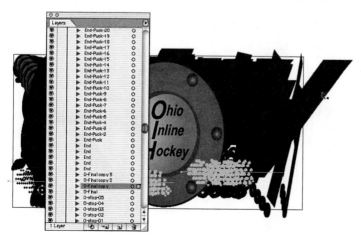

Figure 23.19
The active layer is highlighted, and a box to the far right of its row indicates that an object or group on that layer is selected on the artboard.

Option+clicking [Alt+clicking] the eye icon in the visibility column of the group hides all other layers in the document. (If the intended layer or group disappears with the others, click the visibility icon of any layer to which the sublayer or group belongs.) Figure 23.20 shows the groups that belong to that layer. The Group Selection tool can be used to isolate the offending piece of artwork. Clicking on the extended H with the Group Select tool pinpoints its location in the Layers palette.

Note also that clicking the Layer Targeting icon (the circle to the right on the H's row) in the Layers palette selects a specific object independently of its group on the artboard. In Figure 23.21, the bounding box of the oversized element is adjusted to bring it back in line with the target dimensions of the animation. By adjusting the bounding box, the object is resized. (Working with layers is discussed in Chapter 10.)

Figure 23.20
Because an element of a group has been selected, the selected art indicators for the group and the layer have been changed to smaller boxes. You can think of the concentric circles as a "bounding circle" around the Layer Targeting icon, much as a bounding box surrounds an object or group selected on the artboard.

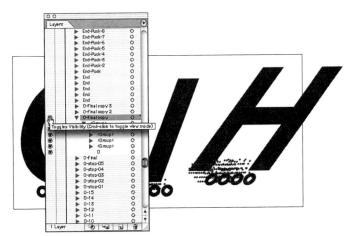

Figure 23.21
Selecting the object through the Layers palette is the same as clicking an object in a group with the Group Selection tool rather than the Selection tool. Using the Selection tool allows resizing and repositioning.

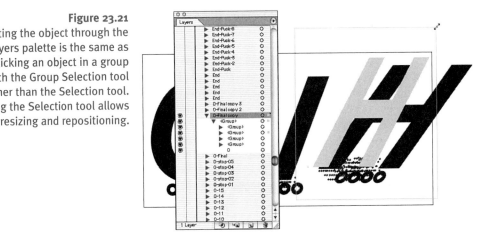

➪ *If you're having trouble activating an individual object in the Layers palette, see "Layers Palette Selections" in the "Troubleshooting" section at the end of this chapter.*

Any additional frames that contain oversized elements are also corrected using this technique. To complete the process, all layers are made visible by again Option+clicking [Alt+clicking] the visibility icon. The Illustrator document is saved, and finally the animation is again exported to SWF, replacing the earlier version. A comparison of Figure 23.22 and Figure 23.23 shows that the ending of the animation was also in need of correction (oversized letters *O* and *H*). The overall size and impact of the animation are improved by reducing the offending elements and so allowing the rest of the animation to play at the size for which it was designed.

Figure 23.22
A number of frames had protruding objects in the original design.

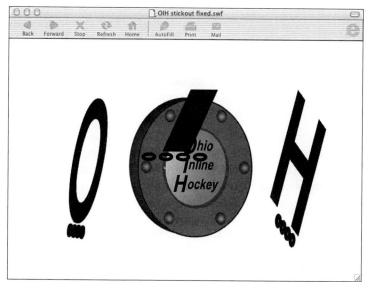

Figure 23.23
All the elements of all the frames are now within the original design boundaries.

EXPORTING TO SWF

After you prepare your animation, you can export it to SWF directly from Illustrator. Choose File, Export and then select the Macromedia Flash (SWF) format from the pop-up menu. Pick a name and location for the file, and then click the Export button. The resulting dialog box is pictured in Figure 23.24.

Figure 23.24

The Flash (SWF) Format Options dialog box contains two parts: Export Options, which determines file format, and Image Options, which determines compression format.

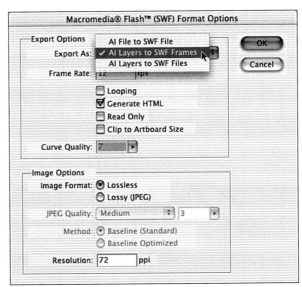

Exporting an Illustrator file to a Flash (SWF) file allows further editing in the Flash program. Choosing AI Layers to SWF Frames produces a Web-ready animation, with each layer of the Illustrator document converted to a single frame of animation. AI Layers to SWF Files produces a series of frames as individual files, which can then be manipulated and combined in Flash. Other items in the dialog box include the following:

- Frame Rate is normally 12 frames per second (fps), although you can change this rate within a large range. This field is active only when AI Layers to SWF Frames has been chosen.

- Auto-Create Symbols is used by Flash to represent elements of an animation, thereby reducing file size. The symbols are automatically added to the Flash symbol library and are required in Flash for each object in the animation. This option also produces additional frames, which you must remove prior to finalizing an animation in Flash.

- Read Only prohibits viewers from modifying the file and also prevents editing in Flash.

- Clip to Artboard Size eliminates any part of the artwork that extends beyond the document edges. Choosing this option is an additional method of controlling inadvertent resizing of an animation. It is effective, of course, only when the artboard is the desired size of the animation.

- Curve Quality is a slider that can reduce file size by compromising the integrity of the image's paths.

- Image Format determines whether the image will be saved with all information, or whether data will be discarded to reduce file size. Saving in JPEG is recommended only when rasterized artwork is present.

- When Lossy (JPEG) is selected, the JPEG Quality pop-up menu is available. It functions like the JPEG quality control in the Save for Web feature, enabling you to balance file size and data inclusion.

  The JPEG Method options are available when JPEG is selected as the file compression scheme. Optimized JPEG is not compatible with all browsers but does produce a smaller file.

- Resolution does not affect screen display or scaling. This is the printer resolution at which the file's graphics are saved. Higher resolution results in larger file sizes and better print quality. If the images are not intended for print, 72ppi is the most acceptable setting. Values can range from 72 to 2400ppi, a range determined by Illustrator rather than Flash.

The biggest factor in determining settings is whether the animation will be further developed in the Flash program. If it will be imported into Flash, the options should include AI File to SWF File, Auto-Create Symbols, High Curve Quality, Lossless compression, and Resolution based on possible print application. If you will not import the image into Flash, choose AI Layers to SWF Frames and uncheck Auto-Create Symbols. The other settings will, of course, depend on your wishes for the individual file.

Before you choose File, Export, ensure that all the layers in your animation are visible. SWF export creates frames only from visible layers and sublayers of your document.

After you export an image to SWF, you can preview it in a Flash-enabled browser. Using the browser's command File, Open (or the equivalent), navigate to the exported file on your hard drive to preview. If, in the export options, you have selected AI Layer to SWF Frames, you see the complete animation in an endless loop. If you choose AI Layers to SWF Files, you see all frames visible at once. Selecting AI Layers to SWF Files creates a series of files, one for each layer, and you can preview each independently in the browser.

When you prepare a file for Flash, you must bring it into the program by using the Import command. Using Flash's Open command prevents you from doing further work on the file.

The complexity of an object can make the difference between a successful export and an error message, as well as the difference between a successful animation and a painfully slow download that plays at the wrong speed. If you're having a problem with an export, see "Overly Complex Flash Exports" in the "Troubleshooting" section at the end of this chapter.

Your ability to place an SWF image into a Web page depends on your Web creation tool. The Flash plug-in must be installed prior to embedding a Flash file. In Adobe GoLive, for example, you embed a Flash file in a page by dragging a plug-in icon from the Basic tab of the Objects palette and then using the Inspector to designate the SWF file. See the specific instructions for your particular Web development tool.

CREATING SVG OUTPUT

Because SVG is a young technology, support for it is still developing. The first proposal for the standard was announced in February 1999, and SVG didn't reach candidate release status with the W3C until October of the following year. One year later, in October 2001, the W3C released the first public draft version of the SVG 1.1 standard. Although SVG Viewers and plug-ins are available, not all the format's capabilities have been implemented.

Creating for SVG starts with defining shapes and text. Theoretically, you could do so strictly in a text editing program because SVG at its core is XML. Using an illustration program has tremendous advantages, not the least of which is visualization. Dragging a tool to create a square in the upper-left corner of a document is also typically faster than writing the code that defines the starting point and parameters of the object.

XML, like HTML, uses opening and closing tags, and allows nested commands. XML goes beyond HTML in the number, variety, and capability of the tags available. XML's greatest advantage over HTML is, arguably, the capability to separate content from presentation. The information within the page therefore can be used as data as well as presentation. It is important to note that XML works in conjunction with HTML rather than instead of the older language. Figure 23.25 shows what an SVG file looks like when opened in a text editor. Experienced HTML coders will see numerous similarities between XML and HTML, as well as a couple of key differences.

Figure 23.25
This is an SVG version of the image shown in Figure 23.1.

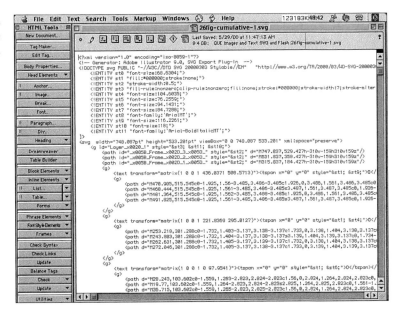

Notice in lines 8 through 11 that the font size is recorded to four decimal places to ensure precise reproduction of the image. (In the original image, the fonts were scaled as part of a group, resulting in the irregular sizes.)

SVG takes advantage of the Document Object Model (DOM), which is a platform- and OS-neutral way to access and update documents. In addition to content, DOM allows updating the style and structure as well. Additionally, XML allows seamless integration with JavaScript, Common Gateway Interface (CGI), and Cascading Style Sheets (CSS). SVG, although developed for the Web, also has print applications. Because it is vector-based, images can be transferred at high enough resolution to allow for quality printing, rather than at the 72dpi that is the limit under HTML.

Among the more sophisticated attributes of an SVG file is the capacity for zooming within a browser window. When using the Adobe SVG Viewer and comparable plug-ins, Control+clicking [right-clicking] opens the contextual menu shown in Figure 23.26.

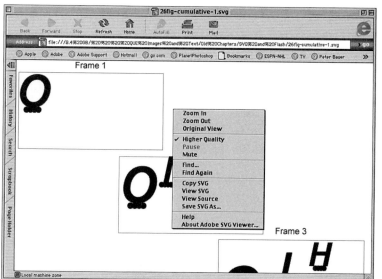

Figure 23.26
Not all features are available at all times. Note that some of the contextual menu features are designed for animation and sound.

Menu items include the following:

- Zoom In and Zoom Out with full quality are possible with vector graphics. Zooming in on an embedded raster image, however, shows pixelization.

- Original View is not the same as Fit to Window. If the image was designed to open in a zoomed mode (in or out), that view is restored.

- Higher Quality slows down the loading of the graphic, usually not by a significant amount.

- Pause is available when an animation is playing. When the animation is paused, the menu item changes to Play.

- Mute silences any soundtrack attached to the SVG file.

- Find and Find Again are used with text in the image. Searchable text is another difference between SVG and HTML. The Find command searches throughout the file, not just that portion that is visible. The image pans to the found text but retains the current zoom level. Hidden, transparent, and moving text are all searchable.

- Copy SVG puts the image on the Clipboard in both Unicode and raster formats. It copies the current view, including the zoom factor.

- View SVG opens a new window containing just the image. It retains all its SVG characteristics in the new window.

- View Source allows access to the XML code itself. The browser's View Source or Source command (under View) is not available for SVG images. The code can be viewed only through the contextual menu.

- Save SVG As allows you to download the file to your hard drive.

- Help and About Adobe SVG Viewer link to Adobe's Web site.

In addition to using the contextual menu, you can zoom with a Zoom tool in Adobe's SVG Viewer. Hold down Cmd [Ctrl] and the cursor becomes the familiar magnifying glass icon. You'll notice one difference from Illustrator's Zoom tool, however. To zoom out, you must press Shift rather than Option [Alt]. You can also drag-zoom using this tool.

SVG also allows for font embedding, which removes the restriction of using only standard system fonts or creating a GIF or JPEG image to retain the text attributes. Embedded fonts can be subsetted in a variety of ways (see "Saving as SVG," later in this chapter). Figure 23.27 shows an SVG file and its code.

Figure 23.27
The inset shows the source code for the page. Note that the first font, Arial, is embedded as the font family Arial MT.

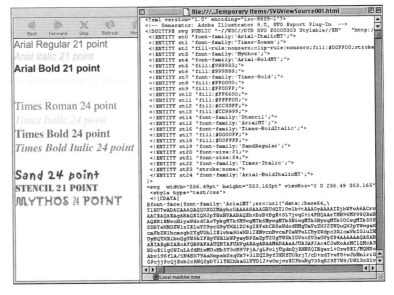

Objects are recorded as paths, with fills and strokes. The path definition begins with a starting point and uses coordinates to describe the shape. The properties of fills and strokes are recorded in XML as well. Opacity, for example, can be a value between 0 and 1 in a command such as

```
<path style="fill-opacity:0.75">
```

Unlike Flash (SWF), strokes can have the standard array of endcaps and joins, and can be dashed. SVG offers full support for gradients; the recording of color values can be hexadecimal values, the color name, or an ICC profile value with corresponding SRGB value. See Figure 23.28 for basic shapes with colored strokes and fills.

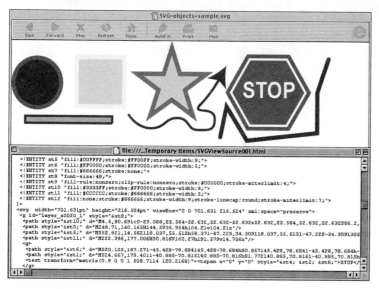

Figure 23.28
Note especially the font size in the description of ENTITY st8, and the availability of linecaps and variable miter limits for ENTITY st12.

Gradients are fully supported in SVG format, with the exception of gradient meshes, which are rasterized. Both a linear and a radial gradient are shown in Figure 23.29.

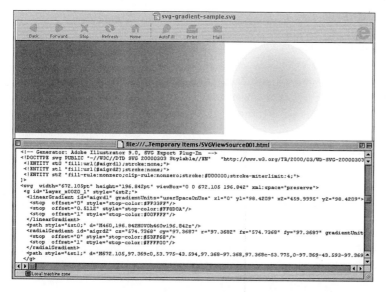

Figure 23.29
Note that the linear gradient has three stops, whereas the radial gradient has but two.

SVG Filters

Found under the Effect menu rather than the Filter menu, the SVG filters are for use only with SVG files. They are actually JavaScripts applied to the image. The advantage to SVG Filters with SVG files is in application. The "filters" are actually JavaScripts that don't actually apply any effect until the image is being downloaded to the viewer's browser. When the SVG image is scaled to the appropriate size, the effect is applied. Using standard filters means that the effect must be scaled with the SVG file, which can result in pixelization.

To apply an SVG filter, select an object on the artboard and use the menu command Effect, SVG Filter, Apply SVG Filter to open the dialog box shown in Figure 23.30.

Figure 23.30
In this example, a Gaussian Blur has already been applied to the object, as you can see in the Appearance palette. Double-clicking the SVG Filter in the palette re-opens the dialog box.

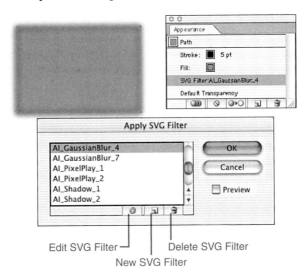

If you know which filter is appropriate, you can bypass the dialog box and select the filter from the Effect, SVG Filter submenu.

At the bottom of the dialog box shown in Figure 23.30 are several buttons similar to those normally found at the bottom of Illustrator's palettes. From the left, the buttons are Edit SVG Filter, New SVG Filter, and Delete SVG Filter.

As you can see in Figure 23.31, SVG filters are actually a series of instructions between tags, much like HTML. Modifying an effect can be as simple as finding the variable and entering a new value. It can also be as complex as writing the effect from scratch.

Dragging an SVG filter to the New SVG Filter button at the bottom of the dialog box automatically assigns a new name (adding _1) and opens the Edit SVG Filter dialog box. You can also click on a filter name in the list and click on the Edit SVG Filter button to edit and replace the original.

Illustrator ships with a variety of SVG filters, and others are available as freeware, shareware, and commercial products.

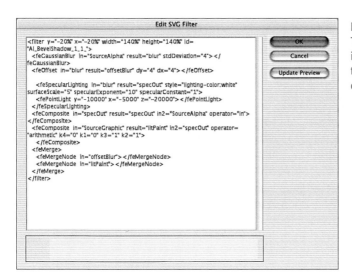

Figure 23.31
The Bevel_Shadow_1 SVG filter is opened as Bevel_Shadow_1_1 to edit and make a copy without overwriting the original.

Raster Images in SVG Files

Raster images (GIF, JPEG, PNG-8, and PNG-24) can be embedded in an SVG image, and 24-bit color images retain their true color values. Clipping paths can also be used in conjunction with raster images. Figure 23.32 has, from left, a JPEG photo, a rasterized logo that contains several gradients, and text as a clipping mask over a rasterized gradient with three stops.

Figure 23.32
The SVG text file for this image, in Courier at 8 point, single spaced, creates a 66-page plain text document. The Illustrator file is 1.1MB, and the SVG file is 432KB (as is the TXT file).

Any object that you can create in Illustrator can be described mathematically in a text file using SVG. It is the interaction between SVG and XML that enables the image to be reproduced in a Web browser's window.

> If you're having trouble with disappearing raster images, check "Embedding Raster Art" in the "Troubleshooting" section at the end of this chapter.

DYNAMIC SVG

SVG promises a tremendous amount of sophistication within the browser. Images can be transformed, animated, linked to mouse or keyboard events, and more. Collectively, these capabilities are referred to as *Dynamic SVG*.

Each object has a transform attribute available in the SVG format. This attribute can control move, scale, rotate, and skew operations. SVG uses a six-number matrix to record the values. The values are applied in reverse order. In order, the six numbers of the matrix are as follows:

- **Scale x-axis**—Using decimal notation, 0.75 would scale to 75% along the x-axis. Scaling automatically occurs from the 0,0 point. To change the center of scale, you must note a location.

- **Skew y-axis**—Uses degrees for skewing. Skews from the 0,0 point along the y-axis.

- **Skew x-axis**—Uses degrees for skewing. Skews from the 0,0 point along the x-axis.

- **Scale y-axis**—Using decimal notation, 0.75 would scale to 75% along the y-axis. If no value is entered, it is assumed to be the same as the Scale x-axis value.

- **Translate (move) x-axis**—The value entered moves that number of units along the x-axis.

- **Translate (move) y-axis**—The value entered moves that number of units along the y-axis.

You can apply animation using SVG's Animation Elements or DOM (Document Object Model). The W3C's SVG Working Group collaborated with the Synchronized Multimedia Working Group (SYMM) to incorporate the Synchronized Multimedia Integration Language (SMIL) Animation specification within SVG. SVG, however, also incorporates additional extensions to the SMIL Animation. Among the additions are the following:

Caution

Using the advanced features of SVG may leave some of your viewers out in the cold. Not all SVG Viewers and browser plug-ins fully support the format for all platforms. Additionally, Microsoft Internet Explorer for Macintosh will not allow a plug-in to access the Java engine. Any viewers using IE for Macintosh will not be able to see any part of your SVG creation that relies on JavaScript. And that includes most of the advanced features. Static images (no motion, no interactivity) will display properly, but the millions of iMac and other Macintosh owners who use IE 4 and IE 5 lose all other SVG features.

SWF, on the other hand, is well supported across platforms, and modern browsers automatically install the plug-in.

One of the keys to implementing SVG's features is the judicious use of layers. When you export to SVG, layers are classified as groups, so you can manipulate and tag them as such.

- Modification of an SVG transform attribute over time

- Full support for SVG's path syntax as attributes for the `animateMotion` element

- A `keyPoints` attribute for `animateMotion` to regulate velocity of motion path animation

- A `rotate` attribute for `animateMotion`

All of SVG's advanced features can be written into a file, but it is early in the development of this young technology, and drag-and-drop simplicity has not yet arrived.

The SVG Interactivity Palette

Interactivity is the capability to respond to a viewer's action. A button click starting an animation or executing a script, zooming, hyperlinking, and changes to the cursor as it moves are all examples of interactivity. Three categories of user (or viewer) events can trigger interactivity: pointer events, keyboard events, and document events. Pointer events include mousing and clicking. They are normally linked to the topmost graphic beneath the mouse cursor at the moment of the event. Keyboard events can include simple keystrokes. Document events can include scrolling, loading, and resizing, among others.

Illustrator implements interactivity through JavaScript. Some knowledge of JavaScript is required to work with the SVG Interactivity palette. Figure 23.33 shows the bare-bones approach to adding interactivity.

Figure 23.33
The "interactivity" of SVG is JavaScript capability. Pre-prepared scripts are attached to the image or an object within the image.

```
document.write("<h1>Verify Date/Time Setting</h1>");
currtime = new Date();
document.write("Your computer shows " + currtime + ")
```

Verify Date/Time Setting

Your computer shows Fri Mar 29 09:25:02 EDT 2002

The SVG Interactivity palette does supply the first part of the code. A list of triggering events has been included in the palette, as shown in Figure 23.34.

When mature, the capabilities of SVG are likely to also have an easier form of implementation within Illustrator. In the meantime, remember that a substantial percentage of Web viewers cannot yet take advantage of SVG's advanced features, but you can code JavaScript to produce magnificent results.

⇨ *Problems previewing Dynamic SVG files? See "SVG and Internet Browsers" in the "Troubleshooting" section at the end of this chapter.*

SAVING AS SVG

To create SVG files from Illustrator, you use the Save As command. The Save As dialog box enables you to choose SVG or SVGZ, a compressed version of the already-small files. SVGZ is not supported by all browser plug-ins or all SVG Viewers; however, an embed tag can direct the browser to an uncompressed version of the file.

SVG Options

Whether you save a file as SVG or SVG Compressed (SVGZ), the same SVG Options dialog box opens. The basic options include the choice of linking or embedding fonts and images. Clicking the Advanced button opens a second dialog box, which offers additional control (see Figure 23.35).

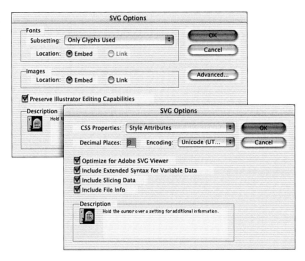

The SVG Options export choices are as follows:

- Font Subsetting is addressed in the following section.

- Images can be embedded or linked. Raster images that contain an alpha channel are embedded as PNG-24, whereas those without an alpha channel are embedded as JPEG. SVG, by the way, automatically rasterizes gradient meshes.

- CSS Property Location offers four methods of saving style attributes (Cascading Style Sheets) with SVG files. Presentation Attributes applies the CSS properties at the top of the hierarchy, allowing the most flexibility for design and implementation. Style Attributes can result in somewhat larger file sizes, but produces a more readable SVG file. Style Attributes (Entity Reference) puts each style sheet into the document at its required location; download speeds are fastest. Style Elements uses CSS, which can format both HTML and SVG documents from a single style sheet; rendering times may be slower.

- Decimal Places determines how accurate the vectors in the artwork will be. The range is from one to seven, with the default of three considered adequate for most purposes. Images that may be printed at high resolution might require a higher decimal value. The higher the number, however, the larger the file.

- Encoding options are ISO 8859-1, UTF-8, or UTF-16. The UTF encoding systems offer better support for languages such as Japanese, Chinese, and Hebrew. SVG has the potential to recognize the language of the browser and deliver the proper version of a file on-the-fly. With UTF encoding, multiple versions of a document can be stored together to fulfill multiple language requirements.

- Optimize for Adobe SVG Viewer doesn't prevent other SVG viewers from displaying the file, but does allow browsers using the SVG Viewer to render the image faster, especially when using filters.

- Include Extended Syntax for Variable Data is designed for use with dynamic data-driven graphics (see Chapter 27) and server scripting languages for programs such as Adobe AlterCast.

- Include Slicing Data should be checked whenever an SVG image is sliced. It maintains the slicing and slice optimization information.

- Include File Info results in a slightly larger file in order to include such information as creation and modification dates and the file author info.

Font Subsetting with SVG

Font Subsetting is designed to both reduce the size of your file (by including only some of the characters) and to ensure that your image is viewed as designed (by the inclusion of those characters required).

Choosing None (Use System Fonts) forces the file to use the system fonts installed on the viewer's computer. If the image was designed with those fonts in mind, no conflict occurs.

Opting for Only Glyphs Used includes the characters (glyphs) required for the image as it is at the time of export. Editing could change the characters needed.

Common English (with or without Glyphs Used) includes those standard letters, numbers, and symbols used in the English-speaking world.

Common Roman (also available with and without Glyphs Used) subsets all the characters common in the world among the languages that use a Roman-based alphabet.

All Glyphs includes the entire font, resulting in a larger file, but no worries about editing or language.

Remember that SVG files are text files, with the exception of embedded raster images. A single embedded raster image can increase the size of the SVG file by more than the size of the original raster image.

SAVE FOR WEB WITH SWF AND SVG

In addition to the Export command for SWF and the Save As command for SVG, Illustrator's Save for Web feature can be used to produce SWF and SVG files. The options are the same as the respective dialog boxes (see Figure 23.36).

Unless an SWF file will be further developed in Flash, remember to select Layers to SWF Frames, even if the image has only one layer. Keep in mind, too, that with large vector artwork, SWF may produce files substantially smaller than even GIF.

Figure 23.36
The SWF options from the Save for Web dialog box are shown to the left; those for SVG are on the right. The Image Size and Layers tabs contain identical options for each.

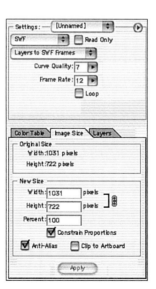

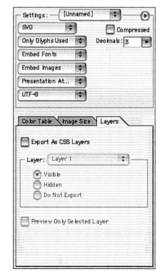

TROUBLESHOOTING

Layers Palette Selections

I can't seem to get the hang of making selections in the Layers palette. Sometimes I get a group instead of an object within that group. Sometimes I see the bounding box around the object I want, but all I can do with the Selection tool is reposition, not resize.

Keep in mind these three factors:

1. A highlighted layer is a selected layer. You can delete, copy, or otherwise affect the layer as a layer when it is highlighted. These actions are primarily Layers palette actions. More than one layer can be selected at a time.

2. A group, object, or layer can be "targeted" for changes by clicking the circle at the right end of a row. This targeting is primarily for use with attributes and appearances, but can be used as a selection tool. More than one row in the Layers palette can be targeted.

3. Only one row in the Layers palette can actually be "active" at a time. This is indicated by the small black triangle in the row's upper-right corner. When you're Shift+clicking to select or target multiple rows, only the last can be active.

If the object you've targeted is not the last thing you've clicked, it's not active and therefore not selected. This can happen, for example, when you click a Layer Targeting icon for a specific object and then Option+click [Alt+click] a Visibility icon for the object's group to hide other layers.

Overly Complex Flash Exports

I've been getting an error message while trying to export my magnificent creation to SWF. What could be wrong?

A file that contains too many complex objects and paths, too many gradients and transparency, or patterned strokes and paths can lead to problems. Check especially any objects that have been copied to appear on several layers. Textures created by drawing many short stroked paths with the Pen tool can be especially troublesome. Although the Pen tool is great for adding depth to a field of grass or a wooden wall, those tiny paths add up to a whole lot of information. Create a pattern and let the texture be rasterized in the export process.

Embedding Raster Art

I had my SVG file all set to go, logged on to my FTP, posted the image on my Web site, and now half of it is missing! All the pictures are gone. What happened?

When you saved as SVG, your options likely said "Raster Image Location: Link to Raster Images." The JPEGs, GIFs, or PNGs used in the SVG image were left behind on your hard drive. When the SVG file looked for them, it no longer had a connection to them. It works just like the hyperlinks and images in your Web pages: If they can't be found, the link is broken and they aren't displayed. Re-save to SVG, and this time opt for Embed Raster Images. You'll get a larger file, but it will have all its parts.

As a side note, the SVG link can bypass the Illustrator file and go directly to the raster image. The Illustrator file can be deleted, but the JPEG, GIF, or PNG has to remain in the original location for the link to work.

SVG and Internet Browsers

I can't seem to get my browser to preview my interactive SVG files, and I'm afraid to post them on my site without previewing.

Good choice! If you're having trouble, it means your site's visitors will, too. First, your browser must have an SVG Viewer plug-in installed. You can download a viewer from Adobe's Web site. Second, you can't use Internet Explorer for Macintosh with Dynamic SVG. Because SVG relies on JavaScript for its more complex features, it is not compatible with Internet Explorer. Explorer does not allow plug-ins (such as the SVG Viewer) to access the Java engine. Microsoft is aware of the issue.

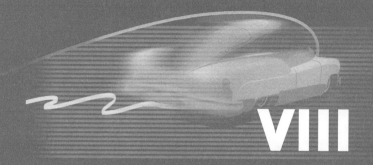

VIII

PRE-PRESS AND FOUR-COLOR PROCESS PRINTING

IN THIS PART

24   Commercial Printing and Trapping Issues   **569**

25   Linking and Embedding Images and Fonts   **603**

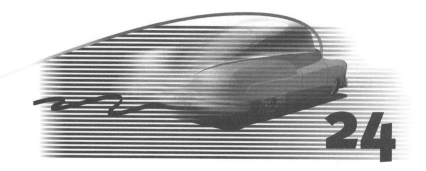

COMMERCIAL PRINTING AND TRAPPING ISSUES

IN THIS CHAPTER

Terms and Concepts **570**

The Basics of Printing **575**

Color Issues **579**

Preparing Artwork for Print **586**

Service Bureaus, Print Brokers, and Printers **595**

Trapping **596**

Troubleshooting **596**

TERMS AND CONCEPTS

Commercial printing is a combination of art and science. Generally, just four inks are used to create the entire range of colors needed to reproduce photographic images. Additional colors, called *spot colors*, can be added, but the bulk of the work is done with just four inks. Knowing how and where to put the ink to correctly re-create an illustration or image requires a substantial level of expertise. General knowledge of principles of printing must be supplemented with specific knowledge of the individual printing presses and the particular inks and paper being used for the job, and sometimes even weather conditions.

Perhaps the most important guideline when preparing artwork for process printing is the simplest: Talk with your printer. In most cases, you are not expected to know (or even understand) the specific tolerances of a huge piece of machinery in another company's building. The people who work directly with that machinery do, theoretically, know its capabilities and foibles and can compensate for them as necessary.

If you are or will be preparing artwork for commercial reproduction, you can benefit from a basic understanding of the process. Clarifying some basic terminology and a closer look at some key aspects of printing will set the groundwork for a discussion of preparing projects for print.

- **Bleed**—In many cases the paper is larger than the print area. To ensure that the ink extends all the way to the area that will be cut from the larger paper, a bleed is used. Without the bleed, a tiny error in trimming the paper can result in an unwanted white line in places where the design should go to the edge. Bleed extends the ink past the crop marks from 0 to 72 points. Illustrator's default is 18 points and can be changed in the Separations Setup dialog box.

- **Blend**—A blend is the artwork that results when two or more objects on the artboard are blended. Illustrator creates a series of intermediary objects to produce the appearance of a smooth transition from one object to another. (Blends were discussed in Chapter 9, "Working with Blends.") Blends are important to printing because of their complexity. Although some blends can be simple, others, especially smooth color blends, can create printing problems. (See also *gradient*.)

Caution

This chapter deals primarily with commercial process and spot color printing, and the techniques and procedures related to such printing. Process printing uses CMYK inks applied by huge mechanical printing presses.

The guidelines and background do not pertain to most inkjet printers. Most inkjets also use CMYK inks, but they use software to convert from RGB colors to the CMYK gamut (with the exception of high-end proofers). Generally, you should not prepare CMYK output for inkjet printers, but rather send only RGB data. See Chapter 11, "Output Options," for a discussion of the difference between inkjet and commercial printing.

For the remainder of this chapter, the terms *printing* and *printer* will be used to refer to the commercial printing process, using process and spot inks, unless otherwise noted.

- **Choke**—In *trapping*, the process of extending the surrounding light color onto an enclosed dark color is called choking. (See also *spread* and *trapping*.)

- **CMYK**—Cyan , magenta (M), yellow (Y), and black (K) are the four *process colors* used in commercial printing. Artwork being prepared for color printing must be in this color mode. RGB illustrations and images cannot be separated for printing. (See "Color Issues," later in this chapter, and Chapter 12, "Understanding and Applying Color.")

- **Color stitching**—Color stitching is the undesirable visibility of the transition from vector to raster artwork in an image. It occurs when a printer handles the two types of artwork differently. You can control color stitching by changing the Quality/Speed slider to a higher setting in the Transparency panel of the Document Setup dialog box. When color stitching appears onscreen rather than from the printer, you can uncheck the Anti-aliased Artwork option in the general preferences (Edit, Preferences, General).

- **Contract proof**—The final approval of a piece of work before printing of the final separations and printing plates is called the contract proof. After the contract proof is approved by the client or other approving authority, the job should roll. The contract proof is the standard against which the final production project will be measured. It is critical that the proofs be prepared properly and using the correct technique. Digital proofs should not be used for a job that will eventually be printed from film-based plates. Likewise, creating a laminate proof for a digital output job opens the door to inaccuracy. Final approval of the contract proof is normally in writing, and the contract proof is used to ensure accurate color during the press check. (See also *press check*.)

- **Duotone**—When only two colors are used to create an image or illustration, it can be considered a duotone. Although Illustrator does not call it such, if only two colors of ink will be used to produce the image, that's what it is. When preparing separations for a duotone, you must ensure that the option Convert to Process is not selected in the Separations Setup dialog box (see Figure 24.1).

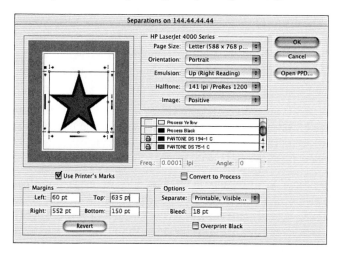

Figure 24.1
The Separations Setup dialog box will be explained fully later in this chapter.

Potential Path Problems

Perhaps the leading cause of errors when you're trying to separate an illustration on an image-setter is complex paths. Extremely large paths can choke a printer or imagesetter, overloading the memory to the point where the machine freezes or aborts the job with an error message. Patterns can also create complex paths.

These four techniques reduce complex path problems:

- **Simplifying**—Choosing Object, Path, Simplify reduces the number of anchor points (and therefore the number of segments) in a complex path.

- **Splitting**—Available through the Printing & Export panel of the Document Setup dialog box, this command breaks extremely complex paths into two or more pieces. Splitting makes future editing of the object difficult, so working with a copy of the document is highly recommended. You can rejoin split paths by eliminating any added segments and using the Pathfinder palette command Unite.

  The split path will preview and print as though nothing had changed. Splitting paths works with unstroked, filled, and closed paths. You should split open paths and unfilled stroked paths manually with the Scissors tool.

- **Changing Resolution**—Specifying a lower print resolution for a specific object can ease printing problems. In the Output field of the Attributes palette, you can change to a lower dpi setting.

- **Rasterizing**—Choosing Object, Rasterize can eliminate printing problems for overly complex objects. Because the object is no longer vector art, editing its path is no longer possible. It is, therefore, a very good idea to make a copy of the original artwork before you rasterize.

One none-too-subtle clue that you may encounter printing problems is the error message shown in Figure 24.16.

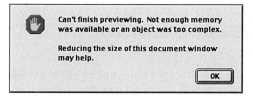

Figure 24.16
When a path is overly complex, this message is a prelude to printing problems.

⇨ *If splitting paths wasn't enough to get a document to separate, see "Simplifying Files for Printing" in the "Troubleshooting" section at the end of this chapter.*

Crop, Trim, and Printer's Marks

Crop marks indicate the edges of the artwork. They show where the paper should be cut after printing. Trim marks function similarly but are used primarily to show the limits of multiple items on a single page. Printer's marks include registration marks, star targets, calibration bars, and separation labels.

Although they serve different purposes, these three types of marks have several things in common:

- They are not part of the artwork.

- They are printed, unlike grids and guidelines.

- They are printed on all the separations (with the exception of the color-specific printer's marks).

- They are important to the proper outcome of your printing project.

You set crop marks by choosing Object, Crop Marks, Make. Either a rectangle must be selected on the artboard or in the Layers palette, or there must be no selection (to use the entire artboard). The rectangle should define the limits of the artwork or the page. Crop marks are shown in Figure 24.17.

Figure 24.17
Crop marks define the desired limits of the artwork, although the art can extend past. This is most common with a bleed.

After you create crop marks, you cannot select, edit, or move them. If you must make changes, choose Object, Crop Marks, Release. Keep in mind that you can have only one set of crop marks per document. Illustrator also offers the option of Japanese crop marks.

You create trim marks by choosing Filter, Create, Trim Marks. There are several differences between crop marks and trim marks:

- Trim marks are treated as artwork. You can select, edit, ungroup, and delete them, and you can even apply effects.

- Unlike crop marks, creating trim marks is a nondestructive process. If you use a rectangle to create the marks, the rectangle will still be on the artboard afterward.

- Trim marks use a selection's bounding box. In Figure 24.18, note that the trim marks on the left, created using the rectangle, fit more closely than the trim marks using the text's bounding box.

- Trim marks can be made from any selection, not just rectangles.

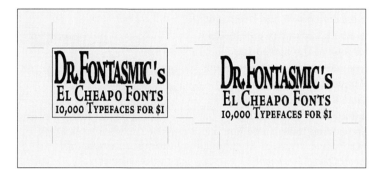

Figure 24.18
The trim marks on the right were created with the text selected. Those on the left were created with only the rectangle selected.

The various printer's marks, which you add or omit by using the Separations Setup dialog box, serve various purposes:

- **Registration marks**—Arguably the most important, these marks are printed outside the crop area and are used by the printer to align the printing plates.

- **Star targets**—A variation of registration marks, star targets are also used to align plates. They are more accurate than standard registration marks but also more difficult to use.

- **Calibration bars**—Samples of the black used for overprinting, the various colors, and a gradient bar are printed. The color swatches appear only on the separation for that color.

- **Labels**—The name of the file, the screen frequency and angle, and the color of the plate are all listed on the individual separations.

Printer's marks not showing up? See "Adding Registration Marks" in the "Troubleshooting" section at the end of this chapter.

Document Info

The Document Info palette supplies a wealth of information about the document and about individual objects. You access it by choosing Window, Document Info. The palette is shown with its menu in Figure 24.19.

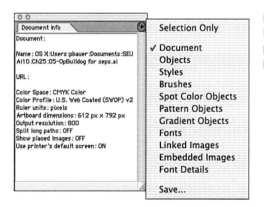

Figure 24.19
Each of the 11 selections opens pertinent information in the palette's window.

While often used as a troubleshooting tool, the Document Info palette can also play an important role in preventing trouble. For example, a quick look at the Linked Images information can serve as a reminder of what files you will need to include with the document. Likewise, the Document Info palette contains a list of all fonts used. (Linking files and embedding fonts are discussed in Chapter 25, "Linking and Embedding Images and Fonts.")

➡️ *Not seeing the data you need? Check "Document Information" in the "Troubleshooting" section at the end of this chapter.*

When you think that an object (or objects) in a document might cause some trouble, you can leave a message for your service bureau or printer. The Attributes palette allows you to annotate any selected object or group. Click the double arrow in the palette's tab to fully expand the palette or use the palette menu command Show Note. The empty rectangular area at the bottom of the palette can hold up to 240 characters of information.

When the file is converted to PostScript, the notation is preceded by the character string *%AI3_Note* and can be found in a text editor.

Resolution Options

The Printing & Export panel of the Document Setup dialog box gives you control over how Illustrator handles transparency when you're printing or exporting a document. When you use the Transparency panel of the Document Setup dialog box, Illustrator provides you with five levels of compromise between quality and printing speed. Illustrator's descriptions of the five levels of Quality/Speed are as follows (from Lower/Faster to Higher/Slower):

- The entire illustration will be rasterized. Use this setting for printing or exporting very complex illustrations with many transparent objects. Ideal for fast output at low resolution; higher resolution will yield higher quality but increase processing time. Size of saved files or print spool files may be large.

- Maintains simpler vector objects, but rasterizes more complex areas involving transparency. Ideal for artwork with only a few transparent objects. Some printers may yield rough transitions between bordering vector and raster objects and make hairlines appear thicker—appropriate for low-memory systems.

- Maintains most objects as vector data, but rasterizes very complex transparent regions. Generally the best setting for printing and exporting most illustrations. With some printers it improves transition issues between bordering vector and raster objects.

- Maintains most of the illustration as vectors, rasterizing only extremely complex areas. Produces high quality output that is generally resolution independent. Higher occurrences of transparent regions will increase processing time. With some printers, improves transition issues between bordering vector and raster objects.

- The entire illustration is printed or exported as vector data, to the greatest extent possible. This produces the highest quality resolution-independent output. Processing of complex illustrations may be very time and memory intensive.

SERVICE BUREAUS, PRINT BROKERS, AND PRINTERS

An illustrator must do several things to prepare artwork for commercial printing. Several other steps, however, may be best left to others. In some cases, one individual serves as designer, illustrator, and prepress specialist. Understanding who is responsible for what steps, and communicating about those steps, is often the key to successful completion of a project.

Service Bureaus

It would be lovely if you had a huge budget and an office equipped with the latest and greatest machinery, ready and waiting for any project that comes along. Unfortunately, the reality is that budgets are usually tight, or at least realistic. Spending tens of thousands of dollars for a piece of equipment that you may use only a few times a year is not efficient. Hiring out that particular piece of work a couple of times a year may be far more practical.

Service bureaus have evolved to fill that niche. The typical service bureau offers drum scanners that can produce the highest quality digital images, imagesetters that can produce the films from which the printing plates are made, calibrated color proofing equipment, and various other hardware and services. Finding (and maintaining a good working relationship with) a good service bureau allows a small operation or independent to offer all the services of a major production house. And, within those major production houses, maintaining good relationships between departments is often critical to mission accomplishment. For contractors and independents, most service bureau costs can be built into a bid, estimate, or contract. In-house project estimators should also build in such expenses.

In the offset printing workflow, service bureaus may be used for initial scans, color correction, color proofs, and separations or film. Most service bureaus can handle Windows as well as Macintosh files and can work with files generated by all major graphics and publishing programs. However, it is always a good idea to ask what file formats, program versions, and platforms are acceptable before you enter into a working relationship with a service bureau.

Print Brokers

Print brokers are middlemen, outside vendors who coordinate a print job for you. Some print brokers are sales representatives with a working knowledge of the business and a stable of clients. Other print brokers may be experts in the field with extensive experience and endless contacts. In either case, they are expected to serve as your representative to and with the printer.

Your communication with print brokers, as with anyone involved with a project, is important. Print brokers need to understand clearly what you (or the client or boss) expect before finding and contracting with a printer. The specific areas of discussion may include color fidelity, image clarity, paper quality, and finishing. If you're using a broker, you'll also want to clearly delineate areas of responsibility. Perhaps you need the broker to price out the job and determine the best printer for the contract. On the other hand, you may need a broker who is able to handle the job from the time it's completed on your computer to the time that it's sent into the distribution channel.

Printers

Some printers have all the capabilities of service bureaus; some printers contract out everything except putting ink on paper. The key to a good printer is twofold: fulfilling your requirements at a good price and communicating with you.

After you've received or conceived the project, determine whether any special inks or papers will be involved. If so, one of your first calls should be to the printer. Find out what requirements (and limitations) could have an impact on your creative or production process. You should also know, if you'll be transferring projects digitally, what file formats and program versions the printer can use.

You may need different printers for different types of jobs, too. One printer may produce superior color fidelity but be too expensive for a two-color insert. Another printer may be able to offer faster turnaround for emergency jobs. Having working relationships with several printers may allow you to save money or, sometimes more importantly, time.

TRAPPING

Trapping can be highly complicated or very simple. If two different colors do not abut in the artwork, trapping isn't necessary. If colors abut in many places, or if several colors abut at one location, trapping may be necessary.

Service bureaus and printers often have dedicated workstations with specialized software to do trapping. Trapping can be extremely time-consuming and, therefore, very expensive. Typically, the workstations and trapping software are run by an experienced professional.

Caution

While an understanding of trapping can be beneficial, it is usually best to leave the actual procedure to specialists. Improper trapping can produce severe output problems. Before attempting to trap an image, speak with your printer or service bureau.

Trapping Software and Plug-ins

Dedicated trapping software falls into two categories: programs that rasterize a PostScript file before identifying edges and those that work with vector objects. Among the trapping programs available are TrapWise from ScenicSoft and Ultimate's Trapeze.

Adobe Systems and Agfa, among others, have been advocating *in-RIP trapping*, especially for PDF documents. This software solution doesn't require a standalone system. This technology is substantially less expensive than proprietary trapping software, which can run up to $5,000 (not counting the workstation's hardware).

Somewhere between dedicated trapping workstations and the capabilities of Adobe Illustrator lie the page layout programs, such as QuarkXPress, Adobe InDesign, and Adobe PageMaker. With integrated capabilities and (for InDesign and QuarkXPress) plug-ins, these programs are capable of automatic trapping, as well as manual. When you're given the option, trapping in a page layout program is usually preferable to doing the work in Illustrator.

General Trapping Techniques

To trap properly in Illustrator, expand the lighter color so that it overlaps with the darker color. Expanding the lighter color minimizes distortion of the image. The darker color's shape remains the same, resulting in less apparent change of the image.

There are two basic types of trapping. A *spread* occurs when the lighter color sits on a darker background, and the lighter color is expanded. A *choke* occurs when the darker color sits on a lighter background, and the lighter color spreads onto the darker. Figure 24.20 shows a simulation of the difference.

Figure 24.20
To the left, the lighter color appears to constrict the darker color, a choke. To the right, the lighter color seems to expand onto the darker, a spread. The dashed lines indicate the actual extent of the letter.

The command Effect, Pathfinder, Trap is one tool for trapping in Illustrator. It can be applied to two or more objects, type and an object, groups, or layers. When you select objects that are not appropriate for trapping, Illustrator displays a warning (see Figure 24.21).

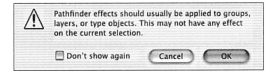

Figure 24.21
Selecting groups in the Layers palette rather than on the artboard will help you avoid this error message.

Choosing Effect, Pathfinder, Trap opens the Pathfinder Options dialog box (see Figure 24.22). In it, you can make a number of decisions about how to trap.

The Soft Mix Settings Mixing Rate, near the top of the dialog box, is not available when you're trapping. You use it with the command Effect, Pathfinder, Soft Mix. The settings that you can use with the Trapping command are listed under Trap Settings.

The Trap Settings options are as follows:

- **Thickness**—This field determines the width of the area affected by the trap. It is always measured in points. This field accepts values in the range from –32,768 to 32,767, although negative numbers do not reverse the trap. The smallest usable value is 0.01 points (anything less is rounded to 0). The default is 0.25 points.

Figure 24.22
The Pathfinder Options dialog box offers several options.

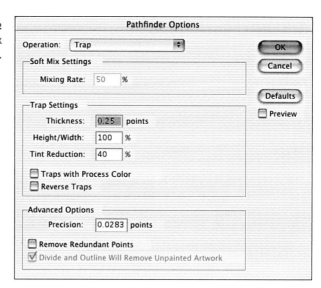

* **Height/Width**—This field allows you to trap vertically or horizontally more or less than the counterpart. If, for example, you expect paper stretching to be a problem during the print run, but the plates will hold their positions perfectly, you might need height rather than width in the trapping. At 100% (the default), the trap extends the same distance in all directions. Values higher than 100% trap vertically (horizontal lines) more than horizontally (vertical lines), as shown in Figure 24.23. Percentages lower than 100% extend the trap sideways more than up and down.

Figure 24.23
The trap here is exaggerated in both size and darkness to show the height/width ratio.

* **Tint Reduction**—This option lightens the lighter color being trapped (only in the trap itself). The darker color is unaffected. Reducing the tint prevents discoloration when two relatively light colors are being trapped. The default is 40%.

* **Traps with Process Color**—When spot colors are trapped, this option creates an over-printed object of the process color equivalent.

• **Reverse Traps**—When two reasonably equivalent colors are being trapped, you may decide that Illustrator chose the wrong color as the lighter of the pair. Reversing the trap makes the correction. You can also use this option to spread or choke a darker color over a lighter color. Figure 24.24 shows reversing a trap.

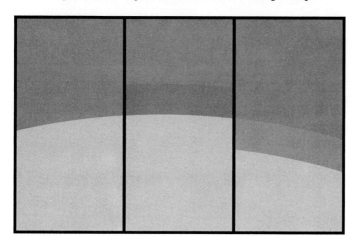

Figure 24.24
To the left, the colors are untrapped. In the center, the lighter color is spread. To the right, the trap is reversed and the darker color is spread.

The Advanced Options at the bottom of the Pathfinder Options dialog box are used with other Pathfinder commands and have no effect on trapping.

Using the Trap command from the Pathfinder palette menu is the other major method of applying trapping in Illustrator. Selecting the Trap command opens the Pathfinder Trap dialog box, as shown in Figure 24.25.

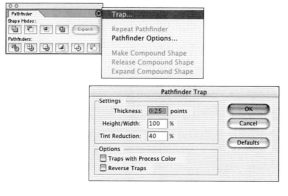

Figure 24.25
The Trap command of the Pathfinder palette menu opens the Pathfinder Trap dialog box.

The options in this smaller dialog box are exactly the same as the trap-related options discussed for the trap effect.

The Pathfinder palette menu also offers Pathfinder Options. This dialog box is not the same as the one discussed in the preceding paragraphs. It contains only the Advanced Options and has no effect on trapping.

Pathfinder Palette vs. Pathfinder Effect

The difference between using the Pathfinder palette and using the Pathfinder effect to trap is the difference between a filter and an effect. If you use the palette, the trap is permanently applied and cannot be changed. If you use the effect, you can remove or change the trap by double-clicking it in the Appearance palette (see Figure 24.26).

Figure 24.26
The Appearance palette is explained in Chapter 14, "Using the Appearance and Styles Palettes."

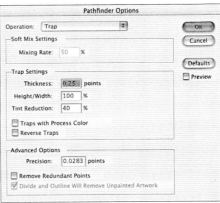

One alternative to trapping is overprinting a stroke. This technique is easiest when you're working with previously unstroked objects.

1. To create a spread, stroke the lighter object with its fill color. That extends the color over the darker color.

2. To choke, stroke the darker object with the lighter object's color.

3. Choose Overprint Stroke in the Attributes palette.

4. Note that the amount of the trap will be one-half the weight of the stroke in points.

5. Be aware that the stroke extends all the way around an object. If an object overlaps or abuts another color on only one side or in only one area, this technique may not be appropriate. Instead, use the Pen tool to create a path along the edge that needs trapping and stroke the path accordingly.

6. When the object to be trapped already has a stroke, you can add another stroke in the Appearances palette and increase its weight to create the trap.

Avoiding the Need to Trap

Among the most popular techniques for avoiding trapping problems is simply to avoid situations that require trapping. Some designers have turned trapless illustration into a science. This can reduce the cost of a project, in some cases substantially. In addition, when you eliminate the need for trapping, the document can be prepared and processed faster, and the margin of error is reduced. You can minimize the need for trapping in a number of ways:

- Separate elements on the page.
- Use only process colors.
- Ensure that neighboring process colors have at least one substantially similar color value.
- Overprint black strokes.

The bottom line is, however, to talk with your printer. If it's a simple matter of manually trapping one element or several, the printer can give you the technical specifications you need to do the job properly. If the trapping requirements are more substantial, the printer or service bureau should handle the job. Under no circumstances should you trap "blind," without knowing the requirements of the specific printing press upon which the job will be run.

TROUBLESHOOTING

Simplifying Files for Printing

I've split my paths, but my document still doesn't print. What else can I do?

Simplifying the file itself may be a good idea. Start by deleting all unused patterns from the Swatches palette. Next, check to see how many fonts you're embedding in the file (and if you need them all). You can, if necessary, also start rasterizing artwork. Start with the most complex.

Adding Registration Marks

My printer is none-too-happy about the separations I sent. He says he won't run the job unless I give him separations with registration marks or sign a release that he's not responsible for lousy work.

Your printer is right. He could try to visually align the plates, but "eyeballing it" could result in misregistration, and you would be very unhappy with the results. Go to File, Separation Setup and check the box Use Printer's Marks. The registration marks will show up.

Document Information

My Document Info palette says that I don't have any fonts in this file, yet I can see the text right onscreen, and I know I chose to embed fonts when I saved the file. What's wrong?

In the Document Info palette menu (which you access through the small triangle in the palette's upper-right corner), you should deselect Selection Only. When that option is checked, the palette shows information only for the object or objects selected on the artboard or in the Layers palette. When you need data for the document as a whole, the option must be unchecked.

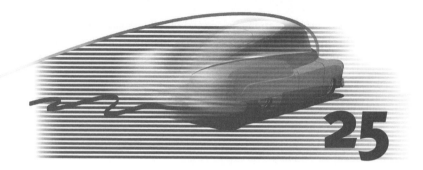

25

LINKING AND EMBEDDING IMAGES AND FONTS

IN THIS CHAPTER

Linking Raster Images   **604**

Embedding Raster and Vector Images   **612**

Embedding Text Files and Fonts   **617**

Troubleshooting   **620**

LINKING RASTER IMAGES

When an illustration includes an image created outside Illustrator, that image is either linked or embedded. Linked images are not part of the Illustrator file, but embedded images are added to the document. Each method has its advantages. The choice often depends on your future plans for the artwork.

When your illustration will spend its entire life on your computer, the difference between linking and embedding is not substantial. If you plan to send out the illustration for printing or place it in a page layout program, you must consider the difference. Failure to include a linked file prevents an illustration from printing correctly. However, file size limitations may prevent images from being embedded.

Illustrator allows you to link and embed a wide range of file types, as you can see in Figure 25.1. The list includes all file formats that Illustrator can open, with the exception of Illustrator's own .AI format (which cannot be placed).

Figure 25.1

You are unlikely to ever work with files of some proprietary formats, such as Pixar and Targa.

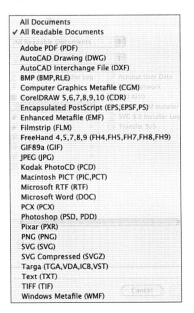

    All Documents
  ✓ All Readable Documents

    Adobe PDF (PDF)
    AutoCAD Drawing (DWG)
    AutoCAD Interchange File (DXF)
    BMP (BMP,RLE)
    Computer Graphics Metafile (CGM)
    CorelDRAW 5,6,7,8,9,10 (CDR)
    Encapsulated PostScript (EPS,EPSF,PS)
    Enhanced Metafile (EMF)
    Filmstrip (FLM)
    FreeHand 4,5,7,8,9 (FH4,FH5,FH7,FH8,FH9)
    GIF89a (GIF)
    JPEG (JPG)
    Kodak PhotoCD (PCD)
    Macintosh PICT (PIC,PCT)
    Microsoft RTF (RTF)
    Microsoft Word (DOC)
    PCX (PCX)
    Photoshop (PSD, PDD)
    Pixar (PXR)
    PNG (PNG)
    SVG (SVG)
    SVG Compressed (SVGZ)
    Targa (TGA,VDA,ICB,VST)
    Text (TXT)
    TIFF (TIF)
    Windows Metafile (WMF)

Fonts, too, can be embedded in an Illustrator file, but there are legal restrictions. If the file will be created, developed, and output from a single computer, you might not need to embed fonts. You may need to include fonts if the illustration will be placed into another file, such as a page layout program's document, or if it will be sent out for commercial printing.

Vector file formats (CGM, WMF, EMF, SVG), AutoCAD files (DWG, DXF), and text files (TXT, DOC, RTF) must be embedded. Illustrator allows you to link only raster images.

Images in raster file formats can be linked to an Illustrator file. (Files in vector formats supported by Illustrator must be embedded rather than linked.) As linked objects, they can be modified in their parent program and updated in your document. Illustrator does, if you choose, automatically update your document to the latest version of the linked file. Two palettes help you keep track of your linked images: Document Info and Links. Using the Links palette, you can also manage and update your linked images.

The Basics of Image Linking

When you place an image in an Illustrator document (using the command File, Place), the default setting is Link. Figure 25.2 shows the Place dialog box.

Figure 25.2
The Link box is checked by default. Unchecking the box results in the image being embedded.

Linking a file simply places a preview of the image (if one is available) in the Illustrator file, with a link to the original file. Just as a hyperlink on the World Wide Web leads you to a different page, so too does a linked image in Illustrator point to a different file.

The linked image appears in the center of the screen, regardless of the zoom factor or whether the artboard is off center. The image is selected on the artboard and added to the Links palette. Placed images are added to the top of the active layer.

That file remains independent of the Illustrator document and can be modified in its parent program. If it is changed, Illustrator can warn you, automatically get the updated version, or ignore the change unless you want to update the image. Illustrator's behavior with linked files is set in the preferences. Figure 25.3 shows the Files & Clipboard panel of the Preferences dialog box.

Illustrator offers a pair of palettes to help you manage your linked images. The Links palette gives you information and allows you to work with the images. The Document Info palette also tracks the linked images.

➩ *Not able to see your placed images on the page? See "Preview Problems" in the "Troubleshooting" section at the end of this chapter.*

Figure 25.3
The Update Links option refers to linked files, not hyperlinks.

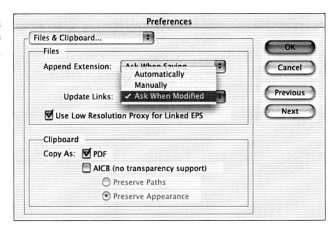

When you make edges visible (by using the command View, Show Edges), linked images in many formats are instantly recognizable. Most linked images have a pair of diagonal lines across the preview. Figure 25.4 shows the visual difference between linked and embedded images.

Figure 25.4
The center image has no preview available. Both the top and center images are linked, but the bottom image is embedded. All are selected on the artboard.

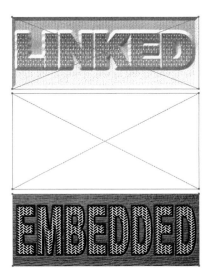

Not all file formats show the diagonal lines when linked. Figure 25.5 tells the tale. Note that the diagonal lines, as part of the edges, are not obscured by artwork higher in the stacking order. Like guides and bounding boxes, the edges are nonprinting.

▷ *Do you find the diagonal lines across linked images annoying? See "Losing Link Lines" in the "Troubleshooting" section at the end of this chapter.*

Caution

If your Illustrator document takes advantage of Illustrator's transparency features, including blending modes, opacity, and certain effects, EPS files should be embedded rather than linked. Linked EPS files in documents with transparency may produce output irregularities.

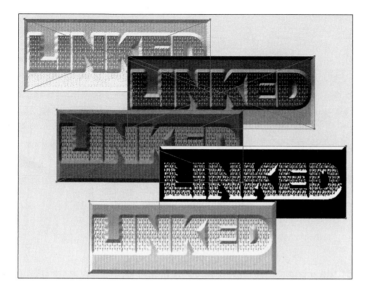

Figure 25.5
The various images are, from the top, EPS, PDF, Photoshop native (.psd), JPEG, and TIFF. As you can see, the JPEG and TIFF previews do not have the crossed diagonal lines. The differences among the images are strictly for illustrative purposes.

Illustrator allows you to view linked (and embedded) images in two ways while you're working in Outline view. The Artboard panel of the Document Setup dialog box, shown in Figure 25.6, contains the option Show Images in Outline.

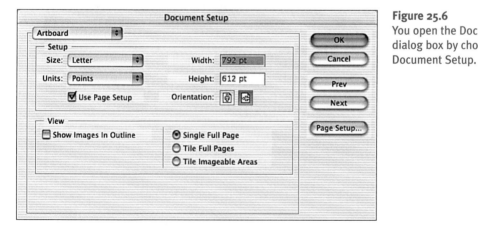

Figure 25.6
You open the Document Setup dialog box by choosing File, Document Setup.

When this option is selected, all linked and placed images are shown with black-and-white previews in Outline view. (Linked images that do not have previews are, of course, shown as empty boxes.) The difference in views is demonstrated in Figure 25.7.

Working with Linked Images

When linked images are raster images, they retain their specific file format qualities. Raster images are composed of pixels and can be manipulated as any rasterized object. When you place a linked image in an illustration, you can edit it in various ways. For example, you can apply transformations and effects.

Figure 25.7
The samples are, clockwise from the top, Preview, Outline, and Outline view with the Show Images in Outline option selected. You can switch between Preview and Outline views by using the View menu.

Figure 25.8 shows several of the images that were placed in Figure 25.5. They have been transformed and had effects applied, just as any other rasterized artwork in Illustrator.

Figure 25.8
From the upper left, Rotate, Feather, Scale, Dry Brush, and Radial Blur are some of the transformations and effects that have been applied to these linked images.

If Illustrator cannot find a linked file or the linked file cannot be opened, you may see a dialog box like the one shown in Figure 25.9.

Figure 25.9
Missing or otherwise unavailable linked files generate this message.

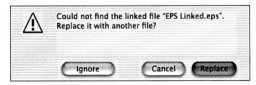

If you get the error message shown in Figure 25.9 and click the Replace button, a dialog box called Replace appears (see Figure 25.10).

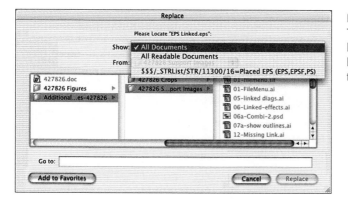

Figure 25.10
This dialog box is similar to both the Open and Place dialog boxes, but you should notice the file type options.

Unsure of what to include with a document headed to the printer? See "Preflighting" in the "Troubleshooting" section at the end of this chapter.

The Replace dialog box indicates that you should locate the original image (notice the message above the Show menu). However, if you must use a different file, the dialog box puts some restrictions on your choices. The choices are not as clear-cut as they may seem:

Caution

If an Illustrator file containing linked images is to be placed into a page layout program's document or will be sent out to a service bureau or printer, you must ensure that copies of the linked files are sent along, too.

- If you select All Documents in the Show menu, you do, indeed, see a list of all documents. Illustrator even allows you to choose any of those documents. However, if the selected document is not appropriate, the file that you are opening continues to open, but the new image is not visible.

- The choice All Readable Documents shows only those files that can be used by the file being opened as a replacement for the missing image. This does not, however, guarantee that your decision will be correct. See Figure 25.11 for verification.

Figure 25.11
Just because an image is available to replace a missing image does not mean that you should use it. Compare this figure to Figure 25.8.

Notice that the transformations and effects applied to the missing files remain in place for the replacements. Also notice, however, that the new images in the upper- and lower-left corners have different dimensions from their predecessors. Their proportions have not been adjusted to those of the missing images.

Caution

EPS files, if missing, should be replaced with like files. Illustrator handles these files somewhat differently from dedicated raster formats, such as TIFF and JPEG.

- The third choice in the Replace dialog box shows you a list of acceptable file formats for substitution. In the case of a missing EPS file, as shown in Figure 25.11, only EPS, EPSF, and PostScript files are listed. If the missing file were, for example, a PDF image, Illustrator's Replace dialog box would show a list of all file formats that can be linked.

Caution

Although you are able to apply filters to linked TIFF and JPEG images, you lose the advantages of linking. After the image is filtered, it is embedded.

Filters should not be used with linked images. Filters, in fact, are available for only some of the linked file formats. Linked JPEG and TIFF images can have most filters applied. Photoshop (.psd), PDF, and EPS, on the other hand, cannot be filtered when placed as linked images. Use effects rather than filters.

The Links Palette

Trying to remember which linked file formats can have filters applied? Select the linked image on the artboard or in the Layers palette, and look for the crossed diagonal edge lines (refer to Figure 25.5). If the lines are there, you cannot apply filters to the linked image.

Using the Links palette is an excellent way to track and control images from external sources. It lists both linked and embedded images. In addition, the palette's menu offers the Information command, which displays details of the placed image. (See the sidebar "Image Info," later in this chapter for details.) The palette and its menu are shown in Figure 25.12.

Icons to the right of an image indicate its status. A yellow warning triangle, like that next to the file EPS Link.eps, indicates that the linked file has been modified. The icon to the right of the next image, Tiff Embed.tif, indicates that the image is embedded rather than linked. A red stop sign with a white question mark (shown in Figure 25.12 next to PDF Link.pdf) indicates that a linked image's original file is missing. The fourth filename in Figure 25.12, JPEG Link.jpg (highlighted in the palette), has no icon to the right. The lack of an icon indicates that the file is linked and that there are no problems.

The buttons at the bottom of the palette are as follows (from the left):

- **Replace Link**—Even if an image is not missing, this button allows you to put another image in its place on the artboard.

- **Go To Link**—When you select a file in the Links palette and click this button, the image is selected on the artboard and centered in the window. This feature is very convenient, especially when the illustration has numerous linked or embedded images.

- **Update Link**—When the preferences are set to Update Links: Manually clicking this button is the way to update it. When you select a linked image in the palette and click this button, the image is updated on the artboard and in the Illustrator file.

- **Edit Original**—If the linked image's originating program is available, it is launched and the image is opened for editing when you click this button.

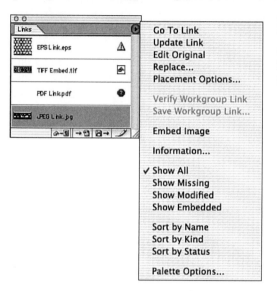

Figure 25.12
The Links palette can display subsets of all linked images, such as those missing, modified, or embedded.

The palette can display all linked or embedded images or display only those with potential problems. Individual problem images can be updated or replaced using the palette menu commands. If you've selected Ask When Modified in the Update Links menu of the preferences, Illustrator may show the dialog box seen in Figure 25.13 when a linked file is missing or modified. When the preferences are set to update manually or automatically, the message will not appear.

Figure 25.13
Clicking Yes updates all images as necessary.

Working within the Links palette, you can click a link and choose Information from the palette menu commands. Figure 25.14 shows the level of information available. You also can access a link's information window by double-clicking the link in the Links palette.

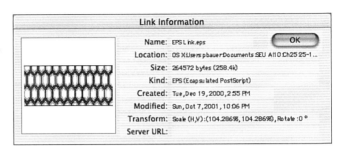

Figure 25.14
New in Illustrator 10 is the addition of the Server URL field for images stored in a database.

You can select a group of contiguous links in the palette by clicking a link at one end of the list and Shift+clicking the farthest link. You can select noncontiguous links by Cmd+clicking (Ctrl+clicking). When one or more links are selected, you can use the palette menu command Go To Link to select the image(s) in the document. The view automatically scrolls to show the images; however, it does not zoom out to accommodate the images.

In the Links palette, you also can edit the original of a linked image. Click the link once in the palette to select it and then use the palette menu command Edit Original. If the program that created the image is available, it is launched and the image is opened for editing. When you return to Illustrator, the warning dialog box shown in Figure 25.13 is displayed, offering you an opportunity to update the linked image.

EMBEDDING RASTER AND VECTOR IMAGES

When the Link option is not selected in the Place dialog box, the selected image is embedded in the Illustrator document. Embedded images become part of the illustration, much like any other element on the artboard. Embedded images, because they become part of the Illustrator document, increase the file size.

Both raster and vector files can be embedded. Photoshop files offer the option of flattening or creating individual objects from the files' layers when embedded.

Embedding Raster Images

Any raster image file format that can be linked can also be embedded. When a file is embedded, it loses its link to the original image and is not updated. Filters, effects, and transformations can be applied to any rasterized artwork. Embedded EPS and PDF files can be edited in Illustrator.

You embed raster images, like linked images, by using the Place command. The difference between the two is simply deselecting the Link option in the Place dialog box (see Figure 25.15).

Embedding images increases the size of your Illustrator document by the size of the placed file. Embedding numerous raster images in a document can result in huge file sizes.

The Links and Document Info palettes offer a wealth of information about embedded images. See the sidebar "Image Info" for details.

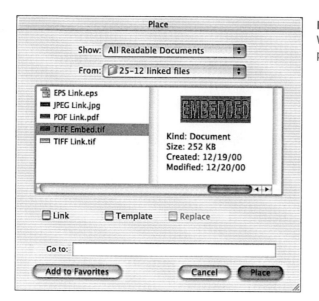

Figure 25.15
When Link is not selected, the placed image is embedded.

Image Info

Between the Information command of the Links palette and the Document Info palette, there's little that you cannot learn about placed raster images (see Figure 25.16).

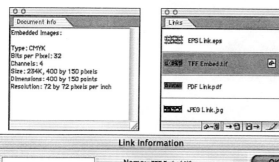

Figure 25.16
The Document Info palette can show details of all linked or embedded images, or those of a selection. You access the Link Information window from the Links palette menu.

Whether an image is linked or embedded, here's what the Document Info palette offers:

- **Type**—This line tells you the image's color mode. It is either the document's color mode (RGB or CMYK) or Grayscale. Remember that Illustrator 10 allows objects of either CMYK or RGB in a document, not both. Placing an image automatically converts it to the document's color mode. Illustrator also converts indexed color images but does not allow you to place images that use the Lab or multichannel color modes.

- **Bits per Pixel**—At eight bits per channel, the number of bits can be 8, 24, 32, or 40. Illustrator allows a single alpha or spot channel in addition to the one (grayscale), three (RGB), or four (CMYK) 8-bit color channels.

- **Channels**—This line, like Bits per Pixel, tells you if the image has an alpha channel or spot channel. If there is not an extra channel, grayscale images have one channel, RGB images have three, and CMYK images have four channels.

- **Size**—The file size is followed by the image's pixel dimensions. They are the original width and height of the image, as placed into the Illustrator document.

- **Dimensions**—This line tells you the size of the placed image in points, measured horizontally and vertically as a rectangle (see Figure 25.17).

Figure 25.17
The upper image has not been transformed and is listed at the top of the Document Info palette. The lower image's dimensions are indicated by the dashed rectangle.

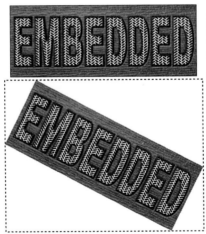

- **Resolution**—If an image has not been transformed, this line tells you its original print resolution. If the image has been transformed, as has the lower image in Figure 25.17, the pixels are redistributed and the print resolution changes.

The Links palette offers additional data about placed objects, either linked or embedded. The palette menu command Information opens a separate window, as shown in Figure 25.18.

The information displayed is that of the image selected in the Links palette, which may not be the same as the object selected on the artboard. Information is available for linked images and for embedded images of certain formats, including Photoshop, JPEG, and TIFF. For other embedded files, including EPS and PDF (and other formats when the original file is no longer available), the Link Information window shows only the transformation information.

The Link Information window shows you information related to the original file, including a thumbnail of what the image looked like before any transformations or effects were applied. In addition, you can see the following:

- **Name**—The placed file's name is listed as it appears in the file itself.

- **Location**—For both linked and embedded files, this is the location of the source file. If the original file of an embedded image is moved from this location, the window shows only transformation data.

- **Size**—The file size in bytes and kilobytes (K) is listed. (Remember that there are 1,024 bytes in a kilobyte.)

- **Kind**—For the Macintosh, the actual file format is shown rather than the filename extension. Macintosh users can open the File Exchange control panel to associate specific formats with the filename extensions used in downloaded files or files copied from a Windows computer. In Windows, the Link Information window shows the filename extension to indicate the file type.

- **Created**—This line shows the creation date embedded in the file.

- **Modified**—This line shows the date and time of the latest changes to the original file.

- **Transform**—The one entry that is present for all placed images, this line relies on information stored in the Illustrator document rather than with the image's original file. It displays the horizontal and vertical scaling in percent and any rotation (in degrees).

- **Server URL**—When a linked image is drawn from a database using Illustrator's dynamic data-driven graphics, this entry will show the source location.

Embedding Vector Images

Unlike linking, embedding allows you to add vector objects from other documents to your illustration. Like embedded raster artwork, these embedded files become part of the Illustrator document and have no ties to the original files. And, as embedded images, they increase the size of the Illustrator document.

The biggest difference between embedding vector artwork and embedding raster images, other than the actual
nature of the files, is how the contents are handled.
Vector objects embedded in an Illustrator object are converted into Illustrator paths. You can then edit them as
you would objects created in Illustrator. This includes vector elements of PDF and EPS images.

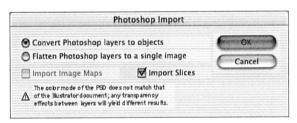

You can easily predict whether
the Link Information window will
have more than just transformation data. If the file is listed by
name in the Links palette, the
information is complete. If the
name of the embedded file is
not listed, you see only transformation information. There's an
exception, however. If an
embedded image's original file
has been moved or is otherwise
not available, Illustrator does
not display the additional information.

Embedding Photoshop Files

Embedding Photoshop files, which is also discussed in
Chapter 28, "Integrating Illustrator 10 and Photoshop,"
gives you some flexibility. You can convert each of the
Photoshop file's layers to an object, or you can flatten the
image and treat it as a single piece of raster artwork. If
the file has slices or image maps, Illustrator can maintain
them or ignore them. In addition, you'll get a warning if
the Photoshop image's color mode does not match that of
the Illustrator document (see Figure 25.19).

Figure 25.19
Converting layers to objects
allows you to edit the
embedded image.

Photoshop Import
⦿ Convert Photoshop layers to objects
◯ Flatten Photoshop layers to a single image
☐ Import Image Maps   ☑ Import Slices
⚠ The color mode of the PSD does not match that of the Illustrator document; any transparency effects between layers will yield different results.

Illustrator will maintain image data on Photoshop layers that can be used to recreate rollovers
and animations (see Figure 25.20).

Figure 25.20
The original Photoshop image
has Web features that can be
recreated in Illustrator.

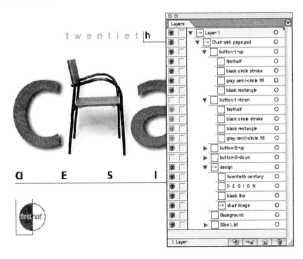

Note, however, that each Photoshop 6 layer is not only a separate raster object in Illustrator's Layers palette, but also a separate unnamed file in Illustrator's Links palette (see Figure 25.21).

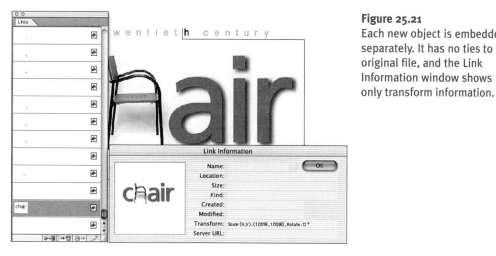

Figure 25.21
Each new object is embedded separately. It has no ties to the original file, and the Link Information window shows only transform information.

EMBEDDING TEXT FILES AND FONTS

Text files can be embedded similarly to vector artwork. The contents of the file become part of the Illustrator document. Text can retain its formatting, including font attributes, when embedded. Unlike raster or vector artwork, however, embedded text files do not appear in the Links palette.

Fonts are not embedded on the artboard like text or artwork. Rather, they are included within the file's data on disk when you so choose. Including the fonts when an illustration is sent to a service bureau or printer ensures that the document will be output correctly—and will output at all. Missing fonts are a major source of problems at service bureaus and printers. There are, however, legal restrictions on font embedding. In addition, fonts can be subset, which includes only part of the font, and can reduce file size.

Embedding Text Files

You can embed text files, including Microsoft Word (.doc), RTF (.rtf), and plain text (.txt) formats, in Illustrator documents by using the Place command. As you can see in Figure 25.22, Illustrator does not allow you to link text files; that option is not available.

Text files embedded in an Illustrator document do not appear in the Links palette (see Figure 25.23). The text is placed in the center of the window in its own text box. It is fully editable, and the text container acts like any other.

Figure 25.22
With the options below grayed
out, text files must be embedded rather than linked.

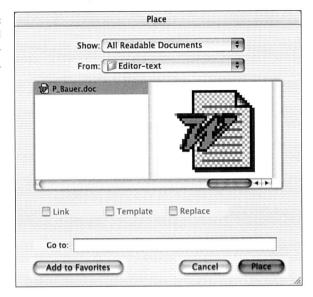

Figure 25.23
The Links palette ignores the
embedded text file, regardless
of file format.

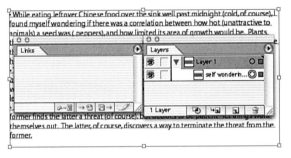

You can wrap the newly placed text, use the spell checker, and even embed formatted text. In
Figure 25.24, you can see that Illustrator accepted text of different font sizes, fonts, styles, and
colors.

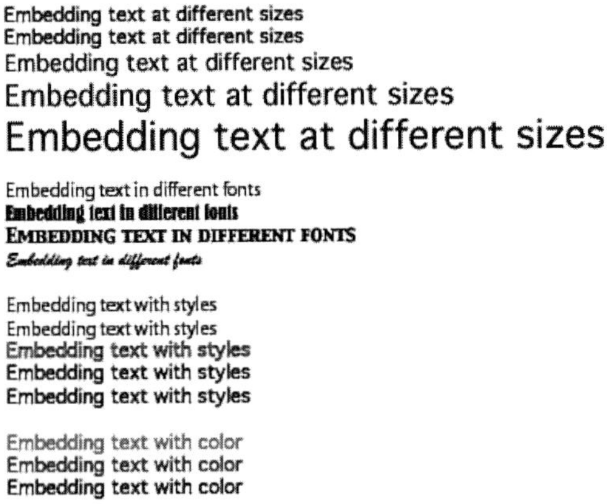

Figure 25.24
Illustrator substitutes a font if
one isn't available.

Embedding text at different sizes
Embedding text at different sizes
Embedding text at different sizes
Embedding text at different sizes
Embedding text at different sizes

Embedding text in different fonts
Embedding text in different fonts
EMBEDDING TEXT IN DIFFERENT FONTS
Embedding text in different fonts

Embedding text with styles
Embedding text with styles
Embedding text with styles
Embedding text with styles
Embedding text with styles

Embedding text with color
Embedding text with color
Embedding text with color

Embedding Fonts

Illustrator allows you to include the fonts that appear in the document when saving files in the Illustrator (.ai), PDF, EPS, and SVG formats. Embedded fonts are available if the illustration is opened on a different computer or in a different program. When a font is not embedded and it is not installed on the computer opening the file, another font is substituted. However, that font may not have the same spacing, appearance, or size as the font originally used and, therefore, the appearance of your image can be altered, sometimes drastically. Additionally, missing fonts can generate PostScript errors, preventing the document from outputting properly at a service bureau or print shop.

Unsure about what fonts need to be embedded? See "Typefaces to Go" in the "Troubleshooting" section at the end of this chapter.

Another aspect of font embedding deserves attention. Fonts are copyrighted. You may or may not have acquired the right to embed a font when you purchased or otherwise acquired the font itself. If you are sending a project to a print shop or service bureau that does not own copies of specific fonts, you must have permission from the copyright holders of the fonts to embed them. Fonts are commercial property, like any other software, and making unauthorized copies for others to use, even when you have paid for the fonts, is illegal. Adobe allows embedding of all its fonts (as long as you have acquired the fonts legally). Other foundries may not. For information on how to determine the ownership of a font, check the Adobe Web site at http://www.adobe.com/type/embedding.html.

Font subsetting is designed to reduce the size of your file by including only that part of the font necessary to reproduce your image. Subsetting is available for Illustrator (.ai), SVG, and PDF formats, but not EPS.

When you're saving a file in Illustrator format, your choices (shown in Figure 25.25) include embedding all fonts and, if embedding, subsetting. You can specify at what level of usage a font will be subset, but that is the extent of the option.

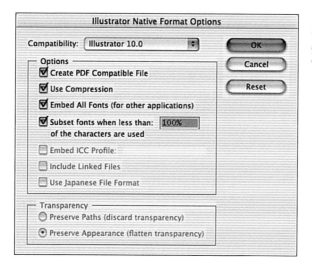

Figure 25.25
Only Illustrator 10 and Illustrator 9 version compatibility allow you to embed fonts.

The SVG file format allows font embedding with far more sophistication. See Chapter 23, "Flash and SVG Support," for details.

TROUBLESHOOTING

Preview Problems

My linked image isn't showing up properly. It prints okay, but I want to be able to see it on the artboard. What's the problem?

It's probable that the image was saved without a preview. Illustrator doesn't open the actual image to show you how it looks. Rather, the preview embedded in the original file is used. Open the file in an image-editing program and resave it with a preview. You can also open many raster image formats directly in Illustrator by choosing File, Open, and then resave them.

Losing Link Lines

I don't like seeing the diagonal lines across my linked images. Can I turn them off?

They are part of the image's edges. You can make them disappear by choosing View, Hide Edges.

Preflighting

I'm sending a document with linked files to a printer. What do I have to do?

The term *preflighting* actually refers to the quality control process used in the prepress industry to ensure that a project can be printed successfully. Entire software programs have been designed to handle the job from top to bottom. A small part of that massive undertaking applies to this particular subject: You should gather together copies of all the linked files in a single folder, along with copies of the fonts used. Unsure what you need in that folder? Use the command File, Document Info. The Document Info palette contains windows that list both fonts and linked images in the document. Change the content of the palette through its menu.

Typefaces to Go

I've heard that I don't need to include the "basic" fonts when I send out a file for printing. Is that true?

As always, when you're sending a file to a service bureau or printer, call to confirm. It's usually better to include (with permission) all the fonts used in a document because fonts, like programs, come in different versions. Although you can easily see the difference between a program named Adobe Illustrator 6 and one named Adobe Illustrator 10, it's not as easy to see the difference between font versions. Variations, however slight, can ruin your layout by changing character spacing.

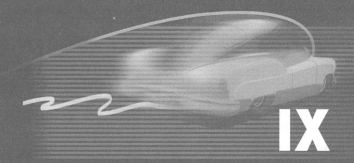

IX

ILLUSTRATOR EFFICIENCY AND INTEROPERABILITY

IN THIS PART

26 Automation Through Actions **625**

27 Dynamic Data-Driven Graphics **645**

28 Integrating Illustrator 10 and Photoshop **655**

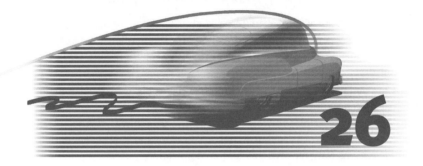

AUTOMATION THROUGH ACTIONS

IN THIS CHAPTER

Actions in Theory and Practice **626**

Recording Custom Actions **632**

Troubleshooting **642**

ACTIONS IN THEORY AND PRACTICE

Illustrator offers a powerful, yet underutilized, method of streamlining your work and improving efficiency. If you perform a task or series of tasks regularly, it's probable that Illustrator's *Actions* can make your work easier, faster, and even more precise by applying identical values, time after time.

Actions are simply prerecorded steps. You can use them to perform a series of tasks with a single click. Illustrator installs, by default, two dozen Actions, and many more are available free or at minimal cost on the Web. However, the true power of Actions comes to the fore when you write your own custom Actions. You can even share your Actions with others and load their Actions for your own use and customization.

Virtually anything you can do in Illustrator, an Action can do for you. Some Actions are completely automated and can be run while you're away from the computer; other Actions require you to enter specific values for certain procedures. Illustrator also enables you to specify whether to use the values originally recorded with an Action or to pause the Action for you to input new values.

You create, store, organize, and play back Actions by using the Actions palette. You can specify how Actions are played back and can even run them on multiple files sequentially as a *batch*. Batch processing of a folder of files can even include subfolders.

What Is an Action?

To appreciate the power of Actions, you need to understand what they are and how they work. Figure 26.1 shows the steps recorded in a simple Action, one of those installed by default by Illustrator. (The Actions palette itself is explained in depth in the section called "The Action Palette," later in this chapter.)

Figure 26.1

The Action Style/Brush/Swatch Cleanup is part of the Default Actions set installed by default with Illustrator 10.

Cleaning up the palettes is a good way to minimize file size and confusion. Unused items are removed from the palettes, making it easier to find those that you need while you're working. It also reduces file size, sometimes significantly. Using this Action makes cleaning up a simple matter rather than a time-consuming step that is likely to be skipped.

When the Action is run, six commands are executed. First, all unused styles are selected and deleted, then all unused brushes are selected and deleted, and finally all unused swatches are selected and deleted.

Performing this cleanup using the Action requires five basic steps:

1. Open the Actions palette, if it's not already visible.

2. Expand the Default Actions folder.

3. Scroll to the Style/Brush/Swatch Cleanup Action and select it.

4. Click the Play button.

5. Click OK to confirm each of the deletions. (You'll have to move the mouse just once. The three dialog boxes appear in exactly the same place, so you can simply click three times.)

This process takes about 10 seconds; 5 seconds if the Actions set is organized properly. Cleaning up manually requires several more steps:

1. Open the Styles palette, if it's not already visible.

2. Open the palette's menu, scroll down to the command Select All Unused, and click it.

3. Open the palette's menu again, scroll down to the command Delete Style, and select it.

4. Confirm the deletions by clicking OK in the dialog box.

5. Click the tab to open the Brushes palette.

6. Open the palette's menu, scroll down to the command Select All Unused, and click it.

7. Open the palette's menu again, scroll down to the command Delete Brush, and select it.

8. Confirm the deletions by clicking OK in the dialog box.

9. Click the tab to open the Swatches palette.

10. Open the palette's menu, scroll down to the command Select All Unused, and click it.

11. Open the palette's menu again, scroll down to the command Delete Swatch, and select it.

12. Confirm the deletions by clicking OK in the dialog box.

This procedure takes approximately 30 seconds, so the time savings are not overwhelming. However, you will discover a tremendous advantage in convenience. The simple step of cleaning up an image's palettes is something you should do with every file. Yet, because of the inconvenience, it's an often-neglected step, even when it does come to mind. Using the Action makes it a realistic part of the workflow for every document.

As you can see, everything in this Action you can do manually. However, recording the steps is far more convenient. An Action is simply a series of Illustrator commands and tools recorded and stored for later playback.

Stop and Go

I have an Action that stops in the middle, but no message appears. I have to click the Play button again to make it continue.

Expand the Action in the Actions palette and look for a Stop at the point where the Action halts. Now look in the second column. An icon must be visible in the Modal Control column for the Stop's warning box to appear.

Showing the Stop

My Actions go right past my Stop messages sometimes, just not showing them at all. What can I do to fix this problem?

Open the Actions palette, click the triangle next to the specific Action to expand it in the palette, and take a look at the first column. If you don't see a check mark, the step is skipped.

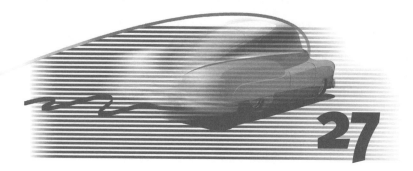

DYNAMIC DATA-DRIVEN GRAPHICS

IN THIS CHAPTER

Dynamic Data-Driven Graphics—Overview   **646**

Templates, Variables, and Data Sets   **648**

Troubleshooting   **654**

DYNAMIC DATA-DRIVEN GRAPHICS—OVERVIEW

Intended for use in large-scale operations, dynamic data-driven graphics offer the capability to automatically update and replace graphics in a layout. Dynamic data-driven graphics can be used in both Web and print operations. They can require considerable expertise in areas beyond the scope of Illustrator.

Working with dynamic data-driven graphics for the Web requires two types of knowledge. In addition to the designer who creates the layout, a developer is required to code the variables and data sets. Dynamic data-driven graphics is a technology that is designed to be a collaborative effort between designers and developers. Print applications of the technology, on the other hand, can be implemented using a working knowledge of XML and Illustrator automation.

In the simplest of terms, dynamic data-driven graphics allows a Web page or a print layout to automatically substitute and update graphic (and text) elements. The Web page or layout becomes a *template* into which the updateable elements are added as *variables*. The variables are filled with elements from a *data set* stored in a database or XML file called a *variable library*.

How They Work

Consider dynamic data-driven graphics to be a highly evolved form of the technology that allows mass mailings to be "personalized," such as the fictional example in Figure 27.1.

Figure 27.1
The template is the form letter shown at the top. It accesses a database to "personalize" the letter for each individual.

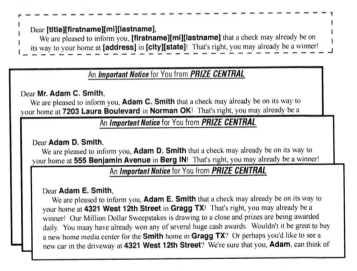

Templates can consist of both variables and static objects. The static objects are the framework of the page, Web, or layout. They are the graphics and text that are not updated, the unchanging, non-dynamic parts of the page.

In Figure 27.2, a Web page is shown that contains both static and dynamic elements.

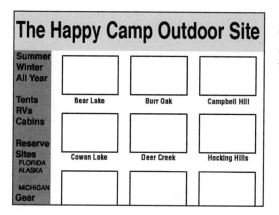

Figure 27.2
This fictional page could use dynamic data-driven graphics to update content.

In this simplified example, the frames, the banner, the menu, and the individual site labels under the boxes can all be static. They need not be updated regularly. The boxes, which could display available camp sites at each area, can be variables. The developer can use XML to access a database that holds the information for each box. The database can be updated independently.

Dynamic Data-Driven Graphics Terminology

There are several terms used with dynamic data-driven graphics that are important to understanding the technology:

- **Template**—The template is the graphic Web page or layout that incorporates all of the elements. It includes both the elements that will change and those that will always appear the same. It is the Illustrator document itself.

- **Variable**—Variables are the elements in the template that change. Variables are identified in the Variables palette. Linked images, graph data, and text strings can be variables. The visibility of an element on the page can also be a variable.

- **Dynamic/Static**—Dynamic objects can be changed or updated. They are the variables. Static objects will remain unchanged. The non-variable objects on a page or in a layout are static objects. They are the same, no matter what content fills the variables.

- **Data Set**—The data set is one or more variables and the associated images, text, or graph data used in the variables. This is the data itself, the collection of content for the elements in the page that will change.

- **Data Source**—The database from which the variables are filled is called the data source.

- **Binding**—A variable is *bound* to the data source. This is the link that connects the variable to the collection of content, the data set. Binding is not done in Illustrator. Rather, the developer uses a Web design tool (such as Adobe GoLive), image serving software (such as Adobe AlterCast), or scripting to do the binding.

The Design Process

While it's possible for a single individual to implement dynamic data-driven graphics, more typically designers and developers work together, integrating their particular skills. Typically, the design staff and the development staff work together to formulate a plan.

The developer can produce specifications for a sample data set, with one or more examples of each object that will fill a variable. The designer can use a sample database in the creation of a template to ensure that each variable appears in the correct place and in the correct dimensions. The template is then passed to the developer, who produces the code that binds the variables to the data set, allowing the variables to be filled from the database.

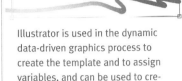

Illustrator is used in the dynamic data-driven graphics process to create the template and to assign variables, and can be used to create data sets. The balance of the work—making dynamic data-driven graphics function with databases, writing XML, integrating with GoLive or AlterCast—is done outside of Illustrator and is beyond the scope of this discussion.

TEMPLATES, VARIABLES, AND DATA SETS

The three parts of dynamic data-driven graphics with which Illustrator works are the templates, the variables, and the data sets.

Creating and Using Templates

The template is an Adobe Illustrator document that contains variables and (optionally) static objects and text. Templates can contain numerous variables, of various types (see Figure 27.3).

Figure 27.3
The graph, the photo, and the name are all variables.

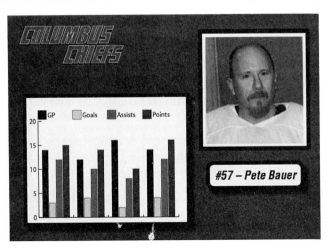

To use a template with Adobe AlterCast or GoLive 6, it should be saved in SVG format. To use a template with Adobe GoLive 6, place it in the GoLive page. The variables must then be bound to the database using dynamic links. AlterCast is used to generate iterations of the page. AlterCast can also be used to bind variables directly to a database.

The Variables Palette

Dynamic data-driven graphics are all about the variables. The concept is about being able to insert images, text, or other content from a database rather than creating separate layouts or Web pages for each variation. The key to working with dynamic data-driven graphics in Illustrator is the Variables palette (see Figure 27.04). This is where elements in the template are designated as variables and where each is affiliated with a particular data set.

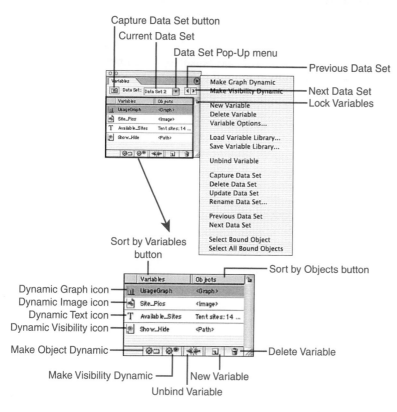

Figure 27.4
The Variables palette is shown with its menu open.

Notice that there are different types of variables shown in the Variables palette, each represented by its specific icon. Double-clicking a variable in the palette opens the Variable Options dialog box.

Understanding the controls can show the power of the Variables palette.

- **Capture Data Set**—This button creates a new data set from the current list of variables in the palette.

- **Current Data Set**—This lists the name of the current set. When the name is shown in italics, the set has been changed since capture or last update. Use the palette menu command Update Data Set.

- **Data Set Pop-up Menu**—A list of all data sets associated with the current document. Change data sets by switching in the list.

- **Previous/Next Data Set**—These buttons enable you to rotate among the data sets in order.

- **Sort Objects by...**—Clicking either of the headings will sort the contents of the Variables palette. If sorted by variables, the contents of the palette will be listed alphabetically by the variable name. When sorted by objects, the contents will be grouped by type, and then listed alphabetically within type.

- **Lock Variables**—This button prevents changes to variables.

- **Make Object Dynamic**—This button will change its name to fit the current selection. For example, it will be called Make Linked Image Dynamic, Make Text Dynamic, or Make Graph Dynamic, depending upon the current selection on the artboard.

- **Make Visibility Dynamic**—Clicking this button establishes whether an object will be visible on the artboard. Visibility is determined by the visibility (eyeball) column in the layers palette.

- **Unbind Variable**—A variable selected in the Variables palette can be unbound (unlinked) from any object on the artboard.

- **New Variable**—Clicking this button produces a new unbound variable in the Variables palette. Until a type is assigned (image, graph, text, or visibility), the icon to the left of the name will be the circle-with-diagonal line symbol. Holding down Option (Alt) when clicking creates a new unbound variable and opens the Variable Options dialog box.

- **Delete Variable**—Deleting a variable removes all occurrences of the variable, but does not affect objects on the artboard.

Creating Variables

There are four types of variables in dynamic data-driven graphics:

- **Linked Images**—Images can be raster or vector, but must be linked, not embedded.

- **Text**—Only point type can be used as a variable, not area type or type-on-a-path.

- **Graph Data**—Appropriate graph data used as a variable will updated a graph dynamically.

- **Visibility**—Any object can be shown or hidden dynamically. Grouped objects and layers can also be tied to a visibility variable.

To create a new variable without associating it with any specific object or text on the artboard, click the New Variable button at the bottom of the Variables palette. To open the Variable Options dialog box (see Figure 27.5) at the same time, hold down the Option (Alt) button when clicking on New Variable.

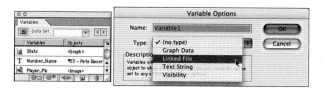

Figure 27.5
The options for an existing variable can be changed by double-clicking it in the Variables palette.

A variable can be named and its type can be assigned from the Variable Options dialog box pop-up menu.

To associate an existing object (or text or graph) with a variable, select it on the artboard, select the appropriate variable in the Variables palette, and click the Make Object Dynamic button. The selection on the artboard and the variable in the Variables palette must be of the same kind.

Illustrator won't let you create a variable from your selection? See "Variable Types" in the Troubleshooting section at the end of this chapter.

One of the keys to dynamic data-driven graphics is the database. It should be ODBC-compliant. That's Open Database Connectivity. ODBC-compliant software that can be used with dynamic data-driven graphics includes Microsoft Excel or Access, FoxPRO, dBase, Oracle, IBM DB2, and SQL.

Working With Data Sets

Data sets are individual collections of variable contents. For example, in Figure 27.6, each player's data set holds one item for each of the variables.

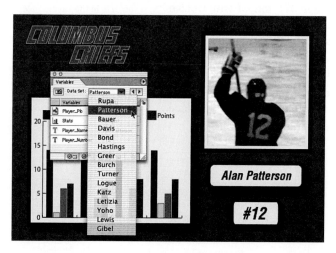

Figure 27.6
Each data set has one picture, one graph, one name, and one number.

As is indicated by the Capture Data Set button in the Variables palette, you can think of a data set as a "snapshot" of the template at that time. To create a data set, add to the template the specific content that you want for each variable. When all of the variables have the content that should be associated with a particular set visible, either Option-click (Alt-click) the Capture Data Set button in the Variables palette or use the palette's menu command. The menu command opens the New Data Set dialog box, which enables you to assign a name to the data set (see Figure 27.7).

Figure 27.7
The only data set option is the name.

If you don't down the Option (Alt) key while clicking the Capture Data Set button, the dialog box will not open and the data set will be given the name Data Set followed by the next available number. To change the name of a data set, make it the active set and either over-type the name in the Variables palette or use the palette menu command Rename Data Set.

As shown earlier in Figure 27.4, you can change among existing data sets by using the data set pop-up menu, the Previous and Next buttons, or the Previous and Next menu commands. If the buttons are grayed out, the document does not have multiple data sets.

➡️ *Can't create your data set? See "Managing Data" in the Troubleshooting section at the end of this chapter.*

XML IDs

Illustrator automatically assigned a valid XML ID to each dynamic object you create. However, keep in mind that if you intend to use a template in SVG format with GoLive or AlterCast, the object names in the Layers palette must conform to XML standards. XML syntax requires that names begin with a letter, an underscore, or a color. Names cannot contain spaces.

In Illustrator's Units & Undo preferences, you have the option of identifying objects by name or by XML ID (see Figure 27.8).

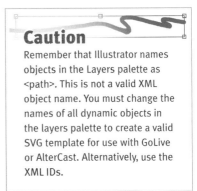

Caution

Remember that Illustrator names objects in the Layers palette as <path>. This is not a valid XML object name. You must change the names of all dynamic objects in the layers palette to create a valid SVG template for use with GoLive or AlterCast. Alternatively, use the XML IDs.

Figure 27.8
Opting for XML IDs affects only dynamic objects.

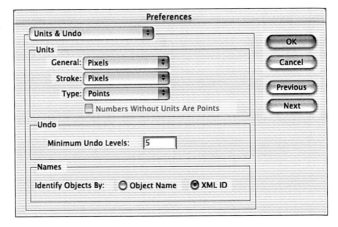

Changing to XML ID automatically updates both the layers palette and the Variables palette. Objects that have been renamed manually will not be updated, nor will static (non-dynamic) objects (see Figure 27.9).

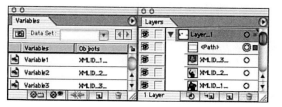

Figure 27.9
Note that one path, which is not a variable, retained its name, while all dynamic objects were automatically changed to the sequential XML ID.

Variable Libraries

Variables and associated data sets can be saved as XML files to be used with multiple documents. The Variables palette menu contains the commands Save Variable Library and Load Variable Library.

Loading a variable library adds the variable names and types to the variables palette, so that they need not be created from scratch. It also makes the data set contents available. However, it adds nothing to the artboard and does not re-create the original template.

Editing Variable Libraries

Variable libraries are XML files. They can be opened in a text editor or word processor. Additional data sets can be defined by editing the text and resaving the XML file (see Figure 27.10). Copying, pasting, and editing the content between the tags is an easy way to create additional data in a set.

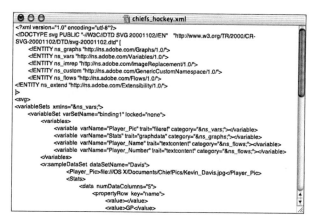

Figure 27.10
XML files use tags, much like HTML.

TROUBLESHOOTING

Variable Types

I'm trying to create a variable from an object on the artboard, but Illustrator won't let me.

First make sure that the object with which you're trying to work is capable of becoming a dynamic object. Point type (not area type or type-on-a-path), an Illustrator graph (that has not be ungrouped), and linked files are the only dynamic objects allowed. You cannot, for example, create a variable from a rectangle or a line or a brush stroke. Move the artwork to a separate Illustrator document and export or save it in any format other than Illustrator's own .ai (which cannot be placed).

Next, make sure that the Lock Variables icon, to the right of the Objects button in the Variables palette, is showing as an open padlock (see Figure 27.11). If the lock icon is closed, you can't make changes to the data set. Click the lock icon to unlock the variables and continue.

Figure 27.11
Locking variables also prevents changes to the current data set.

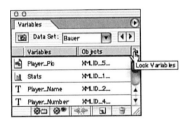

Managing Data

I don't think I have a handle on how to work with data sets. I keep overwriting them, apparently.

Here's the system: Make the artboard look just the way you want the Web page or print layout to look. Option-click (Alt-click) the Capture Data Set button in the Variables palette. Give the data set a name and click OK. Change the variables to make the artboard look like the next version of the Web page or layout. Save the data set. Continue on until all desired variations are saved. Text, images, and graph data will be updated automatically when you next load the data set.

When working with images, it's usually convenient to place all the linked files into the Illustrator document before defining the data sets. Afterward, all but one can be removed from the layers palette.

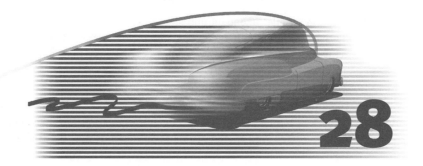

INTEGRATING ILLUSTRATOR AND PHOTOSHOP

IN THIS CHAPTER

Illustrator Versus Photoshop **656**

Moving Artwork from Illustrator to Photoshop **660**

Moving Artwork from Photoshop to Illustrator **668**

Troubleshooting **671**

ILLUSTRATOR VERSUS PHOTOSHOP

Adobe Photoshop is the premier image-editing software. It is, without question, the standard against which all other raster file editors are measured. No illustration or drawing program is better matched with Photoshop than Illustrator. And now the line between the programs has blurred even more.

In addition to sharing major interface components, Photoshop and Illustrator can exchange files with unprecedented ease. Photoshop layers do not have to be flattened when placed in an Illustrator document. Illustrator's vector text can be edited in Photoshop. The appearances of transparency, blending modes, and masks can be maintained as files go back and forth between the two programs.

Before learning how the two programs can work together, you need to understand how they differ. Although their capabilities have started to overlap, they remain two separate programs, with two different purposes.

Illustrator's Vectors, Photoshop's Rasters

Illustrator is primarily a vector art program, whereas Photoshop is designed to work with raster images. (The difference between vector and raster was examined in depth in Chapter 18, "Raster Images and Rasterized Objects.")

Vector file formats record artwork as objects. Each object is described mathematically in relationship to the other objects in the file. Starting point, shape, stroke, fill, and effects are among the data recorded. Because these descriptions are independent of the size of the page, vector art can be scaled to any size and maintain its sharpness and appearance.

Raster images, also known as bitmap images, do not recognize objects. Each file is simply a record of a given number of squares, called *pixels*, each with its particular color. The squares are arranged in rows and columns, a raster. Every raster image is rectangular, although some file formats allow transparency that may make the outline of the image appear to be other than rectangular. Transparent pixels actually fill in the remainder of the rectangle.

You can increase the size of a raster image in two ways: by resampling or scaling. When an image is resampled, the number of pixels is increased to fit the new dimensions. Each pixel remains the same size. When a raster image is scaled, the number of pixels remains the same, but their individual size is changed. (This can occur when you're printing a raster image at a size other than the size at which it was designed.)

Resampling is typically done in an image-editing program, such as Photoshop. Figure 28.1 shows an example.

Figure 28.1
On the left, the original image appears at 100% zoom. In the middle, the image has been scaled to 200%. On the right, the image has been scaled to 400%.

The images in Figure 28.1 are not zoomed-in views. Rather, the image itself was resized in Photoshop. This process is comparable to using Illustrator's command Object, Transform, Scale. In the original object, the vertical and horizontal lines are perfectly straight and clean. The curves are not as smooth as they would be in Illustrator. In the middle, after the object has been doubled in each dimension (and each pixel has been doubled), the straight lines are still sharp, but the curves show the corners of the individual pixels. This condition is known as the *jaggies*. In the third image, even the straight lines are starting to get blurry as new pixels are introduced. Photoshop has added gray pixels to help smooth the edges, a process known as *antialiasing*.

Note also in the right image of Figure 28.1 that the curves are now extremely blocky and jagged. Even antialiasing is ineffective. Keep in mind that antialiasing is available only in color and grayscale images. One-bit black-and-white images (also called *bitmap*) cannot be antialiased because each pixel can be only black or white, with no shades of gray. Figure 28.2 shows what happens when the design shown earlier is resampled as a 1-bit image.

Figure 28.2
Without antialiasing, the jagged edges are much more prominent.

When a raster object is scaled in Illustrator, the number of pixels used to create the object remains constant. To fill a larger area, each pixel is increased in size. Figure 28.3 shows how this change can adversely affect an image.

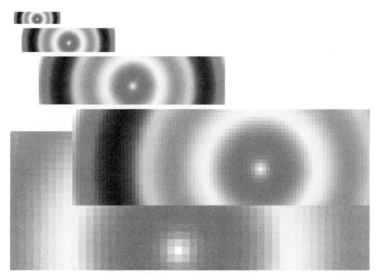

Figure 28.3
The original object is shown in the upper left. It has been scaled to 200%, 400%, 800%, and 1600%.

The original object in Figure 28.3 was created in Photoshop at a size of 100 pixels by 25 pixels. When placed in Illustrator (using the command File, Place), it retained those original pixels. In Figure 28.4, the Document Info palette shows the details.

Figure 28.4
The Document Info palette is available through the Window menu.

In comparison, look at the information for the largest of the scaled copies, shown in Figure 28.5.

Figure 28.5
A copy of the object has been scaled to 1600%.

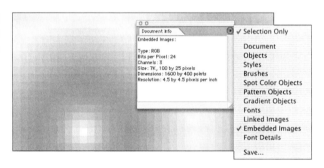

Note that the only differences between the two Document Info listings are Dimensions and Resolution. The size remains 7K, with dimensions of 100 pixels by 25 pixels. No pixels have been added to increase the object's size. The Resolution, however, has dropped from 72 pixels per inch (ppi) to 4.5 ppi.

The Raster Advantage

Despite the potential problems of jaggies with raster images, in some areas, pixels have traditionally outshone vector art. In the past, creating such effects as drop shadows and glows was time consuming and difficult in vector artwork, and often resulted in output problems as numerous gradients and blends were introduced to simulate the interaction of semi-transparent shadows and other effects. The image in Figure 28.6 would be extremely difficult to reconstruct in a program that does not support transparency.

If you wanted to create this image without transparency, the area of overlapping shadows (shown in Figure 28.7) alone would require some two dozen distinct objects.

Figure 28.6
The overlapping transparency is difficult to simulate with non-transparent vector objects.

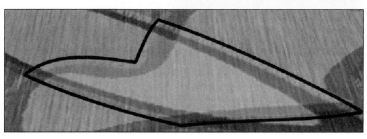

Figure 28.7
Each place where two colors overlap would become a separate object in a vector program that does not support transparency.

The Vector Edge

Vector art's primary advantage over its raster cousin is sharpness. As mentioned earlier, vector art can be scaled to any size, and the edges remain sharp and clean, unlike raster art. In Figure 28.8, the same path used earlier has been imported into Illustrator and stroked and filled. Two additional copies were made and scaled to 200% and 400%. As you can see, they have suffered no degradation in the transformations.

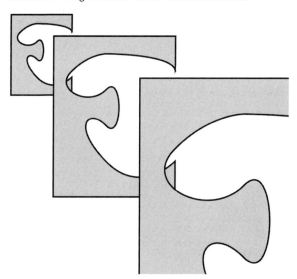

Figure 28.8
The curves are as sharp in the largest copy as they are in the original.

Photoshop's Layers, Illustrator's Objects

As you know, Photoshop works with pixels instead of objects. That doesn't mean that you can't manipulate parts of a Photoshop file independently in Illustrator. The key is understanding the relationship between Photoshop layers and Illustrator objects.

When creating an image in Photoshop, you have the option of working with multiple layers, just as you do in Illustrator. Each Photoshop layer can be treated as a separate entity in Illustrator. (Note the use of the word *entity* and not *object*.) As you'll see shortly, Illustrator enables you to retain Photoshop layers when placing a .psd file into an Illustrator document. You can then edit the contents of each layer as a separate placed raster image.

Conversely, keep layers in mind when exporting from Illustrator in Photoshop's .psd format. If each object is placed on a separate layer, later you can manipulate them individually in Photoshop. Don't overlook the power of Illustrator's Release to Layers (Sequence) command for this task!

➪ *Considering purchasing Photoshop, but not sure whether you need it? See "Catching Up, But Not Quite There" in the "Troubleshooting" section at the end of this chapter.*

MOVING ARTWORK FROM ILLUSTRATOR TO PHOTOSHOP

You can move objects and images between programs in a number of different ways. Copy and paste, drag and drop, Save, Save As, and Export are some of the techniques and commands available. Some have advantages over others. You can also insert Illustrator, EPS, and PDF files into a Photoshop document by using Photoshop's Place command. All three formats produce rasterized images with excellent fidelity to the original Illustrator file's appearance.

Saving as Illustrator, Opening in Photoshop

At its core, the modern Illustrator file format is the Portable Document Format (PDF). Figure 28.9 shows a sample file that was created in Illustrator.

Figure 28.9
The file includes type, slices, an image map, sublayers, and a compound shape.

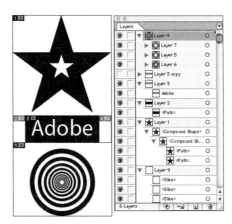

When opened in Photoshop, an Illustrator file is treated as a generic PDF document (see Figure 28.10).

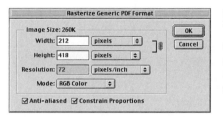

Figure 28.10
The dialog box will, by default, show you the actual size of the artwork. You can scale the image or change its resolution as you open it.

When the image is opened in Photoshop, it will consist of a single layer that contains all artwork. As you can see in Figure 28.11, transparency is maintained, but the original slices are ignored.

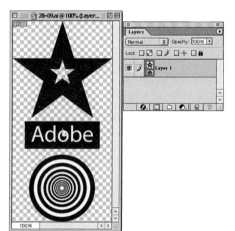

Figure 28.11
The rasterized image has a single layer.

Once in Photoshop, the file can be edited as a typical raster image.

Exporting from Illustrator in Photoshop Format

Transferring artwork from Illustrator to its sister program using the Photoshop format requires two steps. First, you must export the file, and then you must open it.

When your artwork is ready, the first step in creating a Photoshop file from Illustrator is to choose the menu command File, Export. In the dialog box, specify the Photoshop format (see Figure 28.12).

The following discussion of Illustrator/Photoshop compatibility assumes that you are working with Illustrator 10 and Photoshop 6 or later. Earlier versions of Photoshop do not support many of the compatibility features discussed here. Versions of Photoshop prior to 6 do not support, among other features, layer sets or vector type.

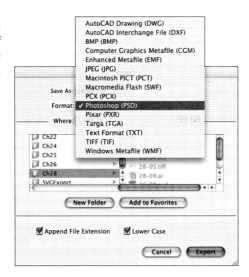

Figure 28.12
Photoshop's .psd is just one of many formats that can be exported from Illustrator.

After you've selected a name and location to go with the file format, Illustrator will present you with a series of options (see Figure 28.13).

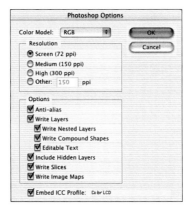

Figure 28.13
Options that are not available will be grayed out and may or may not show a check mark in the selection box.

The options in this dialog box are as follows:

- **Color Model**—RGB, CMYK, and Grayscale are offered. You are not restricted to the document's original color mode.

- **Resolution**—Higher resolution is used for print, whereas Screen is appropriate for the Web. This choice determines how many pixels the Photoshop image will contain and how big the file will be.

- **Anti-Alias**—As discussed in Chapter 18, "Raster Images and Rasterized Objects," antialiasing helps smooth the appearance of curves and text in raster artwork.

- **Write Layers**—If this option is unselected, the Photoshop file will contain a single layer. Remember that Photoshop 6 can handle a virtually unlimited number of layers, but Photoshop 5.5 and earlier are restricted to 99 layers. Three additional layer-related choices are available.

- **Write Nested Layers**—This option preserves Illustrator's sublayers as Photoshop layer sets.

- **Write Compound Shapes**—Illustrator's compound shapes, created through the Pathfinder palette, are converted to Photoshop shape layers.

- **Editable Text**—Checking this box enables you to select and alter the text in Photoshop. If it is unselected, the text is rasterized.

- **Include Hidden Layers**—This option is available only if the document contains layers whose visibility is set to hidden.

- **Write Slices**—If you have designated slices in Illustrator, that data can be included in the Photoshop file. Make sure that slices are visible (View, Show Slices) prior to exporting the document.

- **Write Image Maps**—Image maps can be saved with a .psd file for use with Adobe ImageReady.

- **Embed ICC Profile**—An embedded color profile enables Photoshop to appropriately display the image's colors. A profile can only be embedded when one is selected in the Edit, Color Settings dialog box.

The artwork shown in Figure 28.9 (which was opened in Photoshop as a PDF file in Figure 28.11) was exported to Photoshop's .psd format with all options selected. As you can see in Figure 28.14, Photoshop maintained all the relevant features.

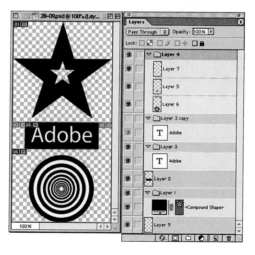

Figure 28.14
The file is shown opened in Photoshop 6.0.1.

As you can see in Photoshop's Layers palette, layers, hidden layers, editable type, and the compound shape were maintained. Notice that the type layers are now parts of layer sets. Remember that type must always be on a separate layer in Photoshop, so the Illustrator layer that contains type becomes a layer set with the set containing the type layer in Photoshop.

Editable Text from Illustrator to Photoshop

Starting with version 6.0, Photoshop has been capable of handling vector type, such as that created in Illustrator. This is considered to be among the most important improvements in recent Photoshop upgrades.

If Illustrator text is to remain editable when exported to Photoshop, it cannot share a layer with anything else. That means you cannot export text on a path as editable text (the path causes the layer to be rendered), nor can you export area type (the container also causes rendering). Applying a stroke to text also keeps it from being editable when exported. When two type objects share a layer, they're split into two separate layers automatically.

⇨ *Text on a path not editable in Photoshop? See "Paths Versus Warping" in the "Troubleshooting" section at the end of this chapter.*

When an exported .psd file with editable type is opened in Photoshop, you'll be asked to update the type (see Figure 28.15).

Figure 28.15
Opening an exported .psd file that contains editable type generates this message in Photoshop.

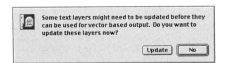

Some text layers might need to be updated before they can be used for vector based output. Do you want to update these layers now?

[Update]   [No]

If the layer is not updated, it will retain its appearance unless edited. Editing the type may result in font substitution or other changes in appearance. For that reason, it's a good idea to click the Update button in the dialog box.

Copy and Paste, Drag and Drop

When you copy a selection in Illustrator to paste into Photoshop, your actions are governed by one of the preferences. Choosing Edit, Preferences, Files & Clipboard opens the dialog box shown in Figure 28.16.

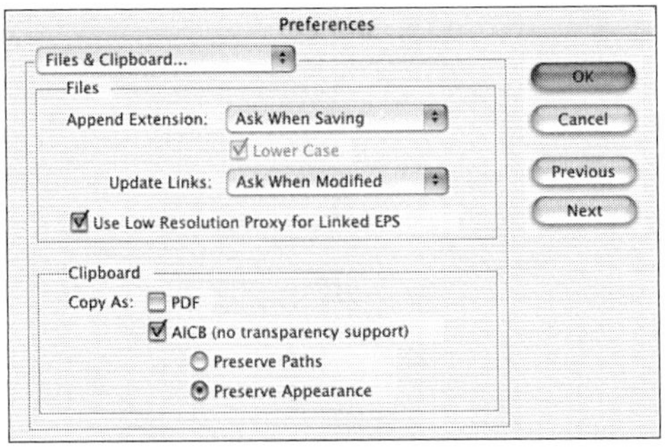

Figure 28.16
The lower half of the dialog box pertains to copying and pasting.

Preferences

Files & Clipboard...

Files
Append Extension: Ask When Saving
☑ Lower Case
Update Links: Ask When Modified
☑ Use Low Resolution Proxy for Linked EPS

Clipboard
Copy As: ☐ PDF
☑ AICB (no transparency support)
○ Preserve Paths
◉ Preserve Appearance

OK
Cancel
Previous
Next

Illustrator copies selections to the Clipboard as PICT files and, if you so choose, PDF or AICB (Adobe Illustrator Clipboard):

- **PICT**—On the Clipboard, this file format is raster only. The selection is converted to pixels and placed in memory. Most programs receive the PICT version of the selection. This version is added to the Clipboard automatically. The other options are in addition to the PICT data. When pasting into Photoshop, a new layer is created and the pixels are added to the layer.

- **PDF**—The PDF version, if available, copies a rasterized version of the selected object or objects to the clipboard. When pasted into Photoshop, the artwork will be placed on a new layer and Free Transform will be active. As you can see in Figure 28.17, the pasted artwork has an active bounding box, which can be used to resize, and when the cursor is positioned just outside the bounding box, it will show as the curved double-arrow icon that indicates that the selection can be rotated.

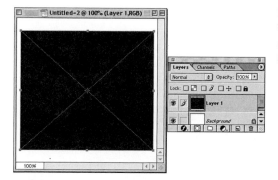

Figure 28.17
With Illustrator's PDF clipboard option active, Photoshop pastes as pixels, ready to transform.

- **AICB**—This format is best used with Photoshop. It offers you a choice of giving preference to the integrity of paths over the look of the illustration, or maintaining the appearance of the selection at the possible expense of editable paths.

Whether Preserve Paths or Preserve Appearance is selected in the preferences, how Illustrator copies is less important than how Photoshop pastes. When you have AICB selected, Photoshop offers you a choice of how to handle the data on the Clipboard (see Figure 28.18).

Figure 28.18
This dialog box appears when pasting into Photoshop with Illustrator's AICB option.

The results of the paste vary widely, depending on your selection:

- **Pixels**—Photoshop pastes a rasterized version of the artwork and activates Free Transform, just as it does when using Illustrator's PDF clipboard option.

- **Path**—As you can see in Figure 28.19, a single work path is generated. The path loses any fill or stroke from Illustrator.

- **Shape Layer**—Photoshop creates a new layer, fills it, and creates a clipping path to expose the fill in the shape of the Illustrator object (see Figure 28.20). While not equivalent to a vector object, Photoshop's shape layers can serve many of the same functions.

Figure 28.19
The Paths palette shows a single work path.

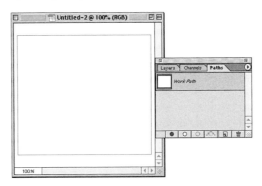

Figure 28.20
The path is selected and therefore visible, but it is unstroked.

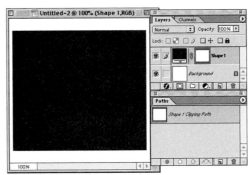

When using Illustrator's AICB clipboard option with selections with appearances more complex than a simple object, expect to paste as pixels. Pasting as a path, of course, removes all appearance characteristics. Pasting as a shape layer results in a single color.

Rasterize in Illustrator

To truly protect the appearance of a selection being copied to Photoshop, rasterize in Illustrator first. After pasting into a Photoshop document, you can return to Illustrator and use the Undo command twice (once for Copy, again for Rasterize). In Figure 28.21, the original Illustrator object is shown at the top (in Illustrator). To the lower left is the result when pasting pixels into a Photoshop document. On the right, the result when the original object is rasterized (at 72ppi) before copying.

Figure 28.21
Rasterizing first, even at low resolution, greatly improves the performance of the Clipboard with complex appearances.

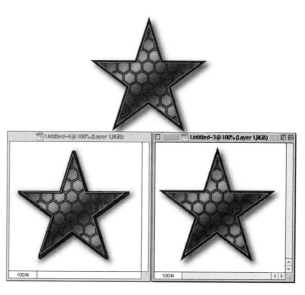

If you press Cmd [Ctrl] while dragging from Illustrator to Photoshop, paths are created, much like pasting with the Path option selected.

Alternative File Formats

Illustrator and Photoshop have a number of file formats in common. Most of them are raster formats. Exporting an Illustrator file in any such format rasterizes all data and flattens the image as well. Both TIFF and EPS do an excellent job of preserving the appearance of the Illustrator file. PDF also works well with the appearance of the file, but the entire image is rasterized, even if Preserve Illustrator Editing Capabilities is selected in the Adobe PDF Format Options dialog box.

MOVING ARTWORK FROM PHOTOSHOP TO ILLUSTRATOR

Once upon a time, bringing a Photoshop image into Illustrator simply meant using an appropriate file format to get a rectangle full of pixels in place. Occasionally, you might have needed to export paths from Photoshop to Illustrator for purposes of alignment or preparation of a trap.

Things changed, however, with the introduction of Photoshop 6. Vector type and shape layers make transferring images between the programs feasible, perhaps even attractive in a variety of situations. Illustrator's capability to maintain Photoshop layers and transparency also adds to the feasibility of moving Photoshop files into Illustrator. Photoshop's opacity masks are converted to layer masks when you open a Photoshop file in Illustrator.

The Photoshop 6 file in Figure 28.22 contains multiple layers, layer effects, several paths, and, for the highlighted layer, reduced opacity.

Figure 28.22

With transparency, layers, a hidden layer, blending modes, and vector text, this image has many features that can no longer be edited if the file is flattened.

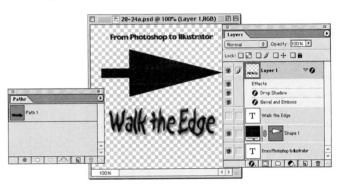

Opening Photoshop Files in Illustrator

When you choose Illustrator's menu command File, Open and select the sample file, you must decide whether to flatten the file or preserve layers, as shown in Figure 28.23.

Figure 28.23

If the Photoshop file contains image maps or slices, you also have the option of retaining them.

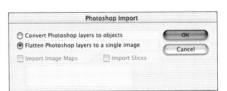

If you elect to flatten the layers of a Photoshop object, the file opens with one rasterized object on one layer, as shown in Figure 28.24.

When you elect to convert each Photoshop layer into an object, Illustrator creates a separate layer for each Photoshop layer and the contents become a single rasterized object (see Figure 28.25).

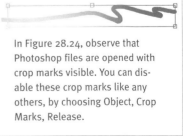

In Figure 28.24, observe that Photoshop files are opened with crop marks visible. You can disable these crop marks like any others, by choosing Object, Crop Marks, Release.

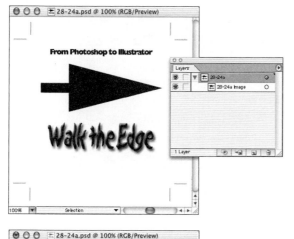

Figure 28.24
The layer and object name are taken from the file name.

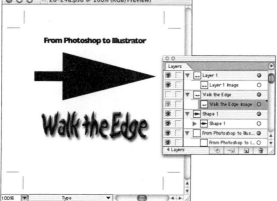

Figure 28.25
Note that the hidden layer remains hidden in Illustrator.

Copy and Paste, Drag and Drop

Using the Copy and Paste commands enables you to move image data between Photoshop and Illustrator, but transparency is lost. When you switch to Illustrator and use the Paste command, the pixels are pasted as a flattened image and transparency effects are lost. This happens regardless of whether PDF is selected in the Illustrator preferences (Edit, Preferences, Files & Clipboards).

When dragging and dropping between a Photoshop window and an Illustrator window, you also lose transparency features, but you do gain some other capabilities. Dragging from Photoshop to Illustrator, for example, enables you to transfer linked layers as a set. (Copying and pasting requires that you put each layer on the Clipboard and transfer it individually.)

Exporting Paths to Illustrator

Photoshop enables you to transfer paths to Illustrator through an export process. Choosing File, Export, Paths to Illustrator opens the dialog box shown in Figure 28.26.

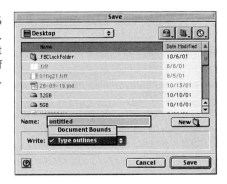

Figure 28.26
This dialog box is labeled Save. Notice that there is no file format choice, but rather a choice of paths to export.

The file is exported as an Illustrator native file (add the file extension .ai to the name) and can be opened directly in Illustrator. The paths will appear in the Layers palette, but will not be visible on the artboard unless selected, because they are unstroked and unfilled (see Figure 28.27).

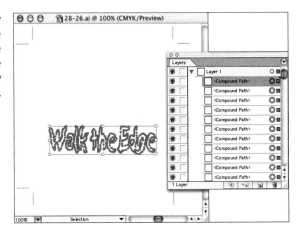

Figure 28.27
The file created when paths were exported from Photoshop can be opened in Illustrator using the File, Open command, just as any other Illustrator file.

Round-Tripping

Sometimes an image must go from Photoshop to Illustrator and then back to Photoshop. (This round-tripping is not as frequent as it was before Photoshop 6's vector type and shapes tools.) Likewise, an Illustrator file may have to go into Photoshop and then back to Illustrator. (This, too, is far less common now that Illustrator has transparency capabilities.)

In Figure 28.28, a Photoshop file has been opened in Illustrator, and a group of Illustrator objects has been added.

You can make several choices at this point:

- You can export the file back to Photoshop format. If you make this choice, the layers are rasterized.

- You can save the file as an Illustrator document. When you reopen it in Photoshop, it is opened as a generic PDF file and rasterized at the resolution and dimension you select.

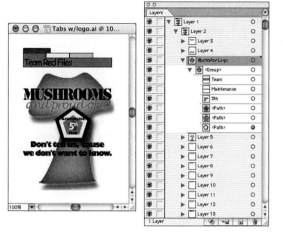

Figure 28.28
The insignia added in Illustrator is a group of vector objects and text, as seen in the Layers palette.

- You can save the file as EPS or PDF. The results are identical to those for an Illustrator file.

- You can export the file in any of a variety of raster formats, including TIFF and JPEG. The image is rasterized and saved according to the capabilities of the individual file format. In all cases, a single layer is created, and the file is flattened.

Files going from Illustrator to Photoshop and back to Illustrator follow the same basic pattern established here. Images saved in Illustrator, EPS, or PDF file formats are rasterized and layers are merged. When you export as Photoshop, the files retain their layers, but all objects are rasterized.

TROUBLESHOOTING

Catching Up, But Not Quite There

I have Illustrator 10, with its transparency capabilities, effects, filters, and Save for Web. Should I still buy Photoshop?

Your decision depends on a couple factors. As always, budget is a concern to many people. In terms of capabilities, Illustrator still has a way to go when it comes to pixel pushing. Photoshop works with some color modes and file formats that remain foreign to Illustrator, including 16-bit color and Lab mode. A substantial number of filters and third-party plug-ins can be fully exploited only in Photoshop. And remember that Photoshop has layer effects capabilities that far outstrip the Stylize effects available in Illustrator. If you don't need the advanced raster-editing capacity, only applying an occasional drop shadow or glow, pass it by. If you want the full power of the pixel in your hands, snap it up.

Paths Versus Warping

Photoshop 6 doesn't let me edit my Illustrator text on a path. Do I have any options?

Remember that text, to remain editable in Photoshop, must be alone on a separate layer. The path upon which your text sits counts as an object, so Photoshop rasterizes the layer. Photoshop itself does not support text on a path. It does, however, have text warping, as shown in Figure 28.29. Although no substitute for text on a path, the warped type remains fully editable in Photoshop.

Figure 28.29
These examples are just some of the possibilities available with the text warping capability of Photoshop 6.

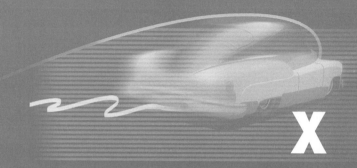

X

APPENDIXES

IN THIS PART

A   Installing Illustrator **675**

B   Illustrator Assistance and Resources **687**

C   Illustrator to Go **697**

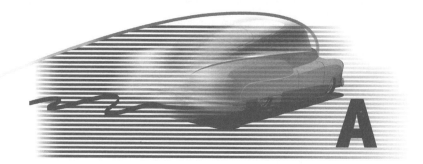

A

INSTALLING ILLUSTRATOR

IN THIS APPENDIX

Illustrator's Easy Installation Process **676**

The Custom Installation Procedure—Basic Files **679**

Macintosh Custom Installation—Additional Files **681**

Windows Custom Installation—Additional Files **683**

What Can Be Skipped? **684**

What Can Be Deleted After Installation? **685**

ILLUSTRATOR'S EASY INSTALLATION PROCESS

Illustrator 10 comes on a single CD with documentation. The program must be decompressed from the CD onto a hard drive to run. The installation process can be very simple, although doing a custom installation requires some planning. Understanding the options and using the custom installation option can save hard disk space, reduce the amount of time required to load and start Illustrator, and streamline the work process. In addition, a custom installation may be required when limited hard drive space is available. (A typical Easy Install requires some 180MB of hard drive space.)

The Easy Install option for the Macintosh is comparable to accepting the installation default settings in Windows. In both cases, the program decides what is required for Illustrator and for you. You are, however, given an option of where to install the program.

Administrator Accounts

Windows XP, Windows 2000, and Windows NT may require you to log in as an Administrator to install software.

Mac OS X also requires that an administrator account be in use before changes can be made to the Applications folder (see Figure A.1).

Figure A.1
Without an appropriate account being active—and a password— you cannot install software under Mac OS X.

Preparing for Installation

To prepare for installation, first quit all other programs. If you have virus-detection software running (which is, of course, recommended), you need to disable it. If you regularly defragment your hard drive, fine. If not, this is a good time to start. Numerous utilities are available to consolidate the information on your drives, which enables the system and the various programs to run more smoothly and less problematically.

Installing Illustrator the Easy Way: Macintosh

Mac OS X users need install Illustrator only once to be able to use the program in both OS X and in the Classic mode. To install Illustrator on the Macintosh, follow these steps:

1. Insert the Illustrator CD into the appropriate drive. Open the Illustrator CD icon by double-clicking it (if it isn't open already) and double-click the Installer icon.

2. The first screen shows the Illustrator logo and a Continue button.

3. The second screen presents you with the software End User License Agreement (EULA). You are encouraged to read the agreement in its entirety. In addition, see the sidebar "Adobe's Licensing Agreement."

4. After accepting the licensing agreement, you'll choose between an Easy Install and a Custom Install (see Figure A.2). You also have the opportunity to modify where the program will be installed.

5. You need to enter registration information in the next screen, including the serial number supplied with the software.

6. You must confirm the registration information before continuing. (This process does not constitute registration. The product isn't registered until you send the information to Adobe, whether electronically or on paper.)

7. After you confirm the registration information, the actual installation process begins. Following installation, you should restart your computer prior to using Illustrator.

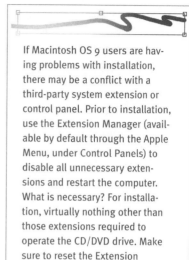

If Macintosh OS 9 users are having problems with installation, there may be a conflict with a third-party system extension or control panel. Prior to installation, use the Extension Manager (available by default through the Apple Menu, under Control Panels) to disable all unnecessary extensions and restart the computer. What is necessary? For installation, virtually nothing other than those extensions required to operate the CD/DVD drive. Make sure to reset the Extension Manager after installation and prior to restarting.

Figure A.2
Custom installation is discussed later in this appendix.

Installing Illustrator the Easy Way: Windows (Generally)

To install Illustrator in Windows, follow these steps:

1. Insert the Illustrator CD into the appropriate drive. Use the Start menu and the Run command. If Setup.exe is not showing, browse to that file on the Illustrator CD.

2. After the InstallShield Wizard runs, and you approve the installation, you'll be advised to shut down all Adobe products so that you don't have to restart your computer.

with the effect? If a command is grayed out (unavailable in the menu), the targeted object might not be suitable (or no target may be designated).

Such questions and evaluation often lead to simple solutions. However, if all the answers indicate that everything should, in fact, be working as planned, Illustrator's Preferences file may have become corrupted. The sidebar "The Fresh Prefs Fix" discusses a possible remedy.

WHERE TO GO FOR HELP

Several resources are available to help solve Illustrator problems. The primary tools are discussed in the following sections.

Special Edition Using Adobe Illustrator 10

This book offers a great deal of information, most of which can be valuable in times of crisis. The extensive and comprehensive index at the end of the volume can lead you to the information you require.

Most of the chapters have "Troubleshooting" sections. These discussions address specific problems pertinent to the chapter's subject.

The Illustrator User Guide

Although better suited to training than troubleshooting, the User Guide does have substantial information on a variety of subjects. Again, as with this volume, the index can help narrow the search.

Illustrator's Help PDF

Illustrator 10 has an additional help document in PDF format. This is more than just an electronic version of the User Guide or a PDF version of Illustrator Help.

Illustrator's Help Menu

As you can see in Figure B.1, the Help menu offers far more than just Illustrator Help.

Figure B.1
The Macintosh and Windows Help menus. For Macintosh, About Illustrator and About Plug-ins are found under the Apple Menu (OS 9) or under the Illustrator menu (OS X).

The primary resource under the Help menu in Illustrator is Illustrator Help. (The Internet-based options will be discussed later.) Illustrator Help offers an index and the capability to search for a specific word or term (see Figure B.2). Help requires an Internet browser (version 4 or higher of Netscape Navigator or Microsoft Internet Explorer) but does not require an Internet connection for basic Help services.

Figure B.2
Illustrator Help offers three
ways to access information:
Contents (Help Topics), Index,
and Search. The question mark
on the left opens the help for
Help ("How to use Help").

- **Contents**—A series of general topics appears in the left frame. When you click a topic, it displays its links in the right frame.

- **Index**—An alphabetical listing of all Help topics appears when you click a letter. Click the number listed next to a topic, and the link appears to the right.

- **Search**—This option opens a field into which you can enter a word or term to search. The results appear by subject below, and content is shown in the right frame.

Internet-Based Help Options

The Help menu offers Internet access to several Adobe- and Illustrator-related Web sites. (A working Internet connection and browser are, of course, required.) Of primary interest for this discussion are those resources devoted to Illustrator.

- **Tips & Techniques**—This area of the Adobe Web site is updated regularly. It contains information and tutorials on various aspects of Illustrator. Typically, several tutorials are available, with various subject areas. You can find articles on prepress and the Web, as well as illustration and production.

- **Online Services**—This opens a page filled with links to a variety of services provided by Adobe and other companies. In addition, several online tools are available.

- **Plug-ins**—Adobe has teamed with third-party developers to make various plug-ins available through this page.

Adobe Online

You can access Adobe Online resources by clicking the image at the top of the Illustrator Toolbox or through the Help menu. Adobe Online provides product-specific access to the Adobe Web site, taking you directly to (in this case) Illustrator-related pages.

Adobe Online can be set to check automatically for updates to Illustrator or for itself. The frequency can be set in the initial Adobe Online dialog box or in the Illustrator preferences. While there is a convenience factor in having Adobe Online automatically search the Adobe Web site, setting the preference to Never is more practical for most users, preventing the program from accessing the Internet without your knowledge.

The Adobe Support Web Site

Available free of charge at `www.adobe.com/support`, the Adobe Support Web site is an Adobe-wide resource. Rather than the Illustrator-specific area opened through the link in Adobe Online, this Web address includes assistance for all Adobe products. The major areas include the following:

- **Top Issues**—Easily accessed and tailored for your needs, this pop-up menu enables you to select Illustrator and go directly to a collection of technical documents. Those tech docs contain the latest and most commonly requested technical information.

- **Adobe Support Marketplace**—This links to the ePeople online technical support service. It is a fee-based system, with competitive bidding for specific assistance requests. Adobe actively encourages Adobe Certified Experts and Adobe Certified Training Providers to participate.

- **User to User Forums**—These bulletin board–style services allow users of various Adobe products to exchange information and opinions and to help each other with problems. (Be forewarned, however, that not all the advice offered is truly helpful. This tool is best used after you have become familiar with the individuals who post regularly.) In addition to Adobe's own staffers, you can find a number of top experts and authors visiting the U2U Forums. (You can find more information on using the forums later in this appendix.)

- **Technical Announcements via E-mail**—These updates arrive regularly in your e-mail Inbox, listing the most recent information available. Links are given for downloading the tech docs.

- **Search the Support Knowledgebase**—The Support Knowledgebase is perhaps the most valuable of the resources; every Adobe technical document and article is included and available. This is the support database used by Adobe's own Technical Assistance teams. (You can find tips on how to find what you're looking for in the next section.)

- **Technical Guides**—These guides are highly informative background articles on major issues. They are grouped into categories by product.

- **Tutorials**—This link leads to some very interesting How To articles. The main page includes the various categories (by product), and you can find a link to the Illustrator-specific tutorials. (You can also reach them through the Tips button of Adobe Online.)

TIPS FOR SEARCHING AND ASKING

Using the Adobe Support Knowledgebase can be a rewarding or a frustrating experience. Likewise, accessing the User to user Forums can produce gold or dross. Here are some tips.

Searching the Support Knowledgebase

You can use several techniques to search the Adobe Support Knowledgebase so that you can find your answer quickly and efficiently:

* Make your first attempt as specific as possible. Include several keywords to narrow the search. If you don't get any hits or the documents returned do not answer the question, drop one or more of the keywords and try again.

* Use the terminology that Adobe uses. For example, search for *overprint* rather than *over-print*. Check the index at the back of the User Guide.

* The search engine is sensitive to case in a flexible way. If you capitalize a word, the search engine returns only documents in which the word is capitalized. If you use a lowercase letter, it returns both upper- and lowercase versions.

* Use the plus symbol before words that must be contained in the document. Also, use this symbol when entering multiple words. The symbol should appear immediately before the word:

    +Illustrator +install

    This example will return all documents that contain both the word *Illustrator* and the word *install*.

* Use the minus symbol before words to be excluded from the search:

    +Illustrator +install -SVG

    This example will return all documents involving Illustrator and installation except those involving the installation of the SVG Viewer.

* Use quotation marks for phrases:

    +Illustrator +error +"The file cannot be found."

    This capability is especially helpful when you're searching after receiving an error message.

* Use an asterisk as a wildcard, substituting for one or more letters. Such a search returns all variations of a word:

    +Illustrator +install*

    This example will find all documents containing the word *Illustrator* and the words *install*, *installation*, *installed*, *installer*, *installing*, *installment*, and *installs*.

Using the User to User Forum

The User to User Forums are separated by product and by platform. You can go to separate forums for Illustrator (Mac) and Illustrator (Windows). Unless you have a platform-specific problem ("I keep getting a .dll error message"), it often pays to check both forums.

Before you gain access to the forum of your choice, Adobe requires that you register. After you've registered, you have access to the forum and can read and post messages, and start new discussions, too.

Always check to see whether a discussion on the subject is underway before you open a new topic. When you click a subject, all the messages in the discussion are shown in the order specified by your preferences.

There can be far more to the user forums than problem solving and technique swapping, too. Using these forums is an excellent way to get your opinions heard by Adobe. You can say what you like and don't like about Illustrator, as well as what features you'd like to see in the future. Professionalism is preferred.

When you're trying to solve a problem with the assistance of others on the User to User Forum, be aware of the credentials of the person offering assistance. Adobe's programmers often monitor and contribute to discussions. However, other individuals posting messages may not have the same level of expertise and experience. Clicking the poster's name opens a link that shows the personal information that the individual entered in the preferences section. Reading through pertinent discussions can give you an indication of someone's background and experience. Be sure to back up files before trying solutions presented on the forums. Always work on a copy of the file. In addition, be very careful when making changes at the program or system level.

Of course, feel free to assist others while you're visiting the Forum. Perhaps you have encountered and solved a problem being experienced by another Illustrator user. Maybe you've developed a neat trick that deserves to be shared. The forum can be an excellent place to "exchange recipes" as well as to seek and offer assistance.

THE ADOBE EXPERT CENTER

The Expert Centers (one for each major Adobe product) require registration and login. Once registered and logged in, you'll have access to a collection of tips and tutorials, support, links, and more.

Updated frequently, you'll find downloadable "goodies," such as banners, brushes, styles, and templates. There are quick links to the latest updates and plug-ins, as well as links to the Adobe support resources discussed earlier in this appendix.

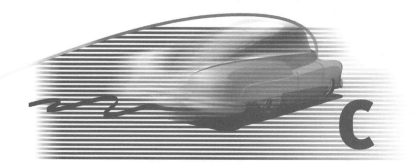

ILLUSTRATOR TO GO

IN THIS APPENDIX

Taking Illustrator with You   **698**

Preparing an Image for the Client's Computer   **699**

Separations and Proofing   **700**

Press Check Checklist   **703**

Web Animation Checklist   **703**

TAKING ILLUSTRATOR WITH YOU

Sometimes you need to be mobile. You need to work on the road, stop by the print shop or service bureau, visit a client, or perhaps try to finish that one last project while traveling to your vacation spot. If you're on the go, you'll find this appendix handy in various situations.

You might need to take Adobe Illustrator with you away from the office sometimes. Whether you own a portable computer or borrow one, you need to keep several points in mind.

Legalities

The document governing the installation of Illustrator on multiple computers is the End User License Agreement (EULA). In the case of individually owned copies of the program, you accepted the terms of the agreement when you installed Illustrator. If you are an employee of a company that purchased Illustrator, you are obligated to ensure that the company is not in violation of the agreement. The EULA is, by default, installed with the software on the hard drive. Section 2 is the applicable part of the agreement. You should make sure that you do not install multiple copies of a single-license program, except as allowed by the agreement.

Preparing a Portable

Assuming you are in compliance with the EULA, you should make sure that a laptop or other additional computer is capable of functioning comparably to your office machine. You might consider the following questions:

- **Are all required fonts installed?** If you move a file from one computer to another, you should make sure that either the document's fonts are present on the second machine or that they are embedded in the document itself.

  The difference is this: Fonts embedded in a document are available to that document only, and only to the extent that they are subsetted. (Subsetting includes only a partial set of characters from the font.) Fonts installed on a computer are available to all current documents and those yet to be created.

- **Are linked images available?** Whether you're taking a laptop on the road to finish some work or to meet with a client, you'll have a hard time accomplishing your goals if linked files are not available. Any time you transfer a document containing linked files to another computer or disk, you must include copies of the linked images. Open the Document Info palette (by choosing Window, Document Info) and select Linked Images from its menu to see a list of the files you'll need to collect (see Figure C.1). Make sure that Selection Only is *not* checked.

- **Is color being converted?** If you have a calibrated CRT monitor on your desk, it and your laptop certainly use different RGB settings. (If your desktop monitor is an LCD, it's still likely that the two screens have different profiles.) In the Color Settings dialog box, under Color Management Policies, you should probably set RGB to Convert to Working Space. This setting preserves the appearance of colors, despite the differences in displays.

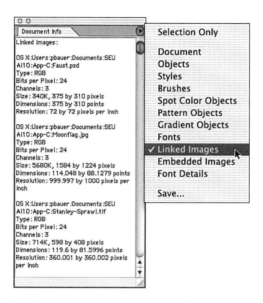

Figure C.1
The Document Info palette lists all linked images.

- **Are you showing your work the best way?** If you plan to show your work on the laptop, let the work be shown without distractions. Clean up the workplace with a couple keystrokes. Press Tab to hide all the palettes. Press F twice to hide the menu bars. Press Cmd+1 [Ctrl+1] to show the image at Actual Size. (If the illustration doesn't fit, press Cmd+zero [Ctrl+zero] for Fit in Window.)

PREPARING AN IMAGE FOR THE CLIENT'S COMPUTER

When you need to take (or send) Illustrator documents to a client, it's likely that you won't have Adobe Illustrator available to open the files. While Adobe Acrobat Reader can open Illustrator format files, it's best to prepare a copy of the file appropriately before you pop it into your briefcase or hand it off to the delivery service. (If you want to send a file in .ai format, make a copy and flatten the artwork first.) You can choose from a number of available file formats:

- Under most circumstances, you can save a copy of your document as a PDF file. Virtually all computers now have Adobe Acrobat Reader available, and the format is multiplatform. In Illustrator, you choose File, Save As and then select Adobe PDF (PDF) for the Format. Name the file, pick a location, click OK, and the Adobe PDF Format Options dialog box opens (see Figure C.2).

  If your intent is to enable the client to see the image and print a working copy, you can start with Screen Optimized. If the client needs to print a high-quality version of the document, begin with Default. You are not likely to need to preserve Illustrator editing capabilities, but embedding fonts (and subsetting them) is usually a good idea. Check Embed ICC Profile, and the Options Set changes to Custom. Leave all other settings as either their Screen Optimized or Default settings.

Figure C.2
This dialog box offers two panels: General and Compression. You usually don't need to change the compression settings.

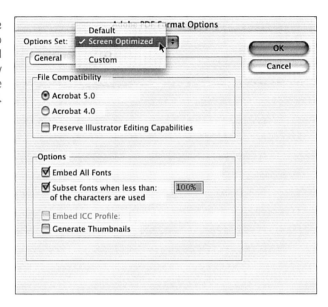

- When you're preparing images that will eventually be viewed on the Web, use the appropriate Web format for still images. (Animation will be discussed in the section "Web Animation Checklist," later in this appendix.) Photographic images and illustrations that contain gradients or blends should be saved as JPEG files. Use the highest quality setting to preserve the image's appearance as much as possible. (Remember to retain the original file for later edits or updating.) Documents that consist solely of large areas of solid color, such as cartoons and many logos, should be saved as GIFs.

- Both Macintosh and Windows computers have built-in capabilities for viewing graphics. The Macintosh PictureViewer supports the file formats TIFF, BMP, and PICT, among others. On Windows computers, the Accessories may include both Imaging (which opens TIFF, BMP, JPEG, GIF, and a variety of other file formats) and Paint (which is best with BMP files). Check with your client to find out what programs are available, and you might want to ask whether the client has a preferred image format.

If color is to be evaluated, ensure that your client is using a properly calibrated monitor.

SEPARATIONS AND PROOFING

Despite the increased number of direct-to-plate printing operations, separations are still a vital step in most press work today. When separations won't output to an imagesetter, you can check several things.

All jobs should be *proofed* in one or more ways and often multiple times. These reviews are an important quality control step in preparing a job for print. (See Chapter 24, "Commercial Printing and Trapping Issues.") You may be doing your proofing at a service bureau or print shop, or you may be proofing with a client at the client's office. It's important that you understand what kinds of proofs you're using and what to look for during the review.

Separation Problem Solving

When the imagesetter can't handle a file, you can check several likely culprits:

- **Complex paths**—If the illustration contains extremely long or complicated paths, the imagesetter may not have enough memory to handle the job. You have several options. Choosing Object, Path, Simplify reduces the number of anchor points, often substantially and with no apparent change in the path. The Printing & Export panel of the Document Setup dialog box offers the option to split long paths. Rasterizing an object eliminates the problem of complex paths. In the Output field of the Attributes palette, you can specify a lower resolution for objects.

- **Gradients and blends**—The subtle transitions between colors can also be overwhelming for imagesetters. Rasterization is the best way to handle problem gradients and blends.

- **Spot colors**—If the imagesetter is not producing individual separations for the spot colors, choose File, Separation Setup. Make sure that the Convert to Process box is not checked, and make sure that, in the list of separations, the printer icon appears next to the spot color's name. If the four-color icon is visible, the spot color is being converted to process colors. If the column is blank, the separation is not being printed.

Types of Color Proofs

Examining the color proofs prior to approving a job for print can take various forms. Remember that the quality of your decisions depends to a large degree on the quality of the proofs that you are reviewing.

- **Soft proofing**—This type of proofing relies on onscreen images. The monitor must be calibrated properly, and appropriate color settings must be used.

- **Digital proofs**—These proofs are produced by high-end inkjet printers. The printer must be appropriately calibrated to the press on which the print job will be run. You might want to request that your printer, if applicable, show you the proofs of and actual prints from previous jobs to assure you that the proofs can accurately predict the press's color.

- **Laminate proofs**—Using the actual films from which the job will be run (assuming no changes are necessary), laminate proofs have a layer of each color applied. The cyan separation is placed over a sheet of paper, and they are exposed. Areas where there should be no cyan ink are either washed or peeled away. The other separations are, in turn, also overlaid on the paper, exposed, and washed or peeled. At the end of the process, four layers of color have been applied to the paper, which can then be laminated for protection and to simulate coated or uncoated paper. These proofs are the most common and usually considered to be highly accurate.

- **Wet proofs**—Actual printing plates are made, and a small printing press produces actual copies of the output. The printing press is set up to duplicate the output of the large presses on which the job will be run. The actual paper to be used for the press run can be used. While extremely accurate, wet proofs are also extremely expensive.

- **Contract proofs**—No matter which method was used to produce them, the contract proofs are the ones that received final approval.

- **Press check**—This stage is the last possible opportunity to correct color problems. It is done at the printer, with the job on the machine. The presses are warmed up, some paper is run through, and when everything seems right, some pages are printed. This is it. The actual printed material. See the "Press Check Checklist" for details.

Color Page Proofs

When you're reviewing samples for approval, the following are some of the things to look for (be sure to use a loupe or a magnifying glass):

- **Color accuracy**—Do the colors of the proofs match the originals? Load up your briefcase with some of the original images and compare them directly to the proofs. Is the color consistent from page to page? If the separations were created at different times, using different methods or settings, or on different machines, variations can result.

- **Color registration**—If slight shadowing of colors is visible, or if one color sticks out from the others, check the registration marks. If the proof was not properly prepared, request another. If the registration is correct and yet the colors are not aligned properly, the problem may be worse.

- **Color blocks**—Areas of solid color must be smooth, not irregular.

- **Gradients and blends**—Transitions between colors should be smooth and regular, not banded or blotchy.

- **Highlights**—The light areas of the proof should still have dots. If, for example, a white shirt or blouse has no color at all, it will be "blown out" on the page, appearing as blindingly white (depending on paper color, of course). The exception may be *specular highlights*, which are those areas of reflection that carry no color at all.

- **Shadows**—When using the loupe, you should be able to see a dot structure in all areas of an image. Even the deepest shadows should not be solid black. In illustrations that do contain areas of solid black (such as logos), look for uniformity.

- **Detail**—Tiny text should be crisp and clean. Images incorporated into the document must have good detail.

- **Trapping**—Examine closely areas where two colors abut. With trapping, a slight overlap should be apparent. (Checking trapping might be easier using properly registered separations on a light table.)

- **Overprinting**—In areas where black should overprint, the colors beneath should not show through. (Do not confuse poor overprinting and *rich black*. Rich black is created by adding cyan, magenta, and/or yellow inks to 100% black ink. Poor overprinting allows you to see the shapes of the images beneath the black.)

- **Bleeds**—If a colored element is to extend to the edge of the printed page, it should extend beyond the crop marks.

- **Crossover**—An image or illustration that extends across two pages must be properly aligned. Align the two page proofs to check. Also, look for bleeds. Normally, both pages have bleeds to the inside.

- **Page order and numbering**—You should review each page proof in order, and they should be in order. Check that no pages have been accidentally skipped.

As you review the proofs, mark any and all errors. Circle the areas in question and write short, specific comments. All requests for correction should be noted on the proofs and these proofs saved for comparison to the corrected versions. When you're checking the new proofs, first check to make sure that the requested corrections were actually done; then start over and look at the new proofs as closely as you did the initial proofs. Make sure that new errors were not introduced when the old ones were fixed.

PRESS CHECK CHECKLIST

At the press check, it's too late to discover typographical errors or decide to change a layout. This round of proofing is the absolute end. The plates are on the machine; the job is about to roll. Remember to take the contract proof with you for side-by-side comparison. Here's what you should be checking:

- **Misregistration**—Look at the registration marks to make sure that each ink is being placed in perfect alignment with the others.

- **Bleedthrough**—Too much ink saturates the paper and shows on the other side.

- **Blurring**—Two possible causes for blurring are paper shifting as it runs through the press and low ink viscosity. The former produces a smeared look; the latter produces irregular halftone dots, creating an out-of-focus appearance.

- **Crossovers**—Make sure the two pages align perfectly.

- **Spotting**—Dirt, clumps of ink, and scraps of paper on the plates can also produce spots (called *hickeys*) on the page.

As you do with page proofs, you should circle problems. Talk with the printer or press operator, and ask questions if you have them. The printer wants you to be a happy (and repeat) customer.

WEB ANIMATION CHECKLIST

Just as prepress work has proofing, so should Web production. The work needs to be checked and double-checked, and final client approval is one of the goals. The best way to proof images created for the Web is to do so on the Web. The best type of check is incorporating the images into the pages for which they were designed and posting those pages. Put the pages on the same server from which they will be downloaded, if possible, perhaps password-protecting the area to restrict access.

You can, of course, preview images and animations before posting them to a Web server. You can show them to a client on your computer or on the client's machine. In either case, the following are some ideas to consider:

- **Is the Web browser capable?** Whether you're using Flash or SVG, make sure that the computer you use has a browser that can handle that form of animation or that it is equipped with the appropriate plug-in. If possible, do a test run in advance—well enough in advance that you have time to execute your backup plan. (You do have a backup plan, right?) Remember that Microsoft Internet Explorer for Macintosh, versions 4 and 5, requires the SVG plug-in. The plug-in is distributed freely, and you can download the latest version from Adobe's Web site. You can find Windows and Macintosh, Internet Explorer and Netscape Navigator versions, together at

  http://www.adobe.com/svg/viewer/install/main.html

  Download all the installers and burn them onto a CD to tuck into your briefcase.

- **Is the monitor calibrated?** For your work to look its best, you should view it on a monitor that will display the colors as you intended them to be seen. Granted, the vast majority of Web visitors have uncalibrated monitors, but you should show your work at its best.

- **Are the raster images and fonts embedded?** Remember to save your SVG creations with the option Embed Raster Images before you take them on the road. If you use the option Link to Raster Images, they'll be left behind on your hard drive. Likewise, embed the fonts that you used.

- **Size equals speed.** Remember that the playback rate of a Flash animation is tied directly to the video card and VRAM of the computer on which the animation is shown. Make sure that the computer to be used has enough horsepower. That old pre-Pentium laptop in the closet may not be the right tool for showing off animation.

INDEX

Numbers

8-bit
colors, 284, 499-500
PNG (Portable Network Graphic), 505
RGB (Red, Green, Blue), color, 479

8.3 naming system, 43

16-bit color, 500

24-bit
color, 499-500
PNG (Portable Network Graphic), 505
RGB (Red, Green, Blue), color, 479

48-bit color, 500

64-bit color, 500

72ppi (pixels per inch), 143

A

About Adobe SVG Viewer command (SVG Viewer), 556

Absolute Colorimetric color profile, 586

accessing
blends, 213
brush patterns, 308
commands, 26
Swatch Libraries, 294
tables, color tables, 516
tools, 32-33

accuracy, colors, 702

Acrobat Reader, PDF, 262

Acrobat, Adobe Acrobat, 46

Action Options command (Actions palette menu), 629

actions, 33, 359, 626

Actions
assigning, 632
Button Mode, 629
combining, 640
commands, nonrecordable, 634-635
copying, 630, 640
customizing, 629
deleting, 640
editing, 640-641
error messages, 632
Export commands, overriding, 632
folders, batch processing, 626
grouping, 629
identifying, 629
loading, 629
managing, 626-629
modal
control, 628, 639
dialog boxes, 629
moving, 640
naming, 640
nesting, 630
opening, 642
paths, 635-636
pausing, 638-639
playing, 629-630
recording, 632-634
Save commands, overriding, 631

sets, 628
saving, 641-642
selecting, 631
sharing, 641-642
steps, 628
stops, adding, 638
storing, 628
Style/Brush/Swatch Cleanup, 627
tools, nonrecordable, 634
troubleshooting, 642

Actions palette, menu commands, 626-628
Action Options, 629
Batch, 630-632
Insert Menu Item, 634
Insert Select Path, 634-635
Insert Stop, 638
New Action, 632
New Set, 632
Playback Options, 630
Save Actions, 641
Select Object, 634-637
Stop Recording, 633

Actual Size command (View menu), 28-29

Add Anchor Point tool, 69, 361

Add Eyedropper Color icon, 511

Add New Fill command (Appearance palette menu), 330, 343

Add New Stroke command (Appearances palette menu), 330

adding
anchor points, 69-70, 191
brushes, 131, 330
colors, Swatches palette, 292-293
flares, images, 92
graphs, 112-113
objects to clipping masks, 377
paths, 68-70
stops, 339-340, 368
style libraries, documents, 335
symbol instances, 486

additive color, 257, 276-279

Adobe
Acrobat, thumbnails, 46
Expert Center, 695
file formats, 262
Illustrator folder, 127
Illustrator Startup_CYMK, 371
Illustrator. *See* Illustrator
licensing agreement, 678
LiveMotion, 535-537
Online, 683-684, 693
PDF Format Options dialog box, 46
Photoshop. *See* Photoshop
Portable Document Format. *See* PDF
Premiere, file formats, 262
products, compatibility, 21
Reader, 46
Support Knowledgebase, search tips, 694-695
Support Web site, 693
Tech Support (searchable database), 694
Type Manager (ATM), multiple master fonts, 162
Version Checker, downloading, 46
Web site, 55, 678

Advanced button, 47

agreements, licensing agreement (Adobe), 678

.ai, Compatibility option or file format, 45

AICB files, 665

aligning
anchor points, 216
artwork, 364
objects, 35
printing plates, 584

alignment
paragraphs, 147
printing, 573-574
text, 36, 140

Alignment box, 149

All Documents (Replace dialog box), 609

All Glyphs (SVG Font Subsetting), 564

All Readable Documents (Replace dialog box), 609

Allow Continue check box, 638

Alpha information (transparencies), 510

anchor points, 33
adding, 69-70, 191
aligning, 216
brush paths, 123
clipping masks, editing, 377
combination points, 65
control points, 65
converting, 69, 73
corner, 65-67
creating, 65
deleting, 69
direction lines, 65
managing, 63-64, 70-71
paths, 61-67, 349
redundant, 109
selecting, 70, 74, 101
shearing, 187
smooth, 65
spines, editing, 226

structure, 65-67
types, 64

angle, artboard (rotating), 360

Angle
field gradients, 339
value, 130

angled corners, 313-315

angles
brushes, 130
objects, 187
paths, 208
rotations, 183

Angles (Smart Guides dialog box), 365

animated GIFs, 535

animations
backgrounds, 544
complex, creating, 220
creating, 540
cumulative, 536
distortion, 547
elements, oversized, 551
file formats, Web images, 482
Flash, 482, 538-543
flickers, troubleshooting, 541
frame-based, 536
frames, 535
images, static, 541
managing, 543
noncumulative, 536
online, 534-536
previewing, 553
reproportioning, 544
resizing, 544, 548-551
screen resolution, 546
size, determining, 545, 548
SVG, 560-564
SWF, exporting to, 552-554
typewriter effects (cumulative animations), 250, 536

video, 536
Web, checklist, 703-704

Animation Elements (SVG), 560

annotations, Attributes palette, 637

Anti-Alias option (Illustrator), 662

Anti-aliased Artwork check box, 361

antialiasing, 507
  artwork, 361
  curves, 202
  images, 657
  JPEG, 504
  pixel edges, softening, 401
  rasterized objects, 401-403
  resolution, 402
  type objects, 15
  Web, 14-15

Appearance palette, menu commands, 324-328, 338
  Add New Fill, 330, 343
  Add New Stroke, 330
  Clear Appearance, 331
  Duplicate Item, 331
  Layer/Group Overrides Color, 331
  New Art Has Basic Appearance, 331
  Reduce to Basic Appearance, 331
  Remove Item, 331
  Replace (Style), 334

appearances
  applying, 331-333
  attributes, layers, 232
  brushes, adding, 330
  characteristics, 324
  copying, 327, 331
  deleting, 331
  troubleshooting, 335-336
  versus attributes, 33
  work area, customizing, 29-31

Append Extension (Files & Clipboard dialog box), 367

Apply button, 113

Apply Last Filter command (Filter menu), 434

applying
  animation, SVG, 560-561
  appearances, 331-333
  artwork, graphs, 116
  blur (images), 521
  brushes, 125-126, 248
  color, 248, 290-291
  effects, 249, 252
  filters, 249, 252
  gradients, 249, 342-343
  Object menu commands, targeting, 249
  patterns, targeting, 249
  registration colors, 584
  strokes, targeting, 248
  styles, 248, 333
  SVG filters, 558
  transformations, 174
  transparency, targeting, 248
  warps, 196

Arc Segment Tool Options dialog box, 90

Arc tool, 17, 89

arcs
  lengths or widths, 90
  point of origin, 90
  rectangles, 86

Area Select check box, 361

area type (text), 37

Area Type tool, 140

Arrange command (Object menu), 155

Arrange, Bring to Back (Object menu), 233

Arrange, Bring to Forward (Object menu), 233

Arrange, Bring to Front (Object menu), 233

Arrange, Send Backward (Object menu), 233

Arrange, Send Backward command (Object menu), 189

arrow keys, 360

art
  brushes, 120
  modifying, 122, 127, 131-133
  vector, 60-61, 535

Art Brush Options dialog box, 131

artboard, 24, 27
  angle, rotating, 360
  graphs, adding, 112
  size, 26
  versus page tiling, 31-32

artifacts, 503, 521

Artistic, Colored Pencil command (Filter menu), 447

Artistic, Cutout command (Filter menu), 448

Artistic, Dry Brush command (Filter menu), 448

Artistic, Film Grain command (Filter menu), 448

Artistic, Fresco command (Filter menu), 449

Artistic, Neon Glow command (Filter menu), 449

Artistic, Paint Daubs command (Filter menu), 450

Artistic, Palette Knife command (Filter menu), 450

Artistic, Plastic Wrap command (Filter menu), 450

Artistic, Poster Edges command (Filter menu), 451

Artistic, Rough Pastels command (Filter menu), 451

Artistic, Smudge Stick command (Filter menu), 452

Artistic, Sponge command (Filter menu), 452

Artistic, Underpainting command (Filter menu), 453

Artistic, Watercolor command (Filter menu), 453

artwork. *See also* symbols
  aligning, 364
  antialiasing, 361
  applying, graphs, 116
  arranging, 239
  brushes, creating or modifying, 127
  designated color, 129
  key color, 129
  layers, 32
  modifying, brushes, 127
  placement, 27
  positioning, 364
  previewing, 29
  printing, preparation, 586
  restricting, 374
  smoothing, 361

aspect ratio, film recorders, 269

ATM (Adobe Type Manager), multiple master fonts, 162

attributes
  appearances, layers, 232
  copying, 248
  dragging, 248
  targeting, 247
  transfering, 248
  type, copying, 159-160
  versus appearance, 33

Attributes palette, 587, 594, 637

auto slices, 494

Auto Trace Tolerance (Auto Trace tool), 80

Auto Trace Tolerance check box, 363

Auto Trace tool, 80-81, 363

Auto-Create Symbols (SWF), 552

AutoCAD, file formats, 262

AutoCAD Drawing, 49

AutoCAD Interchange File, 49

Automatic, PDF option, 264

B

B mode, 288

Background panel, 528

backgrounds
  animations, 544
  colors, PowerPoint, 266-267
  rasterized objects, 400

backward compatibility, 690

banding
  color, 38
  controlling, 501
  rasterizing, 402

bars
  color, shortcut buttons or sliders, 287
  status bar, 24-26

base
  16 system, 289
  color, 415

base-16 notations, 479

baseline
  shifts, 147, 362
  text, 37
  type, 163

Baseline format method (JPEG), 504

Baseline Optimized format method (JPEG), 504

Basic Creation tools, functions, 85

basic interface (Illustrator), 24

Basic Object Creation tools, 85-92

Batch
  command (Actions palette menu), 630-632
  dialog box, 631

batch processing, folders, 626

Bézier curves, 33, 392-394

billions of colors, 499

binary data, 576

binding, dynamic data-driven graphics, 647

bit depth, 479

bitmaps, 499, 657
  color, 38
  fonts, 161
  images. *See* raster images

Bits per Pixel (Document Info palette), 614

black, creating, 276-277

Black, shortcut buttons, 287

black-and-white, color (Web images), 479

bleeds, 570, 584, 703

Blend
  command (Object menu), 540
  menu commands
    Blend Options, 215
    Expand, 215
    Make, 215
    Release, 215
    Replace Spine, 215
    Reverse Front to Back, 215
    Reverse Spine, 215
  tool, 212, 215-216

Blend Options
  command (Blend menu), 215
  dialog box, 215-225

Blend, Expand command (Object menu), 213, 540

Blend, Make command (Object menu), 212, 216-219, 540

Blend, Replace Spine command (Object menu), 228

blending modes, 409
  base color, 415
  blend color, 415
  Color, 422
  Color Burn, 419
  Color Dodge, 418-419
  Darken, 419-420
  Difference, 420
  effects, restricting, 423
  Exclusion, 420
  Hard Lights, 418-419
  Hue, 421
  Lighten, 420
  Luminosity, 423
  Multiply, 416
  Normal, 416
  Overlay, 417-418
  Saturation, 421
  Screen, 417
  Soft Light, 418

blends, 570. *See also* gradients
  accessing, 213
  caps, 214
  color, 214, 415, 702
  complex, 214
  creating, 212-216, 338
  editing, 214
  effects, 214
  expanding, 229
  fills, 214
  joins, 214
  layers, 214
  making, 216, 219
  miter limits, 214
  objects, 212
  opacities, 214
  orientations, 224
  Outline Mode, 214
  paths, 212, 218
  patterns, 214
  points, 214
  Preview Mode, 214
  printing, 214
  rotating, 216
  separations, 701
  smooth color, 216, 219
  Specified Distance,
    222-224

specified steps, 219-222
spines, 226-228
strokes, 214
transforming, 214
troubleshooting, 229
Bloat tool, 208
block, type, 37
blocks, color blocks, 702
Blocks command (Type
  menu), 150
Blocks, Link command
  (Type menu), 154
blur, images (applying), 521
Blur, Gaussian Blur com-
  mand (Filter menu), 454
Blur, Radial Blur command
  (Filter menu), 455
.bmp, file format, 49
body, type, 163
bold, type, 163
borders
  brush patterns, 312
  images, film recorders,
    269
bounding
  boxes, 247
    brush paths, 123
    brush patterns, 310
    corner tiles, 313, 320
    editing, 362
    end tiles, 320
    fill patterns, 303
    handles, 176
    objects, 31, 98
    printing, 583
    text, modifying, 146
    transforming, 176
  circles, 247
boxes. *See also* check
  boxes; dialog boxes
  Alignment, 149
  bounding boxes, 247
    brush paths, 123
    brush patterns, 310

corner tiles, 313, 320
editing, 362
end tiles, 320
fill patterns, 303
handles, 176
objects (selected), 98
printing, 583
text, 146
transforming, 176
Diameter, 130
Flip Along, 132
Proportional, 132
Scale, 126
small colored, sites (laying out), 472
Break Link button, 492
Break Link to Style button,
  334
Break Link to Symbol
  button, 493
brightness, color, 282
brokers, print, 595
browsers, Web
  animation, checklist, 704
  configuration, 545-546
  CSS (Cascading Style
    Sheets), 483
  interface requirements,
    547
  resolution 475
  SVG, 539
Brush Affects Anchor Points
  check box, 209
Brush Libraries
  command (Window
    menu), 127, 135
  folder, 127
  installation choices,
    Windows, 683
Brush Libraries, Other
  Library command
  (Window menu), 121
Brush Options
  command (Brushes
    palette menu), 121, 127
  dialog box, 121, 126

Brush palette menu commands, Duplicate Brush, 126

brush patterns, 315-317
  accessing, 308
  borders, 312
  bounding boxes, 310
  colors, 309
  continuous patterns, 310
  corner tiles, creating, 313-320
  corners, 306
  creating, 307-309
  designing, 310
  end tiles, creating, 320
  naming, 309
  printers, 310
  repeating patterns, 310
  side tiles, creating, 311-313
  sizes, 308
  spacing, 312
  start tiles, creating, 320
  tiles, 310
  versus fill patterns, 302

Brush Strokes, Accented Edges command (Filter menu), 455

Brush Strokes, Angled Strokes command (Filter menu), 455

Brush Strokes, Crosshatch command (Filter menu), 457

Brush Strokes, Dark Strokes command (Filter menu), 457

Brush Strokes, Ink Outlines command (Filter menu), 458

Brush Strokes, Spatter command (Filter menu), 458

Brush Strokes, Sprayed Strokes command (Filter menu), 458

Brush Strokes, Sumi-e command (Filter menu), 459

brushes, 31
  adding, 131, 330
  angles, 130
  applying, 122, 125-126, 248
  art, 120-122, 131-133
  artwork, modifying, 127
  calligraphic, 120-122, 129
  categories, 120
  changing, 121
  creating, 127-135
  custom, Brushes palette, 127
  diameter, 130
  icon, 121
  libraries, 121, 127
  Liquify tools, 208
  loading, 135
  modifying, 127-133, 135
  paths
    anchor points, 123
    bounding boxes, 123
    editing, 123-125
    transforming, 123-125
  pattern, 120
    color, 122
    creating, 133-134
    modifying, 133-134
    tiles, 133
  scatter, 120
    blend orientations, 225
    color, 122
    creating, 130
    modifying, 130
    options, 130
  selecting, 127
  shadows, 125
  sizes, modifying, 126
  storing, 121
  strokes, 122-123, 128
  tools, 122
  troubleshooting, 135

Brushes palette
  custom brushes, 127
  menu commands, 31, 126
    Brush Options, 121, 127
    Duplicate Brush, 121
    New Brush, 129-133, 307-308
    Options of Selected Object, 121, 128
    View By Name, 121
  tab, 308

Button Mode, 629

buttons
  Actions palette, 629
  Advanced, 47
  Apply, 113
  Break Link, 492
  Break Link to Style, 334
  Break Link to Symbol, 493
  Cell Style, 113
  compound shapes, 107
  Copy, 181-183
  Create New Action, 632
  Create New Layer, 234-238
  Create New Set, 632
  Create New Sublayer, 236
  Delete Color, 517
  Delete Selections, 629, 640
  Delete Style, 334
  Delete SVG Filter, 558
  Delete Swatch, 292
  Direction, 131
  Duplicate, 331
  Edit Original, 611
  Edit SVG Filter, 558
  Expand, 107
  Export, 552
  Fill swatch, 291
  Go To Link, 610
  Import Data, 113
  Layers palette, 236

New Action, 629
New Brush, 121, 129-133
New Color, 517
New Design, 115
New Layer, 316
New Style, 333-334
New SVG Filter, 558
New Swatch, 267,
　292-294, 341
New Symbol, 204, 493
Open PPD, 583
Output, 484
Pathfinder palette,
　108-109
Place Symbol Instance,
　493
Preview browser, 511
Remember, 516
Replace, 608
Replace Link, 610
Replace Symbol, 492
Reset, 516
Reset All Warning
　Dialogs, 361-362
Revert, 113, 583
Select Unused, 115
shortcuts
　Black, 287
　color bar, 287
　None, 287
　White, 287
Show All Swatches, 292
Show Color Swatches,
　292
Show Gradient
　Swatches, 292
Show Pattern Swatches,
　292
Stroke swatch, 291
Swatches palette, 292
Switch X/Y, 113
Tips, 128
Transpose Row/Column,
　113
Update Link, 611
Updates, 369

C

Calibration, installation
　choices (Windows), 683
calibration bars (printer's
　marks), 593
Calligraphic Brush Options
　dialog box, 129
calligraphic brushes, 120
　color, 122
　creating, 129
　modifying, 129
cameras, digital (resolu-
　tions), 261
caps
　blends, 214
　height, type, 163
Capture Data Set control
　(Variables palette), 649
Case Sensitive check box,
　636
CcMmYK printing, 297
Cell Style button, 113
.cgm, file format, 50
Change Case command
　(Type menu), 152
channel values, reversing,
　290
Channels (Document Info
　palette), 614
character, type, 164
Character Identification
　(CID), 162-164
Character palette, 146-147,
　161
characteristics, layers, 325
characters
　baseline shifts, 147
　Character palette, 147
　hidden, 153
　oriental sets, Character
　　palette, 147
　paragraphs, 148

check boxes
　Allow Continue, 638
　Anti-aliased Artwork,
　　361
　Area Select, 361
　Auto Trace Tolerance,
　　363
　Brush Affects Anchor
　　Points, 209
　Case Sensitive, 636
　Convert to Process, 282,
　　571, 581-583
　Disable Auto Add/Delete,
　　361
　Display Preview Bounds,
　　182
　Export as CSS Layers,
　　484
　Global, 294
　Grids in Back, 365
　Include GoLive Code,
　　528
　Invert Mask, 380
　Lower Case, 367
　Maintain Envelope
　　Shape, 201
　Numbers Without Units
　　Are Points, 364
　Object Highlighting, 365
　Only Web Colors, 288
　Optimized, 520
　Overprint Black, 584
　Override Action "Open"
　　Commands, 631
　Preserve Appearance,
　　368
　Preserve Color Numbers,
　　586
　Preserve Paths, 368
　Pressure Pen (Symbolism
　　tool option), 490
　Preview, 181
　Progressive, 520
　Random, 193
　Scale Strokes & Effects,
　　362
　Select Same Tint
　　Percentage, 361

Show Font Names in English, 363
Show Layers Only, 236
Show Tool Tips, 292, 361
Standard, 151
Strokes & Effects, 124
Tracing Gap, 363
Transform Pattern Tiles, .362
Transparency, 519
Type Area Select, 363
Use Area Select, 361
Use Precise Cursors, 361
Use Preview Bounds, 362
Whole Word, 636

Check Spelling command (Type menu), 152

checklists
  press checks, 703
  Web animation, 703-704

Chinese-Japanese-Korean fonts. *See* CJK

chokes, 571, 597

CID (Character Identification), 162-164

circles
  bounding, 247
  icons, 246

CJK (Chinese-Japanese-Korean)
  characters, 147
  type, 164
  fonts, 37

Clear Appearance command (Appearances palette menu), 331

Clip to Artboard Size (SWF), 552

Clipboard, objects, pasting, 244

Clipping Mask, Make command (Object menu), 33, 374

Clipping Mask, Release command (Object menu), 376

clipping
  masks, 33
    anchor points, editing, 377
    creating, 374-376
    editing, 376-377
    guidelines, 374-376
    non-object paths, 80
    objects, adding to, 377
    opacity, troubleshooting, 376
    printing, 375
    repositioning, 377
    troubleshooting, 384
    type as, 377-378
  paths, 268, 374
  sets, 374

closed paths, 393
  anchor points, 61
  creating, 87
  endpoints, 61

CMP Files, installation choice (Windows), 683

CMP Folder, installation choice, (Macintosh), 683

CMY (cyan, magenta, and yellow)
  colors, 277
  versus RGB, 257

CMYK (cyan, magenta, yellow, and black), 38, 571
  colors, 279-281, 500, 580
  commercial printing, 256
  fields, numeric values, 288
  gamut, 285
  images, inverting, 290
  inkjet printers, 256
  process, colors or inks, 279
  reflective colors, 279
  versus
    RGB, 580
    RGB and spot colors, 278-282

collapses, objects, 207

collapsing
  groups, 236
  layers, modifier keys, 237
  sublayers, 236

Collect in New Layer command (Layers palette menu), 243

collections, spot colors, 282

color
  8-bit, 284, 499-500
  16-bit, 500
  24-bit, 499-500
  48-bit, 500
  64-bit, 500
  accuracy, 702
  adding, 292-293, 517
  additive, 257, 276-279
  applying, 248, 290-291
  art brushes, 122
  background (sampling), PowerPoint, 266-267
  banding, 38
  bars, shortcut buttons or sliders, 287
  base color, 415
  billions of colors, 499
  bitmap, 38
  black, creating, 276-277
  blending modes, 415
    Color, 422
    Color Burn, 419
    Color Dodge, 419
    Darken, 419
    Difference, 420
    Exclusion, 420
    Hard Light, 418
    Hue, 421
    Lighten, 420
    Luminosity, 423
    Multiply, 416
    Normal, 416
    Overlay, 417
    restricting, 423
    Saturation, 421
    Soft Light, 418
  blends, 214, 415, 702
  blocks, 702
  brightness, 282

brush patterns, 309
calligraphic brushes, 122
changing, text, 126
CMY, 277
CMYK, 279-281, 580
color model, 39
converting, 279, 585
correcting, 584-585
deleting from color
  tables, 517
designated, artwork, 129
displaying, 499
dithering, 286
drag and drop, objects,
  291
duotone, 571
editing, in color tables,
  517
eyedropper, objects, 291
film recorders, 269
gamuts, 39, 257
global, linked, 294
gradients, 38, 572, 702
graphs, 115
grayscale, 39
grids, setting, 365
guides, setting, 364
hexadecimal, 289, 500
highlights, 702
hue, 282
ICC profile, 39
inkjet printers, 285
in-use, viewing, 516
inverting, 287
jaggies, 39
key, 129, 257
knockout, 412, 572
lines, slices, 366
locking, 517
Macintosh, 682
managing, 38-39
matching, 690
mesh points, 350
millions of colors, 499
models, CMYK or RGB,
  256
modes
  determining, 284-286
  gamuts, 278, 580

  grayscale, 282
  HSB, 282
  *preparing raster
    images, 403*
  rotating, 287
  swatches, 293
modifying, Swatch
  Library palette, 295
monitors, 280
numeric values, revers-
  ing, 290
objects, 292
online, 499-500
organizing, Swatches
  palette, 292
out-of-gamut, 580
output, 256-259
overlapping, 414, 572-574
pages proofs, 702-703
Paintbucket, objects, 291
palettes, reducing, 284
Pantone Process, 282,
  581
Pantone Solid, 282, 581
pattern brushes, 122
pixels, 394, 402
presentations, 286
printers, 280
printing, 351
process, 39, 279, 282,
  571, 574, 580-581
profiles, 585-586
proofing, soft proofing,
  29
proofs, 285, 701-702
ranges (gamuts), 39, 257
raster images, 390, 397
rasterized objects, 399
reflective, CMYK, 279
registration, 278, 584,
  702
resulting color, 415
reversing, 290
RGB, 277-281
sampling, 290
saturation, 282
scatter brushes, 122
selecting, in color tables,
  517

selection area, 288
separating, 351
separations, 40, 574
  composites, 577
  duotone, 577
  negatives, 578
  printing, 578
  reading, 578
  settings, 282
  tritone, 577
shadows, 702
shifting, 517
smooth, 216-219
spot, 40, 258, 278-282,
  293-294, 581
storing, Swatches
  palette, 291
strokes, 122
substrative, 257, 277
symbol instances, 488
tables, 516-517
table menu commands
  Load Color Table, 518
  Save Color Table, 518
  Sort by Hue, 517
  *Sort by Luminance,
    517*
  Sort by Popularity, 517
  Unshift All Colors, 517
  Unsorted, 517
text, 141
thousands of colors, 499
tints, 258, 581
trapping, 36, 575, 590
troubleshooting, 297-298
updating, 290
values, 293, 407
viewing, 584-585
Web
  design, 479-480
  images, 280
Web Safe RGB palette,
  285
Web Snap, 520
Web-safe, 40, 286
wheels, Hue, 283
white, creating, 276-277
Color blending mode, 422

Color Burn blending mode, 419

Color Dodge blending mode, 418-419

Color Model, 504, 662

Color palette, 122, 141, 289
  color bar, 287
  colors, updating, 290
  gamuts, 279
  gradients, 338
  menu commands, 519
    Complement, 290
    Hide Options, 287
    Invert, 290
  shortcuts, 286
  spot colors, 258
  stroke color, changing, 126
  tab, 287
  Toolbox, 288

Color Picker, 258, 364, 519
  fractional values, 288
  grayscale objects, 284
  Hue, 282, 288
  opening, 288

Color Settings
  installation choices, Windows, 684
  command (Edit menu), 369, 682, 690

Color Tables, 511, 516-518

Color, Adjust Color command (Filter menu), 294, 435

Color, Blend Front to Back command (Filter menu), 435

Color, Blend Horizontally command (Filter menu), 435

Color, Blend Vertically command (Filter menu), 435

Color, Convert to CMYK command (Filter menu), 435

Color, Convert to Grayscale command (Filter menu), 435

Color, Convert to RGB command (Filter menu), 436

Color, Invert Colors command (Filter menu), 290, 436

Color, Overprint Black command (Filter menu), 436

Color, Saturate command (Filter menu), 436

Colorization, options, 128

columns
  graphs, 110
  layers, 235

combination point, anchor points, 65

commands
  accessing, 26
  Actions palette menu
    Action Options, 629
    Batch, 630-632
    Insert Menu Item, 634
    Insert Select Path, 634-635
    Insert Stop, 638
    New Action, 632
    New Set, 632
    Playback Options, 630
    Save Actions, 641
    Select Object, 634-637
    Stop Recording, 633
  Appearances palette menu
    Add New Fill, 330, 343
    Add New Stroke, 330
    Clear Appearance, 331
    Duplicate Item, 331
    Layer/Group Overrides Color, 331
    New Art Has Basic Appearance, 331
    Reduce to Basic Appearance, 331
    Remove Item, 331

    Replace (Style), 334
    Show Note, 594
  Blend menu
    Blend Options, 215
    Expand, 215
    Make, 215
    Release, 215
    Replace Spine, 215
    Reverse Front to Back, 215
    Reverse Spine, 215
  Brushes palette menu
    Brush Options, 121, 127
    Duplicate Brush, 121, 126
    New Brush, 129-133, 307-308
    Options of Selected Object, 121, 128
    View By Name, 121
  Character palette menu, Show Options, 147
  Color palette menu
    Complement, 290
    Hide Options, 287
    Invert, 290
  color table menu
    Load Color Table, 518
    Save Color Table, 518
    Sort by Hue, 517
    Sort by Luminance, 517
    Sort by Popularity, 517
    Unshift All Colors, 517
    Unsorted, 517
  Edit menu
    Color Settings, 369, 682, 690
    Cut, 377
    Define Pattern, 303-305, 308, 319
    Keyboard Shortcuts, 239, 358, 369
    Paste, 244-245
    Preferences, 32, 360
    Preferences, Files & Clipboard, 664

Preferences, General,
360, 571
Preferences, Guides &
Grids, 476
Select, Same Fill
Color, 361
Select, Same Fill or
Edit, 292
Ungroup, 306
Effects menu
Convert to Shape,
Ellipse, 437
Convert to Shape,
Rectangle, 437
Convert to Shape,
Rounded Rectangle,
437
Distort & Transform,
174
Distort & Transform,
Twist, 189
Path, Offest Path, 158,
441
Path, Outline Object,
441
Pathfinder, Crop, 443
Pathfinder, Divide, 442
Pathfinder, Exclude,
442
Pathfinder, Hard Mix,
443
Pathfinder, Intersect,
442
Pathfinder, Merge, 443
Pathfinder, Minus
Back, 442
Pathfinder, Outline,
443
Pathfinder, Soft Mix,
443
Pathfinder, Trap, 443,
597
Pathfinder, Trim, 443
Pathfinder, Unite, 442
Pixelate, 461
Rasterize, 444
Rasterize, Rasterize,
401, 512
Sketch, 463

Stylize, 464
Stylize, Feather, 445
Stylize, Inner Glow,
445
Stylize, Outer Glow,
445
SVG Filters, 446
Warp, 174, 446
File menu
Document Color
Mode, 284
Document Info, 593
Document Setup, 26,
143
Export, 48-52, 481,
552
Export, Paths to
Illustrator, 669
New, 144, 284
Open, 553, 668
Open File, 471
Open, Page, 471
Place, 605
Save, 44
Save As, 45, 699
Save for Web, 52, 481
Separation Setup, 282,
351, 583
Filter menu
Apply Last Filter, 434
Artistic, Colored
Pencil, 447
Artistic, Cutout, 448
Artistic, Dry Brush,
448
Artistic, Film Grain,
448
Artistic, Fresco, 449
Artistic, Neon Glow,
449
Artistic, Paint Daubs,
450
Artistic, Palette Knife,
450
Artistic, Plastic Wrap,
450
Artistic, Poster Edges,
451

Artistic, Rough
Pastels, 451
Artistic, Smudge Stick,
452
Artistic, Sponge, 452
Artistic,
Underpainting, 453
Artistic, Watercolor,
453
Blur, Gaussian Blur,
454
Blur, Radial Blur, 455
Brush Strokes,
Accented Edges, 455
Brush Strokes, Angled
Strokes, 455
Brush Strokes,
Crosshatch, 457
Brush Strokes, Dark
Strokes, 457
Brush Strokes, Ink
Outliles, 458
Brush Strokes,
Spatter, 458
Brush Strokes,
Sprayed Strokes, 458
Brush Strokes, Sumi-e,
459
Color, Adjust Colors,
294, 435
Color, Blend Front to
Back, 435
Color, Blend
Horizontally, 435
Color, Blend Vertically,
435
Color, Convert to
CMYK, 435
Color, Convert to
Grayscale, 435
Color, Convert to RGB,
436
Color, Invert Colors,
290, 436
Color, Overprint Black,
436
Color, Saturate, 436
Create, Object Mosaic,
437

Create, Trim Marks,
437, 592
Distort, Diffuse Glow,
460
Distort, Free Distort,
438
Distort, Glass, 460
Distort, Ocean Ripple,
460
Distort, Punk & Bloat,
326
Distort, Roughen, 438
Distort, Scribble and
Tweak, 439
Distort, Twirl, 440
Distort, Twist, 189,
382
Distort, Zig Zag, 440
Last Filter, 434
Pen and Ink, Hatch
Effects, 443
Pen and Ink, Library
Open, 444
Pen and Ink, Library
Save As, 444
Pen and Ink, New
Hatch, 444
Pen and Ink, Photo
Crosshatch, 443
Pixelate, Color
Halftone, 461
Pixelate, Crystallize,
461
Pixelate, Mezzotint,
461
Pixelate, Pointillize,
462
Pucker & Bloat, 438
Sharpen, Unsharp
Mask, 462
Sketch, Chalk &
Charcoal, 463
Sketch, Charcoal, 463
Sketch, Chrome, 463
Sketch, Conte Crayon,
463
Sketch, Graphic Pen,
463

Sketch, Halftone
Pattern, 463
Sketch, Note Paper,
463
Sketch, Photocopy,
464
Sketch, Plaster, 464
Sketch, Reticulation,
464
Sketch, Stamp, 464
Sketch, Torn Edges,
464
Sketch, Water Paper,
464
Stylize, 464
Stylize, Add
Arrowheads, 444
Stylize, Drop Shadow,
445
Stylize, Round
Corners, 446
Texture, Craquelure,
464
Video, De-Interlace,
465
Video, NTSC Colors,
465
Gradient palette menu
Linear, 340
Radial, 340
Help menu, Illustrator
Help, 692
Illustrator menu,
Preferences, 360
Layers palette menu
Collect in New Layer,
243
Create New Layer, 239
Create New Sublayer,
239
Flatten Artwork, 46,
243
Hide Others, 244
Locate Object, 242
Lock Others, 244
Merge Selected, 243
Outline Others, 244
Palette Options, 245

Paste Remembers
Layers, 244
Preview All Layers,
244
Release to Layers
(Build), 244, 249-251
Release to Layers
(Sequence), 244,
249-251, 540
Reverse Order, 244
Show All Layers, 244
Template, 244
Unlock All Layers, 244
Links palette menu
Edit Original, 612
Go To Link, 612
Information, 610, 613
nonrecordable (Actions),
634-635
Object menu
Arrange, 155
Arrange, Bring to
Back, 233
Arrange, Bring to
Forward, 233
Arrange, Bring to
Front, 233
Arrange, Send
Backward, 189, 233
Blend, 540
Blend, Expand, 213,
540
Blend, Make, 212,
216-219, 540
Blend, Replace, 228
Clipping Mask, Make,
33, 374
Clipping Mask,
Release, 376
Create Gradient Mesh,
344
Crop Marks, Make,
359, 592
Crop Marks, Release,
592
Envelope Distort,
Create with Warp,
195

Envelope Distort, Edit Contents, 204, 207
Envelope Distort, Envelope Options, 202
Envelope Distort, Expand, 203
Envelope Distort, Make with Mesh, 200
Envelope Distort, Make with Top Object, 201-202
Envelope Distort, Make with Warp, 196
Envelope Distort, Release, 203
Expand, 306, 344-345, 493
Expand Appearance, 330
Graph, Column, 116
Graph, Data, 115
Graph, Marker, 116
Graph, Type, 113
Object, Transform, 315
Path, Join, 124
Path, Simplify, 159, 191, 208, 591
Rasterize, 260, 266, 401, 591
Show Edges, 587
Slice, Create from Guides, 495
Slice, Create from Selection, 494-495
Slice, Make, 495
Slice, Slice Options, 495
Transform, Move, 181
Transform, Reset Bounding Box, 194
Transform, Scale, 185, 218, 657
Transform, Shear, 187
Transform, Transform Again, 191
Transform, Transform Each, 183, 192-194

Paste, paths (creating), 61
Pathfinder palette menu
Crop, 109
Divide, 108
Merge, 109
Minus Back, 109
Outline, 109
Pathfinder Options, 109
Trap, 109, 599
Trim, 108
Unite, 591
Preferences menu
Type & Auto Tracing, 143
Units & Undo, 143
recorded, 33
reversing, 26
Select menu
Deselect, 103
Edit Selection, 106
Inverse, 103
Next Object Above, 103
Next Object Below, 103
Object, 104-105
Object, All, 105
Object, Brush Strokes, 105
Object, Direction Handles, 105
Object, Save Selection, 105
Reselect, 103
Same, 104
Same, Stroke Weight, 104
Save Selection, 105
Select All, 102
Settings menu
Delete Settings, 518
Optimize to File Size, 518
Repopulate Views, 518
Save Settings, 518
Start menu, Run, 677

Status Bar pop-up menu
Current Tool, 26
Date and Time, 26
Document Color Profile, 26
Free Memory, 26
Number of Undos, 26
Styles palette menu
Duplicate Style, 334
Merge Styles, 334
New Style, 333
Select All Unused, 334
SVG Viewer
About Adobe SVG Viewer, 556
Copy SVG, 556
Find, 556
Find Again, 556
Help, 556
Higher Quality, 555
Mute, 556
Originial View, 555
Pause, 555
Save SVG As, 556
View Source, 556
View SVG, 556
Zoom In, 555
Zoom Out, 555
Swatches palette menu
Name View, 292
New Swatch, 293, 341
Select All Unused, 293
Show Find Field, 292
Small Swatch View, 292
Swatch Options, 293-294
Symbols palette menu
New Symbol, 493
Redefine Symbol, 493
Replace Symbol, 492
Transform menu
Move, 181
paths (creating), 61
Rotate, 178
Scale, 178
Transform Pattern Only, 303
transformations, 175

Transparency palette
menu
    Make Opacity Mask,
        379
    New Opacity Masks
        Are Inverted, 380
troubleshooting, 689
Type menu
    Blocks, 150
    Blocks, Link, 154
    Change Case, 152
    Check Spelling, 152
    Create Outlines, 159
    Find Font, 151
    Find/Change, 150
    Fit Headline, 150
    Rows & Columns, 153
    Show Hidden
        Characters, 153
    Smart Punctuation, 37,
        152
    Type Orientation, 153
    Wrap, 150
View menu
    Actual Size, 28-29
    Edit Views, 31
    Fit in Window, 28-29
    Guides, 30
    Guides, Show Guides,
        311
    Hide Edges, 61
    Hide/Show Artboard,
        30
    Hide/Show Bounding
        Box, 30
    Hide/Show Edges, 29
    Hide/Show Template,
        30
    Hide/Show Tiling, 30
    New View, 31
    Outline/Preview, 29
    Overprint Preview, 29,
        587-589
    Pixel Preview, 29, 478,
        508
    Proof, 585
    Proof Colors, 29, 585
    Proof Setup, Custom,
        29, 585

Proof Setup,
    Macintosh RGB, 29
Proof Setup, Monitor
    RGB, 29
Proof Setup, Windows
    RGB, 29
Show Edges, 606
Show Grid, 311
Show Transparency
    Grid, 411
Show/Hide Grid, 30
Show/Hide Page
    Tiling, 478
Show/Hide Rulers, 30
Show/Hide
    Transparency Grid,
    30
Smart Guides, 30, 365
Snap to Grid, 27, 30
Snap to Pixel, 30, 508
Snap to Point, 27, 30,
    305
Zoom In, 28-29
Zoom Out, 28-29
Window menu
    Brush Libraries, 127,
        135
    Brush Libraries, Other
        Library, 121
    Style Libraries, 335
    Styles, Libraries
        Other, 335
    Swatch Libraries,
        294-295, 581
    Swatch Libraries,
        Load Library, 338
    Swatch Libraries,
        Other Library, 295,
        341, 371, 493
commercial printing, 570,
    575, 596
    CMYK, 256
    line screen frequency,
        396
Common English (SVG Font
    Subsetting), 564
Common Roman (SVG Font
    Subsetting), 564

comparing
    anchor points, corner
        and smooth, 65
    HTML and XML, 554
    raster and vector, 42, 60,
        397-399
Compatibility, .ai file for-
    mat, 45
compatibility
    Adobe products, 21
    backward, 690
    filename, ensuring, 367
    Illustrator/Photoshop, 661
Complement command
    (Color palette menu), 290
complex
    animations, creating, 220
    blends, 214
    gradients, creating,
        341-343
    objects, expanding, 229
    paths, 190, 701
Complex Object Creation
    tools, 92-97
components, Web pages,
    saving, 470
composites, color separa-
    tions, 577
compound
    paths
        clipping masks, 376
        type, 150
    shapes, 106
        buttons, 107
        clipping masks, 376
        expanding, 107
        features, new, 19
Compress Text and Line
    Art, PDF option, 265
compression
    controlling, 503
    file formats, 43
    images, 501
    JPG, 505
    lossless, 482, 505
    lossy, 482, 503

LZW (Lempel-Ziv-Welch), 502

RLE (Run Length Encoding), 49

troubleshooting, 505

Web images, downloading, 482

CompuServe, 502

computers, monitors, 259-261

condensed, type, 164

configuration, Web browsers, 545-546

Constraint Angle, setting, 360

Construction Guides (Smart Guides dialog box), 365

containers
  sublayers, 475
  text
    filling, 158
    linking, 154-156
    objects, 155
    stroking, 158

contents
  envelope distortions (editing), 205
  layers
    hiding, 244
    showing, 244
    viewing, 235
  Layers palette, 236

continuous
  patterns, 310, 313
  tone, 50, 503, 514, 572

contract proofs, 571, 702

controlling
  banding, 501
  compression, 503
  images, 498

controls
  modal (Actions), 639
  points, 65, 199

conventions, naming conventions (swatches), 581

Convert Anchor Point tool, 69, 227, 320

Convert to Process check box, 282, 571, 581-583

Convert to Shape, Ellipse command (Effects menu), 437

Convert to Shape, Rectangle command (Effects menu), 437

Convert to Shape, Rounded Rectangle command (Effects menu), 437

converting
  anchor points, 69, 73
  color, 279, 585
  spot colors to process colors, 582
  text, outlines, 158

Copy As AICB (Files & Clipboard dialog box), 368

Copy As PDF (Files & Clipboard dialog box), 368

Copy button, 181, 183

Copy SVG command (SVG Viewer), 556

copyfitting type, 164

copying
  Actions, 630, 640
  appearances, 327, 331
  attributes, 248
  between layers, 543
  mesh points, 199
  objects, 181-183
  stops, gradients, 340
  styles, 334
  swatches, 293
  type attributes, 159-160

copyrights
  fonts, 54, 162, 619
  law, 678

Corner Radius, setting, 361

corner-to-corner tiles, 315

corners
  anchor points, 65-68
  angled, 313-315
  brush patterns, 306
  continuous patterns, 313
  curved, 313
  inner, 313
  mesh points, 348-349
  outer, 313-315
  points, 198
  square, 313
  tiles
    bounding boxes, 313, 320
    brush patterns, 310
    creating, brush patterns, 313-320
    curved, 319
  types, 313

corrupt
  files, opening, 690
  preferences, 689

Create Gradient Mesh command (Object menu), 344

Create New Action button, 632

Create New Layer
  button, 234-238
  command (Layers palette menu), 239

Create New Set button, 632

Create New Sublayer
  button, 236
  command (Layers palette menu), 239

Create Outlines command (Type menu), 159

Create, Object Mosaic command (Filter menu), 437

Create, Trim Marks command (Filter menu), 437, 592

Created (Link Information window), 615

creating
   animations, 539-543
   black, 276-277
   blends, 212, 216, 338
      Blend menu, 215
      gradients, 213
      objects, 213-214
      paths, 213
      spines, 214
   brush patterns, 307-309
   brushes, 127-133, 135
   clipping masks, 375-376
   closed paths, 87
   complex animations, 220
   compound shapes, 106
   corner
      anchor points, 65
      tiles, brush patterns,
      313-320
   CSS (Cascading Style
      Sheets), 483
   curves, 208
   custom
      brush libraries, 127
      envelope mesh
        objects, 200
   end tiles, brush patterns,
      320
   files, startup, 370
   fill patterns, 304
   flares, 93
   frames, 219
   GIF files, 481
   gradients, 340-348
   intermediary objects, 219
   JPEG files, 481
   layers, 238-239
   margins, objects, 158
   masks, clipping, 374
   objects, 35, 84
   opacity masks, 379-380
   output, SVG, 554-559
   paths, 60, 74-76
      Add Anchor Point
        tools, 69
      Convert Anchor Point
        tools, 69
      Delete Anchor Point
        tools, 69
      Pen tools, 68-69
      segments, 89
   patterns, 300
   PNG files, 481
   point of origin, 186
   pointed segments, 208
   rectangles, 85-86
   seamless patterns,
      303-305, 311
   shadows, 189
   side tiles, brush pat-
      terns, 311-313
   smooth anchor points, 65
   squares, 85
   start tiles, brush pat-
      terns, 320
   styles, 333-334
   sublayers, Layers palette,
      238-239
   swatches, 267
   symbols, 485, 493
   target objects, 97
   text
      boxes, 139
      effects, 330
   tiles, 133
   trim marks, 592
   versus modifying
      brushes, 127
   Web
      pages, Layers palette,
      252
      sites, Layers palette,
      252
   Web-based animation,
      219
   white, 276-277
Creation tools, Basic, functions, 85
Crop command (Pathfinder
   palette menu), 109
crop marks, 591
   Japanese, 361
   modifying, 592
   non-object paths, 80
   repositioning, 583
   setting, 592

Crop Marks, Make com-
   mand (Object menu), 359,
   592
Crop Marks, Release com-
   mand (Object menu), 592
cross-platform file formats,
   PDF, 262
crossover (images), 703
Crystallize tool, 208
CSS (Cascading Style
   Sheets)
   creating, 483
   designs, Web, 482-485
   layers, 482-485
   Web, 14
   Web browsers, 483
CSS Property Location (SVG
   Export option), 563
cumulative animations, 250,
   536
Current Data Set control
   (Variables palette), 649
Current Tool command
   (Status Bar pop-up menu),
   26
Curve Quality (SWF), 553
curved
   corner tiles, 319
   corners, 313
   path segments, 68
curves
   antialiasing, 202
   Bézier, 33, 392-394
   creating, 208
   flatness, troubleshooting,
      588
   printing, 572
custom
   brushes, 127
   graphs, Specified Steps,
      220
   installations
      Illustrator, 679-680
      Macintosh, 681-683
      Windows, 683

startup documents, 477
thumbnails, 236

Custom, PDF option, 264

Custom Install (Illustrator), 684

customizing
  Actions, 629
  appearance, work area, 29-31
  graphs, 115
  Illustrator, 358

Cut command (Edit menu), 377

Cyan, Magenta, Yellow, Black. *See* CMYK

D

Darken blending mode, 419-420

data
  binary, 576
  graphs, 113-115
  sets, dynamic data-driven graphics, 647, 651
  sources, dynamic data-driven graphics, 647

Data Set Pop-up Menu control (Variables palette), 649

data-driven graphics, dynamic. *See* dynamic data-driven graphics

databases
  dynamic data-driven graphics, 651
  searchable, Adobe Tech Support, 694

Date and Time command (Status Bar pop-up menu), 26

Decimal Places (SVG Export option), 563

Default, PDF option, 264

Default Language, hyphenation, 366

defaults
  backgrounds, animations, 544
  values, Fill swatch or Stroke swatch, 291

Default_CMYK swatch, 295

Default_RGB swatch, 295

Define Pattern command (Edit menu), 303-305, 308, 319

defining colors
  CMYK, 281, 580
  RGB, 281

defragmenting, hard drives, 676

Delete Anchor Point tool, 69, 361

Delete Color button, 517

Delete Selected Color(s) icon, 511

Delete Selections button, 629, 640

Delete Settings command (Settings menu), 518

Delete Style button, 334

Delete SVG Filter button, 558

Delete Swatch button, 292

Delete Variable control (Variables palette), 650

deleting
  Actions, 640
  anchor points, 64, 69
  appearances, 331
  effects, objects, 326
  files, Preferences, 360
  layers, 243
  locked
    groups, 235
    layers, 235
    objects, 235

mesh
  lines, 199
  points, 350
Preferences file, 689
stops, gradients, 340
styles, 334
swatches, 293
tabs, 149

depth of field, effects, 252

descender, type, 164

Deselect command (Select menu), 103

designated colors, artwork, 129

designing
  brush patterns, 310
  Web, 470-471, 475
    color, 479-480
    CSS (Cascading Style Sheets), 482-485
    file formats, 480-482
    hexadecimal notation, 479
    HTML, 479
    pages (organizing), 474
    sites (laying out), 472-473
    slicing, 494-495
    symbols, 485-494
    troubleshooting, 496
    Web-safe palette, 480

Destination menu, 631

dialog boxes
  Adobe Online, 693
  Adobe PDF Format Options, 46
  Arc Segment Tool Options, 90
  Art Brush, 131
  Batch, 631
  Blend Options, 121, 126, 215-225
  Calligraphic Brush Options, 129
  Document Info, 400
  Document Settings, 338

Document Setup, 149, 351, 411-412, 425, 571, 607

Edit SVG Fitler, 558

Envelope Distort, 200

Envelope Options, 203

EPS Format Options, 46

export, 49

Export JPEG, 506

Files & Clipboard, 367-369

Flare, 93

Flare Tool Options, 93-94

Flash (SWF) Format Options, 552

General Preferences, 360-362

Graph sign, 371

Graph Type, 113

Guides & Grid, 364-365

Hyphenation, 366

Hyphenation Options, 147-148

Insert Menu Item, 634

JPEG Options, 503-504

Keyboard Shortcuts, 239, 358

Layer Options, 235, 239, 245

Layers Palette Options, 236

Line Segment Tool, 89

Make with Mesh, 200

modal (Actions), 629

Move, 181

New Action, 632

New Brush, 129-133

New Document, 26

New Pattern Brush, 308

New Set, 632

New Swatch, 305

Online Settings, 369

Open, 516

Options, 129

Output Settings, 484, 528-530

Page Setup, 583

Paintbrush Tool
 Preferences, 74

Pathfinder Options, 597

Pathfinder Trap, 599

Pattern Brush Options, 133, 308

PDF, 263

Photoshop Options, 50, 663

Place, 605, 612

Plug-ins & Scratch Disk preferences, 366

Preferences, 144, 365, 605

Raster Effects Settings, 399

Rasterize, 49, 399

Record Stop, 638

Reflect, 184

Replace, 608-610

Rotate, 178, 182

Save As, 45, 263, 562

Save for Web, 483, 509-516, 525

Save for Web (SVG), 564

Save for Web (SWF), 564

Save Optimized As, 484, 527, 530

Save Set To, 641

Scale, 124, 185-187

Scatter Brush Options, 130

Separations Setup, 351, 570-571, 581-584

Set Selection, 637

Shear, 187, 189

Slice Options, 495

Smart Guides, 366

Sprayed Strokes, 459

Style Options, 334

SVG Options, 47, 562-563

Swatch Options, 293-294

Symbolism Tool Options, 489-492

Transform Each, point of origin, 192

Type & Auto Tracing preference, 362-363

Units & Undo, 363-364

warning, 53

Warp Options, 201

Warp Tool Options, 208

Wrinkle Tool Options, 209

diameter, brushes, 130

Diameter
 box, 130
 slider (Symbolism tool option), 490

diamond icon, 339

diamonds, mesh points, 198

Dicolor swatch, 295

Difference blending mode, 420

Diffusion dithering (images), 522

digital
 cameras, resolutions, 261
 images, ppi (pixels per inch), 259
 proofing, 577
 proofs, 701

digitized video, 536

dimensions
 objects, 186
 online images, 506
 raster images, preparing, 403

Dimensions (Document Info palette), 614

dingbats (type), 164

Direct Select Lasso tool, 74, 101

Direct Selection tool, 99, 122, 141-142, 158, 226, 320, 377, 381, 393
 anchor points, managing, 70-71
 direction lines, editing, 72-74
 paths, 69-74

direct to plate printing, 578

Direction buttons, 131

direction
  lines, 349
    anchor points, 65-67
    control points, 65
    *editing, 72-74, 198,
      350*
    path segments, 68
    paths, 393
  points, 34
Director, Macromedia
  Director, 535
Disable Auto Add/Delete
  check box, 361
  preferences, 70
disks, scratch disk, 366-367
Display Preview Bounds
  check box, 182
displays
  fonts, 37
  palettes, 232
Distort & Transform com-
  mand (Effect menu), 174
Distort & Transform, Twist
  command (Effect menu),
  189
Distort, Diffuse Glow com-
  mand (Filter menu), 460
Distort, Free Distort com-
  mand (Filter menu), 438
Distort, Glass command
  (Filter menu), 460
Distort, Ocean Ripple com-
  mand (Filter menu), 460
Distort, Punk & Bloat command (Filter menu), 326
Distort, Roughen command
  (Filter menu), 438
Distort, Scribble and Tweak
  command (Filter menu),
  439
Distort, Twirl command
  (Filter menu), 440
Distort, Twist command
  (Fitler menu), 189, 382

Distort, Zig Zag command
  (Filter menu), 440
distortions, 175
  animations, 547
  effects, 174
  envelopes, 194,
    content (editing), 205
    *Edit Contents com-
      mand, 204, 207*
    *Envelope Distort dia-
      log box, 200*
    expanding, 203-204
    features, new, 15
    *Make with Top Object
      command, 201-202*
    *mesh objects (editing),
      198*
    options, 202
    releasing, 203-204
    warping, 195-198
  features, new, 15
  paths, manipulating, 174
  sliders, warps, 196
  troubleshooting, 210
  warp, editing, 200
dithering, 501, 521
  color, 286
  Diffusion dithering, 522
  images, previewing, 511
  Noise dithering, 524
  Pattern dithering, 522
Dithering
  menu, 519
  slider, 519, 522
Divide command
  (Pathfinder palette menu),
  108
dividers, grids, 94-96
docking
  palettes, 32
  Swatch Library palettes,
    294
Document Color Mode com-
  mand (File menu), 284
Document Color Profile
  command (Status Bar pop-
  up menu), 26

Document Info
  command (File menu),
    593
  dialog box, 400
  palette, 593, 605, 613
Document Object Model
  (DOM), 555, 560
Document Raster Effects
  settings, 434
Document Settings dialog
  box, 338
Document Setup
  command (File menu),
    143
  dialog box, 26, 149, 351,
    411-412, 425, 571, 607
  units of measure, 476
documents
  CMYK colors, 279
  custom startup, 477
  events, 561
  managed, storing, 368
  PDF, viewing, 262
  RGB colors, 279
  style libararies, adding,
    335
  tabs, 149
  type, horizontal or verti-
    cal, 139
DOM (Document Object
  Model), 555, 560
dots
  halftone, tint, 572
  per inch (dpi), versus
    pixels per inch (ppi),
    395
double-byte fonts (type),
  164
downloading
  Version Checker, 46
  Web images, 482
dpi (dots per inch)
  resolution, measuring,
    259
  versus pixels per inch
    (ppi), 395

drag and drop, Photoshop, 666

dragging
attributes, 248
eyedropper, 288

drives, hard drives (defragmenting), 676

drop
cap, type, 164
shadows
colored backgrounds, 408
filters, 327
masks, opacity masks, 414
multicolored backgrounds, 408

duotone
color separations, 577
printing, 571

Duplicate Brush command (Brushes palette menu), 121, 126

Duplicate button, 331

Duplicate Item command (Appearances palette menu), 331

duplicate keyboard shortcuts, 359

Duplicate Style (Styles palette menu), 334

.dwg, file format, 49

.dxf, file format, 49

dynamic data-driven graphics
design process, 648
features, new, 20
functionality, 646
templates, 648
terminology, 647
variables, 649-653
XML IDs, 652

Dynamic objects, dynamic data-driven graphics, 647

Dynamic SVG, 560-561

E

Earthtones_1 swatch, 295

Easy Install (Macintosh option), 676

eclipse angle of rotation, 130

edges
images, linked, 606
objects, 587

Edit menu commands
Color Settings, 369, 682, 690
Cuts, 377
Define Pattern, 303-305, 308, 319
Keyboard Shortcuts, 239, 358, 369
Paste, 244-245
Preferences, 32, 360
Preferences, Files & Clipboard, 664
Preferences, General, 360, 571
Preferences, Guides & Grids, 476
Preferences, Online Settings, 369
Select, Same Fill Color, 361
Select, Same Fill or Edit, 292
Ungroup, 306

Edit Original
button, 611
command (Links palette menu), 612

Edit Selected Paths (Paintbrush tool), 75

Edit Selected Paths (Pencil tool), 76

Edit Selection command (Select menu), 106

Edit SVG Filter, button or dialog box, 558

Edit Views command (View menu), 31

Editable Text option (Illustrator), 663

effects, 35
applying, 249, 252, 466
Artistic, 447
blending mode, restricting effects, 423
blends, 214
depth of field, 252
distortions, 174
fill, 328
images, linked, 607, 610
layers, 232
live, 432
objects, managing, 73
opacity masks, 382
orders, 327
paths, 125
raster images, 390
rasterizing, 400
removing, objects, 326
reversing, 401
scaling, 179-180, 187
selecting, raster images, 398
special, Web images, 471
stroke, 328
SVG Effects, Web, 14
text, creating, 330
transformations, 174
typewriter, 250
versus filters, 326, 431
warps, available as, 16

Effects menu commands
Apply Last Effect, 434
Convert to Shape, Ellipse, 437
Convert to Shape, Rectangle, 437
Convert to Shape, Rounded Rectangle, 437
Distort & Transform, 174
Distort & Transform, Twist, 189
Last Effect, 434
Path, Offset Path, 158, 441
Path, Outline Object, 441
Path, Outline Stroke, 442

Pathfinder, Crop, 443

Pathfinder, Divide, 442

Pathfinder, Exclude, 442

Pathfinder, Hard Mix, 443

Pathfinder, Intersect, 442

Pathfinder, Merge, 443

Pathfinder, Minus Back, 442

Pathfinder, Outline, 443

Pathfinder, Soft Mix, 443

Pathfinder, Trap, 443, 597

Pathfinder, Trim, 443

Pathfinder, Unite, 442

Pixelate, 461

Rasterize, 444

Rasterize, Rasterize, 401, 512

Sketch, 463

Stylize, 464

Stylize, Feather, 445

Stylize, Inner Glow, 445

Stylize, Outer Glow, 445

SVG Filter, Apply SVG Filter, 558

SVG Filters, 446

Transform, 439

Warp, 174, 446

efficiency, improving, 358

elements

    moving, Layers palette, 239-240

    oversized, animations, 551

    storing, Web pages, 475

Ellipse tool, 61, 87

ellipsis, type, 164

Embed ICC Profile option (Illustrator), 663

embedded file formats, 53

embedding

    files, text, 617-618

    fonts, 53-55, 162-163, 604, 617-619

        SVG, 556

        troubleshooting, 620

images, 53-55, 604

    raster, 612-615

    troubleshooting, 620

    vector, 615-616

    versus linking images, 606

    Photoshop files, 616-617

    profiles, ICC, 504

    text, formatted, 618

.emf, file format, 50

emulsion, determining, 583

Encapsulated Postscript (.eps), 46

Encoding (SVG Export option), 563

end

    points, 198

    tiles, 320

End User License Agreement (EULA), 677-678, 698

ending paths, 68

endpoints, paths, 61

Envelope Distort dialog box, 200

Envelope Distort, Create with Warp command (Object menu), 195

Envelope Distort, Edit Contents command (Object menu), 204, 207

Envelope Distort, Envelope Options command (Object menu), 202

Envelope Distort, Expand command (Object menu), 203

Envelope Distort, Make with Mesh command (Object menu), 200

Envelope Distort, Make with Top Object command (Object menu), 201-202

Envelope Distort, Make with Warp command (Object menu), 196

Envelope Distort, Release command (Object menu), 203

Envelope Options dialog box, 203

envelopes, distortions, 194

    content (editing), 205

    Edit Contents command, 204, 207

    Envelope Distort dialog box, 200

    expanding, 203-204

    feature (new), 15

    Make with Top Object command, 201-202

    mesh objects (editing), 198

    options, 202

    releasing, 203-204

    warping, 195-198

EPS Format Options dialog box, 46

.eps, file format, 46

equations, numeric fields, 181

Erase tool, paths (managing), 78

errors

    limitcheck, 573

    messages (Actions), 632

EULA (End User License Agreement), 677-678, 698

events, 561

Exceptions, hypenation, 366

Exclusion blending mode, 420

Expand Appearance command (Object menu), 330

Expand

    button, 107

    command

        Blend menu, 215

        Object menu, 306, 344-345, 493

Expand/Collapse, Layers palette, 236

expanding
    blends, 229
    complex objects, 229
    compound shapes, 107
    envelope distortions,
        203-204
    gradients, 345
    groups, 236
    layers, modifier keys, 237
    mesh objects, 203
    objects, 35, 208
    sublayers, 236-237
    symbol, instances or
        sets, 494

Expert Fractions, 153

export, file formats, 48

Export as CSS Layers check
box, 484

Export
    button, 552
    commands, 48-52, 481,
        552, 632
    dialog box, 49

Export JPEG dialog box,
506

Export, Paths to Illustrator
command (File menu), 669

exporting
    animations, to SWF,
        552-554
    files, 44-52, 661-664
    images, to Illustrator, 668
    keyboard shortcuts, 359
    layers, to SVG, 560
    paths, to Illustrator, 669

extended, type, 165

Extensible Markup
    Language. See XML

Extension Manager,
    Illustrator, installing, 677

Extensions plug-ins
    (Illustrator plug-in), 680

eye icon, 241, 245, 550

eyeball
    columns, layers, 235
    icon, 489

Eyedropper, 129
    colors, objects, 291
    dragging, 288
    modifying, 287
    tool, 159, 267, 290, 510

F

face (type), 165

features, new
    Arc tool, 17
    compound shapes, 19
    distortions, 15
    dynamic data-driven
        images, 20
    Flare tool, 18
    Grid tool, 18
    Line tool, 17
    liquifying, 15
    Mac OS X, 20
    Magic Wand, 17
    Rectangular tool, 18
    Slice Select tool, 18
    Slice tool, 18
    tools, 17-19
    warps, 15
    Web, 14-15
    Windows XP, 20

Fidelity (Paintbrush tool),
    75

Fidelity (Pencil tool), 75

Fidelity (Smooth tool), 78

Fidelity slider, 202

fields, numeric values, 181,
    288

File Format plug-ins,
    680-681

file formats
    .ai, 45
    .bmp, 49
    .cgm, 50
    compression, 43
    cross-platform, PDF, 262

.dwg, 49
.dxf, 49
embedded, 53
.emf, 50
.eps, 46
export, 48
film recorders, 269
fla, 537
images, 265
.jpg, 50
linked, 53
menu, 520
output, 262
.pct, 50
.pdf, 46
platforms, 43-44
PowerPoint, 265
print, 43
.psd, 50
raster
    images, 397, 403
    versus vector, 42
rasterization, 49, 481
Shockwave, 50
.svg, 47
.svgz, 48
.tga, 51
.txt, 52
vector, 397, 482, 604
Web, 43, 480-482
.wmf, 52

File menu commands
    Document Color Mode,
        284
    Document Info, 593
    Document Setup, 26, 143
    Export, 48-52, 481, 552
    Export, Paths to
        Illustrator, 669
    New, 144, 284
    Open File, 471
    Open, 553, 668
    Open, Page, 471
    Place, 605
    Save As, 45, 699
    Save for Web, 52, 481
    Save, 44
    Separation Setup, 282,
        351, 583

filename, compatibility (ensuring), 367

files
AICB, 665
corrupt, opening, 690
exporting, 44-52, 661-664
formats, 660, 667
GIF, creating, 481
JPEG, creating, 481
linked, editing or managing, 368
naming, 44
online, 500-501
optimization, 510
PDF, 263-265, 665, 699
Photoshop, 616-617, 668
PICT, 665
PNG, creating, 481
Preferences, 52, 360, 511, 688-689
rescuing, 690
round-tripping, 670-671
saving, 44-52, 367
Setup.exe, 677
sharing, Illustrator/Photoshop, 660, 664-666
size, 482, 501
startup, 370-371
SVG, pizelization, 558
text, embedding, 617-618
useless (Illustrator), 685-686

Files & Clipboard
dialog box, 367-369
preferences, 411

fill
blends, 214
effects, 328
inactive, 287
layering, 330
paths, 393
patterns, 34, 305-306
  bounding boxes, 303
  creating, 304
  repeating patterns, 303
  saving, 303

seamless patterns, 303
storing, 303
tiling, 302
versus brush patterns, 302
text, 141
values, 291

Fill New Brush Strokes (Paintbrush tool), 75

Fill swatches, 279, 291

film
file formats, 262
recorders
  aspect ratio, 269
  colors, 269
  file formats, 269
  images, 269
  output, 269-270
  pixels (addressable dimensions), 269
  printing, 269
  resolution, 269
  sharpness, 269
RGB color model, 259

Filter menu commands
Apply Last Filter, 434
Artistic, Colored Pencil, 447
Artistic, Cutout, 448
Artistic, Dry Brush, 448
Artistic, Film Grain, 448
Artistic, Fresco, 449
Artistic, Neon Glow, 449
Artistic, Paint Daubs, 450
Artistic, Palette Knife, 450
Artistic, Plastic Wrap, 450
Artistic, Poster Edges, 451
Artistic, Rough Pastels, 451
Artistic, Smudge Stick, 452
Artistic, Sponge, 452
Artistic, Underpainting, 453

Artistic, Watercolor, 453
Blur, Gaussian Blur, 454
Blur, Radial Blur, 455
Brush Strokes, Accented Edges, 455
Brush Strokes, Angled Strokes, 455
Brush Strokes, Crosshatch, 457
Brush Strokes, Dark Strokes, 457
Brush Strokes, Ink Outlines, 458
Brush Strokes, Spatter, 458
Brush Strokes, Sprayed Strokes, 458
Brush Strokes, Sumi-e, 459
Color, Adjuct Colors, 435
Color, Blend Front to Back, 435
Color, Blend Horizontally, 435
Color, Blend Vertically, 435
Color, Convert to CMYK, 435
Color, Convert to Grayscale, 435
Color, Convert to RGB, 436
Color, Invert Colors, 436
Color, Overprint Black, 436
Color, Saturate, 436
Colors, Adjust Colors, 294
Colors, Invert Colors, 290
Create, Object Mosaic, 437
Create, Trim Marks, 437, 592
Distort, Diffuse Glow, 460
Distort, Free Distort, 438
Distort, Glass, 460
Distort, Ocean Ripple, 460

Distort, Punk & Bloat, 326
Distort, Roughen, 438
Distort, Scribble and Tweak, 439
Distort, Twirl, 440
Distort, Twist, 189, 382
Distort, Zig Zag, 440
Last Filter, 434
Pen and Ink, Hatch Effects, 443
Pen and Ink, Library Open, 444
Pen and Ink, Library Save As, 444
Pen and Ink, New Hatch, 444
Pen and Ink, Photo Crosshatch, 443
Pixelate, Color Halftone, 461
Pixelate, Crystallize, 461
Pixelate, Mezzotint, 461
Pixelate, Pointillize, 462
Pucker & Bloat, 438
Sharpen, Unsharp Mask, 462
Sketch, Chalk & Charcoal, 463
Sketch, Charcoal, 463
Sketch, Chrome, 463
Sketch, Conte Crayon, 463
Sketch, Graphic Pen, 463
Sketch, Halftone Pattern, 463
Sketch, Note Paper, 463
Sketch, Photocopy, 464
Sketch, Plaster, 464
Sketch, Reticulation, 464
Sketch, Stamp, 464
Sketch, Torn Edges, 464
Sketch, Water Paper, 464
Stylize, 464
Stylize, Add Arrowheads, 444
Stylize, Drop Shadow, 445

Stylize, Round Corners, 446
Texture, Craquelure, 464
Video, De-Interlace, 465
Video, NTSC Colors, 465
filters, 35
    applying, 249, 252
    Artistic, 447
    drop shadows, 327
    justification of, 432
    objects, managing, 73
    opacity masks, 382
    paths, Actions, 636
    SVG, naming, 558
    versus effects, 326, 431
Find Again command (SVG Viewer), 556
Find command (SVG Viewer), 556
Find Font command (Type menu), 151
Find/Change command (Type menu), 150
Fit Headline command (Type menu), 150
Fit in Window command (View menu), 28-29
fixed pitch, type, 165
.fla file fomat, 537
Flare
    dialog box, 93
    tool, 18, 61, 92-94
Flare Tool Options dialog box, 93-94
flares
    creating, 93
    editing, 94
    halos, 94
    images, 18, 92
Flash, 535. *See also* SWF
    Adobe LiveMotion, 537
    animations, 482, 538-543
    Illustrator, 537
    limitations, 539
    symbols, 543, 552

troubleshooting, 565-566
vector file format, 43
Flash (SWF) Format Options dialog box, 552
flatness
    calculating, 588
    curves, troubleshooting, 588
    printing, 572
Flatten Artwork command (Layers palette menu), 46, 243
flexographic printing, 579
flexography, 572
flickers, animations, troubleshooting, 541
Flip Across option, 309
Flip Along
    box, 132
    option, 309
floating palettes, 24, 32
focal points, 184-185
FOCOLTONE swatch, 295
folders
    Adobe Illustrator, 127
    batch processing, 626
    Brush Libraries, 127
    Fonts, 162
    Photoshop Formats, 48
    Plug-ins, 48, 152, 367
    Text Filters, 152
Font Subsetting (SVG Export option), 563
fonts, 160
    bitmap, 161
    Character palette, 146
    CID (Character Identification), 162
    CJK (Chinese-Japanese-Korean), 37
    classifications, 151
    copyrights, 54, 162, 619
    display fonts, 37
    double-byte, type, 164

embedding, 53-55, 162-163, 604, 617-620
families, 161, 165
multiple master, 38, 148-150, 161, 166
OpenType, 162
ownership, determining, 619
single-byte, type, 168
size
    Character palette, 147
    type, 165
subsetting, 53-54, 163, 619
SVG, 47
    embedding, 556
    subsetting, 563
text, 150
type, 145, 165
Web animation, checklist, 704
weights, 161
Fonts
    folder, 162
    installation choices, Windows, 683
Format menu, 520
Format Method (JPEG Options dialog box), 504
formats. See file formats
fractional values, Color Picker, 288
Frame Rate (SWF), 552
frame-based animation, 536
frames
    animations, 535
    creating, 219
    orders, reversing, 251
Free Memory command (Status Bar pop-up menu), 26
Free Transform tool, 175, 180
full-motion video, 536

G

G mode, 288
gamuts
    CMYK, 285
    color, 39, 257, 278, 580
    Color palette, 279
    Fill swatch, 279
    RGB, 279, 285
    Stroke swatch, 279
Gap (Auto Trace tool), 80
General Preferences
    dialog box, 360-362
    effects or strokes, scaling, 180
GIF (Graphical Interchange Format), 501-503
    animated, 535
    compression, 43
    file formats, Web images, 481
    files, creating, 481
    lossless compression, 482
    optimization settings, 518-520
    raster file format, 43
global
    colors, linked, 294
    swatches, 293-294
    tints, linked, 294
Global check box, 294
glyphs
    OpenType fonts, 162
    type, 165
Go To Link
    button, 610
    command (Links palette menu), 612
Gradient Mesh tool, 344
Gradient
    palette
        gradients, 338
        menu commands, Linear or Radial, 340
    tool, 343

gradients, 34
    Angle field, 339
    applying, 249, 342-343
    blends, creating, 213
    color, 38, 702
    complex, creating, 341-343
    creating, 340
    editing, 340
    expanding, 345
    linear, 342-343
    loading, 338
    managing, 338
    meshes, 343
        creating, 344-348
        direction lines, 349
        guidelines, 346
        lines, 202, 349
        modifying, 348-350
        patches, 349
        path anchor points, 349
        points, 348-349
        printing, 347, 350-351
        simulating, 348
        size, 346-347
    modifying, 341
    opacity, 343
    PowerPoint, 268
    printing, 350-351, 572
    radial, 342
    rasterizing, 338
    saving, 338, 341
    separations, 701
    shaped, smooth colors, 218
    sliders, 340-341
    spot colors, 581
    stops
        adding, 339-340
        copying, 340
        deleting, 340
        locations, 341
        managing, 339
        modifying, 340
        moving, 339
    SVG (Scalable Vector Graphics), 557
    transparency, 406

troubleshooting, 352-353
vector images, 397
Graph
sign dialog box, 371
tools, 61, 219
Graph Type dialog box, 113
Graph, Column command
(Object menu), 116
Graph, Data command
(Object menu), 115
Graph, Marker command
(Object menu), 116
Graph, Type command
(Object menu), 113
Graphical Interchange
Format. *See* GIF
graphical user interface
(GUI), 358
graphics. *See* images
graphs
artboards, adding, 112
artwork, applying, 116
blends, making, 219
colors, 115
column, 110
custom, Specified Steps,
220
customizing, 115
data, 113-115
modifying, Specified
Steps, 221
symbols, 115
tools, 110-112
types, 110-115
Grated Moon, style, 324
grayed eye icons, 244
grayscale, 39
color, 282, 479
images, inverting, 290
objects, 279, 284
greeked text, 144
greeking type, 165, 363
Greeking, type preference,
144

Grid tool
feature (new), 18
paths, creating, 61
Gridline Every, 365
gridlines, subdivisions, 365
grids, 27
color, setting, 365
dividers, 94-96
managing, 94-96
mesh, 200
style, setting, 365
transparency, 411
Grids in Back check box,
365
Group Select tool, 214
Group Selection tool, 99,
122, 377
groups, 240, 244-245
annotating, 594
appearances, applying,
331-333
clipping, 374
collapsing, 236
expanding, 236
locating, 242
locked, 235
managing, 241
objects, duplicating, 35,
219
Outline view, 246
selecting, 241-243
targeting, 232, 236,
246-249, 410
transparency, 410
troubleshooting, 253
viewing, 236
guidelines, clipping masks,
374-376
guides, 31
color, setting, 364
inserting, 27
selections, slices, 495
smart guides, activating,
365
style, setting, 364

Guides & Grid dialog box,
364-365
Guides command (View
menu), 30
Guides, Show Guides com-
mand (View menu), 311
GUIs (graphical user interfaces), 358

H

halftones, 575
dots, tint, 572
options, setting, 583
halos, flares, 94
Hand tool, 510
handles, bounding boxes,
176
hanging
indents, type, 165
punctuation, 148, 165
hard
drives, defragmenting,
676
proofing, 574
Hard Light blending mode,
418-419
Harmonies_1 swatch, 295
head/headline (type), 165
Height/Width (trapping),
598
heights, cap (type), 163
Help
Adobe, 693
command (SVG Viewer),
556
Illustrator User Guide,
691
menu, 691-692
online, 692
PDF formats, 691
Helpers Option, installation
choices (Macintosh), 682

hexadecimal
colors, 500
base 16 system, 289
HTML, 289
names, 289
notation, colors (Web images), 479
values, 288

hidden characters, 153

Hide Edges command (View menu), 61

Hide Options command (Color palette menu), 287

Hide Others command (Layers palette menu), 244

Hide/Show Artboard command (View menu), 30

Hide/Show Bounding Box command (View menu), 30

Hide/Show Edges command (View menu), 29

Hide/Show Template command (View menu), 30

Hide/Show Tiling command (View menu), 30

high luminosity, 378

Higher Quality command (SVG Viewer), 555

highlighting
layers, 236
text, 145

highlights, 702

hinting type, 165

HKS E swatch, 295

HKS K swatch, 296

HKS N swatch, 296

HKS Z swatch, 296

hollow eyeballs, columns (layers), 235

horizontal
reflections, 184
type, 139

How All Layers command (Layers palette menu), 244

HSB (Hue, Saturation, and Brightness), 282
color mode, 282
fields, numeric values, 288
images, inverting, 290

HTML (Hypertext Markup Language), 289
base-16 notation, 479
colors, Web images, 479
hexadecimal colors, 289, 500
saving (Save Optimized As dialog box), 527
versus XML, 554

Hue
blending mode, 421
color wheel, 283
mode, 288

Hue Color Picker, 282

hues, color, 282

hypenation
exceptions, 366
languages, default, 366

Hypertext Markup Language. *See* HTML

Hyphenation dialog box, 366

Hyphenation Options dialog box, 147-148

hyphens (-), 144

I

ICC (International Color Consortium), 39, 504, 538, 682

icons
Add Eyedropper Color, 511
brushes, 121
circles, 246
Delete Selected Color(s), 511
diamond, 339
eye, 241, 245, 550

eyeball, 489
greyed icons, 244
Illustrator CD, 676
images, 54
Layer Targeting, 247-248, 550
Lock, 235
Lock Color, 511
Locked, 245
modal controls, 639
out-of-gamut, 286
Selected Art, 240
Snap to Web Palette, 511
stop sign, 610
targeting, 122
templates, 235, 245
troubleshooting, 689
Web-safe color, 285-286

Identify Objects By, 364

illustrations, rasterizing, 594

Illustrator
10, installing, 680
Anti-Alias option, 662
CD icon, 676
Color Model option, 662
Easy Install (Macintosh option), 676
Editable Text option, 663
Embed ICC Profile option, 663
File Formats plug-ins, 680
Filters plug-ins (Illustrator plug-in), 680
Help command (Help menu), 692
Include Hidden Layers option, 663
menu commands, Preferences, 360
Resolution option, 662
User Guide, 691
Write Compound Shapes option, 663
Write Image Maps option, 663
Write Layers option, 662

Write Nested Layers
  option, 663
Write Slices option, 663
Image Format (SWF), 553
Image Quality (JPEG
  Options dialog box), 503
imagemapping, JPEG, 504
images. *See also* dynamic
  data-driven graphics;
  raster images; vector,
  images
    8-bit RGB, 479
    24-bit RGB, 479
    animated GIFs, 535
    antialiasing, 507, 657
    artifacts, 503
    banding, controlling, 501
    bitmap, 156, 499, 657
    black-and-white, 479
    blur, applying, 521
    borders, film recorders,
      269
    checklist, 481, 704
    CMYK, inverting, 290
    color ranges, 285
    compression, 501
    continuous tone, 50, 503,
      514, 572
    controlling, 498
    crossover, 703
    digital, ppi (pixels per
      inch), 259
    dithering, 501, 511,
      521-524
    embedding, 53-55, 604,
      612, 620
    exporting, to Illustrator,
      668
    file formats, 265
    film recorders, 269
    flares, 18, 92
    fonts, 53-55
    grayscale, 290, 479
    HSB, inverting, 290
    icons, 54
    interlacing, 519
    jaggies, 506
    linked, 612, 620

  linking, 53-55, 604
    edges, 606
    effects, 607, 610
    filtering, 610
    managing, 605-609
    missing images, 610
    transformations, 607,
      610
    versus embedding,
      606
    viewing, 607
  maps, creating (slices),
    495
  matting, 521
  moving, 236, 669
  online
    color, 499-500
    dimensions, 506
    GIFs, 501-503
    JPEGs, 503-504
    PNGs, 505
    SVGs, 505
    SWFs, 506
    uncolored areas, 426
  opacity, 408
  optimizing, 52, 512-514
  pixelization, 261
  pixels, 538, 656
  preparing for creation,
    Web, 475-478
  quality menu, 520
  rasterization, 506-508,
    512
  resampling, 260
  resolution, 259
  RGB, reversing channel
    values, 290
  saving (Save Optimized
    As dialog box), 527
  scalable, 505
  sharing, preparation,
    699-700
  sizes, film recorders, 269
  slices, optimizing,
    525-527
  Specified Steps, 221
  static, animations, 541
  SVG, displaying, 538
  SWF, placing in Web
    pages, 554

  symbols, replacing, 492
  thumbnail, masks, 381
  tiling, 575
  transparency
    blending mode, 409
    changing, 409
    opacity, 407
    simulating, 406
    theory of, 406
    Transparency palette,
      409
  tritone, 575
  Web
    animations, 482
    basics, 470-471
    colors, 280
    downloading, 482
    files, 481-482
    page setup, 477-478
    pixels, 475-476
    preferences, 476-477
    preparing, 471, 700
    previewing, 471
    special effects, 471
    symbols, 485
    view option, 478
  Web Safe RGB palette,
    285
  zooming, 27-29, 513, 657
imagesetters, 578
Import Data button, 113
in-RIP trapping, 596
in-use colors, viewing, 516
inactive, fill or stroke, 287
Include Extended Syntax for
  Variable Data (SVG Export
  option), 563
Include File Info (SVG
  Export option), 563
Include GoLive Code check
  box, 528
Include Hidden Layers
  option (Illustrator), 663
Include Slicing Data (SVG
  Export option), 563

indenting
  paragraphs, 147-149
  type, 165

indents, hanging (type), 165

InDesign, file formats, 262

Index number, 510

indicators
  Layer Targeting, 243
  Selected Art, 236, 239

Information command
  (Links palette menu), 610,
  613

inkjet printers
  CMYK, 256
  colors, 285
  proofing, 256, 285

inks, process, CMYK, 279

inner corners, 306, 313

Insert Menu Item
  command (Actions
    palette menu), 634
  dialog box, 634

Insert Select Path command
  (Actions palette menu),
  634-635

Insert Stop command
  (Actions palette menu),
  638

Install SVG, installation
  choices (Macintosh), 682

installation, custom,
  681-683

installing, Illustrator
  10, 680
  custom installation,
    679-680, 684
  Macintosh, 676-677
  preparations, 676
  Windows, 677-678

InstallShield Wizard, 677

instances
  managing, 14
  objects, 14

symbols, 485
  adding, 486
  color, 488
  expanding, 494
  managing, 493
  moving, 487
  randomizing, 487
  repositioning, 486
  rotating, 487
  size, 487

integration, XML, 555

Intensity (Symbolism tool
  option), 490

interactivity
  SVG, 538
  triggering, 561

Interactivity palette (SVG),
  561

interfaces
  Illustrator, 24-26
  requirements, Web
    browsers, 547

interlacing images, 519

intermediary objects
  creating, 219
  orientations, 215
  smooth colors, 217
  spacing, 222-224
  vertical orientations, 224

International Color
  Consortium (ICC), 538

interoperability, color
  matching, 690

interpolation, 535

Inverse command (Select
  menu), 103

Invert command (Color
  palette menu), 290

Invert Mask check box, 380

inverting
  colors, 287
  images
    CMYK, 290
    grayscale, 290
    HSB, 290

opacity masks, 380
  RGB sliders, 290
  Web-safe RGB values,
    290

invisible, paths, 61

Isolate Blending option
  (Transparency palette),
  423

italic (type), 165

J

jaggies, 506, 538
  color, 39
  pixel edges, 402

Japanese crop marks, 361

JavaScript, interactivity
  (implementing), 561

JFIF (JPEG File Interchange
  Format), 503

joins, blends, 214

JPEG (Joint Photographic
  Experts Group)
  antialiasing, 504
  compression, 43, 482,
    505
  files, 480-481
  imagemapping, 504
  limitations, 503
  optimization settings,
    520-521
  PDF option, 264
  raster file format, 43

JPEG File Interchange
  Format (JFIF), 503

JPEG Options dialog box,
  503-504

.jpg, file format, 50

justification
  text, 37
  type, 163, 165

K

Kbps (kilobits per second), 500

Keep Selected
Paintbrush tool, 75
Pencil tool, 76

kerning
letters, 362
paragraphs, 147
text, 37
type, 144, 147, 166
versus tracking, 37-38

key colors, 129, 257

Keyboard Increment, setting, 360

keyboard
events, 561
shortcuts
A, 99
Alt+Ctrl+[, 103
Alt+Ctrl+], 103
assigning, 358-359
B, 74
C, 79
Cmd+A, 102
Cmd+C, 158
Cmd+D, 191
Cmd+F, 158, 316
Cmd+K, 360
Cmd+L, 239
Cmd+M, 147
Cmd+N, 284
Cmd+O, 471
Cmd+Option+Shift+K, 358
Cmd+S, 358
Cmd+Shift+, 144
Cmd+Shift+<, 144
Cmd+T, 146
Cmd+X, 316
Cmd+Z, 146, 510
Ctrl+A, 102
Ctrl+Alt+Shift+K, 358
Ctrl+C, 158
Ctrl+D, 191
Ctrl+F, 158, 316
Ctrl+K, 360

Ctrl+L, 239
Ctrl+M, 147
Ctrl+N, 284
Ctrl+O, 471
Ctrl+S, 358
Ctrl+Shift+<, 144
Ctrl+T, 146
Ctrl+X, 316
Ctrl+Z, 146, 510
duplicate, 359
E, 175
exporting, 359
functions, 360
L, 87
M, 85
N, 75
Option+Cmd+[, 103
Option+Cmd+], 103
R, 182, 315
saving, 358
T, 138
troubleshooting, 372
V, 98, 316
Y, 99

Keyboard Shortcuts
command (Edit menu), 239, 358, 369
dialog box, 239, 358
installation choices, Windows, 684

keys
arrow keys, 360
modifier
eyedropper, 287
layers, 237-239
sublayers, 237

kilobits per second (Kbps), 500

Kind (Link Information window), 615

Knife tool, paths (managing), 79

knocking out objects, printing, 589

knockout, 35, 412, 572

Kodak Photo CD Support, installation choices (Macintosh), 682

L

labels (printer's marks), 593

laminate proofs, 701

Large Swatch View, 293

Lasso tool, 102

Last Filter command (Filter menu), 434

law, copyright, 678

Layer Options dialog box, 235, 239, 245

Layer Targeting
icon, 247-248, 550
indicator, 243

Layer/Group Overrides
Color command
(Appearance palette menu), 331

layering
fills, 330
strokes, 330, 410

layers, 32, 242. See also sublayers
appearances, 232, 324, 331-333
arranging, 233
blends, 214
characteristics, viewing, 325
collapsing, modifier keys, 237
columns, 235
contents, 235, 244
copying between, 543
creating, 328-239
CSS (Cascading Style Sheets), 482-485
deleting, 243
effects, 232
expanding, modifier keys, 237
file formats, raster images, 397
flattening, 668
highlighting, 236
Layers palette, 232

levels, 238
locations, 238
locked, 235
merging, Layers palette,
    243
naming, 235
nesting, 234
objects, 36, 249
Photoshop, 660
selecting, 243
shape layers, pasting,
    666
styles, 324
SVG (Scalable Vector
    Grahics), exporting to,
    560
targeted, 232, 236,
    246-249
templates, 235, 245
transparency, 232, 410
triangles, 234
troubleshooting, 253
viewing, 241
Web pages, 474, 482
Layers palette, 122, 214
    arranging palette, 233
    blends, making, 216
    buttons, 236
    contents, 236
    effects, applying, 252
    elements, moving,
        239-240
    Expand/Collapse, 236
    features, 232
    filters, applying, 252
    groups, 241-243
    layers
        contents, 244
        creating, 238-239
        deleting, 243
        highlighting, 236
        merging, 243
        selecting, 243
        viewing, 241
    Lock/Unlock, 235
    menu commands
        Collect in New Layer,
            243
        Create New Layer, 239

Create New Sublayer,
    239
Flatten Artwork, 46,
    243
Hide Others, 244
Locate Object, 242
Lock Others, 244
Merge Selected, 243
Outline Others, 244
Palette Options, 245
Paste Remembers
    Layers, 244
Preview All Layers,
    244
Release to Layers
    (Build), 244, 249-251
Release to Layers
    (Sequence), 244,
    249-251, 540
Reverse Order, 244
Show All Layers, 244
Template, 244
Unlock All Layers, 244
    objects
        locating, 242
        modifying, 241
        selecting, 241-243
    rows, 236
    Selected Art indicators,
        236
    Show/Hide, 235
    sublayers
        creating, 238-239
        selecting, 243
        viewing, 241
    Thumbnails, 236
    Web pages, 252
Layers Palette Options dia-
    log box, 236
Layers tab, 483
leading
    setting, 362
    text, 37
    type, 144, 147, 166
legalities, Illustrator (porta-
    bility), 698
Lempel-Ziv-Welch (LZW)
    compression, 502

lengths, arcs, 90
letterform, type, 166
letters
    kerning, 362
    spacing, type, 166
    tracking, 362
levels
    layers, 238
    Minimum Undo Levels,
        364
Libraries, installation
    choices (Windows), 684
libraries. *See* Swatch
    Libraries
    brushes, 121, 127
    styles, 334-335
    swatches, spot colors,
        258
    symbols, saving, 485
Library of Congress Web
    site, 678
licensing agreement
    (Adobe), 678
ligature
    text, 37
    type, 166
Lighten blending mode, 420
limitcheck error, 573
line
    breaks, smart, 148
    of reflection, 184
    screen frequency, 396,
        573
Line Segment tool, 89
Line Segment Tool dialog
    box, 89
Line tool, 17, 61
Linear command (Gradient
    palette menu), 340
linear gradients, 342-343
lines
    color, slices, 366
    direction, 349
        anchor points, 65
        control points, 65

corner anchor points,
67
editing, 72-74, 198,
350
path segments, 68
paths, 393
per inch (lpi), 396, 573
mesh, 343, 349
deleting, 199
gradients, 202
guidelines, 198-199
Link Information window,
615
linked files
editing, 368
formats, 53
managing, 368
linking
global, colors or tints,
294
images, 53-55, 604
edges, 606
editing, 612
effects, 607, 610
filtering, 610
managing, 605-609
missing, 610
transformations, 607,
610
troubleshooting, 620
versus embedding
images, 606
viewing, 607
opacity masks, 380
raster images, 604
slices, 495
text, 150
text containers, 154-156
type, 150
links
selecting, 612
symbols, 492-493
Links palette, menu com-
mands, 54, 605, 611, 614
Edit Original, 612
Got To Link, 612
Information, 610, 613

Liquify tool, 16, 206
brushes, 208
options, 208-209
preferences, 207
liquifying, features, 15
live effects, 432
LiveMotion, 535-537
Load Color Table command
(color table menu), 518
loading
Actions, 629
brush libraries, 121
brushes, 135
gradients, 338
selections, 106
style libraries, 334-335
symbols, 14
Locate Object command
(Layers palette menu), 242
locating
anchor points, 63-64
groups, 242
objects, 242, 292
Swatch Libraries, 297
swatches, 292
Location (Link Information
window), 615
locations
layers, 238
stops, gradients, 341
Lock Color icon, 511
Lock icon, 235
Lock Others command
(Layers palette menu), 244
Lock Variables control
(Variables palette), 650
Lock/Unlock, Layers palette,
235
locked
groups, 235
layers, 235
objects, 235
Locked icon, 245

locking
colors, 517
objects, 35
templates, 245
Lossiness slider, 519
lossless compression, 43,
482, 505
lossy compression, 43, 482,
503
Lossy (JPG) (SWF), 553
Lower Case check box, 367
lpi (lines per inch), 396, 573
luminosity, high, 378
Luminosity blending mode,
423
LZW (Limpel-Ziv-Welch),
compression, 502

M

Macintosh
72ppi (pixels per inch),
144
custom installation,
681-683
Easy Install, 676
files, naming, 44
installing Illustrator,
676-677
OS 9, 677, 680
OS X, 20, 44, 680
PictureViewer, 700
Macromedia Director, 535
Macromedia Shockwave, 50,
535
Macs. *See* Macintosh
Magic Wand
palette, 17, 100
tool, 17, 99, 101
Maintain Envelope Shape
check box, 201
Make command (Blend
menu), 215

Make Object Dynamic control (Variables palette), 650

Make Opacity Mask command (Transpareny palette menu), 379

Make Visibility Dynamic control (Variables palette), 650

Make with Mesh dialog box, 200

managing
    Actions, 626-629
    anchor points, 63-64, 70-71
    animations, 543
    color, 38-39, 571
    folders, plug-ins, 367
    gradients, 338
    grids, 94-96
    images, linked, 605-609
    instances, 14
    linked files, 368
    mesh patches, 199
    objects, 73
    palettes, 25
    path segments, 70-71
    spirals, 91-92
    stops, gradients, 339
    symbols, 485, 493
    transformations, 175
    transparency, 594
    Web pages, 470

maps, image (creating), 495

margins
    creating, objects, 158
    setting, 583
    type, 166

marks
    crop marks, 80, 591-593
    printer's marks, 583, 591-593
    registration, 584
    trim marks, 80, 591-592

masking
    objects, 413
    with text, 376

masks
    clipping masks, 33, 374
        adding objects, 377
        anchor points, 377
        creating, 374-376
        editing, 376-377
        guidelines, 374-376
        non-object paths, 80
        printing, 375
        repositioning, 377
        troubleshooting, 376, 384
        type as, 377-378
    opacity masks, 34, 378
        creating, 379-380
        disabling, 380
        drop shadows, 414
        editing, 380-382
        effects, 382
        filters, 382
        inverting, 380
        linking, 380
        planning, 413-414
        reducing opacity, 382
        repositioning, 380-382
        transparency, 413-414
        troubleshooting, 384
        type as, 383
    thumbnail images, 381
    unlinking, 380

matching, color matching, 690

matrix, SVG, 560

Matte selection menu, 519

Mbps (megabits per second), 500

megabits per second (Mbps), 500

memory, supporting, 366

menus, 24. See also pop-up menus
    Destination, 631
    Effects, 433
    Filters, 433
    Layers palette, 239
    pop-up, Method, 491
    Stop Recording, 633

symbols, overriding, 359
Transform palette, 191

Merge command (Pathfinder palette menu), 109

Merge Selected command (Layers palette menu), 243

Merge Styles (Styles palette menu), 334

mesh
    gradient meshes, 343
        creating, 344-348
        direction lines, 349
        editing, 348-350
        guidelines, 346
        printing, 347, 350-351
        simulating, 348
        size, 346-347
        guidelines, 346
        size, 347
        troubleshooting, 352-353
    grids, 200
    lines, 198-199, 202, 343, 349
    objects, 197-200, 203
    patches, 199, 349
    points, 197-199, 343, 348-350

messages, error (Actions), 632

Method pop-up menu (Symbolism tool option), 491

Microsoft PowerPoint, file formats, 262

millions of colors, 499

Minimum Undo Levels, 364

Minus Back command (Pathfinder palette menu), 109

misregistration, 573, 590

miter limits, blends, 214

MM (Multiple Master)
    Design palette, 148, 161

modal
  controls, 628, 639
  dialog boxes (Actions),
    629

models, color models
  (CMYK or RGB), 256

modes. *See also* color,
  modes
  B, 288
  blending modes, 414-415
    Color, 422
    Color Burn, 419
    Color Dodge, 418-419
    Darken, 419-420
    Difference, 420
    Exclusion, 420
    Hard Light, 418-419
    Hue, 421
    Lighten, 420
    Luminosity, 423
    Multiply, 416
    Normal, 416
    Overlay, 417-418
    restricting effects, 423
    Saturation, 421
    Screen, 417
    Soft Light, 418
  G, 288
  Hue, 288
  Outline, 214, 244
  Preview, 214, 244
  R, 288
  S, 288
  view, 28

Modified (Link Information
  window), 615

modifier keys
  eyedropper, 287
  layers, 237-239
  sublayers, 237

modifying
  Actions, 640-641
  anchor points, clipping
    masks, 377
  art brushes, 127, 131-133
  blends, 214
  bounding boxes, 146, 362
  brushes, 123-135

calligraphic brushes, 129
clipping masks, 376-377
colors, Swatch Library
  palette, 295
content envelope distor-
  tions, 205
crop marks, 592
direction lines, 198, 350
eyedropper, 287
files, 368, 371
flares, 94
global swatches, 294
gradients, 340-341,
  348-350
graph data, 113-115
images, linked, 612
mesh, objects or points,
  198
object transparency, 409
objects, bounding box,
  31
opacity masks, 380-382
paths, 70-74, 207
pattern brushes, 133-134
patterns, 305
resolution, paths, 591
scatter brushes, 130
selections, 106
settings, Rounded
  Rectangle tool, 361
spines, 226-227
stops, gradients, 340
swatches, 293
symbols, 492
text, 664
tiles, 133
vector images, 390
versus creating brushes,
  127
warp distortions, 200

monitors
  colors, 280
  computers, 259-261
  resolutions, 259
  Web animation, check-
    list, 704

monospace, type, 166

Move
  command (Transform
    menu), 181
  dialog box, 181
  tool, 126, 181-182

moving
  Actions, 640
  anchor points, 63-64
  elements, Layers palette,
    239-240
  images, 236, 669
  mesh points, 198, 350
  objects, 181, 397
  pixels, raster images, 397
  stops, gradients, 339
  swatches, 295
  symbol instances, 487
  transformations, 176

MS-DOS, files (naming), 44

multiple
  master fonts, 38, 148-150,
    161, 166
  startup files, 371

Multiply blending mode,
  416

Mute command (SVG
  Viewer), 556

N

Name (Link Information
  window), 615

Name View, 292-293

names
  hexadecimal, 289
  swatches, 292-293

naming
  Actions, 640
  brush patterns, 309
  conventions, swatches,
    581
  files, 44
  layers, 235
  styles, 334
  SVG filters, 558
  swatches, 294
  tints, 294

Navigator palette, zooming with, 28

negative color separations, 578

nesting
Actions, 630
layers, 234

New Action
button, 629
command (Actions palette menu), 632
dialog box, 632

New Art Has Basic Appearance command (Appearances palette menu), 331

New Brush
button, 121, 129-133
command (Brushes palette menu), 129-133, 307-308
dialog box, 129-133

New Color button, 517

New command (File menu), 144, 284

New Design button, 115

New Document dialog box, 26

New Entry, hypenation, 366

New Layer button, 316

New Opacity Masks Are Inverted command (Transparency palette menu), 380

New Pattern Brush
dialog box, 308
option, 307

New Set
command (Actions palette menu), 632
dialog box, 632

New Style
button, 333-334
command (Style palette menu), 333

New SVG Filter button, 558

New Swatch
button, 267, 292-294, 341
command (Swatch palette menu), 293, 341
dialog box, 305

New Symbol
button, 204, 493
command (Symbols palette menu), 493

New Variable control (Variables palette), 650

New View command (View menu), 31

Next Object Above command (Select menu), 103

Next Object Below command (Select menu), 103

Noise dithering (images), 524

noncumulative animations, 536

None, shortcut buttons, 287

nonglobal, swatches, 293-294

nonlinear paths, objects (rotating), 224

nonprinting templates, 245

nonrecordable
commands (Actions), 634-635
tools (Actions), 634

Normal blending mode, 416

notations
base-16, 479
hexadecimal, Web images, 479

notes, entering, 638

Number of Undos command (Status Bar pop-up menu), 26

numbering, proofing, 703

Numbers Without Units Are Points check box, 364

numeric
fields, 181
values
CMYK fields, 288
HSB fields, 288
reversing, colors, 290
RGB fields, 288

O

Object
command (Select menu), 104-105
menu commands
applying (targeting), 249
Arrange, 155
Arrange, Bring to Back, 233
Arrange, Bring to Forward, 233
Arrange, Bring to Front, 233
Arrange, Send Backward, 189, 233
Blend, 540
Blend, Expand, 213, 540
Blend, Make, 212, 216-219, 540
Blend, Replace, 228
Clipping Mask, Make, 33, 374
Clipping Mask, Release, 376
Create Gradient Mesh, 344
Crop Marks, Make, 359, 592
Crop Marks, Release, 592
Envelope Distort, Create with Warp, 195
Envelope Distort, Edit Contents, 204, 207
Envelope Distort, Envelope Options, 202

Envelope Distort, Expand, 203
Envelope Distort, Make with Mesh, 200
Envelope Distort, Make with Top Object, 201-202
Envelope Distort, Make with Warp, 196
Envelope Distort, Release, 203
Expand, 306, 344-345, 493
Expand Appearance, 330
Graph, Column, 116
Graph, Data, 115
Graph, Marker, 116
Graph, Type, 113
Path, Join, 124
Path, Simplify, 159, 191, 208, 591
Rasterize, 260, 266, 401, 591
Show Edges, 587
Slice, Create from Guides, 495
Slice, Create from Selection, 494-495
Slice, Make, 495
Slice, Slice Options, 495
Transform, Move, 181
Transform, Reset Bounding Box, 194
Transform, Rotate, 315
Transform, Scale, 185, 218, 657
Transform, Shear, 187
Transform, Transform Again, 191
Transform, Transform Each, 183, 192-194
Object Creation tools, 84-97
Object Highlighting check box, 365

Object, All command (Select menu), 105
Object, Brush Strokes command (Select menu), 105
Object, Direction Handles command (Select menu), 105
Object, Save Selection command (Select menu), 105
object-based slicing, 14, 495
objects. *See also* selections
   aligning, 35
   angles, 187
   annotating, 594
   appearances, 324, 327
   arranging, 155
   blends, 212-214
   changing into pixels, 401
   collapses, 207
   color, 290-291
   complex, expanding, 229
   copying, 181
   creating, 35, 84
   dimensions, 186
   distorting, 181, 184
   edges, 587
   effects, removing, 326
   expanding, 35, 208
   filters, 35, 326
   flipping, 184
   focal points, 184
   gradient mesh, 343-350
   grayscale, 279, 284
   grouped, duplicating, 219
   grouping, 35
   instances, 14
   intermediary, 215-219, 222-224
   knockout, 35
   layers, 36
   locating, 242, 292
   locked, 235
   locking, 35
   managing, 73
   margins, creating, 158
   masking, 413
   mesh, 197-200, 203
   modifying, 31, 241

   moving, 181, 397
   opacity, 408
   Outline view, 246
   overlapping, knockout, 35, 412, 572
   pasting, 244-245
   placing, 249
   point of origin, 35, 186
   positioning, 181
   previewing, 181
   printing, knocking out, 589
   proxies, 182
   rastered
      antialiasing, 401-403
      backgrounds, 400
      colors, 399
      padding, 400
      resolution, 400-403
      troubleshooting, 403
   rasterizing, 399-403
   reflecting, 180, 184
   resolutions, fineness or courseness, 261
   rotating, 180-183, 224
   scaling, 362
   segments, distorting, 185
   selected
      bounding boxes, 98
      points, 184
   selecting, 98-99, 180, 241-243, 292
   shaded, smooth colors, 218
   shearing, 180, 187
   showing, 306
   size, 185
   slanting, 187
   stacking order, 36, 215, 249
   styles, 324, 334
   SVG, recording, 557
   symbol sets, 14
   target, creating, 97
   targeted, 236
   targeting, 246-247, 249
   text
      containers, 155
      wrapping, 156-158

transforming, 178
transparency, 36
  blending mode, 409
  changing, 409
  opacity, 407
  simulating, 406
  theory of, 406
  Transparency palette,
    409
transparent, spot colors
  (overlapping), 582
type, antialiasing, 15
ungrouping, 35, 229
unlocking, 35
vector images, 392
rasterizing, 402
viewing, 236

ODBC-compliant, databases
(dynamic data-driven
graphics), 651

offset printing, 573

old-style figure (type), 166

online
  Adobe Online, help, 693
  animation, 534-536
  color, CMYK or Web
    Safe, 500
  files, size, 500-501
  help, 692
  images, 426
    color, 499-500
    dimensions, 506
    GIFs, 501-503
    JPEGs, 503-504
    PNGs, 505
    SVGs, 505
    SWFs, 506
  resolution, 506
  transparency, 426

Online Help, installation
choices, 682-684

Online Settings dialog box,
369

Only Web Colors check box,
288

opacity, 406, 410. *See also*
  transparency
  blends, 214
  clipping masks, trou-
    bleshooting, 376
  color value (comparison),
    407
  colored backgrounds, 408
  gradients, 343
  masks, 34, 378
    creating, 379-380
    disabling, 380
    drop shadows, 414
    editing, 380-382
    effects, 382
    filters, 382
    inverting, 380
    linking, 380
    opacity, reducing, 382
    planning, 413-414
    repositioning, 380-382
    transparency, 413-414
    troubleshooting, 384
    type as, 383
  multicolored back-
    grounds, 408
  overlapping objects, 408
  symbols, adding or
    instances, 488

Open
  command (File menu),
    553, 668
  dialog box, 516

Open File commands (File
menu), 471

open paths, 61, 393

Open PPD button, 583

Open, Page command (File
menu), 471

opening
  Actions, 642
  Color Picker, 288
  files, corrupt, 690

OpenType
  fonts, 162
  type, 166

optical size (type), 167

optimization, 52, 510-511,
  516-518
  GIF, 518-520
  images, 512-514
  JPEG, 520-521
  PNG-8, 520
  PNG-24, 521
  slices, 525-527
  SVG, 521
  SWF, 521

Optimize for Adobe SVG
  Viewer (SVG Export
  option), 563

Optimize to File Size command (Settings menu), 518

Optimized check box, 520

Opting for Only Glyphs
  Used (SVG Font
  Subsetting), 564

options
  Colorization, 128
  envelope distortions, 202
  halftone, setting, 583
  Liquify tools, 208-209
  Paintbrush tool, 74
  scatter brushes, 130
  Symbolism tools, 489-492
  view, Web images, 478

Options (General), PDF
  option, 264

Options dialog box, 129

Options of Selected Object
  command (Brushes palette
  menu), 121, 128

orders
  effects, 327
  frames, reversing, 251
  stacking, objects, 215,
    249

Orientation, Blend Options
  dialog box, 224

orientations
  blends, 224
  intermediary objects, 215
  vertical, intermediary
    objects, 224

Original View command
(SVG Viewer), 555

out-of-gamut
colors, 580
icon, 286

outer corners, 306, 313-315

Outline
command (Pathfinder
palette menu), 109
mode, 244
view, groups or objects,
246

Outline Mode, blends, 214

Outline Others command
(Layers palette menu), 244

Outline Stroke command
(Effect menu), 442

Outline/Preview command
(View menu), 29

outlines, text (converting
to), 158

output
colors, 256-259
file formats, 262
film recorders, 269-270
options, 265-270
PDF, 262, 265
print, 256
resolution, 259-261
SVG, creating, 554-559
troubleshooting, 270

Output button, 484

Output Settings dialog box,
484, 528, 530

overlapping
colors, 414, 572-574, 582
objects, knockout, 35,
412, 572
spot colors, 582

Overlay blending mode,
417-418

Overprint Black check box,
584

Overprint Preview com-
mand (View menu), 29,
587-589

overprinting, 574, 702
assigning, 587
curves, flatness, 588
objects, edges, 587
paths, reversing, 587
RGB, 587
strokes, 600

Override Action "Open"
Commands check box, 631

overriding
Export commands,
Actions, 632
menu symbols, 359
Save commands, Actions,
631

oversized elements, animations, 551

ownership, fonts, determining, 619

P

Page Graphics Markup
Language (PGML), 538

Page Setup dialog box, 583

PageMaker, file formats, 262

pages
order, proofing, 703
organizing, Web design,
474
PostScript PDF, 262
proofs, color, 702-703
setup, Web images,
477-478
tiling, 27, 31-32
Web
components (saving),
470
creating (Layers
palette), 252
elements (storing), 475
layers, 482
managing, 470
SWG images, 554

Paint Bucket tool, 159

Paintbrush tool, 76
brushes, 122
options, 74
paths, creating, 74-75

Paintbrush Tool Preferences
dialog box, 74

Paintbucket, colors, objects,
291

Palette Options command
(Layers palette menu), 245

palettes
Actions, 626-629
Appearance, 324-328,
338
Attributes, 587, 594, 637
Brushes, 31, 121, 126-127,
308
Character, 146, 161
cleaning up, 627
Color, 122, 141, 258, 289
changing stroke color,
126
color bar, 287
gamuts, 279
gradients, 338
menu, 519
shortcuts, 286
spot colors, 258
tab, 287
Toolbox, 288
updating colors, 290
displays, 232
docking, 32
Document Info, 593, 605,
613
Fill, default values, 291
floating, 24, 32
Gradient, gradients, 338
Layers, 122, 214
blends, making, 216
buttons, 236
contents, 236
effects, applying, 252
elements, moving,
239-240
Expand/Collapse, 236
features, 232
filters, applying, 252

groups, *241-243*
layers, *233, 236-244*
Lock/Unlock, *235*
objects, *241-243*
row, *236*
Selected Art indica-
    tors, *236*
Show/Hide, *235*
sublayers, *241-243*
Thumbnails, *236*
Web pages, creating,
    252
Links, 54, 605, 610-614
Magic Wand, 17, 100
managing, 25
MM (Multiple Master)
    Design, 148, 161
Navigator, zooming with,
    28
Paragraph, 140, 147
Pathfinder
    buttons, 108-109
    compound shapes,
        106-107
    troubleshooting, 108
reducing, 284
Stroke, 122, 291
Styles, 122, 324, 333-334
SVG, Interactivity, 561
Swatch Library, 294-295
Swatches, 141, 295-297
    buttons, 292
    colors, 291-293
    creating swatches,
        267
    global swatches, 294
    gradients, 338
    nonglobal swatches,
        294
    sliders, 293
    spot colors, 258
    storing fill patterns,
        303
Symbol, 485
Symbols, symbols (stor-
    ing), 14
Tab Ruler, 149
Toolbox fly-out, 69

Transform, 124, 175
    menu, 191
    point of origin, 177
Transparency, 300, 379,
    409
    gradients, 338
    Isolate Blending, 423
troubleshooting, 689
Web-safe, 284-285,
    479-480, 499
panels
    Background, 528
    Printing & Export
        (Document Setup dialog
        box), 594
    Saving Files, 529
PANTONE Coated swatch,
    296
PANTONE Matte swatch,
    296
Pantone Process, 282, 581
PANTONE Process swatch,
    296
Pantone Solid, 282, 581
PANTONE Uncoated
    swatch, 296
Paragraph palette, 140, 147
paragraphs
    alignment, 147
    characters, 148
    hanging punctuation, 148
    indenting, 147, 149
    kerning, 147
    smart line breaks, 148
    text
        attributes, 160
        spacing, 148
    tracking, 147
    words, hyphenating, 148
Paste command, 61, 244-245
Paste Remembers Layers,
    244-245
Pastels swatch, 296
pasting
    layers, shape layers, 666
    objects, 244-245

paths, 666
pixels, 665
text, Photoshop, 664-666
patches, mesh, 349
Path Type tool, 140-142
Path, Join command (Object
    menu), 124
Path, Offset Path command
    (Effect menu), 158, 441
Path, Outline Object com-
    mand (Effects menu), 441
Path, Simplify command
    (Object menu), 159, 191,
    208, 591
Pathfinder Options
    command (Pathfinder
        palette menu), 109
    dialog box, 597
Pathfinder palette
    buttons, 108-109
    compound shapes,
        106-107
    menu commands
        Crop, 109
        Divide, 108
        Merge, 109
        Minus Back, 109
        Outline, 109
        Pathfinder Options,
            109
        Trap, 109, 599
        Trim, 108
        Unite, 591
    troubleshooting, 108
Pathfinder Trap dialog box,
    599
Pathfinder, Crop command
    (Effects menu), 443
Pathfinder, Divide command
    (Effects menu), 442
Pathfinder, Exclude com-
    mand (Effects menu), 442
Pathfinder, Hard Mix com-
    mand (Effects menu), 443
Pathfinder, Intersect com-
    mand (Effects menu), 442

Pathfinder, Merge command (Effects menu), 443

Pathfinder, Minus Back command (Effects menu), 442

Pathfinder, Outline command (Effects menu), 443

Pathfinder, Soft Mix command (Effects menu), 443

Pathfinder, Trap command (Effect menu), 443, 597

Pathfinder, Trim command (Effects menu), 443

Pathfinder, Unite command (Effects menu), 442

paths. *See also* spines
    Actions, 635-636
    adding to, 68
    anchor points, 33, 61
    angles, 208
    blends, 212-213, 218
    brushes, 122-125, 128
    clipping, 268, 374
    closed, 61, 87, 393
    closing, 68, 124
    complex, printing, 190
    compound, 150, 376
    creating, 60, 68-69, 74-76
    cutting, 124
    direction lines, 393
    editing, 70-74
    effects, 125
    ending, 68
    exporting, to Illustrator, 669
    fills, 393
    intermediary objects, spacing, 223
    invisible, 61
    manipulating, 174
    non-object, 80
    nonlinear, rotating objects, 224
    objects, vector images, 392
    open, 61, 393
    pasting, 666

rasterizing, 591
resolution, modifying, 591
reversing, 587
segments, 34, 61, 65-73, 89, 207
selecting, 122
separating, troubleshooting, 591
shaping, anchor points, 62-67
showing, 306
simplifying, 191, 208, 591
splitting, 573-574, 591
starting points, starting, 124
strokes, 34, 393
text, 141, 156, 158
troubleshooting, 81-82
types, 61
vector art, 60-61
viewing, 236

Pattern Brush Options dialog box, 133, 308

Pattern dithering (images), 522

patterned backgrounds, animations, 544

patterns, 34. *See also* brush patterns; fill, patterns
    applying (targeting), 249
    blends, 214
    continuous, 310, 313
    creating, 300
    editing, 305
    flipping, 134
    printers, 306
    repeating, 303, 310
    rotating, 178, 183
    rules, 300, 303
    scaling, 178, 187
    seamless, 303-305, 311
    tiling, 300-302
    transforming, 178
    transparency, 300
    troubleshooting, 321-322

Pause command (SVG Viewer), 555

PC Paintbrush, 50

.pct, file format, 50

PDF (Portable Document Format)
    dialog boxes, 263
    documents, viewing, 262
    file format, 46, 481, 660
    files, 263-265, 665, 699
    options
        Automatic, 264
        Compress Text and Line Art, 265
        Custom, 264
        Default, 264
        JPEG, 264
        Screen Optimized, 264
        Zip, 264
    PostScript pages, 262
    raster images, 262
    vector images, 262

Pen and Ink, Hatch Effects (Filter menu), 443

Pen and Ink, Library Open (Filter menu), 444

Pen and Ink, Library Save As (Filter menu), 444

Pen and Ink, New Hatch (Filter menu), 444

Pen and Ink, Photo Crosshatch (Filter menu), 443

Pen tool, 67-70, 122, 316, 349, 361

Pencil tool, 75-76, 122

percents, scaling, 186

Perceptual color profile, 586

performance, troubleshooting, 688-689

permanence, effects/filters comparison, 431

PGML (Page Graphics Markup Language), 538

Photoshop, Adobe Photoshop
  Additional Photoshop Effects, 681
  alternate file formats, 667
  compatibility, 661
  drag and drop, 666
  exporting images to Illustrator, 668
  file formats, comparing, 42
  files, embedding, 616-617
  Illustrator compatiblity, 21
  manipulating file parts in Illustrator, 660
  opening files in Illustrator, 668
  text, 664-666
  versus Illustrator
    moving images between, 669
    raster images, 656-658
    resampling, 260
    round-tripping, 670-671
    sharing files, 660, 664-666
    vector images, 656-659

Photoshop Effects, 681

Photoshop File Formats plug-ins, 681

Photoshop Filters & Effects package, 681

Photoshop Filters, 681

Photoshop Formats folder, 48

Photoshop Options dialog box, 50, 663

pica, type, 167

PICT files, 665

PictureViewer (Macintosh), 700

Pixar, 51

Pixel Preview, 29, 478, 506-508

pixel space (file size), 501

Pixelate, Color Halftone command (Filter menu), 461

Pixelate, Crystallize command (Filter menu), 461

Pixelate, Mezzotint command (Filter menu), 461

Pixelate, Pointillize command (Filter menu), 462

pixelization, 538
  images, 261
  SVG files, 558

pixels, 34, 656
  addressable dimensions, 269
  banding, colors, 402
  calculating, 395
  color, 394
  edges, 401-402
  interpolation, 535
  jaggies, 538
  moving, raster images, 397
  objects, changing into, 401
  pasting, 665
  points (type), 143
  raster
    advantage, 658
    images, 394-396, 535
  resampling, 260
  resolutions, 259, 395
  Web images, 475-476

pixels per inch (ppi), versus dots per inch (dpi), 395

Place
  command (File menu), 605
  dialog box, 605, 612

Place Symbol Instance button, 493

placeholders, text, 363

placement, artwork, 27

plates, printing, 578-579, 584

platforms, file formats, 43-44

Playback Options command (Actions palette menu), 630

Plug-in folder, 152

plug-ins, 366
  File Format, 680-681
  folders, managing, 367
  Illustrator, 680
  SVG Viewer, 539
  trapping, 596

Plug-ins & Scratch Disk preferences dialog box, 366

Plug-ins folder, 48, 367

plus (+) signs, 139

PNG (Portable Network Graphic), 505
  8-bit, 505
  24-bit, 505
  compression, 43
  files, 481
  lossless compression, 482
  raster file format, 43

PNG-8, optimization settings, 520

PNG-24, optimization settings, 521

point of origin
  arcs, 90
  creating, 186
  objects, 35, 186
  proxies, 177
  relocating, 177
  rulers, 27, 302
  shearing, 187
  Transform Each dialog box, 192
  transformations, 176-178
  troubleshooting, 372
  versus rule origin, 32

point type text, 38

point-to-point tiles, 315

pointed segments, creating, 208

pointer events, 561

points. *See also* anchor points
  blends, 214
  combination, anchor points, 65
  control, 65, 199
  corner, 198
  direction, 34
  end, 198
  focal, 184-185
  mesh, 343
    color, 350
    copying, 199
    corner, 348
    deleting, 350
    diamond, 198
    editing, 198
    guidelines, 198-199
    moving, 198, 350
    objects, 197
    points, corner, 349
    selecting, 199, 350
  path anchor points, 349
  pixels (type), 143
  rotation, 183, 190
  selected, objects, 184
  starting (paths), starting, 124
  type, 143, 167

Polar Grid tool, 95-97

Polygon tool, 87-88

pop-up menus, Method (Symbolism tool option), 491

portability
  Illustrator, 698-699
  images (sharing), preparation, 699-700
  press check, checklist, 703
  separations, 700-703
  Web animation, checklist, 703-704

Portable Document Format. *See* PDF

Portable Network Graphic. *See* PNG

PostScript
  pages, PDF, 262
  printers, errors, 573

PostScript Printer Description (PPD), 574, 583

PowerPoint
  background colors, sampling, 266-267
  clipping paths, 268
  file formats, 262, 265
  gradients, 268
  transparency, 266

PPD (PostScript Printer Description), 574, 583

ppi (pixels per inch), 259, 359

Preferences
  Auto Trace tool, 80-81
  command, 32, 360
  corrupt, 689
  dialog box, 144, 365, 605
  Disable Auto Add/Delete, 70
  Files & Clipboard, 411
  files, 52, 360, 511, 688-689
  Illustrator, 360, 368-369
  Liquify tools, 207
  menu commands
    Type & Auto Tracing, 143
    Units & Undo, 143
  troubleshooting, 360
  units of measure, changing, 476
  Web images, 476-477

Preferences, Files & Clipboard command (Edit menu), 664

Preferences, General command (Edit menu), 360, 571

Preferences, Guides & Grids command (Edit menu), 476

Preferences, Online Settings command (Edit menu), 369

Premiere, file formats, 262

preparing
  artwork, for printing, 586
  images, for Web, 700
  raster images, 403
  spot colors, for print, 581-582
  Web images, 471, 475-478

presentations
  colors, 286
  programs, PowerPoint, 265, 268

Preserve Appearance check box, 368

Preserve Color Numbers check box, 586

Preserve Paths check box, 368

Presets package, installation choices (Macintosh), 681

press checks, 574, 702-703

Pressure Pen check box (Symbolism tool option), 490

Preview
  browser button, 511
  check box, 181
  mode, 244

Preview All Layers command (Layers palette menu), 244

Preview Mode, blends, 214

previewing
  animations, 553
  artwork, 29
  dithering, images, 511
  objects, 181
  printing, 589
  Web images, 471

previews
.eps files, 46
Pixel Preview, 506-508
TIFF, 46

Previous/Next Data Set control (Variables palette), 650

Primary (plug-ins), 367

print
brokers, 595
colors, 256-259
file formats, 43, 262
output, 256
resolution, 259-261

printer's marks, 583, 591-593

printers
brush patterns, 310
colors, 280
commercial, 596
inkjet, 256, 285
patterns, 306
PostScript, errors, 573
resolution, 573
slide. *See* film, recorders
Swatch Libraries, 297

printing
alignment, 573
artwork, preparation, 586
bleeds, 570, 584, 703
blends, 214, 570
bounding boxes, 583
CcMmYK, 297
colors, 351
proofs, 701-702
separations, 577-578
commercial, 570, 575
CMYK, 256
line screen frequency, 396
complex paths, 190
contract proofs, 571
crop marks, 591-592
curves, 572
digital proofing, 577
direct to plate, 578
duotone, 571
film recorders, 269

flatness, 572
flexography, 572, 579
gradients, 347, 350-351, 572
halftones, 572, 575
images, continuous tone, 572
imagesetters, 578
knockout, 572
limitcheck error, 573
line screen frequency, 573
lpi (lines per inch), 573
masks, clipping, 375
misregistration, 573, 590
objects, knocking out, 589
offset, 573
outsourcing, 596
overprinting, 574, 587-588, 702
pages, dpi (dots per inch), 259
paths
splitting, 574
troubleshooting, 591
PDF files, 263
plates, 578-579, 584
PPD (PostScript Printer Description), 574
press checks, 574, 702-703
previewing, 589
printer's marks, 591-593
process colors, 571, 574
proofs, 574-577, 585, 702-703
raster images, pixels, 396
resolution, 594
separations, 701
service bureaus, 595
soft proofing, 576
spot colors, 258, 280, 575, 581-582
tiling, 575
transparency, 406, 424-426, 575
trapping, 575, 590, 596-601

trim marks, 591-592
tritone, 575
troubleshooting, 601
vector images, 392
Web, RGB, 256
wet proofing, 576

Printing & Export panel (Document Setup dialog box), 594

Printing & Export slider, 425-426

process
colors, 39, 282, 574
CMYK, 279, 571
versus spot colors, 580-581
inks, CMYK, 279
swatches, 293

processing, batch processing, 626

profiles
colors, 585
Absolute Colorimetric, 586
Perceptual, 586
Relative Colorimetric, 586
Saturation, 586
selecting, 586
ICC, embedding, 504

programs
crashing, 688
freezing, 688
presentations, PowerPoint, 265, 268

Progressive
check box, 520
format method (JPEG), 504

proof, color, 285

Proof Colors command (View menu), 29, 585

Proof command (View menu), 585

Proof Setup, Custom command (View menu), 29, 585

Proof Setup, Macintosh RGB command (View menu), 29

Proof Setup, Monitor RGB command (View menu), 29

Proof Setup, Windows RGB command (View menu), 29

proofing
digital, 577
hard, 574
inkjet printers, 256, 285
numbering, 703
page order, 703
printing, 574
soft, 29, 574-576, 585, 701
wet, 576

proofs
color, 701-703
contract proofs, 571, 702
digital, 701
laminate, 701
printing, 574-577
wet proofs, 701

proportional, type, 167

Proportional box, 132

proxies
objects, 182
point of origin, 177

.psd, file format, 50

Pucker & Bloat command (Filter menu), 438

Pucker tool, 207

punctuation, hanging, 148, 165

Q-R

Q, type, 143

Quality slider, 520

QuarkXPress, file formats, 262

R mode, 288

Radial command (Gradient palette menu), 340

radial gradients, 342

raised cap, type, 167

Random check box, 193

randomized transformations, 194

ranges, colors (gamuts), 39, 257, 285

Raster Effects Settings dialog box, 399

Raster Image Location (SVG Export option), 563

raster images, 499, 535
Adobe Photoshop, 390
advantages, 658
color, 390, 397
definition, 34
effects, 390, 398
embedding, 612-615
file formats, layers, 397
gradient meshes, creating, 346-348
Illustrator versus Photoshop, 656-658
linking, 604
PDF, 262
pixelization, 538
pixels, 34, 394, 397, 535
preparing, 403
printing, pixels, 396
resampling, 656
resolution, 259
scaling, 656
SVG, 559
transparency, 398
troubleshooting, 403
versus vector images, 42, 60, 390, 392-394, 396-399
Web animation, checklist, 704

rasterization, 506-508
file formats, 49, 266, 481
images, 512

Rasterize
command, 260, 266, 401, 444, 591
dialog box, 49, 399

Rasterize, Rasterize command (Effect menu), 401, 512

rasterizing
banding, 402
effects, 400
gradients, 338
illustrations, 594
objects, 399-403
paths, 591
vector objects, 402

ratios, aspect, 269

Read Only (SWF), 552

Record Stop dialog box, 638

recorded commands, 33

recorders, film
aspect ratio, 269
colors, 269
file formats, 269
images, 269
output, 269-270
pixels (addressable dimensions), 269
printing, 269
resolution, 269
sharpness, 269

Rectangle tool, 61, 85, 315

rectangles, 85-86

Rectangular Grid tool, 94

Rectangular tool, feature (new), 18

Red, Green, Blue. See RGB

Redefine Symbol command (Symbols palette menu), 493

Reduce to Basic Appearance command (Appearances palette menu), 331

reducing
artifacts, 521
opacity, opacity masks, 382
palettes, 284
size, files, 501

redundant anchor points, 109

Reflect
dialog box, 184
tool, 175, 179, 184, 303

reflections, 184

reflective colors, CMYK, 279

registration
color, 278, 584, 702
confirming, 678
marks, 584, 593
software, 36

regular (type), 167

Relative Colorimetric color profile, 586

Release command (Blend menu), 215

Release to Layers (Build) command (Layers palette menu), 244, 249, 251

Release to Layers (Sequence) command (Layers palette menu), 244, 249-251, 540

Remember button, 516

Remove Item command (Appearances palette menu), 331

repairs, troubleshooting, 688

repeating patterns, 303, 310

Replace (Style) command (Appearnce palette menu), 334

Replace
button, 608
dialog box, 608-610

Replace Link button, 610

Replace Spine command (Blend menu), 215

Replace Symbol
button, 492
command (Symbols palette menu), 492

Repopulate view command (Settings menu), 518

Reselect command (Select menu), 103

Reset All Warning Dialogs button, 361-362

Reset button, 516

Reshape tool, 175-177, 184

resolution
antialiasing, 402
browsers, Web, 475
computer monitors, 261
courseness, 261
film recorders, 269
fineness, 261
images, 259
imagesetters, 578
measuring, 259
monitors, 259
online, 506
output, 259-261
paths, modifying, 591
pixels, 259, 395
printers, 573
printing, 594
raster images, 259
rasterized objects, 400-403
screen, animations, 546

Resolution (Document Info palette), 614

Resolution (SWF), 553

Resolution Depth (JPEG Options dialog box), 504

Resolution option (Illustrator), 662

Reverse Front to Back command (Blend menu), 215

Reverse Order command (Layers palette menu), 244

Reverse Spine command (Blend menu), 215

Reverse Traps (trapping), 599

Revert button, 113, 583

RGB (Red, Green, Blue), 40
additive colors, 279
colors, 277-281
computer monitors, 259
fields, numeric values, 288
gamut, 279, 285
images, 290, 479
overprinting, 587
sliders, inverting, 290
values, Web-safe, inverting, 290
versus CMY, 257, 580
versus CMYK and spot colors, 278-282
Web printing, 256

RLE (Run Length Encoding), 49

Roman, type, 167

Rotate
command (Transform menu), 178
dialog box, 178, 182
tool, 175, 179, 182-183, 303, 315

rotating
angle, artboard, 360
blends, 216
color modes, 287
objects, 180-182, 224
patterns, 178, 183
symbol instances, 487

rotations
angles, 183
points, 183, 190

round-tripping, files, 670-671

Rounded Rectangle tool, 86, 361

Roundness value, 130

rows, Layers palette, 236

Rows & Columns command (Type menu), 153

rulers, 27
  origin, versus point of origin, 32
  point of origin, 27, 32, 302
  ruler origin, 32
  tab, 149
  units of measure, changing, 476
rules (type), 167
Run command (Start menu), 677
Run Length Encoding (RLE), 49

S

S mode, 288
Same command (Select menu), 104
Same, Stroke Weight command (Select menu), 104
Sample Files, installation choices (Windows), 684
Sample Files Folder, installation choices (Macintosh), 682
Saturation
  blending mode, 421
  color profile, 586
saturations, color, 282
Save Actions command (Actions palette menu), 641
Save As
  command (File menu), 45, 699
  dialog box, 45, 263, 562
Save Color Table command (color table menu), 518
Save command, 44, 631
Save for Web
  command (File menu), 52, 481
  dialog box, 483, 509-516, 525, 564

Save Optimized As dialog box, 484, 527, 530
Save Selection command (Select menu), 105
Save Set To dialog box, 641
Save Settings command (Settings menu), 518
Save SVG As command (SVG Viewer), 556
saving
  Actions, sets, 641-642
  animations, as SVG, 562-564
  brushes as styles, 122
  components, Web pages, 470
  files, 44-52, 367
  fill patterns, 303
  gradients, 338, 341
  HTML (Save Optimized As dialog box), 527
  Illustrator files, opening in Photoshop, 660
  images (Save Optimized As dialog box), 527
  optimizations, 516
  PDF files, 263-265
  selections, 105
  strokes as styles, 122
  styles, 333
  swatches, 292
  symbols, 485
  tints, 294
Saving Files panel, 529
scalable
  images, 505
  vector images, 545
Scalable Vector Graphics. See SVG
Scale
  box, 126
  command (Transform menu), 178
  dialog box, 124, 185-187
  tool, 175, 185-187, 303
    guidelines, 186
    patterns, transforming, 179

Scale Strokes & Effects check boxes, 362
Scale x-axis (SVG matrix), 560
Scale y-axis (SVG matrix), 560
scaling
  effects, 179-180, 187
  images, raster, 656
  numerically, 186
  objects, 362
  patterns, 178, 187
  percents, 186
  strokes, 179-180, 187
  transformations, 176
  type, 167
  vector images, 390, 392
Scallop tool, 208
scanners, resolutions, 261
Scatter Brush Options dialog box, 130
scatter brushes, 120
  artwork, modifying, 127
  color, 122
  creating, 130
  modifying, 130
  options, 130
  orientations, blends, 225
Scissors tool, 79, 124
scratch disks, 366-367
screen, halftone dots, 572
Screen (Symbolism tool option), 491
Screen blending mode, 417
Screen Optimized, PDF option, 264
screening. See halftones
screens
  computers, 259-261
  resolutions, animations, 546
Scrunch (Symbolism tool option), 491
seamless patterns, 303-305, 311

searchable databases,
Adobe Tech Support, 694

Secondary (plug-ins), 367

segments
objects, distorting, 185
paths, 61, 67
adding, 70
*corner anchor point,
65*
curved, 68
direction lines, 68
editing, 69, 73, 207
straight, creating, 89
pointed, creating, 208
spines, editing, 226

Select All command (Select
menu), 102

Select All Unused com-
mand, 293, 334

Select menu commands
Deselect, 103
Edit Selection, 106
Inverse, 103
Next Object Above, 103
Next Object Below, 103
Object, 104-105
Object, All, 105
Object, Brush Strokes,
105
Object, Direction
Handles, 105
Object, Save Selection,
105
Reselect, 103
Same, 104
Same, Stroke Weight, 104
Save Selection, 105
Select All, 102

Select Object command
(Actions palette menu),
634-637

Select Same Tint
Percentage check box, 361

Select Unused button, 115

Select, Same Fill Color command (Edit menu), 361

Select, Same Fill or Edit
command (Edit menu), 292

Selected Art
icon, 240
indicator, 236, 239

selected points, objects, 184

selecting
Actions sets, 631
anchor points, 63-64, 70,
74, 101
brushes, 127
color profiles, 586
effects, raster images,
398
focal points, 185
folders, plug-ins, 367
groups, 241-243
layers, 243
links, 612
mesh points, 199, 350
objects, 98-99, 180,
241-243, 292
paths, 122, 636
Pen tools, 70
PostScript Printer
Description (PPD), 583
styles, 334
sublayers, 243
swatches, 292
tools, 25

Selection tool, 98-99, 122,
139, 142, 176, 316, 397

selections
editing, 106
loading, 106
reversing, 103
saving, 105
slices, guides, 495
slicing, 494

Separation Setup command
(File menu), 282, 351

separations
blends, 701
colors, 40, 574
composites, 577
duotone, 577
negatives, 578
printing, 578
reading, 578
settings, 282
tritone, 577
complex paths, 701
gradients, 701
portability, 700-703
spot colors, 701
troubleshooting, 701

Separations Setup
command (File menu),
583
dialog box, 351, 570-571,
581-584

serif, type, 167

Server URL (Link
Information window), 615

service bureaus (printing),
595

Set Selection dialog box,
637

sets
Actions, 628
playing, 630
saving, 641-642
selecting, 631
sharing, 641-642
clipping, 374
symbols, 485, 490
expanding, 494
objects, 14

setting
baseline shifts, 362
color, 364-365
crop marks, 592
halftone options, 583
leading, 362
margins, 583
point of origin (rulers),
27
preferences, Illustrator,
360
style, 364-365
type, 364
units of measure,
363-364

Setting Size (Symbolism tool
option), 491

settings
color separations, 282
Macintosh, 682
Optimization, 511
GIF, 518-520
JPEG, 520-521
PNG-24, 521
PNG-8, 520
SVG, 521
SWF, 521
transparency, 411-412
Trap, 597, 599

Settings
installation choices,
Macintosh, 683
menu commands, 520
Delete Settings, 518
*Optimize to File Size,
518*
Repopulate View, 518
Save Settings, 518

setups, pages (Web
images), 477-478

shaded objects (smooth colors), 218

shades, grayscale objects,
284

shadows, 702
brushes, 125
creating, 189
drop
filters, 327
*shadows, opacity
masks, 414*

shaped gradients, smooth
colors, 218

shapes
compound, 106
buttons, 107
clipping masks, 376
expanding, 107
features (new), 19
layers, pasting, 666

shaping, paths (anchor
points), 62-67

sharing
Actions, sets, 641-642
files,
Illustrator/Photoshop,
660, 664-666
images, preparation,
699-700

Sharpen, Unsharp Mask
command (Filter menu),
462

Shear
dialog box, 187-189
tool, 175, 179, 187-189

shearing
anchor points, 187
objects, 180, 187
point of origin, 187

Shockwave, Macromedia
Shockwave, 50, 535

Shockwave Format. *See*
SWF

shortcuts. *See also* key-
board shortcuts
buttons
Black, 287
color bar, 287
None, 287
White, 287
Color palette, 286

Show All Swatches button,
292

Show Color Swatches but-
ton, 292

Show Edges command, 587,
606

Show Find Field command
(Swatch palette menu),
292

Show Font Names in
English check box, 363

Show Gradient Swatches
button, 292

Show Grid command (View
menu), 311

Show Hidden Characters
command (Type menu),
153

Show Layers Only check
box, 236

Show Note command
(Attributes palette menu),
594

Show Options command
(Character palette menu),
147

Show Pattern Swatches button, 292

Show Slice Numbers, 366

Show Tool Tips check box,
292, 361

Show Transparency Grid
command (View menu),
411

Show/Hide Grid command
(View menu), 30

Show/Hide Layers palette,
235

Show/Hide Page Tiling command (View menu), 478

Show/Hide Rulers command
(View menu), 30

Show/Hide Transparency
Grid command (View
menu), 30

side tiles, 311-313

Simulate Colored Paper
option (Document Setup
dialog box), 412

Simulate Paper setting, 427

single-byte fonts, type, 168

sites, laying out, 472-473.
See also Web, sites

size
animations, determining,
545, 548
artboard, 26
brush patterns, 308
brushes, modifying, 126

files, 482, 500-501

gradient meshes, 346-347

images, film recorders, 269

objects, 185

side tiles, 311

symbol instances, 487

Web animation, checklist, 704

Size (Document Info palette), 614

Size (Link Information window), 615

Size/Leading, type preference, 144

Sketch, Chalk & Charcoal command (Filter menu), 463

Sketch, Charcoal command (Filter menu), 463

Sketch, Chrome command (Filter menu), 463

Sketch, Conte Crayon command (Filter menu), 463

Sketch, Graphic Pen command (Filter menu), 463

Sketch, Halftone Pattern command (Filter menu), 463

Sketch, Note Paper command (Filter menu), 463

Sketch, Photocopy command (Filter menu), 464

Sketch, Plaster command (Filter menu), 464

Sketch, Reticulation command (Filter menu), 464

Sketch, Stamp command (Filter menu), 464

Sketch, Torn Edges command (Filter menu), 464

Sketch, Water Paper command (Filter menu), 464

Skew x-axis (SVG matrix), 560

Skew y-axis (SVG matrix), 560

Slice Options dialog box, 495

Slice Select tool, feature (new), 18

Slice Selection tool, 526

Slice tool, 18, 494

Slice, Create from Guides command (Object menu), 495

Slice, Create from Selection command (Object menu), 494-495

Slice, Make command (Object menu), 495

Slice, Slice Options command (Object menu), 495

slices
auto, 494
guides, selections, 495
image maps, creating, 495
line color, 366
linking, 495
optimizing, 525-527
types, 494
user, 494

slicing
object-based, 14, 495
selections, 494
Web design, 494-495

slide printers. *See* film, recorders

sliders
color bars, 287
Diameter (Symbolism tool option), 490
distortion, warps, 196
Dither, 522
Dithering, 519
Fidelity, 202
gradient, 340-341
hiding, 287

Lossiness, 519

Printing & Export, 425-426

Quality, 520

RGB, inverting, 290

Swatches palette, 293

Tint, 294

Tolerance, 100

small caps, type, 168

Small Rows view, 543

Small Swatch View, 292-293

smart line breaks, 148

Smart Guides
command (View menu), 30, 365
dialog box, 366

Smart Punctuation, 37, 152-153

Smart Quotes, 152, 168

Smart Spaces, 152

smooth
anchor points, 65, 68
colors
blends, 216, 219
intermediary objects, 217
shaded objects, 218
shaped gradients, 218
tool, paths, managing, 78

Smooth Color, Blend Options dialog box, 216, 219

Smoothness
Paintbrush tool, 75
Pencil tool, 76
Smooth tool, 78

Snap to Grid command (View menu), 27, 30

Snap to Pixel command (View menu), 30, 508

Snap to Point command (View menu), 27, 30, 305

Snap to Web Palette icon, 511

Snapping Tolerance (Smart Guides dialog box), 366

Soft Light blending mode, 418

soft proofing, 29, 574-576, 585, 701

software
registration, 36
trapping, 596

Sort by Hue command (color table menu), 517

Sort by Luminance command (color table menu), 517

Sort by Popularity command (color table menu), 517

Sort Objects by control (Variables palette), 650

space, white (type), 168

spacing
brush patterns, 312
intermediary objects, 222-224
letter, type, 166
text, 148
type, 168

special effects, Web images, 471

Specified Distance
Blend Options dialog box, 222-224
blends, 222, 224

Specified Steps, Blend Options dialog box, 219-222

Specified Steps, 222
complex animations, creating, 220
custom graphs, 220
frames, creating, 219
graphs, modifying, 221
grouped objects, duplicating, 219
images, 221
Web-based animation, creating, 219

Spin (Symbolism tool option), 491

spines
blends, creating, 214
curving, 227
editing, 226-227
replacing, 228
reversing, 228

Spiral tool, 91-92

spirals, 91-92

spot colors, 40, 258, 570
blending, 582
gradients, 581
overlapping, 582
printing, 280, 575, 581-582
separations, 701
swatches, 293-294
to process colors, converting, 582
versus
process colors, 580-581
RGB and CMYK, 278-282
white, 582

Sprayed Strokes dialog box, 459

spreads, trapping, 575, 597

squares. *See also* pixels
corners, 313
creating, 85

stacking order, objects, 36, 215, 249

Stain (Symbolism tool option), 491

Standard check box, 151

Star tool, 88-89

stars
measuring, 88
targets (printer's marks), 593

Start menu commands, Run, 677

start tiles, creating, brush patterns, 320

starting points, paths, 124

startup files, 370-371

Startup.exe file, 677

static images, animations, 541

Static objects, dynamic data-driven graphics, 647

status bar, 24-26

Status Bar pop-up menu commands
Current Tool, 26
Date and Time, 26
Document Color Profile, 26
Free Memory, 26
Number of Undos, 26

steps, Actions, 628

Stop Recording
command (Actions palette menu), 633
menu, 633

stop sign icons, 610

stops
Actions, adding, 638
gradients
adding, 339-340
copying, 340
deleting, 340
locations, 341
managing, 339
modifying, 340
moving, 339

storing
Actions, 628
brushes, 121
colors, Swatches palette, 291
fill patterns, 303
managed documents, 368
PPD (PostScript Printer Description), 574
symbols, 14, 485
Web pages, elements, 475

Strata VideoShop, file formats, 262

streaming video, 536

stroke, 34
  applying (targeting), 248
  blends, 214
  brushes, 122-123, 128
  color, 122
  effects, 328
  inactive, 287
  intermediary objects, spacing, 224
  layering, 330, 410
  overprinting, 600
  paths, 393
  scaling, 179-180, 187
  text, 141
  units of measure, setting, 364
  values, 291
  weights, brushes, 122

Stroke
  palette, 122
  swatches, 279, 291

Strokes & Effects check box, 124

Style (Symbolism tool option), 491

Style Libraries
  command (Window menu), 335
  installation choices, Windows, 684

Style Libraries, Other command (Window menu), 335

Style Options dialog box, 334

Style palette menu commands, New Style, 333

Style/Brush/Swatch Cleanup Action, 627

styles
  applying, 248, 333
  brushes, 122, 330
  copying, 334
  creating, 333-334
  deleting, 334

Grated Moon, 324
grids, setting, 365
guidelines, 333-334
guides, setting, 364
libraries, 334-335
naming, 334
objects, 334
replacing, 331
saving, 333
selecting, 334
strokes, 122
swatches, 334
troubleshooting, 335-336
type, 168

Styles palette, menu commands, 122, 324, 333
  Duplicate Style, 334
  Merge Styles, 334
  Select All Unused, 334

Stylize command (Filter menu), 464

Stylize, Add Arrowheads command (Filter menu), 444

Stylize, Drop Shadow command (Filter menu), 445

Stylize, Feather command (Effects menu), 445

Stylize, Inner Glow command (Effects menu), 445

Stylize, Outer Glow command (Effects menu), 445

Stylize, Round Corners command (Filter menu), 446

subdivisions (gridlines), 365

sublayers, 240-245
  collapsing, 236-237
  container, 475
  creating, Layers palette, 238-239
  expanding, 236-237
  Layers palette, 232
  objects, placing, 249
  selecting, 243
  targeted, 236, 241
  troubleshooting, 253

viewing, 236, 241
Web pages, organizing, 474

subscript, 37
  negative baseline shift, 362
  type, 168

subtractive color, 257, 277

superscript, 37
  positive baseline shift, 362
  type, 168

SVG (Scalable Vector Graphics), 505, 535
  Animation Elements, 560
  animations, 560-564
  DOM, 555, 560
  dynamic, 560-561
  files, 47, 481, 558
  filters, naming, 558
  fonts, 556, 563
  gradients, 557
  images, 538, 559
  interactivity, 538
  layers, exporting to, 560
  matrix, 560
  objects, recording, 557
  optimization settings, 521
  output, creating, 554-557, 559
  palettes, Interactivity, 561
  Save for Web dialog box, 564
  SVG Viewer plug-in, 539
  troubleshooting, 565-566
  vector file format, 43
  Web browsers, 539
  XML, 554
  zooming, 555-556

SVG Effects, SVG, 14

SVG Filter, Apply SVG Filter command (Effect menu), 558

SVG Filters command (Effects menu), 446

SVG Options dialog box, 47, 562-563

SVG Viewer commands
  About Adobe SVG
    Viewer, 556
  Copy SVG, 556
  Find, 556
  Find Again, 556
  Help, 556
  Higher Quality, 555
  Mute, 556
  Original View, 555
  Pause, 555
  Save SVG As, 556
  View Source, 556
  View SVG, 556
  Zoom In, 555
  Zoom Out, 555

SVG Working Group, 538

.svgz, file format, 48

Swatch Libraries, 294-297, 581
  accessing, 294
  command (Window
    menu), 294-295, 581
  locating, 297
  palette, 294-295
  printers, 297
  spot colors, 258

Swatch Libraries, Other
  Libraries command
  (Window menu), 295, 341, 371

Swatch Library, Load
  Library (Window menu), 338

Swatch Options
  command (Swatches
    palette menu), 293-294
  dialog box, 293-294

Swatch palette, 141, 295-297
  buttons, 292
  colors, 291-293
  fill patterns, storing, 303
  global swatches, 294
  gradients, 338

menu commands
  Name View, 292
  New Swatch, 293, 341
  Select All Unused, 293
  Show Find Field, 292
  Small Swatch View,
    292
  Swatch Options,
    293-294
  nonglobal swatches, 294
  sliders, 293
  spot colors, 258
  swatches, creating, 267

swatches, 35
  color, 293
  copying, 293
  creating, 267
  Default_CMYK, 295
  Default_RGB, 295
  deleting, 293
  Dicolor, 295
  drag and drop, 293
  Earthtones_1, 295
  editing, 293
  Fill, 279, 291
  FOCOLTONE, 295
  global, 293-294
  Harmonies_1, 295
  HKS E, 295
  HKS K, 296
  HKS N, 296
  HKS Z, 296
  Index number, 510
  locating, 292
  moving, 295
  names, 292-294, 581
  navigating, 292
  nonglobal, 293-294
  PANTONE Coated, 296
  PANTONE Matte, 296
  PANTONE Process, 296
  PANTONE Uncoated, 296
  Pastels, 296
  process, 293
  saving, 292
  selecting, 292
  spot colors, 293-294
  Stroke, 291, 279
  styles, 334

System (Macintosh or
  Windows), 296
Toyo, 296
Trumatch, 296
updating, 290
viewing, 292-293
Visibone2, 296
Web, 296

SWF (Shockwave Format), 506
  animations, exporting to, 552-554
  Auto-Create Symbols, 552
  Clip to Artboard Size, 552
  Curve Quality, 553
  file formats, Web images, 481
  Frame Rate, 552
  Image Format, 553
  images, placing in Web
    pages, 554
  Lossy (JPG), 553
  optimization settings, 521
  Read Only, 552
  Resolution, 553
  Save for Web dialog box, 564

Switch X/Y button, 113

Symbol Library, Other
  Library command
  (Window menu), 493

Symbol Set Density
  (Symbolism tool option), 490

Symbol Sprayer, Symbolism
  tool, 486

Symbolism Tool Options
  dialog box, 489-492

Symbolism tools, 485-492

symbols
  custom, creating, 493
  editing, 492
  Flash, 543, 552
  graphs, 115

instances, 485
   adding, 486
   color, 488
   expanding, 494
   managing, 493
   moving, 487
   opacity, 488
   randomizing, 487
   repositioning, 486
   rotating, 487
   size, 487
links, 492-493
loading, 14
managing, 485
menu, overriding, 359
redefining, 493
replacing, images, 492
sets, 14, 485, 490, 494
storing, 14
text overflow, 140
type, 168
updating, 492-493
Web, 14-15
Web design, 485-494

Symbols palette, menu com-
  mands, 14, 485
  New Symbol, 493
  Redefine Symbol, 493
  Replace Symbol, 492

System (Macintosh) swatch,
  296

System (Windows) swatch,
  296

T

Tab Ruler palette, 149
tables
  Color Tables, 511,
    516-518
  color tables, 516-517
tabs
  Brushes palette, 308
  Color palette, 287
  deleting, 149
  documents, 149
  Layers, 483

Targa, 51
targeted
  groups, 236
  layers, 236
  objects, 97, 236
  sublayers, 236
targeting
  attributes, 247
  brushes, applying, 248
  color, applying, 248
  effects, applying, 249
  filters, applying, 249
  gradients, applying, 249
  groups, 246-249
  icon, 122
  layers, 246-249
  Object menu commands,
    applying, 249
  objects, 246-249
  patterns, applying, 249
  strokes, applying, 248
  styles, applying, 248
  sublayers, 241
  transparency, applying,
    248

Template command (Layers
  palette menu), 244
templates
  dynamic data-driven
    graphics, 647-648
  icons, 235, 245
  layers, 235, 245
  locking, 245
  nonprinting, 245
text
  alignment, 36, 140
  area type, 37
  baseline, 37
  block type, 37
  bounding boxes, modify-
    ing, 146
  boxes
    containers, 154
    creating, 139
    resizing, 139
  brushes, applying,
    125-126
  color, 126, 141

containers
  filling, 158
  linking, 154-156
  objects, 155
  stroking, 158
converting to outlines,
  158
effects, creating, 330
files, embedding, 617-618
fill, 141
flipping, 142
flows, 142
fonts, 150
formatted, embedding,
  618
greeked, 144
highlighting, 145
justification, 37
kerning, 37
leading, 37
ligature, 37
linking, 150
masking with, 376
modifying, in Photoshop,
  664
overflow symbol, 140
pasting, Photoshop,
  664-666
paths, 141
placeholders, 363
point type, 38
repositioning, 142
spacing, 148
stroke, 141
subscript, 37
superscript, 37
tracking, 38
troubleshooting, 169
vector images, 398
wrapping, 141, 150,
  156-158

Text Filters
  folder, 152
  plug-ins (Illustrator plug-
    in), 680

Text Label Hints (Smart
  Guides dialog box), 365

Texture, Craquelure com-
  mand (Filter menu), 464

textured backgrounds, animations, 544

.tga, file format, 51

Thickness (trapping), 597

thousands of colors, 499

thumbnails
   Adobe Acrobat, 46
   custom, 236
   hiding, 237, 331
   images, masks, 381
   Layers palette, 232, 236
   showing, 331

TIFF, previews, 46

TIFF Options, 52

tilde (~), 179, 302

tiles
   brush patterns, 310
   corner
      bounding boxes, 313, 320
      brush patterns, creating, 313-320
      curved, 319
   corner-to-corner, 315
   creating, 133
   end
      bounding boxes, 320
      brush patterns, creating, 320
   modifying, 133
   pattern brushes, 133
   point-to-point, 315
   seamless patterns, 303
   side
      sizes, 311
      brush patterns, creating, 311-313
   start, brush patterns, creating, 320
   types, 133

tiling
   fill patterns, 302
   images, 575
   pages, 27, 32
   patterns, 300-302

Tint Reduction (trapping), 598

Tint slider, 294

tints, 575
   colors, 258, 581
   global, linked, 294
   halftone dots, 572
   naming, 294
   saving, 294

Tints and Shades colorization option, 309

tips, searching (Adobe Support Knowledgebase), 694-695

Tips button, 128

Tolerance sliders, 100

Tool Tips, viewing, 361

Toolbox, 24, 32-33
   Color palette, 288
   fly-out palette, 69
   stroke color, changing, 126
   transformation tools, 175

tools
   accessing, 32-33
   Add Anchor Point, 69, 361
   Arc, 17, 89
   Area type, 140
   Auto Trace, 80-81, 363
   Basic Creation, function, 85
   Basic Object Creation, 85-92
   Blend, 212, 215
   Bloat, 208
   brushes, 122
   Complex Object Creation, 92-97
   Convert Anchor Point, 69, 227, 320
   Crystallize, 208
   Delete Anchor Point, 69, 361
   Direct Select Lasso, 74, 101
   Direct Selection, 69, 99, 122, 141-142, 158, 226, 320, 377, 381, 393

editing, 70-74
Ellipse, 61, 87
Erase, paths (managing), 78
Eyedropper, 159, 267, 290, 510
features, new, 17-19
Flare, 18, 61, 92, 94
Free Transform, 175, 180
Gradient Mesh, 344
Gradient, 343
Graph, 61, 219
graphs, 110-112
Grid, 18, 61
Group Select, 214
Group Selection, 99, 122, 377
Hand, 510
Knife, paths (managing), 79
Lasso, 102
Line Segment, 89
Line, 17, 61
Liquify, 16, 206-209
Magic Wand, 17, 99, 101
managing, 70-71
Move, 126, 181-182
nonrecordable (Actions), 634
Object Creation, 84
Paint Bucket, 159
Paintbrush, 74-76
Path Type, 140-142
Pen, 67-70, 316, 349, 361
Pencil, 75-76
Polar Grid, 95-97
Polygon, 87-88
Pucker, 207
Rectangle, 61, 85, 315
Rectangular Grid, 94
Rectangular, 18
Reflect, 175, 179, 184, 303
Reshape, 175-177, 184
Rotate, 175, 179, 182-183, 303, 315
Rounded Rectangle, 86, 361

Scale, 175, 179, 185-187, 303

Scallop, 208

Scissors, 79, 124

selecting, 25

Selection, 98-99, 122, 139, 142, 176, 316, 397

Shear, 175, 179, 187-189

Slice Select, 18

Slice Selection, 526

Slice, 18, 494

Smooth, paths (managing), 78

Spiral, 91-92

Star, 88-89

switching, 185

Symbolism, 485-492

Transform, 365

transformations, 175

troubleshooting, 689

Twirl, 207

Twist, 175-177, 189-190

Type, 126, 138-140, 143-146, 377

Vertical Area Type, 140

Vertical Path Type, 141-142

Vertical Type, 139-140

Warp, 206

Wrinkle, 208

Zoom, 28, 510

Tools plug-ins (Illustrator plug-in), 680

Toyo swatch, 296

Tracing Gap check tool, 363

tracking
letters, 362
paragrahs, 147
text, 38
type, 144, 147, 168
versus kerning, 37-38

tranformations, randomized, 194

Transform (Link Information window), 615

Transform
command, 61, 439
menu commands
  Move, 181
  Rotate, 178
  Scale, 178
palette, 124, 175
  menu, 191
  point of origin, 177
  pop-up menu commands, Transform Pattern Only, 303
tools (Smart Guides dialog box), 365

Transform Each dialog box, point of origin, 192

Transform Pattern Only command (Tranform palette pop-up menu), 303

Transform Pattern Tiles check box, 362

Transform, Move command (Object menu), 181

Transform, Reset Bounding Box command (Object menu), 194

Transform, Rotate command (Object menu), 315

Transform, Scale command (Object menu), 185, 218, 657

Transform, Shear command (Object menu), 187

Transform, Transform Again command (Object menu), 191

Transform, Transform Each command (Object menu), 183, 192-194

transformations
applying, 174
basics, 175-180
calculating, 176
commands, 175
effects, 174
Free Transform tool, 180

images, linked, 607, 610

managing, 175

Move tool, 181-182

moving, 176

paths, manipulating, 174

point of origin, 176-178

Reflect tool, 184

Reshape tool, 184

Rotate tool, 182-183

Scale tool, 185-187

scaling, 176

Shear tool, 187-189

tools, 175

troubleshooting, 210

Twist tool, 189-190

transforming
blends, 214
bounding boxes, 176
brush paths, 123-125
effects, 179
objects, 178
patterns, 178
Selection tool, 176
strokes, 179

Translate x-axis (SVG matrix), 560

Translate y-axis (SVG matrix), 560

transparency, 36, 406, 410, 575. *See also* opacity
Alpha information, 510
applying (targeting), 248
blending mode, 409
changing, 409
grids, 411
groups, 410
layers, 232, 410
maintaining, 519
managing, 594
multiple, 427
online, 426
outputting, 424
patterns, 300
PowerPoint, 266
printing, 424-426
raster images, 398
settings, 411-412
simulating, 406

theory of, 406
TIFF previews, 46
Transparency palette, 409
troubleshooting, 519

Transparency
check box, 519
palette, 300, 409
gradients, 338
Isolate Blending option, 423
menu commands, 379-380

transparent
objects, spot colors (overlapping), 582
backgrounds, rasterized objects, 400

Transpose Row/Column button, 113

Trap
command (Pathfinder palette menu), 109, 599
settings, 597-599

trapping, 36, 599, 702
choke, 571, 597
in-RIP trapping, 596
misregistration, 590
plug-ins, 596
software, 596
spread, 575, 597
troubleshooting, 600-601

Traps with Proces Color (trapping), 598

triangles, layers, 234

Trim command (Pathfinder palette menu), 108

trim marks, 80, 591-592

tritone, 575-577

troubleshooting
backward compatibility, 690
brushes, 135
commands, 689
effects, applying to groups and layers, 466

files, rescuing, 690
icons, 689
interoperability, 690
palettes, 689
preformance, 688-689
printing, transparency, 424
procedures, 690-691
repairs, 688
separations, 701
tools, 689
transparencies, multiple, 427
transparency, 519

Trumatch swatch, 296

Twirl tool, 207

Twist tool, 175, 189-190
anchor points, adding, 191
point of origin, 177
rotation points, 190

.txt, file format, 52

type
attributes, copying, 159-160
baseline, 163
body, 163
bold, 163
cap height, 163
character, 164
CID (Character ID), 164
CJK (Chinese-Japanese-Korean), 164
clipping masks, 377-378
compound paths, 150
condensed, 164
considerations, 143, 146
copyfitting, 164
descender, 164
dingbats, 164
double-byte fonts, 164
drop cap, 164
ellipis, 164
em dash, 164
em space, 164
en dash, 164
en space, 164
extended, 165

face, 165
fixed pitch, 165
font families, 165
font sizes, 165
fonts, 145, 165
glyph, 165
greeking, 165, 363
handing indents, 165
handing punctuation, 165
head/headline, 165
hinting, 165
horizontal, 139
indenting, 165
italic, 165
justification, 163, 165
kerning, 144, 147, 166
leading, 144, 147, 166
letter spacing, 166
letterform, 166
ligature, 166
linking, 150
margin, 166
measuring, 143
monospace, 166
multiple master fonts, 166
objects, antialiasing, 15
old-style figure, 166
opacity masks, 383
OpenType, 166
optical size, 167
pica, 167
points, 143, 167
preferences, 143, 146
proportional, 167
Q, 143
raised cap, 167
regular, 167
Roman, 167
rules, 167
scaling, 167
serif, 167
single-byte fonts, 168
sizes, 150
small caps, 168
Smart Quotes, 168
spacing, 168
styles, 168
subscript, 168

superscript, 168
symbols, 168
terms, 163-169
tracking, 144, 168
troubleshooting, 169
typeface, 168
underline, 168
units of measure, setting, 364
unjustified, 168
vertical, 139
white space, 168
widths, 168
wingdings, 164
word spacing, 169
WYSIWYG (What You See Is What You Get), 169
x-height, 169

Type & Auto Tracing command (Preferences menu), 143
preference dialog box, 362-363

Type (Document Info palette), 614

Type Area Select check box, 363

Type
menu commands
Blocks, 150
Blocks, Link, 154
Change Case, 152
Check Spelling, 152
Create Outlines, 159
Find Font, 151
Find/Change, 150
Fit Headline, 150
Rows & Columns, 153
Show Hidden Characters, 153
Smart Punctuation, 37, 152
Type Orientation, 153
Wrap, 150
tools, 126, 138-140, 143-146, 377

Type Orientation command (Type menu), 153
typeface (type), 168
types
colors, Web design, 479
corners, 313
graphs, 110-115
slices, 494
tiles, 133
typewriter
animations (cumulative animations), 250, 536
effect, 250

U

Unbind Variable control (Variables palette), 650
uncolored areas, images, online, 426
underline, type, 168
Undo, 36
Ungroup command (Edit menu), 306
Unite command (Pathfinder palette menu), 591
Units & Undo
command (Preferences menu), 143
dialog box, 363-364
units of measure
changing, 476
general, setting, 363
Gridline Every, 365
stroke, setting, 364
type, setting, 364
Unix, files, naming, 44
unjustified (type), 168
unlinking masks, 380
Unlock All Layers command (Layers palette menu), 244
Unshift All Colors command (color table menu), 517

Unsorted command (color table menu), 517
Update Link button, 611
Update Links (Files & Clipboard dialog box), 368
Updates button, 369
updating
colors, 290
Macintosh OS, 9 or X, 680
swatches, 290
symbols, 492-493
Use Area Select dialog box, 361
Use Precise Cursors check box, 361
Use Preview Bounds check box, 362
useless files (Illustrator), 685-686
User Guide (Illustrator), 691
user slices, 494
User to User Forums, 695
utilities folder, installation choices, Macintosh, 683
Utility Files, installation choices, Windows, 684

V

values
Angle, 130
channels, reversing, 290
CMYK colors, 281
colors, swatches, 293
defaults, Fill swatch or Stroke swatch, 291
fill, 291
fractional, Color Picker, 288
hexadecimal, 288
HSB, 282
numeric, 288
reversing, colors, 290
fields, 181

RGB
  colors, 281
  Web-safe, inverting, 290
  Roundess, 130
  stroke, 291

variables, dynamic data-driven graphics, 647, 649
  data sets, 651
  libraries, 653
  types of, 650
  Variables palette controls, 650

Variables palette, controls, 649

vector
  art, 60-61 535
  file formats, viewing, 482
  images, 35, 604
    Bézier curves, 392
    editing, 390
    embedding, 615-616
    file formats, 397
    gradients, 397
    Illustrator versus Photoshop, 656-659
    objects, 392, 397
    PDF, 262
    printing, 392
    scalable, 545
    scaling, 390, 392
    text, 398
    translating, 390
    versus raster images, 390-399
  objects, rasterizing, 402
  versus raster, 42, 60

Vector Markup Language (VML), 538

Version Checker, downloading, 46

versions, Illustrator, 688

Vertical Area Type tool, 140

vertical
  orientations, intermediary objects, 224
  reflections, 184
  type, 139

Vertical Path Type tool, 141-142

Vertical Type tool, 139-140

video, 536
  digitized, 536
  file formats, 262
  full-motion, 536
  RGB color model, 259
  streaming, 536

Video, De-Interlace command (Filter menu), 465

Video, NTSC Colors command (Filter menu), 465

view
  modes, 28
  Outline, 246

View By Name command (Brushes palette menu), 121

View menu commands
  Actual Size, 28-29
  Edit Views, 31
  Fit in Window, 28-29
  Guides, 30
  Guides, Show Guides, 311
  Hide Edges, 61
  Hide/Show Artboard, 30
  Hide/Show Bounding Box, 30
  Hide/Show Edges, 29
  Hide/Show Template, 30
  Hide/Show Tiling, 30
  New View, 31
  Outline/Preview, 29
  Overprint Preview, 29, 587, 589
  Pixel Preview, 29, 478, 508
  Proof Colors, 29, 585
  Proof Setup, Custom, 29, 585
  Proof Setup, Macintosh RGB, 29
  Proof Setup, Monitor RGB, 29

Proof Setup, Windows RGB, 29
Proof, 585
Show Edges, 606
Show Grid, 311
Show Transparency Grid, 411
Show/Hide Grid, 30
Show/Hide Page Tiling, 478
Show/Hide Rulers, 30
Show/Hide Transparency Grid, 30
Smart Guides, 30, 365
Snap to Grid, 27, 30
Snap to Pixel, 30, 508
Snap to Point, 27, 30, 305
Zoom In, 28-29
Zoom Out, 28-29

View Source command (SVG Viewer), 556

View SVG command (SVG Viewer), 556

viewing
  colors, 516, 584-585
  images, linked, 607
  layers, 235, 241, 325
  PDF documents, 262
  reflections, 184
  swatch names, 292
  swatches, 292
  Tool Tips, 361
  vector file formats, 482

views
  Large Swatch View, 293
  Name View, 293
  options, Web images, 478
  Small Rows, 543
  Small Swatch View, 293
  swatches, 293

visible layers, CSS (Cascading Style Sheets), 484

Visibone2 swatch, 296

VML (Vector Markup Language), 538

W

warning dialog box, 53

warnings
  disabling, 361
  hiding, 287
  restoring, 362

Warp
  command (Effect menu),
    174, 446
  tool, 206

Warp Options dialog box,
  201

Warp Tool Options dialog
  box, 208

warps
  applying, 196
  availability, effects, 16
  distortions, 196, 200
  features, new, 15

Web
  animation, checklist,
    703-704
  antialiasing, 14-15
  browsers, 545-547
    CSS (Cascading Style
      Sheets), 483
    resolution, 475
    SVG, 539
  colors, 256-259
  CSS (Cascading Style
    Sheets), 14
  design, 470-471, 475
    colors, 479-480
    file formats, 480-482
    hexadecimal notation,
      479
    HTML, 479
    pages (organizing), 474
    sites (laying out),
      472-473
    slicing, 494-495
    troubleshooting, 496
    Web-safe palette, 480
  designs
    CSS (Cascading Style
      Sheets), 482-485
    symbols, 485-494

features, new, 14-15
files
    formats, 43, 262
    naming, 44
images, 700
    animations, 482
    basics, 470-471
    colors, 280
    downloading, 482
    files, 481-482
    page setup, 477-478
    pixels, 475-476
    preparing, 471,
      475-478
    previewing, 471
    special effects, 471
    symbols, 485
    view options, 478
object-based slicing, 14
pages
    components (saving),
      470
    elements (storing), 475
    layers, 482
    managing, 470
    SWG images, 554
PDF files, 263
printing, RGB, 256
resolution, 259-261
Safe palettes, 284
Safe RGB palette,
  284-285
sites
    Adobe, 55, 678
    Adobe Support, 693
    dynamic data-driven
      graphics. See
      dynamic data-driven
      graphics
    Library of Congress,
      678
SVG Effects, 14
swatch, 296
symbols, 14-15
Web Safe color, online, 500
Web Snap, 520
Web-based animation, cre-
  ating, 219

Web-safe
    color, 40, 285-286
    RGB values, inverting,
      290
Web-safe palette, 479-480,
  499
weights
    fonts, 161
    stroke, brushes, 122
wet
    proofing, 576
    proofs, 701
What You See Is What You
  Get (WYSIWYG), type, 169
wheels, color (Hue), 283
white
    backgrounds, rasterized
      objects, 400
    creating, 276-277
    space, type, 168
White, shortcut buttons,
  287
Whole Word check box, 636
widths
    arcs, 90
    type, 168
wind, spirals, 92
Window menu commands
    Brush Libraries, 127, 135
    Brush Libraries, Other
      Library, 121
    Styles Libraries, 335
    Styles, Libraries Other,
      335
    Swatch Libraries,
      294-295, 581
    Swatch Libraries, Load
      Library, 338
    Swatch Libraries, Other
      Libraries, 341, 371
    Swatch Libraries, Other
      Library, 295
    Symbol Library, Other
      Library, 493

Windows
  72ppi (pixels per inch), 144
  custom installation, 683
  files, naming, 44
  installing Illustrator, 677-678
windows, Link Information, 615
Windows Metafile, 50-52
Windows XP, 20
wingdings type, 164
wizards, InstallShield, 677
.wmf, file format, 52
word spacing (type), 169
words, hyphenating, 148
work area, appearance, 29-31
Wrap command (Type menu), 150

wrapping
  embedded text files, 618
  text, 141, 150, 156-158
Wrinkle tool, 208
Wrinkle Tool Options dialog box, 209
Write Compound Shapes option (Illustrator), 663
Write Image Maps option (Illustrator), 663
Write Layers option (Illustrator), 662
Write Nested Layers option (Illustrator), 663
Write Slices option (Illustrator), 663
WYSIWYG (What You See Is What You Get), type, 169

X-Z

x-height, type, 169
XML (Extensible Markup Language), 505, 535
  advantages, 554
  integration, 555
  SVG, 554
  versus HTML, 554
XML IDs, dynamic data-driven graphics, 652

Zip, PDF option, 264
Zoom In command
  SVG Viewer, 555
  View menu, 28-29
Zoom Out command
  SVG Viewer, 555
  View menu, 28-29
Zoom tool, 28, 510
zooming, 657
  images, 27-29, 513
  SVG, 555-556
  with Navigator palette, 28